PUBLIC ENEMIES

PUBLIC ENEMIES
America's Criminal Past, 1919–1940

William Helmer
with
Rick Mattix

Checkmark Books™
An imprint of Facts On File, Inc.

Public Enemies: America's Criminal Past, 1919–1940

Checkmark Books
An imprint of Facts On File, Inc.
11 Penn Plaza
New York NY 10001

Library of Congress Cataloging-in-Publication Data

Helmer, William J.
Public enemies : America's criminal past, 1919–1940 / William Helmer and Rick Mattix.
p.   cm.
Includes bibliographical references and index.
ISBN 0-8160-3160-6.—ISBN 0-8160-3161-4 (pbk.)
1. Crime—United States—History—20th century. 2. Criminals—United States—History—20th century.
3. Organized crime—United States—History—20th century. I. Mattix, Rick. II. Title.
HV6783.H395   1998
364.973'0904—dc21
98-5032

Checkmark Books are available at special discounts when purchased in bulk quantities for businesses, associations, institutions or sales promotions. Please call our Special Sales Department in New York at (212) 967-8800 or (800) 322-8755.

You can find Facts On File on the World Wide Web at http://www.factsonfile.com

Text design by Robert Yaffe
Cover design by Matt Galemmo

Printed in the United States of America

MP FOF 10 9 8 7 6 5 4 3 2 1
  (pbk) 10 9 8 7 6 5 4 3 2 1

This book is printed on acid-free paper.

CONTENTS

For Marjorie Eker McDougall . . .

. . . . Who as an attractive, young student at the Worsham College of Embalming helped one of her professors make a death mask of the notorious outlaw John Dillinger, only to have it confiscated by an officious Chicago cop, Sergeant Mulvaney. In the crowded, carnival atmosphere of the Cook County Morgue, she then kept Mulvaney flattered, distracted and out of the "cool room" while her colleagues made a second mold of Dillinger's face and slipped it out undetected —as she revealed for the first time while being interviewed at a retirement home in Peoria, Illinois.

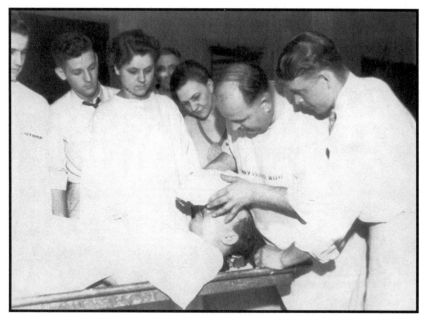

Marjorie Eker McDougall (third from left) *(Authors' collection)*

ACKNOWLEDGMENTS

Several individuals deserve special thanks for their particularly important or ongoing contributions to this project: Jeff Maycroft, Henry Scheafer, Ed Baumann, Mike Webb, Sandy Jones, Bob Fischer, Art Bilek, Rick Cartledge, Roseanne Keefe, Jeffery King, Brad Smith, Jacqueline Kleppe, Richard Lindberg and especially, Patterson Smith, bookseller and publisher, whose expert knowledge of materials on crime history helped make this volume's bibliography the most comprehensive yet published on gangsters, bandits and crime control during this remarkable period of American history.

For sharing their information, recollections and valuable suggestions, our lasting gratitude goes to William Balsamo, Bruce Barnes, Kent Bartram Jr., Bob Bates, Paula Berinstein, Ken Bruce, Tony Brucia, Marian Caporusso, Victoria Cerinich, Val Christmann, Dr. Jim Conway, Dee Cordry, Don Costello, Randy Cozens, Nora Cramer, Dennis Crider, Jonathan Davis, Dennis DeMark, Rob Dickman, Brian Downes, Mike Duffy, Bob Ernst, Leif Ernst, Bill Fiedler, Les Field, Keith Fletcher, Verla Geller, Anita Gold, Bruce Hamilton, Kathi Harrell, Chris Hegle, Gordon Herigstad, Kenan Heise, Karen Henrickson, Tracie Hill, Prof. Dennis Hoffman, Tom Hollatz, Ken Holmes, Mari Allyn Huff, Tom Joyce, Paul Kavieff, Bill Kelly, Mike Koch, Joe Kozenczak, Bill Krueger, Dr. Jonathan Lewis, Mark Levell, Robert Livesey, Paul Maccabee, Paul Meridith, Dale Meyer, Rose Barker Nations, Steve Nickel, Burt Nielson, John O'Brien, Jim Perkins, Tony Perrin, the late Joe Pinkston, Ellen Poulsen, Tom Prior, Ron Rosner, Joe Saccomonto, James Sammons, Tamara Shaffer, Jeff Scalf, Chuck Schauer, Dick Shaw, Cheryl Slaugh, Tom Smusyn, Phillip Steele, Jim Sterling, Keith Taylor, Bill Trible, Neal Trickel, Sid Underwood, Robert Unger, Todd von Hoffman, Charles Wallace Jr., Keith White, Terry Whitehead and Bud Young, among whom many belong to an expanding network of writers, researchers and collectors know on the Web as Partners in Crime (Dr. Horace Naismith, C.E.O.).

Our greatest admiration goes to editor Jim Chambers, whose monumental patience, perseverence and skill quelled a riot of facts and figures into an orderly mob of research material.

INTRODUCTION

If American crime enjoyed a golden age, it would have been from 1920 to 1940—two decades bracketed by great wars, roller-coaster years when a rural nation became urbanized and the 19th century finally gave way to the 20th. The automobile came of age. So did the airplane, the telephone, radio and motion pictures. After a period of fragile prosperity, economic disaster crippled state and municipal agencies and gave rise to centralized national government. It was a time when technological, political and cultural changes occurred so rapidly that many American institutions, including the criminal justice system, were slow to understand and adapt to their significance.

Law enforcement was only beginning to emerge from a tradition of regional independence. In the West public safety generally had been a do-it-yourself proposition; and crime control, the job of local sheriffs, marshals, rangers, posses, vigilance committees and private agencies such as the Pinkertons, who divided their efforts between breaking strikes and catching bank and train robbers. In cities, police departments were replacing watchmen and guards by the 1850s, but these often amounted to little more than untrained, nonuniformed and sometimes competing teams of muscular mercenaries paid and more or less controlled by the ruling political organization, maintaining the peace with as much brutality as

public opinion would tolerate. Full-time uniformed policemen serving under a captain of a district or precinct and a separate "detective" force under a central chief or superintendent represented the first steps toward police professionalism that took place near the end of the century and slowly developed into a unified and organized city service.

The same forces that reshaped society also changed the face of crime. With the settlement of the West, the industrial revolution combined with waves of immigration to create an urban version of the frontier in rapidly growing and poorly managed cities. Slums, violence, disease, vice and corruption spawned a progressive movement that began battling urban decay, the most conspicuous signs of which were labor unrest, street crime and public drunkenness. An unprecedented reform effort called Prohibition seemed imperative to the survival of the traditional American value system, but like other panaceas it demonstrated the doctrine of unintended consequences. Outlawing intoxicants gave America not the era of "clear thinking and clean living" that idealists promised. Instead it vastly increased political and police corruption, transformed drunkenness from a working-class vice into a form of middle-class rebellion and laid the foundation for nationally organized crime. Compared with modern racketeers, the bootleggers of the 1920s seem as grand and gaudy as the cars they drove. Both were primitive by later standards, but they had novelty and a style that evoked as much excitement as fear. They were symbols of their era.

The Roaring Twenties and Prohibition gave way, one after the other, to the Great Depression, a period no less memorable for conditions of a different and frightening kind. After 1930, people who pitied the "poor working stiff" considered themselves lucky to find jobs, and men in breadlines could no longer identify with swaggering gangland toughs. It was easier to condone the exploits of a Robin Hood, or a reasonable facsimile. If bootlegging was the respectable crime of the twenties, Americans in the Depression found something to admire in the bold and desperate men who only "stole from the banks what the banks stole from the people."

The big-city gangsters who corrupted government and turned city streets into battlegrounds were often foreign-born with foreign-sounding names. But the Depression desperadoes were red-blooded, all-American outlaws in the Jesse James tradition who "came from good homes" and were "driven to crime" by circumstances. They were underdogs in a nation of underdogs, "people's bandits" who shook their fists in the face of corrupt authority and attacked the symbols of wealth. Daring, colorful, sometimes gallant, they led the cops a merry chase and died with their boots on.

At least so go their legends, created partly by the press and partly by badly outclassed lawmen to explain their inability to bring them down. These "gangsters" worked as teams instead of in syndicates, used force instead of bribes, lived as fugitives instead of businessmen and soon fell victim to the technological and legal changes they themselves helped bring about.

Sanitized by the passage of time, the urban mobsters of the 1920s like Al Capone can now be glamorized as classic criminals, the first of a new breed that came in with Prohibition, while a Depression-era bandit like John Dillinger represents the last of an old one that now substituted automobiles for horses. In both categories, those best remembered had an outrageous style that mocked authority and enthralled a largely apathetic public whose main source of entertainment was a shamelessly sensational press. To combat the increasing gangster chic, serious crime fighters countered by declaring them Public Enemies, which newspapers seized on just as eagerly as a major killing and need for reforms, but the public's continued fascination with crime, its perception of criminals and its remarkably flexible value system remain a fairly good index to the average citizen's priorities and sense of right and wrong. Celebrity criminals of the Public Enemy era taught Americans that while "Crime Does Not Pay," it can be a shortcut to immortality.

That simplistic summary implies that the crime problem of the past was a manageable one compared with the mindless murder and mayhem that confronts the country presently. With the doubling of the national population, the problem has predictably worsened in many respects, but not to the degree assumed by the fans of true-crime "cop" programs on television, and by lawmakers whose apprehensions are shaped more by journalists and entertainers than by historians. This phenomenon is not uniquely American, but here it combines with a political process that is averse to historical comparisons. As a result, crime and violence are invariably proclaimed a national peril instead of being viewed as a national norm.

The dynamics of this are simple enough:

Crime, violence and corruption are the legitimate concerns of a free press in a democratic society, whose citizens need an awareness of these problems to make informed decisions and shape public policy. As it happens, crime, violence and corruption also sell newspapers and TV shows, which by their nature report on them as novel and newsworthy events rather than as simply the latest manifestation of social problems that have plagued this country since it was settled. Among readers whose memories are as short as a cub reporter's, the impression created by the daily press and reinforced by television news is that conditions are bad and getting worse, and that the end is near.

At the opposite end of the information spectrum, textbook historians describe great movements, great leaders and great wars that have altered the course of world events. Even social historians, with the clarity of hindsight, record the perils of the past without hysteria, as storms that either never materialized or were successfully weathered, once the problem was confronted sensibly. It's not their job (or the desire of their publishers, for that matter) to reassure the contemporary reader that, for instance, the murder and mayhem of the 1990s is proportionately about the same as that of the 1970s or the 1930s, and even less than in some earlier times and places; that our streets are safer now than a hundred years ago; or that the fatality rate for handguns, say, is about the same as it is for birth control pills, an otherwise meaningless comparison that only illustrates the importance of viewing perils in perspective.

Europeans, from the vantage point of experience, have long observed this country's continual reform efforts with interest and sometimes amusement, marveling at three traits that seem to be uniquely American: a penchant for equating sin with crime, a greater ability to perceive problems than to correct them and a limited sense of history affirming the adage that people who do not learn from their mistakes tend to repeat them.

Foreign intellectuals in particular note a fundamental conflict between two of our most cherished principles: that America has "a government of laws, and not of men," with its goals of equal opportunity and equal justice; and a passion for personal freedom embodied in the expression, "that government is best which governs least." Attracted to whichever proposition serves their immediate purpose, Americans demand action and the quick fix, and have never subscribed to the more realistic view of theologian-philosopher Reinhold Niebuhr that "Democracy is finding proximate solutions to insoluble problems."

So while representative government is expected to maximize individual freedom, it is also expected to solve the nation's problems. This makes reform possible, but sometimes impossibly slow. Totalitarian governments need not submit controversial issues to public debate. But the democratic process compels the office seeker and office holder to either exaggerate or minimize the problems of the day and, like a physician with a good bedside manner, prescribe new laws that either topically treat the symptoms, or promise a cure for a condition that in fact is chronic.

The country's political leadership thus includes many faith healers whose nostrums sometimes actually work through a placebo effect, or because a given problem resolves itself naturally. But it remains a standard campaign practice to depict any recurring evil as an imminent peril, blame it on the wrongheaded policies of the incumbent and call on voters to throw the rascal out.

Many historical, demographic and political factors have combined to create a U.S. population that is at once the most lawmaking and lawbreaking in the world—a country whose citizens still believe in the magical powers of legislation to foster a safe and just society, but readily exempt themselves from any rules they consider inapplicable to themselves or an infringement on their rights. Many laws that are eminently ignorable or patently unenforceable are enacted chiefly for their symbolic value, as a statement of lofty moral principle or to "send a message," though their usual effect is only to create more statutory criminals and complicate police work. During Prohibition, the prisons filled up with bootleggers; today the majority of inmates are drug users, not even convicted of dealing.

An increasing number of social scientists are looking at the national record of more than 200 years and concluding that many of the country's problems are simply intractable; that some traits are too ingrained in the national character even for police-state remedies; that with our historic enthusiasm for laws goes an almost moral obligation to break them. These are scholars and intellectuals whose admonitions will be largely ignored, if American politics runs true to form. But occasionally they may persuade an "honest politician" that if sin cannot be abolished by making it a crime, and if

crime cannot be abolished by even draconian punishment, the next best thing is to separate the two. Take the profit out of vice through regulation, and otherwise craft enforceable statutes aimed only at reducing to tolerable levels the crime and violence that history suggests can never be totally eliminated.

So the "golden age" is not a measure of actual crime and violence, which fluctuate wildly depending on many factors, but of public excitement over the celebrity criminal spawned by Prohibition and by the revival of banditry made possible by motor cars. The new-style, 1920s "gangster" was essentially a businessman who mocked the law through bribery and could flaunt his wealth in public, while the successful outlaw committed crimes of violence and exploited primitive police methods to avoid identification and capture. It took lawmakers more than a decade to acknowledge the failure of Prohibition, by which time the organized gangs were learning what happens to Public Enemy racketeers. The armed robbers, who had thrived on anonymity, were netted almost as soon as new police technology could put names to faces and apply the Public Enemy treatment to them.

Supreme Court Justice Charles Evans Hughes once described this country as "the greatest law-making factory the world has ever known." He might have added that some laws are more enforceable than others, and that recognition of a problem does not always mean that it has a solution.

PUBLIC ENEMIES

1

MOBSTERS VS. OUTLAWS

Using the terms *gangster* and *public enemy* to describe both Al Capone and John Dillinger reflects a fundamental misunderstanding about crime that has characterized the U.S. legal system from the start and continues to confuse lawmakers, law enforcers and the public. The confusion lies in the failure to distinguish between consensual crime and violent crime, and to recognize that the strategies for combating one are almost totally ineffective against the other.

Capone was in the business of supplying illegal goods and services to willing consumers. This is consensual crime, which involves violence only to the extent that the business is unlawful and any territorial or personal disputes between competitors require settlement "out of court." Laws against gambling, prostitution, drunkenness, drugs, private sexual acts and even illegal firearm ownership are difficult to enforce because the only complainants are the law enforcers themselves; there is no "victim" in the legal sense of the word, only customers, if the crime goes undetected. As Capone once complained, "When I sell liquor, they call it bootlegging; when my patrons serve it on silver trays on Lake Shore Drive, they call it hospitality."

Robbery, on the other hand, is by definition a violent crime from which an unconsenting victim seeks the protection of the police. Dillinger was a professional criminal who could be declared a "public enemy," but he was not a gangster in the style of Al Capone. More precisely, he was an outlaw—indeed, among the last of the outlaws—in the Jesse James tradition, a fugitive whose survival depended on avoiding recognition and capture. Bandit gangs were not business organizations but raiding parties.

So while the term *gangster* is loosely applied to both racketeers and bank robbers, this clouds the fact that the two types of crimes differ greatly in method, in the ways they threaten the community and in the kinds of laws and enforcement strategies required for their control.

That said, it's true that the criminal community in the 1920s and early '30s had not yet clearly divided into separate populations. The neighborhood bootlegger might be more an adventurer than a career criminal, but he did business with professionals, including gunmen, and some who were professional robbers also did their share of bootlegging. So whether they worked together or not, the gangsters and outlaws often knew each other socially from frequenting the same taverns and roadhouses, and from patronizing the same group of doctors, lawyers, bail bondsmen, mechanics and fences who constituted an underworld support group. Professional courtesies and services were readily exchanged, and some criminals, especially several in the Barker-Karpis gang, divided their time between armed robbery, kidnapping and working for the crime "syndicate."

The following brief biographies include both gangsters and outlaws who achieved notoriety in one type of crime or the other. But their notoriety, like the crimes listed in the chronology, more often reflected the public's perception of the crime problem than actual crime conditions. Some of the most successful bandits operated for long periods during Prohibition, when the country was preoccupied with bootleggers and beer wars and police had not yet developed effective criminal-identification systems. With Repeal and the police professionalism promoted by the FBI, national excitement

shifted to outlaws whom the Bureau could readily name and widely publicize, partly to demonstrate the inability of local police agencies to deal with interstate crime.

Ironically, it was Prohibition that hampered local crime control by closing the saloons where criminals routinely congregated, and where police and their informants could keep tabs on thieves, burglars and stickup artists without sophisticated means. And following Repeal, it was the FBI's preoccupation with interstate banditry and new law enforcement technology that enabled local racketeering to expand into nationally organized crime.

The country's first "public enemies" were organized criminals, the products of Prohibition. After Repeal and the arrival of federalized crime control, they were bank robbers whose careers were as short as they were colorful, thanks to the New Deal Justice Department and its different set of priorities. So the criminal celebrities who earned a place in the history books did not necessarily represent the type or extent of lawlessness occurring at the time they were making news.

Midwest Gangsters and Outlaws, 1919–1940

Adams, Edward J. "Eddie" (true name possibly W.J. Wallace) (1887–1921)
Probably born near Hutchinson, Kansas. Prison escapee from Missouri and Kansas, convicted murderer and bank robber. Led gang that terrorized Kansas, Missouri and Iowa with bank, store and train robberies, committing seven murders in 1921. Killed by police at Wichita, Kansas, November 22, 1921.

Aiello, Joseph (1891–1930)
Born in Castellammare del Golfo, Sicily. Chicago bootlegger, alky cooker (the urban version of moonshiner), and de facto leader of local Sicilian community whose small "kitchen" stills produced most of the raw alcohol used in the manufacture of illegal liquor, the cutting of smuggled liquor and the "needling" of legal "near beer" to bring it back to full strength.

Joe Aiello, center, periodically controlled Little Sicily on Chicago's Near Northwest Side, battling Al Capone for control the Unione Siciliana, whose members operated small home stills to produce most of the raw alcohol needed to make bogus booze, cut imported booze and "needle" so-called near beer back up to proof. Outgunned, he teamed up with neighbor Bugs Moran's North Side "Irish" who were likewise fighting Capone to retain control of Chicago's lucrative lakefront. Moran lost most of his best men in the St. Valentine's Day Massacre of 1929, and Aiello, despite plans to leave the city, died the following year in a machine-gun ambush. *(Capone's Chicago)*

Resented Capone's efforts to control the Unione Siciliana in Chicago's "Little Sicily" on the Near North Side, and so ultimately allied himself with the North Side O'Banions then controlled by George "Bugs" Moran. The refusal of national Unione head Frankie Yale in New York to support Capone's candidates for the local Unione presidency led to several killings in what became known as the "War of the Sicilian Succession" and probably was one of several factors that led to the St. Valentine's Day Massacre in 1929. Yale's murder in 1928, followed by the Massacre a few months later, left Aiello without North Side associates, and he himself was then murdered by Capone machine gunners at 205 Kolmar Avenue, Chicago, on October 23, 1930.

Alterie, Louis "Two-Gun" (true name Leland Varain) (1896–1935)

Leading member of Chicago's North Side mob in 1920s. Well-known gunman, bootlegger and labor racketeer. Originally from California, he owned ranches in Colorado, to which he would retire when Chicago got too hot. Returned to Chicago and was shot to death by unknown killers outside his apartment at 926 Eastwood Terrace, July 18, 1935.

Anselmi, Albert, and Scalise, John

Both born in Sicily. Known as the "Homicide Squad" who worked first for the Gennas and then for Capone. Suspected (along with Frankie Yale and the Gennas) of murdering Dean O'Banion and Hymie Weiss. On June 13, with Mike Genna, they killed policemen Harold Olson and Charles Walsh and wounded detective Michael Conway in a gun battle at Western Avenue and 59th Street in Chicago. Genna mortally wounded in the same battle. Anselmi and Scalise captured and acquitted in 1927, after three trials, on grounds of self-defense. Prominent West Side Italian businessmen, including Harry Spignola, Augustino and Antonio Morici, and Vito Bascone allegedly murdered for refusing to contribute to the Scalise-Anselmi defense fund. Later suspected, with many others, of participating in the St. Valentine's Day Massacre; Scalise indicted but never tried. Both found murdered, with associate Joseph "Hop Toad" Guinta, at Wolk Lake near Hammond, Indiana, May 8, 1929. First presumed to be victims of Moran revenge, the story has since been generally accepted (but never substantiated) that they were killed by Al Capone personally during a formal gang dinner at a roadhouse after he discovered their part in a plot to depose him as head of the Chicago mob.

Bailey, Harvey John (later changed to John Harvey Bailey) (1887–1979)

Born at Jane Lew, West Virginia, August 23, 1887, son of John and Amanda Bailey. Probably America's leading bank robber in 1920s. Participated in approximately two dozen large bank robberies across U.S., 1922–23, with various partners, including Killer Burke, Gus Winkeler, Verne Miller, Frank Nash, Pretty Boy Floyd, Machine Gun Kelly, Alvin Karpis, Fred Barker and Wilbur Underhill. Prime suspect in the so-called Denver Mint robbery of December 18, 1922 (actually the robbery of a Federal Reserve Bank truck parked outside the Mint), and the $2 million robbery of the Lincoln (Nebraska) National Bank & Trust Company on September 17, 1930 (Bailey always denied involvement in either of these crimes). Captured by FBI agents and police at Kansas City, Missouri, July 7, 1932. Convicted of Fort Scott, Kansas, bank robbery and sentenced to 10 to 50 years. With Wilbur Underhill, led mass breakout of 11 convicts from state prison, Lansing, Kansas, May 30, 1933. Erroneously suspected of involvement in Kansas City Massacre of June 17, 1933. Captured at Shannon ranch, near Paradise, Texas, August 12, 1933, during FBI roundup of the Urschel kidnapping gang. Escaped from Dallas (Texas) County Jail, September 4, 1933; recaptured same day at Ardmore, Oklahoma. Mistakenly convicted of involvement in Urschel kidnapping and sentenced to life in federal prisons. Served time in Leavenworth, Alcatraz and the Federal Correctional Institution at Seagoville, Texas, before being paroled on July 24, 1961. Rearrested by Kansas authorities, who still wanted him for his 1933 prison escape. Paroled, March 31, 1965. Died at Joplin, Missouri, March 1, 1979.

Barker, Arizona Donnie "Arrie" Clark (alias Kate "Ma" Barker) (1872?–1935)

Born near Ash Grove, Missouri. Mother of the notorious Barker brothers. In her later years traveled with her sons and was used by them as a cover. Killed by the FBI in a four-hour gun battle with son Fred in a house near Oklawaha, Florida, January 16, 1935. A Thompson submachine gun was found next to her body (not in her hands, as newspapers reported), but that she participated in the fight is doubtful. Some reports have her shot by Freddy himself, once it became apparent they would not be taken alive. Worried that his agents had killed somebody's mother who was thus far unknown to the general public, J. Edgar Hoover instantly publicized her as an evil genius and mastermind of the murderous Barker-Karpis gang, and her offspring the vicious criminal product of parental overindulgence. Alvin Karpis would later claim that while she knew her sons were criminals, she was too slow-witted to participate in their crimes, much less plan them.

Barker, Arthur "Dock" (or "Doc")
(1899–1939)
Born at Aurora, Missouri, June 4, 1899, to George and Ma Barker. Convicted of murder in 1922 and sentenced to life in state prison at McAlester, Oklahoma. Paroled in 1932, allegedly through bribery of state officials by gang associates. With brother Fred, Alvin Karpis and others, committed bank robberies, several murders, and ransom kidnappings of William A. Hamm, Jr., and Edward G. Bremer, 1932–34. Arrested by FBI at 432 Surf Street, Chicago, January 8, 1935, the same day G-men killed one member of the gang and captured others in Courtyard apartment building gun battle at 3912-20 North Pine Grove. Convicted of Bremer kidnapping and sentenced to life. Killed while attempting to escape from Alcatraz, January 13, 1939.

Barker, Frederick "Freddie" (1902?–1935)
Born at Aurora, Missouri, to George and Ma Barker and co-leader, with Alvin Karpis, of the Barker-Karpis gang. Paroled in 1931 from state prison at Lansing, Kansas, where he had met Alvin Karpis while serving time for burglary. Became a notorious bank and payroll robber, killer, and a kidnapper of wealthy St. Paul businessmen William Hamm and Edward Bremer. Died, with his mother, during prolonged gun battle with FBI near Oklawaha, Florida, January 16, 1935.

Barker, Herman (1893–1927)
Born at Aurora, Missouri, October 30, 1893, to George and Ma Barker. Member of Kimes-Terrill gang, leading bank burglars and bandits in the Southwest in late 1920s. Known to have murdered two law officers: Deputy Sheriff Arthur E. Osborne, near Pine Bluffs, Wyoming, August 1, 1927, and Patrolman J.E. Marshall, at Wichita, Kansas, August 29, 1927. Wounded by police and committed suicide at Wichita, August 29, 1927.

Barker, Lloyd "Red" (1896–1949)
Born at Aurora, Missouri, 1896, to George and Ma Barker. Convicted of mail robbery at Baxter Springs, Kansas, and sentenced to 25 years. at Leavenworth Federal Penitentiary beginning January 16, 1922. Paroled in 1938 (though various published accounts state that he served his full sentence). Worked as a cook at a P.O.W. camp at Ft. Custer, Michigan, during World War II; honorably discharged from the army with a good conduct medal. Later assistant manager of a bar and grill in Denver. Killed by his wife, Jennie Barker, outside their home at Westminster, Colorado, near Denver, March 18, 1949.

Barrow, Clyde Champion (true name Clyde Chestnut Barrow) (1909–1934)
Born at Teleco, Texas, March 24, 1909, the son of Henry and Cumie Barrow. Paroled from state prison at Huntsville, Texas, 1932. With girlfriend Bonnie Parker, led the Barrow gang, often called the "Bloody Barrows," a motley collection of small-time thieves who robbed grocery stores, gas stations and small banks throughout the Southwest and Midwest, murdering at least a dozen men, between 1932 and 1934. Bonnie and Clyde were betrayed by a relative of an accomplice and killed May 23, 1934, in an ambush set up by former Texas Ranger Frank Hamer on a country road between Gibsland and Sailes, Louisiana.

Barrow, Marvin Ivan "Buck" or "Ivy" (1905–1933)

Born at Teleco, Texas, March 14, 1905; older brother of Clyde Barrow and member of Barrow gang. Mortally wounded by police near Platte City, Missouri, July 19, 1933, and captured with wife, Blanche, near Dexter, Iowa, July 24. Died at Perry, Iowa, July 29, 1933.

Bentz, Edward "Eddie" Wilheim (alias Wilhelm or "Doc") (1895?–1965)

Probably born in Pipestona, South Dakota; father later killed by a runaway horse. Moved with his mother and siblings to Tacoma, Washington. Despite superior intelligence and cultural interests, Bentz spent time in a Washington reformatory for burglary while still in his teens, then graduated to safecracking and eventually took up robbery in the early 1920s (he committed up to 150 around the country without being identified). While his increasingly notorious colleagues enjoyed high-profile post-robbery sprees, he changed crime partner's frequently and lived in quiet luxury, amassing a small fortune in rare books and coins and even dabbling in legitimate business. He cased jobs thoroughly and prepared detailed getaway charts that made him a legend in the criminal community, especially as the reputed leader of Nebraska's Lincoln National Bank robbery, the largest then on record. By the time he moved to Long Beach, Indiana, in 1933, he had semi-retired and acted mostly as a consultant, but was dragged into the nearly bungled holdup of the bank in Grand Haven, Michigan, by Baby Face Nelson. Nelson, who also had moved to Long Beach, knew Bentz by reputation and at his suggestion drove to San Antonio to buy submachine guns and specially modified machine pistols from gunsmith and gunrunner

H.S. Lebman. Nelson was believed to have later killed the gang's getaway driver who had fled at the sight of a police car, causing Earl Doyle to be captured and leaving Nelson and Bentz to escape from Grand Haven in a second, planted car. Bentz's brother Theodore was wrongly identified and sentenced to prison for the robbery, but was eventually exonerated. After passage of the new federal anti-crime laws in 1934, Bentz made the mistake of robbing a bank at Caledonia, Vermont—the FBI's first "federal" bank job—and some clever sleuthing led to his arrest on March 13, 1936. Agents found him hiding in a dumbwaiter at 1492 Bushwick Avenue in Brooklyn. Supposedly he surprised them by saying he wanted to be sent to Alcatraz, "Because all my friends are there."

Bentz got his wish, but never identified his partner in the Caledonia bank holdup except as a "Smitty" from Chicago. Eventually a tip sent Chicago police looking for the elusive "Smitty," better known as Clyde Nimerick, allegedly the killer of local mob-connected sportsman and government informant Edward J. O'Hare, for whose naval aviator son, an early World War II hero, the city's O'Hare airport is named.

Birger, Charles "Charlie" (true name Shachna Itzik Birger) (1880–1928)

Born at Gambany (or Guainbainy), Russia, either January 1 or 11, in 1880 or 1883, according to different records. Colorful 1920s gang leader who fought Shelton brothers for control of bootlegging and rackets centered in "Bloody Williamson" County in southern Illinois. Their warfare was notable for its military-style use of machine guns, homemade "tanks," and even efforts (not very successful) at aerial bombing. Arrested with several members of his gang for murder in 1927. Convicted of killing Mayor Joe Adams of West City, Illinois, and sentenced to death. Hanged at Marion, Illinois, April 19, 1928.

Brady, Alfred James (Al) (1910–1937)

Born at Kentland, Indiana, October 25, 1910, and reportedly boasted he would "make John Dillinger look like a piker." With Rhuel James Dalhover and Clarence Lee Shaffer, Jr., comprised the "Brady gang," which terrorized Indiana, Ohio and Wisconsin during 1935–37 with numerous bank and store robberies and several murders. Killed with Shaffer by FBI agents and police at Bangor, Maine, October 12, 1937. (Dalhover arrested at same time; later convicted of murder and executed at Indiana state prison on November 18, 1938.)

Burke, Fred "Killer" (true name probably Thomas Camp) (1885–1940)

Reportedly born in Mapleton, Kansas. Highly professional, noted for his police impersonations and early use of submachine guns in bank robberies. A graduate of the old "Egan's Rats" gang of St. Louis and a hired killer in the employ of Al Capone during late 1920s. Wanted across United States for numerous bank and payroll robberies and some 20 murders, including the St. Valentine's Day Massacre of the Bugs Moran gang in 1929. Burke's actual participation is generally assumed, but one bank-robbing associate, Harvey Bailey, claims with annoyance that the two were actually drinking beer in Calumet City at the time of the murders, which, true or not, made him too "hot" to work with thereafter. However, Burke was indeed a Capone gunman, and the two Thompsons used in the Massacre were found in his house near St. Joseph, Michigan, when it was raided by the Berrien County Sheriffs' Department. As Fred Dane, Burke had just killed Patrolman Charles Skelly following a traffic altercation in December 1929 but managed to escape. Arrested near Green City, Missouri, March 26, 1931, on a farm rented from relatives of Harvey Bailey, Burke was extradited to Michigan, convicted of the Skelly murder and sentenced to life imprisonment, without facing trial for his alleged role in the Massacre. He had enough payoff money to live in relative luxury at the Marquette state prison, where he became fat and diabetic and died on July 10, 1940.

John Callahan (1866–1936)

Wichita, Kansas–based bootlegger and drug trafficker. For years probably the largest receiver of stolen goods in the Southwest, whose "treaty" with Wichita police made the city a safe haven for visiting outlaws. A former bank robber from horseback days, Callahan reportedly served as a Fagin figure to young apprentice criminals of later notoriety, including 1920s bank and train robber Eddie Adams and Pretty Boy Floyd, who began his career hauling booze for Callahan. Convicted of smuggling narcotics in the late twenties, he served seven years of a 25-year sentence and died at his home in Wichita, June 8, 1936.

Capone, Alphonse (Al, "Scarface") (1899–1947)

Born January 17, 1899, the son of Gabriel and Theresa Capone, in Brooklyn (not Italy, as often reported). History's most notorious mobster. Graduate of a Brooklyn faction of New York's Five Points Gang who worked as a waiter-bouncer for Frankie Yale's Harvard Inn at Coney Island in the summer of 1917, where his face was scarred in a knife attack by Frank

Galluccio, angered by Capone's flirtation with his sister. Wanted by police for an attempted murder, Capone moved to Chicago about 1919 to work for former Brooklynite and Yale associate Johnny Torrio, now managing the interests of local vice lord Big Jim Colosimo, also from Brooklyn. Following the murder of Colosimo in 1920 (probably by Yale, but sometimes attributed to Capone himself), he rose from the lowly positions of pimp and saloon bouncer to become the most powerful and prominent underworld leader of the Prohibition era—the "Babe Ruth of American Gangsters."

In partnership with Torrio, Capone forged or forced alliances with other gangs (including the Saltis-McErlane gang, who introduced the

An older and mellower Al Capone poses for pictures with his nephew, Ralph, Jr. *(Authors' collection)*

Thompson submachine gun in gang warfare) to form the Chicago Syndicate, or Outfit, which dominated bootlegging, gambling, vice, and business and labor racketeering, first on Chicago's South Side and in the town of Cicero, and eventually throughout the city and several of its suburbs. Presumed responsible for the murder of North Side gang leader Dean O'Banion in December 1924, which set off five years of gangland killings known as the Chicago Beer Wars.

Inherited leadership of the mob after Torrio was shot in retaliation in January 1925, and retired to New York. Two of O'Banion's successors were subsequently killed (Hymie Weiss by the Capone gang, and Vincent "The Schemer" Drucci by a Chicago policeman). The warfare culminated in the St. Valentine's Day Massacre of February 14, 1929, in which six North Side gang members and one visiting optometrist were lined up facing the north wall of a garage at 2122 North Clark Street and machine-gunned by Capone gangsters, some wearing police uniforms. Bugs Moran, the intended target, was not present, but the Massacre finished him as an underworld power. His chief ally, Joe Aiello, was machine-gunned by Capone's men the following year. The Massacre generated public outrage and pressure against the underworld, particularly Capone, who had been acquiring celebrity status with his colorful style and antics. Consequently, Capone found himself declared Public Enemy Number One in a stunt thought up by the Chicago Crime Commission to turn public sentiment against him. The Massacre created such political turmoil both locally and nationally that the country's principal gang leaders convened in Atlantic City in May 1929, holding what amounted to a peace conference to reestablish a degree of underworld harmony. This meeting led to agreements and alliances and procedures for the peaceful settlement of disputes, and the beginning of nationally organized crime. Upon leaving the conference, Capone and his bodyguard were arrested, probably by prearrangement, in Philadelphia. Within hours, Capone was serving his first and unexpectedly long jail sentence of one year for gun possession; and by the time he returned to Chicago he was facing the might of a federal government determined to destroy him as a symbol of underworld power. Convicted of income tax evasion on October 17, 1931, he was sentenced to 11 years in the Atlanta Federal Penitentiary, and fined $50,000, plus $30,000 in court costs. The FBI also charged Capone with contempt of federal court, as a result of his failure to appear and give testimony in a bootlegging case. Other leaders of the original Capone Syndicate were convicted of tax violations until the familiar names were no longer making headlines. Partly for that reason, partly because of Repeal, and partly because the Depression would usher in a new political philosophy and preoccupation with outlaws instead of racketeers, the Capone organization would not only endure but prosper under the leadership of Frank Nitti. Only Capone the individual was destroyed. Imprisoned first at Atlanta, he was transferred to the new federal prison on Alcatraz on August 22, 1934, and finally paroled on November 16, 1939, with mental problems resulting from untreated syphilis. He died at his palatial estate at Palm Island, Florida, January 25, 1947, eight days past his 48th birthday.

Chase, Vivian (alias Gracie Chase, Gracie Adams) (1902–1935)

Reportedly born in southern Missouri. Married in 1922 to a bank robber named George Chase, with whom she was arrested on "suspicion" charges by Kansas City, Missouri, police December 23, 1923. George Chase probably was killed about 1924. Vivian later was implicated with robbers Lee Flournoy, Lyman Ford and Charles Mayes, and bankers G.C. Robertson and Clarence R. Howard, in the prearranged robbery of the Montgomery County National Bank in Cherryvale, Kansas, May 26, 1926. She was acquitted March 14, 1928. With boyfriend Luther Jordan she robbed two banks in the Kansas City area, and was suspected of several gas station holdups during April and May of 1932. Captured with Jordan at North Kansas City, April 9, 1932, both were charged with robbing the National Bank and Trust Company there on June 7, 1932. Jordan was tried, convicted and sentenced to 25 years; Vivian escaped in October 1933 from the Clay County Jail at Liberty, Missouri, and linked up with remnants of the "Egan's Rats" gang of St. Louis and the gang of "Irish" O'Malley. With O'Malley, she allegedly masterminded the kidnapping of August Luer, a 78-year-old retired Alton, Illinois, banker and meat packer in July 1933. Luer was released unharmed and without payment of ransom when the kidnappers became concerned for his health. Most of the gang were soon apprehended. O'Malley was captured in Kansas City, May 27, 1935, pleaded guilty to kidnapping and was sentenced to life. Vivian returned to Kansas City about June 1935; although suspected of seven robberies in the area in the following months, she and a male accomplice were never

NEW YORK VS. CHICAGO

What Chicago lacked in class and understatement it made up for in a quirky combination of Midwest cornpone and ostentation. The simple business card was New York's key to a speakeasy, which inside might have a small band, gambling and booze, but outwardly looked like a respectable brownstone—sometimes compelling neighbors to post signs on their doors or sidewalk gates to the effect that "This is NOT a speakeasy."

Chicago, on the other hand, might stop short of putting a large beer sign out front, but otherwise blatantly advertised its places of booze, dancing and floor shows in entertainment guides, complete with goofy typography, dancing cooks and singing waiters, and euphemisms like "Bottle Goods and Special Drinks not listed." It saw nothing inconsistent in combining a barnyard theme with a "Monsieur François" to add what Midwesterners might think was a touch of class. The *New Yorker*'s trademark character Eustace Tilly, the foppish dandy who makes his appearance on the magazine's cover once a year, would never have visited Chicago voluntarily and could not have been forced into Bert Kelly's Stables except at gunpoint. If wearing his standard *New Yorker* outfit, he might have passed for one of the entertainers. But as a prospective customer he would have been the butt of jokes, beaten up, thrown out, or all three, and hurried back to Gotham happy that the only souvenir of his

In Chicago, and probably elsewhere, a few "soft drink parlors" actually sold soft drinks, but the term became the telephone directory euphemism for onetime taverns and saloons, which sold "near beer" over the counter and real beer or hard liquor from under it. Usually unlisted were the protected speakeasies, and the even less formal "beer flats," which moved around like floating crap games. *(Author's collection)*

apprehended. She was found bound with rope and shot to death in a parked car outside St. Luke's Hospital in Kansas City, November 3, 1935.

Colbeck, William P. "Dint" or "Dinty"
Early 1920s boss of "Egan's Rats," notorious St. Louis bootlegging and robbery gang, graduates of which included St. Valentine's Day

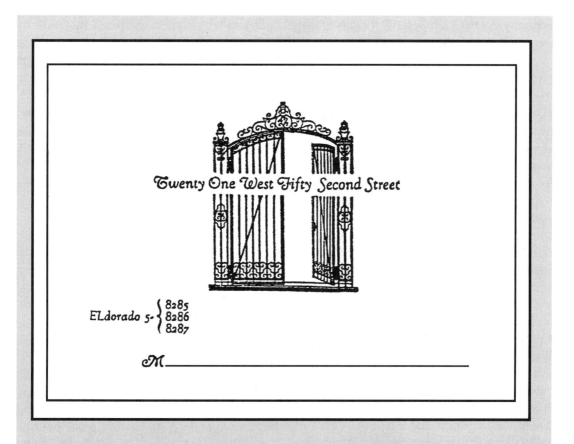

Twenty One West Fifty Second Street

ELdorado 5- {
8285
8286
8287
}

Chicago visit was a bullet hole fired in sport through his top hat.

By the same token, few Chicagoans would have had a clue to how to find, gain entrance to, or comport themselves in a New York "speak"; they would probably have gawked like hayseed tourists, or otherwise embarrassed the regulars until politely asked to leave. New York gave rise to the "nightclub," which operated more or less discreetly in place of the hotel or auditorium ballroom. Chicago had huge ballrooms, too, but also "joints" with jazz bands, South Side black-and-tan clubs where "race mixing" was customary, and grubby "beer flats" and taverns where many carried pistols unless the management insisted that they be checked at the door.

Massacre suspects Fred "Killer" Burke, Gus Winkeler and Claude Maddox. Convicted of Staunton, Illinois, mail robbery, November 1924, and sentenced to 25 years in federal prison. Convicted of St. Louis mail robbery, January 1825 and sentenced to 15 years. Paroled in 1941. Victim of machine-gun murder —by then a rare occurrence—in St. Louis on

February 17, 1943, supposedly for muscling in on gambling operations in southern Illinois.

Colosimo, James "Big Jim" (1878–1920)

Born in Cosenza, Italy. Came to America in 1895 with his father Luigi, passing through Brooklyn where they had relatives and settling in the old Levee district on Chicago's Near South Side where vice abounded. As bagman for notoriously corrupt aldermen "Bathhouse John" Coughlin and "Hinky Dink" Kenna, young James made the acquaintance of a homely but prosperous madam who liked his style and decide the two had a future together. Soon James was Big Jim Colosimo, vice lord of the Levee, whose riches from prostitution and gambling permitted him to refine his tastes. In 1910 he opened Chicago's most opulent nightclub, Colosimo's Cafe, at 2126 South Wabash, which featured the best entertainment and the best clientele, who enjoyed the excitement of rubbing shoulders with some of the most prominent criminals in the city. When threatened by Black Hand extortionists, Colosimo sent to Brooklyn for a quietly tough relative, John Torrio, whose suave manners belied his efficiency at killing his uncle's tormentors. Torrio became manager of Colosimo's vice empire and was shopping for an assistant when he learned that a young scar-faced hoodlum from back home needed a new start in life. Meanwhile, Big Jim had outgrown the frumpy wife who had sponsored his early enterprises and dumped her for a beautiful young songbird named Dale Winter, then performing at his cafe. While recapturing his lost youth, Big Jim not only left Torrio and Capone in charge of his vice empire but displayed no interest in the vast opportunities presented by Prohibition. Love smitten, he married Dale, and barely two weeks later, on May 11, 1920, was found shot to death in the vestibule of his cafe. Police initially suspected the brothers of the wife who had been scorned, divorced and generally humiliated, but their discovery that Frankie Yale happened to be in town persuaded most that he had been summoned by Torrio and Capone, who soon expanded Big Jim's local operations into a bootlegging and racketeering empire of a magnitude the country had never imagined possible.

Daugherty, Roy (alias "Arkansas Tom" Jones) (1870–1924)

Last survivor of the 1890s Bill Doolin gang of Oklahoma train and bank robbers. After serving prison sentences for murder and bank burglary, resumed his criminal career until killed by police in Joplin, Missouri, August 18, 1924.

Dillinger, John Herbert (1903–1934)

Born in Indianapolis, Indiana, June 22, 1903, the son of Molly and John Wilson Dillinger. Most notorious as well as glamorous of all the Depression outlaws and the only one besides Pretty Boy Floyd to acquire some of the folk-hero status enjoyed by Jesse James. After Dillinger's release from the state prison at Michigan City, Indiana, in May 1933, his criminal career lasted only 14 months but captured the public's imagination, and his exploits did much to both popularize and embarrass the FBI. He robbed at least a dozen banks, was blamed for dozens more, raided police stations for guns, shot his way out of police and FBI traps, was twice captured and escaped. His use of a wooden pistol to bluff his way out of the supposedly escape-proof jail in Crown Point, Indiana, stealing the woman sheriff's car in the process, guaranteed him a permanent place in American criminal history—even if the escape was later revealed to have been facilitated with bribes. He was set up by former Indiana madam Anna Sage, "the woman in red," who expected to collect the reward money and avoid deportation on morals charges. New evidence reveals Dillinger attorney Louis Piquett already knew Mrs. Sage, and sent Dillinger to stay with her. All were well acquainted with the northern Indiana criminal community. Seeing her chance, she contacted friends in the East Chicago Police Department, who contacted the FBI and insisted on participating in the ambush to make sure Dillinger was killed so he wouldn't learn of their betrayal and expose their corruption. He was shot from behind on the night of July 22, 1934, as he left the Chicago's Biograph Theatre on Lincoln Avenue in the company of Anna Sage and his girlfriend Polly Hamilton, after watching the Clark Gable gangster movie *Manhattan Melodrama.* Contrary to the usual accounts, Dillinger met Polly through Sage instead of the other way around. She was not in on the setup; Piquett may have been, and had made a point of being out of the city when Dillinger was shot.

Drucci, Vincent "The Schemer" (true name Di Ambrosio or D'Ambrosio) (1895–1927)

Succeeded Dean O'Banion and Hymie Weiss as leader of Chicago's North Side gang. Shot during a police raid on his office, he recovered and refused to press charges. Killed April 4, 1927, in the backseat of a police car en route to headquarters for questioning, by a policeman who claimed Drucci had tried to disarm him.

Durkin, James Martin "Marty" (1901–1981)

Born in Chicago, Marty Durkin committed many minor crimes before going into car theft in a big way, shooting it out with police when necessary and acquiring notoriety in the process.

Before hooking up with ex-con Ed Singleton to attempt—and bungle—his first holdup of a Mooresville grocer, which landed him in prison, John Dillinger (standing behind the batboy) regularly played on local baseball teams and, even as a notorious fugitive, insisted on attending Chicago Cubs games, to the dismay of his lawyer, Louis Piquett, whom he'd sometimes encounter and wave at, shouting "Hi, Counselor!" *(Author's collection)*
Inset: Early in his life, John Dillinger showed signs of wanting to settle down. He met and married Beryl Hovious (pictured here for the first time), who expected to be decently supported and was probably a factor in the commission of her husband's first serious crime—the bungled attempt with ex-con Ed Singleton to rob a Mooresville, Indiana, grocer, who after closing up for the day was walking to a nearby bank. *(Authors' collection)*

On October 11, 1925, in a garage at 6237 Princeton Avenue, he shot and killed federal agent Edward C. Shanahan, then escaped after another shoot-out in Chicago and was finally captured on January 20, 1926, by federal agents and local detectives on a train coming into St. Louis. Convicted in two Chicago trials of killing Shanahan and of interstate car theft, he received sentences totaling 50 years but avoided the death penalty partly because Shanaham, the first Justice Department agent to die in the line of duty, had not identified himself.

Fleagle, William Harrison "Jake" (1890–1930)

Born in Iowa but moved at an early age to Garden City, Kansas. Leader of the notorious Fleagle gang of bank robbers who committed several large holdups in the Midwest and West, but were not identified until the spectacular $200,000 robbery of the First National Bank at Lamar, Colorado, May 23, 1928, in which four men were killed. Fleagle was shot and mortally wounded by police and postal inspectors while boarding a train at Branson, Missouri, October 14, 1930, and died the next day at Springfield, Missouri.

Floyd, Charles Arthur "Pretty Boy" (1904–1934)

Born Adairsville, Georgia, February 3, 1904, the son of Walter and Mamie Floyd. Colorful outlaw regarded as something of a Robin Hood figure in his adopted state of Oklahoma, but elsewhere considered a dangerous career criminal. Accused of 10 murders and approximately 40 bank robberies. Convicted of highway robbery in Missouri in 1925, and sentenced to five years in the state prison at Jefferson City. Convicted of bank robbery in Ohio but escaped December 10, 1930, from a train taking him to prison. Accused by the FBI of participating in the Kansas City Massacre of June 17, 1933, but some historians remain unconvinced. Also known as the Union Station Massacre, this was an unsuccessful attempt to free captured bank and train robber Frank Nash from police custody at the railroad station in Kansas City. Killed in the shooting were FBI agent Raymond Caffrey, an Oklahoma police chief, two Kansas City police detectives and Nash himself. The other attackers were alleged to be Adam Richetti, Floyd's chief crime partner at the time, and Verne Miller, a Kansas City gunman and bank robber considered an associate of Nash. Floyd was killed by FBI agents on a farm near Clarkson, Ohio, October 22, 1934, while fleeing across a field, according to the official version. Another version, told by former East Liverpool, Ohio, police officer Chester Smith in 1974, was that the wounded and disabled Floyd was simply "executed" by another FBI agent on orders from Melvin Purvis, when he refused to talk. The last surviving FBI agent declares the story false, as might be expected. According to the widow of a gangster who knew several of the criminals involved and robber Harvey Bailey, Pretty Boy was in fact one of the gunmen, along with Verne Miller, but Richetti, although captured and executed for the crime, was actually innocent—for the simple reason that a night of excessive drinking had left him too hungover to participate. While the death of Nash is usually ascribed to bad shooting by the attackers, new evidence indicates that the battle began when a federal agent sitting behind Nash killed him and probably two other officers while trying to work the action of an unfamiliar shotgun.

Genna brothers

Six brothers from Marsala, Sicily, known as the "Terrible Gennas," whose South Side gang controlled a large community of alky cookers, as they were called in the city, operating small stills in their homes and apartments. Originally allies of Torrio and Capone, the Gennas became a liability when their territorial disputes with the North Side O'Banion gang led to the murder of O'Banion and open conflict between the North Siders and the Torrio-Capone Syndicate. "Bloody Angelo" Genna was murdered by O'Banion's successors, the Weiss-Drucci-Moran gang, May 25, 1925. Mike "The Devil" Genna was fatally shot by police who interrupted another gang battle, June 13, 1925. Tony "The Gentleman" Genna was murdered, allegedly by a disgruntled gang member named Giuseppe Nerone, July 8, 1925. The remaining Gennas (Sam, Pete and Jim) all fled Chicago and went into hiding. They eventually returned but retired from the rackets. Capone inherited the services of John Scalise and Albert Anselmi, two murderous torpedoes allegedly imported from Sicily by the Gennas.

Guzik, Jake "Greasy Thumb" (1887–1956)

Former pimp who became gambling boss, chief accountant and treasurer for the Capone Syndicate. Served short sentence for income tax evasion in 1930s. Died of natural causes, February 21, 1956.

Hamilton, Raymond (Ray) (1913–1935)

Born near Schulter, Oklahoma, May 21, 1913, the son of John H. and Alice Hamilton. Sometime partner of Clyde Barrow, Hamilton also pursued his own career as a major bank robber and jailbreaker. Captured at Bay City, Michigan, December 5, 1932; convicted of murder and several robberies, and sentenced to 263 years at Eastham, Texas, prison farm. Using guns planted by Bonnie and Clyde, killed a prison guard and escaped from a road gang with Joe Palmer and others on January 16, 1934. Recaptured near Howe, Texas, April 25, 1934. Convicted of murder and sentenced to death along with Joe Palmer, the two again obtained smuggled pistols and managed to escape from the Texas state prison's death house on July 22, 1934, the same date John Dillinger was killed by federal agents in Chicago. Recaptured at Grapevine, Texas, April 6, 1935, and, with Palmer, executed on May 10.

Holden, Thomas James (Tommy) (1896–1953)

With partner Francis Keating, robbed U.S. mail train of $135,000 at Evergreen Park, Illinois, in 1926. Both convicted of mail robbery and sentenced to 25 years. Received at Leavenworth in 1928, both escaped on February 28, 1930. Over the next two years they committed a series of major bank robberies in the Midwest, usually in partnership with Harvey Bailey, Frank Nash, George "Machine Gun" Kelly, Verne Miller, Fred Barker and Alvin Karpis. Captured with Keating and Bailey at Old Mission Golf Course, Kansas City, Missouri, July 7, 1932. Returned to Leavenworth; later transferred to Alcatraz. Paroled November 28, 1947. Murdered his wife, Lillian, and her two brothers, at their Chicago apartment, June 5, 1949, and again became a fugitive. First man named to FBI's "Ten Most Wanted," list March 14, 1950. Captured by FBI at Beaverton, Oregon, June 23, 1951. Convicted of murder and sentenced to life in the Illinois state prison at Joliet, where he died on December 18, 1953.

Humphreys, Murray "The Camel" (true name Llewelyn Morris Humphreys) (1899–1965)

Robber and kidnapper who became a prominent labor racketeer for the Capone Syndicate. For years he remained top-ranking member of the Chicago mob, and was sometimes regarded as Capone's successor. Died of natural causes, Chicago, November 23, 1965.

Jones, Ezra Milford (1896–1932)

Milford Jones, despite his frail looks and schoolboy face, was a graduate of the "Egan's Rats" and Cuckoo gangs of East St. Louis, Illinois, and so well connected with both politicians and powerful gambling interests that he exceeded the notorious Fred "Killer" Burke in his murdering and other lawbreaking but avoided attracting the notoriety he richly deserved. He worked "snatching" other gangsters for ransom and killing for hire, and between 1913 and 1927 he was arrested some 130 times by St. Louis police for everything from bank robbery to rape, but spent only a few months in prison for a holdup. He had a special animosity for Italian mobsters, murdering many and kidnapping many others to Detroit, where he and Burke moved their "snatch racket." He continued feuding with the Italians until they shot him to death in a speakeasy on January 15, 1932.

Karpis, Alvin "Old Creepy" (true name Francis Albin Karpaviecz) (1908–1979)

Born Montreal, Canada, August 10, 1908, the son of John and Anna Karpaviecz (FBI spelling). Co-leader, with Fred Barker, of the Barker-Karpis gang. Burglar, bank, mail and train robber. Obtained a total of $300,000 in ransom money from the kidnapping of two wealthy St. Paul businessmen—William A. Hamm, Jr., on June 15, 1933, and Edward G. Bremer, on January 17, 1934. From 1931 to 1936, Karpis and his partners stole over a million dollars and killed approximately 10 men. Captured by FBI director J. Edgar Hoover in New Orleans, May 1, 1936 (Karpis later claimed he was disarmed and held at gunpoint by federal agents so Hoover could arrest him personally). Pleaded guilty to Hamm kidnapping and sentenced to life in federal penitentiary. Spent 33 years in prison, mostly on Alcatraz. Paroled January 14, 1969, and deported to Canada. Moved to Spain in 1973 and died in the town of Torremolinos on August 26, 1979, from an overdose (possibly accidental) of sleeping pills. Collaborated on two books, *The Alvin Karpis Story* (1971), published in Canada under the title *Public Enemy No. 1,* and *On the Rock* (1980).

Kelly, George "Machine Gun" (true name George F. Barnes, Jr.) (1900–1954)

Born in Chicago, July 17, 1900 (not July 18, 1895, as often reported), the son of George and Elizabeth Kelly Barnes. Moved at an early age to Memphis, Tennessee, and briefly attended the University of Mississippi. Despite a good family background, Kelly dabbed in bootlegging and was arrested for smuggling liquor onto an Indian reservation. He later committed several bank robberies without attracting much attention and might have remained an obscure, small-time criminal but for a weakness for "wilder" kinds of women. A particularly attractive one named Kathryn became his wife and introduced him to friends with criminal records and inclinations. With them he participated in a sensational $200,000 kidnapping of Oklahoma City oilman Charles F. Urschel on July 22, 1933. The FBI quickly captured all the gang members but the Kellys, whose reputations grew—or were exaggerated by the Justice Department—far out of proportion to their dangerousness or criminal histories. The two were captured without incident by police and FBI agents at Memphis, Tennessee, September 26, 1933 (the same day 10 inmates escaped from the Indiana State Prison using guns supplied by John Dillinger). It became official FBI legend that Kelly coined the Bureau's enduring nickname when, confronted by federal agents, he supposedly cried, "Don't shoot, G-men!" although local newspaper accounts don't bear this out. Convicted on October 12, 1933, Kelly received a life sentence, and was transferred from Leavenworth to Alcatraz in September 1934. He was returned to Leavenworth in 1951, and died there of a heart attack on July 18, 1954.

Kimes, Matthew (Matt) (1906–1945)
Co-leader, with Ray Terrill, of the Kimes-Terrill gang, major bank robbers in the Southwest and Midwest during the 1920s who allegedly swore a blood oath to free any captured gang members or die trying. Their more memorable deeds included robbing two banks in one day, and winching bank safes onto stolen trucks. Captured near Rudy, Arkansas, August 28, 1926. Convicted of murdering Deputy Perry Chuculate at Sallisaw, Oklahoma, and sentenced to 35 years. Gang rescued Kimes from the Sallisaw jail, November 21, 1926, but he was recaptured at the Grand Canyon in Arizona, June 24, 1927. Retried for Chuculate slaying and received a sentence of death that was later reduced to life imprisonment. Received another life sentence for the murder of Marshal J.N. McAnally at Beggs, Oklahoma. Granted a leave of absence in 1945, he allegedly robbed a bank at Merton, Texas, only to be run over by a truck at North Little Rock, Arkansas, on December 1, 1945. Died two weeks later in a Little Rock hospital.

Klutas, Theodore "Handsome Jack" (1900?–1934)
Attended University of Illinois and sometimes worked for Capone. In 1930s led the "College Kidnappers," a Chicago-area gang that specialized in kidnapping underworld figures for ransom. Betrayed by a member of his gang and killed by police at Bellwood, Illinois, January 6, 1934.

Lamm, Hermann K. "Baron" (1890?–1930)
Reportedly a former Prussian army officer who immigrated to U.S. and became a bank robber. Served a term in Utah state prison, then successfully robbed banks across the country in 1920s. Killed by a posse, near Sidell, Illinois, December 16, 1930, following a robbery at Clinton, Indiana. Two survivors of Lamm's gang, Walter Dietrich and James "Oklahoma Jack" Clark, served time in Indiana with John Dillinger, who adopted Lamm's system of carefully casing banks well in advance of a robbery and planning escape routes using detailed notes and practice runs.

Lazia, John (1897–1934)
Boss of North Side Italian mob in Kansas City and politically affiliated with Tom Pendergast's Democratic machine. Allegedly furnished the machine guns used in the Kansas City Massacre. Killed outside the Park Central Hotel at 300 East Boulevard on July 10, 1934, with one of the same machine guns, according to ballistics tests.

McErlane, Frank (1894–1932)

Chicago-born co-leader, with Polack Joe Saltis, of the Saltis-McErlane gang, bootleggers who were allied at times with Al Capone. Once shot a lawyer in a Crown Point, Indiana, tavern as a display of marksmanship, but murder charge was dropped after the key witness was found clubbed to death. Apparently murdered his own mistress, Elfrieda Rigus, along with her two dogs, who were found in his car at 8129 Phillips Avenue, on October 8, 1931. Case dismissed to lack of evidence. The alcoholic gangster had health as well as mental problems, was considered dangerously demented even by underworld standards, and died of pneumonia in a Beardstown, Illinois, hospital, October 8, 1932.

McErlane was evidently the first to introduce the Thompson submachine gun in gangland warfare in an unsuccessful effort to kill bootlegging rival Edward "Spike" O'Donnell who had invaded Saltis-McErlane territory on Chicago's South Side. In a classic drive-by shooting at the busy corner of Western Avenue and 63rd Street on September 25, 1925, a machine gunner aiming at O'Donnell missed him but took out the plate-glass windows of a large drugstore. That attack and two others in quick succession caused the Capone gang and soon others to acquire the new weapon, possession

Frank McErlane's life was such a stormy one that it's hard to imagine him teaming up with Polack Joe Saltis or anyone else. He had a tacit alliance with Capone forces on Chicago's South Side, but when his territory was encroached on by Spike O'Donnell and his brothers (the South Side O'Donnells, as opposed to Klondike O'Donnell and his West Side O'Donnell brothers), he evidently borrowed one of the new Thompson submachine guns that Dean O'Banion had discovered on a trip to Colorado and went to war. Nor was McErlane's domestic life peaceful. He drank too much of what he sold, and his girlfriend, Elfrieda Rigus (often spelled Elfreda, but she preferred the name Marion Miller), put a bullet in his leg during one of their quarrels. While recuperating in traction, his hospital room was invaded by rivals bent on finishing the job, but McErlane also had a pistol and the hospital's normal tranquility was shattered by a gun battle. After his release, with three additional but minor wounds, he killed Elfrieda as well as her two pet dogs, leaving the bodies in his car. Police once arrested him for firing a shotgun at imaginary foes on Chicago's South Shore Drive. In 1932 he was back in a hospital, where he died in a state of pneumonia-induced delerium. *(Authors' collection)*

Frank McErlane's mistress/wife, Elfrieda Rigus, aka Marion Miller, shot to death, along with her two dogs, in the back of McErlane's car. Chicagoans were more upset by the killing of the dogs than of Elfrieda. *(Goddard Collection)*

of which was in fact legal because it did not violate the city's concealable-weapon law. The use of machine guns helped make Chicago the "gangster capital of the world."

McGurn, "Machine Gun" Jack (true name Vincenzo or Vincent Gebardi, possibly changed from Gibaldi, but also used James DeMora or DeMory, the name of his stepfather) (1904–1936)

Al Capone's chief lieutenant, bodyguard and torpedo, and a prime suspect in the St. Valentine's Day Massacre. Indicted but never tried due to lack of evidence. Frustrated authorities later convicted both him and his girlfriend, Louise Rolfe (his "blond alibi" for the Massacre), of conspiring to violate the Mann Act by transporting themselves across state lines for "immoral purposes." The convictions were eventually reversed by the U.S. Supreme Court, which found that the law did not anticipate a woman conspiring to victimize herself. Thus McGurn's conspiracy conviction had to be voided as well for lack of a co-conspirator. McGurn fell on hard times after Capone went to prison, and was shot to death in a bowling alley at 805 Milwaukee in Chicago, just after midnight on February 15, 1936, probably on orders of Frank Nitti, who killed several potential rivals for leadership of the Chicago Syndicate. Years later, an FBI wiretap on Murray "The Camel" Humphreys as he talked about the good old days, revealed that one of the shooters was Claude Maddox, once a close associate whose Circus Cafe on North Avenue was found to have been the staging area for the 1929 Massacre.

Miller, Vernon C. (Verne or Vern) (1896?–1933)

Former South Dakota sheriff and convicted embezzler turned gangster, bootlegger, bank robber and professional killer. Hired to rescue Frank Nash in what became the Kansas City Massacre. Regarded as a trigger-happy psychopath. According to a statement later given to the FBI by Machine Gun Kelly, it was Miller, on a mission of personal revenge, rather than Capone or other gangsters, who shoved a machine gun through the back window of Manning's resort hotel near the Wisconsin border and killed or wounded several bootleggers in the so-called Fox Lake Massacre in 1930, although some accounts suggest he and others were paid. Shunned by former associates, Miller was found murdered near Detroit, November 29, 1933, probably by Longy Zwillman's New Jersey mob who had harbored him following the Kansas City Massacre until he allegedly killed one of them in the course of an argument.

George "Bugs" Moran inherited leadership of the North Siders following the deaths of Dean O'Banion, Vincent "Schemer" Drucci and Earl "Hymie" Weiss. He was presumably the main target in the St. Valentine's Day Massacre of 1929, but Capone lookouts across the street mistook him for another gang member and summoned the machine gunners prematurely, or the body count (including the two men with him) would have been 10. *(Authors' collection)*

Moran, George Clarence "Bugs" (1893–1957)

Reportedly born in St. Paul to Julius and Diana Moran, sometimes using Gage as an alias. Moran was the last of Chicago's North Siders to oppose Al Capone, but the St. Valentine's Day Massacre and the murder of Joseph Aiello a year later left him without a gang and without allies, and his criminal career quickly spiraled downward to burglary, theft and other small-time offenses. Finally convicted of bank robbery in 1946, he was sentenced to 25 years at Leavenworth, where he died of cancer on February 25, 1957.

Murphy, Timothy "Big Tim" (1886–1928)

One-time Illinois legislator turned big-time labor racketeer. Allegedly masterminded $385,000 mail train robbery at Chicago's Polk Street station on April 6, 1921. Convicted and sentenced to six years in Leavenworth, Murphy claimed he was framed by William Fahy, the "ace" postal inspector who sometimes solved cases in just this manner and was himself later convicted of being the inside man on the $2 million Rondout train robbery in 1924. Big Tim became a major figure in Chicago gambling and bootlegging, and attempted to take over the Cleaners and Dyers Union. Machine-gunned, probably by Capone gangsters, outside his home at 2525 West Morse on June 26, 1928.

Nash, Frank "Jelly" (1887–1933)

Bank and train robber with Al Spencer gang in 1920s. Convicted of mail robbery, 1924, and sentenced to 25 years in Leavenworth. Escaped in 1930 and worked with Barker-Karpis gang and others. Recaptured at Hot Springs, Arkansas, June 16, 1933; killed the next day in Kansas City Massacre.

Nelson, George "Baby Face"; Jimmy
Williams; etc (true name Lester Joseph Gillis,
although the FBI repeatedly listed him as
Lester M. Gillis on wanted posters) (1908–1934)
Born in Chicago at 942 North California on
December 6, 1908, son of Joseph and Mary
Gillis. Car thief, bootlegger, bank robber; escaped from train en route to state prison at
Joliet, Illinois; later associated with John Dillinger. Close to several rising Chicago mobsters
and may have occasionally worked as a syndicate gunman. Killed several men, including
three FBI agents during his brief and bloody
career. Mortally injured in battle with federal
agents at Barrington, Illinois, November 27,
1934, but escaped with wife and accomplice
and reached the house of friends in Niles Center
(now Skokie), where he died a few hours later
from his 17 wounds. His body was found the
next day, wrapped in a blanket and lying in the
grass at the northeast corner of St. Paul's cemetery not far away.

Newton brothers
Originally cowboys and ranchers from Uvalde,
Texas, Willis, Jess, William ("Dock") and Joe
Newton became experts at robbing trains and
looted as many as 80 small banks in Texas and
neighboring states, usually without violence,
between 1914 and 1924. On June 12, 1924, they
joined some hoodlums from Chicago and St.
Louis in committing the largest, and one of the
last, train robberies in U.S. history when they
commandeered the Chicago, Milwaukee & St.
Paul mail train near Rondout, Illinois, making
off with over $2 million. The perfectly executed
crime failed when one of the brothers was mistakenly shot by a fellow robber, and Chicago
police, responding to reports of a wounded
man, captured him and one of the ringleaders,

a politician-bootlegger named James Murray,
whose "inside man" on the job was none other
than "ace" postal inspector and bandit-catcher
William J. Fahy, now suspected of framing Chicago's Big Tim Murphy for an earlier train job.
The wounded Newton survived, and, with
Murray, traded much of the hidden loot for
shortened sentences. Surviving injuries and
their prison terms, the brothers thereafter went
straight, although "Dock" Newton came out of
retirement at age 77 and robbed the bank at
Rowena, Texas (incidentally the hometown of
Bonnie Parker), in 1968. He was shot and spent
a few months in a prison hospital before entering a nursing home, where he died in 1974. Jess
Newton had already died of lung cancer in
1960, and Willis and Joe Newton lived without
further criminal excitement until 1979 and
1989, respectively.

Nitti, Frank "The Enforcer" (true name
Francesco Raffele Nitto) (1889–1943)
Born in Augori, Italy, January 27, 1889. After
Capone's imprisonment in 1931, Nitti conspired with friends to kill several rivals in his
own mob and emerge as head of the Chicago
Syndicate in the middle 1930s. Involved in
post-Prohibition racketeering, he was indicted
in a movie extortion case that would probably
have sent him to prison. Facing that prospect
and reportedly suffering from cancer, he committed suicide on March 19, 1943.

O'Banion, Charles Dean (often spelled Dion
—his baptismal name— O'Bannion) (1892–1924)
Born at Maroa (not Aurora, as usually reported), Illinois, July 8, 1892, the son of Charles
and Emma O'Banion. Split with Torrio and
Capone in the early '20s to become independent
leader of Chicago's North Side gang, which was

considered Irish, though more in attitude than in fact. Safecracker, bootlegger and hijacker alleged to have killed a dozen or more. Operated out of Schofield's flower shop at 738 North State Street, directly across from the Holy Name Cathedral, controlling the wealthy "Gold Coast" and northern lakefront neighborhoods. Personal contempt for the South Side Italians led him to swindle Torrio in a brewery deal—a scheme cooked up by his buddy Hymie Weiss —which led to Torrio's arrest and imprisonment as a second-time violator of the Volstead law. In retaliation, O'Banion was killed in his flower shop on November 10, 1924, in the famous "handshake murder," probably by New York gangster Frankie Yale, suspected of killing Big Jim Colosimo four years earlier, also as a favor to Torrio and Capone, former Brooklyn colleagues. This was the first murder of a major gang chieftain and set off five years of "beer wars" between the different bootlegging factions, represented mainly by the Capone interests and O'Banion's successors, until the North Siders were routed in the St. Valentine's Day Massacre of 1929.

Oberta, John "Dingbat" (1903–1930)

Bootlegger and gunman for Saltis-McErlane gang, sometimes spelling his name O'Berta when it suited him to sound Irish. Married widow of Big Tim Murphy. Murdered with bodyguard Sam Malaga, Chicago, March 6, 1930.

O'Connor, Thomas "Terrible Tommy" (1886–?)

Notorious Chicago robber and murderer convicted in October 1921 of killing a policeman. Sentenced to hang on December 15, but escaped from Cook County Jail just prior to exe-

cution and was never recaptured. Presumed to have fled back to his native Ireland.

Parker, Bonnie (1910–1934)

Born in Rowena, Texas, October 1, 1910, the daughter of J.T. and Emma Parker. Married hoodlum Roy Thornton, who ended up in prison. Became girlfriend and accomplice of Clyde Barrow, given to writing inspired doggerel and having snapshots taken of herself and Clyde clowning around with guns. Despite her petite size (under 100 pounds, and Clyde barely 150), the two typically relied on relatively heavy Browning Automatic Rifles (the BAR) stolen from National Guard armories and sometimes cut down, instead of the smaller and lighter Thompson. Regarded by other outlaws of the day as two-bit killers and robbers of gas stations and grocery stores, and glamorized mainly as a boy-and-girl bandit team. Died with Barrow in a roadside ambush by Texas and Louisiana peace officers near Sailes, Louisiana, May 23, 1934.

Remus, George (1876?–1952)

Born in Germany and settled in Chicago, where he obtained a license to practice law before moving to Cincinnati in 1920. There he organized drug companies to obtain huge supplies of "medicinal spirits" from bonded warehouses, dispensed graft to hundreds of officials, and became known as "King of the Bootleggers" because of the size of his operations. Served short prison term during 1926–27 for violation of Volstead Act. On October 6, 1927, shot and killed his estranged wife Imogene, who had left him for Franklin Dodge, a federal agent instrumental in Remus's conviction. Tried for murder and acquitted by reason of insanity. Briefly institutionalized. Died at Covington, Kentucky, January 20, 1952.

Richetti, Adam "Eddie" (1909?–1938)

Oklahoma bank robber and partner of "Pretty Boy" Floyd. Only man convicted for Kansas City Massacre, on entirely circumstantial evidence. Captured by police near Wellsville, Ohio, October 21, 1934, and sentenced to death for the killing of Kansas City police detective Frank Hermanson, one of the Massacre victims who in fact was probably shot accidentally by the same federal agent who killed prisoner Frank Nash in the gun battle. Died in gas chamber at Missouri state prison, October 7, 1938, protesting that this was one crime of which he was innocent because he had stayed up all night drinking and was too hungover to participate.

Saltis, Joseph "Polack Joe" (also spelled Soltis) (1894–1947)

Co-leader, with Frank McErlane, of Southwest Side Chicago bootlegging gang allied with Al Capone. Regarded as a violent thug who supposedly had once clubbed a woman to death for refusing to sell his beer in her ice cream parlor. Amassed a considerable fortune and retired to a resort estate at Barker Lake, Wisconsin, but died a pauper at the county hospital in Chicago in August 1947.

Sankey, Verne (1890–1934)

Former Canadian Pacific railroad employee and South Dakota rancher became one of the country's most wanted criminals in 1933–34. With partner Gordon Alcorn, reportedly robbed several banks in U.S. and Canada before kidnapping Haskell Bohn, son of a St. Paul refrigerator manufacturer on June 30, 1932. Demanded only $35,000 in ransom and re-

leased Bohn unharmed after payment of $12,000. Kidnapped Denver millionaire Charles Boettcher II, February 12, 1933, transporting him to Sankey's turkey ranch near Chamberlain, South Dakota, and releasing him unharmed upon payment of $60,000 ransom. Wrongly suspected of Hamm and Bremer kidnappings, which were carried out by the Barker-Karpis gang. Arrested by police and FBI agents at a Chicago barbershop January 31, 1934. Removed to South Dakota to trial in the Boettcher kidnapping and held in the state prison at Great Falls, where he hanged himself with his necktie on the night of February 8, 1934. Sankey's partner, Alcorn, was captured in Chicago on February 2, 1934, and received a life sentence.

Seadlund, John Henry (alias Peter Anders) (1910–1938)

Born in Ironton, Minnesota, and spent his youth drinking, hunting, fishing and stealing until he had a chance encounter with Tommy Carroll of the Dillinger gang in March 1934. Briefly harbored Carroll in a fisherman's cabin near Ironton and afterward aspired to become a major criminal. Committed several small holdups of stores, gas stations and taverns in St. Paul and Brainerd, Minnesota, and was captured near Brainerd in July 1934. Escaped from Crow Wing County Jail in Brainerd on July 25, 1934. Led the life of a hobo, petty thief, drug addict and occasional lumberjack, but managed to rob banks in Milltown and Eagle River, Wisconsin, and in Shakopee, Minnesota. Briefly owned a lumber camp near Spokane, Washington, but remained dedicated to crime, sensible and otherwise. With partner James Atwood Gray, plotted to kidnap major league baseball players for ransom. When this proved unfeasible, they instead kidnapped Olive Borcia, wife of a

Chicago nightclub owner, near Lake Geneva, Wisconsin, on September 2, 1937. Unable to collect the ransom, they released Mrs. Borcia on her promise that her husband would later pay $2,000. On September 25, 1937, Seadlund and Gray kidnapped retired businessman Charles S. Ross on Wolf Road, near Chicago, demanding a ransom of $50,000. Seadlund collected the money but then murdered both his accomplice and Ross, concealing their bodies at the place of Ross's captivity, an underground pit in a wooded area near Spooner, Wisconsin. Seadlund buried $30,000 of the money and exchanged some of the rest for clean bills at the betting windows of racetracks. Arrested by federal agents at the Santa Anita track near Los Angeles on January 14, 1938, he received a death sentence in Illinois and was electrocuted at the Cook County Jail in Chicago on July 14, 1938.

Shelton brothers

Bootlegging partners of Charlie Birger in early 1920s who later became his chief rivals. On November 12, 1926, hired an Iowa cropduster to drop homemade dynamite bombs on Charlie Birger's heavily fortified "Shady Rest" headquarters near Harrisburg, Illinois, in what probably qualifies as the first aerial bombing in the U.S. However, the only bomb to explode was far off its target. The Birger and Shelton gangs also employed machine guns and specially made armored cars in their numerous battles in southern Illinois until 1927, when Birger had Carl, Earl and Bernie Shelton framed for mail robbery and sentenced to 25 years in Leavenworth. Sheltons were later freed when a Birger gang member confessed to perjury. The Sheltons moved back to East St. Louis, Illinois, and operated rackets there until the late 1940s, when

their former henchman, Frank "Buster" Wortman, took control, allegedly with the backing of the Chicago Syndicate. Carl Shelton was murdered on his farm near Fairfield, Illinois, October 23, 1947. Bernie Shelton was killed outside his tavern near Peoria, July 26, 1948. Roy Shelton was shot to death on his farm in Wayne County, June 7, 1950. Earl Shelton survived a murder attempt and fled the state.

Spencer, Ethan Allen (Al) (1893–1923)

Notorious Southwestern outlaw born near Lenapah, Oklahoma, and reputedly a one-time member of Henry Starr's over-the-hill gang. With Frank Nash and others, credited with robbing some 42 banks during 1922–23. Robbed Katy Limited mail train of $20,000 near Okesa, Oklahoma, on August 21, 1923. Killed by police and federal officers on Osage Indian Reservation near Bartlesville, Oklahoma, on September 16, 1923.

Starr, Henry ("Buck," or "The Bearcat") (1873–1921)

Born near Fort Gibson, Indian Territory, December 2, 1873, the son of George "Hop" Starr and Mary Scott Starr, and nephew of Sam and Belle Starr. "Halfbreed Cherokee outlaw" and a transitional figure between the outlaws of the "Old West" and the "motorized bandits" of the '20s. Often but erroneously credited as the first American bank robber to switch from horse to automobile. After a long criminal career that included several prison terms, Starr was mortally wounded while robbing a bank at Harrison, Arkansas, on February 18, 1921, and died four days later.

John Torrio moved from Brooklyn to Chicago about 1909 to help Big Jim Colosimo fend off so-called Black Hand extortionists, who he simply killed. *(Authors' collection)*

Torrio, John *(Johnny)* (1882–1957)

Born in Orsara di Puglia, Italy, near Naples, January 20, 1882, the son of Thomas and Maria Torrio. Entered U.S. with his widowed mother in 1884, and was "discovered" a few years later by Brooklyn gangster Frankie Yale. Related to Chicago brothel-owner Victoria Moresco, he was commissioned to deal with local Black Hand extortionists threatening Victoria's husband, Big Jim Colosimo, and became his second in command. About 1919 Torrio provided employment for young Brooklyn fugitive Alphonse Capone, who had become a murder suspect while working for Yale. Soon he conspired with Capone to eliminate Colosimo, who

not only had left his wife to marry singer Dale Winter, but was indifferent to the bootlegging opportunities afforded by Prohibition. Brooklyn mobster Frankie Yale was suspected of the murder, as was Capone himself. In any case, Torrio and Capone took over Colosimo's organization, expanded into large-scale bootlegging and racketeering, and then used persuasion and violence to forge a citywide crime cartel known as the Chicago Syndicate, or the Outfit. Following the Sieben Brewery swindle that led to Torrio's arrest and Dean O'Banion's murder in 1924, Torrio himself was nearly killed by O'Banion's successors on January 24, 1925, outside his apartment at 7011 Clyde Avenue. He recovered, turned the organization over to Capone, served a brief jail sentence stemming from the Sieben Brewery raid and fled to Italy. He later returned to U.S. as gangster emeritus, remaining active in New York rackets but also working to shape the future of U.S. organized crime. In 1939 he pleaded guilty to income tax evasion, was sentenced to two and a half years in Leavenworth, and then evidently retired. Died of a heart attack in Brooklyn, April 16, 1957.

Touhy, *Roger* (1898–1959)

Best known of five gangster brothers (collectively called the "Terrible Touhys") whose father was a Chicago policeman. Roger became a major bootlegger and labor racketeer who controlled the Northwest suburbs in defiance of the Capone Syndicate. The Touhy mob also included several men, including brother Tommy, who were wanted for a number of mail and bank robberies and who allegedly worked with the Chicago kidnapping gang of Handsome Jack Klutas. Arrested after car wreck near Elkhorn, Wisconsin, on July 19, 1933, Roger was charged, tried and acquitted of kidnapping

THE MACHINE-GUN NEST

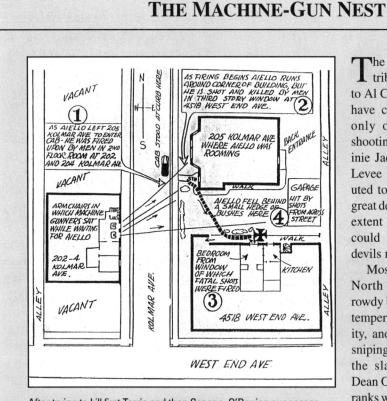

As firing begins Aiello runs around corner of building, but he is shot and killed by men in third story window at 4518 West End Ave.

VACANT

① As Aiello left 205 Kolmar Ave to enter cab - he was fired upon by men in 2nd floor. Room at 202 and 204 Kolmar Ave.

VACANT

Armchairs in which machine gunners sat while waiting for Aiello

202-4 Kolmar Ave.

VACANT

N W S E

Cab stood at curb here

205 Kolmar Ave where Aiello was rooming

Back entrance

Walk

Garage Hit by shots from across street

④ Aiello fell behind a small hedge of bushes here

Bedroom from window of which fatal shots were fired

③ 4518 West End Ave.

Walk

Kitchen

Kolmar Ave.

ALLEY

ALLEY

WEST END AVE.

After trying to kill first Torrio and then Capone, O'Banion successor Hymie Weiss died in the first machine-gun-nest murder, when gunmen in apartment windows covered the front, side and back of Schofield's flower shop. Joe Aiello died in an even more diabolic ambush, shown above *(Authors' collection)*

The press and the police attributed dozens of murders to Al Capone and he may well have committed several. But only one—the face-to-face shooting of Joe Howard in Heinie Jacob's saloon in the old Levee district—can be attributed to him personally with a great degree of certainty. To the extent he ordered others, he could have claimed that the devils made him do it.

Most of the devils were the North Siders, a thoroughly rowdy bunch who were Irish in temperament if not in nationality, and who spent five years sniping at Capone to avenge the slaying of their leader, Dean O'Banion, after he broke ranks with Capone's boss, John Torrio, swindling him in a brewery deal that also sent him to jail. The difference was that they (and others) continually

William Hamm, who was actually abducted by the Barker-Karpis gang. The following year Touhy was convicted of kidnapping Jake "The Barber" Factor, a Capone associate and international confidence man, and sentenced to 99 years in Joliet. Touhy always maintained that he had been framed by the Capone mob in collusion with State's Attorney Tom Courtney, his corrupt investigator Dan "Tubbo" Gilbert ("the world's richest cop") and Factor to put him out of business. Convinced his case was hopeless, he joined Basil "The Owl" Banghart, Eddie Darlak and others in a successful prison break on October 9, 1942. He was recaptured at 5116 Kenmore Avenue in Chicago on December 28, 1942, by FBI agents led by J. Edgar Hoover (performing his last "personal" arrest). Two other escapees, James O'Connor and St. Clair

missed their target, and Capone, in carefully planned retaliation, did not. That Bugs Moran survived the St. Valentine's Day Massacre was pure luck, and the result of Capone leaving the job to others. More typical was the 1926 killing of O'Banion's successor, Hymie Weiss, after he used a convoy of cars loaded with gunmen to lay siege to Capone's headquarters, then in the Hawthorne Hotel on the main street of Cicero. Three weeks later, Weiss and four others went down in a hail of bullets form a machine-gun nest in the building next to O'Banion's flower shop, across from the Holy Name Cathedral, and police then found a second, backup nest covering the flower shop from the other side as well as the alley behind it. The main shooter's Thompson had jammed after 35 rounds because the bullet from a faulty cartridge failed to clear the barrel, but those slugs plus several loads of buckshot from the same window were fatal to Weiss and bootlegger/bodyguard Patrick Murray.

In 1930 an equally sophisticated trap took out Capone's main adversary, Joe Aiello, who had teamed up with the North Siders before the Massacre and also coveted leadership of the Unione Siciliana, the principal source of Chicago's home-distilled grain alcohol. Leaving an

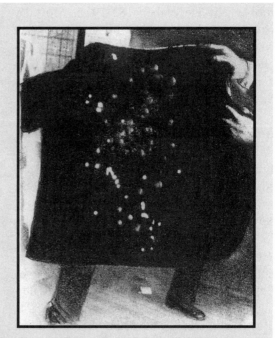

Police examining Aiello's overcoat estimated he had taken 59 slugs, possibly setting a beer-war record. *(Authors' collection)*

apartment building at 205 Kolmar, Aiello walked into a blaze of machine-gun fire from a nest across the street, and ran for a place of shelter that was directly under a second nest in the building next door. Police found he had taken 59 slugs, possibly setting a record.

McInerney, were killed by FBI agents the same day, just around the corner at 1254 Leland. The escape cost Touhy an additional 199 years. In 1954 federal judge John P. Barnes reviewed the case, concluded that the Factor kidnapping was in fact a hoax and set Touhy free, but state authorities soon returned him to prison on his escape conviction. His sentence finally was commuted and he was paroled in November

1959, but was shot to death on December 16 outside his sister's Chicago home at 125 North Lotus. Co-author of *The Stolen Years* (1959).

Trainor, Nicholas "Chaw Jimmie" (alias J.S. Sloane) (1887–1922)

Midwest bank robber and sometime partner of Harvey Bailey. Only man every positively identified as a participant in the Denver Mint robbery of December 18, 1922. Mortally wounded in battle with Mint guards, one of whom was killed. Carried off by his accomplices, Trainor's body was found in the abandoned getaway car in a garage at 1631 Gilpin Street in Denver, January 14, 1923.

Underhill, Wilbur "Mad Dog" (true name Wilbur Underhill, Jr.) (1901–1934)

Born in Joplin, Missouri, the son of Wilber and Nancy Almira Underhill. Violent bank robber known as the "Tri-State Terror" who was supposedly kicked out of the Kimes-Terrill gang in 1920s for his homicidal ways. Twice convicted of murder but escaped from state prisons in both Oklahoma and Kansas. Robbed banks with Harvey Bailey and others in Oklahoma and Kansas during 1933. One of many suspects in Kansas City Massacre. Mortally wounded by police and FBI agents near Shawnee, Oklahoma, on December 30, 1933. Died at prison hospital, McAlester, Oklahoma, January 6, 1934.

Weiss, Earl "Hymie" (true name Earl Wajiechowski) (1898–1926)

Born in Poland, immigrated to the U.S. at an early age, and succeeded Dean O'Banion as leader of Chicago's North Siders. Spurned Capone's peace offers and made several attempts on his life, prompting Capone to buy his famous armored Cadillac limousine and retaliate in self-defense. On October 11, 1926, three weeks after Weiss had sent several carloads of gunmen to attack Capone's Cicero headquarters in the Hawthorne Hotel, he and bootlegger Patrick Murray were killed and two others wounded by Capone machine gunners firing from the upstairs window of an apartment building next to Schofield's flower shop, where O'Banion had been killed in 1924 and which had remained headquarters for the North Side gang.

Winkeler, Gus "Big Mike" (true name August Henry Winkeler, often spelled Winkler) (1900–1933)

Born in St. Louis, Missouri, March 28, 1900. Graduate of St. Louis's "Egan's Rats" gang and longtime partner of Fred "Killer" Burke in bank and payroll robberies. With Burke, joined Capone Syndicate as a special-assignment gunman who probably helped kill New York's Frankie Yale when he turned against Capone and his Unione Siciliana candidate. This supposedly qualified him and his murder squad to perform the big one: the St. Valentine's Day Massacre. Wrongly suspected in the $2 million bank robbery at Lincoln, Nebraska, September 1930, but knew the perpetrators and avoided prosecution by arranging the return of a large part of the loot. Rose in the ranks of the Capone organization as one of his "American boys" and was rewarded with control of much of Chicago's prosperous North Side, once Moran's hold was broken and Joe Aiello killed. Opened several popular night spots, including the 225 Club, managed by Edward Lebensberger, whose death was ruled a suicide despite suspicions he was murdered. Part owner of 22nd Street garage of Joe Bergl, who supplied cars specially equipped with armor plating, sirens, and smoke-screen devices to major mobsters and outlaws, including Machine Gun Kelly and the Barker-Karpis gang. Lived in luxury at 3300 North Lake Shore Drive and enjoyed a measure of respectability as his holdings expanded, including his interest in the beer distributing company of Charles H. Weber, whose drivers raced the Prima Brewery trucks to supply the first legal brew to Chicagoans when the Volstead Act was amended in 1933 to permit 3.2 percent beer. Murdered on October 9, 1933, by shotgun blasts from a panel truck parked outside the Weber distributing company at 1414 Roscoe Street on Chicago's Mid-North Side. Killers were probably sent by Frank Nitti in his campaign to take over the Capone organization by eliminating his potential competition, especially from the "American boys." Winkeler was also talking with federal agents, to Nitti's alarm, although Gus's main intention may have been to distance himself from the likes of Miller, Burke and other former colleagues whose crimes of violence interested the FBI more than the bootlegging and gambling operations of the mob. Winkeler's loyal and long-suffering wife Georgette had been urging her husband to abandon violent crime, at least, due to the constant stress, but following his death she became seriously depressed and tipped her hand by telephoning the wife of Fred "Killer" Burke, who had moved into the neighborhood after her own husband had gone to prison. Bonnie Burke perceived Georgette's state of mind and reached the apartment in time to call the fire department's rescue squad.

Ziegler, "Shotgun" George (true name Fred Goetz) (1896–1934)

World War I army pilot who attended the University of Illinois and later became a robber, kidnapper and Capone Syndicate hitman. Arrested for attempted rape of a seven-year-old girl in Chicago, 1925. Took part in the St. Valentine's Day Massacre, according to a young accomplice, Byron "Monty" Bolton, who had been one of the Massacre lookouts. (Bolton had carelessly left behind a letter addressed to himself in one of the lookout rooms, and years later correctly recalled the false name he had used to buy one of the cars used by the killers.) Later Ziegler also worked for the Barker-Karpis gang, participating in robberies and the Hamm and Bremer kidnappings. Shot to death in front of 4811 West 22nd Street, Cicero, on March 21, 1934. His pockets contained, among other things, a $1,000 bill.

Zuta, Jack ("Jake")

Prominent North Side gangster involved in bootlegging, gambling and prostitution, and allied with Bugs Moran and Joe Aiello against the Capone Syndicate. A suspect in the Jake Lingle murder, of which Leo Brothers, represented by Dillinger's future lawyer Louis Piquett, was convicted on flimsy evidence and given a relatively light sentence of 14 years. Zuta was machine-gunned in spectacular fashion on the dance floor of the Lake View Hotel, near Delafield, Wisconsin, on August 1, 1930, presumably on orders of Capone.

Major East Coast Gangsters and Outlaws, 1920–1940

Adonis, Joe (true name Giuseppe Dato, Americanized to Joseph Doto) (1902–1971)

Born in Montemarano, Italy, November 22, 1902, son of Michele and Maria Dato (birth record falsified in 1933 to Passaic, New Jersey, November 5, 1901). Headed "Broadway Mob" of rumrunners during Prohibition. Lieutenant of Charles "Lucky" Luciano and suspect in

1931 murder of Joe "the Boss" Masseria. Brooklyn waterfront racketeer, loan shark, suspected narcotics trafficker, partner of Frank Costello and Meyer Lansky in illegal gambling casinos in New York, New Jersey and Florida, 1930s–'50s. Convicted in 1951 of gambling conspiracy and sentenced to two to three years in New Jersey state prison. Deported to Italy, January 3, 1956. Arrested in Milan, June 1971 in anti-Mafia drive by Italian police. Exiled to Serra de Conti, Italy. Died at Ancona, Italy, November 26, 1971.

Amberg brothers

Small-time Brooklyn gangsters involved in loan-sharking in competition with Dutch Schultz, and narcotics. Joe Amberg, at age 43, was executed with his chauffeur, Morris Kessler, by an underworld firing squad at a Brooklyn warehouse on September 30, 1935. His 36-year-old brother, Louis "Pretty" Amberg, probably joined others in supporting the October 23, 1935, Newark massacre of the Schultz mob, but was killed the same day. He was hacked up with an ax and left in a burning car near Brooklyn's Navy Yard.

Anastasia, Albert (true name Umberto Anastasio) (1902–1957)

Born in Tropea, Italy, September 26, 1902. Entered U.S. in 1919. Brooklyn waterfront racketeer closely allied to Louis "Lepke" Buchalter. Called by the press the "Lord High Executioner of Murder, Inc." and known in the underworld as "The Executioner" and "The Mad Hatter." Convicted with Joe Florina, alias Speranza, of the 1920 murder of George Terillo (or Tirello) and sentenced May 25, 1921, to be executed. Both ordered retried on December 6, 1921. Charges dropped, after four witnesses were shot to death and a fifth was sent to a mental institution. Convicted in 1923 of gun possession and sentenced to two years. A suspect in numerous murders over the years, including the 1931 assassination of Joe the Boss Masseria. Anastasia allegedly headed the eastern Syndicate's execution squad, known in the press as "Murder, Inc." For years controlled Local 1814 of the International Longshoreman's Union through his brother, Anthony "Tough Tony" Anastasio. Identified by informers Abe Reles and Albert Tannenbaum as instigator of the 1939 slayings of Teamsters official Morris Diamond and longshoreman Peter Panto. Charged with Diamond slaying, he became a fugitive, joining the army under an assumed name. Charge dropped when witness Abe Reles, under suspicious circumstances, fell or was pushed out the window of a hotel room where he was being held in protective custody by New York police. Said by less-than-reliable informer Joe Valachi to have ordered the 1952 murder of Arnold Schuster, who had turned in bank robber Willie Sutton. Underboss of Vincent Mangano crime family from 1931 to 1951, when Mangano disappeared, presumably murdered, and Anastasia assumed leadership. Shot to death October 25, 1957, in barbershop of Park Sheraton Hotel (formerly Park Central, where Arnold Rothstein had been killed in 1928). His murder was attributed to Vito Genovese's takeover of the Costello crime family (Anastasia was an ally of Costello) but also of Meyer Lansky's efforts to muscle in on pre-Castro Cuban gambling operations.

Anderson, George "Dutch" (true name Ivan Dahl Von Teller) (1879–1925)

Born in Denmark of a noble family. Reportedly a graduate of the Universities of Uppsala and

Heidelberg, he was fond of music and literature, and spoke several languages. Came to U.S. about 1899 or 1900. Attended the University of Wisconsin but did not earn a degree. Began a life of petty crime about 1907 and served prison sentences in Ohio, Wisconsin and Illinois. Arrested in Rochester, New York, in 1917 for a 1913 burglary, convicted, and sentenced to five years in Auburn prison, where he met "Gentleman Gerald" Chapman. Both paroled in 1919. After working briefly as bootleggers in Detroit, Toledo and New York, Anderson and Chapman joined Charles Loeber, another Auburn parolee, in robbing a U.S. mail truck on Leonard Street in New York City, October 24, 1921, taking $2.4 million in cash, bonds and jewelry. All three captured in New York July 3, 1922. Anderson and Chapman each sentenced to 25 years in Atlanta Federal Penitentiary. Chapman escaped April 5, 1923, and Anderson escaped December 30, 1923. Both later suspected of numous bank robberies and other crimes. Though Chapman was the more notorious, Anderson was regarded as the leader. When Chapman was recaptured, Anderson murdered the informer Ben Hance and his wife near Muncie, Indiana, August 11, 1925. On October 31, 1925, in Muskegon, Michigan, Detective Charles DeWitt Hammond attempted to arrest Anderson for passing counterfeit money and was shot. Though fatally wounded, Detective Hammond wrested away Anderson's gun and killed him with it.

Antinori, Ignacio
Reputed Mafia leader in Tampa, Florida, allegedly active in gambling and narcotics. Murdered on October 22, 1940.

Ashley, John (1895–1924)
Everglades-based bank robber, bootlegger, hijacker and pirate whose gang terrorized Florida for a decade, becoming folk heroes in the process. His criminal career may have begun with the murder of a Seminole Indian in 1911, and he became one of the first "motorized bandits," using cars in his robberies. In addition to bank jobs, the Ashley gang is said to have disrupted rumrunning between the Bahamas and Florida in the early '20s with their frequent hijackings and to have raided liquor warehouses at Bimini. Ashley and three of his gang were ambushed and killed by police at Sebastian, Florida, November 1, 1924.

Avena, John "Big Nose" (alias John Nazzone)
Reputed boss of Italian crime family in Philadelphia. Murdered by gunmen on August 17, 1936.

Bazzano, John
Allegedly succeeded Joseph Siragusa as boss of Pittsburgh Mafia family. Found strangled and stabbed to death and sewn into a burlap bag on a street in Brooklyn, August 8, 1932.

Buchalter, Louis "Lepke" (1897–1944)
Infamous New York labor racketeer and narcotics trafficker, reputed to have ordered the murders of dozens of enemies and potential witnesses against him. Suspect in 1927 murder of Jacob "Little Augie" Orgen and wounding of bodyguard Jack "Legs" Diamond. Probably planned the 1935 murder of Dutch Schultz. Arranged through radio personality Walter Winchell to surrender in person to J. Edgar Hoover in New York City on August 24, 1939. Convicted of narcotics conspiracy in 1939 and

sentenced to 14 years in Leavenworth. Convicted of murder in New York, 1941, and sentenced to death. Died in electric chair at Sing Sing prison on March 4, 1944, the first crime syndicate boss ever to be legally executed.

Chapman, Gerald (1888?–1926)
Convicted of grand larceny in 1907 and served one year of a 10-year sentence. Convicted of burglary in 1908 and served three years. Convicted of armed robbery in 1911 and sent to Auburn prison, where he met George "Dutch" Anderson, his future partner in crime. Both paroled in 1919. Chapman, Anderson and Charles Loeber achieved national notoriety as the decade's first "super-bandits" when they robbed a U.S. mail truck of $2.4 million on Leonard Street in New York City on October 24, 1921. All three captured July 3, 1922. Chapman and Anderson sentenced to 25 years in the federal penitentiary at Atlanta. Shot in escape attempt March 27, 1923. Escaped April 5, 1923. Anderson escaped on December 30, 1923. With Anderson, suspected of bank and mail robberies and various major crimes in 1924. With Walter Shean, attempted to burglarize a store in New Britain, Connecticut, October 12, 1924, killing policeman James Skelly. Shean later captured and named Chapman as his accomplice. Chapman and Anderson harbored at Muncie, Indiana, by Ben Hance, who later turned informer, causing Chapman's capture at Muncie on January 18, 1925 (for which Hance was later murdered by Anderson). Convicted of Skelly murder and sentenced to death. Chapman's attorneys appealed, questioning the state's right to execute Chapman when he still owed the federal government 24 years on his mail robbery conviction. President Coolidge mooted that issue by commuting the federal

sentence and Chapman was hanged at Wethersfield, Connecticut, April 26, 1926.

Coll, Vincent "Mad Dog" (1909–1932)
Gunman for New York's Dutch Schultz mob, who broke away in 1930 to form his own gang and wage war on Schultz. Later teamed with Diamond mob against Schultz. Hijacked liquor, and kidnapped other mobsters for ransom, including George "Big Frenchy" DeMange, partner of Owney Madden. Allegedly contracted by Mafia boss Salvatore Maranzano to murder Lucky Luciano and Vito Genovese in 1931, though this never came off. Accused of Harlem "Baby Massacre," the shooting of five children, one fatally, during an unsuccessful attempt to kill gangster Joe Rao in front of the Helmar Social Club at 208 East 107th Street, July 28, 1931. This earned him the nickname "Mad Dog," but was acquitted when attorney Samuel Liebowitz proved witness George Brecht gave perjured testimony. Machine-gunned on orders of Schultz in a telephone booth in the London Chemist's drugstore, 314 West 23rd Street, February 8, 1932.

Coppola, Michael "Trigger Mike" (1900–1966)
Born near Salerno, Italy, July 29, 1900, son of Giuseppe and Angelina Coppola. Moved at an early age to New York where he became notorious as a gunman reputedly associated at various times with Vincent "Mad Dog" Coll, Louis "Lepke" Buchalter, and Jack "Legs" Diamond. Suspected of masterminding the robbery of guests (mostly politicians and gangsters) at a democratic club's supper honoring Judge Albert Vitale, at the Roman Gardens restaurant in the Bronx, December 7, 1929. The supper apparently had been organized by Ciro Terranova,

Harlem crime boss and lieutenant of Joe the Boss Masseria. Sided with Salvatore Maranzano against Masseria in the "Castellammarese War" of 1930–31, later became lieutenant of Lucky Luciano, replacing Ciro Terranova in mid-thirties as boss of the Harlem numbers racket. Prime suspect in the beating death of East Harlem Republican leader Joseph R. Scottoriggio on election day, November 5, 1946. In later years involved in Brooklyn waterfront racketeering and Florida gambling. Pleaded guilty to income tax evasion in 1962 and served a short prison sentence. His former wife, Ann Drahmann Coppola, who suspected Mike of murdering his first wife and who had cooperated with the IRS investigation, apparently committed suicide six months later in Rome,

Italy. Trigger Mike died in a Boston hospital October 1, 1966.

Costello, Frank (true name Francesco Castiglia) (1891–1973)

Born in Lauropoli, Italy, January 26, 1891, the son of Luigi and Maria Castiglia. With partner William Vincent "Big Bill" Dwyer, ran largest rumrunning operation in New York in 1920. Expanded into slot machines in 1928, becoming known as the "Slot Machine Czar." Apparently inherited control of Tammany Hall political machine after the murder of Arnold Rothstein in 1928. Succeeded Lucky Luciano as boss of New York's largest Italian crime family in 1937, after Luciano was convicted of controlling prostitution and his underboss, Vito

The huge crowds and costly funerals enjoyed by many prominent gangsters were denied New York's Vincent Coll, who earned his nickname "Mad Dog" by trying to kill a rival outside the Helmar social club on Manhattan's Upper East Side, but hitting instead a group of children, one of whom died. He beat the rap, but not a burst of tommy gun bullets that riddled him in the telephone booth of a drugstore on 23rd Street in 1932. *(Authors' collection)*

Genovese, fled to Italy to avoid prosecution for murder. Involved for years in both illegal and legal casino operations with Meyer Lansky, Joe Adonis and others, in New York, New Jersey, Florida, Kentucky, Louisiana and Nevada. Apparently retired from the rackets after May 2, 1957, when he survived an assassination attempt by Vincent "The Chin" Gigante, a soldier of Vito Genovese, who then assumed control of the family. Costello served a term for income tax evasion, was denaturalized for lying on his citizenship application, but avoided deportation. Died of a heart attack in a New York hospital, February 18, 1973.

Crowley, Francis "Two-Gun" (1912–1932)

Born in New York City October 31, 1912, the illegitimate son of Dora Dietz; father reputed to have been New York City policeman. Francis' brother, John Crowley, was killed by New York police while resisting arrest for disorderly conduct in 1925. Francis became a juvenile gunman and cop killer who terrorized New York City in the spring of 1931. Involved in numerous holdups and several shootings. Suspected participant in robbery of Huguenot Trust Company, New Rochelle, New York, in March 1931. Shot and killed Patrolman Frederick Hirsch at North Merrick, Long Island, May 6, 1931. Captured by New York police following a spectacular gun battle at an apartment building at 303 West 90th Street. Convicted of murder and executed at Sing Sing prison, January 21, 1932. (Crowley's partner, Rudolph "Fats" Duringer, also known as "Tough Red," was captured at the same time, convicted of murdering dance hall hostess Virginia Brannen, and executed at Sing Sing December 10, 1931.)

Cugino, Anthony "The Stinger"

Philadelphia's Public Enemy Number One in 1934. Gang leader, bandit and murderer, allegedly affiliated with the Tri-State Gang. Most noted for the extreme treachery he displayed by murdering some of his own crime partners to avoid sharing the loot. Betrayed by an accomplice and captured in New York City, September 8, 1935. Confessed to eight murders, then committed suicide by hanging himself in his cell.

Diamond, John Thomas (Jack or "Legs")
(Birth name probably John T. Noland)
(1898–1931)

Born in Philadelphia, Pennsylvania, July 11, 1898. Bodyguard and gunman for Arnold Rothstein and Jacob "Little Augie" Orgen. Bootlegger, narcotics trafficker, hijacker, bank robber, suspected of numerous murders. Reputedly a onetime rumrunning partner of Al Capone. Later allied with Vincent "Mad Dog" Coll's mob in unsuccessful gang war against Dutch Schultz. Arrested over two dozen times and survived at least four assassination attempts, which led newspapers to call him the "clay pigeon" until he was murdered on December 17, 1931, in his sleep while in a rooming house at 67 Dove Street, Albany, New York, where he was intending to expand his operations.

Dwyer, William Vincent "Big Bill" (1883–1946)

Ex-stevedore who became a bootlegger during Prohibition, then established the largest rumrunning syndicate on the East Coast with help of boyhood friends from the "Gophers" and "Hudson Dusters" street gangs. First to engage in wholesale bribery of U.S. Coast Guard crews and employ some as rumrunners. Partner in Phoenix Brewery with Owney Madden and Waxey Gordon. Also worked with Frank

Costello, Frankie Yale, Larry Fay and Charles "Vannie" Higgins. Convicted of bootlegging in 1926 and sentenced to two years in the Atlanta Federal Penitentiary. Succeeded by Frank Costello, who was acquitted in the same case. Dwyer traded liquor interests to his associates for racetrack interests, gaining reputation as a millionaire sportsman. Original owner of Brooklyn Dodgers football team. Brought professional hockey to New York. Acquitted of incometax evasion in 1934. Convicted on another tax charge in 1939 and died penniless in 1946.

Eastman, "Monk" (true name Edward Osterman) (1873?–1920)

Notorious early 1900s New York gang leader. Sent to prison in 1904 for shooting a Pinkerton detective in a holdup. Later a bodyguard and collector for Arnold Rothstein. Shot to death in New York, December 26, 1920. A Prohibition agent later pleaded guilty to manslaughter in this case, claiming to have shot Eastman in an argument over tipping a waiter.

Fay, Larry (1888–1933)

New York cabdriver who smuggled bottles of whiskey in from Canada in 1920, making enough money eventually to become a prominent mobster, rumrunner, nightclub operator and owner of a large fleet of taxis. Chiefly remembered as an early promoter and financial backer of Texas Guinan, the "Hello, Sucker!" girl who served as hostess of Fay's El Fey Club. In addition to his other interests, Fay took over the New York Chain Milk Association and monopolized the milk industry in New York. He was shot to death at his Club Casa Blanca, January 1, 1933, by Edward Maloney, the club's drunken doorman, whose wages had been cut.

Genovese, Vito "Don Vitone" (1897–1969)

Born in Naples, Italy, November 21, 1897. Entered U.S. in 1913. Murderous New York gangster, chief lieutenant and heir apparent to Lucky Luciano. Prominent figure in the Castellammarese War of 1930–31 and allegedly one of the killers of Joe the Boss Masseria. The Genovese faction is also credited in FBI records with the murder of Legs Diamond. Presumably ordered the New York murder of Gerard Vernotico, March 16, 1932, marrying Vernotico's widow 12 days later. Eventually Anna Genovese would divorce Vito, testifying that he was a millionaire gambling and narcotics boss. Genovese fled to Italy before World War II to avoid prosecution for the murder of Ferdinand "The Shadow" Boccia. Became an intimate of Mussolini and reportedly ordered the 1943 murder of Carlo Tresca, publisher of an anti-Fascist Italian-language newspaper in New York. Organized extensive black market operations in cooperation with the Sicilian Mafia and the Neapolitan Camorra during the war, but may also have spied on Mussolini for the American OSS. Later an official in Allied Military Government. Arrested in 1944 by U.S. Army CID investigator Orange C. Dickey, who brought Genovese, over protests of his superiors, back to U.S. to face trial for murder. Murder charge dropped in 1946 after key witness Peter LaTempa was poisoned in a Brooklyn jail. Assumed leadership of former Luciano-Costello crime family in 1957, following the attempted murder of Frank Costello. Convicted of narcotics conspiracy in 1959 and sentenced to 15 years. Died in prison February 14, 1969.

Gordon, "Waxey" (true name Irving Wexler) (1886–1952)

One of New York's most powerful Prohibition-era mobsters. Former pickpocket and member of pre–World War I "Dopey" Benny Fein mob of labor racketeers. Reputedly organized the city's first large-scale rumrunning operation in early 1920s, financed by Arnold Rothstein. Established huge brewery operations in New Jersey, supplying beer to that state, New York and Pennsylvania. Fought gang wars with Dutch Schultz and the Bugs & Meyer Mob, headed by Bugsy Siegel and Meyer Lansky. Convicted of income-tax evasion, 1933, sentenced to 10 years in Leavenworth, and fined $20,000; paroled in 1940. Convicted of selling narcotics, December 13, 1951, and sentenced to 25 years to life in New York state prison; then indicted on federal narcotics conspiracy charge and temporarily detained on Alcatraz, where he died, June 24, 1952.

Higgins, Charles "Vannie" (1897–1932)

Notorious New York bootlegger and murderer. Onetime lieutenant of Big Bill Dwyer. Briefly allied with Legs Diamond, Mad Dog Coll and Little Augie Pisano against Dutch Schultz, but later an enemy of Diamond. Suspect in murders of gangsters Samuel Orlando and Robert Benson and in the October 1930 shooting of Diamond at New York's Hotel Monticello. Once knifed in Baltimore. Wounded in gun battle at Blossom Heath Inn speakeasy in New York, 1931. Amateur aviator who once angered Governor Franklin Roosevelt by flying to the state prison to dine with the warden. Fatally shot by rival gangsters outside the Knights of Columbus clubhouse in Prospect Park, June 18, 1932.

Kaplan, Nathan "Kid Dropper" or "Jack the Dropper" (1895–1923)

Major pre-Prohibition New York mobster. Member of Five Points Gang, headed by Paolo Antonini Vaccarelli, alias Paul Kelly. Fought celebrated gun duel in 1911 with rival gangster Joseph Weyler, alias Johnny Spanish. Convicted of robbery same year and sentenced to seven years in Sing Sing. Paroled in 1917 and formed his own gang, the "Rough Riders of Jack the Dropper." Suspected in the murder of Johnny Spanish, July 29, 1919. Later fought Jacob "Little Augie" Orgen's gang in laundry workers' union dispute. Participated in August 1923 gun battle in which Orgen gang member Jacob "Gurrah" Shapiro was wounded and two bystanders killed. Arrested soon after on weapons charge. Shot to death while leaving Essex Market Courthouse under police guard, August 28, 1923, by Louis Cohen, alias Kushner, an Orgen gangster subsequently convicted of manslaughter (Cohen would be murdered by Louis "Lepke" Buchalter's gang on January 24, 1939).

Kastel, Philip "Dandy Phil" (1894–1962)

Bucket-shop operator and henchman of Arnold Rothstein in 1920s. Later Frank Costello's partner in slot machine operations in New York and New Orleans. Brought slot machines to New Orleans in 1930s at invitation of Huey Long, following Mayor Fiorello LaGuardia's anti-gambling crusade in New York. Headed Costello's gambling operations in Louisiana and later founded Beverly Club casino near New Orleans in partnership with Costello, Meyer Lansky and others. Going blind and suffering from abdominal cancer, committed suicide by shooting himself at his Claiborne Towers apartment in New Orleans, August 16, 1962.

Lansky, Meyer (true name Maier Suchowljansky) (1902–1983)
Born in Grodno, Russia, either July 4 or August 28, 1902, or August 28, 1900, the son of Max and Yetta L. Suchowljansky (July 4 birthday claimed in Lansky's 1921 Declaration of Intention to become a U.S. citizen). With Bugsy Siegel, headed the Bugs & Meyer Mob in New York in 1920s, but committed murders, hijackings and strong-arm activities for other gangs. Closely associated with Lucky Luciano, Frank Costello and Joe Adonis in bootlegging and gambling. Suspected of being a Bahamian rum-running partner of Al Capone in late '20s. Attended 1929 gangster convention in Atlantic City. Named by New York press in 1935 (along with Siegel, Luciano, Buchalter and Shapiro, Costello, Adonis, Johnny Torrio and Abner "Longy" Zwillman) as one of the leaders of a New York syndicate that ordered the murder of Dutch Schultz and took over his gang. Moved to Miami in 1930s and became a major gambling figure in Florida and Cuba. In later years was noted for pioneering international casino operations and the laundering of mob money through foreign banks. Successfully avoided prosecution over the years (though he briefly fled to Israel in the early 1970s) and died of natural causes at Miami Beach, Florida, January 15, 1983.

Lonergan, Richard "Peg Leg"
Last leader of Irish "White Hand" gang who battled Frankie Yale's Italian gang for control of the Brooklyn waterfront. Shot to death, with henchmen Cornelius "Needles" Ferry and Aaron Harms at the Adonis Social Club, an Italian mob hangout, December 26, 1925. Several Italian gangsters present, including Chicago's Al Capone, were arrested and released.

Luciano, Charles "Lucky" (true name Salvatore Lucania) (1897–1962)
Born in Lercarra Friddi, near Palermo, Sicily, November 24, 1897, son of Antonio and Rosalia Lucania. Entered U.S. in 1907. Arranged murders of Joe the Boss Masseria and Salvatore Maranzano in 1931 and succeeded them as New York's most powerful Mafia boss. One time member of Legs Diamond gang in 1920s. Ran gambling, bootlegging and narcotics operations. Closely associated with Frank Costello, Bugsy Siegel, Meyer Lansky, Dutch Schultz and others. Convicted of controlling prostitution (in a case many now believe was a frame-up) and sentenced to 30 to 50 years at Dannamora prison, Clinton, New York. This conviction greatly advanced the political career of the prosecutor, Thomas E. Dewey, who, as governor, pardoned Luciano in 1946 for the mobster's alleged role in preventing waterfront sabotage during World War II. Deported to Sicily, February 9, 1946. Moved to Cuba in 1946 but ousted under pressure from U.S. government. Resettled in Naples, Italy, where he died, January 26, 1962. In his later years, Luciano was under constant surveillance by Italian police and the U.S. Federal Bureau of Narcotics, who maintained he was running an international heroin smuggling network. Despite his close association with American and Italian underworld figures, no hard evidence permitted his conviction.

Madden, Owen Vincent "Owney the Killer" (1891–1965)
Born in Leeds, England, December 18, 1891, son of Francis and Mary Madden. Immigrated to U.S. at early age and became leader of the Gophers street gang. Arrested 44 times before Prohibition. Convicted in 1914 of murdering

Little Patsy Doyle, a member of the rival Hudson Dusters, and sentenced to 10 to 20 years in Sing Sing prison. Paroled in 1923 and became prominent New York bootlegger, known as the "Duke of the West Side." Closely associated with other old-time mob leaders, such as Waxey Gordon and Larry Fay, who were left out when New York mobs syndicated in early 1930s. Madden's close friend and lieutenant Big Frenchy DeMange was once held for ransom by the Coll mob, and Madden allegedly placed a $50,000 bounty on Coll's head. Along with Dutch Schultz, was suspected of instigating Coll's murder in 1932. Returned to prison for parole violation, July 7, 1932. Released, July 1, 1933, and "retired" to Hot Springs, Arkansas, then a notoriously corrupt city popular with big-time criminals. Reportedly ran illegal gambling operations in Hot Springs until the 1960s. Died of natural causes, April 24, 1965.

Magaddino, Stefano (Steve) (1891–1974)

Born in Castellammare del Golfo, Sicily, October 10, 1891. Long-time boss of Italian crime family in Buffalo, New York, until his death from natural causes on July 10, 1974. Cousin of Brooklyn mobster Joseph "Joe Bananas" Bonanno. Magaddino's sister, Mrs. Nicholas Longo, who lived next door, was killed by a bomb blast probably intended for him on May 19, 1936.

Mais, Robert Howard (1906–1935)

With Walter Legurenza, alias Legenza, led the so-called Tri-State Gang, which actually operated in several eastern states in the early 1930s, committing bank and payroll robberies, hijackings and murders. Captured by Baltimore police, Mais and Legenza were extradited to Virginia, tried and convicted of murdering a bank messenger and sentenced to death. Using a smuggled pistol, they escaped from the Richmond jail, September 29, 1934, killing a policeman. Reorganizing their gang, Mais and Legenza staged other robberies and the ransom kidnapping of Philadelphia racketeer William Weiss, whom they murdered. Captured by FBI agents in New York City in January 1935, Mais and Legenza were returned to Richmond, Virginia, and died in the electric chair there on February 2, 1935.

Mangano, Vincenzo (Vincente or Vincent) (1887–1951)

Born in Villabati, Palermo, Sicily. Reportedly entered U.S. in 1922 with father Gaetano and friend Joseph Profaci. One of 23 Sicilian gangsters arrested in conference at a Cleveland hotel in December 1928. Maranzano ally in Castellammarese War. Became boss of a Brooklyn crime family in 1931, assisted by brother Philip and underboss Albert Anastasia. Reportedly served for years as chairman of the "national commission" of Italian-American crime families and also as a liaison to representatives of the Sicilian Mafia. Disappeared in 1951, allegedly murdered by or on orders of Anastasia, who took over the family. Mangano's body was never found. His brother Philip was shot to death in Brooklyn on April 19, 1951.

Maranzano, Salvatore (1868–1931)

Born in Castellammare del Golfo, Sicily. Battled Giuseppe "Joe the Boss" Masseria for control of the Italian underworld in New York in the Castellammarese War of 1930–31. After Masseria's murder, Maranzano set himself up as the "boss of bosses" of the Italian crime families and reportedly plotted to murder any organized crime figures unwilling to submit to his rule.

THE CASTELLAMMARESE WAR

While Chicago's gangs volleyed and thundered at one another in the absence of a strong city government, New York's Tammany Hall had evolved from the days of Boss Tweed into a political machine that was thoroughly corrupt but so centralized and powerful that its police could keep a lid on the kind of open warfare engaged in by the rowdies in Chicago and southern Illinois. During the 1920s, most New York gang killings had been conducted without Chicago-style spectacle in outlying boroughs between rival factions in Italian and Sicilian communities that were difficult for both police who were predominantly Irish and reporters to penetrate, and of relatively little interest to either. Toward the end of the decade the mounting number of murders was discovered to be the fallout of a feud between one Giuseppe Masseria, self-proclaimed boss of bosses, and Salvatore Maranzano, a contender from Castellammare del Golfo, Sicily, who was not only challenging Maranzano in Brooklyn but branching out to Buffalo, Cleveland and other cities. When the local murders were proclaimed a "Mafia" war—"Mafia" having become the reporters' name for Italian and Sicilian crime families—the public began to take an interest. Each of the two leaders had a following of young gangsters who would eventually acquire underworld prominence. Masseria's camp included Lucky Luciano, Frank Costello, Albert Anastasia, Carlo Gambino and Joe Adonis, among others. In Maranzano's organization the rising stars were Tommy Lucchese, Joe Bonanno and Joe Profaci.

The killings between Masseria and Maranzano forces became known as the Castellammarese War, which seemed not only pointless to the young combatants born and raised in the U.S. but also perpetuated the rule of two old "Mustache Petes" in a personal vendetta that ignored opportunities for serious racketeering. Luciano, already in league with Meyer Lansky, Bugsy Siegel and other non-Italian gangsters, secretly contacted Lucchese, who agreed that Masseria and Maranzano had to go. The murders of both in 1931 were engineered by Luciano, who then implemented the form of post-Prohibition, nationally organized, equal-opportunity racketeering advocated by gang leaders from other cities at a historic meeting in Atlantic City two years earlier.

These potentially included Lucky Luciano, Vito Genovese, Frank Costello, their non-Italian ally Dutch Schultz and Chicago mob boss Al Capone. Any such plot was ended when gunmen of the Bugs & Meyer Mob, allies of Luciano, shot and stabbed Maranzano to death at his office in New York's Eagle Building Corporation, 230 Park Avenue, on September 10, 1931. The group may have included Schultz gunman Abe "Bo" Weinberg, who supposedly got separated from the others during their escape, found himself in a crowded Grand Central Station, and ditched his gun by slipping it into the coat pocket of an unsuspecting commuter, to his own great amusement. According to an enduring legend that may have started with Weinberg, Masseria's killing signaled the start of a concerted nationwide slaughter of 40 or more of Maranzano's contemporaries in what many popular crime historians still call the

"Night of the Sicilian Vespers," which supposedly purged the Sicilian-dominated Mafia of the old "greasers" and "Mustache Petes." Thus emerged a modernized "American" Mafia ruled by a new generation of Italian-American organized-crime figures led by Luciano, but closely associated with Jewish and other prominent underworld figures. The Mafia did acquire new leadership in the early thirties, but several scholars have since debunked the colorful "bloodbath" story, discovering only three or four other killings around this time that might be linked to that of Maranzano.

Marlow, Frankie (true name Gandalfo Civito)
Important New York bootlegger, reputedly chief lieutenant for Frankie Yale. Owned Silver Slipper nightclub at Broadway and 48th Street in partnership with Owney Madden and Bill Duffy. Also a partner, with gangster Larry Fay and comedian Jimmy Durante, in Les Ambassadeurs club. Owned racehorses and managed several boxers, including Jack Gannon, Ricardo Bertalazzo, and middleweight world champion Johnny Wilson. Shot to death by unknown gunmen at 166th Street and Queens Avenue, Flushing, June 24, 1929. Suspects included Ciro Terranova, Joe the Boss Masseria and Boston gangleader Charles "King" Solomon.

Masseria, Giuseppe "Joe the Boss"
(1880–1931)
Defeated the Morello brothers in the early 1920s to emerge as boss of the largest Italian crime family in New York during Prohibition. By 1930 was being challenged by the crime family of Maranzano, composed largely of recent immigrants from the area around Castellammare del Golfo, Sicily, which inspired the term "Castellammarese War." This feud centered mainly in the New York–New Jersey area, though Nicola Gentile, Joe Valachi, Joe Bonanno and others have linked it to the struggles of the Italian underworld in other parts of the country, claiming that Al Capone's archenemy in Chicago, Joseph Aiello, who sought control of the Unione Siciliana, supported Maranzano while Capone backed Masseria. The "war" ended April 15, 1931, when Masseria was betrayed by his underboss, Charles "Lucky" Luciano, and murdered at Gerardo Scarpato's Coney Island restaurant, allegedly by Benjamin "Bugsy" Siegel, Joe Adonis, Albert Anastasia and Vito Genovese.

Mock Duck (1878–1942)
Most notorious of Chinese gang leaders. Gambler, opium addict and allegedly chief hatchetman for the Hip Sing tong. Principal figure in Chinatown wars in San Francisco and New York between rival tongs, or associations, the Hip Sing and the On Leong, for control of gambling, prostitution and opium trafficking from about 1900 to 1930. Arrested many times and survived many attacks, but eventually died of natural causes in Brooklyn.

Morello, Giuseppe (alias Joe or Peter "The Clutching Hand" Morello; Terranova)
(1863–1930)
Born in Corleone, Sicily. Immigrated to U.S. in 1892 after being charged with murder and counterfeiting. Reputedly first boss of New York Mafia, assisted by brothers Antonio, Vincent and Nicholas, half-brother Ciro Terranova and brother-in-law Ignazio "Lupo the Wolf" Saietta. Engaged in Black Hand extortion in the Italian community and counterfeiting and warfare against the Brooklyn branch of the Camorra, a Neapolitan criminal society whose

members began immigrating to this country around the 1890s. Prime suspect in "barrel murders" of Joseph Catania, July 23, 1902, and Benedetto Madonia, April 14, 1903. Convicted of counterfeiting in 1910 and sentenced to 25 years in the Atlanta Federal Penitentiary. Paroled in 1921 and eventually became a lieutenant of Joe the Boss Masseria, who named him puppet "boss of bosses" of the Italian crime families. Shot to death with Giuseppe Pariano by members of the Maranzano crime family in his office at 362 East 116th Street, August 15, 1930.

Moretti, Quarico "Willie" (alias Willie Moore) (1894–1951)

Born in New York City June 4, 1894. Operated from New Jersey with Longy Zwillman, Waxey Gordon, Lucky Luciano, Joe Adonis and Frank Costello. Named as murderer in 1931 deathbed statement by victim William Brady, a Hackensack, New Jersey, cab driver who had informed police about a still. Charge dropped when Brady's statement disappeared. Sided with Masseria faction in Castellammarese War. After Prohibition, Moretti became a prominent gambling figure in New Jersey. Admitted to Kefauver Committee his acquaintance with many notorious gangsters, including Al Capone, whom he described as "well charactered" like himself. By that time, Moretti was reportedly syphilitic, losing his faculties and talking too much for the comfort of his associates, who shot him to death at Joe's Elbow Room, 793 Palisades Avenue, in Cliffside Park, New Jersey, October 4, 1951.

Orgen, Jacob "Little Augie" (true name Orgenstein)

Member of old "Dopey" Benny Fein mob of pre–World War I labor racketeers in New York, and Fein's apparent successor following the 1923 murder of rival gangleader Nathan "Kid Dropper" Kaplan. Early lieutenants included Louis "Lepke" Buchalter, Jacob "Gurrah" Shapiro, Jack "Legs" Diamond and Irving "Waxey Gordon" Wexler. Murdered at Delancey and Norfolk Streets, New York, October 15, 1927, allegedly by Buchalter and Shapiro, who had formed their own opposing factions in a painters' union dispute. One of the wounded was bodyguard Legs Diamond.

Pisano, "Little Augie" (true name Anthony Carfano)

With Joe Adonis, succeeded Frankie Yale as principal Italian gangleader in Brooklyn and rumrunning partner of Al Capone. Sometimes associated with Legs Diamond, whom he briefly joined in gang war against Dutch Schultz. Later a lieutenant of Joe the Boss Masseria, Lucky Luciano and Frank Costello. Increasing legal pressure forced him to move to Miami in 1933, where he invested in hotels and illegal gambling. Shot to death in Queens, New York, with friend Janice Drake, September 25, 1959, apparently a victim of Vito Genovese's takeover of the former Luciano-Costello crime family.

Profaci, Joseph (1897–1962)

Born in Villabati, Palermo, Sicily, October 2, 1897. Reportedly entered U.S. in 1922 with Vincent Mangano. Boss of a Brooklyn crime family from the 1920s until his death. Arrested at Hotel Statler in Cleveland, December 5, 1928, along with 22 other Sicilian gang leaders. Ally of Salvatore Maranzano in Castellammarese War. Long suspected of bootlegging, narcotics trafficking and other major crimes but never convicted. In later years a multimillionaire

and the country's major importer of olive oil and tomato paste, Profaci allegedly collected $25 in monthly dues from each member of his crime family. Attended Apalachin, New York, mob conference in 1957. Died of cancer at the South Side Hospital, Long Island, New York, June 7, 1962.

Reina, Gaetano (Tom) (1890–1930)

Boss of an Italian crime family allied to Joe the Boss Masseria. Allegedly held a near monopoly on ice distribution in New York City. Shotgunned to death on Masseria's orders, February 26, 1930, causing many members of the family secretly to defect to Salvatore Maranzano in what would become the Castellammarese War between the two factions. Reina's daughter later married Joe Valachi.

Reles, Abe "Kid Twist" (1907–1941)

Chief executioner for "Murder, Inc." as newspapers termed the Brooklyn gang that handled enforcement duties for the Syndicate. Alleged to have personally participated in at least 30 murders. Turned informant in 1940, providing insights into the organization of the national crime cartel and solutions to dozens of gang killings. Reles's testimony encouraged other mob informers to come forth and doomed Louis "Lepke" Buchalter, to date the only Syndicate boss ever legally executed. States' witness Reles mysteriously fell to his death from his well-

Gentleman gangster Arnold Rothstein was accused of helping to throw the 1919 World Series. Whether he did so or only capitalized on the fix remains open to question, but he bankrolled much of New York's organized crime and helped the popular but corrupt Mayor Jimmy Walker keep the lid on that city's violence until he himself was murdered in a downtown hotel room in 1928. *(Authors' collection)*

guarded room on a high floor of the Half Moon Hotel in Coney Island, November 12, 1941, earning him a footnote in underworld history as "the canary who could sing but couldn't fly."

Rothstein, Arnold "The Brain" (1882–1928)

Born in New York City, son of Abraham and Esther Rothstein. Big-time gambler, controller of Democratic political machine at Tammany Hall, suspected narcotics trafficker and underworld financier known as "The Big Bankroll." Allegedly masterminded the 1919 World Series fix (the "Black Sox" scandal) by bribing eight members of the Chicago White Sox to throw games to the Cincinnati Reds. Rothstein's guilt in this has never been proven and is doubted by some historians, though he certainly knew the games were rigged and bet accordingly. Alleged to have financed Waxey Gordon and Big Maxey Greenberg in the first rumrunning operations from Europe in the early 1920s. Suspected of masterminding the theft of $5 million in bonds in Wall Street robberies, for which his lieutenant Nicky Arnstein went to prison. Fatally shot at the Park Central Hotel in Manhattan, November 4, 1928, possibly as the result of unpaid debts owed from high-stakes card games, or of the ambitions of his former bodyguard, Jack "Legs" Diamond.

Saietta, Ignazio "Lupo the Wolf" (1877–1944)

Born in Corleone, Sicily. Fled to New York to escape murder charge in 1899. Brother-in-law of Giuseppe Morello and Ciro Terranova and most infamous of the early Italian gang leaders in New York. Underboss of Morello crime family in early 1900s. Suspect in 1903 barrel murders. Active in Black Hand extortion, counterfeiting and narcotics. Suspected kidnapper. Proprietor of so-called Murder Stable at 323 107th Street in Harlem, where 23 men allegedly were killed between 1900 and 1917. Victims were supposedly hung on meat hooks or burned alive in the stable's furnace. Convicted of counterfeiting in 1910 and sentenced to 30 years in Atlanta. Paroled in 1921. Parole revoked by President Roosevelt in 1936 after New York State authorities discovered Lupo was running a lottery and extorting the bakery and grape industries. Died in 1944, soon after release from prison.

Schultz, Dutch (true name Arthur Flegenheimer) (1902–1935)

Born August 6, 1902, at 1690 Second Avenue, New York City, the son of Herman and Emma Neu Flegenheimer. One-time gunman for Legs Diamond; became a speakeasy owner in the 1920s, expanded his operation to become beer baron of the Bronx, then branched out into labor racketeering and gambling. Muscled black operators and seized control of Harlem numbers racket. Gained much notoriety in 1930–32 period during a violent gang war with his former henchman, Vincent "Mad Dog" Coll. Indicted for income-tax evasion in 1933 and became a federal fugitive. Surrendered at Albany, New York, November 28, 1934. Acquitted after two trials in 1935. Fatally shot, with three gang members, at the Palace Chop House, Newark, New Jersey, October 23, 1935, by Charles "The Bug" Workman. Allegedly, the Schultz murder was ordered by Lucky Luciano and Lepke Buchalter, who feared that the pressure to clean up local corruption would only become more intense if the hot-headed Schultz carried out his plan to assassinate Special Prosecutor Thomas E. Dewey.

Shapiro, Jacob "Gurrah" (1897–1947)

Born in Minsk, Russia, May 5, 1897. New York labor racketeer and longtime partner of Lepke Buchalter. Suspect in 1927 murder of Little Augie Orgen and later his bodyguard, Legs Diamond. Convicted in October 1936, and sentenced to two years for violating federal anti-trust laws by conspiring to restrain trade in rabbit skins. Freed on $10,000 bond, he jumped bail and became a fugitive. Later indicted by New York County on numerous counts of extortion in the garment and baking industries. Surrendered to authorities on April 14, 1938. Convicted in 1943 on 32 counts of extortion and sentenced to 15 years to life. Died in Sing Sing state prison on June 9, 1947.

Siegel, Benjamin "Bugsy" (1906–1947)

Born in Brooklyn, February 28, 1906, son of Max and Jennie Siegel. With Meyer Lansky, led the Bugs & Meyer Mob in New York in 1920s. Later closely associated with Lucky Luciano. Prime suspect in several murders, reportedly boasted of having killed 12 men. Moved to Los Angeles in 1930s and allegedly organized and ran West Coast branch of the national crime syndicate. Best known as the underworld founder of Las Vegas. With financial backing from eastern mobsters, built the Flamingo, first of the luxury hotel-casinos on the "Strip," which failed to pay off while he was living. Suspected of skimming the funds, Siegel was murdered June 20, 1947, at the mansion of his mistress, Virginia Hill, at 810 North Linden Drive in Beverly Hills.

Solomon, Charles "King" (1884–1933)

Native New Yorker who became New England's premier bootlegger during Prohibition, but also dabbled in morphine and cocaine smuggling, prostitution, receiving stolen goods and bail bonds. Shot to death by Irish gangsters at his Cotton Club in Boston, January 24, 1933.

Sutton, William Francis "Willie the Actor" (1901–1980)

Noted for using trickery instead of violence, Sutton supposedly stole over $2 million during his long criminal career. His elaborate disguises included makeup and uniforms (police, fire, messenger, etc.), which also helped him escape. Convicted of bank burglary in New York, 1926, and sentenced to 5 to 10 years; served time at Sing Sing and Dannamora. Paroled in 1929. Worked briefly for Dutch Schultz. Convicted of bank robbery in 1931 and sentenced to 30 years in Sing Sing. Escaped in December 1932. Recaptured in Philadelphia, 1934, convicted of another bank robbery there, and sentenced to 25 to 50 years at Eastern State prison in Philadelphia. Transferred to Holmesburg prison after another escape attempt. With several others, escaped from Holmesburg, February 10, 1947. Suspected in Boston Brink's robbery in 1950 and named to FBI's "Ten Most Wanted" list. Robbed his last bank in New York in March 1950. Captured last time in Brooklyn, February 18, 1952, on a tip from Brooklyn clothing salesman Arnold Schuster, who was murdered on March 9. Given long sentence for two counts of gun possession and for bank robbery, added to previous 30-year sentence. Released from Attica prison, December 24, 1969. Died at his sister's home in Spring Hill, Florida, November 2, 1980.

Terranova, Ciro "The Artichoke King" (alias Ciro Morello) (1891–1938)

Sicilian gang boss in Harlem and member of the large Morello-Terranova clan. Half-brother of Joe Morello, alleged founder of first New York

Mafia family. Notorious produce racketeer who monopolized the artichoke market in New York before Prohibition. Indicted in 1918 for ordering murders of Charles Lombardi and Joe Di-Marco; indictment dismissed. Alleged Italian lottery boss and narcotics trafficker, later bootlegger. Allied with Dutch Schultz in late twenties and became a partner with Schultz in Harlem numbers racket formerly controlled by black operators. Hosted banquet for Judge Albert Vitale in Roman Gardens restaurant in the Bronx, December 7, 1929, where guests were held up and robbed by gunmen. New York police later claimed, absurdly, that Terranova masterminded the robbery in order to recover a "murder contract" which had actually been put in writing by a Chicago mobster for the killings of Frankie Yale and Frankie Marlow. By other accounts, the robbery was committed by underworld rivals, possibly working for Salvatore Maranzano, to embarrass Terranova. Terranova's notoriety supposedly forced him to turn over his artichoke business to a lieutenant, Joseph Castaldo. His artichoke racket ended in 1936 when Mayor Fiorello LaGuardia took the unusual step of banning their sale. Terranova's power had already declined, however, and he was forced into retirement by Lucky Luciano. The murder of Schultz removed Terranova's most important ally and he was replaced as Harlem gang leader by Trigger Mike Coppola. Died of coronary thrombosis in 1938.

Trafficante, Santo, Sr. (1886–1954)

Born in Sicily, immigrated to the U.S. in 1904, naturalized in 1925, and took up residence in Tampa, Florida, where he ruled gambling, narcotics and other criminal enterprises until the 1950s. Died of natural causes on August 11, 1954, and was succeeded by his son, Santo, Jr.

Uffner, George (alias George Hoffman)

During the twenties, specialized in narcotics with Arnold Rothstein, Legs Diamond and Lucky Luciano. Arrested with Luciano and Thomas "Fats" Walsh in November 1928 as a suspect in the Rothstein murder. Convicted of forgery and grand larceny in 1933 and sentenced to serve four to eight years. After release became a partner of Frank Costello in Texas and Oklahoma oil deals. Killed in plane explosion over Texas on September 29, 1959, with 33 other passengers. Wreckage yielded over $200,000 in diamonds believed to have been Uffner's.

Weinberg, Abe "Bo"

Chief gunner for Dutch Schultz, and also a close partner who often acted as Schultz's goodwill ambassador to smooth things over after the temperamental "Dutchman" had managed to insult or otherwise upset his erstwhile underworld friends. Allegedly a member of the group who flashed fake badges to gain entrance to the office of Salvatore Maranzano before shooting and stabbing him to death. Joined Luciano when the government appeared to have Schultz on the ropes for income-tax evasion, and was killed for his apparent disloyalty when Schultz beat the rap. Body never found.

Yale, Frankie (true name Francesco Iole; Americanized to Uale or Yale) (1893–1928)

Born in Calabria, Italy, and led New York's Five-Points Gang and its affiliates, whose most famous graduates were Johnny Torrio and Al Capone. Continued his association with Torrio and Capone after their move to Chicago, both in bootlegging and allegedly as a killer. Yale was a principal suspect in the murders of Chicago crime figures Big Jim Colosimo in 1920

GANGSTER AND OUTLAW QUOTATIONS

You can get much farther with a smile, a kind word and a gun than you can with a smile and a kind word.

—Al Capone

This is probably the most colorful remark attributed to Al Capone, and has appeared in several "famous quotations" books without source or citation. It is probably also apocryphal, the invention of some writer who decided that if Capone didn't say it, he could have said it, or should have said it. But during his reign as the country's most notorious gangster, Capone could not resist entertaining reporters with comments and commentary they found highly quotable, and which now seem to reveal a person more complex than the vicious, flamboyant thug usually portrayed in gangster films. Other criminals were as capable and crafty, but either they lacked Capone's capacity for introspection, or they learned from his example that the notoriety he obviously enjoyed only made him the most conspicuous symbol of Prohibition-era crime and thus an ever larger target for reformers and rivals alike.

At least as well known is the quote attributed to Willie Sutton when asked why he robbed banks. Supposedly he answered, "Because that's where the money is." Sutton later denied he ever said that, and credited it to a reporter who simply made it up.

"We can't all be saints" is a memorable quip probably made by John Dillinger to a reporter who has so far eluded researchers.

The following quotes are better substantiated, taken mainly from newspaper stories and magazine articles.

AL CAPONE:

I'm a businessman. I've made my money supplying a popular demand. If I break the law, my customers are as guilty as I am.

I've seen gambling houses, too—in my travels, you understand—and I never saw anyone point a gun at a man and make him go in. I've never heard of anyone being forced to go to a place to have some fun.

I never stuck up a man in my life. Neither did any of my agents ever rob anybody or burglarize any homes while they worked for me. They might have pulled plenty of jobs before they came with me or after they left me, but not while they were in my outfit.

Ninety percent of the people of Cook County drink and gamble, and my offense has been to furnish them with those amusements. Whatever else they may say, my booze has been good and my games have been on the square. Public service has been my motto.

When I sell liquor, they call it bootlegging. When my patrons serve it on silver trays on Lake Shore Drive, they call it hospitality.

Graft is a byword in American life today. It is law where no law is obeyed. It is undermining this country. The honest lawmakers of any city can be counted on your fingers. I could count Chicago's on one hand.

A crook is a crook, and there's something healthy about his frankness in the matter. But the guy who pretends he's enforcing the law and steals on his authority is a swell snake.

The worst type is the Big Politician who gives about half his time to covering up so that no one will know he's a thief. A hard-working crook can buy these birds by the dozens, but he hates them in his heart.

Union members look at dues the same way they look at taxes: just something you got to pay the thieves who run things.

There's always some wiseacre who stands in the wings and criticizes. You've got two choices. You either buy these wiseacres off by giving them jobs . . . or you scare them off. If they don't scare, you take them in the alley. When they get out of the hospital, if they still want to squawk, you get rid of them.

People who respect nothing dread fear. It is upon fear, therefore, that I have built up my organization. But understand me correctly, please. Those who work with me are afraid of nothing. Those who work for me are kept faithful, not so much because of their pay as because they know what might be done with them if they broke faith.

Every time a boy falls off a tricycle, every time a black cat has gray kittens, every time someone stubs a toe, everytime there's a murder or a fire or the Marines land in Nicaragua, the police and the newspapers holler, 'Get Capone!' I'm sick of it. As soon as I possibly can, I'll clear out of here.

They've hung everything on me but the Chicago fire.

Nobody was ever killed except outlaws, and the community is better off without them.

I have always been opposed to violence, to shootings. I have fought, yes, but fought for peace. And I believe I can take credit for the peace that now exists in the racket game in Chicago. I believe that

the people can thank me for the fact that gang killings here are probably a thing of the past.

I'm tired of gang murders and gang shootings. It's a tough life to lead. You fear death at every moment, and worse than death, you fear the rats of the game who'd run around and tell the police if you don't constantly satisfy them with money and favors.

I came to Chicago with forty dollars in my pocket. . . . My son is now twelve. I am still married and I love my wife dearly. We had to make a living. I was younger than I am now, and I thought I needed more. I didn't believe in prohibiting people from getting the things they wanted. I thought Prohibition was an unjust law and I still do.

Now get me right. I'm not posing as a model for youth. I've had to do a lot of things I don't like to do. But I'm not as black as I'm painted. I'm human. I've got a heart in me.

I'm out of the booze racket now and I wish the papers would let me alone.

Let the worthy citizens of Chicago get their liquor the best way they can. I'm sick of the job. It's a thankless one and full of grief.

You gotta have a product that everybody needs every day. We don't have it in booze. Except for the lushes, most people only buy a couple of fifths of gin or Scotch when they're having a party. The workingman laps up half a dozen bottles of beer on Saturday night, and that's it for the week. But with milk! Every family every day wants it on the table. The people on Lake Shore Drive want thick cream in their coffee. The big families out back of the yards have to buy a couple of gallons of fresh milk every day for the kids. . . . Do you guys know there's a bigger markup in fresh milk than there is in alcohol? Honest to God, we've been in the wrong racket right along.

"Scarface" Al Capone, knifed by angry, inebriated Frank Galluccio at Frankie Yale's Harvard Inn in Brooklyn in 1917, sometimes had his wounds enhanced in newspaper pictures. An unretouched version appears on the *Time* magazine cover, p. 163. *(Goddard Collection)*

If Capone had the morals and mind-set of a robber baron, his outlaw counterpart was John Dillinger, a daredevil bandit less articulate but also concerned with his public image. He differed from most other "public enemies" in seeming to possess a fairly conventional value system—one that included a basic sense of right and wrong, tempered with a flexibility that was also an American trait. Unlike some contempo-

raries who displayed a sadistic streak, he viewed himself as a professional bank robber engaged in crimes against property, and who faced the same occupational hazards as those paid to kill or capture him. As a fugitive he was less accessible to the press, but when in custody he, like Capone, would banter with reporters.

JOHN DILLINGER:

I don't smoke much, and I drink very little. I guess my only bad habit is robbing banks.

I stick by my friends and they stick by me.

Never trust a woman or an automatic pistol.

Maybe I'll learn someday, Dad, that you can't win in this game.

We can't all be saints.

I'd like to have enough money to enjoy life; be clear of everything—not worry, take care of my old man and see a ball game every day.

MARY KINDER (about Dillinger):

Johnnie's just an ordinary fellow. Of course he goes out and holds up banks and things, but he's really just like any other fellow, aside from that.

J. EDGAR HOOVER (about Dillinger):

He had his weaknesses—women, for one thing, and a flair for the spectacular.

INDIANA SHERIFF LILLIAN HOLLEY
(from whose jail Dillinger escaped with a wooden pistol):

We do not expect to have any trouble with our newest prisoner. Of course, I warned him the first thing that we would stand for no monkey business.

Most criminals were not particularly inclined to introspection or self-expression, but a few had memorable remarks.

BUGSY SIEGEL:

We only kill each other.

MICKEY COHEN:

I never killed a guy who didn't deserve it.

JACK "LEGS" DIAMOND:

I'm just a young fellow trying to get ahead.

PRETTY BOY FLOYD:

They'll get me. Sooner or later I'll go down full of lead. That's how it will end.

RAYMOND HAMILTON:

I'm Raymond Hamilton and I don't intend to give you any trouble. I'm just fresh out of ammunition, money, whiskey and women. Let's go to jail.

MACHINE GUN KELLY:

My people are good people even if I turned out to be an awful heel. [Kelly's most famous quote, "Don't shoot, G-men!" appears to have been a fabrication of the FBI.]

BABY FACE NELSON:

Tell my children I said good-bye.

BUGS MORAN:

I hope, when my time comes, that I die decently in bed. I don't want to be murdered beside the garbage cans in some Chicago alley.

BONNIE PARKER:

Tell the public I don't smoke cigars. It's the bunk.

HARRY PIERPONT:

I'm not like some bank robbers—I didn't get myself elected president of the bank first.

ARNOLD ROTHSTEIN:

Look out for Number One. If you don't, no one else will. If a man is dumb, someone is going to get the best of him, so why not you? If you don't, you're as dumb as he is.

ROGER TOUHY: (dying of shotgun wounds after 25 years in prison);

The bastards never forget.

FRANK GUSENBERG (mortally wounded in the St. Valentine's Day Massacre):

Nobody shot me.

WILBUR "TRI-STATE TERROR" UNDERHILL (mortally wounded by FBI agents):

Tell the boys I'm coming home.

ARTHUR "DUTCH SCHULTZ" FLEGENHEIMER:

If I'd stuck to Flegenheimer, I'd never be in trouble like this. Schultz is a short word, and swell for the headlines. You'd-a never stuck Flegenheimer in the headlines, and nobody'd ever heard of me.

and Dean O'Banion in 1924, presumably to accommodate Torrio and Capone. National president of the Unione Siciliana until July 1, 1928, when he became New York's first tommy gun victim. Use of submachine guns led police to believe the killers were from Chicago, which in fact they were. Yale supposedly had allowed the hijacking of Chicago liquor shipments, and had further antagonized Capone by opposing his candidate for president of the Chicago branch of the Unione, whose members supplied much of the home-produced alcohol used to make illegal liquor. Probably murdered by Fred "Killer" Burke and Gus Winkeler, originally outlaws from St. Louis, who became the special assignment squad known in Capone camp as his "American boys," and Louis "Little New York Louie" Campagna. One Thompson was tossed, but another, found at Burke's home in Michigan, would be linked ballistically to both the murder of Yale and Chicago's St. Valentine's Day Massacre the following year.

The same year Arnold Rothstein was mortally shot, Brooklyn's Frankie Yale, onetime friend and colleague of both John Torrio and Al Capone, crossed his Chicago friends and, in 1928, became New York's first submachine-gun victim. *(Partners in Crime Archive)*

TRADE EXPANSION
—Enright in the New York *World*.

The machine-gun murder of Frankie Yale marked the expansion of Chicago-style crime, or as one cartoonist put it, Chicago-style trade, to New York. *(Authors' collection)*

Zwillman, Abner "Longy" (1904–1959)

Born in Newark, New Jersey, July 27, 1904, the son of Avraham and Anna Zwillman. Bootlegging and gambling boss of northern New Jersey during Prohibition, founding member of the national crime syndicate and a major organized crime figure in the East until his death. Fought 1930 gang war with Ruggiero "Richie the Boot" Boiardo. Boiardo was seriously wounded in a murder attempt in Newark on November 26, 1930. Either Al or Ralph Capone reportedly went to Newark to help settle differences between Zwillman and Boiardo, who eventually became close allies. Zwillman harbored outlaw Verne Miller after the Kansas City Massacre of July 1933, until Miller allegedly killed a member of Zwillman's mob. Miller was found murdered in Detroit on November 29 of that year, almost certainly on Zwillman's orders. Zwillman ended his own remarkably long crime career on February 26, 1959, by hanging himself in the basement of his mansion at West Orange, New Jersey, but many believe he was murdered.

2

CHICAGO'S BOOTLEGGING GANGS AND ITS FIVE YEARS OF "BEER WARS"

When national Prohibition became the law of the land, the city's most prominent saloons seemed to join the public and the press in grudgingly accepting the idea of a dry America. Wartime prohibition was already in place, pushed through as a patriotic measure to keep farm products in the food chain for eating instead of drinking; and while this had already disrupted public drinking habits, most of the political quarrelling concerned exemptions, exceptions, local option matters, special closing laws in the cities, and the amount of alcohol permissible in beer. So on January 17, 1920, a day widely celebrated (or mourned) in the press and major drinking establishments, the 18th Amendment became enforceable under the Volstead Act, legally creating a dry America and inspiring Chicago's colorfully corrupt Alderman "Hinky Dink" Kenna to ceremoniously donate his giant personal beer stein to the Chicago Historical Society.

The general assumption was that the Volstead Act, which created a National Prohibition Bureau with federal police powers, and which obligated state authorities to cooperate, could be enforced. No one doubted it could and would be violated, but buttressed by the moral authority of a Constitutional Amendment, Chicago's existing criminal and quasi-criminal gangs, thinking small, regarded bootlegging merely as a new and welcome source of illegal revenue, without appreciating Prohibition's incredible potential.

The murder of Big Jim Colosimo in 1920 freed John Torrio to expand into bootlegging, and his first efforts were to bring to it some semblance of order. With hundreds of breweries closing or converting to tepid "near beer," he masterminded the purchase of dozens of these plants, usually in collusion with their former owners and usually in partnership with other gang leaders, which created a *pax Torrio* of interlocking financial interests as everyone worked like beavers to develop his allocated territory.

Ironically, this reduced the city's crime rate. The enormous profits in illicit beer and liquor provided a new and less risky occupation for

SUMMER SHACK OF A STRUGGLING YOUNG BOOTLEGGER

The enormous profits in bootlegging provided many Italian, Irish and other immigrants who had the stomach for the risks their quickest escape from poverty. *(Goddard Collection)*

safecrackers, burglars and thieves, as well as for gunmen who became bodyguards and the underworld's police force. Now they provided security against independent hijackers too lazy or contrary to become team players, sometimes working with off-duty cops who could earn a month's police pay just for shepherding a truckload of booze through hostile neighborhoods, or from an illegal distillery to a distribution point. They could defend their cargo against rival gangs, but more often, they would negotiate a reasonable toll expected by brother officers working the streets.

By 1923, the low-key, unheralded Torrio had emerged as head of a loosely knit liquor syndi-

cate that included formerly law-abiding brewers, Prohibition agents and many police. He was also the recognized leader of the local criminal community that included Dean O'Banion, Hymie Weiss, George Moran, Terry Druggan, Frankie Lake, Frank McErlane, Dapper Dan McCarthy, Walter Stevens, Danny McFall, Louis "Two-Gun" Alterie, the West Side O'Donnells and even the notorious Genna brothers—a veritable equal-opportunity Godfather who had taken the city's safecrackers, Black-Handers, burglars, teenage gang members and put them gainfully to work. Even young Al Capone, on the lam from murder charges in New York, was acquiring business skills, despite occasional slipups.

With a few exceptions, this harmony prevailed during the first three years of Prohibition, then unravelled because of forces beyond Torrio's control.

The kind of young men inclined to crack safes and crack heads for politicians, newspaper and cab companies, could not always resist the temptation to hijack a load of booze, challenge the sovereignty of another gang or get into personal disputes that led to shootings. An outbreak of such violence in 1923, combined with election violence led to the defeat of Big Bill Thompson by William E. Dever, a reform candidate (though not a dedicated "dry") who pledged to strictly enforce the largely ignored Prohibition law and purge the city of its flamboyant corruption.

Among Dever's unprecedented actions was a well-orchestrated raid on the Sieben Brewery, which O'Banion, tipped off in advance, had just sold to Torrio for a reported half million dollars in cash. That O'Banion regarded this as a grand prank meant that Torrio was losing not only control of his affiliates but also the political protection his operations had enjoyed under the Thompson administration. Battles already had broken out in several parts of the city, and with O'Banion's declaration of independence inspiring even more revolts, Torrio felt obliged to roll out his own forces, captained by Al Capone. A series of killings failed to restore order, leading newspapers to start counting casualties among rival gangs, which came to a head when the primary elections of 1924 turned into a bloodbath. Harrassed by Dever, the South Siders had moved their operations a few miles west along 22nd Street to the adjoining town of Cicero. Capone's brother Frank was killed near a polling place by Chicago police sent in by Dever to restore order, making O'Banion's treachery in the Sieben raid all the more intolerable, especially when the North Sider would scornfully refer to his Italian colleagues as "greaseballs" and "spaghetti benders." Two days after the natural death of the city's underworld peacekeeper, Mike Merlo, level-headed leader of the Sicilian Union respected by O'Banion and Torrio alike, three men walked into Schofield's flower shop and blew O'Banion away. The *Chicago Tribune*'s banner headline read:

North Side Gang Chief O'Banion Killed

This was the first assassination of a Chicago gang "chieftain," a man who had left the Torrio fold to take personal control of the city's wealthy Gold Coast neighborhood and most of the North Side. It was correctly viewed as the opening shot in what would become known as the Chicago "beer wars," which would rage for nearly five years. The press and the public, who had previously regarded bootleggers as perhaps a civic problem but an interesting one, and

important providers of a public service, found themselves witnessing spectacular intergang gun battles that amounted to an underworld series whose spectators rarely were injured by foul balls.

The murder of O'Banion in such a conspicuous manner and place—at noontime in a State Street flower shop across from the Holy Name Cathedral, seat of the local archdiocese, following the unprecedented Sieben Brewery raid staged by the city's new reform administration, and the takeover of Cicero by Torrio and Capone—came as an awakening to the city's newspapers. Bootlegger killings were no longer viewed as border skirmishes or personal retaliations but evidence that the gangs were far better organized than previously supposed and now had gone to war.

One indication of this was the swift response of the North Siders to the death of their leader. Within the next few weeks they shot up the car of Al Capone, hitting his chauffeur, and then badly wounded Torrio, who passed the torch to young "Scarface" and retreated to New York as gangster emeritus. Their attacks on what were now Capone-affiliated gangs had the paradoxical effect of enhancing Capone's reputation as a ruthless killer. The North Siders were rowdy Irish in temperament if not in fact, and their repeated efforts to get at him usually involved more fireworks than careful planning. One attempt—which probably still holds the record for drive-by shootings—involved a midday motorcade of several cars filled with gunmen who poured over a thousand rounds into Capone's Hawthorne Hotel headquarters on the main street of Cicero. Capone emerged unscathed but not unimpressed, and even paid the medical bills of a bystander injured in the action. Three weeks later O'Banion's successor Hymie Weiss and four others were mowed down by machine-gun and shotgun fire from an upstairs window in the flat next to O'Banion's flower shop. Weiss and a bootlegger friend died in front of the cathedral, whose bullet-scarred cornerstone became a tourist attraction. The killers and their presumed backups in parked cars departed quickly, and investigating officers later discovered a second machine-gun nest in another apartment covering the flower shop's alley. Capone left nothing to chance.

Unless one counts the killing of Assistant State's Attorney William McSwiggin. For reasons never satisfactorily explained McSwiggin had accompanied two bootlegger buddies to a speakeasy in Capone's home territory of Cicero, and was in the group when it was sprayed with machine-gun bullets fired from a passing car.

McSwiggin's murder first was considered a flagrant disregard of the tacit understanding, shared by police and citizens alike, that gangsters shooting gangsters was only good for the gene pool, with public officials a protected species. Several grand juries investigated the case without establishing that McSwiggin was the intended target. McSwiggin's choice of friends did raise eyebrows, especially when one of his fellow victims turned out to have been a defendant acquitted in a murder case he had tried. Nevertheless, McSwiggin's death was regarded as a rare case of poor planning by Capone, who went into hiding until the furor subsided.

Another indication that gangs were acquiring political control over their former masters was the enormous wealth they were reaping from Prohibition. Street punks who had once depended on trolley transportation now dressed like the nouveau riche they were, employed chauffeurs to drive them about in the most luxurious or sporty of automobiles and thumbed their noses at the criminal justice system through generous bribes to police and judges, or intimidation of potential jurors and witnesses. Nor could many public officials reject a payoff that might represent an entire year's salary, especially knowing that such gratuities could come on a regular basis.

Indeed, a poorly paid policeman sometimes had the wisdom to hoard his wealth, using it later to move to a better neighborhood and give his children a college education. Many a prominent Chicagoan owes his prosperity to a father who saw the folly of Prohibition first-hand and considered bootlegger bribes his family's only means of social and economic advancement. Likewise, at least some bootleggers contented themselves simply to flee the slums, invest in honest enterprises and put their kids through school. Daniel Bell was among the first to recognize such crime as a ladder of upward social mobility, without going into much detail. Perhaps it was sufficiently obvious that a cop could lose his job, a bootlegger his life, and either could go to prison if he lacked good judgment or good luck. Ironically, national Prohibition filled the country's prisons with mostly harmless lawbreakers, while providing others with opportunities rarely encountered in the course of honest labor. A special talent for risk management probably made the difference.

This situation prevailed nationwide. Where Chicago and New York differed greatly was in their toleration of the violence that accompanied Prohibition. By the 1920s New York regarded itself as cultured and cosmopolitan; and if crime had been common it genuinely worried the local Establishment enough to close down its vice district, vanquish its "fighting gangs" and promote the city as America's undisputed leader in the fine arts and civilized living. Its handsome and colorful mayor, Jimmy Walker, was forced to resign, but his stylishness had compensated for his corruption; and until Arnold Rothstein's murder in 1928, he had been a gentleman gangster who bankrolled criminal enterprises while discouraging public gun battles.

By contrast, Chicago's mayor was Big Bill Thompson, a slobbish onetime cowboy elected mainly because his political incompetence and toleration of gang wars made up for his embarrassing public pronouncements. He had less couth than Al Capone in a city that attracted so much attention with the Thompson submachine gun that it became known as the "Chicago typewriter."

Despite Chicago's magnificent lakefront, creative post-fire architecture, world-class museums, and commercial importance, the average citizen regarded New Yorkers as pansies. Rather than enter a cultural competition they would have lost, they agreed with Carl Sandburg to be the city of broad shoulders and hog butcher to the world, and to the annoyance of civic leaders took a certain perverse pride in the outrageousness of their gangsters. Most agreed with the wisecrack of Al Capone: "When I sell liquor, they call it bootlegging; when my patrons serve it on silver trays on Lake Shore Drive, they call it hospitality."

Unlike New York, Chicago took a certain pride in its tough reputation, as reflected in a local newspaper's amazingly casual coverage of one election day's action:

Gunmen Fight Election War; Other Violence

One man was killed and two were wounded, one probably fatally, during election disturbances yesterday.

Voters and precinct workers in some sections of the city were slugged, intimidated and even kidnapped. There were narrow escapes from death as rival gunmen in fast automobiles fired volleys while near polling places.

A gun battle between two groups of gangsters in automobiles ended almost in front of a polling place at 405 South Hoyne Street, when John Mackey, 1224 West Madison Street, a well known police character, was shot and killed. Eleven bullets were found in Mackey's head and body.

Two Others Wounded

One of his companions, Claude Maddox, was shot in the back and a second, Anthony Kissane, another notorious character, was found huddled in an alley nearby a few minutes later, splattered with the blood of his dead friend and nursing a sprained ankle which he suffered in the leap from Mackey's car. Mackey and Kissane were arrested ten days ago as the bandits who robbed a northwest side bank, but were freed when they established alibis. . . .

Even the *Chicago Tribune*, smarting from the disparaging remarks that New York and other cities enjoyed heaping on the "Gem of the Prairie," found a poetic way to shrug off critics. Referring to the publicity generated when the governor of Illinois decided National Guard troops might be needed to keep the peace, the

"Trib," tongue firmly in cheek, found the silver lining in an April 1927 editorial:

The Terrifyng Chicagoan

. . . Our officialdom, local and state, did something to help [Chicago's reputation] along. The National Guard touch, a few days before the voting, indicated that each voter might go to the polls under the protection of bayonets. The police machine gun squads and the riot details helped out the picture. . . .

Thus far the most inspired picture of political life in Chicago has been given in London by the London Daily News: *"Three thousand hooligan gangs are carrying on a campaign of brigandage and murder," etc. Machine guns, bullet swept streets, death lists and the casualties all over the place.*

It may be for the best. A Chicagoan soon will be regarded as a person who is alive because of particular individual hardihood, courage and markmanship. He will be known as the hard boiled egg of the world. He has survived. That is sufficient. He may have a quiet, even chastened, appearance, but no one, particularly no one abroad, will rely on that. The man probably can shoot from six pockets at once and will if annoyed. . . .

Under the eccentric leadership of publisher "Colonel" McCormick (who modestly billed the *Tribune* "The World's Greatest Newspaper" beneath its front page logo, and required it to "Americanize" the spelling of many English words), the "Trib" battled Mayor "Big Bill the Builder" Thompson, trumpeted against his corruption, championed reform as a matter of principle, but above all defended Chicago against its detractors, especially those in New York. And in a city whose newspapers had fought circulation wars with the same sluggers and gunmen used by its politicians, and condoned nearly any trick or scam a reporter might use to scoop the opposition (giving rise to the "Chicago school of journalism"), the *Tribune*'s staunch opposition to Prohibition mitigated its view of bootlegging as a crime. This forced the paper to agree on some issues with Chicago's clown mayor, who named pet rats after his political enemies, threatened to burn history books uncritical of the British and "punch King George in the nose." The middle ground that most Chicago papers took was to condemn crime in general but blame it largely on a foolishly conceived and badly enforced law; and beyond that simply to report every gangland killing for the benefit of its readers.

The Landesco Report

After the middle 1920s the Chicago gang wars (as well as the Birger-Shelton feud in southern Illinois) were attracting so much national attention that several business and civic organizations joined forces to sponsor the most comprehensive study of the problem yet attempted. Experts were called in from around the country, and over a period of about three years delivered themselves of a massive 1,100-page *Illinois Crime Survey* that state and local politicians all but ignored. The only part to catch the eye of scholars and criminologists was a section by John Landesco, a University of Chicago sociologist who went beyond the study's simplistic theme of blaming crime on criminals and a faulty criminal justice system,

"They Are Spoiling an Otherwise Inspiring Picture," John T. McCutcheon's 1928 Chicago Tribune *cartoon, depicts the tolerance of public officials for gangs as a blight on Chicago. CHS, ICHi-13902.*

Collusion between criminal gangs, politicians and police had been commonplace for years but worsened dramatically during Prohibition, leading one discouraged reformer to remark, "Chicago is unique. It is the only totally corrupt city in America." *(Authors' collection)*

and sought to explore the social roots of criminal behavior. What became known as the Chicago school of sociology had already attracted much attention and some disapproval by abandoning the "outhouse counting," which had characterized that discipline nationally; instead it examined urban problems (including criminality) from the new perspective of "cultural relativism" pioneered by progressive anthropologists of the period. As adapted by the Chicagoans, this was the notion that cultures or subcultures, in urban as in primitive societies, should be examined on their own terms rather than judged by an outsider's value system. Contrary to conventional thinking, the adult criminal was not necessarily abnormal or maladjusted, but was in fact a conformist. In his world, only the maladjusted might aspire to become, say, a doctor.

Of equal importance, Landesco virtually coined the term "organized crime" to describe the kind of institutionalized or systematic lawbreaking that was so common in Chicago and elsewhere as to have escaped recognition, except as targets for specific reforms. The crime Landesco referred to was organized locally, and had been for decades, enduring through the simple practice of bribing police, politicians or both. And if Landesco could see that bootleggers were fostering this corruption to an unprecedented degree, it was still too soon to appreciate that Prohibition would result in the networking of gangs throughout the country. Following Repeal, the avenues created for distributing booze would be traveled less obviously by racketeers who used the next few years of armed-robber hysteria to evolve nearly unmolested into nationally organized crime.

But in mapping the rise of the Syndicate that would eventually control Chicago, Landesco

himself became caught up in the gangland battles and sometimes studied them less like a scholar than a war correspondent. He presented a detailed report on the machine-gun murder of Assistant State's Attorney McSwiggin and his bootlegger friends as a case study in political corruption and police incompetence, whose solution defied a coroner's jury and six grand juries, one after the other, because of conflicting agencies, investigations and agendas. His hope was that this example would awaken citizens to the need for reform and professionalism. He then proceeded to cover the fighting in a manner

The World's Most Impudent Criminal

By the late 1920s Al Capone wielded more actual power than anyone else in the city, and Chicago politicians and civic leaders had to enlist his support in nearly all matters involving crime, such as curtailing the bombings and shootings that marked 1928's "Pineapple Primary." *(Authors' collection)*

that he thought reflected the existing gangs and rivalries and alliances. Landesco became tangled up in his civic geography and oft-changing gang affiliations, sometimes putting a murder in the wrong "casualty" list. This was especially true with the Gennas, a family of old-world Sicilians who were alternately allied with or fighting the South Siders, the West Siders and the North Siders, sometimes on the principle that any enemy of my enemy is my friend. Such a policy worked both ways, of course, until most of them were killed or had fled Chicago. So Landesco's efforts to differentiate among rival bootlegger battles probably reflect fast-breaking news stories, police reports that were often inaccurate or misleading, and some guesswork, but at least provide historians with a sense of how confusing things were at the time. Landesco's recognition of separate and concurrent gang wars reflected the efforts of a scholar to apply scientific method to improve on the journalistic reporting that tried to link the killings chronologically. In his summary, he correctly observed that the election of a reform mayor, Dever, who tried to enforce an unpopular law (of which he personally disapproved) as a matter of principle, had the contrary result of displacing an orderly system of corruption with something close to anarchy. Commenting on the failings of the criminal justice system, he said: "The gang code of silence and personal vengeance rather than legal redress was so compelling that of the 215 murders of gangsters during four years of armed strife, only a handful of arrests and no convictions were secured by the law enforcing agencies. But the police, forced apparently to resort to shooting it out in running battle, succeeded in killing 160 gangsters during this same period."

Noting that Chicago exceeded all other cities in gangland violence, Landesco decided this could not be explained simply by the failure of the majority of citizens to support national Prohibition. "In the first place, other cities have not experienced so violent a disorder in the enforcement of prohibition. In the second place, this defiance of law and order by the gunman and

LOOKS AS IF WE GOT THE OLD FORT REBUILT JUST IN TIME

Chicago officials began looking ahead to the Century of Progress World's Fair in 1933 about the same time the city had secured its undisputed reputation as the country's gangster capital. At a secret meeting Capone, who had tried more than once to establish a gangland truce, considered the continual violence bad for the city and bad for business. He said he could order the "dagos" to behave, but wanted to know how far he should go with the "micks" and other gangsters who were shooting each other on sight. When the head of the Chicago Crime Commission did not advocate their murder, as Capone seemed to be suggesting, Big Al magnanimously agreed to call his friends in the police department and simply have any troublemakers locked up. Keeping order was all but impossible, but the presidential election of 1928 was one of the city's first to involve no killings, kidnappings or voter intimidation. *(Authors' collection)*

his immunity from punishment by the orderly processes of law are not limited in Chicago to the field of prohibition," but prevail in every field of criminality as a result of institutionalized collusion between criminals, politicians and to a large degree the police.

The Wickersham Commission

In May 1929, President Hoover, moved by the spectacle in Chicago, the Illinois Crime Survey with its Landesco report and the expansion of Chicago-style violence to other cities, established the National Commission on Law Enforcement and Observance, chaired by onetime attorney general George W. Wickersham. This was a federal version of the Illinois study and became popularly known as the Wickersham Commission which went on a nationwide tour like a great circus, holding much-publicized hearings in every major city and systematically describing Prohibition-enforcement conditions almost county by county. But its final report, issued in 1931, dismayed both wets and dries with its failure to reach conclusions that either side could use to its advantage; thus it joined other mammoth and costly government studies quickly entombed in the bowels of libraries that hold Congressional records, investigations and hearings as a matter of policy, immortalized only as footnotes in graduate theses and dissertations.

So much for the Wickersham Report, a monument to equivocation that had but one interesting feature. While surveying most states, including New York, in only a few pages, it devoted an entire volume to Illinois, with a separate section concentrating on Chicago, where the action was.

Its local investigator, Bureau of Prohibition agent Guy L. Nichols, described the Chicago situation with the enthusiasm of a cub reporter, taking it upon himself to skulk about the city with car, camera and bodyguards, sneaking pictures of notorious gangster headquarters, hangouts and saloons, referring to himself in the third person and describing his adventures with great excitement:

> . . . *Leaving the Metropole [a Capone stronghold at 2300 South Michigan Avenue, a block south of the Lexington Hotel, where he headquartered from 1928 to 1932] your investigator, in a large, closed car, accompanied with a bodyguard of three in civilian clothes, stopped in the center of the street and from the middle side car window photographed the Paddock Grill, 2507 South Wabash Avenue. . . . At the time it was snapped a lookout was seen through the window. He immediately stepped aside and Jack Heinan, a former pugilist and a present partner of Ralph Capone, came to the window.*
>   . . . *After snapping the picture from inside the car, we sped on to other scenes, but had not proceeded over two blocks when it was discovered that a car had put out through curiosity from the Paddock and was following us. The chase was given up in the maze of traffic. . . .*

While touring the valley of the shadow of death, investigator Nichols and his bodyguards penetrated to the heart of the enemy camp in

THE NOBLE EXPERIMENT

Chronic drinking, like chronic violence, had its own origins. In Colonial America alcohol was considered nutritious, an aid to digestion, a convenient substitute for water that not only lacked "food value," but also was often contaminated. It was essential to farm animals (which further diminished its appeal), but otherwise useful mainly for cooking, washing and navigation. Liquor also reflected the increasing abundance of grain whose most manageable and marketable form was whiskey, preferred over sour wines and bitter brews, and sometimes a victual necessity for washing down salty, greasy and rancid food. Getting somewhat drunk in the process was a cross one had to bear.

With the development of new grain products and markets, the upheaval of the Civil War, and then an Industrial Revolution with its opportunities for progress and economic prosperity, the United States' feeble and religious-oriented "temperance" movement began finding more and more allies. The social cost of widespread drunkenness was conspicuous in city streets that looked like battlefields littered with dead and wounded, and in the destruction of families dependent on meager wages to pay for food and rent instead of the transient solace provided by the saloon. "Drink is the curse of the working class," declared the captains of industry, plagued with absenteeism and reeling workmen, and if they were supported first by extremists like Carrie Nation whose flailing hatchet destroyed saloons (often to the merriment of spectators), the new Progressive Movement worked hard to remedy every urban ill from alcoholism to poverty to ignorance to disease, all of which ravaged the urban slums.

By the turn of the century, many states, especially in the South and West, had enacted their own prohibition laws, following the lead of a spreading Temperance Movement that now could win state and local elections and even nominate presidential candidates. This campaign might have failed in the major cities, whose large immigrant populations considered beer and wine a birthright and also depended on the neighborhood tavern or saloon for many personal and community services not yet provided by the city. Besides being the only source of recreation for the working poor, the saloon functioned as a post office, message center, first-aid station, counseling clinic, soup kitchen and a campaign headquarters for ward bosses and aldermen.

The temperance movement had its roots in Kansas, as a poorly organized women's campaign led by women such as Carrie Nation who could get away with destroying saloons on the ground that they were technically illegal under state law. But even as her campaign evolved into a movement supported by less violent but more influential organizations, such as the Women's Christian Temperance Union, it remained a moral crusade. An Anti-Saloon League that originated in Ohio as a nonsectarian organization included some high-minded politicians who initially opposed saloons and taverns as a practical matter to reduce public and on-the-job drunkenness, but discovered it had strong support among businessmen and industrialists. It soon expanded from a state to a national movement and in the process found itself (with changes in leadership and policies) absorbing local prohibitionist groups, which transformed it into the country's most powerful lobby for banning the sale of booze wherever and whenever possible.

A complete standoff was averted by the First World War and appeals to patriotism. The idea that supposedly scarce grain and other foodstuffs were being denied starving orphans in Europe so that Americans might drink inspired image-conscious politicians to enact a special and presumably temporary wartime prohibition law giving the president authority over agricultural production.

With so many drinking-age citizens in the military, and the remainder either accommodating wartime prohibition or ignoring it, the last few states ratified the 18th Amendment in January 1919, barely two months after the armistice, without giving much thought to its enforcement. It was sincerely believed that a decree enshrined in so hallowed a document as the U.S. Constitution would be observed by nearly everyone as a matter of principle. To deal with those few who might think they could ignore such a powerful mandate, Congress passed a criminal law called the Volstead Act which gave distillers, brewers and taverns a transitional period of exactly one year before the law took effect. Congress also allocated only a modest sum to establish a federal enforcement agency, partly because the law also required the states to pass their own versions of the Volstead Act.

The flush of victory did not last long. The opportunities afforded by Prohibition provided the urban poor with what historian Daniel Bell would one day call a "queer ladder of social mobility" that accomplished precisely the opposite of what the Prohibitionists intended. Liquor Prohibition, like drug criminalization later, transformed many relatively harmless neighborhood gangs into wealthy underworld organizations that corrupted government from top to bottom, including the police, who had never

been much more than thinly disguised goon squads controlled by the ruling ward boss.

The 18th Amendment banned the manufacture, transportation, sale—everything but the actual drinking—of any beverages containing more than one half of one percent of alcohol. At last awakening to what this meant, several states belatedly rebelled, only to have their efforts to circumvent or modify the law quickly knocked in the head by the U.S. Supreme Court. So one minute after midnight of January 16, 1920—a day remembered for the desperate efforts of countless Americans using everything from wagons to baby carriages to stock their cellars with the last legal booze—the Volstead Act officially created a dry America; and each time it was challenged, the Supreme Court only tightened its provisions.

Promoted as an unprecedented national reform that would introduce an "era of clear thinking and clean living," Prohibition was much more than that. It was a major victory for an ascetic rural and Protestant value system over the vice and depravity associated with the city, one that was somehow expected to magically change the lifelong social habits of tidal waves of immigrants, at that time predominantly Catholics from Italy and Ireland (who had only their religion in common), but also Germans, Poles and Jews, all of whom were seen as rejecting traditional American values in favor of hedonistic, criminal or mercenary ones of their own.

Prohibition reduced per capita drinking for a time, but turned it from a working-class vice into a form of safe, middle-class rebellion against stodginess and respectability. Worse, it made drunkenness fashionable and humorous, and that, combined with the proliferation of automobiles, created an even greater national problem. With Repeal 13 years later the local gangs that had prospered from bootlegging lost that source of wealth and concentrated on racketeering, traveling the intercity routes established in the twenties for the distribution of liquor. What began as a collaboration with their criminal counterparts around the country evolved into a much more powerful and profitable nationwide confederation that by the 1950s represented modern organized crime.

In 1920, before the "noble experiment" blew up in the country's face, the *Literary Digest* sampled opinion from newspapers of the day expressing varying degrees of hope, righteousness, apprehension, disgust and fatalistic acceptance of a legal reality.

New Haven Courier-Journal: *"We are about to enter upon the greatest social experiment any civilized nation ever undertook [and] of all the civilized nations on the earth this nation is best calculated to make it a success—if a success can be made."*

New York Evening Post: *"No one who assists in violating the prohibition law can be called a good citizen; the buyer of a drink is no better than the seller."*

Providence Journal: *"No law-abiding citizen will think of attempting to evade the Volstead Act, which, strictly construed, is a criminal statute."*

Washington Post: *"Involved in the problem of making people both temperate and happy is the fact that a large proportion of the industrial population is made up of aliens or new naturalized citizens whose lifelong habits differ from those of native Americans."*

New York Evening World: *"The people of the United States are in the grip of a law which a majority of them do not approve and which large numbers of them do not respect. A law can be constitutional without being the will of the people—if misrepresentatives turn their backs on the people.*

"The enforcement of nationwide prohibition can only continue to be what it already is—a costly and unsuccessful effort productive of evasion, subterfuge, and hypocrisy."

Boston Herald: *"The Prohibition Amendment may have been unwise; it may or may not express actually the majority sentiment of the people, but the act was passed and ratified—and there you are."*

The Price of Prohibition

The cost of the noble experiment in money, lives and permanent disabilities was impossible to calculate since both wets and drys were equally willing to distort any data available. In 1929 a "dry" Justice Department abandoned the effort in the face of some truly grim statistics. The Hearts newspapers reveled in Prohibition's failure, and ran a series of feature articles listing the name of every Prohibition fatality, without always describing the circumstances. Its count in 1929 was 1,360 dead, illustrated by a grim cartoon of Roland Kirby–style Prohibitionists with guns riding gaunt horses past endless rows of corpses. At the time of Repeal, with the new Roosevelt administration in office, the government was pleased to issue a report declaring Prohibition had cost an average of a billion dollars a year in lost federal and local taxes and federal appropriations for enforcement—10 times the expense of the country's participation in the World War. Those killed by the end of 1932 included 2,089 civilians and 512 state and local dry-law enforcers. Prisons overflowed with small-time bootleggers, including a few who received "life for a pint" under a drastic state law passed in Michigan. Wet and dry leaders would continually dispute how many thousands were permanently maimed, blinded or killed by industrial alcohols deliberately poisoned by the previous administration in its search for denaturing methods that would defy rectification by "alky-cookers" [not many of whom had degrees in chemistry or, for that matter, lost much sleep over the purity of their product].

The safest source of good booze was the local pharmacist, who could issue cold-sufferers (or anybody else) up to a pint a week of "medicinal spirits" on a doctor's prescription —which could often be issued on the pretense of treating a head cold, whose symptoms could not yet be detected—or even merely as a sensible precaution against colds going around. This led to a few hundred thousand doctors and pharmacists obtaining licenses to dispense "medicinal spirits," and to the prosecution of many for turning this loophole into their major source of income. It also profiled several large distilleries, some of which did little more than add "for medicinal purposes only" to the label on their booze bottle.

The following tables taken from the November 1933 issue of the news publication *Mida's Criterion* offer some statistics on the final cost of Prohibition.

Cost of the "Noble Experiment" for the Thirteen Years:

Congressional enforcement appropriations	$132,958,530
State appropriations (8 years only)	5,585,850
Assessed value of property seized	186,867,322
Subsistence for jailed violators	111,103,870
Court costs for violators	111,103,870
Coast guard appropriations for enforcement	152,503,464
Customs service enforcement	93,232,230
Criminal court costs to state and municipal governments	2,922,622,000
Rental lost to padlocked landlords	303,615,000
Federal liquor revenue lost	11,988,000,000
State and municipal liquor revenue lost	6,540,620,000
Loss to consumers on excessive liquor bills, bootleg profits and protection	15,000,000,000

The thirteen-year cost is more than one-third greater than the national debt of 22 billions. It is more than two and one-half times the amount owed us by foreign governments. It is 10 billions greater than the cost of America's participation in the war, which was $26,361,000,000.

Table, complete to 1932, of Prohibition Killings, as Compiled from Federal Records and the Daily Press:

	Agents killed	Citizens killed	Total
1920	20	40	60
1921	38	75	113
1922	44	67	111
1923	33	66	99
1924	42	106	148
1925	49	97	140
1926	37	79	110
1927	56	97	158
1928	41	87	128
1929	59	110	169
1930	65	62	127
1931	14	15	33
1932	15	18	33
Estimated killed by local and state agents		1,170	1,170
Total	512	2,089	2,602

Life

Teacher: NOW WHICH OF YOU KNOWS WHAT THAT SIGN MEANS?
Small Bobby: I KNOW, TEACHER! IT MARKS THE SPOT WHERE THE BODY WAS FOUND.

X marks the spot entered the language of the twenties when newspaper photographers reached a murder scene after a body had been removed, or when a particular paper considered itself too family-oriented to publish crime-scene pictures that were especially gruesome. While Hearst's evening *Chicago American* spread a gory photograph of the St. Valentine's Massacre corpses across the entire width of its front page, McCormick's *Chicago Tribune,* for all its other excesses, had its retoucher cover the bodies with an opaque gray. Being "taken" or "put on the spot" still connotes trouble of one kind or another, although few know how the expressions evolved. *(Authors' collection)*

visiting the Anton (later Alton) Hotel in neighboring Cicero, living not only to tell the tale but also to draw a ground-floor plan of the place. Since the Anton's restaurant, bar and gaming rooms were heavily patronized by a public that enjoyed these amusements with no fear of being murdered, it's likely that Investigator Nichols and his men were the most conspicuous party in the place, and possibly a source of amusement. But his work certainly would not have been complete had he failed to attempt a survey of the gangs and their members. With even less insider knowledge than Landesco's, he assembled an impressive list of some "330 alleged gangsters" and their affiliations, using yet a different scheme that again illustrated the difficulty in trying to figure out the structure of the criminal community.

Both Landesco and the Wickersham investigator overlooked the members of the Capone gang who would one day follow in the "Big Fellow's" footsteps. At the time, Frank Nitti, Joey Aiuppa, Paul Ricca, Tony Accardo and Sam Giancana were merely young drivers, advisers and gunmen toiling in the vineyards of Prohibition, but over the next 30 or 40 years they would become the leaders of the Chicago mob.

3

CRIME CHRONOLOGY, 1919-1929

Crime reporting is less likely to reflect the seriousness of the crime problem at any given time than public perception; and perceptions are often shaped by press coverage based less on muddled statistics than on pronouncements of elected and appointed officials.

In the two or three decades that led to and included the First World War, crime and violence had become serious problems in urban areas but still were localized, consisting mainly of thievery, burglary, shopkeeper extortion, one-man stickups, and interpersonal violence of the bedroom and barroom variety. Compared with the present, even fewer ventured out at night alone or without arms, especially in certain neighborhoods that were understood to be free-fire zones. As *Gem of the Prairie* author Herbert Asbury described conditions in Chicago during the crime wave of 1905–06:

> . . . *The average citizen, and especially the average woman, was probably in greater danger of being robbed and murdered than at any other time in the history of Chicago . . . . With nothing to stop them, bands of thugs and hoodlums prowled the streets from dusk to dawn. They robbed every*

> *pedestrian they encountered, and many of these holdups were remarkable for brutality; sometimes the footpads stripped their victims, tied them to lamp posts, and cut shallow slits in their flesh with razors and knives. They broke into stores and residences, held sex orgies and drinking parties on the lawns and porches of private homes, and pursued every woman they saw. . . .*

Still, such crime presented no challenges that were new to urban life at the turn of the century, or could not be controlled or at least confined by municipal policemen or county sheriffs. Even gang crime could be suppressed, when political considerations demanded, by conventional police methods, however primitive they were.

By 1920, however, the automobile alone was revolutionizing crime. It had revived the kind of hit-and-run robbery that had greatly declined with better neighborhood policing, improved security measures, telephone communications and travel by railroad instead of stagecoach. The cities were the first to experience a dramatic rise in daylight holdups of banks, jewelry stores and payroll messengers by gangs of "strangers" who might have been the James brothers or the Daltons except for their use of cars. The police and the press, for want of new terminology, labeled these raiding parties "highwaymen," a relic of the 19th century. Their use of automobiles soon popularized the term "motorized bandits," but that lacked formality for law-enforcement purposes, and as the use of getaway cars became standard procedure, the term "armed robbery" was adopted by most agencies.

It quickly became apparent that traditional police methods were all but useless against criminals in cars. Even when city governments conceded the need to equip their departments with cars and motorcycles, they were so parsimonious that a district or precinct might rate only one or two vehicles, usually Model T Fords that made a police force look like Keystone Kops compared with their adversaries in Lincolns, Packards and Cadillacs. The central detective force enjoyed the prestige of patrolling the city in high-powered machines, but these served little purpose other than getting them to the scene of the crime rapidly and in style.

While inventors and visionaries came up with some truly goofy ideas to achieve parity with the crooks, such as armored chase cars with ramming features and motorcycles equipped with sidecar-mounted machine guns, the more typical situation was that which prevailed in Chicago on the morning of February 14, 1929. The neighborhood police station's two Model A Fords were already out, and the one officer on enforcement duty had to hitch a ride with a civilian to the scene of the St. Valentine's Day Massacre. (Coincidentally, several Chicago police officials had just arrived in Detroit to inspect the country's first two-way police radio system.)

Even with improved equipment, poor criminal-identification methods limited police effectiveness throughout the twenties. This helped the anonymous "motorized bandits" of that decade enjoy relatively long careers and far greater profits than the celebrated "public enemies" of the 1930s, who by then could be identified quickly, pursued doggedly and barely made expenses before earning posterity in the annals of American crime.

Police were slow to appreciate how well the earlier gangs were organized or how professionally they worked until some were tripped up through the fencing industry. Much loot in the form of jewelry, furs and securities had to be transformed into cash; by infiltrating the fencing business, police "detectives" were able to stamp out several major criminal operations. For example, New Yorkers were impressed to learn that the Whittemore and "Cowboy" Tessler gangs (unheralded until their capture) had maintained staffs of jewelers, and garages to store and service their automobiles, used guns with silencers, and otherwise represented state-of-the-art criminality. A number of gangs plundered the Midwest throughout the 1920s, robbing banks in one state and harboring in another, until they were taken by local authorities for perhaps a single job that satisfied their captors but hardly did "justice" to the quantity or quality of their long criminal careers.

Consequently, the press focused its attention on the criminal phenomenon that was most conspicuous, easily understood and had the virtue of novelty—the bootlegging gangs, whose leaders did not need anonymity to avoid prosecution, but only money to enrich politicians and pay off police. The corruption fueled by Prohibition made them nearly invulnerable, except to the gunfire of rivals.

Paradoxically, then, the newsmakers of the twenties were not the major and often deadly robberies by unidentified gunmen (though these were duly reported), but crimes associated with Prohibition—gang wars, political and police corruption and Prohibition itself. In truth, the celebrity bootleggers of the twenties were merely the vanguard of the nationally organized crime that would begin to flourish (again with anonymity) only after the Depression, the fall of Capone and the passage of Repeal signaled the end of the "Roaring Twenties." In 1933, the New Deal Justice Department, with a different agenda, fostered that notion by declaring a "war on crime" against public enemies in the form of bank robbers and kidnappers, some of whom were much less for-

midable than their predecessors, and made relatively easy targets once J. Edgar Hoover's new G-men had learned from their early mistakes.

The FBI can be credited with revolutionizing police work the way the car had revolutionized crime, and for restoring a measure of confidence in the federal government. It did so by means of new federal anti-crime laws that were long overdue in the age of the interstate fugitive, but which failed to address or even recognize nationally organized crime in the form of racketeering that grew nearly unmolested until the 1950s.

Like a catalogue of the criminals who gained lasting notoriety during the public enemy era, a chronology of crime is more an indicator of its news or publicity value, and the public's fears or fascinations, than an accurate measure of the menace crime presented at any given time.

PROHIBITION-ERA CRIME CHRONOLOGY
1919-1929

1919

January 16, 1919   Thirty-six states ratify the 18th Amendment to the Constitution, banning the manufacture, transportation and sale of alcoholic beverages.

January 19, 1919   "Auto bandits" rob a Philadelphia jewelry store of $10,000 in gems. L.J. Gale is arrested in New York City. This and several other large robberies begin attracting national attention to the new problem of "gas bandits" or "motorized bandits" who have little difficulty eluding the police who use only telephone communications and still rely largely on neighborhood foot patrols.

January 21, 1919   Policeman foils robbery of the Water-Tower Bank in St. Louis. One bandit is slain.

February 4, 1919   "Auto bandits" rob Frank Sternberger's saloon in the Bronx.

March 3, 1919   Robbers dynamite the First National Bank safe in Ansted, West Virginia.

March 7, 1919   New York bank messenger robbed of $65,800.

March 8, 1919   New York bandits rob Sinclair Valentine Company messengers of a $3,800 payroll.

March 9, 1919   Four bandits rob the Southside Bank in Kansas City, Missouri, killing cashier G.M. Shockley.

May 19, 1919 A Lehigh & Hudson freight train is robbed near Maybrook, New York.

July 28, 1919 Race riots occur in Chicago, lasting three days and killing 36. Similar riots occur the same summer in Washington, D.C., St. Louis and Arkansas.

July 29, 1919 East Side gang leader Joseph Weyler, alias Johnny Spanish, is shot to death by rival gangsters outside a restaurant at 19 Second Avenue in New York.

August 20, 1919 Railway Express truck stolen in New York City; driver and helper kidnapped.

September 13–14, 1919 New York Mayor Hylan suggests Police Commissioner Enright use automobile squad to intercept suspicious night gangs; Enright forms special automobile squad.

October 1–9, 1919 Eight members of the Chicago White Sox, bribed by gamblers, throw the World Series to the Cincinnati Reds. New York gambler and underworld financier Arnold Rothstein will be accused of organizing the World Series fix, though his involvement may have been marginal.

October 16, 1919 "Motor bandits" rob the First National Bank at Roselle, New Jersey, of $25,482, shooting police sergeant F. Keenan.

November 25, 1919 Chicago records 250 robberies in one week.

December 8, 1919 Morris Klein's jewelry shop in Chicago is robbed of $100,000.

December 30, 1919 Dean O'Banion hijacks truckload of Grommes and Ullrich whiskey outside Bismarck Hotel in Chicago.

1920

January 16, 1920 The Volstead Act goes into effect, providing for enforcement of the 18th Amendment.

In Chicago, six masked gunmen seize watchmen and railroad employees and loot two freight cars of $100,000 worth of whiskey. Attributed to West Side Hershie Miller gang.

February 3, 1920 Maurice "Mossy" Enright, Chicago labor racketeer, is shot to death in front of his home at 1110 West Garfield Boulevard. Attributed to fight for control of Street Cleaners Union.

February 5, 1920 *New York Times* notes revival of "highway robbery" by bandits using motor cars.

April 1, 1920 Dennis "Dinny" Meehan, leader of Brooklyn's Irish "White Hand" gang, is shot to death in his home on Warren Street and his wife is seriously wounded. The White Hand is at war with the Italian "Five Points Gang," headed by Francesco "Frankie Yale" Iole, for control of the Brooklyn waterfront.

April 22, 1920 Eddie Coleman, head of the Chicago Teamsters Union, is fatally shot by an unidentified gunman hiding in his office at 184 West Washington St.

April 26, 1920 Seven bandits rob the First National Bank at Sandy Springs, Maryland.

May 7, 1920 The Drovers National Bank in East St. Louis, Illinois, is robbed. One bandit is killed and another captured.

May 11, 1920 James "Big Jim" Colosimo, South Side Chicago vice lord and restaurateur, is shot to death in the vestibule of his famous cafe at 2126 South Wabash Avenue by a gunman hiding in the check room. Police suspect the killer was Brooklyn gangster Frankie Yale, former associate and employer of Johnny Torrio and Al Capone, who could not interest Colosimo in exploiting the opportunities afforded by Prohibition because he was already wealthy

Smitten by Dale Winter, a young songbird performing at his popular cafe and nightclub at 2126 South Wabash in the old Levee district just below the "Loop," Chicago vice lord Big Jim Colosimo ignored bootlegging in favor of lovemaking, turned most of his operations over to John Torrio (who apprenticed Al Capone), and in 1920 was "retired" by a gunman in the vestibule of his restaurant, shortly after he had dumped his frumpy wife from their earlier whorehouse days and married the unsullied Dale. His ex-wife's brothers were suspected until police discovered that New York's Frankie Yale was in town the day of the killing. *(Goddard Collection)*

and newly in love, and violating the Volstead Act was a federal offense he couldn't easily "fix."

June 6, 1920   New York jeweler Samuel Schonfeld attacked and robbed of $100,000 in gems.

June 16, 1920   Bandits rob the Dressel Commercial and Savings Bank in Chicago, killing a bank customer and wounding a policeman.

August 3, 1920   The Commercial Savings Bank at Moline, Illinois, is robbed of $20,000.

September 5, 1920   Eddie Adams and Ray and Walter Majors, notorious Wichita, Kansas, criminals, attempt to rob Harry Trusdell's gambling house at 1209 Grand Avenue in Kansas City, Missouri. In the resulting gun battle, gambler Frank Gardner is killed and Adams and the Majors brothers are captured. Adams will be convicted of murder and sentenced to life in the state prison at Jefferson City, Missouri. The Majors brothers will receive five-year sentences for robbery.

September 9, 1920   New York judge McIntyre announces he will sentence all holdup men to 20 years.

September 16, 1920   "Wall Street Bomb" explodes in horse-drawn wagon at the corner of Wall and Broad Streets in New York City, killing 38 in the blast, injuring hundreds, and shattering windows for several blocks; never explained or solved.

September 28, 1920   Grand jury in Chicago indicts eight members of the White Sox baseball team for allegedly throwing the 1919 World Series to the Cincinnati Reds.

October 1, 1920   In New York, a paymaster and guard for the American Cigar Company are beaten and robbed of $10,000.

November 4, 1920   Detroit bank messengers are robbed of $20,000.

November 10, 1920   Ottawa, Illinois, police call state prison at Joliet looking for safecrackers who can rescue a teller believed locked in the National City Bank's vault.

November 17, 1920   New York City home invaders rob Mrs. C.K. Palmer of jewelry worth $400,999.

THE BLACK HAND

Ignorance of the history and traditions in Sicilian and Italian immigrant communities, as well as silence on the part of the immigrants, led most American reporters to regard the Black Hand as a secret organization along the lines of the Sicilian Mafia and the Italian Camorra, about which neither they nor the police had much understanding. In actuality, Black-Handers in this country were simply extortionists, sometimes a small group, sometimes a single individual, whose messages threatening kidnapping, murder or other harm to individuals often employed excessively polite and flowery language demanding money, signed with a black handprint or drawing, with a few knives, crosses and other cryptic decorations designed to evoke the fear that organized Black-Handers commanded in the old country. A potential target, usually a prosperous businessman, didn't always know how to treat such threats, since many would-be extortionists operated mainly on the hope they would be taken seriously. Among those who had lived in the U.S. for many years and who knew the difference, this could backfire. When Chicago's Big Jim Colosimo was threatened, he sent for a Brooklyn relative, Johnny Torrio, who met with three Black-Handers in a South Side railroad underpass ostensibly to pay them off and instead simply killed them. That message was clear enough that Colosimo, with his already famous restaurant and major vice operations in the old Levee district, was left in peace.

Confusing the issue among the general public were groups calling themselves "white handers." In New York these were Irish toughs who emulated the Italian and Sicilian extortionists, while in Chicago Americanized Italians, often lacking much police protection, formed a White Hand group that for a time dealt with Black-Handers vigilante style.

(Authors' collection)

December 12, 1920 Buffalo jeweler kidnapped and robbed of $70,000 in gems.

December 16, 1920 New York jeweler murdered by bandits who escape with $50,000 in gems.

December 17, 1920 Baltimore reports 100 holdups and burglaries in two months; robbers loot passengers of a trolley car in Elizabeth, New Jersey.

December 22, 1920 New Jersey legislature will vote on bill providing life terms for armed robbers.

December 24, 1920 Prohibition agents J.F. McGuiness is found murdered in Bayonne, New Jersey.

December 26, 1920 "Monk" Eastman, bodyguard and collector for gambler Arnold Rothstein, is found shot to death outside the Blue Bird Cafe at 62 East 14th Street in New York. Eastman had previously led a powerful East Side street gang. Prohibition agent Jerry Bohan will receive a three-to-10-year prison sentence after pleading guilty to manslaughter, saying he shot Eastman in the course of an argument.

December 29, 1920 Bootlegger Salvatore Mauro is shot dead at 222 Chrystie Street in New York. His rival, Giuseppe "Joe the Boss" Masseria, is arrested but discharged for lack of evidence.

Five bandits hold up State Exchange Bank in Culver, Indiana, and are captured by local citizens.

1921

January 4, 1921 New York transit officials confer with police after series of robberies of subway stations and passengers.

January 9, 1921 Pennsylvania Railroad towerman held up in Kearny, New Jersey; police commandeer engine to pursue robber.

January 24, 1921 Five bandits hold up two trolley cars in Summit, New Jersey.

January 27, 1921 As Al Brown, Al Capone is indicted in the Criminal Court of Cook County, Illinois, for keeping a disorderly house and slot machines.

February 1921 Convicted murderer Eddie Adams escapes from a train en route to the Missouri state prison.

February 5, 1921 $10,000 bank robbery in Hamilton, Indiana.

February 8, 1921 New York City police will begin guarding United Cigar Store chain as these businesses become favorite target of armed robbers.

February 11, 1921 Eddie Adams and Julius Finney rob a bank and store in Cullison, Kansas.

February 17, 1921 Eddie Adams and Julius Finney are captured by possemen near Garden Plains, Kansas. Adams will be convicted of bank robbery and sentenced to 10 to 30 years in the state prison at Lansing, Kansas.

February 18, 1921 Notorious bank robber Henry Starr is fatally shot while robbing the Peoples National Bank at Harrison, Arkansas. Two accomplices escape by automobile and leave it burning outside of town.

February 26, 1921 One trolley bandit shot and two others captured in Townley, New Jersey; they confess to 21 holdups and burglaries since December 12.

March 8, 1921 Paul Labriola, Municipal Court bailiff for 15 years, is shot down near his home at 843 West Congress Street in Chicago.

THE MAN WHO CARVED CAPONE

It would have taken an unusually gutsy reporter to ask Al Capone in person how he earned the nickname "Scarface." Rumored explanations included a childhood fight in a Brooklyn schoolyard, a dispute with a New York barber (Capone's father had operated a barbershop), and the one Capone himself preferred—shrapnel wounds while fighting with the "Lost Batallion" in France. This explanation was accepted by his first biographer, Fred Pasley, possibly as a courtesy, and newsmen researching Capone's early years did in fact discover that an Al Capone had enlisted in the army at Atlantic City during World War I. This turned out to be another and unrelated Al Capone, though the coincidence of names would one day inspire a series of detective magazine articles whose author became convinced, mainly on the basis of differing fingerprints, that the "real" Capone had been killed sometime in the twenties, and that an obscure look-alike relative had been recruited to masquerade as the world's most notorious mobster. That idea gained enough currency that the FBI was called upon to check it out, and resolved the mystery to its satisfaction.

Variations on the knife-fight story remained in circulation, but the details of the incident probably were revealed for the first time by William Balsamo, a retired longshoreman turned crime researcher who had relatives in the Brooklyn Mafia and managed to arrange a personal, though long unreported, interview with an aging member of the Genovese crime family named Frank Galluccio who had actually wielded the blade. His youthful scrap with Capone left the future Chicago mob boss with three deep scars on

the left side of his face that probably enhanced his image as a ruthless gangster, but also embarrassed him the rest of his days. How Capone's attacker lived to tell the tale is a significant part of the story.

Blasamo met with Galluccio at Lento's Bar & Grill at 39th Street and Third Avenue in Brooklyn in the fall of 1965. He agreed not to divulge the details of their conversation published here with his permission until after Galluccio's death, which occured from natural causes several years ago.

An otherwise little-known gangster, Frank Galluccio's only claim to fame is that he gave Al "Scarface" Capone his notorious scars. Galluccio cut the infamous mobster, who was working as a waiter before he made the big time, during a knife fight that erupted after Capone insulted Galluccio's sister. *(Authors' collection)*

FRANK GALLUCCIO: *One thing I want you to do for me, Bill. Whatever I tell you now, I don't want you to say anything about it till I'm long gone.*

BALSAMO: *Mr. Galluccio, I will respect your wishes.*

GALLUCCIO: *I heard from Esposito and several dockworkers that you wanted to talk to me about Al Capone.*

BALSAMO: *Yes, I do.*

GALLUCCIO: *The first thing I want to ask you, what was Battista Balsamo's son's name?*

BALSAMO: *Vito. He was my mother's first cousin.*

GALLUCCIO: *Yes, that's right. That makes you the great nephew of Battista Balsamo from Columbia and Union Street. . . . I hope you don't mind me asking about your family, Bill, but it's for my own satisfaction.*

BALSAMO: *I understand. Now about Capone. I've heard that you are the man who cut Al Capone's face. Is that right?*

GALLUCCIO: *Well, I would never admit that to the detectives or anyone connected with newspapers, but the answer is yes, I did it. I had every right to do it. Nobody insults my sister like that. Especially in public at a dance hall, when I was with my date.*

BALSAMO: *When did this happen and where?*

GALLUCCIO: *It happened in the summer of 1917 at a dance hall that was owned by Frankie Yale. You ever heard of him?*

BALSAMO: *Of course. What was the name of the dance hall?*

GALLUCCIO: *The Harvard Inn, on the Bowery in Coney Island. Al was just a bartender-bouncer in those days. He was a disappointed gangster.*

BALSAMO: *He was a nobody then. Why did you cut his face? What did he do to your sister? By the way, what was her name?*

GALLUCCIO: *Lena. I was with Maria Tanzio. I took both of them out that evening to dine and dance at the Harvard for a good time. Capone was trying to put the make on Lena, and Lena ignored him every time, and every time he would pass our table he would try to talk to her. It seemed to me she didn't want to be bothered with him, she was getting mad. Whenever he passed the table, he would try to say something. I thought she knew him, so I asked her, you know that guy? or something like that. My sister told me she never saw him before, and he had a lot of nerve. She said, "He won't give up, Frank. He can't take a hint. But I don't like him, he is embarrassing me. Maybe you could ask him to please stop in a nice way." Capone was passing by the table again, and I was about to ask him to leave my kid sister alone, in a nice way, of course. And he leans over and tells her that she had a nice ass.*

BALSAMO: *Did you hear that or did she tell you what he said?*

GALLUCCIO: *You kidding? He said it loud enough that people sitting at a table next to ours overheard the insult, too. "You got a nice ass, honey, and I mean it as a compliment. Believe me." When I heard that, I jumped up from the table and said to him, "I won't take that shit from nobody. Apologize to my sister now, you hear?" He smiled and came toward me with his arms out and his palms open as if to say, Come on, buddy, I'm only joking. I shouted back that that is no fucking joke, Mister. Capone wasn't smiling anymore after that. He still came toward me. I called for the owner. He just kept coming toward me. So I whipped out a pocket knife and went for the son of a bitch's neck.*

BALSAMO: *How come you got his face instead?*

GALLUCCIO: *Well, I was drinking that night, and I was a little drunk. I think maybe my aim was not good because of the booze, you know. But I think I sliced him two or three times. I don't remember. It was a long time ago. But fuck him, he deserved it. I'm sure if it was the other way around, he would do the same thing I did. I mean, that was my kid sister, you know. Nobody likes to be insulted. Especially at a dance.*

BALSAMO: *Then what did you do after that?*

GALLUCCIO: *I grabbed my sister and Maria and ran out of the joint right away. Later I find out from some neighborhood guys that this big guy is looking for me.*

BALSAMO: *How big was he then?*

GALLUCCIO: *To me, he looked like at least five-feet-eleven or six feet. But you got to remember, I was a little under the booze. So to me he looked big and stocky, and I'm only five-feet-six. I must have been about 148 pounds then. This guy looked like he was 200 pounds. Hey, this guy could hurt me bad if I let him get me. I better strike first and quick, and I knew that a punch was not enough to stop him, so fuck that. I had to use what I learned in the streets. A few days later I still keep hearing that this guy is looking for me. He's telling people that he is with Frankie Yale.*

BALSAMO: *What did he mean, he was with Frankie Yale?*

GALLUCCIO: *It means he belongs to Yale's crew. Then about a week later I went to see my friend from the East Side, Albert Alterio. He was related to Two Knife Willie in some way. I told Albert about this problem, so he takes me to see Giuseppe Masseria—"Joe the Boss"—and Charley Luciano.*
   Albert pleaded my case and Joe the Boss and Charley agreed nobody should insult another man in front of his own family and get away with it.

What happened then was a sit-down at the Harvard Inn between me, Charley, Frankie and Capone. You know, I was really sorry what I did to his face. But I was a little drunk, and he insulted Lena. So I did what I thought was right at the time. The decision at the sit-down was Al Capone was ordered by Luciano and Yale not to look for revenge, and I was ordered to apologize. As a matter of fact, the look of the cuts I put on his face kind of shook me up, because I was really sorry for what I had done to him. Jesus, Bill, Capone had to go through life with those scars.

BALSAMO: *Did you ask him how many stitches he got that day?*

GALLUCCIO: *No, not personally. But Charley later told me it was close to 30. Luciano said they took him to Coney Island Hospital to get patched up.*

BALSAMO: *How were things after that?*

GALLUCCIO: *The few times we saw each other face-to-face, he would smile like he was trying to be nice to me. He did say to me that he was wrong when he insulted my sister in public. We never associated together while he was still living in Brooklyn.*

BALSAMO: *Would you say Luciano and Yale made Capone understand that if he went looking for you, it would be his funeral?*

GALLUCCIO: *You could put it that way. I guess that was the understanding. Now remember, Bill. Don't tell anyone about this till I am long gone. Capeesh?*

BALSAMO: *No problem. I swear on my mother, not a word.*

Galluccio never acquired prominence in the Genovese crime family, but Balsamo heard that on Capone's trips to Brooklyn in the 1920s he would request the services of Galluccio as chauffeur and bodyguard.

The same day Harry Raimondi is shot and killed at his cigar store at 910 Garibaldi Place. Both had supported 19th Ward alderman John "Johnny de Pow" Powers in his successful re-election campaign, and probably were killed by the Genna gang, working for Powers's opponent, Anthony D'Andrea.

April 6, 1921 A U.S. mail truck is robbed of $385,000 in cash and bonds after leaving the Dearborn Street railroad station in Chicago. Big Tim Murphy, labor racketeer and former state legislator, will be convicted of organizing the robbery.

April 8, 1921 The State Bank at Malden, Illinois, is robbed by men hired to install a burglar alarm.

April 14, 1921 Al Capone pleads guilty to keeping a disorderly house and slot machines, is fined $150, plus $110 costs.

April 15, 1921 One bandit is killed and two are wounded in holdup of the Cicero State Bank in Cicero, Illinois.

Two Chicago bank messengers robbed of $638,000—in canceled checks.

May 11, 1921 Anthony D'Andrea, defeated for alderman by "Johnny de Pow" Powers in Chicago's "Bloody 19th" ward, shot to death while entering his home at 902 South Ashland.

May 21, 1921 The Hunterstown Bank in Hunterstown, Indiana, is robbed of $21,500.

May 24, 1921 The Union National Bank in Newcastle, Pennsylvania, is robbed of $40,000. Police use a machine gun–equipped automobile in futile pursuit of the bandits.

June 3, 1921 In Minneapolis, Millers and Traders Bank messengers are robbed of $16,000.

June 7, 1921 Bandits use occasion of local police parade to hold up Merchants' Ice & Coal Company in St. Louis.

June 10, 1921 One bandit captured following $40,000 messenger robbery in Pittsburgh.

August 8, 1921 A Jefferies State Bank messenger is robbed of $10,000 in Chicago.

August 12, 1921 Three policemen are killed and four wounded in the robbery of a Ford Motor Company paymaster in Memphis, Tennessee.

August 13, 1921 After sabotaging the prison's electric plant, Eddie Adams and fellow convicts Frank Foster, George Weisberger and D.C. Brown scale walls of the Lansing, Kansas, state prison and escape. Brown is soon recaptured, but the others, with Billy Fintelman, form the new Adams gang.

The Kincaid Loan & Trust Company at Kincaid, Illinois, is robbed of $114,000.

August 26, 1921 The Huntington Park branch of the Los Angeles Trust Company is robbed of $20,000.

August 28, 1921 In Chicago, vaults of the Security Trust & Deposit Company are looted of $250,000. Two guards are suspected.

August 30, 1921 Armed robber arrested during holdup of United Cigar Store on Lexington Avenue; 31 of the stores robbed in New York City since first of the year.

September 1921 Eddie Adams murders Wichita, Kansas, policeman A.L. Young; the Adams gang robs banks in Haysville and Rose Hill, Kansas, stealing $10,000. In the Haysville holdup, Adams fatally pistol-whips 82-year-old James Krievell.

September 29, 1921 Robbers take $25,000 payroll of the Western Coal and Mining Company at Herrin, Illinois.

October 8, 1921 The Adams gang battles officers near Anoly, Kansas, wounding Deputy Benjamin Fisher.

Sheriff W.S. McPherson is killed by bootleggers in Monarch, Wyoming.

October 10, 1921 A Grand Avenue Bank messenger is robbed of $17,650 in St. Louis.

Five men are captured after robbing the Spring City National Bank in Spring City, Pennsylvania, of $17,500.

October 19, 1921 The Adams gang robs an Osceola, Iowa, bank of $500 in silver, then battles a posse near Murray, Iowa, killing C.W. Jones before making their escape in a car stolen from Sheriff E.J. West.

October 20, 1921 En route to Wichita, stealing and abandoning cars, the Adams gang robs 11 stores at Muscotah, Kansas. Near Wichita, they abduct and rob two motorcycle patrolman, setting fire to their motorcycles.

October 24, 1921 "Gentleman Gerald" Chapman, George "Dutch" Anderson and Charles Loeber rob a U.S. mail truck of $2.4 million in cash, bonds and jewelry on Leonard Street in New York.

October 31, 1921 Four persons shot during $5,000 robbery of Niagara Falls Trust Co.

November 2, 1921 Chicago jewelry salesmen robbed of $100,000 in uncut diamonds.

November 5, 1921 The Eddie Adams gang robs Santa Fe express train of $35,000, near Ottawa, Kansas.

November 9, 1921 Detroit bandit leaps from one moving car to another and escapes with $4,000 payroll.

November 20, 1921 Joy-riding with prostitutes in Wichita, the Adams gang are stopped by police. Gang member Frank Foster murders Patrolman Robert Fitzpatrick and the gang escapes. Later that night, the gang attempts to steal a car from Cowley County farmer George Oldham, who is shot to death by Adams.

November 22, 1921 Eddie Adams is slain by police in a gunfight at a Wichita, Kansas, garage. Detective Charles Hoffman is mortally wounded.

December 4, 1921 Robbery victim who kills bandit is charged with homicide and violation of New York's Sullivan gun law; murder charge later dropped, but remains charged with illegal possession of handgun.

December 7, 1921 Two policemen are slain by bandits during the robbery of the Grand Rapids Savings Bank at Grand Rapids, Michigan. Robert Leon Knapp, alias Walker, and Frank "The Memphis Kid" McFarland are suspected. Both will later be accused of the Denver Mint robbery.

December 11, 1921 Four days before his scheduled hanging, Chicago cop killer Terrible Tommy O'Connor escapes from the Cook County Jail and is never recaptured.

December 28, 1921 $30,000 worth of whiskey is stolen from La Montagne's Sons' warehouse in Lexington, Kentucky.

1922

January 17, 1922 Robbers bind clerks and steal $25,000 in diamonds from the Star Loan Bank in Chicago; two bank messengers shot and robbed of $9,600.

January 26, 1922 United Cigar Store at 92nd Street and Second Avenue, New York, held up for third time in one month.

January 27, 1922 Notorious bank robber Al Spencer escapes from the state prison at McAlester, Oklahoma. In coming months Spencer will gain notoriety for making the transition from horses to automobiles.

January 28, 1922 Hoboken police lieutenant fatally shot during $21,000 robbery of First National Bank messenger.

March 1, 1922 A Palmolive Company paymaster is robbed of $19,000 in Milwaukee.

March 14, 1922 $500,000 in checks saved by New York bank messenger despite bullet through his coat.

March 20, 1922 Nierman jewelry store in Chicago robbed of $100,000 in gems.

March 28, 1922 The Commonwealth State Bank in Detroit is robbed of $75,000.

April 4, 1922 In Chicago, Pennsylvania Railroad cashier loses $75,000 to robbers who escape but drop their loot.

May 8, 1922 Vincent Terranova, brother of Harlem crime boss Ciro "The Artichoke King" Terranova, is shot to death on East 116th Street in New York. Later in the day, Terranova's bootlegging partner, Joseph Peppo, is murdered on Broome Street, near police headquarters.

Italian gangsters in a gun battle at 194 Grand Street hit four bystanders. Umberto Valenti escapes unharmed, but Silva Tagliagamba is fatally wounded. Giuseppe "Joe the Boss" Masseria is captured nearby after a detective sees him throw away a pistol (for which he has a permit). Masseria will be charged with the Tagliagamba slaying but never tried. The shootings are the result of a power struggle between Masseria and the Morello-Terranova family for control of the New York Mafia.

May 16, 1922 George Remus, Cincinnati's biggest bootlegger, is convicted of conspiracy to violate the Volstead Act, sentenced to two years in a federal prison, and fined $10,000.

May 24, 1922 One bandit killed and three captured in Bridgeport, Connecticut, during attempted robbery of $19,000 payroll.

June 25, 1922 150 cases of whiskey are stolen from the American Distillery in Pekin, Illinois.

June 30, 1922 Philadelphia policeman prevents bank messenger robbery in shootout that leaves six wounded.

July 3, 1922 Million-dollar mail robbers Gerald Chapman, George "Dutch" Anderson and Charles Loeber are captured by New York police.

July 5, 1922 St. Louis bank messenger robbed of $99,200.

August 7, 1922 Ko Low, national president of the Hip Sing tong, a Chinese criminal society, is shot to death outside the Delmonico Restaurant on Pell Street in New York's Chinatown. The Hip Sing tong has carried on periodic warfare for years with the rival On Leong tong for control of gambling, opium dens and brothels in the nation's Chinatowns.

August 30, 1922 After his car collides with a taxi at Randolph and Wabash and he threatens the driver with a gun, Al Capone is arrested by Chicago police (who spell his name Caponi) and charged with drunken driving, assault with an automobile and carrying a concealed weapon. The charge is dropped and expunged from the record.

September 28, 1922 Harvey Bailey, Nicholas "Chaw Jimmie" Trainor and others hold up the Hamilton County Bank in the Cincinnati suburb of Walnut Hills and escape with $265,000 in bonds and cash.

December 18, 1922 Five bandits rob a Federal Reserve Bank truck of $200,000, killing guard Charles Linton outside the U.S. Mint in Denver. One of the gang is wounded and carried away by his partners. Although the attack is on a delivery truck, this becomes known as the Denver Mint Robbery.

December 30, 1922 Paymasters of the Buick Automobile Company and the Ferry Cap and Screw Company are robbed in Cleveland.

1923

January 14, 1923 The frozen corpse of Mint robber Nicholas "Chaw Jimmie" Trainor is found in a bullet-riddled car in a garage at 1631 Gilpin Street in Denver.

January 15, 1923 Dan Culhane, described as a member of a "million dollar gambling syndicate," is arrested in Chicago as a suspect in the Denver Mint robbery. Ted Hollywood is also sought.

January 23, 1923 In New York, four bandits hijack a Municipal Bank car carrying $50,000, throw the guards out and escape. The car is later found abandoned, still containing $3,700.

February 1, 1923 Owney "The Killer" Madden, New York gang leader, is released from Sing Sing prison in Ossining, New York, after serving nearly eight years of a 10-to-20-year sentence for the murder of rival gangster Little Patsy Doyle.

February 17, 1923 $80,000 from the Denver Mint robbery, and $73,000 worth of bonds from the Hamilton County Bank job in Walnut Hills, Ohio, are recovered by authorities in Minneapolis. The Mint robbers elude capture.

February 24, 1923 Chicago jeweler robbed in elevator of diamonds worth $100,000.

March 26, 1923 The Al Spencer gang robs the Mannford State Bank at Mannford, Oklahoma. In a running fight with possemen, citizen J.B. Ringer and gang member Bud Maxwell are killed. Spencer is wounded but escapes with others into the Osage Hills.

March 27, 1923 Gerald Chapman is shot and wounded while attempting to escape from the Atlanta Federal Penitentiary.

April 2, 1923 The "Egan's Rats" gang robs a U.S. mail truck in St. Louis of $2.4 million in bonds.

April 4, 1923 Minneapolis grand jury indicts some 20 persons as part of nationwide ring dealing in stolen bonds.

April 5, 1923 Gerald Chapman escapes from Atlanta Penitentiary.

April 20, 1923 St. Louis police raid the home of "Egan's Rats" gangster William "Whitey" Doering and recover loot from the million-dollar mail robbery.

April 29, 1923 New York police charge one Dennis Murphy with theft of ukeleles.

July 2, 1923 Seven gunmen rob the United Railways Company at 39th Street and Park Avenue in St. Louis of $38,306. Fred "Killer" Burke will be arrested, tried and acquitted.

July 24, 1923 Six bandits rob 14 bank messengers in Toronto of $130,000, shooting four people. Toronto police suspect that the same gang committed the Denver Mint robbery.

July 30, 1923   One killed and three wounded as seven bandits hold up a Moosic, Pennsylvania, trolley car to get $70,000 payroll.

August 1, 1923   The Baltimore Trust Company in Baltimore is robbed of $16,000.

August 19, 1923   Seven gunmen rob 150 guests of $25,000 at the Allendale Inn in Detroit, killing a policeman and wounding six customers.

August 20, 1923   In Oklahoma's last train robbery, Al Spencer, Frank "Jelly" Nash and others loot the Katy Limited near Okesa of $20,000 in bonds and cash.

August 28, 1923   Despite a police guard, New York labor racketeer Nathan "Kid Dropper" Kaplan is shot to death while leaving Essex Market Courthouse by Louis Cohen, a member of the rival gang headed by Jacob "Little Augie" Orgen.

September 5, 1923   Chicago police arrest Al Capone for carrying a concealed weapon. Discharged by Judge O'Connell of the Municipal Court.

September 7, 1923   Jerry O'Connor, one of Edward "Spike" O'Donnell's bootleggers, is shot to death in Joseph Kepka's saloon at 5358 South Lincoln in Chicago by Torrio-Capone gunmen. O'Conner's death opens a series of killings by Chicago's bootlegging gangs.

September 13, 1923   The Indiana National Bank in Indianapolis is robbed of $40,000 in securities.

September 15, 1923   Train robber Al Spencer is slain by police and federal agents on the Osage Indian reservation near Bartlesville, Oklahoma.

September 17, 1923   The Torrio-Capone gang kill George Meeghan and George "Spot" Bucher of the O'Donnell gang, which has been trying to expand its operations on Chicago's South Side.

September 27, 1923   Some 40 men raid a Philadelphia distillery and escape with $30,000 worth of "medicinal" liquor.

October 10, 1923   Burglars steal a safe containing $12,000 from the Mechanics State Bank in Cedar Springs, Michigan.

October 11, 1923   Gang loots New York City warehouse of $125,000 in furs during four-hour robbery.

Brothers Roy, Ray and Hugh De Autremont attempt to rob a Southern Pacific mail train near Siskiyou, Oregon. They dynamited the mail car, setting it afire and killing a mail clerk, shot three railroad employees to death, and fled with no loot. The Postal Department would offer a reward of $15,900 in gold for their apprehension.

October 20, 1923   In Oakland, Illinois, burglars shoot the watchman, blow the safe of the First National Bank and escape with $15,000.

October 28, 1923   Fifth robbery of a United Cigar Store on Second Avenue in New York.

October 31, 1923   William "Wild Bill" Lovett, successor to Dennis Meehan as boss of Brooklyn's "White Hand" gang, is murdered in the Lotus Club speakeasy at 25 Bridge Street.

November 2, 1923   The Jake Fleagle gang robs the First National Bank at Ottawa, Kansas, of $150,000.

November 9, 1923   In Detroit, Ford Motor Company messenger saves $25,000 from bandits by throwing payroll onto passing locomotive.

Frank "Jelly" Nash, last of the Okesa train robbers, is arrested by U.S. Marshal Alva McDonald near Sierra Blanca, Texas, after hiding in Mexico.

THE TALE OF MORTON'S HORSE

Gangster Nails Morton died in 1923 after a fall from a horse that he rode for pleasure on the bridle paths of Chicago's Lincoln Park. That any gangster would be an equestrian, or be killed accidentally, had enough news value to receive substantial coverage in the local press. The thing that earned Morton a permanent place in Prohibition-era history is what supposedly happened next. Legend holds that Morton's grieving friends, sometimes led by Dean O'Banion, sometimes by Ox Riesner, but usually by Louis "Two-Gun" Alterie, later took the same horse from the Parkway Riding Academy at 2153 North Clark in the same block as the Massacre garage, and executed it, either in Lincoln Park or outside of town, and then told the stable owner where he could retrieve the saddle.

There's no disputing how Morton died, but the murder of the horse appears to be pure myth, possibly based on a passing comment by Charles Gregston in the Chicago *Daily News* for November 19, 1924, in a short feature on Torrio when O'Banion's death was still in the news. Killing a horse that someone needed in his business was already a practice of extortionists, and even after the automobile was commonplace, a city's horse population was large enough for some to die of natural causes. So dead horses were not exactly rare, and this may have inspired the Morton horse story, especially if it started out as a joke that turned into a rumor and seemed entirely plausible, given the North

Nails Morton, who formed his young gang to protect Jewish merchants from marauding "dagoes" in the Maxwell Street neighborhood before teaming up with O'Banion—only to be killed by his own horse, which was then supposedly executed for its "crime." *(Authors' collection)*

Siders' penchant for pranks. At least nobody has been able to verify that it happened, and in those glory days of the Chicago school of journalism, newspapers were not shy about printing higher truths which transcended mere fact.

November 15, 1923 At his Halfway resort, between Marion and Johnston City, Illinois, bootlegger Charlie Birger kills his bartender, Cecil Knighton, in a gunfight.

Birger will be acquitted on grounds of self-defense.

November 18, 1923 Charlie Birger kills St. Louis gangster William "Whitey" Doering in another shooting at his Halfway resort. A member of "Egan's Rats," Doering was free on appeal from a mail robbery conviction. Birger again will be acquitted on a plea of self-defense.

November 22, 1923   New York police capture four burglars, but also file assault charges against two shopkeepers who shot at them.

December 1, 1923   Thomas "Morrie" Keane and William Egan, beer runners of the Spike O'Donnell gang, are murdered by the Torrio-Capone gang.

December 3, 1923   Owney Madden and two others charged with theft of 200 cases of whiskey from New York City warehouse.

December 4, 1923   The Vandergrift Distillery warehouse near Frederickstown, Pennsylvania, is looted for the fifth time.

December 16, 1923   New York City robbery victim rings fire bell for help and is arrested for turning in a false alarm.

December 17, 1923   Chicago gang boss Johnny Torrio pleads guilty to Prohibition law violation and is fined $2,500.

December 22, 1923   Prohibitionist vigilantes of the Ku Klux Klan, led by former federal agent S. Glenn Young, stage massive liquor raids in southern Illinois. Other raids follow on January 5 and 7, 1924.

December 30, 1923   George "Dutch" Anderson, serving 25 years for mail robbery, escapes from the federal penitentiary in Atlanta.

1924

January 17, 1924   New York City gunmen rob three Thom McAn shoe stores in one day.

February 2, 1924   New York police capture "Broadway Navy" gang of dishonorably discharged sailors.

February 1924   New York police assign 500 detectives to catch a woman robber known as the "Bob-Haired Bandit."

March 3, 1924   Train robber Frank "Jelly" Nash enters Leavenworth under a 25-year sentence for mail robbery.

March 8, 1924   Philadelphia church sexton shoots poor-box thief.

March–April 1924   Over 200 alleged liquor violators, including gang leader Charlie Birger, are tried in federal court at Danville, Illinois. Convicted of bootlegging and possession of liquor and counterfeit tax stamps, Birger receives concurrent sentences of one year and 10 months in jail and fines of $2,800, plus costs.

April 1, 1924   During the municipal election at Cicero, Illinois, Salvatore (Frank) Capone, Al's brother, is killed by police while terrorizing voters. Al Capone and cousin Charlie Fischetti escape.

May 8, 1924   Chicago bootlegger Joe Howard is shot to death in Heinie Jacobs' saloon at 2300 South Wabash Avenue by Al Capone after slapping around Jake "Greasy Thumb" Guzik, Capone's bookkeeper. Capone briefly becomes a fugitive until several witnesses suffer memory loss.

May 9, 1924   William J. Burns, director of the U.S. Justice Department's Bureau of Investigation, resigns in the aftermath of government corruption scandals.

May 10, 1924   New U.S. Attorney General Harlan Fiske Stone appoints J. Edgar Hoover as "acting director" of the Bureau of Investigation. In eight months he will be named director.

May 19, 1924   Johnny Torrio is arrested in a raid on the Sieben Brewery at 1470 North Larrabee in Chicago, after being set up by North

Side gang boss Dean O'Banion. The Volstead Act conviction is Torrio's second, mandating jail time, for which O'Banion will soon pay with his life.

May 21, 1924 Outlaw Dick Gregg, a former member of the Al Spencer gang, robs the Farmers State Bank at Burbank, Oklahoma.

In Chicago, 13-year-old Bobby Franks is kidnapped and killed by university students Richard Loeb and Nathan Leopold, Jr.

May 22, 1924 Dick Gregg is captured after a gun battle at Lyman, Oklahoma.

May 23, 1924 Driving to East St. Louis from a Ku Klux Klan rally in Harrisburg, Illinois, Prohibition vigilante S. Glenn Young is ambushed by gunmen in a passing car. Young is wounded in the leg and his wife, Maude, permanently blinded by bullets.

May 24, 1924 Jack Skelcher, of the Shelton brothers' gang, is killed by Ku Klux Klansmen near Herrin, Illinois, in retribution for the ambush of S. Glenn Young.

May 31, 1924 The Argentine State Bank in Kansas City, Kansas, is robbed of $20,000.

In the southern Illinois county known as Bloody Williamson for its labor violence and Ku Klux Klan activities, the bootlegging gangs of Carl Shelton and Charlie Birger (here sitting on the front part of the car roof with a tommy gun) worked together until they reportedly had a falling out over a woman. In the mid-twenties they turned on one another with military ferocity, using everything from bomb-dropping airplanes to homemade tanks. Finally convicted of a murder, Birger went to the gallows in 1928—the last public hanging in Illinois—cracking jokes. *(Chuck Webb)*

June 11, 1924 Gunmen escape with a $100,000 gem shipment after a truck robbery at Eighth Avenue and 12th Street in New York.

June 12, 1924 Well-organized bandits commandeer the Chicago, Milwaukee & St. Paul mail train, force it to stop where their cars are waiting at the Buckley Road crossing near Rondout, Illinois, some 32 miles north of Chicago, and steal over $2 million in what becomes the last major train robbery in the U.S. The well-executed crime unravels when one of the robbers mistakenly shoots an accomplice in the dark. Chicago police routinely nab Dean O'Banion, who is tired of constant harassment and sends them to an apartment at 53 North Washtenaw, where they find the wounded man. Postal Inspector William J. Fahy will receive a 25-year prison sentence for providing inside information to the gang organized by Chicago politician-bootlegger James Murray. The actual robbers, including the outlaw Newton brothers from Texas, and Murray will exchange a large portion of the loot for early release. Murray will resume his life of crime, harboring fugitives, including members of the Dillinger gang.

Jack "Legs" Diamond, Eddie Diamond, John Montforte and Eddie Doyle are arrested by New York police for a $100,000 jewel robbery. Discharged, June 14.

June 14, 1924 Babe Pioli, a member of Diamond's gang, murders prizefighter Bill Brennan at his Tia Juana Club on Manhatten's West Side. Pioli will plead guilty to manslaughter.

June 27, 1924 Guard killed during $9,500 robbery of Brinks Express Company in New York City.

July 2, 1924 Irwin "Blackie" Thompson, Joe Clayton and Bill Donald rob the Avery State Bank at Avery, Oklahoma, then kill Police Chief Jack Ary and Officer U.S. Lenox in a gun battle near Drumright, Oklahoma.

July 24, 1924 Mazer Company of Detroit robbed of $125,000 in jewels.

August 18, 1924 Bank robber Roy "Arkansas Tom" Daugherty is killed by police at Joplin, Missouri.

Coney Island freak show robbed of $13,500.

Police arrest 381 "negro excursionists" following robbery of a store in Richmond, Virginia.

August 29, 1924 North Ward National Bank messengers in Newark are robbed of $112,000 in checks.

September 25, 1924 Bank messenger for Union Trust Company of Springfield, Massachusetts, disappears with $100,000 shipment of currency.

October 1, 1924 Chicago jewelry salesman robbed of $200,000 in gems.

October 1924 While driving along Fifth Avenue, New York gangster Jack "Legs" Diamond is slightly wounded by shotgun pellets from a passing car. Diamond drives himself to Mount Sinai Hospital.

October 12, 1924 Gerald Chapman murders policeman James Skelly in an attempted store burglary in New Britain, Connecticut.

October 30, 1924 Pittsburgh police called to six holdups in 15 minutes.

November 1, 1924 Bank robber and bootlegger John Ashley, "King of the Everglades," is killed, along with gang members Hanford Mobley, Ray Lynn and Bob Middleton, in a police ambush at Sebastian, Florida.

Bill Tilghman, famous deputy U.S. marshal of the territorial days but still an active lawman at age 70, is shot to death in Cromwell, Oklahoma, by Wylie Lynn, a drunken and corrupt Prohibition agent.

November 8, 1924 Mike Merlo, head of the Chicago branch of the Unione Siciliana, dies of cancer. A much respected Sicilian gang leader, Merlo had served as peacemaker between the Torrio-Capone syndicate, the Genna brothers and the O'Banion gang.

November 10, 1924 Dean O'Banion, leader of Chicago's North Side gang, is shot to death by three gunmen who commit the "handshake

Schofield's flower shop at 738 North State Street, across from Chicago's Holy Name Cathedral, where the "handshake murder" of North Side gang leader Dean O'Banion in 1924 set off five years of "beer wars" in which hundreds were killed before Capone forces shocked the entire country with the machine-gun murder of seven North Siders under Bugs Moran in the St. Valentine's Day Massacre. *(Authors' collection)*

murder" in his flower shop at 738 North State Street. Police suspect Brooklyn gangster Frankie Yale, friend of Torrio and Capone, who once again is discovered to be in the city, ostensibly for the funeral of Mike Merlo. Earl "Hymie" Weiss succeeds to the leadership of the North Side gang.

November 23, 1924 Eddie Tancl and Leo Klimas are shot and killed in a pistol duel with gangsters at Tancl's cabaret, the Hawthorne Inn in Cicero. Myles O'Donnell and James Doherty will be tried and acquitted.

December 6, 1924 Two killed and five wounded in bandit raid on saloon in South Bend, Indiana.

December 19, 1924 Bandits burn most of town after robbing two banks in Valley View, Texas.

December 24, 1924 Bandits take over Paradise, Texas, and rob every store and bank.

December 25, 1924 Milford, Indiana, bank cashier reported missing with $200,000.

United Cigar Store at 42nd Street and Second Avenue, New York, reports sixth holdup.

1925

January 2, 1925 Bandit captured during $18,000 robbery of American Express Co. payroll in Chicago.

January 5, 1925 Robbers hold up Kearny, New Jersey, cab driver, escape in locomotive.

January 12, 1925 Al Capone's car is riddled with shotgun and pistol fire by North Side gangsters at State and 55th Streets in Chicago and chauffeur Sylvester Barton wounded. Capone orders a $20,000 armored Cadillac with bulletproof glass.

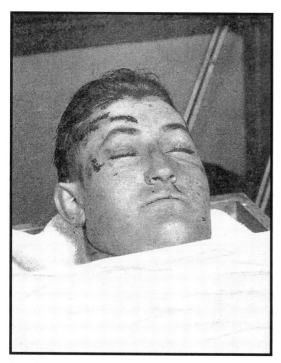

Dean O'Banion split from the Torrio-Capone combine, and following his murder his successors kept sniping at Big Al. *(Goddard Collection)*

January 18, 1925 Gerald Chapman is captured at Muncie, Indiana.

January 24, 1925 Johnny Torrio is seriously wounded by members of the North Side gang outside his apartment at 7011 Clyde Avenue in Chicago. Torrio will survive, serve his short jail term resulting from the Sieben Brewery arrest, and then leave Chicago, turning the organization over to Al Capone.

Bootlegger and deputy sheriff Ora Thomas and Klan vigilante S. Glenn Young and two of his henchmen are killed in a gun battle in Herrin, Illinois.

January 27, 1925 Mail messenger at Collinsville, Illinois, is robbed of a $21,000 mine payroll.

February 5, 1925 Atlanta grocery chain, after 21 robberies in a month, designates three stores for robbers to visit.

February 20, 1925 Robber Richard Reese Whittemore escapes from the Maryland state penitentiary, killing guard Robert H. Holtman.

February 24, 1925 Richard Reese Whittemore and gang rob a Western Maryland Dairy Company car in Baltimore of $16,304, shooting the driver and guard.

March 16, 1925 In Baltimore, the Whittemore gang robs J. Wahl Holtzman, American Banking Company messenger, beating him and stealing $8,792 in cash, plus securities.

March 20, 1925 Local posse, tipped off to robbery of Farmers' Bank of Steeleville, Missouri, kill two bandits and capture two others.

March 26, 1925 Posters hung on Mott and Doyer Streets in New York's Chinatown announce peace between the Hip Sing and On Leong tongs.

March 30, 1925 Thom McAn shoe store chain in New York City reports 55th robbery in six months.

April 5, 1925 The Whittemore gang robs the Metro Sacks jewelry store at 43 West 125th Street in New York of $16,000.

April 10, 1925 As Al Brown, Al Capone is arrested for carrying a concealed weapon in Chicago. He will be discharged the next day.

April 17, 1925 Walter O'Donnell, brother of Spike O'Donnell, and Harry Hassmiller are shot to death in an Evergreen Park, Illinois, roadhouse.

April 19, 1925   Murderer Midget Fernekes captured in Chicago.

April 26, 1925   Five bandits rob 75 patrons of the Cafe de l'Europe in New York City.

April 29, 1925   Chicago police find $50,000 in loot at boys' club that made stealing an initiation test.

May 9, 1925   Richard Reese Whittemore and his gang rob jeweler Jacques Ross, at 290 Grand Street in New York, of $25,000 in diamonds.

May 22, 1925   United Cigar Store at 1357 First Avenue, New York, reports 11th robbery.

May 26, 1925   Gang leader Angelo Genna, who succeeded Mike Merlo as Chicago presi-

THE ONE-WAY RIDE

It would have required no great leap of imagination to conceive the idea of killing someone in a car instead of on the street, but in the early twenties the automobile itself was enough of a novelty that taking someone for a "ride" seemed like a significant advance in murder strategy. Accordingly, writers of the day declared a number of different gangsters, all Chicagoans, to be the "inventor" of the "one-way ride." Modern writers, all cribbing from the same few books, whose authors had cribbed from even fewer sources, are virtually unanimous in attributing the first "ride" murder to Hymie Weiss, as if this were gospel. (Different newspaper writers of the day named Nails Morton, Frank McErlane, Dean O'Banion and others.) In fact, a survey of killings finds instances of bodies dumped from cars, in New York rather than Chicago, as early as 1918, and careful research would probably push the date back even further. While there had to be a first time that someone was murdered in a car, it would be historically interesting to discover which writer launched the legend that credits Weiss with originating the "one-way ride."

Another gangland practice was the disposal of murder victims in lakes and rivers, giving rise to another item of gangster lore—the "concrete overshoes," or kimona, a technique that involved planting someone's feet in a washtub (or its equivalent) of fresh cement to be later pushed off a pier or the back of a boat. If this was a common practice, New York's East River, Chicago's Lake Michigan, and many other bodies of water should be cluttered with hundreds if not thousands of rusty washtubs with legbones sticking up like potted plants. A fairly thorough search of books on gangster history as well as the *New York Times* Index reports the occasional corpse in a sunken car, but no divers engaging in their popular sport, or searching for shipwrecks or artifacts, have found the remains of a gangster scuttled in the classic movie manner. The fact is, bodies are hard to dispose of in water. They tend to bloat and float to the surface, as in the case of one mobster, suspected of skimming, who was weighted with heavy slot machines and dumped in a lake in the Catskills. Eventually he came bobbing to the surface in spite of the slot machines. Similarly, crewmen on a ship in Boston Harbor were surprised to discover a female murder victim, still-secured in a full-size bathtub where her homicidal husband had left her, when she surfaced in her porcelain vessel, and was deemed an obstruction to shipping.

dent of the Unione Siciliana, is killed by four men with sawed-off shotguns after a car chase that ends in a crash at Ogden and Hudson Avenues. Police attribute the murder to the North Side gang, in retaliation for the slaying of Dean O'Banion.

June 1, 1925   The Whittemore gang robs the Levy Jewelry Co. at 483 Main Street in Buffalo of $50,000 in gems.

June 13, 1925   Gangster Mike Genna and Chicago police detectives Charles Walsh and Harold Olson die following a gun battle at South Western Avenue and 59th Street, and detective Michael Conway is badly wounded. Genna's associates, John Scalise and Albert Anselmi, are captured and charged with murder but, after two bizarre trials, are acquitted on grounds of self-defense.

July 8, 1925   Chicago gang leader Tony Genna is lured to a meeting with three men at the corner of Curtis and Grand Avenues and fatally shot in a "handshake murder." The remaining Genna brothers, Sam, Pete and James, go into hiding.

July 16, 1925   The Whittemore gang robs Stanley's jewelry store at 269 West 125th Street in New York of $50,000 in gems.

July 18, 1925   Chicago gangsters James Vinci and Joe Granata kill one another in a gun duel in the saloon of John Genaro at 2900 South Wells.

August 6, 1925   Attempted holdup on 125th Street craps game in New York results in gun battle with police who shoot three robbers, killing one and fatally wounding another.

August 11, 1925   Ben Hance and his wife are murdered near Muncie, Indiana, apparently for informing on mail bandit Gerald Chapman. The slayings are attributed to Chapman's partner, Dutch Anderson.

September 11, 1925   Charles Arthur Floyd, Fred Hilderbrand and Joe Hlavaty rob the Kroger Grocery & Baking Company in St. Louis of $11,934. Police confuse Floyd with another criminal named "Pretty Boy" Smith and the nickname usually credited to prostitute Beulah Baird, sticks.

September 13, 1925   Charles "Pretty Boy" Floyd and Fred Hilderbrand are arrested in Sallisaw, Oklahoma. They will be returned to St. Louis on September 17, where Hilderbrand will confess to the Kroger Grocery robbery, implicating Floyd and Hlavaty.

September 14, 1925   The Whittemore gang robs David Bick's store at 360 Third Avenue in New York of $50,000 in jewelry.

September 25, 1925   The Saltis-McErlane gang attempts to kill gang leader Edward "Spike" O'Donnell at 63rd Street and Western Avenue in Chicago, using a Thompson submachine gun. O'Donnell escapes unharmed in this first known tommy-gun attack in gang warfare.

October 4, 1925   The Saltis-McErlane gang sprays the Chicago headquarters of the Ralph Sheldon gang at 5142 South Halsted with machine-gun fire that kills Charles Kelly, making him presumably the tommy gun's first gangland fatality.

Yeggs, safecrackers, blow three safes at Jewelers' Exchange on New York's Bowery.

October 5, 1925   The Whittemore gang robs Mrs. J. Linherr's store at 193 Sixth Avenue in New York of $30,000 in jewelry.

"THE GUN THAT MADE THE TWENTIES ROAR"

The Thompson Submachine Gun

The timing could not have been worse—or better, as the case may be. In 1920, the same year that Prohibition became the law of the land, the Auto-Ordnance Corporation of New York contracted with the Colt's Patent Firearms Manufacturing Company of Hartford, Connecticut, to produce 15,000 Thompson submachine guns. At the time no one knew what a "submachine" gun was, but five years later it would become a world-recognized symbol of American gangland violence—the mobster equivalent of the cowboy's six-shooter.

Intended for the army, the tommy gun was the brainchild of Brigadier-General John Taliaferro Thompson, a retired Ordnance Department officer with an inventive streak who believed that Allied infantrymen needed more individual firepower in the European war. After a false start on an automatic rifle in 1916, he produced the first "submachine" gun—a term he coined to describe a small, fully automatic firearm that used pistol instead of rifle ammunition and could be shot from the hip by a soldier on the run. It was an odd-looking weapon, weighing only 10 pounds, with pistol grips front and rear, and it fired the army's standard .45-caliber Automatic Colt Pistol cartridge at a rate of 800 per minute from 20-shot straight magazines or circular drums holding 50 or 100 rounds. Thompson called it his "trench broom," and had completed a working prototype just as the war ended. That was only the start of the Auto-Ordnance Corporation's long run of bad luck.

With a small fortune already invested in the project, Auto-Ordnance tried to market the gun commercially. At demonstrations in 1920, weapons experts acclaimed its revolutionary design, reliability and enormous firepower, and one dazzled police official predicted it would either kill or cure the country's gunmen, rioters and "motorized bandits." But that early enthusiasm never translated into sales, and the gun slipped back into obscurity until 1926, when a *Collier's* writer described it less approvingly:

> *This Thompson submachine gun is nothing less than a diabolical engine of death . . . the paramount example of peace-time barbarism . . . the diabolical acme of human ingenuity in man's effort to devise a mechanical contrivance with which to murder his neighbor. . . .*

The reason for that outburst was the machine-gun murder of an assistant state's attorney in Cicero and the otherwise increasing use of tommy guns by Chicago's bootleggers, for whom subtlety and public image were never major considerations. In 1929, the St. Valentine's Day Massacre sealed Chicago's reputation as gangster capital of the world, and the gun's reputation as a gangster weapon. Called in to work on the Massacre, ballistics expert Col. Calvin Goddard wrote that the Thompson was being used in 11 percent of gangland killings, meaning that "the usefulness of such weapons in gang warfare has been grasped by the lower element, which has put them to extremely practical use during the past few years."

The "beer wars" that broke out in Chicago following the "handshake" murder of North Side gang leader Dean O'Banion in December 1924 were already attracting national attention because many of the killings and gun battles were taking place in broad daylight on the city's busiest streets and in residential neighborhoods, with seeming indifference to the police. But what secured Chicago's reputation as the country's gangster capital was the introduction of the Thompson submachine gun, which signaled a major escalation in the fighting.

Ironically, the gun seems to have been discovered by Dean O'Banion on his last "vacation" trip to Colorado, where he and his men regularly amused themselves with rodeos and other horseplay at the "Diamond D" Ranch of fellow mobster Louie "Two-Gun" Alterie. While a handheld machine gun seemed mainly a novelty to both the police and the peacetime military when first demonstrated, it had found a market among private security guards and agencies hired by certain large industries, including Colorado mining companies, to deal with labor violence. On his return to Chicago, O'Banion and his entourage stopped in Denver to stock up on weapons which, a local paper reported, included three of the "baby" machine guns. A few days later the city's then-most-colorful gangster was murdered in his flower shop on North State Street. In reporting on his lavish funeral, Chicago papers published rumors that the South Side gang of Joe Saltis and Frank McErlane had drifted away from the Torrio-Capone outfit to form a secret alliance with O'Banion, and a few months later they would be the first to thrill and chill America with a revolutionary weapon that would soon become known as the "Chicago Typewriter."

Saltis and McErlane probably obtained their Thompson from the North Siders to use on Spike O'Donnell, a dapper but particularly pesky poacher whose fainthearted brothers had allowed themselves to be gerrymandered out of their rightful South Side territory while Spike

Retired General John T. Thompson, who developed the first submachine gun at end of the First World War, was dismayed that the deadly firearm he had envisioned as a "trench broom" for Allied soldiers instead gained fame as a gangster weapon. He died in 1940 regretting the invention that bore his name, and only weeks before every Allied army was clamoring for Thompson guns for the military use he had always intended.   *(Authors' collection)*

was cooling his heels in prison. Unintimidated by McErlane's threats, O'Donnell was standing at the busy northwest corner of 63rd Street and Western Avenue on the evening of September 25 when a barrage of bullets from a passing car missed him and took out the plate-glass windows of a large drugstore (now a currency exchange). With typical savoir faire, Spike went inside to

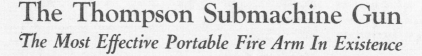

The Thompson Submachine Gun
The Most Effective Portable Fire Arm In Existence

THE ideal weapon for the protection of large estates, ranches, plantations, etc. A combination machine gun and semi-automatic shoulder rifle in the form of a pistol. A compact, tremendously powerful, yet simply operated machine gun weighing only *seven* pounds and having only *thirty* parts. Full automatic, fired from the hip, 1,500 shots per minute. Semi-automatic, fitted with a stock and fired from the shoulder, 50 shots per minute. Magazines hold 50 and 100 cartridges.

THE Thompson Submachine Gun incorporates the simplicity and infallibility of a hand loaded weapon with the effectiveness of a machine gun. It is simple, safe, sturdy, and sure in action. In addition to its increasingly wide use for protection purposes by banks, industrial plants, railroads, mines, ranches, plantations, etc., it has been adopted by leading Police and Constabulary Forces, throughout the world and is unsurpassed for military purposes.

Information and prices promptly supplied on request

AUTO-ORDNANCE CORPORATION
302 Broadway   *Cable address: Autordco*   **New York City**

the soda fountain and asked for a drink of water, but had nothing to say to the police. Newspapers duly recorded another skirmish in the South Side beer war, and ascribed the unusually large number of bullet holes to "shotguns and repeating rifles."

His second time out, McErlane at least managed to score with his new gun and get it mentioned in the papers. On the Saturday night of October 4 the headquarters of the Ralph Sheldon gang was strafed with .45 bullets that killed one Charles Kelly (presumably the Thompson's first gangland victim) and wounded a Thomas Hart. This time the police figured out what all the bullet holes meant, as reported in the *Chicago Daily News:*

> *A machine gun, a new note of efficiency in gangland assassinations, was used to fire the volley from the black touring car, killing one man and wounding another in front of the Ragen Athletic club . . . at 5142 South Halsted St. last Saturday night. Captain John Enright of the stockyards police said today his investigation satisfied him that a machine gun had been used, and that the same gun had been used in an attack on Spike O'Donnell at 63rd St. and South Western Ave.*

Despite the machine gun, the story was buried on an inside page. The wire services picked it up as a short human-interest item—the latest wrinkle in Chicago gangland warfare. But that was all. Nor did McErlane get rave reviews on October 16 when he riddled Spike O'Donnell's car, wounding his brother Tommy.

Finally, Chicago's tommy-gun pioneer made the front page. Despite the usual poor marksmanship, it rated a banner headline in the *Chicago Tribune* for February 10, 1926:

MACHINE GUN GANG SHOOTS 2

The story reported an attack on the speakeasy of Martin (Buff) Costello, 4127 South Halsted, which had left two men wounded. This caused Chicago Police Captain John Stege to grump that "McErlane and Saltis have one of these guns" and therefore "It is imperative that [the police] be armed accordingly."

Not to lag behind in the underworld arms race, the South Siders (now led by Al Capone) and the North Siders (now led by Hymie Weiss) quickly obtained Thompsons of their own and started using them against one another in spectacular shootouts. Their open warfare culminated in the grandest bloodfest of all—the St. Valentine's Day Massacre of 1929, which took out seven men in a garage at 2122 North Clark Street.

Opposite: A 1920 advertisement for the Thompson, the first handheld "submachine" gun, completed too late for the First World War and which might have remained an obscure ordnance novelty had Chicago's North Side gang leader Dean O'Banion not discovered it on a vacation trip to Colorado shortly before his death in 1924. There it was being used by mining company security forces to intimidate strikers. O'Banion included at least two in a major arms purchase made in Denver on his way home. Probably these guns went to the Saltis-McErlane gang, who had quietly defected from the Torrio-Capone group on the city's South Side to join forces with Hymie Weiss, O'Banion's successor. After some efforts to kill Spike O'Donnell the following year, both the police and other mobs became aware of the Thompson and used it widely in the city's beer wars that made Chicago the country's undisputed "gangster capital," especially when Capone stocked up on them from local hardware and gun dealer Alex Korecek on 18th Street in the South Side tough "Valley" district, the Near North Side sporting good and police supply shop of Peter von Frantzius, the major underworld armorer at 608 West Diversey Parkway and other sources. Because the "tommy gun" technically was not a "concealable weapon" regulated by law, it could be sold over the counter—at least for a time—to anyone with $175. Later newspaper accounts, probably exaggerated, declared that Chicago gangsters had acquired some 500 of the weapons. The Thompson's first recorded fatality was one Charles Kelly, killed October 25, 1925, when Saltis-McErlane gunmen riddled the Ragen Colt's clubhouse, headquarters of a rival gang at 5142 South Halsted Street. *(Authors' collection)*

A page from the catalogue of Peter von Frantzius in the late 1920s, displaying Elliott Wisbrod's "bulletproof" vest as well as the Thompson. *(Neal Trickel Collection)*

By this time, the Thompson's worldwide notoriety had inspired rumors that the Auto-Ordnance Corporation was giving them free to gangsters for promotional purposes. In fact, the company was nearly bankrupt, with most of its guns still stacked in a Colt warehouse.

Repeal ended the Chicago beer wars, but not the gun's evil reputation. By 1933, John Dillin-ger, Baby Face Nelson, Machine Gun Kelly and other Depression outlaws were either buying submachine guns on the black market or stealing them from police stations, and using them to drive the last few nails in the Auto-Ordnance coffin. In 1939, the nearly defunct company was forced to sell to a shady Connecticut industrialist named Russell Maguire for only $529,000

—about the wholesale value of the 4,700 guns still in inventory, with manufacturing equipment thrown in.

Before he died in 1940 at the age of 79, General Thompson wrote a last melancholy note to one of the young engineers who had helped design the submachine gun in the closing days of the Great War. It said, in part,

I have given my valedictory to arms, as I want to pay more attention now to saving human life than destroying it. May the deadly T.S.M.G. always "speak for" God and Country. It has worried me that the gun has been so stolen by evil men and used for purposes outside our motto, "On the side of law and order."

That note was received on August 1, 1939, after Thompson had lost the company to Maguire. Exactly a month later, the German Wehrmacht invaded Poland behind their version of the submachine gun, the 9mm MP-40, popularly called the "Schmeisser." Suddenly, every Allied army was clamoring for submachine guns, and the only one ready for mass production was the Thompson. Maguire sold over 2 million in both commercial and military models before the end of World War II, becoming wealthy and famous as America's "Tommygun Tycoon."

October 10, 1925   Two gunmen sentenced to death for murder committed during robbery of Chicago's Drake Hotel.

October 11, 1925   Special Agent Edward C. Shanahan, of the U.S. Justice Department's Bureau of Investigation, is shot dead in Chicago by car thief Martin James Durkin. Shanahan is the first agent of what will later be called the FBI to die in the line of duty.

October 17, 1925   New York police department's experienced fence squad charge 11 men and one woman member of notorious Cowboy Tessler gang with 80 holdups and one murder.

October 18, 1925   Arrest of Rothenberg gang, suspected of one quarter of New York's burglaries during past six months, considered another triumph of police department's "older," more experienced detectives following their capture of the Tessler gangsters.

October 20, 1925   The Whittemore gang robs John Sandford, salesman for Larter & Sons, stealing $25,000 worth of watches and jewelry from his car at 84th Street and Broadway in New York.

October 29, 1925   Six bandits rob a Federal Reserve Bank car in Buffalo of $93,000, killing the driver and a guard. The crime is variously attributed to Dutch Anderson, the Whittemore gang and others.

October 31, 1925   Bootlegger Edwin "Spike" Kenny is shot in a Baltimore roadhouse and names Richard Reese Whittemore as his attacker. The shooting was apparently motivated by Kenny's romantic involvement with his assailant's wife, Margaret "Tiger Lil" Whittemore.

Mail robber Dutch Anderson mortally wounds police detective Charles DeWitt Hammond in Muskegon, Michigan. The dying officer wrests away Anderson's gun and kills him.

November 24, 1925   Six bandits hold up Drovers' National Bank money car for $57,760 in Chicago; two gunmen and one policeman shot.

December 1925 Charlie Birger and the Shelton brothers, later enemies, form slot machine partnership in southern Illinois.

December 2, 1925 The Whittemore gang robs M.G. Ernest's jewelry store at 566 Columbus Avenue in New York of $75,000 in diamonds.

December 8, 1925 Pretty Boy Floyd pleads guilty to first degree robbery and is sentenced to five years in the state prison at Jefferson City, Missouri, where he will be received on December 18.

December 21, 1925 Simon Gilden, a member of the Whittemore gang, is found shot to death in New York.

December 22, 1925 Gangster Dynamite Joe Brooks and ex-policeman Edward Harmening are found shot to death in Marquette, Illinois. Saltis-McErlane gang suspected.

December 23, 1925 The Whittemore gang robs Folmer Prip, jeweler at 90 Nassau Street in New York, of $10,000.

December 26, 1925 At the Adonis Social Club, an Italian mob hangout in Brooklyn, Richard "Peg Leg" Lonergan, head of the Irish "White Hand" gang, is shot to death, along with gang members Cornelius "Needles" Ferry and Aaron Harms. Several Italian gangsters, including visiting Chicago mob boss Al Capone, are arrested and questioned.

Joseph Ross, a member of the Whittemore gang, is found shot to death near Elizabeth, New Jersey.

1924–25 More than 80 murders, in the Chinatowns of New York, Boston and Chicago, are attributed to the latest war between the Hip Sing and On Leong tongs.

1926

January 10, 1926 Chicago lawyer Henry Spignola, brother-in-law of Angelo Genna, is shot to death while leaving Amato's Restaurant on South Halsted, allegedly for refusing to contribute to a gangland defense fund of cop killers Albert Anselmi and John Scalise.

January 11, 1926 At 22 West 48th Street in New York, the Whittemore gang robs Belgian diamond merchants Albert Goudvis and Emanuel Veerman of $175,000 in gems.

January 26, 1926 Brothers Agostino and Antonio Morici are ambushed and slain on Ogden Avenue in Chicago. Wealthy wholesale grocers in competition with Capone mobster Antonio Lombardo, the Moricis also allegedly refused to contribute to the Scalise and Anselmi defense fund.

At Webster Grove, Missouri, near St. Louis, police and Bureau of Investigation agents board the Katy "Texas Special" train from San Antonio and arrest Martin James Durkin, killer of federal agent Shanahan. Durkin will be convicted and sentenced to life imprisonment.

February 9, 1926 Martin "Buff" Costello's saloon at 4127 South Halsted Street in Chicago is raked with machine gun fire by the Saltis-McErlane gang. William Wilson and John "Mitters" Foley are wounded.

February 10, 1926 Al Capone's gang orders three tommy guns from South Side hardware and sporting goods dealer Alex Korecek.

February 13, 1926 Two bandits who robbed Chicago's Drake Hotel are hanged for murder.

February 15, 1926 Orazio "The Scourge" Tropea, collector for the Anselmi-Scalise defense fund, is shotgunned to death on Chicago's Halsted St.

February 23, 1926 Ecola "The Eagle" Baldelli, a Tropea henchman, is found shot to death in an alley at 407 North Curtis in Chicago.

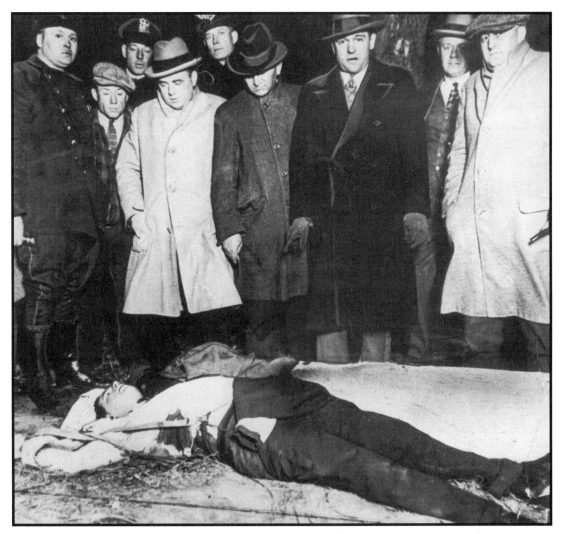

Chicago's first "mini-massacre" occurred on April 27, 1926, when the now-traditional touring car containing several Capone gunmen and possibly Capone himself, roared down Cicero's 12th Street (now West Roosevelt Road) and several men standing in front of a saloon went down in a hail of machine-gun bullets. Among the fatalities was State's Attorney William McSwiggin, whose association with known bootleggers (one of whom he had recently tried for murder) was never satisfactorily explained. Newspapers eventually concluded that the intended targets were the two bootleggers, encroaching on Capone territory, and it was simply McSwiggin's bad luck to be hobnobbing with them at the time.   *(Goddard Collection)*

February 24, 1926   Vito Bascone, another Tropea collector for the defense fund, is found dead in a ditch in Stickney, Illinois, shot between the eyes.

March 19, 1926   Samuzzo "Samoots" Amatuna, successor to Angelo Genna as chief of Chicago's Unione Siciliana, is shot to death in a Roosevelt Road barber shop.

Richard Reese Whittemore and gang members Bernard Mortillaro, Pasquale Chicarelli, Morris "Shuffles" Goldberg, Jake and Leon Kramer, Anthony Paladino and Margaret "Tiger Lil" Whittemore are captured by New York police; suspected of murdering holdup witness.

April 23, 1926 Capone machine gunners riddle Pearl Hruby's beauty shop at 2208 South Austin Boulevard in Cicero with 92 bullets, wounding Pearl's boyfriend, James "Fur" Sammons.

April 26, 1926 Gerald Chapman is hanged for murder at Wethersfield, Connecticut.

April 27, 1926 Assistant State's Attorney William H. McSwiggin and gangsters James Doherty and Thomas Duffy, of the Klondike O'Donnell gang, are killed by machine gun bullets in front of Madigan's saloon at 5613 West Roosevelt Road in Cicero. The killings are attributed to the Capone gang, and Capone himself is said to have wielded the tommy gun.

A Buffalo jury is discharged after failing to reach a verdict in the murder and bank car robbery trial of Richard Reese Whittemore. He will not be retried.

April 30, 1926 Whittemore is turned over to Baltimore authorities, to be tried for the murder of a prison guard.

May 21, 1926 Richard Reese Whittemore is convicted of murder in Baltimore. He will be sentenced to death on June 10.

June 7, 1926 Captured driving a stolen car in Fort Scott, Kansas, Herman Barker and Elmer Inman are extradited to Oklahoma to face robbery charges. Both are soon free on bond. Barker is the oldest son of Kate "Ma" Barker.

June 30, 1926 Matt and George Kimes rob their first bank, at Depew, Oklahoma.

July 2, 1926 Al Capone is indicted in Chicago for conspiring to swear falsely to qualify voters. Indictment will be quashed in December.

July 12, 1926 Boyd "Oklahoma Curley" Hartin is killed in a gunfight in a Herrin, Illinois, roadhouse—probably an early casualty in Birger-Shelton gang war.

July 29, 1926 In Chicago, criminal complaint against Al Capone (as "Alphonse Caponi," alias "Scarface Brown") for the murder of Assistant State's Attorney William McSwiggin, is dismissed by Judge Thomas J. Lynch.

August 3, 1926 An Al Capone chauffeur is found tortured and shot to death in a southwest Chicago cistern.

August 10, 1926 Four Capone gangsters attack Earl "Hymie" Weiss and Vincent "The Schemer" Drucci with pistols in front of the Standard Oil Building at 910 South Michigan Avenue. No one is hit, but Chicago police arrest and question Drucci and Capone gunman Louis Barko. May have been a holdup attempt.

August 12, 1926 Richard Reese Whittemore is hanged.

August 15, 1926 Hymie Weiss and Schemer Drucci are again attacked—and missed—by Capone gunmen outside the Standard Oil Building.

August 20, 1926 Joseph "The Cavalier" Nerone, alias Antonio Spano, suspect in the murder of Tony Genna, is shot to death by unknown killers on Division Street in Chicago.

Matt and George Kimes and an accomplice

rob the Farmers National Bank at Beggs, Oklahoma, of $5,000.

August 22, 1926 Harry Walker and Everett Smith, of the Shelton brothers' gang, are shot to death in a roadhouse near Marion, Illinois.

August 26, 1926 Matt and George Kimes and their gang rob both the American State Bank and the Covington National Bank in Covington, Oklahoma.

August 27, 1926 The Kimes brothers kill Deputy Perry Chuculate in a gun battle at Sallisaw, Oklahoma, take Chief of Police J.C. Woll and farmer Wesley Ross as hostage, and flee into Arkansas. The hostages are released unharmed.

August 28, 1926 Matt and George Kimes are wounded and captured at the home of their cousin, Ben Pixley, near Rudy, Arkansas. George Kimes will be convicted of bank robbery and sentenced to 25 years in the state prison at McAlester, Oklahoma. Matt will be convicted of murder and sentenced to 35 years, pending an appeal.

August 30, 1926 Girls lead bandit raid on Chicago "car barn" cashier; seven persons shot, two fatally.

September 12, 1926 While leaving a roadhouse between Herrin and Johnston City, Illinois, Shelton gangster Wild Bill Holland is machine-gunned to death and two others wounded by the Charlie Birger gang.

September 20, 1926 A motorcade of Hymie Weiss gangsters riddles the Hawthorne Hotel in Cicero with machine-gun and shotgun fire in an unsuccessful attempt to kill Al Capone.

Four unidentified boy bandits rob First National Bank of Columbus, Wisconsin, of over $1 million.

September 27, 1926 Arrested for burglary, Ray Terrill and Elmer Inman overpower a jailer and escape from the Carter County Jail at Ardmore, Oklahoma.

October 1, 1926 Federal Grand Jury in Chicago indicts Al Capone for conspiracy to violate the National Prohibition Act.

October 4, 1926 Shelton gangsters in a specially armored truck open fire on Birger gangster Art Newman's car, near Harrisburg, Illinois. Mrs. Newman is wounded.

October 11, 1926 Hymie Weiss and bodyguard Patrick Murray, brother-in-law of James, are killed in front of the Holy Name Cathedral by Capone machine gunners firing from an upstairs window in the building next to the late Dean O'Banion's State Street flower shop, which has remained headquarters for the North Siders. Gangsters Sam Pellar and Benny Jacobs and mob attorney W.W. O'Brien are wounded. Vincent "The Schemer" Drucci succeeds Weiss as boss of the North Side gang.

October 14, 1926 Seven bandits, armed with tommy guns rob a U.S. mail truck in Elizabeth, New Jersey, of $161,000, killing the driver and wounding his assistant and a policeman. Because of the machine guns, the killers are assumed to be Chicago gangsters, but will soon be identified as a New York gang headed by James "Killer" Cunniffe.

October 16, 1926 President Coolidge discusses the New Jersey mail robbery with his Cabinet. On the following day, 2,500 Marines will be assigned to guard mail shipments.

Thompson guns are stolen from the Rosiclare Spar Mining Company at Rosiclare, Illinois. Attributed to the Charlie Birger gang.

The Jake Fleagle gang robs the Exchange

Bank of Schmidt and Koester at Marysville, Kansas, obtaining only $741.

October 21, 1926 A peace conference, called by Al Capone and attended by 30 Chicago gang leaders, results in a temporary truce.

October 26, 1926 Burnett "High Pockets" McQuay is found machine-gunned in a car near Herrin, Illinois, and the bullet-riddled body of Ward "Casey" Jones is found in the Saline River, near Equality, Illinois. Both were members of the Birger gang. The Shelton gang is blamed.

October 27, 1926 The Post Office announces that U.S. Marines will acquire 250 Thompsons, making that branch of the armed forces the first to acquire the submachine gun, which it will soon use in Nicaragua against rebels headed by Augusto César Sandino.

In Chicago, the trial of Albert Anselmi and John Scalise for the slaying of Detective Harold Olson begins.

October 31, 1926 William "Ice Wagon" Crowley, one of the New Jersey mail robbers, kills James "Killer" Cunniffe and his girlfriend in an argument at the Highland Court Apartments, 257 Highland Avenue, in Detroit. Police arrive to investigate, and in the resulting gun battle Crowley and Patrolman Ernest Jones are also slain.

November 6, 1926 Jeff Stone, mayor of Colp, Illinois, and John "Apie" Milroy are shot to death in the Birger-Shelton gang war. A tripod-mounted machine gun is reportedly used. Both gangs attribute the killings to the other.

November 12, 1926 First "aerial bombing" in the U.S. A crop-duster pilot is hired by the Shelton gang to drop three dynamite bombs on rival Charlie Birger's well-fortified "Shady Rest" headquarters near Marion, Illinois. One bomb misses the target, the others fail to explode.

In Chicago, Albert Anselmi and John Scalise are convicted of manslaughter in the killing of Detective Harold Olson and sentenced to 14 years in the state prison at Joliet. Both appeal.

Harvey Bailey and others rob the Peoples Trust and Savings Bank at LaPorte, Indiana, of $140,000 in cash and bonds.

November 21, 1926 A gang of gunmen, later alleged to include notorious bank burglar Ray Terrill, force their way into the Sallisaw, Oklahoma, jail and free convicted murderer Matt Kimes.

November 28, 1926 Theodore "The Greek" Anton, owner of the Anton Hotel in Cicero and manager of Capone's Hawthorne Hotel headquarters next door to it, is kidnapped and tortured to death. Usually attributed to North Side gang, though some accounts indicate Capone had Anton killed after an argument.

November 30, 1926 The Charlie Birger gang robs the Bond County State Bank at Pocahontas, Illinois, of $5,000.

December 4, 1926 The Harvey Bailey gang robs the Olmsted County Bank and Trust Company at Rochester, Minnesota, of $30,000.

Luther Bishop, ace investigator for the Oklahoma State Crime Bureau, is murdered in his home at 1515 Northwest 28th Street in Oklahoma City. His wife will be tried and acquitted, but Bishop was probably killed by one of the many outlaws he pursued. Ex-convict Burt Meredith will testify at Mrs. Bishop's trial that Ray Terrill admitted killing Bishop.

December 12, 1926 Mayor Joe Adams, a Shelton ally, is murdered by the Birger gang at West City, Illinois.

Wilbur Underhill and Ike "Skeet" Akins shoot Fred Smythe in a holdup in Picher, Oklahoma.

December 23, 1926 The Illinois Supreme Court grants Albert Anselmi and John Scalise a retrial for the killing of Chicago policeman Harold Olson.

December 25, 1926 Wilbur Underhill and Ike "Skeet" Akins attempt to rob the Purity Drug Store in Okmulgee, Oklahoma, and murder a 19-year-old customer, George Fee.

December 27, 1926 Kimes-Terrill gang member Elmer Inman is captured while burglarizing a store in Oklahoma City.

December 28, 1926 Charlie Birger is charged with the murder of Joe Adams.

1927

January 7, 1927 $80 million worth of legally stored whiskey stolen from New York Chemical Co. warehouse.

Wilbur Underhill and Ike "Skeet" Akins, wanted for murder and robbery, are captured in Tulsa.

January 8, 1927 The Shady Rest roadhouse, headquarters of the southern Illinois Birger gang, is destroyed by fire. Three bodies are found in the ruins.

January 10, 1927 Matt Kimes, Ray Terrill and others rob the State Bank at Sapulpa, Oklahoma, of $40,000.

January 17, 1927 The Kimes-Terrill gang attempts to burglarize the bank in Jasper, Missouri, but flees in two cars when a posse arrives. One car, believed to contain Matt Kimes, another man and a woman, escapes to Kansas. Two other gang members, Ray Terrill and Herman Barker (a son of Ma Barker), are trailed to

a house at 602 East Main in Carterville, near Joplin, and captured after a gun battle in which Barker is wounded.

January 19, 1927 Ray Terrill escapes from a car while being returned to the state prison at McAlester, Oklahoma, from which he has previously broken out.

Illinois Highway Patrolman Lory Price and his wife Ethel disappear. Price was allegedly a partner of Charlie Birger in a stolen car racket.

January 21, 1927 Herman Barker is transferred from Joplin, Missouri, to Fayetteville, Arkansas, to face charges of robbing a West Fork bank.

January 25–27, 1927 Albert Anselmi and John Scalise are freed on $25,000 bond, pending their new trial for the killing of Detective Olson.

January 30, 1927 Wilbur Underhill, Ike "Skeet" Akins, Duff Kennedy and Red Gann escape from the Okmulgee County Jail in Okmulgee, Oklahoma.

January 31–February 5, 1927 Carl, Earl and Bernie Shelton are tried and convicted of the 1925 Collinsville, Illinois, mail robbery, largely on the perjured testimony of Birger gang members. The Sheltons are sentenced to 25 years in a federal penitentiary.

February 5, 1927 The body of Highway Patrolman Lory Price, shot to death by the Birger gang, is found in a field near Dubois, Illinois. His wife's body will be recovered from an abandoned mine on June 13.

February 9, 1927 Elmer Inman is convicted of burglary in Oklahoma City and sentenced to seven years in the state prison at McAlester.

Oklahoma murderer Ike "Skeet" Akins is captured in Lamar, Missouri.

February 10, 1927 After winning their appeal, Albert Anselmi and John Scalise are retried in Chicago for the murder of Detective Charles Walsh.

February 12, 1927 While being returned to Okmulgee County, Oklahoma, Ike "Skeet" Akins attempts to escape and is killed by Sheriff John Russell.

February 13, 1927 Wilbur Underhill robs a Picher, Oklahoma, theater of $52 but is caught by Constable George Fuller. Underhill seizes Fuller's gun, kills deputized citizen Earl O'Neal, and escapes.

February 25, 1927 Gang leader William Duffy is killed in Philadelphia's first machine-gun murder. Attributed to Duffy's rival, Max "Boo Boo" Hoff.

March 5, 1927 Bootlegging gang members captured using hose to siphon whiskey from government warehouse.

March 11, 1927 An armored truck carrying a $104,250 payroll of the Pittsburgh Terminal Coal Company is dynamited and robbed by the "Flatheads" gang near Coverdale, Pennyslvania. Five guards are seriously injured in the nation's first armored car robbery.

Saltis-McErlane gangsters Frank "Lefty" Koncil and Charles "Big Hayes" Hubacek are shot to death in Chicago. Attributed to the Ralph Sheldon gang.

March 16, 1927 Chicago gamblers Frank Wright, Joseph Bloom and Reuben Cohen are machine-gunned to death in the "Milaflores Apartment Massacre" in Detroit. Attributed to former St. Louis gangster Fred "Killer" Burke on assignment from Detroit's "Purple Gang."

March 17, 1927 Elmer Inman escapes from guards near Bolton, Oklahoma, while en route to the state prison.

March 18, 1927 Anselmi and Scalise are acquitted of the Walsh slaying.

March 20, 1927 Murderer Wilbur Underhill is captured in Panama, Oklahoma.

March 24, 1927 Moy Sing and Moy Yuk Hong, members of the On Leong tong, are murdered in Chicago.

March 30, 1927 Herman Barker and forger Claude Cooper saw the bars of their cell and escape from the Washington County Jail at Fayetteville, Arkansas.

April 4, 1927 Vincent "The Schemer" Drucci is arrested, then killed in a scuffle with Detective Daniel Healy in a squad car at Clark Street and Wacker Drive in Chicago. George "Bugs" Moran succeeds to leadership of the North Siders.

May 12, 1927 Bandits haul away a safe containing $207,000 in cash and securities from the McCune State Bank at McCune, Kansas. Ray Terrill is suspected.

May 18, 1927 Matt Kimes and eight other members of the Kimes-Terrill gang stage simultaneous raids on the Farmers National Bank and the First National Bank in Beggs, Oklahoma, stealing about $18,000 and killing Marshall W.J. McAnally.

May 23, 1927 Birger gangster Harvey Dungey admits giving perjured testimony in the Shelton brothers' mail robbery trial. The Sheltons are granted a new trial and released on bond.

May 25, 1927 New York gangster Tony Torchio is machine-gunned to death in Chicago, after responding to Joe Aiello's offer of a

$50,000 bounty on Al Capone. Aiello and Capone war over control of the Unione Siciliana, whose members supply much of the city's home-distilled alcohol.

May 27, 1927 Roy "Blackie" Wilson and Owen Edwards, members of the Kimes-Terrill gang, are captured by Texas Rangers at Borger, Texas, and extradited to Oklahoma for the murder of Marshal W.J. McAnally. Three other men and a woman are in custody for the same crime.

June 1, 1927 Aiello gangster Lawrence LaPresta is killed by the Capone gang.

June 3, 1927 Wilbur Underhill is convicted of murder at Okmulgee, Oklahoma, and sentenced to life imprisonment.

June 9, 1927 In Chicago, Albert Anselmi and John Scalise are again tried for the killing of Detective Harold Olson. They will be acquitted on June 23, by reason of self-defense.

June 24, 1927 Matt Kimes and associate Raymond Doolin are captured near the Grand Canyon in Arizona. Kimes will be sent to the Oklahoma state prison on two life sentences for murder.

June 29–30, 1927 Diego Attlomionte, Numio Jamericco and Lorenzo Alagna, Aiello gangsters, are gunned down by the Capone gang.

July 9, 1927 Police and federal agents arrest Legs Diamond on narcotics smuggling charge in Mount Vernon, New York.

July 11, 1927 Giovanni Blandini (Blaudini, Baludin), an Aiello gangster, is shot to death in Chicago.

July 17, 1927 Dominic Cinderello, an Aiello gangster, is murdered in Chicago.

Legs Diamond had worked for Arnold Rothstein, operated New York's Hotsy Totsy nightclub (a term popularized in that city) and acquired a measure of fame with not only his own shooting but his remarkable ability to survive gunshot wounds. After several failed attempts on his life, his enemies tracked him to a boardinghouse upstate where he had hoped to move his operations without being shot by rivals and hassled by the police. Nevertheless, he was murdered in his sleep in 1931. *(Authors' collection)*

August 1, 1927 Herman Barker kills Deputy Arthur Osborne, near Pine Bluffs, Wyoming. The crime is at first erroneously attributed to Elmer Inman, another former Kimes-Terrill outlaw.

August 10, 1927 Anthony K. Russo and Vincent Spicuzza, St. Louis gangsters attracted by Joe Aiello's $50,000 bounty on Capone, are machine-gunned in Chicago.

August 19, 1927 Harvey Bailey and gang rob the Farmers National Bank at Vinton, Iowa, of $70,000 in cash and Liberty Bonds.

August 29, 1927 Fleeing from a Newton, Kansas, robbery, Herman Barker kills Patrolman J.E. Marshall at Wichita. Wounded by other officers, Barker commits suicide. One accomplice, Charles Stalcup, is captured. Another, Porter Meeks, will be slain by Wichita police the following day.

September 13, 1927 First theft of seaplane in Boston raises legal issue of whether an aircraft can also be a vessel.

September 24, 1927 Sam Valente, Cleveland gangster hired by Joe Aiello to kill Capone, is machine-gunned in Chicago.

October 6, 1927 Cincinnati bootlegger George Remus murders his estranged wife, Imogene. Remus will be acquitted by reason of insanity and briefly institutionalized.

October 13, 1927 Mobster "Big Joe" Lonardo is shot to death in a Cleveland barber shop. Attributed to a power struggle between Lonardo and the Porello brothers for control of the Cleveland Mafia.

October 15, 1927 Labor racketeer Jacob "Little Augie" Orgen is shot to death and bodyguard Jack "Legs" Diamond wounded at Delancey and Norfolk Streets in New York, allegedly because of a painters' union dispute with rival mobsters Louis "Lepke" Buchalter and Jacob "Gurrah" Shapiro.

November 9, 1927 "Machine Gun" Jack McGurn shot and wounded by the Moran gang's Gusenberg brothers, Pete and Frank, in the cigar store of Chicago's McCormick Hotel.

November 10, 1927 Robert and Frank Aiello, rivals of Al Capone, are shot to death at Springfield, Illinois.

November 20, 1927 Bombs damage restaurant owned by gangster Jack Zuta at 323 North Ashland and real estate office of John P. Remus at 5315 Fullerton Avenue in Chicago.

November 22, 1927 Al Capone is arraigned in Chicago on charges of vagrancy and disorderly conduct. Discharged by Judge William E. Helander.

November 23, 1927 Bomb damages headquarters of Jack Zuta–Billy Skidmore–Barney Bertsche vice syndicate, at 823 West Adams in Chicago.

Chicago police engage in a running gun battle with gangsters surprised in front of Tony Lombardo's home at 4442 West Washington. Lombardo is the Capone-backed head of the Unione Siciliana. A machine-gun nest is discovered opposite Lombardo's home.

November 26, 1927 Ray Terrill and Elmer Inman are captured by police in Hot Springs, Arkansas.

November 29, 1927 Carmen Ferro, wire wholesaler and alleged bootlegger, is shot to death and his body thrown into a ditch near Bensenville, Illinois.

December 17, 1927 The Haymarket Hotel, at 734 West Madison, is damaged in Chicago's 108th bombing of the year.

Al Capone arrives in Chicago from Los Angeles in an armored car, delayed by his arrest in Joliet the previous day.

December 23, 1927 Four bandits, one wearing a Santa Claus suit, rob the First National Bank at Cisco, Texas. In the resulting gun battle, Police Chief G.E. "Bit" Bedford and Officer

George Carmichael are slain, along with gang member Louis Davis. Six citizens and two bandits are wounded, and Marshall "Santa Claus" Ratliff, Henry Helms and Robert Hill will be captured the following day. The incident makes local history as the "Santa Claus Bank Robbery."

December 28, 1927   St. Louis gang leader Vito Giannola is machine-gunned to death by rivals at his girlfriend's house.

1928

January 1, 1928   Burglars raid 32 stores in town of Galesburg, Illinois.

January 3, 1928   Bombs damage the Forest Club, an alleged gambling resort at 7214 Circle Avenue, Forest Park, Illinois, and the Newport Hotel, a Zuta-Bertsche-Skidmore gang hangout, at 2351 West Madison in Chicago.

January 5, 1928   Capone gangsters shoot up the Aiello Bros. Bakery at 473 West Division Street in the Capone-Aiello war. Dago Lawrence Mangano and Phil D'Andrea, Capone lieutenants, are sought by the police.

January 26, 1928   Chicago homes of Dr. William H. Reid, 1257 West Garfield Boulevard, and Charles C. Fitzmorris, 5533 Hyde Park Boulevard, two members of the Mayor Thompson cabinet, are bombed by gangsters —possibly the mayor's, intending the blame to fall on his political opponents.

January 27, 1928   Marshall Ratliff, leader of the "Santa Claus Bank Robbery," is convicted and sentenced to 99 years.

January 31, 1928   Watchman H. Bermish is shot to death by a gang attempting to burglarize the Herman Gabbe and Company Fur Company on West 22nd Street in New York.

February 2, 1928   New York police raid the Paramount Building at Broadway and 42nd Street, recover $20,000 worth of stolen furs, and arrest Legs and Eddie Diamond along with 14 others. Legs Diamond is held on suspicion of murder but discharged the next day.

February 5, 1928   Al and Ralph Capone are arrested in New Orleans on "suspicion" and then released.

February 6, 1928   The Harvey Bailey gang robs the Peoples and Drovers Bank at Washington Court House, Ohio, of $225,000 in cash and bonds.

February 20, 1928   Henry Helms, of the "Santa Claus Bank Robbery" gang, is tried for murder at Eastland, Texas. He will be convicted and sentenced to death.

February 21, 1928   Bomb damages Chicago home of Lawrence A. Cuneo, brother-in-law and secretary to State's Attorney Robert E. Crowe at 2917 Pine Grove.

February 25, 1928   Armed with tommy guns, Charles "Limpy" Cleaver and his gang rob a U.S. mail train of $135,000 near Evergreen Park, Illinois. The machine guns were purchased from the Auto-Ordnance Corporation in New York by a bogus "Mexamerica Company."

March 19, 1928   Robert Hill, of the "Santa Claus" gang, is tried at Eastland, Texas, and will be sentenced to life.

March 21, 1928   Diamond Joe Esposito, prominent Italian politician and bootlegger, is killed by shotgun blasts almost in front of his Chicago home at 800 South Oakley Boulevard.

March 26, 1928   Bombs damage the Chicago homes of Senator Charles S. Deneen, and of Circuit Judge John A. Swanson, running against

BOMBS AND BOMBAST

Chicago's "Pineapple Primary"

Chicago became the American underworld's bombing capital well before the turn of the century, and by the late 1920s the practice had evolved into a cross between an art and a science thanks to the greater precision demanded by a new breed of criminal known as the racketeer.

In the city's Italian neighborhoods, Black Hand extortionists had long used bombs against shopkeepers just as they used kidnappings against those whose wealth was not in the form

Elected mayor in 1923, William E. Dever broke with long and hallowed Chicago tradition by trying to stamp out graft and corruption and enforce Prohibition as a matter of principle. His efforts threw the city's politicians and criminal community into turmoil that included five years of "beer wars" and the so-called Pineapple Primary of 1928, marked by violence unmatched in the history of Chicago or any other American metropolis, before or since. In the mayoral election that followed, Big Bill Thompson was restored to power, at least in theory, when civic leaders prevailed on Al Capone to command his gunmen to help the police restore the Chicago version of law and order. *(Authors' collection)*

of business property. In other neighborhoods, particularly the Irish, extortionists also used bombs but refined their threats from simple ultimatums to offers of "protection" (mainly against the protectors).

But the bomb also was a popular means of exposing a small-scale brothel or gambling parlor that was demonstrating too much independence. With painted ladies running around in housecoats, or clouds of smoke and betting slips billowing out of a gutted storefront, the arriving police had no choice but to announce the discovery of an illegal establishment. During the Chicago gambling war of 1907, pool halls and whist clubs, the usual fronts for gambling operations, were popping like champagne corks.

The bombs used to expose rival vice or gambling operations usually were little more than large, homemade firecrackers—a sizable cardboard container filled with homemade flash powder or black gunpowder. Such "cannon crackers," as they were called, produced much noise, concussion and smoke but usually did only superficial damage and rarely hurt anyone. However, a few serious Black Hand bombers might add bolts, nuts, nails, glass and other shrapnel to their cannon crackers to make them genuine antipersonnel devices. (In the commercial-fireworks trade, any unusually large firecracker still is known as a Dago bomb.)

Crime had been "organized" at the local level long before the twenties, but the arrival of Prohibition in 1920 led to the proliferation of rival bootlegging gangs, and as these expanded into vice and racketeering, bombs became more sophisticated and more lethal. Cannon crackers gave way to dynamite, the longtime favorite of labor radicals, and to the homemade pipe bomb, a length of three- or four-inch pipe threaded and capped at both ends, drilled for a fuse and

charged with ordinary black powder from any gunshop.

The typical dynamite bomb consisted of two to five sticks taped together and detonated by a blasting cap and commercial fuse; the more powerful devices could dismantle a brick building.

The pipe bomb had only a fraction of the power of dynamite, but its size and weight would carry it through a plate-glass window when thrown from a passing car, and the metal casing fragmented into sharp projectiles, especially if serrated with a file or hack saw. The professional version of the pipe bomb was the Army's Mark I Mills hand grenade—the traditional "pineapple" which was regularly stolen from Army and National Guard armories.

The more exotic types of military and industrial explosives—TNT, nitroglycerin and the like—were never widely used by gangsters, for the simple reason that they were harder to come by, more dangerous to handle and dynamite or black powder would usually do the job. (Safecrackers often used nitro because of its shearing power, and the fact that it could be poured into a safe door through seams or a drilled hole, but the usual means of obtaining it—literally by cooking it out of dynamite sticks over a stove—made safe-blowing a fairly hazardous business.)

Chicago bombing reached its all-time high in the late twenties, when rival gangs were not only competing for territorial control, extorting businesses and seizing labor locals, but also terrorizing political-reform candidates on behalf of the Mob-controlled machine. The local election of April 1928 made history of sorts as the Pineapple Primary, for actual political power as well as civic policy, city jobs and police priorities were determined by the winning faction, for whom the general election in November was little more than a formality. This

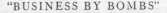

252   IT'S A RACKET   "BUSINESS BY BOMBS"

Sept. 30—Jackson Park, Parked Automobile. Revenge or racket.
Sept. 30—5425 Broadway. Taxi Cab Garage. Revenge.
Sept. 30—3300 N. Halsted St. Taxi Cab Garage. Revenge.

OCTOBER

Oct. 3—5345 Cottage Grove Av. Garage. Max Finkel. Racket.
Oct. 12—101 Wacker Drive (lower level). Soft Drink Parlor. Joseph Ryan. Prohibition.
Oct. 13—8041 St. Lawrence Av. M. E. Daily. Private garage. Unknown.
Oct. 14—4154 W. 16th. Kazimir Lipkin. Chicken store. Racket.
Oct. 14—5620 Stony Island Av. W. T. Woodley. Garage Racket.
Oct. 16—2050 W. Roosevelt Rd. Kenard Shoe Store. Racket.
Oct. 16—4032 W. Roosevelt Road. Irving Wittenberg. Bakery Shop. Racket.
Oct. 17—5507 So. Michigan Av. Speedway Tire Service. Racket.
Oct. 17—2354 So. Crawford Av. Kostka Bros. Auto Accessory & Battery Shop. Racket.
Oct. 18—4032 W. Roosevelt Road. Irving Wittenberg. Bakery Shop. Racket.
Oct. 20—4065 Sheridan Road. Apt. House. Earl Leatherman. Racket.
Oct. 24—220 No. Clark. Wacker Grill—Steffeo & Kaplin. Prohibition.

(Above) This was a business establishment until the proprietor refused to "go along" with the racket. *(Right)* A dynamite bomb whose time fuse failed to explode it, examined by a police detective; it could have razed a large building.

A two-page spread from *It's a Racket!* by Hostetter and Beesley, 1929, discussing Chicago's bombing war that reached all-time heights during the "Pineapple Primary" of 1928 when Mayor Dever's crackdown on bootlegging had failed and gangsters were developing more sophisticated "time" bombs for "racketeering." *(Authors' collection)*

particularly violent period inspired one journalist to write:

The rockets' red glare,
The bombs bursting in air,
Gave proof through the night
That Chicago's still there.

The bombings in the Prohibition category, like those in the old vice and gambling wars, were used to flush out a rival. Explosives were often planted in the furnace area of a clandestine brewery or distillery, and for a time police assumed that such blasts were caused by boilers blowing up.

By the end of the twenties, Chicago bombers were taking professional pride in their work. In one rare instance of prosecution, a defendant indignantly explained to a judge that the absence of injuries to upstairs residents of a blasted building was no accident: "It was technical skill. I build a bomb to do its work and quit."

In the thirties, with the rise of the Syndicate and its more subtle and businesslike forms of crime, Chicago-style terror bombing declined; but for certain hard cases who could not be moved by friendly persuasion, or who were too wily and well guarded to be removed by bullets, the bomb in the car remained a popular tactic.

Because dynamite was powerful yet relatively easy to obtain and handle, and because it could be detonated by either a burning fuse or an electrical blasting cap shoved into the stick, it always has been the explosive of choice for car bombers. One lead of an electrical blasting cap is grounded by a clamp to some part of the car frame; the other is clipped onto a terminal in the electrical system to trigger the charge when the key is turned on or the starter is engaged. However, some bombers hooked charges to car horns, headlights or even homemade switches installed in the suspension system to conceal the connections from prospective victims who might check under the hood for any strange wires.

In his review of Prohibition-era bombings, Landesco came up with the following figures:

1920	51
1921	60
1922	69
1923	55
1924	92
1925	113
1926	89
1927	108
1928	116

While bombings were a communal Chicago tradition—one reporter quipped that without a pre-dawn explosion to wake them up, many citizens would be late getting to work, and another observed that the main service performed by the police bomb squad was to record the dimensions of the window glass that would need replacement—the election of reform Mayor William Dever in 1924 upset the city's acceptable level of corruption and doubled the work load of Chicago's "bomb trust," as reporters called it, which included one James Belcastro, "king of the bombers."

The Dever victory and his crackdown on speakeasies, combined with the death of peacekeeper Mike Merlo and Dean O'Banion's decision to branch out on his own, ended nearly four years of relative harmony known as the *pax Torrio* after John Torrio, who had persuaded rival gangs to respect each other's territories. O'Banion's murder triggered nearly five years of "beer wars" as the city's booze cartel fragmented and sought to expand their territories. First swindled by O'Banion in the Sieben Brewery bust and then badly wounded by his former North Side colleagues, Torrio (who had been blamed for O'Banion's murder), took the jail term mandated by a second Volstead Act conviction, and turned his own expanding beer, vice and gambling empire over to Al Capone, an organization-minded young understudy who had come a long way since Brooklyn. Mostly for show, he shrugged off Mayor Dever's closing of his cramped offices in the Four Deuces club (at 2222 South Wabash) and rented several floors of the Metropole Hotel at Michigan and 23rd Street. However, he moved his main headquarters a few miles west to the Chicago suburb of Cicero, residing first at the Anton (later Alton) until its sister hotel, the Hawthorne, was rehabbed to his specifications.

Big Bill Thompson's defeat by Dever's reformers did not diminish his news value, however. He amused the press by ordering construction of a large yawl for a South Seas expedition to capture an elusive "tree-climbing fish" he'd heard about somewhere and believed might be anthropology's missing link. That vessel and venture made it only as far as New Orleans before it foundered on a reef of cash flow problems, but by then Capone was making up for any shortage of headlines with spectacular gun battles, including a mini-massacre whose victims included—probably by an unlucky coincidence—Assistant State's Attorney William McSwiggin. New York's Lucky Luciano supposedly returned from a business trip to Chicago declaring the city "a goddam crazy place. Nobody's safe on the streets."

Actually, the streets were safe enough for the average citizen, because one thing Capone demanded of his troops was that they abandon the predatory crime on which many had subsisted and enjoy the prosperity that came with working for Big Al, who paid well for obedience. Capone had to continually remind businessmen and short-sighted officials that any truly determined effort to close down his booze operations would lead to a serious revival of street crime by unemployed bootleggers.

The daytime and downtown gun battles that Dever could not control had made Chicago the gangster capital of the country, even the world, and with the introduction of the tommy gun, the killing of State's Attorney William McSwiggin, and the Pineapple Primary, the peaceful majority of citizens decided they'd had enough of the well-intentioned Dever. In 1927 they reelected Big Bill Thompson, who was thoroughly but at least predictably corrupt, and could therefore revive systematic graft as a means of restoring order. Thompson reassured his supporters (much to the delight of city's gambling, drinking and entertainment interests) that he was "wetter than the Atlantic Ocean," and Al Capone decided it was once more safe to relocate his main headquarters from the Hawthorne Hotel in Cicero to the luxurious Lexington at Michigan and 22nd Street. One disgruntled reformer had already conceded the situation hopeless. "Chicago is unique," he declared. "It is the only totally corrupt city in America."

The bombing war subsided on orders of Capone, to whom city leaders and officials had been forced more than once to go hat in hand with their special requests. Following the wild Pineapple Primary, Frank J. Loesch, president of the Chicago Crime Commission and an ardent foe of Capone, decided he had no choice but to arrange a secret meeting at the Lexington where he all but begged the Big Fellow to rein in his hoodlums for the sake of a peaceful national election in November. No doubt personally flattered, but also mellowing with age, power and fatherhood, Capone conceded that the city needed to spruce up its image for a presidential-election year, as well as for the Century of Progress World's Fair that Chicago businessmen were beginning to fear might suffer from the city's gangster reputation. He reportedly said, in a display of magnanimity, that he could control the "dagoes" by simple edict; and as for his competitors and independents, "I'll have the cops send over squad cars the night before the election and jug all the hoodlums and keep them in the cooler until the polls close."

Thus Chicago enjoyed not only a peaceful election, but a jolly one. A story filed by the *New York Sun*'s Chicago bureau reported that Big Bill's pre-election "street parade, augmented by last hour recruiting of additional tumbling clowns, bucking horses and yipping cowboys, was well up to the average of such demonstrations when undertaken by any of the big traveling circuses." Thompson forces virtually commandeered the Loop, one reporter said, and "inside the theaters his Chicago Police Quartet regularly interspersed with Big Bill's patriotic favorites the following ditty:

Happy days are here again,
The gang is feeling swell again,
The mayor's coming back again . . .
He was out for while,
But he's back with a smile,
And he'll shove the others all about,
Just like they took his appendix out!"

The paper also quoted Big Bill in his customary third-person style: "Those steamboat whistles from New Orleans ought to be heard in Chicago inside of six months. But unless Bill Thompson goes up there to prod them into action it will take two years."

Meanwhile, New York, its own machine working smoothly, had taken the ingenuous position that the worst of its criminal element had been nightsticked into leaving town, and were causing a ruckus in places like Philadelphia, Buffalo, Cleveland, Toledo and especially Chicago. But that same year Manhattan's gentleman gangster Arnold Rothstein had been fatally shot in a downtown hotel room by someone who pitched the pistol out the window; and its less gentlemanly gangster, Frankie Yale, had been blown away Chicago-style as he motored to his home in Brooklyn. His was New York's first machine-gun murder, and New Yorkers had to assume that the last few years of comparative

Copyright, 1928, by the Chicago *Tribune*
HE WOULD PLAY WITH MATCHES
—Orr in the Chicago *Tribune*.

(Authors' collection)

tranquility were coming to an end as Chicago's "Big Bill the Builder," himself on the brink of a breakdown, was making Capone his unofficial chief of police.

Chicago could not be fathomed by the rest of the country, as illustrated in a full-page *Tribune* ad paid for by supporters of Thompson rival Anton J. Cermak, who portrayed himself as more of a reformer than he was. By 1931 Capone controlled the city, using his own methods, and suffered the embarrassment of his link to Thompson. Midwestern newspapers editorialized:

If [Thompson] wins in April, decent Chicagoans might as well take to the trees....
Daily Advertiser, Tiffin, Ohio

Mayor Thompson has served three terms and during these years lawlessness has become one of the most highly specialized and profitable industries in the Windy City....
Chronicle, Augusta, Georgia

No city in the atlas has earned itself as much ridicule in Bill's time as our strident sister on the lake.
News, Detroit, Michigan

The present mayor of Chicago is the master ballyhooer, showman and four flusher in the politics of America today—bar none. He knows his Chicago better, perhaps, than he knows his A, B, C's. He has earned from long experience to place his reliance in the rabble, the underworld, the self-seeking, office-holding and office hungry politicians, and they have yet to fail him in the pinches.
News, Springfield, Missouri

[The prospective World's Fair visitor] is a class that is disposed to think of Thompson and Capone as representatives of the spirit of Chicago, to regard

Chicago as a place so wicked, vile and abominable that it should be avoided by decent people. If Chicago expects to retain Thompsonism and Caponeism and yet attract this host with a glittering exposition, it has one more guess coming....
State Tribune Leader, Cheyenne, Wyoming

Big Bill Thompson, the blustering, bellicose, boisterous, belligerant Chicago bull-slinger....
Eve Union, Springfield, Massachusetts

Chicago will hardly fail to have both Mayor Thompson and Al Capone on exhibition at its World's Fair in 1933. It would be almost impossible to overestimate their advertising value.
News, Springfield, Missouri

Of the more than 200 names sponsoring the ad, only one was obviously Italian. And only one newspaper seemed to grasp the fundamental craziness of Chicago politics that the average local citizen, if not its better element, took for granted and probably enjoyed for the notoriety that made them objects of conversation and curiosity wherever they went. The Nebraska City *News Press* wrote:

Outsiders, apparently, do more worrying about the plight of Chicago than the residents themselves....

Unfortunately for Capone, the Internal Revenue Service had been pressured by the press and the business community to get him, his brother Ralph, and some other top mobsters, one way or another, for violating U.S. income tax laws. This, plus the Public Enemy label hatched by the Chicago Crime Commission, distracted him from his civic duties. But by then the Depression had set in, Capone had been sent to prison, and his chosen mayoral candidate,

Anton J. Cermak, had been killed in Miami by a bullet aimed at president-elect Roosevelt.

With both Capone and Prohibition out of the headlines, Chicago arbitrarily declared its gangster era over, and was smiling at the gang wars brewing in New York. In the early thirties an obscure Edward Kelly and his Irish crony Patrick Nash rode the national Democratic land-

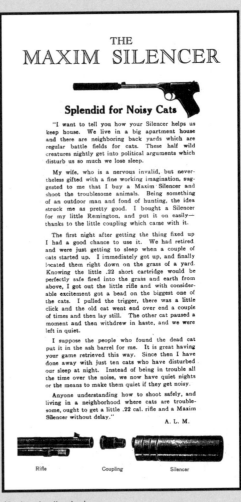

(Authors' collection)

slide to victory in the race for mayor, and created Chicago's first truly functional political machine that would survive until recent times.

Without Capone to make news, his successors, particularly Frank Nitti, consolidated the crime syndicate without fanfare or excessive gunfire, and turned the avenues originally used for the intercity distribution of beer and booze into turnpikes of nationwide racketeering. From Capone, everyone had learned the hazards of notoriety; and from Tammany Hall, the Kelly-Nash machine had learned how to make Chicago "the city that worked"—one way or another, using the same anonymous community of sluggers against rebellious unions that the city's newspapers once had used against each other.

Gangland bombings largely ceased in favor of discreet shootings that didn't wake up a residential neighborhood, and the depositing of bodies in the trunks of cars stolen for that specific purpose. Instead of employing mad bombers like Belcastro, the mob turned to its friends, many of whom were cops with basement workshops and inventive streaks, interested in the design and modification of firearms. After World War II, Chicago became the country's principal source of homemade silencers, more properly called suppressors. Some of these were substantial improvements on the commercial versions, which could still be purchased from properly licensed dealers but qualified as Class Three ordnance strictly controlled under both state and federal laws.

By the time New York crime families had revived Chicago-style warfare in the 1950s and '60s, Chicago had learned to maintain the outward appearance of tranquility, quietly (with a few major exceptions) dispatching hard cases with professionally fabricated silencers threaded onto the barrel of the common .22 Long Rifle target pistol, then stashing the body in the trunk of a stolen car left in the long-term parking lot at O'Hare airport, or on some remote side street to ripen until the neighbors called the cops.

incumbent Robert E. Crowe for the office of State's Attorney.

Marshall Ratliff, leader of the "Santa Claus Bank Robbery," is tried at Abilene, Texas, for the murder of Police Chief Bit Bedford. He will be convicted on March 30, sentenced to death, then returned to Eastland County Jail to be tried on another charge of robbery with firearms (punishable by death in Texas).

April 10, 1928   Octavius C. Granady, a black attorney running against Capone ally Morris Eller for boss of Chicago's 20th Ward, is machine-gunned to death at 13th Street and Hoyne Avenue.

April 16, 1928   Gus Winkeler, Fred Goetz, alias "Shotgun" George Ziegler, Ray "Crane-Neck" Nugent, Bob "Gimpy" Newberry and Charles J. Fitzgerald kill a policeman while robbing an American Express Company truck in Toledo of $200,000.

April 19, 1928   Charlie Birger, cracking jokes on the gallows, is publicly hanged for murder at Marion, Illinois.

April 22, 1928   Ben Newmark, former chief investigator for State's Attorney Crowe, is killed by a shot through a bedroom window of his bungalow at 7316 Merrill Avenue in Chicago.

May 23, 1928   The Jake Fleagle gang robs the First National Bank at Lamar, Colorado, of $200,000, killing bank president A.N. Parrish and his son John, a cashier. Teller Everett Kessinger is taken hostage and later murdered in Kansas. Dr. William Winneger at Dighton, Kansas, is forced to treat wounded gang member Herbert Royston, then also is murdered.

June 26, 1928 Gangster and racketeer Big Tim Murphy is machine-gunned to death outside his home at 2525 Morse on Chicago's northwest side.

July 1, 1928 Brooklyn crime boss Frankie Yale is killed in New York's first tommy gun murder. The slaying is attributed to the Capone mob because of disputes over control of the Chicago Unione Siciliana and hijacking of Capone liquor shipments.

July 20, 1928 Dominic Aiello, uncle of Joe Aiello, is murdered in front of his store at 928 Milton Street in Chicago.

September 7, 1928 Tony Lombardo, Capone-backed head of the Unione Siciliana, and bodyguard Joseph Ferraro are shot to death at the corner of Madison and Dearborn Streets in the heart of Chicago.

Dago Lawrence Mangano, a Capone gangster, is charged with bombing the home of Chicago Police Captain Luke Garrick at 1473 Summerdale Avenue.

September 17, 1928 Men disguised as armored car guards rob New York company of $18,000.

October 10, 1928 Brooklyn Mafia boss Salvatore "Toto" D'Aquila is shot to death by unknown gunmen.

October 15, 1928 Joey Noe, bootlegging partner of Arthur "Dutch Schultz" Flegenheimer, is shot to death outside the Chateau Madrid on West 54th Street in New York. Attributed to the Legs Diamond gang.

October 25, 1928 The Bailey gang robs the Whitney Loan and Trust Company in Atlantic, Iowa, of $55,000.

November 4, 1928 Gambler Arnold Rothstein is fatally shot in Manhattan's Park Central Hotel. Gambler George "Hump" McManus is sought as a suspect.

THE MACHINE-GUN MURDER OF FRANKIE YALE

The daylight shooting of Brooklyn's Frankie Yale on July 1, 1928, was the first time a machine gun had been used in New York, and this caused a major uproar. Because of the tommy gun, police attributed the killing to Chicagoans, who already had made the Thompson notorious as a "gangster" weapon, and the press viewed it ominously as the spread of Chicago-style violence to New York. Both were right. Ballistics tests later established that one of the submachine guns used on Yale was also used in Chicago's St. Valentine's Day Massacre a few months later by Fred Burke, Gus Winkeler, and others in Capone's organization. Capone had learned that Yale, his onetime boss and mentor, and national head of the Unione Siciliana, was sabotaging his booze shipments from the East and supporting his rivals for leadership of the Chicago Unione. The murder of Frankie Yale seemed to persuade New York's gangsters that they were lagging behind in the arms race, and soon the warring forces of Dutch Schultz, Vincent Coll and Legs Diamond adopted the Thompson as standard gangland issue.

(Authors' collection)

November 6, 1928   Eddie Diamond, brother of Jack "Legs" Diamond, escapes injury when his car is riddled by machine-gun fire on a Denver street. Denver police arrest Eugene Moran and James Piteo, former bodyguards of Arnold Rothstein, and charge them with assault. Moran and Piteo are released on $15,000 bond and skip town. Frank "Blubber" Devlin is also a fugitive on this charge.

November 16, 1928   John G. Clay, secretary of the Laundry and Dyehouse Chauffeurs Union, is shot in his office at 29 South Ashland Avenue in Chicago. Attributed to Capone-Moran labor rackets war.

November 17, 1928   Charles "Lucky" Luciano, George Uffner and Thomas "Fats" Walsh are charged with robbery by New York police, questioned about the Rothstein murder and released.

November 27, 1928   George McManus surrenders to New York police.

December 1, 1928   State of Texas reports only three bank robberies for year; all robbers captured.

December 4, 1928   George McManus is indicted for the Rothstein murder but later acquitted. Slaying will be attributed to Legs Diamond

Patsy Lolordo was murdered in his home on North Avenue, a victim of the "War of Sicilian Succession" for control of Chicago's Unione Siciliana. The killers probably were Joe Aiello's men, in league with Bugs Moran and a factor leading up to the St. Valentine's Day Massacre. *(Goddard Collection)*

or Dutch Schultz, in retribution for the murder of Joey Noe.

December 5, 1928 Car bomb kills St. Paul crime boss "Dapper Danny" Hogan.

Twenty-three Sicilian gangsters, from New York, Chicago, Buffalo, Tampa, Detroit, St. Louis and Newark are arrested while meeting at the Statler Hotel in Cleveland. Newspapers describe the event as a meeting of the "Grand Council" of the Mafia, presumably the first, and probably convened in response to Chicago's war over leadership of the local Sicilian Union.

December 17, 1928 The Harvey Bailey gang robs the Sturgis National Bank at Sturgis, Minnesota, of $80,000.

December 24, 1928 The Bailey gang robs the Citizens State Bank at Clinton, Indiana, of $52,000 in cash and Liberty Bonds.

December 31, 1928 Hugh "Stubby" McGovern and William "Gunner" McPadden, of the Danny Stanton mob, are the year's last gangland murder victims in Chicago. George Maloney, of the Bubs Quinlan mob, will be convicted and sentenced to 14 years.

1929

January 8, 1929 Pasqualino (Patsy) Lolordo, successor to Tony Lombardo as Chicago head of the Unione Siciliana, is shot to death in his home at 1921 West North Avenue. Attributed to the combined Moran-Aiello gangs.

January 10, 1929 Harry Vesey, Queens beer runner formerly associated with Arnold Rothstein, is found shot to death near the Hoboken waterfront. Legs Diamond is suspected.

January 21, 1929 Garage in Bronx held up twice in half hour; first robbers get $300, leaving none for second group.

February 14, 1929 The St. Valentine's Day Massacre: Six members of the Bugs Moran gang and a visiting optometrist are mowed down by Capone machine-gunners, some disguised as policemen, in the S.M.C. Cartage Company garage at 2122 North Clark Street in Chicago. The victims are Frank and Peter Gusenberg, James Clark, Adam Heyer, John May, Albert Weinshank and Dr. Reinhart Schwimmer.

February 22, 1929 Two safes in Camillus, New York, cracked by a yegg, who phones police to brag of his feat.

March 3, 1929 Frank "Blubber" Devlin, wanted for the Denver machine-gun attack on Eddie Diamond, is found shot to death on a farm near Somerville, New Jersey. Legs Diamond is suspected.

March 7, 1929 Thomas "Fats" Walsh, former henchman of Arnold Rothstein, is shot to death at the Biltmore Hotel in Miami.

Pretty Boy Floyd is released from the state prison at Jefferson City, Missouri.

March 9, 1929 Pretty Boy Floyd is arrested by police of Kansas City, Missouri, for investigation.

March 20, 1929 Dick Gregg robs the Wynona National Bank in Wynona, Oklahoma.

April 12, 1929 Five robbers hold up Irvington (New Jersey) Smelting & Refining Company for $18,000 in bar gold.

April 17, 1929 Five men with machine guns rob payroll of New York's Bell Telephone Laboratories.

May 6, 1929 Police in Kansas City, Kansas, arrest Pretty Boy Floyd for vagrancy and suspicion of highway robbery. He is released the following day.

THE ST. VALENTINE'S DAY MASSACRE

The crime most closely associated with Prohibition was the firing-squad-style execution of six Chicago bootleggers and one optometrist "groupie" on February 14, 1929, by rival gangsters masquerading as police. The St. Valentine's Day Massacre was so well planned and cold blooded that it made the front page of virtually every major newspaper in the country, and probably did more than any other single event to tip public opinion in favor of Repeal. The mass murder confirmed what most Americans already believed—that Prohibition had not only failed to solve the country's chronic alcohol problem, it had actually aggravated it, corrupted government at every level and brought gangland violence to intolerable proportions.

The Massacre caused total turmoil as Chicago police, in a rare spasm of law enforcement, clamped down on thousands of speakeasies and issued almost daily declaration that the case was all but solved. However, this amounted to rounding up the usual suspects against whom they had no evidence, declaring the murders a Capone-sponsored bloodbath intended to complete the conquest of Chicago (although Capone himself was in Miami) and naming the shooters largely on the basis of their presumed grievances against the Bugs Moran gang.

Moran had inherited leadership of the North Siders following the deaths of Dean O'Banion, Hymie Weiss and Vincent Drucci during four years of beer wars, which had encompassed hundreds of gangland murders and introduced Americans to the previously unknown Thompson submachine gun (soon dubbed the "Chicago typewriter").

The Massacre remains unsolved, but the standard account has it engineered by Capone's right-hand man, "Machine Gun" Jack McGurn, who supposedly tricked the Moran gang into assembling at their Near North Side booze depot, 2122 North Clark Street, to take delivery of a load of Old Log Cabin whiskey they believed had been hijacked from Capone. This may have been pure speculation based on remarks of a federal Prohibition official who had learned of a recent hijacking. But he also thought the killers might well be crooked Chicago cops on a personal mission—an accusation he later denied making, but which still caused his banishment to another city.

In any case, about 10:30 A.M. on February 14, 1929, the Moran men were drinking coffee in their unheated garage (innocuously identified as the S.M.C. Cartage Co.), when they were interrupted by two men in police uniforms who arrived in what looked like a Chicago detective car. Annoyed but not particularly worried at what they assumed would be a routine shakedown, they surrendered their weapons, and were ordered to line up facing the north wall, about the only place not cluttered with cars and trucks used in their particular line of "cartage." Before a payoff could be discussed, two or three men in expensive overcoats entered the garage and raked the group with 70 bullets from two Thompsons, plus a couple of shotgun blasts. The killers then handed their now-empty guns to the men in uniform, who marched them, as if arrested, back outside to the phoney police car and left.

By most accounts, Bugs Moran, the intended target, survived only because he and two fellow bootleggers arrived a few minutes late, saw the phoney police car, and ducked into a corner coffee shop. If not, the death toll would have been 10. It would later appear that one or both of his companions had secretly defected to the Capone gang and had helped set up their colleagues.

A woman neighbor heard what sounded like gunfire and the howling of a dog, and asked her roomer to investigate. In the back of the garage, still reeking with gunsmoke, he found six dead men and one who would die a short time later.

The mass murder horrified Chicago and the rest of the country. Police later arrested McGurn in a room at the luxurious Stevens Hotel on Michigan Avenue (now the Hilton Towers), but his girlfriend, Louise Rolfe, whom he later married, would always stick to her story that Jack had been with her in bed all morning, presumably making St. Valentine's Day love. He used his interest in the huge Guyon Hotel at 3000 West Washington to post bond and ultimately was set free for lack of evidence.

In the months following the Massacre, a coroner's jury of prominent Chicagoans met several times without developing enough evidence to prosecute anyone, though police work established that the killers had headquartered at Maddox's Circus Cafe at 1857 West North Avenue while awaiting the word from at least two lookouts who had rented rooms across the street from the S.M.C. Cartage Co. The jury decided that the gunmen included a notorious St. Louis hoodlum named Fred Burke and other veterans of that city's Egan's Rats who had moved to Chicago, where they operated as Capone's special-assignment squad of "American boys." Further evidence that the killers were not the "usual suspects" came from a woman in nearby Lincoln Park whose horseback-riding companion had noticed them earlier and described them as "West Side gangsters," as opposed to Moran's North Siders.

A major blunder on Burke's part later confirmed his involvement in the Massacre. The following December, while lying low as "Frederick Dane" in the lakeside town of St. Joseph, Michigan, Burke panicked following a minor traffic accident and killed a policeman named Charles Skelly. He escaped, but sheriff's officers ransacking his lavishly furnished bungalow uncovered a cache of weapons that included two Thompson submachine guns. These were sent to Chicago for ballistics tests by firearms-identification expert Colonel Calvin Goddard, a pioneer in that field personally hired by some prominent local businessmen to work on the case. Using comparison microscopes and other new techniques, Goddard convinced the coroner's jury that the 70 .45-caliber bullets used on the Moran gang could have been fired only by Burke's Thompsons, one fitted with a 50-round drum and the other a straight 20-round box magazine (possibly used because drum magazines had a greater tendency to misfeed). Goddard discovered, moreover, that one of the Valentine's Day guns had been previously used to kill New York gangster Frankie Yale in 1928, just as the authorities there suspected, since the Thompson was new to that city but had been standard issue in Chicago for at least three years.

For reasons not entirely clear, Michigan authorities refused to extradite Burke to Illinois even for questioning, and he eventually died in the Michigan state prison while serving life for the murder of Officer Skelly. Ironically, while a man resembling Burke took part in the Massacre, fellow crook Harvey Bailey gave him an alibi of sorts. In a book coauthored by Texas historian J. Evetts Haley, Bailey complains that he and Burke were in fact drinking beer in Calumet City at the time of the killings, and were forced to abandon their lucrative bank-robbing partnership once Burke became the object of a nationwide manhunt. The implication was that Burke had merely done his Chicago friends a favor by stashing the guns safely out of state, not realizing they could be linked to the crime by the new science of forensic ballistics, which courts before then had not considered conclusive evidence.

Whether or not Burke was personally involved in the Massacre, the real story did not come out for another five years—and then, thanks partly to J. Edgar Hoover, the inability of a mobster's wife to find a publisher and reluctance of the Chicago police to reopen the case. Only the original version made it into history books.

Nevertheless, in January 1935, several members of the Barker-Karpis gang were captured in an FBI raid on a courtyard apartment building at 3920 North Pine Grove Avenue. One was Byron Bolton, charged with kidnapping; while in federal custody he (probably through a lawyer, and probably because he thought the Capone mob had tipped off the FBI to their hideout) gave a considerably different version of the Massacre to the *Chicago American.* He revealed that he, not the Keywell brothers from the Detroit Purple Gang, had been one of the Clark Street lookouts; that some of the planning had taken place at a Capone hideaway in Wisconsin, with two state legislators present; that he had been the errand boy who not only catered the meeting but also purchased one of the *two* cars used by the principal gunmen, who were not the suspects named by the police and reported by the press, but rather the "American boys." Bolton correctly remembered the phoney name he had used to buy the car some five years earlier. Though he had left his post to use a phone when he thought he saw Moran, he guessed the killers to be Burke, Gus Winkeler,

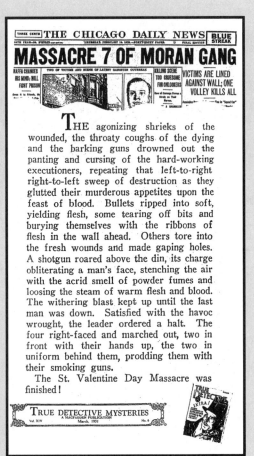

The vivid, often lurid writing style in popular detective magazines left little to the imagination. *(Authors' collection)*

Fred Goetz (alias Shotgun George Ziegler), Murray Humphreys and Claude Maddox, though the newspaper's anonymous source had obtained the details secondhand and may have confused Bolton's plotters with the actual shooters. He even left behind, by accident, either a bottle of prescription medicine (according to Mrs. Winkeler), or a letter addressed to him from his downstate family, or both—which gave the police an unfamiliar name they ignored at the time. The newspaper devoted its front page to this scoop, but since Bolton had not shared any Massacre information with his FBI captors, J. Edgar Hoover immediately declared it false, and other papers took Hoover at his word.

Though scotched by Hoover at the time, Bolton's "confession" in the *Chicago American* was largely confirmed a short time later by a most unlikely source. After reading the paper, the widow of Gus Winkeler, one of several "American boys" involved in the Massacre and since murdered by the mob's Frank Nitti faction, told what she knew to the FBI. With minor differences, her version supported Bolton's story and added new details, including the name Ray Nugent (in place of Humphreys or Maddox), another St. Louis gunman, whom the papers may have called James Ray. She said Fred Goetz was the man who brought the police uniforms to her and Gus's home, and who had amused himself by wearing one to answer knocks on the door.

The standard story describes one bogus detective car arriving at the S.M.C. Cartage Co., but the woman in the building next door had looked out her bay window, noticed both cars and wondered what was going on. Whether this preceded or followed the shooting isn't clear, but police at the time dismissed the confirming report by a neighborhood youngster who said he had seen one of the cars in the alley behind the garage, and that men dressed as police had first gone in the back double doors when they were opened to admit a truck. Sensing that some excitement would soon occur, he hurried around to the front, probably about the time of the shooting, and there witnessed the scene described by others: Two armed men in uniform marching two or three men in civilian overcoats, hands raised, to another detective car, which then sped away. This would suggest that the phoney cops slipped in through the back, disarmed the occupants and then let the plainclothes machine-gunners in through the front.

Eventually the Chicago police decided that their witnesses had missed most of the activity, and an officer who stayed on the case almost as a hobby later calculated that as many as 11 to 14 men participated in the Massacre one way or another, some remaining in the getaway cars, others leaving through both front and rear doors, as well as several lookouts who would have been parked up and down Clark Street to block any pursuit in case a real police squad happened by. A name added to the group in more recent times was that of Tony Accardo, then a young rookie who drove for Jack McGurn but who would one day boss all organized crime in Chicago.

Most of these random facts went unnoticed or unreported at the time, but some came together a few days later when a car fitted out to resemble a detective Cadillac exploded on February 21 in an alley garage on Wood Street, about a block from Maddox's Circus Cafe and maybe a 10-minute drive from Clark Street. Arriving firemen found a siren, police gong and a Luger pistol in the wreckage, and police decided that the garage had been rented by Maddox himself, using a phoney name and an address next door to his Circus Cafe (which had suddenly gone out of business). Both buildings were vacant, but the one next to the cafe obviously had served as a meeting place for Maddox's Circus gang, which included his St. Louis friends and amounted to a Capone beachhead on Chicago's Near North Side.

Someone had seen a burned man run from the garage toward a nearby hospital, but he left minutes later without waiting for treatment or possible questioning by police. That minor mystery was cleared up some 40 years later when outlaw Alvin Karpis published his biography. The burn victim was one "Tough Tony" Capezio, friend of Karpis, ally of Capone and a co-owner of the Circus Cafe, who had been tediously dismantling the 1927 Cadillac, unaware that the fuel system included a canister of gasoline attached to the firewall to gravity-feed the carburetor. The blast ended that project, but the leads it provided were not diligently pursued. On February 27, a second murder car, a 1926 Peerless, exploded in a garage in the suburb of Maywood, where firemen found another police-type gong and gun rack, as well as a pocket notebook apparently belonging to Albert Weinshank, one of the Massacre victims. Maddox lived in Maywood, but nothing came of that lead, either, possibly because the town was a stronghold of Capone.

The role of Capone is perhaps the greatest mystery—whether he personally ordered the Massacre out of a murderous megalomania (as popular history would have it); approved the killing of Moran, partly in self-defense; or if he truly was exasperated with the continuing gangland violence (as he claimed) and left the matter to his "American boys," expecting them to use good judgment. Those are some of the complex possibilities, for there were several other factors involved.

The North Siders had recently teamed up with gangster Joe Aiello in his war with Capone for control of the Unione Siciliana, originally an immigrants' benevolent society which had turned small-scale distilling into a major cottage industry in "Little Sicily" which bordered Moran's territory on Chicago's Near North Side. Meanwhile, Moran had discovered the enormous profit potential in both racketeering and gambling, which pitted him against Capone allies (including the "American boys") invading his own North

May 9, 1929 John Scalise, Albert Anselmi and Joseph "Hop Toad" Guinta are found murdered near Hammond, Indiana. Police first attribute the slayings to the Moran-Aiello gang, in revenge for the St. Valentine's Day killings, but informants soon claim that the three were beaten to death at a gang dinner party by Al Capone personally after he learned they were plotting to betray him.

Police in Pueblo, Colorado, arrest Pretty Boy Floyd for vagrancy. He is fined $50 and sentenced to 60 days in jail.

May 13–15, 1929 Midwestern and East Coast mobsters meet at the President Hotel in Atlantic City to devise a system for peacefully arbitrating their disputes. This is usually considered the official beginning of a national crime syndicate. Delegates include Al Capone, Frank Nitti, Jake "Greasy Thumb" Guzik, Frank McErlane and Polack Joe Saltis of Chicago; Johnny Torrio, Charles "Lucky" Luciano, Frank Costello, Dutch Schultz, Meyer Lansky, Joe Adonis, Owney "The Killer" Madden, Larry Fay and Frank Erickson of New York; Joe Bernstein from the Detroit "Purple Gang"; John Lazia and Solly "Cutcher-Head-Off" Weissman of Kansas City; Max "Boo Boo" Hoff and Harry "Nig Rosen" Stromberg of Philadelphia; Abner "Longy" Zwillman of Newark; Moe Dalitz, Louis Rothkopf and Chuck Polizzi of Cleveland; and Atlantic City political boss Enoch "Nucky" Johnson.

May 15, 1929 Detective Raymond Martin of the Chicago Police Department is killed by gangsters on Laramie Avenue while acting as a

Side. His unruly gang had never ceased sniping at Capone since the murder of Dean O'Banion in his flower shop in 1924; and Capone had lately deeded North Side gambling operations to Gus Winkeler and his friends, if they could muscle out Moran.

According to one police scenario, the threat of killing was all that was ordered. But when Pete Gusenberg saw some familiar South Side faces enter the garage, he assumed the worst, went for a gun in a nearby desk drawer, and the shooters opened up with their Thompsons. That seems unlikely, considering all the planning and effort involved. More plausible is that the gunmen did not anticipate the crowd they had lined up, and didn't know what to do except kill them. One can only imagine Capone in Miami getting the phone call from Chicago and thinking to himself, If you want anything done right, you have to do it yourself.

For the St. Valentine's Day Massacre was a public-relations disaster that cost the Chicago Syndicate millions in a reluctant crackdown on speakeasies (which numbered 8000 to 10,000) and countless gambling joints, ranging from handbooks to betting parlors to casino-size clubs. It caused economic turmoil in the business community that had thrived on out-of-town visitors, and left the city with a scar as conspicuous as those on Capone's left cheek. It also blackened the name of Capone, who had rather enjoyed his improving image as the Babe Ruth of American gangsters. And it inspired two wealthy businessmen to fund the establishment of the country's first full-scale crime lab, to be operated by Northwestern University because Chicago's police were so notoriously corrupt.

decoy in a $50,000 kidnapping plot. He was impersonating Moses L. Blumenthal, who was to pay a $10,000 ransom for his brother Philip, a former bootlegger.

May 16, 1929   Returning from the Atlantic City meeting, Al Capone and bodyguard Frank Rio are arrested in Philadelphia on gun-carrying charges, probably by prearrangement. Expecting a short sentence while Chicago cooled down, they are surprised to receive the maximum—a year in prison.

May 22, 1929   Chicago police detective Joseph Sullivan, looking for the killers of Detective Martin, is shot to death in Red Bolton's saloon at 1610 Polk Street.

May 24, 1929   Messenger car for American First National Bank of Oklahoma City held up for $75,000 by Russell "Slim Gray" Gibson, James "Cowboy" Hayes and Neal Merritt. Gibson will be arrested but escape from the county jail in Oklahoma City.

June 11, 1929   Salvatore "Black Sam" Todaro, successor to Big Joe Lonardo, is shot to death in Cleveland. Joe Porello succeeds to leadership of local Italian crime family.

June 13, 1929   Jack "Legs" Diamond and bodyguard Charles Entratta kill William "Red" Cassidy, Peter Cassidy and Simon Walker in a gun battle in Diamond's Hotsy Totsy Club, 1721 Broadway, New York. Diamond and Entratta become fugitives.

June 20, 1929   Bridgeport, Connecticut, burglar gives up attempt after spending six hours under bed occupied by talking girls.

"MACHINE GUN" JACK McGURN

Jack McGurn, aka Gebardi or Gibaldi, or De-mora or DeMory, lost his stepfather to a gunman before the outbreak of Chicago's beer

Jack McGurn and Louise Rolfe *(Capone's Chicago)*

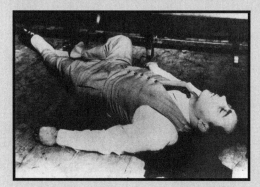

The body of "Machine Gun" Jack McGurn, whose killers had sent this blackly humorous card addressed to him at the bowling alley he frequented at 805 North Milwaukee Avenue. One of his killers would turn out to be Claude Maddox, who helped him set up the Massacre exactly seven years before. *(Goddard Collection; Authors' collection)*

wars and eventually drifted from the North Sid-ers into the Capone camp, where he became the right-hand triggerman of the "Big Fellow" him-self. He had adopted the name McGurn as a young prizefighter in a sport dominated by the Irish, and that name is on his tombstone at Mt. Carmel Cemetery; how he picked up the nick-name "Machine Gun" isn't clear, since most of the killings attributed to him were carried out with a pistol, and most of the victims were local or imported bounty hunters gunning for his boss. Supposedly his trademark was a nickel,

(Authors' collection)

June 22, 1929 Using a .30-caliber Brown-ing machine gun, Frank Ellis (alias Frank Smith), Charles Berta and James Sargert rob a Southern Pacific mail train of $16,000, near

put in the hand of the deceased to proclaim him a "cheap hood." In public, however, McGurn exemplified the Roaring Twenties "sheik," a spiffy dresser in the style of actor George Raft, who favored light blue outfits, strummed the ukulele, had his pick of showgirls (despite a marriage and children), and survived more than one shooting. He supposedly ordered the almost-fatal knifing of popular comedian Joe Brown, at the North Sider–owned Commonwealth Hotel on Diversey when Brown and his act jumped ship at the Green Mill nightclub (in which McGurn held an interest) for the newly opened Rendezvous, a nearby Moran-sponsored club at the intersection of Clark, Diversey and Broadway. He was Capone's chief torpedo until Capone went to prison and he fell on hard times.

Although indicted for the St. Valentine's Day Massacre, the charge had to be dropped for lack of evidence, especially when his "blond alibi," Louise Rolfe, insisted they had spent the entire morning in his suite at the Stevens Hotel making St. Valentine's Day love.

In frustration, local authorities prevailed on the Justice Department to charge McGurn and girlfriend Louise with conspiring to violate the Mann Act—transporting a woman across state lines for "immoral purposes" when visiting Capone in Florida. Both were convicted and sentenced under a law originally intended to suppress organized prostitution rather than hassle consenting individuals. Angry at the misuse of the law, McGurn and Rolfe took their appeals all the way to the U.S. Supreme Court, where justice of a sort prevailed. The Court concluded that the law, as worded, did not contemplate a woman victimizing herself, and reversed the

conviction of Louise, whom Jack had since married. This left McGurn with no one to have "conspired" with, and thus his conviction also had to be vacated. So thanks to McGurn and his blond alibi, federal prosecutors now find it hard to convict an unmarried couple of engaging in "white slavery" when they travel together, or when the motel they find happens to be a few miles down the road in a neighboring state.

After Capone's income-tax conviction, Frank Nitti maneuvered for control of the Chicago "Outfit," which included purging those who had been especially close to the Big Fellow or were rapidly expanding their North Side operations in the vacuum left by the demise of the Moran gang. Possibly seen as a threat to the new order, McGurn was gunned down in a bowling alley at 805 Milwaukee Avenue in 1936, a few minutes after midnight of the seventh anniversary of the St. Valentine's Day Massacre. Evidently the comic card was waiting for him when he arrived, not dropped on his body by the shooters, as most accounts state. To some, the card suggested he was killed to avenge the Massacre by patient remnants of the North Side gang. Years later, however, on telephone-surveillance tapes made by the FBI, Murray "The Camel" Humphreys talked about the killing of McGurn and others, and remarked that one of the shooters was McGurn's longtime colleague in crime, Claude Maddox, in whose Circus Cafe on North Avenue the Massacre crew presumably waited for the phone call that sent them to the S.M.C. Cartage Co. garage. Maddox was one of the few "American boys" to survive and prosper after Nitti became the de facto leader of the Chicago mob in the 1930s.

McAvoy, California. Jake Fleagle is also suspected.

June 24, 1929   Gandalfo Civito, alias Frankie Marlow, a follower of the late Frankie

Yale, is shot to death by unknown gangsters at 166th Street and Queens Avenue in New York.

July 19, 1929   Hotsy Totsy Club waiter Walter Wolgast is found murdered at Bordentown, New Jersey. About 10 other witnesses to the Hotsy Totsy Club murders reportedly disappear.

July 31, 1929   James "Bozo" Shupe, an ex-convict and machine-gun supplier, and Thomas McNichols, a former court bailiff, kill one another in a pistol duel at the corner of Madison and Aberdeen in Chicago.

August 4, 1929   Yee Sun, a member of the Hip Sing tong, is murdered in Chicago following an attack in Boston on another Hip Sing member. War briefly erupts in Chinatowns of the East and Midwest between the Hip Sings and On Leongs.

August 6, 1929   Mafia boss Steve Monastero is murdered by gunmen outside the Allegheny General Hospital in Pittsburgh.

August 10, 1929   Man found shot and burned in a car in Newark city dump. The body will eventually be identified as that of Eugene Moran, jewel thief and former bodyguard of Arnold Rothstein. Legs Diamond gang suspected.

August 12, 1929   Paul E. Reynolds, special agent in the El Paso Field Office of the U.S. Bureau of Investigation, is found shot to death in a canal near Phoenix, Arizona. The murder is never solved.

August 29, 1929   The Harvey Bailey gang robs the Emmet County State Bank at Estherville, Iowa, of $5,350.

Bank robber Dick Gregg and Tulsa County Highway Patrolmen Abraham Bowline and Ross Darrow are killed in a highway gun battle between Sand Springs and Tulsa, Oklahoma.

September 2, 1929   Gangster Henry "Hoop-a-Daisy" Connors is shot to death by unknown killers in the C & O Restaurant at 509 North Clark Street, Chicago.

Under the alias of Joe Scott, Charles "Pretty Boy" Floyd is arrested in Kansas City, Missouri, for investigation.

September 6, 1929   Henry Helms, of the "Santa Claus" gang, is executed in the electric chair at Huntsville, Texas, state prison.

September 26, 1929   Frank Smith, aka Ellis, and gang rob the Rodeo, California, branch of the Bank of Pinole of $28,000, killing Constable Arthur McDonald.

September 27, 1929   Fleagle gang arrested on suspicion of Lamar, Colorado, bank holdup in which four were killed.

October 6, 1929   Palm Gardens Road House near Lansing, New York, held up for fifth time in three months; robbers dance with guests.

October 17, 1929   New York gangster Charles "Lucky" Luciano is abducted, beaten and dumped from a car on Staten Island by plainclothes detectives searching for fugitive murderer Legs Diamond. Luciano is hospitalized and the legend begins that he has survived a one-way ride at the hands of gangland rivals.

Brinks Express Company armored truck with 10 payrolls stolen in New York.

October 18, 1929   Fred "Killer" Burke and Gus Winkeler are suspected in the $93,000 robbery of the First National Bank at Peru, Indiana.

November 7, 1929   The Farmers and Merchants Bank at Jefferson, Wisconsin, is robbed of $319,850 in bonds. The loot will later be recovered from the Michigan hideout of Fred "Killer" Burke, but the robbery will be attributed by Mrs. Gus Winkeler to Harvey Bailey's gang.

November 18, 1929 "Santa Claus" bank robber Marshall Ratliff shoots and mortally wounds popular jailer Uncle Tom Jones while attempting to escape from Eastland, Texas, county jail. A lynch mob drags Ratliff from the jail and hangs him.

Kansas City, Missouri, police arrest Pretty Boy Floyd for investigation in a holdup. Floyd is released the next day.

December 2, 1929 After several trial delays, the indictment against Machine Gun Jack McGurn for the St. Valentine's Day Massacre is dismissed.

December 7, 1929 Guests at banquet for Judge Albert Vitale, hosted by Harlem racketeer Ciro Terranova, are robbed by gunmen at the Roman Gardens restaurant in the Bronx.

December 14, 1929 Patrolman Charles Skelly is shot to death while investigating an auto accident in St. Joseph, Michigan. The slayer, using the name Fred Dane, escapes, but his home is raided by Berrien County deputies who discover an arsenal, including two Thompson guns. Dane is soon identified as Fred "Killer" Burke, wanted for the St. Valentine's Day Massacre and numerous other crimes. Ballistics tests by Col. Calvin Goddard, director of the country's first "full-service" scientific crime detection laboratory, will establish that Burke's machine guns were used in the Massacre, and one had been used in the 1928 murder of New York's Frankie Yale.

4

John Dillinger, Baby Face Nelson, Pretty Boy Floyd, Machine Gun Kelly and the Barker-Karpis gangs who made headlines and history during the Depression can be considered the last representatives of an outlaw tradition dating to the closing days of the Civil War, but that view still raises issues of definition and semantics.

History's "highwaymen" had operated successfully in sparsely settled areas of continental Europe and England as soon as the plow horse was supplemented by the riding horses traditionally owned by the aristocracy. Eventually they also became a commoner's form of transportation; and in the American West the horse enabled outlaws to hold up stages, trains and banks even after the turn of the century. Civil War veterans who engaged in robbery had learned during the war the value of prior planning and organization, especially in the face of possible resistance, giving rise to the Jameses, the Daltons and other outlaw gangs who essentially were civilian versions of military raiding parties. But not until the early 1920s did American language abandon the term "highway robbery" in favor "armed robbery" to describe a general situation where armed men used the element of surprise, and usually the automobile, to steal money or other valuables at gunpoint.

Horseback outlawry was eventually suppressed by mounted posses of sworn and armed citizens and by professional security forces such as the Pinkertons, whose pursuit of fugitives across state lines made them in some ways private-enterprise versions of the future FBI. Even in the late 1800s the effectiveness of organized "vigilance" committees and Pinkerton-type "detective" agencies had made commando-style robbery a sufficiently risky proposition that daylight attacks by gangs on horseback were giving way to bank burglaries, which pitted safecrackers, or yeggs, against safe makers, who themselves were competing to develop thief-resistant designs.

As historical chance would have it, advances in locks and vault design exceeded the skills of the average "yegg," or safecracker, about the same time that the transportation industry developed relatively fast and reliable automobiles. The result was a post–World War I revival of daylight armed robbery by James-style gangs now using cars instead of horses, at a time when law-enforcement was again in the hands of local police who found themselves no match for the new "motorized bandits."

Compounding the problem was the advent of Prohibition, which not only ushered in an era of unprecedented graft, but dismantled the principal means used by police to put a lid on crime. In the absence of anything resembling a central criminal records file, district and precinct cops depended heavily on their network of informants who patronized popular hoodlum hangouts to identify suspects and fugitives. The closing of the more notorious saloons and taverns dispersed the criminal community to speakeasies that came and went like floating craps games, and (thanks to the automobile) to a growing number of roadhouses that ringed every city, catered to big-spending crooks and enjoyed police protection—from other police.

The result was a police preoccupation with bootleggers who had little to fear from the courts even when prosecuted, and the opportunity for better-equipped armed robbers to regroup as gangs who could resume raiding banks, payroll messengers and even trains with virtual impunity. Many of the jobs made banner headlines because of the size of the loot, but identification methods were so primitive and uncoordinated that newspapers could only report that some unrecognized strangers had easily vanished after pulling a "daring daylight robbery." Thus some of the country's all-time greats, including Eddie Bentz, Baron Lamm and Harvey Bailey, plundered the Midwest with an anonymity that cost them status in the annals of crime, while lesser outlaws became Depression-era celebrities once Al Capone went to prison and new federal laws unleashed a publicity-conscious FBI.

Nevertheless, since crime waves are largely a matter of public perception, a number of robbers, kidnappers and their cohorts were deliberately transformed into symbols of the national crime problem, whether or not they constituted "gangs" in the historic sense. Sometimes all it took was a memorable nickname, supplied either by the press or by the Justice Department, which understood that public support for its "war on crime" was directly proportional to the notoriety of its opponents.

Other factors were the refinement of wire-service journalism that linked newspapers nationwide and the competitiveness of publishing magnates, epitomized by William Randolph Hearst. Crime and scandal were the biggest headline makers, especially in cities like Chicago, and the larger papers even had their own syndicates that fed the country's appetite for crime news. About the same time, "detective magazines" that began as pulps abandoned crime fiction for crime "fact" in articles about gangsters, murders, robberies and kidnappings that were making daily headlines. Some became slick, well-edited and generous enough to attract good writers whose research was far better than that of the harried newspaper reporter racing to meet a particular edition's deadline. They became barbershop staples and actually led to the capture of quite a few criminals whose faces became more familiar to their readers than to the police.

So it was timing, as much as anything, that fostered the notoriety of certain criminals who composed "gangs" in the minds of the public and went into the history books as such.

For instance there was never a "Dillinger gang," but rather a criminal community that included several robbers he worked with when possible, and others when necessary, all of whom came and went as luck and the law allowed. Whether they were close confederates or simply filling in on a particular job, some qualified as "members" of the gang only to the extent that any association with Dillinger was their one claim to fame.

What constituted a gang "moll" was pretty vague. The extent to which Bonnie participated in Clyde's crimes remains a matter of disagreement. That she considered herself his crime partner is clear, but she may have been less active than generally portrayed. Some killings may have been attributed to her by former accomplices to save their own skins. Ma Barker's role in gang affairs is now known to have been greatly exaggerated, whereas Edna "The Kissing Bandit" Murray seems to have thrived on the risk and excitement of robbing banks with boyfriend Volney Davis, after which she'd often kiss her victims. Machine Gun Kelly's wife Kathryn fostered his criminal career and reputation, bought him a machine gun and even involved her own family by hiding the kidnapped Urschel at their farm, but she took no active part in that crime or his robberies, so far as is known. (The fact that the FBI's reading room contains thousands of pages on Dillinger, Nelson, Floyd and others, but nothing on the Urschel kidnapping that launched the Bureau nationally, raises some questions. One is that its quick solution of case may have depended less on Urschel's noting of an airliner's daily flights than on a tip from some crooked cops the kidnappers thought would participate. Another is that disgruntled former agent William W. Turner, in his book *Hoover's F.B.I.*, published interoffice memos noting that the handwriting evidence used to convict Kathryn later proved to be erroneous; and presumably for that reason the Bureau refused to release case files that could have caused it and Hoover "embarrassment." Unaware of this, the judge hearing

Kathryn's appeal in 1959 may have wondered at Hoover's lack of cooperation, for the director had always and adamantly opposed the paroling of "public enemies." But in the absence of case records, he released Kathryn after more than 25 years in prison.)

In any event, newspapers of the day made few distinctions between a woman who was either an ignorant or thrill-seeking girlfriend, a loyal wife, a willing accomplice, or a full-fledged crime partner, and tended to describe anyone associated with a halfway prominent criminal as a "moll."

JOHN DILLINGER (WITH "GUN MOLLS" IN PARENTHESES)

John Dillinger (Mary Longnaker, or Longacre, Evelyn "Billie" Frechette, Rita "Polly" Hamilton Keele)

William Shaw

Noble "Sam" Claycomb

Paul "Lefty" Parker

Hilton Crouch

Harry Copeland

Homer Van Meter (Marie Conforti)

Sam Goldstein

Frank Whitehouse

George Whitehouse

Clifford "Whitey" Mohler

Glen "Big Foot" Zoll

Fred Bremen

John Vinson

Merrit Longbrake

Harry "Pete" Pierpont (Mary "Shorty" Kinder)

Charles "Fat Charlie" Makley

John "Red" Hamilton (Elaine Dent, Patricia Cherrington)

Russell "Boobie" Clark (Opal "Mack Truck" Long, alias Bernice Clark)

John Dillinger, with machine and wooden pistol, on a visit to his home in Mooresville at the height of the country's largest manhunt. *(John Dillinger Museum)*

Edward Shouse

Leslie "Big" Homer

Lester Joseph Gillis, alias Jimmy Williams, but best known as "Baby Face" Nelson (Helen Gillis)

Thomas Leonard "Tommy" Carroll (Jean Delaney Crompton)

Edward W. "Eddie" Green (Bessie Green)

Albert W. "Pat" Reilly (Helen "Babe" Delaney Reilly)

John Paul Chase (Sally Bachman)

Joseph Raymond "Fatso" Negri

PRETTY BOY FLOYD

Charles Arthur "Pretty Boy" Floyd

Adam "Eddie" Richetti, shortened from Ricchetti

Vernon C. "Verne" Miller

George Birdwell

Bill "The Killer" Miller

Bob Amos

Jack Atkins

James Bradley

Fred Hildebrand

MACHINE GUN KELLY

George Barnes, alias George "Machine Gun" Kelly (Kathryn Kelly)

Albert W. Bates (Clara Feldman)

Robert "Boss" Shannon (Ora Shannon)

Armon "Potatoes" Shannon (Oleta Shannon)

Frank Nash

Eddie Doll

Francis Keating

Eddie Bentz

Thomas Holden

["Kelly" owed most of his notoriety to the FBI.]

BARKER-KARPIS GANG

Arizona Donnie Clark Barker, alias Kate "Ma" Barker

Fred Barker (Paula "Fat-Witted" Harmon)

Arthur "Dock" [or "Doc"] Barker (Mildred Kuhlman)

Alvin "Old Creepy" Karpis (Dorothy Slayman Karpis, Dolores Delaney, Edith Barry, Jewell LuVerne Grayson, alias Grace Goldstein)

Jimmie Creighton

Joe Howard

William Weaver, alias Bill "Lapland Willie" Weaver, "Phoenix Donald" (Myrtle Eaton)

Jimmie Wilson

Harry Sandlovich, alias Harry "Dutch" Sawyer (Gladys Sawyer)

Thomas James "Tommy" Holden (Lillian Holden)

Francis "Jimmy" Keating (Marjorie Keating)

Lawrence "Larry" DeVol

Bernard Phillips, alias "Big Phil" Courtney (Winnie Williams)

GANG INTERCONNECTIONS

As the Midwest's geographic crossroads and burgeoning trade center, Chicago provided heartland America with gambling and prostitution that became organized and politically protected long before Prohibition gave rise to the Roaring Twenties "gangster." It was also the target of reform movements which came in a steady succession like waves off Lake Michigan, sometimes wetting politicians' feet but leaving the established vice districts high and dry. The police used nightstick law to keep most of the city safe for both its permanent residents and for criminals who were politically protected, outwardly respectable and commuted to their workplaces in the red-light and night-life districts.

St. Paul lacked Chicago's wide-open wickedness, but probably exceeded it in systematic corruption. The police there didn't ignore organized crime; they *were* organized crime, and employed a law-and-order strategy that bordered on genius. Fugitives from other states could use the city as a sanctuary so long as they tipped the right officials and behaved themselves, which made St. Paul a combination of vacation and convention center for some of the most active felons in the country. This interesting method of local crime control had been formulated at the turn of the century by police chief John J. O'Conner who reigned on and off until his final resignation in 1920. It worked so well that his successors, in and out of the department, carried on the tradition, to the utter frustration of the U.S. Justice Department.

By the time Hoover's G-men were empowered by a New Deal Congress in 1934 to carry guns and catch crooks worse than interstate car thieves (the Dyer Act) and fornicators (the Mann Act), the man supervising the so-called O'Conner system was a saloon keeper, fence and racketeer named Harry Sawyer, who served not only as St. Paul's primary fixer but also as underworld banker, and was so well connected he could also secure protection for criminals in several other cities. He was a mutual contact of the Dillinger and Barker-Karpis gangs, for instance, and some of the ransom money paid in the Edward Bremer kidnapping, which Sawyer had set up for the Barker-Karpis gang, was later found at the lodge in northern Wisconsin where the FBI nearly captured Dillinger.

Sawyer's Green Lantern saloon was patronized by a host of celebrity criminals, and managed by Albert "Pat" Reilly. Reilly's wife, Helen, had sisters who were the girlfriends of Dillinger gang members Tommy Carroll and Alvin Karpis. Two other Green Lantern employees had once been housekeepers for bank robber Frank Nash, who had worked with the Barker-Karpis gang before he was killed in the Kansas City Massacre. The same two were arrested by the FBI while trying to deliver luggage to Dillinger gang member Eddie Green, onetime member of the Barker-Karpis gang.

The FBI discovered that the Barker-Karpis gang also had close ties with a Reno gambling syndicate connected with San Francisco bootleggers, including a former Chicagoan named Lester Gillis, better known as Baby Face Nelson. Nelson had escaped from a guard while en route to Joliet state prison following his second bank robbery conviction, and was introduced to the West Coast underworld by Chicago mobsters William "Klondike" O'Donnell and

William "Three-fingered Jack" White. Later, as a driver-gunman for the Reno mob, he became friends with Alvin Karpis and Fred Barker. He may have already known Karpis, who had grown up in the same part of Chicago, for they had mutual friends in Anthony "Tough Tony" Capezio and Rocco De Grazio (or DeGrazia), both rising members of the Capone syndicate and suspects in the St. Valentine's Day Massacre. Two others involved in the Massacre were Byron Bolton and Fred Goetz, who later teamed up with the Barker-Karpis gang in both the Bremer and Hamm kidnappings.

As a crime that came under federal jurisdiction in 1932, these kidnappings were the means by which the FBI discovered the extent of St. Paul police involvement in criminal activities. The bureau would later use the new federal laws to prosecute both individuals and local officials. Its investigations not only crippled the so-called O'Conner system, but gradually provided a clearer picture of the criminals who constituted full-fledged gangs, the extent to which they associated or collaborated and the ties they had with syndicate crime in various other cities.

When finally captured in 1936, Alvin Karpis admitted meeting Bonnie and Clyde, who were peddling guns stolen from a National Guard Armory, and Pretty Boy Floyd, who had come out of deep hiding since the Kansas City Massacre looking to join an established gang of bank robbers, preferably Dillinger's. Byron Bolton, who testified against his former associates in the Bremer and Hamm kidnapping cases, named Anthony "Soap" Moreno as a West Coast contact of Alvin Karpis and other members of the Barker-Karpis gang. Moreno was convicted of harboring Baby Face Nelson, as was Frank Cochran of Reno, an air service operator who worked on cars for both Nelson and the Barker-Karpis gang.

Thomas "Tobe" Williams, ex-convict owner of the Vallejo General Hospital in Vallejo, California, was also a mutual contact of Baby Face Nelson and the Barker-Karpis gang and later was convicted of harboring Nelson. Helen Gillis, Nelson's wife, had been treated at Williams' hospital for an illness, and Williams was considered the main West Coast health-care provider for other fugitives.

Another mutual contact of the Dillinger and Barker-Karpis gangs was Joseph Aiuppa, alias Joey O'Brien, Chicago gambling and nightclub operator who would one day rule the Capone syndicate. Aiuppa reportedly supplied guns and ammunition to the Dillinger and Barker-Karpis gangs, who frequented his Chicago nightspots, the Hi-Ho Club and the Moulin Rouge. Jack Perkins, a close friend of Baby Face Nelson, allegedly owned a piece of the Hi-Ho Club and is also alleged to have provided the bulletproof vests used by the Dillinger gang in the South Bend robbery.

Aiuppa was one of several persons arrested in suburban Bellwood, Illinois, near the house where Handsome Jack Klutas, leader of a Chicago kidnapping gang, was slain by police in January 1934. Walter Dietrich, a member of the Klutas gang also captured there, was one of the 10 convicts who had used guns smuggled in by Dillinger to escape from Indiana state prison the previous September. Klutas had a rumored connection with Dillinger, and reportedly had bought the gun found on Dietrich at the time of his arrest. Klutas was also a close associate of Fred Goetz, William J. Harrison, Big Homer Wilson and Gus Winkeler, all of whom were connected to both the Capone syndicate and the Barker-Karpis gang.

Louis Cernocky's notorious roadhouse at Fox River Grove, Illinois, was a popular gathering spot for both the Dillinger and Barker-

Karpis gangs, and it was Cernocky who reportedly sent Dillinger and Nelson to Emil Wanatka's Little Bohemia Lodge in northern Wisconsin with a letter of introduction. Wanatka had operated a Little Bohemia restaurant on Chicago's South Side in the early twenties, and had moved to Wisconsin after beating a murder rap and selling his place to West Side "beer barons" Terry Druggan and Frankie Lake, bootlegging rivals of Capone. One of Wanatka's attorneys is thought to have been future Dillinger lawyer Louis Piquett, a one-time city prosecutor who later worked for a Chicago abortion ring, where he probably became acquainted with brothel keeper Anna Sage. As appointed fixer for a North Side police district, he had once quashed the stolen jewelry charges against Russell Gibson, alias Slim Grey, later a member of the Barkis-Karpis gang.

Another gang hangout was the O.P. Inn in Melrose Park, Illinois, operated by Louis "Doc" Stacci, alias Stacey, a Capone gangster convicted of conspiracy to obstruct justice in the Kansas City Massacre case. Those harbored by Stacci included Frank Nash, Verne Miller, Eddie Green, Alvin Karpis, Fred and Dock Barker and other prominent criminals. Stacci was reportedly a golfing companion of notorious Capone gangster Vincent Gebardi, alias Ma-

chine Gun Jack McGurn, a suspect in the St. Valentine's Day Massacre, and cited in some FBI records as a friend and possible contact of Baby Face Nelson.

Also serving both the Dillinger and Barker-Karpis gangs was Chicago doctor Joseph P. Moran, who had served time for illegal abortions, achieved considerable notoriety as an underworld physician who patched up local gangsters and outlaws (including John Hamilton of the Dillinger gang), and successfully removed the fingerprints of Alvin Karpis. Dr. Moran helped pass ransom money from the Bremer kidnapping, but also drank and talked too much. He disappeared in Toledo in July of 1934 while in the company of the Barker-Karpis gang, and in differing accounts was either taken for a one-way boat ride on Lake Erie or simply killed and buried.

The Seafood Inn in Elmhurst, Illinois, was another contact point for the Dillinger and Barker-Karpis gangs. Dillinger and Homer Van Meter took John Hamilton there to contact Doc Moran after Hamilton was badly wounded by deputies near South St. Paul, Minnesota, following the Little Bohemia battle in April 1934. Moran refused him medical attention, probably on orders of the Chicago syndicate, which by then was distancing itself from the outlaws who

Harvey John "Shotgun Tom" Bailey

Frank "Jelly" Nash (Frances Nash)

Jesse Doyle (Helen Murray, Doris O'Connor)

Earl Christman (Helen Ferguson)

Vernon C. "Verne" or "Vern" Miller (Vivian Mathias)

Volney "Curley" Davis (Edna "Rabbits" Murray, alias "The Kissing Bandit")

Harry Hull

John P. "Jack" Peifer (Viola Nordquist)

Charles J. Fitzgerald, alias "Old Charley," "Big Fitz" (Isabelle Born)

"Old Gus," alias "Jack," "Schnozzle" (possibly Gus Stone or Stevens)

Fred Goetz, alias "Shotgun" George Ziegler (Irene Dorsey)

William Bryan Bolton, alias Byron "Monty" Bolton, Monte Carter

Elmer Farmer

Edmond Bartholmey

Harry Campbell (Wynona Burdette)

William J. "Willie" Harrison (Ruth Heidt)

Russell "Rusty" Gibson, alias Roy "Slim" Gray (Clara Fisher Gibson)

were generating too much heat from both police and the FBI. Unable to find a doctor, Barker-Karpis gangster Volney Davis drove Hamilton to his apartment at 415 Fox Street in Aurora, Illinois. According to the FBI and Edna "The Kissing Bandit" Murray, Davis's girlfriend who stayed with him, Hamilton died on or about April 30, 1934, and was buried by Dillinger, Van Meter and members of the Barker-Karpis gang, including Davis, Dock Barker, Harry Campbell and William Weaver, in a shallow grave near a gravel pit outside Oswego, Illinois. (The body wasn't found for nearly two years, and some plausible evidence exists that it wasn't Hamilton's, who may have survived, recovered in northern Indiana and eventually made it to Canada.)

Edna Murray was the sister of Doris O'Connor, alias Vinita Stanley, the moll of Barker-Karpis gangster Jess Doyle. The Barker-Karpis and Dillinger gang molls included three sets of sisters. In addition to Edna Murray and Doris O'Connor and the Delaney sisters, Opal Long (alias Bernice Clark), and Patricia Cherrington were also sisters. Opal Long was the wife or mistress of Dillinger gangster Russell Clark. Patricia Cherrington was a sometime mistress of John Hamilton.

Before he and Dillinger teamed up, Nelson had worked with Eddie Bentz, a major 1920s bank robber turned planner and caser, and Chicago mobster Tommy Touhy of the Roger Touhy gang. Through Bentz, he met San Antonio gunsmith and dealer H.S. Lebman, who had devised a means of converting Colt semiautomatic pistols and Winchester autoloading rifles into remarkably effective, fully automatic weapons. Probably through Nelson, Lebman's customized guns, most with Thompson-style foregrips, compensators and extra-capacity magazines, made their way to some of the most prominent criminals of the day, including Dillinger, the Touhy mob, and even Pretty Boy Floyd. He supplied Thompsons to some of the same groups. Arrested under a new Texas machine-gun law that predated the National Firearms Act of 1934, he beat the rap on a hung jury; the continuing efforts of federal authorities to secure a retrial proved fruitless. After several years, Texas authorities, citing the deaths of most of Lebman's customers and the disappearance of important witnesses, dropped the charges, and Lebman, whose family was locally influential, stayed at the same location another 40 years. However, he put most of his efforts into the other side of his business, boot- and saddle-making.

Fred Hunter (Ruth Hamm Robison, alias Connie Morris)
"Pinky" Mitchell
Joe Rich
Sam Coker
John Brock
Benson Groves, alias Ben Greyson

BARROW GANG

Clyde Barrow (Bonnie Parker Thornton)
Marvin Ivan "Buck" Barrow (Blanche Caldwell Barrow)

Raymond Hamilton (Mary "The Washerwoman" O'Dare)
Ralph Fults
Frank Clause
Everett Milligan
Hollis Hale
Frank Hardy
William Daniel Jones, alias W.D. Jones, "Deacon"
Monroe Routon
Joe Bill Francis
S.J. "Baldy" Whatley
James Mullen

Joe Palmer
Henry "Boodles" Methvin

BRADY GANG

Alfred James "Al" Brady (Margaret Larson, Jo Raimondo)
Clarence Lee Shaffer, Jr. (Christine Puckett, Minnie Raimondo)
Rhuel James "Jim" Dalhover (Marie "Babe" Meyers, Mary Raimondo)
Charles Geiseking

BAILEY-UNDERHILL GANG

Harvey John "Shotgun Tom" Bailey
"Mad Dog" Wilbur Underhill (Hazel Jarrett Hudson)
Robert "Big Bob" Brady (Leona Brady)
Jim Clark (Goldie Johnson)
Sebron Edward "Ed" Davis
Frank Sawyer
Jess Littrell
Bill Shipley

KLUTAS GANG
("THE COLLEGE KIDNAPPERS")

Theodore "Handsome Jack" Klutas
Edward Doll, alias Eddie LaRue
Russell Hughes
Gale Swolley
Frank Souder
Eddie Wagner
Julius "Babe" Jones

Walter Dietrich
Earl McMahon
Ernest Rossi

TRI-STATE GANG

Walter Legurenza, alias Legenza
Robert Howard Mais (Marie McKeever)
Anthony "The Stinger" Cugino
Salvatore Serpa
John Zukorsky (Ethel Marshall)
Edward "Cowboy" Wallace (Florence Miller)
Johnny Horn
Anthony "Musky" Zanghi
William Benjamin "Big Bill" Phillips (Marie McKeever)
Morris Kauffman
John Kendrick
Arthur Misanas
Herbert Myers
Martin Farrell
Roy Willey
Robert Eckert
Joseph Coffey

CRETZER-KYLE GANG

Joseph "Dutch" Cretzer (Edna Kyle Cretzer, alias Kay Wallace)
Arnold Kyle, alias "Shorty" McKay (Thelma Cretzer Kyle)
Milton Hartman, alias James Courey
John Oscar Hetzer

5

The Rise and Fall of the
Last Great Outlaw Band

After 1933, Capone was in prison, and Repeal was ending the Prohibition Era of big-city bootleggers. As Roosevelt's New Deal administration declared a federal "war on crime" spearheaded by a newly empowered FBI, a new peril confronted the American public in the form of kidnappers and bandit gangs "terrorizing the Midwest." In fact, the most successful armed robbers had been operating for years with virtual immunity from law enforcement because of their anonymity, mobility and the uncoordinated efforts of state and local authorities. Newspapers frequently headlined the raids of "daring daylight bank robbers," but in the absence of an effective central criminal-records agency the bandits usually went unrecognized, and a fast escape to another state frustrated pursuit. Harvey Bailey, the Newton Brothers, Baron H.K. Lamm and Eddie Bentz knocked over hundreds of banks, payrolls and even trains in the 1920s without local police knowing who they were; and the "snatch racket" that involved criminals kidnapping one another did not concern the public, the police or the press.

By 1932, only Pretty Boy Floyd and Bonnie and Clyde had earned any national publicity, usually because they were locally known or left calling cards in one form or another. But while all had one or more partners in crime, they didn't lead gangs in the usual sense of the word. In 1933, Machine Gun Kelly became a household name not because he led a gang (despite newspaper accounts), but because he was involved in the most sensational "civilian" kidnapping since the Lindbergh case and eluded authorities long enough to earn personal notoriety.

The famous outlaw gangs of the Depression were largely the invention of the FBI, with two conspicuous exceptions. The Dillinger gang, consisting mainly of convicts he helped break out of the Michigan City prison, worked closely as a group, but only from September 1933 until

137

the following January, when most were arrested in Tucson when a fire in their hotel led to their recognition. After Dillinger himself escaped from the Crown Point, Indiana, jail two months later, using bribes and a wooden pistol, he was forced to team up with Baby Face Nelson, who had put together his own small band of robbers and of course resented greatly the identification of his group as the "Dillinger gang" by the national press. Dillinger's criminal career lasted only another four months before he was set up by supposed friends and killed by federal agents outside Chicago's Biograph Theatre.

The only group that qualified as a bona fide gang in the traditional sense of the word was the one headed by Alvin Karpis and the Barker brothers, mainly Dock and Freddie, and supposedly captained by the notorious Ma Barker. Despite two more civilian kidnappings, many burglaries, several murders and dozens of bank, train and payroll holdups since the 1920s, the FBI did not even know of their existence as a group until the Bureau captured a talkative associate of the Dillinger gang in the spring of 1934. Their depredations spanned the entire "public enemy" era; and while the Barkers and Alvin Karpis were always the principals, they teamed with many criminals from other gangs and also worked with organized crime groups in several cities, especially Chicago.

In truth, the headline-making "gangs" of Floyd, Kelly, and Bonnie and Clyde, were far more loosely structured than suited headline writers, the FBI or the general public to believe.

✪ ✪ ✪

The nucleus of the Barker-Karpis gang was the Barker family, who came from a part of Ozark backwoods that was isolated from the main-

Arthur Dunlap with "Ma" Barker   *(Authors' collection)*

stream of American culture and a longtime breeding ground of desperadoes. Ma Barker's role in the gang is a matter of dispute. Legend based largely on FBI publicity has it that she deliberately groomed her sons as lawbreakers and managed their criminal careers. There's no doubt she knew of her sons' crimes, which necessitated constant moving to elude the police. But she never participated in their robberies or kidnappings, and no member of the gang ever named her as their leader. Alvin Karpis would characterize her as an ignorant old hillbilly who traveled with her sons because they were "family," and she came in handy as camouflage.

A later member of the gang, Harvey Bailey, told author L.L. Edge in *Run the Cat Roads:* "The old woman couldn't plan breakfast. When we'd sit down to plan a bank job, she'd go in the other room and listen to Amos and Andy or hillbilly music on the radio." Bailey found laughable the idea that the Barkers, Alvin Karpis, Frank Nash and other professionals would depend on Ma Barker to plan their crimes. She may have been overly indulgent, protective and possessive of her sons, and would harbor their friends from the law; in return they treated her regally, kept her in fancy clothes and cars, without her questioning the source of their prosperity. However, the image of Ma Barker as a cunning, ruthless gang leader appears to be as exaggerated as the largely mythical exploits of Belle Starr, to whom she has often been compared.

J. Edgar Hoover's early characterization of her, as "a monument to the evils of parental indulgence," is likely more accurate than the *Bloody Mama* figure familiar to many moviegoers, comic book fans, and devotees of crime literature, factual and otherwise. The latter image, too, was created by Hoover. Ma Barker's troubles seem rooted in a blind devotion to her sons, whom she chose to believe were driven to crime by hard times and constant police persecution. In this respect, she was similar to the mothers of the Jameses, the Youngers, the Daltons, the Barrows and countless other bandit brothers of the rural Southwest. She probably qualified as a fairly dense and nonjudgmental matriarch of a clannish tribe of Ozark hillbillies whose careers just happened to be in crime instead of oil.

"Ma Barker," according to an FBI report, dated November 18, 1936, "in the formative period of her sons' lives was probably just an average mother of a family which had no aspirations or evidenced no desire to maintain any high plane socially. They were poor and existed through no prolific support from Ma's husband, George Barker, who was more or less a shiftless individual. . . . The early religious training of the Barkers . . . was influenced by evangelistic

and sporadic revivals. The parents of the Barkers and the other boys with whom they were associated did not reflect any special interest in educational training and as a result their sons were more or less illiterate. . . ."

Years later, J. Edgar Hoover would write that "over the backyard fence Ma boasted to neighbors: 'I got great days ahead of me, when my children grow up. Silk dresses. Fur coats and diamond rings.'" This hardly sounds like someone without aspirations to wealth, but by then the mythmaking was in full swing and J. Edgar its leading propagator.

Had she not died with her son Fred in battle with the FBI, Ma Barker might have gotten off with a short jail sentence for harboring her murderous offspring, as did the mothers of Bonnie and Clyde. But once the Bureau ended its siege of their hideout in January 1935 and discovered it evidently had killed an old lady who would turn out to be Ma, she had to be instantly villainized. And if Americans had found something almost romantic in a boy-and-girl bandit team despite their murderous ways, the notion of a mother-and-son bandit team also appealed to the country's streak of rebellion against duly constituted authority, especially when most police of the day were regarded as only a cut above the crooks they were supposed to catch.

Ma was born Arizona Donnie Clark near Ash Grove, Boone Township, northwest of Springfield, in "about" 1872, instead of 1875. When she married George Elias Barker, some 13 years older, at Aurora, Missouri, on September 14, 1892, she listed her name on the marriage license as "Arrie Clark" but adopted the name Kate. They made their home in Aurora, where her first pregnancy resulted in a miscarriage, according to relatives. Between 1893 and 1902 they had four sons, Herman, Lloyd, Arthur (called "Doc" or "Dock") and Fred, before moving to Webb City, near Joplin. There George reportedly found work in the area's lead and zinc mines and left the child-rearing to Ma.

In 1935, crime reporter Harrison Moreland interviewed Webb City residents who remembered the Barkers' early years. One of Herman's favorite antics, said Moreland, was riding a pinto pony into the town's saloons, in imitation of his hero, Jesse James, who was supposed to have ridden into saloons, shooting. The Barker boys soon went beyond mere rowdyness, however, acquiring reputations as petty thieves. They, especially Freddie, also associated closely with an older boy, Herbert Allen Farmer, who would likewise develop an extensive criminal record. Legend has it that neighbors who complained to George Barker about his sons' activities were shrugged off with, "You'll have to talk to Mother. She handles the boys." Ma Barker would then rage at the accusers, call them liars, and send them packing. A widespread impression was that she had an almost paranoid belief that the community had singled out her sons as scapegoats.

On March 5, 1915, Herman Barker was arrested by Joplin police for highway robbery. Reportedly, Ma got him released, then declared that she could no longer abide living in such an intolerant town. The whole family soon moved to Tulsa, Oklahoma, setting into a two-room shack at 401 North Cincinnati Avenue, at least according to FBI files and most popular accounts. Strangely, census records show that George and Ma were residing in 1920, without the boys, in Stone County, Missouri. Either the move to Tulsa occurred later than commonly supposed, or George and Kate returned to Missouri for a time, leaving their sons in Oklahoma.

The boys soon ingratiated themselves with other young hellions who hung around Old Lincoln Forsythe School and the Central Park district. The result was an aggregation of delinquents called the "Central Park Gang," which in time reportedly numbered some 22 young thieves and hoodlums. Alleged members included Volney "Curley" Davis, Harry Campbell, Sam Coker and Russell "Rusty" Gibson (later important members of the Barker-Karpis gang), William "Boxcar" Green and Ray Terrill. Terrill would join Matt and George Kimes on a series of spectacular bank robberies, shootings and jailbreaks in the late twenties. Green would play a leading role in a 1931 mass breakout from Leavenworth, and then commit suicide to avoid recapture.

Herman Barker left the Tulsa area during the 1915–20 period and traveled around the country as a small-time robber and swindler. Sentenced in 1916 to two years for burglary and larceny, Herman escaped from the Greene County Jail at Springfield, Missouri, before he could be transferred to the penitentiary. He was arrested several more times, in Montana, Iowa, Minnesota and Tennessee, and served sentences for burglary in Montana and grand larceny in Minnesota. He remained in contact with the family, probably sending home some of his criminal earnings. Fred Barker also left home for a time, returning to Joplin to visit Herb Farmer, a former Webb City neighbor. Herbert Allen Farmer, also known as Black, Snyder, "Deafy" Farmer, Harry J. Garner, William Hilary Baker, etc., was a confidence man and pickpocket with a long record of arrests. He had just been released from McAlester, Oklahoma, state prison, after receiving a five-year sentence for assault with intent to kill. Herb had long been a close friend of the Barkers, particularly

Fred, and an FBI report would later note that "it is safe to assume that Fred Barker received considerable education in the school of crime from Farmer." The chicken ranch near Joplin, where Farmer lived with his wife, Esther, was used as a contact place by numerous ex-cons. Fred reportedly met many of these men, inviting them to drop by any time at the Barker home in Tulsa.

Herb Farmer continued his association with the Barkers for years afterward. He harbored many southwestern outlaws, including Bonnie and Clyde. Farmer would eventually serve two years at Alcatraz as one of the Kansas City Massacre conspirators.

Arthur "Dock" Barker displayed a streak of patriotism on the Fourth of July in 1918, by getting arrested for theft of a government-owned car in Tulsa. He escaped, was recaptured in Joplin in 1920, and returned to Tulsa, then escaped again. On January 15, 1921, as Claud Dale, Dock was arrested for attempted bank burglary in Muskogee. Ray Terrill was arrested at the same time, under the alias of G.R. Patton. Both were transferred to McAlester for safe-keeping. Dock was discharged by court order on June 11, 1921. Terrill was later sentenced to three years for second-degree burglary and released on March 1, 1923. He was subsequently arrested for other crimes but either "beat the rap" or escaped. On August 26, 1921, James J. Sherrill, a nightwatchman at Tulsa's St. John's Hospital, was killed by burglars. Dock was arrested for this murder, tried and convicted. On February 10, 1922, he was sentenced to life at McAlester.

Nearly a year later, Volney Davis, a member of the Barkers' "Central Park Gang," was also sent to prison for life for the Sherrill slaying. Davis escaped from McAlester in January 1925, but was recaptured 13 days later in Kansas City.

Lloyd "Red" Barker was picked up by Tulsa police for vagrancy in 1921. He was later implicated in a mail robbery at Baxter Springs, Kansas, for which he was tried and convicted. On January 16, 1922, as inmate 17243, Lloyd was received at Leavenworth facing a 25-year sentence. This marked the end of Lloyd Barker's criminal career. Paroled in 1938, he went straight, working as a cook at a P.O.W. camp at Fort Custer, Michigan. During World War II, he received an honorable discharge from the army, married and became an assistant manager of a bar and grill in Denver. On March 18, 1949, his wife killed him with a shotgun at their home in Westminster, Colorado. She was subsequently placed in an insane asylum.

On January 27, 1922, Al Spencer, reputedly a former member of Henry Starr's outlaw gang, escaped from the prison at McAlester. Fleeing into the Osage Hills, Spencer organized a new band of bank robbers. They included Frank "Jelly" Nash, Grover Durrill, Earl Thayer and several others. By some accounts, Ray Terrill was also a member, and the Spencer gang may have used the Barkers' Tulsa home as a hideout. During 1922–23, the gang was credited with robbing 42 banks. On August 20, 1923, the Spencer gang robbed the Katy Limited mail train of $20,000 in bonds and cash at Okesa, Oklahoma, which led to their undoing. Federal officers and railroad investigators joined in the gang's pursuit and huge rewards were offered for their capture. On September 16, 1923, Al Spencer was killed while resisting arrest on the Osage Indian Reservation near Bartlesville, Oklahoma. Other participants in the train robbery were likewise apprehended. Frank Nash fled to Mexico but was arrested the following year when he returned to the United States. Nash was sentenced to 25 years in Leavenworth for assaulting a mail custodian.

Ray Terrill, not involved in the train robbery, was soon operating with a new gang, burglarizing banks and stores throughout the Southwest. This group probably included Herman Barker, Elmer Inman, Wilbur Underhill, Alvin Sherwood, Joe Howard, Bill Munger, Ralph Scott, Danny Daniels, Charles Stalcup (alias Pale Anderson) and others. Their favorite technique, credited to Terrill, was to back a stolen truck up to a bank, winch out its portable safe, and drive away to crack it at their leisure. For a time, the gang used the Radium Springs Health Resort near Salina, Oklahoma, as a hideout. Radium Springs was owned by Herman Barker and his wife, Carol, who operated it as a cover under the names of Mr. and Mrs. J.H. Hamilton. The resort was fortified and equipped with a powerful electric light that served as a warning beacon if law officers came to visit. Safes stolen by the gang were emptied and dumped off a nearby bridge over the Grand River.

From brotherly love or a need for career counseling, or both, Fred Barker soon joined his older brother at the resort. Fred had been arrested for "investigation" at Miami, Oklahoma, September 5, 1922. A month later he was picked up for vagrancy in Tulsa and jailed for 30 days. In June 1923, he was convicted of armed robbery and sentenced to five years in the state reformatory at Granite, Oklahoma. Fred made parole only to be arrested soon afterward for robbing a bank. He was later arrested as a fugitive from justice at Little Rock, Arkansas, for burglary in Ponca City, Oklahoma, and was wounded in a battle with Kansas City police. Under the alias of Ted Murphy, Fred was arrested at Winfield, Kansas, November 8, 1926,

for burglary and grand larceny. He was again convicted and sentenced to five to 10 years in the state prison at Lansing, Kansas. Investigators discovered that Herman Barker, who avoided arrest on that occasion, likely had participated in the Winfield burglary. The car Fred was driving at the time of his arrest had been bought by Herman from a Nash agency in Tulsa.

Winfield Police Chief Fred C. Hoover told the FBI (then known as the Bureau of Investigation) that the sheriff of Mayes County, Oklahoma, site of the Radium Springs Health Resort, was a friend of the Barkers. He also believed that Herman Barker and Elmer Inman often frequented Wetumps Road House, near Ponca City, operated by Fred "Wetump" Tindle. Barker and Inman were wanted for interstate car theft, which made them federal fugitives under a special law passed in 1924 (the Dyer Act) to facilitate the return of cars stolen in one state and recovered in another.

Barker and Inman had driven a Paige coupe, stolen from Henry Ward of Fairfax, Oklahoma, to Fort Scott, Kansas, on or about June 6, 1926. They were arrested the next day and extradited to Oklahoma, where both were also wanted for robbery. They didn't remain in custody long. Herman Barker, charged with robbing the county attorney at Miami, Oklahoma, of approximately $600 in money and valuables, was released on bond on June 22. Elmer Inman, former son-in-law of Kansas state prison warden J.K. Coddings, was charged with bank and post office robbery at Ketchum, Oklahoma, but also made bond. Inman was again arrested at Ardmore, Oklahoma, with Ray Terrill, for burglary. Together they overpowered a county jailer at Ardmore on September 27, 1926, and escaped.

About this time, Ray Terrill went into partnership with Matt Kimes and branched out into armed bank robbery. The Kimes-Terrill gang made headlines in the Southwest with their daring daylight raids and spectacular jailbreaks, but typically the police were rarely clear on who should be charged with what.

On June 29, 1926, Matt Kimes broke out of jail in Bristow, Oklahoma, where he was facing charges of car theft. The following day, he and his brother George robbed their first bank at Depew, Oklahoma. On August 20, they hit the Farmers National Bank at Beggs, Oklahoma, for $5,000. With three other men, the Kimes boys robbed two banks in Covington, Oklahoma, on August 25, and two days later killed Deputy Sheriff Perry Chuculate in a gun battle at Sallisaw, home grounds of Pretty Boy Floyd. They also took the police chief and another man hostage, and fled to Arkansas, where they were wounded and captured at a cousin's home near the town of Rudy. The Kimeses were returned to Oklahoma where George was sentence to 25 years and Matt to 35 for bank robbery and murder. George was sent to the state prison, but Matt remained in the Sallisaw jail pending an appeal. On November 21, 1926, members of the gang, possibly including Terrill, Barker and Inman, raided the jail and set Kimes free.

Elmer Inman was recaptured on December 27, 1926, while burglarizing a store in Oklahoma City. For this he was convicted and sentenced to seven years for burglary, but escaped on March 17, 1927, en route to McAlester, by leaping from a train. On January 10, 1927, Matt Kimes and Ray Terrill were named as members of a gang who had robbed the State Bank at Sapulpa, Oklahoma, of $42,950.

On January 17, about 5 A.M., the gang attempted to burglarize the First National Bank at Jasper, Missouri, near Joplin. Arriving in two cars and a truck, they entered the bank by cutting the bars from a rear window, stole the bank's safe and wheeled it out the back door. A baker spotted them and phoned the night telephone operator, who alerted the town marshal. Police in Joplin and Carthage quickly deputized a posse of citizens to ambush the gang. The would-be burglars had to abandon their truck but still managed to escape in two cars.

One car, believed to contain Matt Kimes, another man and a woman, fled west into Kansas. Herman Barker and Ray Terrill were in the other car. They returned to their hideout, a house at 602 East Main in Carterville, Missouri, which Joplin and Webb City police were watching on a tip that it was "the headquarters of an organized band of outlaws." A gun battle followed, in which Barker was wounded and he and Terrill taken into custody.

Herman Barker was extradited to Fayetteville, Arkansas, on charges of robbing a Westfork bank. On January 19, Ray Terrill, a McAlester escapee who still owed Oklahoma 20 years on his earlier bank robbery conviction, was returned to that state but again escaped, leaping from a moving car as it neared the prison. On March 30, Herman also escaped, sawing the bars of his cell and taking along a suspected forger named Claude Cooper.

More bank jobs followed. On May 12, bandits stole a safe containing $207,000 in securities and cash from the State Bank at McCune, Kansas. Ray Terrill was named as a suspect. On May 18, two carloads of gunmen, led by Matt Kimes, robbed two banks at Beggs, Oklahoma, and escaped after a gun battle in which they killed Marshal W.J. McAnally. Soon after these robberies, several gang members were arrested in Texas and Oklahoma. Matt Kimes

$5,000 REWARD
For DEAD Bank Robbers

$5,000 cash will be paid for each Bank Robber legally killed while Robbing this bank

THE Texas Bankers Association, a corporation, offers a standing reward of $5,000 for each bank robber legally killed while robbing and holding up a reward subscribing member bank in Texas with firearms during the daytime. Limits of the place and time of such killing are: in the banking house, or as the robbers and holdups leave the bank, while the robbery and holdup and threats are being committed; and as they flee from the bank with the property taken, and are resisting legal pursuit and arrest, within twenty miles of the bank robbed and within six hours after the robbery and holdup. This reward does not apply to night attacks on Texas banks. It is expressly provided that the Texas Bankers Association shall determine whether or not payment of this reward shall be made hereunder, and to whom (if anyone) such payment shall be made, and such determination and judgment shall be final, conclusive and not reviewable.

¶ The Association will not give one cent for live bank robbers. They are rarely identified, more rarely convicted, and most rarely stay in the penitentiary when sent there—all of which operations are troublesome, burdensome and costly to our government.

¶ In order to protect the lives of people in such banks and to protect the property of such banks, the Association is prepared to pay for any number of such robbers and holdups so killed, while they are robbing and holding up its reward subscribing member banks with firearms in the daytime, at $5,000 apiece.

¶ This reward is effective April 1st, 1930, and all other rewards, offers and statements are cancelled and superseded hereby.

TEXAS BANKERS ASSOCIATION

$5,000 in cash will be so paid for the legal killing of any robber and holdup WHILE ROBBING THIS BANK with firearms in the daytime

(Authors' collection)

was captured in Arizona, near the Grand Canyon, on June 24.

On August 1, 1927, a man appeared at the American National Bank in Cheyenne, Wyoming, using the name R.D. Snodgrass, and cashed three American Express Travelers' Cheques. "Snodgrass" then left the bank and entered a blue Chrysler coach with Idaho license plates. A woman, with dark hair and a dark complexion, was also in the car. The teller quickly identified the checks as having been stolen in a Buffalo, Kansas, bank robbery in December 1926. He chased after "Snodgrass," who simply ignored him and drove away. "Snodgrass" was actually Herman Barker and the woman was his wife, Carol, known as Carol Hamilton, who was part Cherokee.

Herman was stopped at Pine Bluffs, about 40 miles east of Cheyenne, by Deputy Sheriff Ar-

thur E. Osborne. As the deputy approached the car, his own gun still holstered, Barker drew a .32 automatic and shot him twice, then sped off. A half hour later Osborne was found unconscious and dying along the highway by a Nebraska deputy who just happened along. At first, Osborne's killer was mistakenly identified as Elmer Inman.

On August 29, after robbing an icehouse in Newton, Kansas, Herman Barker and two other men shot it out with police in Wichita. In that gunfight, Herman killed another officer, Patrolman J. E. Marshall, but was so badly wounded in the exchange that he shot himself rather than be taken alive. One of his companions, Charles Stalcup, alias Pale Anderson, was taken into custody. The other man, first thought to be Inman, escaped. He was actually another Oklahoma outlaw named Porter Meeks, killed the next day by Wichita policeman Merle Colver, who would himself be slained in 1931 by Wilbur Underhill, soon to be dubbed the "Tri-State Terror."

Ray Terrill and Elmer Inman were captured at Hot Springs, Arkansas, November 26, 1927. They soon joined the Kimes brothers at the Oklahoma state prison.

Carol Hamilton Barker subsequently pleaded guilty as an accessory to the Osborne murder and admitted it was Herman, not Elmer Inman, who had killed Deputy Osborne. She was sentenced to two to four years but, since Wyoming had no separate facility for female prisoners, served her time in the Colorado state prison at Canon City. She was received there on September 29, 1927, and was paroled on October 2, 1929. Soon afterward, she was working as a prostitute out of the Carlton Hotel in Sapulpa, Oklahoma, and briefly became the mistress of Alvin Karpis. Karpis would later marry her niece, Dorothy Slayman.

George and Kate Barker buried their oldest son at the Williams Timberhill Cemetery near Welch, Oklahoma, where they and two other sons would eventually join him. They separated about 1928, apparently because Ma and a friend were dating other men in Tulsa. George moved back to Webb City, Missouri, and spent his remaining years operating a filling station. Ma soon moved in with an alcoholic billboard painter named Arthur W. Dunlop.

Dunlop spent more time drinking than painting; and with Herman dead and the other boys in prison, the family income fell dramatically. Ma became dependent on her daughter-in-law, Carol Hamilton, for groceries. She despised Carol, whom she considered a "hussy," as she did all her sons' women. Throughout her life, Ma Barker would vainly attempt to discourage or sabotage her sons' relationships with other women. J. Edgar Hoover would call her a "jealous old battle-ax." According to Alvin Karpis: "Ma didn't like female competition. She wanted to be the only woman who counted with her boys."

Alvin Karpis, born in Montreal in 1908, met Fred Barker at the Kansas state prison in 1930. Received at the State Industrial Reformatory at Hutchinson, Kansas, on February 25, 1926, under a five-to-10-year sentence for burglary, Karpis became a prison protégé of Lawrence DeVol, an expert safecracker and a cop killer. The two escaped from Hutchinson on March 9, 1929, and engaged in a burglary spree. Recaptured in Kansas City on March 23, 1930, Karpis was returned to the reformatory but soon transferred to the penitentiary when officials there found knives in his possession. Still, he earned time off his sentence by working in the coal mine and hiring lifers to mine coal for him—another trick he had learned from DeVol. Karpis and Fred Barker became close friends and agreed to form a criminal partnership.

When Fred was paroled on March 20, 1931, and Karpis the following May 10, they contacted Carol Hamilton and Ma Barker in Tulsa. Ma sent a telegram to Fred, then living at 701 Byers in Joplin with another ex-convict named Jimmie Creighton, alias Jones, wanted in Hastings, Nebraska, for kidnapping, robbery and attempted murder. Creighton was also a suspect, with Lawrence DeVol, in the April 1930 murders of two businessman brothers at the Hotel Severs in Muskogee, Oklahoma. Fred soon joined Karpis in Tulsa, and they committed a series of small burglaries.

On the night of May 16, 1931, Fred's former roommate, Creighton, shot and killed a local man, Coyne Hatten, outside the Morgan drugstore in Webb City, apparently over Hatten's failure to apologize profusely for bumping into him on the street. Creighton was convicted of murder and sentenced to life imprisonment. Interestingly, one of Creighton's companions at the time of the slaying was Mickey Carey, through whom Karpis would later meet Clyde Barrow and Bonnie Parker, at the home of Herb Farmer.

On June 10, 1931, Tulsa police arrested Fred Barker, Alvin Karpis, Sam Coker and Joe Howard. Karpis was transferred to Henryetta, Oklahoma, to face charges of burglarizing a jewelry store. He returned the stolen jewelry, pleaded guilty to burglary on September 11, 1931, and was sentenced to four years, but paroled for having already served three months in the county jail and making restitution. Barker was transferred to Claremore, Oklahoma, on another burglary charge, but escaped. Coker

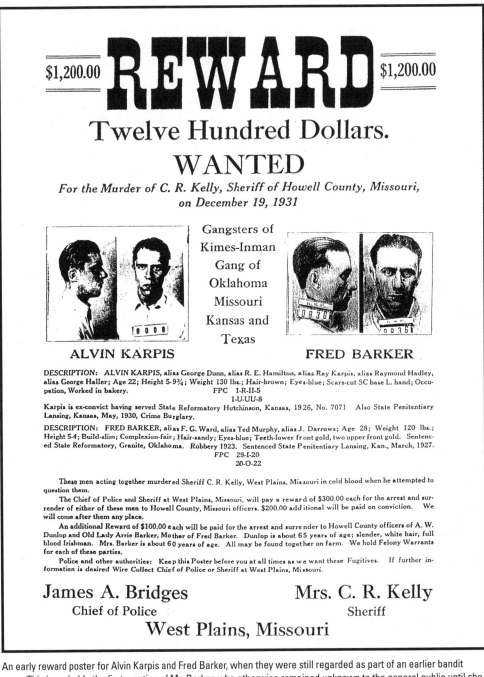

An early reward poster for Alvin Karpis and Fred Barker, when they were still regarded as part of an earlier bandit gang. This is probably the first mention of Ma Barker, who otherwise remained unknown to the general public until she died in a Florida gun battle with federal agents in January 1935 and became an instant legend. *(Authors' collection)*

was returned to the McAlester prison to complete a 30-year sentence for bank robbery. Howard was released on bond and disappeared.

Karpis joined Fred and Ma Barker and Arthur Dunlop on a rented farm near Thayer, Missouri. On June 20, 1931, Bill Weaver, alias "Phoenix Donald" or "Lapland Willie," had been paroled from McAlester after serving six years of a life sentence for murder and bank robbery, and was residing on another rented farm only two miles away. On October 7, 1931, Karpis, Fred Barker, Weaver and one Jimmie Wilson robbed the Peoples Bank at Mountain View, Missouri, of $14,000 in cash and securities. In November, Fred Barker murdered Night Constable Albert Manley Jackson at Pocahontas, Arkansas, a crime for which three local men would be wrongly arrested, convicted, and imprisoned.

On the night of December 18, McCallon's Clothing Store in West Plains, Missouri, was burglarized. Two strangers in town, driving a 1931 DeSoto, had aroused enough suspicion that some residents noted their license plate numbers. The following day, three men drove a 1931 DeSoto into the Davidson Motor Company garage in West Plains to get two flat tires repaired. A repairman noticed the tires' tread matched treadmarks left by the burglars' car and told his boss. The suspicious garage owner stepped out of the building and called Sheriff C. Roy Kelly and Clarence McCallon, owner of the clothing store. When they arrived, two of the DeSoto's occupants opened fire, killing the sheriff, then fled. The murderers were subsequently identified as Alvin Karpis and Fred Barker. Karpis probably fired the fatal shots with a .45 automatic, putting four bullets into Kelly's chest. Barker, armed with a .38 revolver, shot the sheriff in the right arm.

The third man in the garage was arrested and released. He was J. Richard Gross, a 20-year-old college student picked up by Karpis and Barker while hitchhiking from Jonesboro, Arkansas, to Springfield.

Area law officers raided the farm near Thayer, only to find it deserted. The house stood on a hill, with a good view in every direction. It was surrounded by barbed wire, the front gate hooked to an electric alarm bell. In the house, officers found photos of the Barkers, Karpis and Dunlop, as well as letters, including one to Ma from Lloyd Barker in Leavenworth thanking her for Christmas gifts and an interior drawing of the First National Bank of West Plains, Missouri. The farm rented by Bill Weaver was also abandoned.

West Plains Police Chief James A. Bridges and Howell County Sheriff Lula Kelly, succeeding her murdered husband, offered a $1,200 reward: $500 each for the arrest and conviction of Alvin Karpis and Fred Barker and $100 each for the arrest of "A.W. Dunlop and Old Lady Arrie Barker, Mother of Fred Barker." This was the first official notice of Ma Barker, who would make no further news until she was killed by federal agents three years later. Fred Barker and Karpis were listed on "wanted" posters as "Gangsters of the Kimes-Inman Gang of Oklahoma, Missouri, Kansas and Texas."

Just after Sheriff Kelly's murder, a red-headed woman with a "hardboiled appearance" arrived in West Plains on a bus from Chicago, looking for a Raymond Hamilton. She gave her name as Lee Hamilton but turned out to be Dorothy Slayman Karpis (Alvin had been known in the area as R.E. or Ray Hamilton, which may have added to official confusion of Karpis with Ray Hamilton, connected with the

Barrows). Dorothy was questioned, jailed for a while and released. She did not see her husband again until 1935, when he visited her in Tulsa, gave her some money, and told her to get a divorce. By this time Dorothy had followed in Aunt Carol's footsteps and become a prostitute.

The Barkers, Karpis, Weaver and Dunlop had fled to the home of their old friend Herb Farmer, near Joplin. Farmer advised them to go to St. Paul and contact Harry Sawyer. Coincidentally, Karpis's trigger-happy friend, Lawrence DeVol, arrived in St. Paul at about this time. Considered by Karpis a mentor and teacher, DeVol had murdered a policeman in Kirksville, Missouri, in November 1930 and was suspected of several other killings in Muskogee, Oklahoma; Omaha, Nebraska; and Washington, Iowa.

For years, St. Paul had been a "safe town" for criminals. Out-of-town fugitives could harbor there, with no interference from the police, so long as they paid a modest protection fee and committed no crimes within the city limits. In 1928 the manager of this layover system, fixer and bootlegger "Dapper Dan" Hogan, had been killed by a car bomb, and his successor, Harry Sawyer, imposed fewer requirements. He no longer enforced the rule forbidding crimes within the city. Sawyer even condoned local crimes, so long as he shared in the proceeds. The police department was as corrupt as ever, visiting criminals were still safe from arrest, but a city that had been nearly crime-free since the turn of the century was now tolerating more and more robberies, gang murders and even kidnappings.

After checking in with Sawyer, as was the custom, the Barker-Karpis group rented an apartment at 1031 South Robert Street in West St. Paul. Fred and Karpis again busied themselves with small burglaries, holdups and hijackings. In December of 1931 and January 1932, they and some accomplices staged well-planned night raids on the Minnesota towns of Pine River and Cambridge, taking several citizens hostage and systematically looting the major businesses and several private homes. Furthermore, through Harry Sawyer, Barker and Karpis soon made their most important future business connections.

The formation of the Barker-Karpis gang as such might be dated to December 31, 1931. Karpis and Fred Barker attended a gala New Year's Eve party at Harry Sawyer's Green Lantern saloon, 545½ Wabasha, where they met some of the elite of the Midwest underworld. These included Minneapolis crime boss Isadore "Kid Cann" Blumenfeld, Capone gangster Gus Winkeler and several leading bank robbers, including Harvey Bailey, Tommy Holden and Francis "Jimmy" Keating, Big Homer Wilson and Frank "Jelly" Nash, a former member of the old Al Spencer gang who may have known the Barkers during their Tulsa days. Nash has escaped from Leavenworth on October 19, 1930.

Holden and Keating had also escaped from Leavenworth. Sentenced to 25 years for a $100,000 mail train robbery at Evergreen Park, Illinois, they were welcomed back to Leavenworth in May 1928, soon meeting and befriending Frank Nash and other Spencer gang veterans. Another new friend was a minor Oklahoma bootlegger named George Kelly, who had been serving a short sentence for smuggling liquor onto an Indian reservation. Kelly, whose real name was George Barnes, would later make headlines as Machine Gun Kelly, but at the time he worked in the photographic section of the prison's records room. On February 28, 1930, Holden and Keating walked out of

Leavenworth, using trusty passes allegedly forged by Kelly. They fled to Chicago and then St. Paul, where they were joined later that year by Kelly and Nash.

In St. Paul, Holden and Keating teamed up with Harvey Bailey, who had been committing major and minor bank robberies for nearly a decade. A former bootlegger, Bailey had been arrested only once and had served no time in prison, but was considered the nation's top bank robber by law enforcement agencies that bothered to keep score. He was suspected of participating in the "Denver Mint robbery" of December 18, 1922, which actually involved the robbing of a Federal Reserve Bank truck parked outside the Mint. Bailey's regular associates included Big Homer Wilson, another longtime bank robber once arrested by Seattle police as a train robbery suspect, but otherwise unknown; Charles J. Fitzgerald, a criminal in his sixties who had Chicago mob connections, many aliases and an extremely long arrest record; Verne Miller, a First World War hero and former South Dakota sheriff turned bootlegger, bank robber and professional killer, and whose increasing mental instability (possibly aggravated by drug use, advanced syphilis or both) eventually led to his murder by other underworld characters endangered by his erratic stunts); and Bernard Phillips, alias Big Phil Courtney, a onetime Chicago policeman turned bandit. A loose aggregation of criminals, with floating membership, soon developed. Though Bailey seems to have been the real leader, the group became known as the "Holden-Keating gang."

This gang, or members of it, committed a number of spectacular crimes: the $70,000 robbery of a bank in Willmar, Minnesota, on July 15, 1930; the $40,000 robbery of a savings bank at Ottumwa, Iowa, on September 9, 1930; the record-breaking $2.7 million robbery of the Lincoln National Bank and Trust Company in Nebraska on September 17, 1930; and the $40,000 robbery of the Central State Bank at Sherman, Texas, on April 8, 1931. On October 2, 1931, Holden and Keating robbed First American National Bank messengers in Duluth of $58,000. On October 20, the same two and others robbed the Kraft State Bank at Menomonie, Wisconsin, of $130,000. Cashier James Kraft, son of the bank's president, was taken hostage and murdered. Two gang members, Charlie Harmon and Frank Weber, were found shot to death, along with Kraft; one theory holds that other gang members murdered them for shooting the hostage. Harmon's widow, Paula, known as Fat-Witted, later joined Fred Barker.

The deaths of Harmon and Weber left vacancies in the gang. On December 11, 1931, seven federal prisoners escaped from Leavenworth, taking Warden Thomas White hostage. They seized White in his office as he was granting an interview to inmate Lloyd "Red" Barker. This may have been only a coincidence, as Lloyd didn't join in the escape and may have had no prior knowledge of it, but the escapees included Grover Durrill, George "Whitey" Curtis and Earl Thayer of the old Spencer gang, and William "Boxcar" Green, a onetime member of the Barkers' Tulsa gang. Durrill, Curtis and Green were cornered by police in a nearby farmhouse and committed suicide. The others soon were caught, and the warden survived his ordeal. As it turned out, the break had been financed and engineered by Frank Nash, who had smuggled guns and explosives into the prison.

The gang soon acquired new recruits. Alvin Karpis and Fred Barker joined Tommy Holden, Bernard Phillips and Lawrence DeVol, on

March 29, 1932, in the well-planned holdup of the North American Branch of the Northwestern National Bank in Minneapolis. No one was killed and the gang escaped with $266,500 in cash, coins and bonds, fleeing in a fast Lincoln stolen especially for the job. The car had belonged to an executive of the National Lead Battery Company of St. Paul.

A few weeks prior to this robbery, a double homicide occurred, which may have been connected with the gang's activities. Two women were found shot to death in a burning Buick at Turtle Lake, Wisconsin, on March 5, 1932. One was Margaret Perry, alias Indian Rose Walker, Margaret Burns, Maggie Shecog, etc., a Chippewa Indian and the former mistress of Denver Bobby Walker, a suspect in the Denver Mint robbery. The other was her recent jailmate, a prostitute named Marjorie Schwartz or Sadie Carmacher, with other aliases. The car had been borrowed by Bernard Phillips from Alvin Karpis, who had stolen it from one O.S. Werner on January 5, when the gang ransacked the town of Cambridge, Minnesota. In later years Karpis claimed that Harry Sawyer was offered $50,000 by a St. Paul banker to have the women murdered. By other accounts, the women had threatened to inform on the gang.

Nick Hannegraf, their landlady's son, recognized pictures of Alvin Karpis and Fred Barker in *True Detective Mysteries,* and dutifully called the police. St. Paul Police Chief Tom Brown, who was on Harry Sawyer's payroll, advised Hannegraf to report this information at the Central Police Station. The desk sergeant there told Hannegraf he would have to come back later and see Inspector James Crumley, another Sawyer flunky. Seven hours after the call to Chief Brown, St. Paul police raided the house on South Robert Street, by which time the Barkers, Karpis and Arthur Dunlop were long gone.

Dunlop was found dead the following day on the shore of Lake Frestead, near Webster, Wisconsin. He had been shot three times at close range. The FBI later would theorize, probably correctly, that Karpis and Fred Barker had killed him as a suspected informer.

Heat from the Dunlop killing caused the gang temporarily to shift its base to Kansas City. The Barkers and Karpis stayed at the Longfellow Apartments in Kansas City from May 12 until July 5, 1932, as "Mrs. A.F. Hunter and sons," then rented an apartment at 414 West 46th Terrace. Harvey Bailey, Frank Nash, Holden and Keating, Bernard Phillips and Lawrence DeVol also rented apartments in the area.

On June 17 this group (probably including Keating) robbed the Citizens National Bank at Fort Scott, Kansas, of $47,000. Jess Doyle was released on parole from the Kansas state prison on the same day, met Fred in Kansas City and joined the gang. Proceeds from the robbery were spent on a lavish "coming out" party for Doyle at the Barker-Karpis apartment.

On July 7 Kansas City police officers, accompanied by Special Agent Raymond Caffrey of the FBI, arrested Harvey Bailey, Tommy Holden and Francis Keating on the Old Mission Golf Course in Kansas City after letting them play a few holes. A fourth gang member, Bernard Phillips, escaped to warn the others. Phillips was later suspected of betraying the trio, particularly after other gang members learned he was a former policeman. Phillips disappeared later in the year on a trip to New York with Frank Nash and Verne Miller, and is believed to have been murdered.

A Liberty Bond from the recent bank robbery was found in Bailey's pocket and turned over to Fort Scott authorities for use as evidence at his trial. Holden and Keating were returned to Leavenworth.

The rest of the gang returned to Minnesota. The Barkers, Karpis and Frank Nash rented cottages on White Bear Lake. FBI files indicate that Fred Barker and Alvin Karpis associated there with a Tulsa lawyer named J. Earl Smith, who was supposedly retained by the gang to defend Bailey.

Smith took the money but not the case, and Bailey was defended by a court-appointed lawyer named James G. Shepperd. On August 17 he was sentenced to 10 to 50 years in the Lansing, Kansas, state prison. The following day, Attorney Smith was found shot to death at the Indian Hills Country Club near Tulsa.

Most accounts indicate that Smith was murdered by Fred Barker and Alvin Karpis, for failing to defend Bailey. Some earlier, and more believable, versions have it that Smith either informed on the gang or cheated them out of money. Karpis and Barker seem to have been in St. Paul during this period, however, and some FBI reports name Smith's murderers as Harry Campbell, Jimmie Lawson and Jew Eddie Moss.

Bailey would escape from the Kansas state prison on Memorial Day, 1933, along with Wilbur Underhill and nine others, using smuggled guns. Frank Nash and the Barker-Karpis gang would later be suspected of arranging the breakout. After a brief bank-robbery spree, Bailey was recaptured in the summer of 1933 and accused of involvement in both the Kansas City Massacre and the kidnapping of Oklahoma oilman Charles Urschel. No solid evidence linked him to the Kansas City killings, and he apparently had no personal involvement in the Urschel kidnapping, but was unlucky enough to be laying low, and fast asleep, at the farm of Albert Bates when it was raided by federal agents looking for the kidnappers, and he took the blame with Bates, George and Kathryn Kelly and their associates.

This left Fred Barker and Karpis running the gang, though Karpis at first deferred to Fred, considering him the real leader. The on-the-job training they had received from Bailey, Holden and Keating had made them big-time but little-known criminals.

On July 25, 1932, Karpis, DeVol, Fred Barker, Jess Doyle and Earl Christman robbed the Cloud County Bank at Concordia, Kansas, of $250,000 in bonds and cash. On August 8, Fred Barker, correctly or not, was identified as one of three men who robbed the Citizens Security Bank at Bixby, Oklahoma, of $1,000.

Arthur "Dock" Barker was paroled from his life sentence at McAlester on September 10, 1932, on the condition he leave Oklahoma forever. The parole was secured by an agent of the gang named Jack Glynn, a corrupt private detective at Leavenworth, Kansas, who knew whom to bribe. Dock visited with his father in Missouri, then joined the gang in St. Paul.

The Barker-Karpis gang robbed the State Bank and Trust Company at Redwood Falls, Minnesota, on September 23, 1932, escaping with $35,000. On September 30, they robbed the Citizens National Bank at Wahpeton, North Dakota, of $7,000. They had planned to rob the bank at nearby Brekenridge, Minnesota, on the same day, but decided not to push their luck. On October 18, Lawrence DeVol was identified as a robber of a bank in Amboy, Minnesota, which had lost $4,400 to several gunmen.

Dock Barker wanted a parole for his "rap buddy," Volney Davis, still in McAlester for the Sherrill murder. Karpis later claimed in his autobiography that he contacted "a big operator in St. Paul" who said he could arrange an early release for $1,500. However it was accomplished, Volney Davis, convicted murderer and former escapee, was released from the Oklahoma state prison on November 3, 1932, not on parole but on a two-year "leave of absence." Davis was due back at McAlester on July 1, 1934, but instead joined the gang in St. Paul and soon accompanied Ma Barker on a trip to California to visit her sister.

Davis's girlfriend, Edna "The Kissing Bandit" Murray, escaped from the women's state prison at Jefferson City, Missouri, on December 13, 1932. It was her third prison break, which earned her the additional nickname of Rabbits. Edna had been serving a 25-year sentence for highway robbery, and when Davis learned of her escape he returned to the Midwest to join her and her teenage son, Preston Patton.

The Barker-Karpis gang, now including Bill Weaver and Verne Miller, robbed the Third Northwestern Bank in Minneapolis on December 16, killing two policemen and a bystander. They escaped with $22,000 in cash and $92,000 in bonds, using the same Lincoln they had driven in the bloodless March robbery. Following the Minneapolis job, Verne Miller returned to Kansas City, and the rest of the gang, except for Lawrence DeVol, headed to Reno.

DeVol got drunk, crashed a party at 298 Grand Avenue in St. Paul and was arrested, still in possession of $17,000 of the bank loot. He was convicted of robbery and murder and sentenced to life in the state prison at Stillwater, Minnesota. (Three years later he was transferred to the St. Peter Hospital for the Criminally Insane and escaped with 15 other inmates on June 6, 1936. After a series of crimes, he died a month later in a gun battle with police at Enid, Oklahoma, taking an officer with him.)

So far John Dillinger was still an inmate at the Indiana state prison, while the equally unknown Barker-Karpis gang wintered in Reno and San Francisco, making good contacts through the Reno gambling syndicate headed by Bill Graham and Jim McKay. It was probably there that Karpis met Illinois prison escapee Lester Gillis, who had grown up in the same general part of Chicago and preferred the name Jimmy Williams to his later alias of George "Baby Face" Nelson. Karpis sometimes dined with Gillis, his wife, Helen, and their children, Ronald and Darlene, in their apartment at 126 Caliente Street. Gillis introduced Karpis to the ex-convict owner of a private hospital in Vallejo, California, also named Williams, a hatchet-faced doctor known as Thomas or "Tobe," who treated Gillis's wife, Helen, as a regular patient, performed illegal abortions and took care of sick or wounded fugitives under any name they chose. He removed Karpis's tonsils in February 1933, shortly before the gang returned to the Midwest.

Another useful contact was Frank Cochran, a Reno airplane mechanic and garage owner who serviced cars for criminals, putting a siren on Nelson's ostensibly to facilitate escapes, or because he just liked sirens. In return for favors rendered, Karpis lined up Gillis, aka Nelson, with a gang of experienced bank robbers headquartered in Long Beach, Indiana, near the Michigan City pen where Dillinger was awaiting parole. These included the aristocratic Eddie Bentz, semiretired collecter of rare books and coins, and such younger disciples as Tommy Carroll and Homer Van Meter, a prison friend of Dillinger's who already had been released. It was here that Nelson and Dillinger, who patronized the same army-navy store operated by a local underworld character, probably became acquainted shortly after Dillinger made parole that summer.

The gang returned to St. Paul in February, but a month later moved back to the Chicago area after Harry Sawyer's police informants tipped him that a gang apartment was scheduled to be raided. Needing to replenish their protection money, they planned another robbery.

On April 4, 1933, Alvin Karpis, Fred and Dock Barker, Frank Nash, Volney Davis, Earl Christman, Jess Doyle and Eddie Green robbed the First National Bank at Fairbury, Nebraska, of $151,350 in cash and bonds. They escaped after a wild gun battle in which a deputy and two citizens were wounded. Earl Christman was also wounded and taken by the gang to Verne Miller's home at 6612 Edgevale Road in Kansas City. Miller called an underworld doctor, but Christman died anyway and was buried by the gang outside the town.

Returning to St. Paul, Karpis and Fred Barker were summoned by bootlegger Jack Peifer to a meeting at his Hollyhocks nightclub. Peifer introduced them to two friends, Fred Goetz, and Byron "Monty" Bolton. Goetz and Bolton were members of the Capone syndicate who had participated in the St. Valentine's Day Massacre, Goetz as one of the gunmen and Bolton as a not-too-bright lookout who mistook another gangster for Bugs Moran, and also left behind a letter, or possibly a medicine bottle, with his name on it. Both occasionally worked with the Capone syndicate but also moonlighted as freelance crooks, and now they had a business proposition for the Barker-Karpis gang. They were hiring help for a Sawyer-

sponsored kidnapping in St. Paul. Fred and Karpis agreed, with much urging, and soon they were joined by Dock Barker and Charles Fitzgerald.

They abducted William A. Hamm, Jr., head at the well-known St. Paul brewery, on June 15, 1933. Hamm was blindfolded and driven all the way to the Chicago suburb of Bensenville, where he was held at the home of Edmund Bartholmey, the town's future (and soon deposed) postmaster, until the family raised a ransom of $100,000. The bills, whose serial numbers had been recorded, were fenced through the Graham-McKay syndicate in Reno. Chicago beer baron Roger Touhy and members of his gang were arrested on general principles, tried amidst great hoopla and acquitted for lack of evidence, to the embarrassment of the FBI. Later, with the help of competitor Al Capone, Touhy was convicted of kidnapping local underworld figure Jake "The Barber" Factor in what the courts, after 25 years, decided was a frame-up. He wrote a book on the case (*The Stolen Years*) shortly before his release, and soon afterward was killed on the front porch of his sister's home by shotgun blasts from a passing car. He died quickly from loss of blood, but not before gasping some famous last words: "The bastards never forget!"

On the same day as the Hamm kidnapping, Frank Nash was captured by the FBI in Hot Springs, Arkansas. Two days later, as he was being returned to Leavenworth, Nash and his captors were ambushed by gunmen at the Union Station in Kansas City. In an apparent release attempt gone wrong, or possibly to silence him, Nash and four law officers were shot to death, though the battle may have been set off more or less accidentally when a federal agent blasted Nash while trying to operate an unfamiliar shotgun. In any case, Verne Miller led the mission, and the FBI would first name Harvey Bailey and Wilbur Underhill as his accomplices before evidence found at Miller's house pointed instead to Pretty Boy Floyd and Adam Richetti. Several underworld figures in Hot Springs, Joplin, Chicago and Kansas City would eventually be convicted of conspiracy in the Kansas City Massacre case. One was the Barkers' friend, Herb Farmer. According to later statements to the FBI by Byron Bolton and Edna Murray, a small portion of the Hamm ransom was set aside as a defense fund for Farmer.

At the South St. Paul post office on August 30, 1933, the Barker-Karpis gang robbed Stockyards National Bank payroll messengers of $33,000, killing one policeman and wounding another. On September 22, driving a car equipped with smoke-screen and oil-slick devices, they robbed Federal Reserve Bank messengers on Jackson Boulevard in Chicago, killing another policeman and wrecking their car but still managing to escape, only to discover the bags they took contained useless checks.

The car was traced to the shop of one Joe Bergl at 5346 West Cermak Road (formerly 22nd Street) in Cicero, next door to Ralph Capone's Cotton Club. Bergl's customers, the FBI would learn, included members of the Capone mob and such visiting outlaws as Machine Gun Kelly. Some may have had steel plates installed in their cars to protect the occupants from gunfire, while the economy versions had their trunks and backseats "bulletproofed" with thick Chicago telephone directories. (Bergl's competitor on Chicago's Near North Side was Clarence Lieder's Oakley Auto Construction Co., 2300 W. Division, who serviced, supplied and modified cars for Baby Face Nelson and his cronies, stored the dirt-track racer

Nelson sometimes drove at Chicago's Robey Speedway on the city's South Side, and who also developed a smoke-screen device, probably consisting of a tube-and-valve arrangement that would squirt motor oil into a car's hot exhaust manifold. The Capone mob had used a similarly equipped car, probably from Bergl, in an unsuccessful effort to kill Dean O'Banion's successor, Vincent "Schemer" Drucci.)

After another vacation in Reno, the Barker-Karpis gang returned to St. Paul, where Harry Sawyer, annoyed at his smallish share from the Hamm job, convinced the gang to pull another kidnapping, this one to be more profitable for him. The target was Edward G. Bremer, president of the Commercial State Bank of St. Paul. Sawyer apparently had a personal grudge against Bremer, and since business still was business his percentage was upped accordingly. Bremer was abducted on January 17, 1934, and, like Hamm, transported to Bensenville, Illinois, where he was held for nearly a month at the home of former bootlegger Harold Alderton, until his family raised a ransom of $200,000.

Things didn't go so smoothly this time. Gasoline cans used by the kidnappers were found along the route of the ransom drop and one bore a fingerprint of Dock Barker. Flashlights used by the gang to signal the payoff location were also found and traced to a St. Paul store, where a clerk identified Alvin Karpis as the purchaser. Dock and Karpis were added to the FBI's wanted list. This money was so hot that the Reno gamblers who had laundered the Hamm ransom refused to touch it. Soon it began turning up in Chicago, and some of the money-changers there as well as crooked politician John J. "Boss" McLaughlin were arrested.

By March 1934 Karpis and Fred Barker (if not the gang as a whole) paid a call on their favorite family physician, Dr. Joseph Moran, Chicago's leading underworld health specialist. Moran had offices at the city's leading underworld hotel, the Irving, on Irving Park Boulevard, near where police had failed to trap Dillinger at another doctor's office the previous November. Once a skilled practitioner and still competent when sober, Moran had served time for one or more botched abortions and had met some high-powered felons, who helped him find his true calling—drinking bootleg booze and treating wounded gangsters, particularly members of the Syndicate. He tried to alter the faces of Karpis and Barker through plastic surgery, without great success, but did manage to remove the fingerprints of Alvin Karpis by the painful use of a scalpel instead of caustic chemicals. When soused, which was often, Moran tended to brag about his medical accomplishments to prostitutes, and unwisely suggested to members of the criminal community that his talents were indispensable. As a result, he was taken for the traditional one-way ride—either by boat on Lake Erie, where he was killed and scuttled, or (from other accounts) by car, to be bumped off and buried in a desolate part of Michigan.

Fred Goetz who divided his time between the Capone mob and the Barker-Karpis gang, was also talkative when drunk. Late on March 21, 1934, his head was blown off by shotgun blasts outside the Minerva Restaurant in Cicero, Illinois, about a block west of the Hawthorne Hotel (which remained the local mob headquarters even after one-term reform mayor Dever lost to Big Bill Thompson, and Capone took over several floors of Chicago's mammoth Lexington Hotel in the city's longtime vice district a few blocks south of the Loop). The generally accepted theory is that Goetz was losing his mar-

bles and babbling about past crimes. It remains uncertain whether his killers were the Barker-Karpis gang, friends of Bugs Moran (for Goetz was a principal in the St. Valentine's Day Massacre) or Frank Nitti, who succeeded Al Capone and was purging the Outfit (as it was often called) of Capone loyalists.

In April, Dillinger gangster Eddie Green, formerly a member of the Barker-Karpis mob, was shot by FBI agents in St. Paul. He died eight days later in a hospital, after deliriously bobbling the details of past crimes while agents took notes. His wife, Bessie, captured at the same time, also provided much information. The Greens gave the FBI its first real knowledge of the Barker-Karpis gang as a cohesive group. From Bessie Green, the Bureau learned that Karpis and the Barker brothers usually traveled in the company of a dowdy old woman who at least "posed" as their mother. Enter Ma Barker, so far unimportant and mentioned only in passing by the West Plains police.

By the end of the year, the Barker-Karpis gang was scattered across the country, dodging the FBI while trying to pass the Bremer ransom. Various gang members were captured and Bremer money was recovered as far away as Havana, where Karpis lived briefly with his pregnant girlfriend ("paramour" was the Bureau's favorite term), Dolores Delaney. Dolores was one of three sisters with similar tastes in men. One was married to Albert "Pat" Reilly, a St. Paul hoodlum employed by Harry Sawyer. Another was the girlfriend of Tommy Carroll, then identified with Dillinger, whose Crown Point escape and worldwide name recognition had robbed Nelson of credit for forming the gang originally.

Dillinger, Floyd, Bonnie and Clyde and Nelson—the most publicized public enemies—

Unlike some of his colleagues, Dillinger's manner charmed much of the press and the public, who had mixed feelings when he was betrayed by a woman he trusted and shot in the back by officers. *(Jeff Maycroft Collection)*

were all killed in 1934, leaving only the Barker-Karpis gang to make Director Hoover famous. On January 8, 1935, an army of agents raided a courtyard apartment building at 3920 North Pine Grove, without telling the police. They created such a commotion with gas and gunfire that city cops rushed to the scene without knowing what to expect. A G-man waving credentials prevented a general bloodbath, and the cops joined the spectators, who were rooting for both sides after agents had thoroughly terrified residents and lobbed tear-gas shells into wrong apartments. Byron Bolton, Clara Fisher Gibson and Ruth Heidt, widow of a recently murdered gang member, surrendered as soon as they could, but Clara's husband, Russell Gibson, alias Roy "Slim" Gray, chose to fight. He donned a bulletproof vest, armed himself with a Browning Automatic Rifle and .32 automatic pistol and tried to escape out the back. Gibson barely made it onto a rear fire escape before an FBI agent with a high-velocity .351 Winchester rifle sent a slug through Gibson's chest that flattened against the inside back of his vest. He died a short time later, a Bureau report stated, "with a curse on his lips for all law enforcement officers." Gibson was an old pal of the Barkers from their Tulsa days, and had been wanted since 1929 for a $75,000 bank messenger robbery in Oklahoma City. He had also been arrested for possession of stolen jewelry, but Chicago police, who had long since streamlined the local criminal justice system, told his distraught wife to give her bail-bond cash to Louie Piquett, the designated fixer and future Dillinger attorney, who cleared the matter up without any bothersome paperwork.

The same day as the battle on Pine Grove Avenue, which angered the police as well as the newspapers, Dock Barker and his girlfriend

Mildred Kuhlman were arrested by the FBI outside their apartment at 432 Surf Street. Inside, agents found a Florida map with the Ocala region circled. Dock had no comment, but Byron Bolton told his interrogators that Ma and Fred Barker, and possibly other gang members, were living on a lake in Florida, where Fred had been using his submachine gun to hunt a huge alligator nicknamed Old Joe by the locals.

Eight days later, on January 16, 1935, a small army of federal agents surrounded a house on Lake Weir, at Oklawaha, Florida, and called on the occupants to surrender. They were answered by machine-gun fire. During a prolonged battle

Our New National Guard.

Thanks to J. Edgar Hoover's publicity campaign emphasizing scientific crime detection and the FBI's incorruptibility, his "G-men," while often scorned by the police, soon were idolized by most people as model crime-fighters. *(Authors' collection)*

the G-men poured more than 1,500 rounds into the two-story structure. Some 45 minutes after the return fire had ceased, Inspector E.J. Connelly sent Willie Woodbury, the Barkers' black handyman (whom the Barkers presumably would spare as a noncombatant), into the house to see what was left of any residents. Woodbury found Ma and Fred Barker dead in an upstairs bedroom. Fred had 14 bullets in him. Nearby lay Ma, dead of a single gunshot wound, which may or may not have been self-inflicted, or fired by Fred when capture seemed imminent.

According to FBI reports, a Thompson was found on the floor between her and Fred. The newspapers, using Hoover's account, embellished this considerably, arming her with a "smoking" submachine gun. Hoover would later declare that her gallant son Fred had given her the Thompson with a 100-round drum, making do himself with one whose magazine held only 50 cartridges. Agents also found two shotguns, two .45 automatics, a .380 automatic, a Winchester rifle, a large quantity of ammunition, several bulletproof vests and cash totaling $14,293. The arsenal was carefully arranged on the front steps of the house for the benefit of photographers.

The bodies of Ma and Fred were allowed to mummify in the Ocala morgue until October, when George Barker could afford to bring his wife and son home for burial. George had successfully sued for recovery of the cash seized at Oklawaha, since the government could not prove any of it was ransom money.

Dock Barker and other members of the gang were convicted of the Bremer kidnapping and sentenced to life, partly on the testimony of Byron Bolton, who pleaded guilty to both the Hamm and Bremer kidnappings and received concurrent sentences of three to five years.

Dock was sent to Leavenworth, then Alcatraz. On Friday, January 13, 1939, guards killed him with rifle fire in what prison officials called an escape attempt, though some witnesses said he was merely trying to retrieve an errant baseball. In any case, his last words were, "I'm all shot to hell!"

Dock first was buried at Olivet Memorial Park Cemetery in Colma, California, identified only by his prison number. His father later moved his body to the family plot at Timberhill Cemetery.

George Barker died on February 28, 1941, at his home at 1201 East Seventh Street in Webb City, Missouri. He also was buried at Timberhill, leaving no one to bring Lloyd home. George, Kate, Herman, Dock and Fred Barker lie today in the isolated northwest corner of Timberhill Cemetery. Only Herman's grave has a monument.

Following the killing of Ma and Fred Barker, Alvin Karpis and Harry Campbell fled north to Atlantic City. Cornered by police at the Dan-Mor Hotel, on January 20, 1935, they shot their way out and escaped. Their girlfriends, Dolores Delaney and Wynona Burdette, were captured and later sentenced to five years for harboring federal fugitives. Dolores gave birth to a son while in prison, named him Raymond Alvin Karpis, and gave him to Karpis's parents in Chicago to raise.

Karpis and Campbell kidnapped a doctor in Pennsylvania and stole his car, releasing him unharmed in Ohio and abandoning the car in Michigan. They later organized a new gang, robbed a mail truck of $72,000 in Warren, Ohio, on April 24, 1935, and a mail train at Garrettsville, Ohio, of $34,000 the following November. One member of the new but unsung gang was the Barkers' old friend Sam Coker,

Karpis wisely kept quiet at the time but later pointed out that the Plymouth coupe he was driving had no backseat where the G-men had claimed they found a rifle, that the agents had forgotten to bring handcuffs, that they didn't know where the federal building in New Orleans was, and that Hoover, smarting from criticism that he was only a desk cop who let his men take all the risks, had hidden in an alley until Karpis was in custody and he could make a formal arrest. *(Authors' collection)*

whose parole from the Oklahoma state prison was allegedly bought by Karpis.

After a long pursuit and some embarrassing blunders, the FBI finally tracked Karpis to a rooming house in New Orleans. J. Edgar Hoover, smarting from criticism that he lacked police experience and let his men take all the risks, rushed there by plane and took personal credit for arresting Karpis on May 1, 1936. Karpis later remarked that Hoover had stayed safely out of range until agents were holding him at gunpoint, then took charge for the benefit of news cameras. Since no one had remembered to bring handcuffs, Karpis was shackled with a necktie, then had to give the visiting G-men directions to the federal building, which housed a bank he had planned to rob. Arrested with him was Fred Hunter, who would be convicted of mail robbery. Five days later, Hoover led another squad of agents in capturing Harry Campbell and Sam Coker in Toledo. Coker's Oklahoma parole was revoked, and Campbell would receive a life sentence for the Bremer kidnapping.

Flown to St. Paul, Karpis pleaded guilty to the Hamm kidnapping and received a life sentence. Altogether he spent some 33 years in federal prisons, mostly Alcatraz, before he was paroled in 1969 and deported to Canada. He later moved to the estate of a friend in Spain and died there on August 26, 1979, of an overdose of sleeping pills, which some believe was accidental. Karpis's New Orleans capture, stage-managed or not, proved J. Edgar Hoover a man of action after all, and marked the end of what most Americans thought of as the "public enemy" era.

Dillinger had made Melvin Purvis a household name, to Hoover's great displeasure and Purvis's regret. Far more deliberately but less successfully, Hoover tried to establish his own crime-fighting reputation by destroying the Barker-Karpis gang. That group was far more formidable than Dillinger's desperadoes, but also far less likable, and hard as he tried, Hoover seemed to understand he could never get the mileage out of Karpis that he had gotten out of Ma. This required popular crime writer and Hoover's private publicist, Courtney Ryley Cooper, to engage in major exaggeration, but Cooper had no qualms in that regard. In a book and one of the dozen or so articles ghost-written or coauthored by Cooper for *American* magazine, Hoover portrayed Ma in prose both purple and fanciful, as if the two had battled it out nose to nose. Wrote Hoover, with a little help from his friend,

> The eyes of Arizona Clark Barker, by the way, always fascinated me. They were queerly direct, penetrating, hot with some strangely smouldering flame, yet withal as hypnotically cold as the muzzle of a gun.

After mopping up a few last fugitives in the late 1930s, the FBI would concentrate on subversives, spies and saboteurs, while racketeering came of age.

6

1930

January 6, 1930 Lester Gillis, alias Baby Face Nelson, and four accomplices rob Mr. and Mrs. Charles M. Richter of $25,000 worth of jewelry in their mansion at 1418 Lake Shore Drive in Chicago.

January 22, 1930 Nelson and three accomplices rob the Lake Forest, Illinois, home of lawyer Stanley J. Templeton, taking $5,000 worth of jewelry.

February 5, 1930 Charles Arthur "Pretty Boy" Floyd and others rob the Farmers and Merchants Bank at Sylvania, Ohio.

February 28, 1930 Thomas Holden and Francis Keating, convicted mail train robbers, escape from Leavenworth Federal Penitentiary, using trusty passes forged by fellow inmate George F. Barnes, Jr., alias Machine Gun Kelly.

March 2, 1930 Clyde Barrow is arrested in Waco, Texas, for burglary and car theft.

March 8, 1930 Marvin "Buck" Barrow, brother of Clyde and convicted burglar, escapes from Huntsville, Texas, state prison. Patrolman

Harland F. Manes is fatally shot in Akron, Ohio, by bank robber James Bradley, alias Bert Walker, an associate of Pretty Boy Floyd. Bradley, Bob Amos, alias John King, and Floyd are arrested on suspicion.

March 10, 1930 After months as a fugitive on murder charges, Jack "Legs" Diamond surrenders to New York police. He will be discharged by Judge Levine on March 21.

March 11, 1930 Clyde Barrow, William Turner and Emory Abernathy escape from Waco, Texas, jail using a gun smuggled to them by Barrow's girlfriend, Bonnie Parker.

March 17, 1930 In Philadelphia, Chicago mob boss Al Capone is paroled from a one-year sentence on gun-carrying charges.

March 18, 1930 Clyde Barrow, William Turner and Emory Abernathy are recaptured in Middleton, Ohio, and extradited to Texas.

March 23, 1930 Alvin Karpis, convicted burglar and Kansas State Reformatory escapee, is recaptured in Kansas City, Missouri. Karpis's partner, Lawrence DeVol, is arrested at the same time.

March 31, 1930 With accomplices Stanton Randall and Harry Lewis, Baby Face Nelson robs Count and Countess Von Buelow in their home at 5839 Sheridan Road in Chicago, taking $95 in cash and over $50,000 worth of jewels.

A temporary federal injunction is granted at Miami, preventing the sheriff from arresting Al Capone.

April 1, 1930 Alvin Karpis's partner, Lawrence DeVol, posts a $1,000 bond in Kansas City, is released and jumps bail.

April 20, 1930 Three Capone gangsters are shot to death by a lone gunman in the "Easter Massacre" in a bar at 2900 South Wells Street in Chicago.

April 21, 1930 Clyde Barrow is received at Huntsville, Texas, state prison, under a 14-year sentence for burglary and car theft.

April 24, 1930 The Chicago Crime Commission publishes its first list of Public Enemies, with Al Capone in the number one position. "Public Enemy No. 1" becomes a popular headline phrase and other law enforcement agencies will soon adopt their own "public enemy" lists.

April 25, 1930 Federal Judge Halsted L. Ritter makes permanent an injunction preventing the Miami sheriff from arresting Al Capone as (essentially) a bad influence.

April 26, 1930 Elderly brothers David and George Smith, wealthy loan brokers from Connecticut, are shot to death in an apparent robbery attempt in Room 817 of the Hotel Severs in Muskogee, Oklahoma. The double homicide is never solved but prime suspects include four gunmen known to have been in the Muskogee area: Lawrence DeVol, his brother Clarence, Jimmie Creighton (later an associate of Fred Barker) and Pat McDonald.

May 8, 1930 Despite his federal injunction, Al Capone, his brother John and two gang members are picked up by Miami police for "investigation."

May 9, 1930 Al Capone's injunction against Miami police is reversed.

May 13, 1930 Al Capone, Nick Circella and former Chicago Alderman Albert Prignano are arrested by Miami police while attending a prizefight. They will be released on a writ of habeas corpus the following day.

May 15, 1930 Anna Urbas, girlfriend of murdered New York gangster Eugene Moran, is strangled and thrown into the East River. Legs Diamond gang suspected.

May 19, 1930 Al Capone and Albert Prignano are arrested by Miami police while on their way to an American Legion boxing match. They are released on $100 bond.

May 20, 1930 Pretty Boy Floyd is turned over to Toledo authorities on a bank robbery charge.

May 21, 1930 Floyd associate Bert Walker is sentenced to death for murder.

In Miami, vagrancy charges against Al Capone and Albert Prignano are dismissed by Judge Frank P. Stoneman.

June 1, 1930 Three Capone-affiliated gangsters and their friends are machine-gunned to death and two wounded in the "Fox Lake Massacre" at Manning's, a popular waterfront resort hotel in Lake County, Illinois. Though murders are reported as a revival of Capone-Moran war, George "Machine Gun" Kelly will later tell the FBI that Verne Miller did the shooting for mainly personal reasons when he heard that his friend, Eugene "Red" McLaughlin, had been taken for a "ride."

The featuring of Al Capone on its cover in 1930 riled many readers of *Time* who objected to the magazine giving such prominence to a criminal already regarded by many as the "Babe Ruth of American Gangsters."   *(Authors' collection)*

June 5, 1930 McLaughlin's body found in the Chicago River, bound with baling wire and weighted down with 75 pounds of metal.

June 7, 1930 Three men and one woman rob Clinton Avenue Branch of the South Side Bank and Trust Company in Newark of $14,000. Legs Diamond gang suspected.

June 9, 1930 Prominent *Chicago Tribune* crime reporter Alfred "Jake" Lingle murdered by gunman in pedestrian underpass at Randolph Street and Michigan Avenue, creating a city-wide uproar until Lingle's mob connections are revealed.

June 14, 1930 Florida's petition to have Al Capone's Palm Island estate padlocked as a public nuisance is dismissed by Miami Judge Paul D. Barnes. Capone is arrested minutes later on two counts of perjury, allegedly committed in warrants issued by S.D. McCreary, Florida's director of public safety whom Capone charged with false arrest.

June 26, 1930 After stealing a car from an Ottumwa, Iowa, garage, Theodore "Handsome Jack" Klutas and Walter Dietrich are spotted by officers near Washington, Iowa. In the ensuing gun battle Klutas kills Night Marshal Aaron Bailey and Sheriff Fred Sweet.

July 10, 1930 Ralph Fleagle, of the early Fleagle gang of bank robbers, is hanged for murder at the Canon City, Colorado, state prison.

July 15, 1930 Harvey Bailey, Thomas Holden, Machine Gun Kelly and others rob Bank of Willmar at Willmar, Minnesota, of $70,000. Three gang members, Jew Sammy Stein, Frank "Weinie" Coleman and Mike Rusick, are killed, possibly by their accomplices, and dumped at White Bear Lake.

July 19, 1930 Herbert Royston and George Abshier, other members of the Fleagle gang, are also hanged for murder at the Colorado state prison.

July 23, 1930 Radio newscaster Gerald Buckley is assassinated by gangsters in the lobby of Detroit's LaSalle Hotel.

August 1, 1930 Moran-Aiello gangster Jack Zuta is machine-gunned by Capone mobsters on the dance floor of a crowded resort at Delafield, Wisconsin.

Capone is cleared of a minor perjury charge in Miami, on a court-directed verdict of acquittal.

August 6, 1930 State Supreme Court Justice Joseph Force Crater becomes and remains New York's most famous "missing person."

August 22, 1930 Catskills bootlegger Harry Western disappears after meeting Legs Diamond and attending a party at Haines Falls, New York. Western's bloodstained Buick turns up in a Brooklyn garage and two members of the Diamond gang are arrested, but his body is never found.

September 1930 Legs Diamond sails to Europe. Denied entry to England, he is arrested at Antwerp, Belgium, and deported to Germany. German authorities deport him back to the United States aboard the freighter *Hanover.*

September 9, 1930 The Harvey Bailey gang robs the Ottumwa Savings Bank in Ottumwa, Iowa, of $40,000.

September 13, 1930 Three men rob the Merchants Trust Company at South Paterson, New Jersey, of $18,000. Chicago gangsters Fred "Killer" Burke and Gus Winkeler are identified by witnesses as two of the holdup men. Both are also suspects in the St. Valentine's Day Massacre.

September 17, 1930 The Bailey gang robs the Lincoln National Bank & Trust Company at Lincoln, Nebraska, of over $2,870,000 in bonds and cash. Tom O'Connor, Howard "Pop" Lee and Jack Britt will be wrongly arrested for this crime, and O'Connor and Lee convicted of it.

September 22, 1930 Arriving in Philadelphia from Hamburg, Germany, Legs Diamond is arrested as a "suspicious" character.

October 3, 1930 Baby Face Nelson, Stanton Randall and Harry Lewis rob the Itasca State Bank at Itasca, Illinois, of $4,600.

October 10, 1930 Disguised as a Western Union messenger, Willie "The Actor" Sutton attempts to rob the Bay Ridge, Brooklyn, branch of the National City Bank in New York. Attempt foiled by watchman.

October 12, 1930 In a third known murder attempt, Legs Diamond is shot and wounded by rival gangsters at the Hotel Monticello in New York City.

October 14, 1930 Gangleader Jake Fleagle is shot by police while boarding a train at Branson, Missouri. He died the next day at a Springfield hospital.

October 19, 1930 Frank "Jelly" Nash, former member of the Al Spencer gang and convicted murderer and bank and train robber, escapes from Leavenworth, where he has been serving a 25-year sentence for mail robbery.

October 23, 1930 Chicago mob boss Joseph Aiello dies of some 59 wounds in a double machine-gun ambush by Capone gangsters outside the apartment of his henchman Pasquale "Presto" Prestigiocomo at 205 Kolmar Avenue in Chicago.

October 28, 1930 Gambling boss Solly "Cutcher-Head-Off" Weissman is shot to death in Kansas City.

Disguised as a Western Union messenger, Willie "The Actor" Sutton robs M. Rosenthal & Sons jewelry store at 1637 Broadway in New York of $130,000 in gems.

November 7, 1930 Baby Face Nelson and an accomplice attempt to rob the State Bank at Plainfield, Illinois, but are thwarted by cashiers' cages of bulletproof glass.

November 9, 1930 Frank Smith, Charles Berta and James Sargert, armed with a .30 caliber Browning machine gun, rob a Southern Pacific mail train of $56,000 at Noble, California.

November 10, 1930 Bert Walker, accomplice of Pretty Boy Floyd, is executed for murder of Columbus, Ohio, state prison.

November 17, 1930 Lawrence DeVol, future Barker-Karpis gang member, murders policeman John Rose in Kirksville, Missouri, following a theater robbery in Hannibal, Missouri.

November 22, 1930 Baby Face Nelson, Stanton Randall and Harry Lewis rob the Hillside State Bank in Hillside, Illinois, of $4,000.

November 24, 1930 Pretty Boy Floyd is convicted of a Sylvania, Ohio, bank robbery and sentenced to 12 to 15 years in the Ohio state prison.

December 1, 1930 Frank Smith, alias Frank Ellis, wanted for bank, train and postal robberies from California to Vancouver since 1928, is captured by police at his Oakland, California, home and killed when he attempts to escape.

December 10, 1930 Pretty Boy Floyd escapes from a train taking him to prison.

December 16, 1930 The Baron Lamm gang robs the Citizens State Bank at Clinton, Indiana, of $15,567, but is trapped by a posse near Sidell, Illinois. Hermann K. Lamm, who has successfully committed bank robberies across the United States for years, is killed, along with W.H. Hunter. G.W. "Dad" Landy commits suicide and two other gang members, Walter Dietrich and James "Oklahoma Jack" Clark, the latter a suspect in the 1922 Denver Mint robbery, are captured. Dietrich and Clark will receive life sentences at the Indiana state prison, where they will teach Lamm's bank-robbing methods to John Dillinger and his friends. (The same bank had been previously robbed by the Harvey Bailey gang in December 1928; Bailey was also a Mint robbery suspect.)

1931

January 13, 1931   Stanton Randall, accomplice of Baby Face Nelson, is arrested by Chicago police in his apartment at 6236 North Mozart. Police also arrest Nelson accomplice Harry Lewis at the Diversey Arms Hotel.

January 15, 1931   Lester Gillis, alias Baby Face Nelson, is arrested by Chicago police in an apartment at 6109 West 25th Street in Cicero, Illinois.

January 24, 1931   Bronx beer baron Arthur "Dutch Schultz" Flegenheimer and Charles "Chink" Sherman, a member of the rival Waxey Gordon mob, are wounded in a gun battle at the Club Abbey on West 54th Street in New York.

February 21, 1931   Francis "Two-Gun" Crowley and two other youths crash the American Legion's Washington's Birthday dance at 290 Bonner Place in the Bronx. When Legionnaires attempt to throw them out, Crowley shoots and wounds two, then flees with his companions.

February 25, 1931   Chicago police arrest Al Capone for vagrancy.

February 26, 1931   Vice case witness Vivian Gordon is found strangled in Van Cortlandt Park in the Bronx.

March 3, 1931   Benita Bischoff, 16-year-old daughter of murdered prostitute Vivian Gordon, committs suicide by inhaling gas in Audubon, New Jersey.

March 9, 1931   Pretty Boy Floyd, Bill "The Killer" Miller and George Birdwell rob the Bank of Earlsboro, at Earlsboro, Oklahoma, of $3,000.

March 13, 1931   Two-Gun Crowley avoids arrest in an office building at 369 Lexington Avenue in Manhattan by shooting police detective Ferdinand Schaedel, who is seriously wounded.

March 15, 1931   Five men rob the Huguenot Trust Company at New Rochelle, New York. Francis "Two-Gun" Crowley later named as a suspect.

March 16–April 2, 1931   St. Louis gangster Leo Brothers is tried in Chicago for the murder of reporter Jake Lingle. Brothers is convicted but sentenced to only 14 years.

March 25, 1931   Pretty Boy Floyd and Bill "The Killer" Miller murder William and Wallace Ash at Kansas City, Kansas, either for informing to the police or in a dispute over the Ash Boys' women.

March 26, 1931   Fred "Killer" Burke, industrious bank robber and Capone Syndicate hitman wanted for the 1929 St. Valentine's Day Massacre, is captured in Green City, Missouri. He will later receive a life sentence in Michigan for the murder of a policeman.

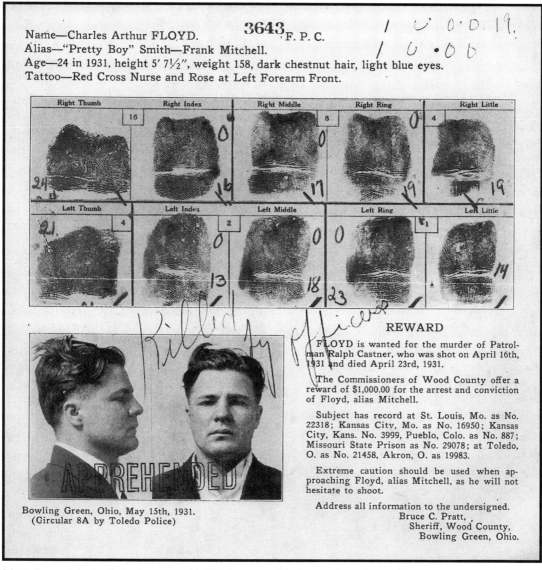

Name—Charles Arthur FLOYD. 3643, F. P. C.

Alias—"Pretty Boy" Smith—Frank Mitchell.

Age—24 in 1931, height 5′ 7½″, weight 158, dark chestnut hair, light blue eyes.

Tattoo—Red Cross Nurse and Rose at Left Forearm Front.

Bowling Green, Ohio, May 15th, 1931.
(Circular 8A by Toledo Police)

REWARD

FLOYD is wanted for the murder of Patrolman Ralph Castner, who was shot on April 16th, 1931 and died April 23rd, 1931.

The Commissioners of Wood County offer a reward of $1,000.00 for the arrest and conviction of Floyd, alias Mitchell.

Subject has record at St. Louis, Mo. as No. 22318; Kansas City, Mo. as No. 16950; Kansas City, Kans. No. 3999, Pueblo, Colo. as No. 887; Missouri State Prison as No. 29078; at Toledo, O. as No. 21458, Akron, O. as 19983.

Extreme caution should be used when approaching Floyd, alias Mitchell, as he will not hesitate to shoot.

Address all information to the undersigned.
Bruce C. Pratt,
Sheriff, Wood County,
Bowling Green, Ohio.

Prior to the new federal anti-crime laws enacted in 1934, the common 8-inch-square (post-office size) "wanted" poster distributed by local authorities was largely ignored by law enforcers outside the county or state where the crime occurred for lack of jurisdictional authority. *(Neal Trickel Collection)*

March 30, 1931 Fred Barker, son of Kate "Ma" Barker and convicted robber and burglar, is paroled from the Lansing, Kansas, state prison.

April 6, 1931 Pretty Boy Floyd and Bill "The Killer" Miller rob Mt. Zion Deposit Bank at Elliston, Kentucky, of $2,262.

April 8, 1931 Harvey Bailey, Frank Nash, Verne Miller, Machine Gun Kelly and others rob the Central State Bank at Sherman, Texas, of $40,000.

April 14, 1931 Pretty Boy Floyd and Bill "The Killer" Miller rob the Bank of Whitehouse at Whitehouse, Ohio, of $1,600.

April 15, 1931 Mafia boss Guiseppe "Joe the Boss" Masseria is assassinated in Gerardo Scarpato's Coney Island restaurant at 2715 West 15th Street. His lieutenant, Charles "Lucky" Luciano, tells police he was in the men's room at the time and saw nothing. Luciano ascends to leadership of the former Masseria crime family. Masseria's killers will be later named by informer Abe Reles as Benjamin "Bugsy" Siegel, Joe Adonis, Albert Anastasia and Vito Genovese, all close associates of Luciano. Masseria's death ends the power struggle between his family and that of rival Salvatore Maranzano for control of the Italian underworld in New York.

Two-Gun Crowley and two accomplices break into the basement apartment of real estate man Rudolph Adler at 133 West 90th Street in New York. Crowley robs and shoots Adler, who survives five wounds. Crowley and accomplices are driven away by Adler's dog, Trixie.

April 16, 1931 Pretty Boy Floyd murders Patrolman Ralph Castner in a gun battle at Bowling Green, Ohio. Floyd's partner, Bill "The Killer" Miller, is also slain and the outlaws' molls, Rose Ash and Beulah Baird, are captured. Floyd escapes.

April 26, 1931 John Schrinsher, alias Paul Martin, the last known member of the Kimes-Terrill gang which terrorized the Southwest in the 1920s, is captured at a tourist camp near Joinersville, Texas. The gang's leaders, Ray

Terrill and Matt and George Kimes, are serving long prison terms in Oklahoma for murder and bank robbery.

April 27, 1931 While joy-riding in New York with Francis "Two-Gun" Crowley and Rudolph "Fats" Duringer, dance-hall hostess Virginia Brannen resists Duringer's sexual advances. He fatally shoots her, and he and Crowley dump the body at St. Joseph's Seminary on Valentine Street in Yonkers.

Legs Diamond is wounded by gunmen at the Aratoga Inn in Acra, New York.

April 29, 1931 Two-Gun Crowley is spotted driving a green Chrysler sedan on 138th Street in the Bronx, near the Morris Avenue Bridge. Crowley escapes in a running gun battle. Bullets lodged in the police car match those used in the Virginia Brannen murder and other recent shootings.

April 30, 1931 Crowley's green sedan, with bullet holes and bloodstains, is found abandoned at 288 East 155th Street in the Bronx.

May 6, 1931 Patrolmen Frederick Hirsch and Peter Yodice discover Two-Gun Crowley and his 16-year-old girlfriend, Helen Walsh, parked on Morris Lane in North Merrick, Long Island. Crowley fatally shoots Hirsch and escapes with Helen.

May 7, 1931 About 150 New York police, armed with rifles, machine guns and tear gas, lay siege for two hours to the rooming-house apartment of Two-Gun Crowley, his girlfriend Helen Walsh and Rudolph "Fats" Duringer, at 303 West 90th Street. A huge crowd watches the battle. While Helen and Duringer stay down and do the reloading, Crowley trades shots with police and tosses back tear-gas bombs. He surrenders after being wounded four times, but two pistols are found strapped to his legs.

May 10, 1931 Alvin Karpis is released on parole from Lansing, Kansas, state prison. He will later join Ma and Fred Barker in Tulsa to form the Barker-Karpis gang.

May 29, 1931 At Mineola, Long Island, Francis "Two-Gun" Crowley is convicted of murdering Patrolman Frederick Hirsch.

May 30, 1931 Peter Coll, brother of Vincent Coll, is shot to death in New York. The Coll brothers are former employees of mobster Arthur Flegenheimer, alias Dutch Schultz, who have broken away from the Schultz organization to form their own gang. A series of murders and hijackings of Schultz beer trucks follows, attributed by police to Vincent Coll, who soon will earn the nickname "Mad Dog."

May or June 1931: Alvin Karpis, Fred Barker and Sam Coker stage a nighttime burglary raid on Coffeeville, Kansas, ransacking a drugstore, shoe store, pool hall and gas station for about $150.

June 1, 1931 Two-Gun Crowley is sentenced to death, as is Rudolph "Fats" Duringer, convicted of murdering Virginia Brannen.

June 10, 1931 Alvin Karpis, Fred Barker, Sam Coker and Joe Howard are arrested by Tulsa police for burglary. Karpis is held on burglary charge. Barker is transferred to the Claremore, Oklahoma, jail and escapes. Coker is returned to Oklahoma state prison to complete a 30-year sentence for bank robbery. Howard is released on bond and disappears.

June 15, 1931 To finance his war against Dutch Schultz, Vincent Coll kidnaps George "Big Frenchy" DeMange, henchman of another New York gang leader, Owney "The Killer" Madden, from DeMange's Club Argonaut, at West 50th Street and Seventh Avenue. De-

Mange is released after Madden pays about $35,000 in ransom. Madden and Schultz reportedly each place a $50,000 bounty on Coll's head.

June 18, 1931 At 1212 Fifth Avenue in Manhattan, Dutch Schultz bodyguard Danny Iamascia is killed by police detectives after drawing a gun in the mistaken belief they are members of the Coll mob. Schultz is arrested.

July 14, 1931 Wilbur Underhill, known as the Tri-State Terror, escapes from McAlester, Oklahoma, state prison, where he has been serving a life sentence for murder.

July 16, 1931 State troopers and New York City police detectives raid a farm in Coxsackie, New York, near the Acra estate of Legs Diamond. Eight men and six women, alleged members of the Coll gang, are captured, along with an arsenal of weapons. Later in the day, the troopers find a dismantled, bloodstained Buick in a Cairo garage. The Diamond and Coll gangs are reported to have joined forces against Schultz.

July 17, 1931 Lester Gillis (Baby Face Nelson) is convicted of armed robbery and enters the Illinois state prison at Joliet under a sentence of one year to life.

July 21, 1931 Pretty Boy Floyd escapes after killing Federal Prohibition Agent Curtis C. Burks and a spectator, M.P. Wilson, during a gun battle at the Noto-Lusco Flower Shop in Kansas City, Missouri.

July 28, 1931 Gunning for Schultz mobster Joey Rao outside the Helmar Social Club at 208 East 107th Street in Harlem, Vincent Coll acquires his nickname Mad Dog when he misses Rao but hits five children with shotgun fire, killing five-year-old Michael Vengalli.

August 4, 1931 Pretty Boy Floyd and George Birdwell rob the Citizens Bank at Shamrock, Oklahoma, of $400.

August 6, 1931 Gus Winkeler of St. Louis, now with Al Capone but still wanted as a bank robber and murder suspect, is injured in an auto accident near St. Joseph, Michigan. Taken to a Benton Harbor hospital, Winkeler is erroneously identified by witnesses as a participant in the million-dollar Lincoln bank robbery. Winkeler will be charged with the robbery but freed on $100,000 bond put up by Capone.

August 13, 1931 Wilbur Underhill murders policeman Merle Colver in Wichita, Kansas, but is wounded and captured by Wichita police the same day.

September 4, 1931 Underhill enters the Kansas state prison at Lansing under a life sentence for murder.

September 8, 1931 Pretty Boy Floyd and George Birdwell rob the Morris State Bank at Morris, Oklahoma, of $1,743.

September 10, 1931 Salvatore Maranzano, self-appointed "boss of bosses" of the Italian crime families in New York, is shot and stabbed to death in his Park Avenue office by killers from the Jewish "Bugs and Meyer" mob, employed by Lucky Luciano. Luciano will shortly organize a national commission consisting of representatives of major crime families.

September 11, 1931 Alvin Karpis pleads guilty to burglary at Henryetta, Oklahoma, and receives a four-year suspended sentence. He rejoins the Barkers at Thayer, Missouri.

September 16, 1931 Joseph Lebold, Joseph Sutker and Hymie Paul, members of the "Little Jewish Navy" gang, are shot to death by rival bootleggers in an apartment at 1740 Collingwood Avenue in Detroit. Three members of the notorious Purple Gang, Harry Keywell, Irving Milberg and Ray Bernstein, will be convicted of the Collingwood Massacre and sentenced to life in the state prison at Marquette, Michigan.

September 29, 1931 Pretty Boy Floyd and George Birdwell rob the First National Bank at Maud, Oklahoma, of $3,850.

October 2, 1931 Members of Mad Dog Coll's gang raid a Schultz "beer drop" at a 151st Street garage in the Bronx and murder Schultz employee Joe Mullins.

October 7, 1931 Alvin Karpis, Fred Barker and others rob the Peoples Bank at Mountain View, Missouri, at $14,000 in cash and securities.

October 14, 1931 Pretty Boy Floyd and George Birdwell rob the Bank of Earlsboro, at Earlsboro, Oklahoma, for the second time, taking $2,498.

October 17, 1931 Chicago gang leader Al Capone is convicted of income tax evasion and failure to file tax returns.

October 18, 1931 Matt Kolb, bootlegging colleague of Roger Touhy, is shot to death at his Morton Inn speakeasy in Morton Grove, Illinois. Suspects include Capone gangsters Frank Rio and Claude Maddox.

October 19, 1931 Edward Popke, alias Fats McCarthy, a member of the Coll mob, kills police detective Guido Passagno in a Manhattan gun battle.

October 20, 1931 The Holden-Keating gang robs the Kraft State Bank at Menomonie, Wisconsin, of $100,000. Two gang members, Charles Harmon and Frank Weber, are killed. Another man, Bob Newborne, will be wrongly charged with the crime, convicted and sentenced to life imprisonment.

October 24, 1931   Al Capone is sentenced to 11 years in prison and fined $50,000, plus court costs of $30,000.

November 2, 1931   First American National Bank messengers at Duluth, Minnesota, are robbed by Frank Nash, Thomas Holden and Francis Keating.

November 5, 1931   Pretty Boy Floyd and George Birdwell rob the First National Bank at Conowa, Oklahoma, of $2,500.

November 6, 1931   The Citizens State Bank at Strasburg, Ohio, is robbed of $50,000. Pretty Boy Floyd is mistakenly suspected.

November 8, 1931   Fred Barker murders Night Marshal Albert Manley Jackson at Pocahontas, Arkansas. Two local men, Lige Dame and Earl Decker, will be wrongly convicted and imprisoned for this crime.

November 11, 1931   Alexander Jamie, chief investigator for the Secret Six, an anti-crime group of anonymous Chicago businessmen representing the "action arm" of the Chicago Crime Commission and who are sometimes accused of vigilante tactics, tells the press that 135 men are working together in a nationwide network of bank robbers. Chicago mobster Gus Winkeler is named as a leader of the organization.

New York police raid the Hotel Franconia, arresting nine Jewish mobsters, including Louis "Lepke" Buchalter, Jacob "Gurrah" Shapiro and Benjamin "Bugsy" Siegel.

November 30, 1931   In New York, Frank Giordano and Dominic "Toughy" Odierno, members of the Coll gang, are convicted of murdering Joe Mullins, a Dutch Schultz henchman, and sentenced to death.

December 10, 1931   Rudolph "Fats" Duringer is executed in the electric chair at New York's Sing Sing Prison.

December 11, 1931   Several federal prisoners, including former members of the Al Spencer gang, escape from Leavenworth, using guns and dynamite smuggled to them by Frank Nash. William "Boxcar" Green, Grover Durrill and George "Whitey" Curtis are soon trapped at the nearby farm of E.C. Salisbury and commit suicide to avoid capture. Tom Underwood, Charles Berta and Stanley Brown are recaptured the same day.

December 12, 1931   Earl Thayer, last of the Leavenworth escapees, is recaptured.

December 16–28, 1931   Vincent "Mad Dog" Coll's trial for the Harlem "Baby Massacre" ends in acquittal after his lawyer, Samuel Liebowitz, proves that the state's star witness, George Brecht, gave perjured testimony.

December 17, 1931   Found innocent after a kidnapping trial, gangster Legs Diamond is shot to death by unknown killers in a rooming house at 67 Dove Street in Albany, New York.

December 18, 1931   Store is robbed at West Plains, Missouri, by Fred Barker and either Alvin Karpis or Bill "Lapland Willie" Weaver.

December 19, 1931   Sheriff C. Roy Kelly is murdered at West Plains by Barker and either Karpis or Weaver. Authorities offer a reward of $1,200 for information leading to the arrest of Alvin Karpis, Fred Barker, A.W. Dunlop and "Old Lady Arrie Barker, mother of Fred Barker." The suspects are erroneously described in the reward posters as members of the "Kimes-Inman Gang" (see page 146). This appears to be the first official notice taken of "Ma" Barker, who otherwise escaped attention until she is killed with Fred in a Florida gun battle some three years later and instantly transformed by FBI publicists into the archcriminal leader of the gang. The Barker-Karpis group flees to St. Paul.

December 27, 1931   Escapee Marvin "Buck" Barrow returns to the Texas state prison and surrenders to finish his sentence.

December 29, 1931   Six bandits, one armed with a machine gun, abduct the town constable and several citizens and ransack a drugstore, hardware store and the store-owners' homes in an early morning raid in Pine River, Minnesota. Possibly an early Barker-Karpis raid.

1932

January 2, 1932   Harry and Jennings Young, minor criminals, are surrounded at their mother's farm near Springfield, Missouri, and escape after a gun battle in which six law officers are slain. A surviving officer identifies Fred Barker as an accomplice of the Youngs. A third brother, Paul Young, and Pretty Boy Floyd are also wanted for the massacre, though all but Harry and Jennings Young will be later exonerated.

January 5, 1932   Harry and Jennings Young allegedly shoot one another to avoid capture, at the end of a gun battle with police at a Walker Avenue bungalow in Houston, Texas.

In a night raid on Cambridge, Minnesota, Alvin Karpis, Fred Barker and others kidnap Night Marshal Frank Whitney and garage attendant Mark Dunning, and ransack the town, looting at least four stores of about $3,000 in merchandise and cash. Authorities note similarity to December 29 raid on Pine River, Minnesota.

The amount of $583,000 in bonds, stolen in the $2 million bank robbery of September 17, 1930, are turned over to officials of the Lincoln National Bank & Trust Company by Capone gangster Gus Winkeler after negotiations with the Chicago Crime Commission's "Secret Six," the Commission's unofficial action arm. Robbery charges against Winkeler, who was not involved but knew the robbers, are dropped.

January 14, 1932   Pretty Boy Floyd, George Birdwell and an unidentified man rob the Castle State Bank at Castle, Oklahoma, of $2,600. The same day, three other men rob the First National Bank at Paden, Oklahoma, of $2,500, but Floyd and Birdwell are blamed.

January 21, 1932   Francis "Two-Gun" Crowley is executed in the electric chair at Sing Sing.

January 22, 1932   Pretty Boy Floyd and accomplices rob the State Bank at Dover, Oklahoma, of $800.

January 27, 1932   Raymond Hamilton, in custody for car theft at McKinney, Texas, saws the bars of his cell and escapes.

January 27–28, 1932   Local manufacturer Howard Woolverton is kidnapped at South Bend, Indiana, by George "Machine Gun" Kelly and Eddie Doll (alias LaRue). He is released unharmed when unable to raise the $50,000 in ransom.

February 1, 1932   Patsy Del Greco and Fiori Basile, henchmen of Vincent "Mad Dog" Coll, are machine-gunned to death in a Bronx apartment, along with Mrs. Emily Torrizello. Another man and woman are wounded. Police attribute the killing to the Schultz mob.

February 2, 1932   Clyde Barrow is paroled from Texas state prison at Huntsville.

February 4, 1932 After two trials, Rose Ash and Beulah Baird, Floyd gang molls, are acquitted of complicity in the Elliston, Kentucky, bank robbery.

February 6, 1932 Five bandits, armed with a machine gun and rifles, fight an hourlong battle with residents of Waveland, Indiana, and flee after unsuccessfully attempting to blast the vault of the town bank.

The Pilot Point National Bank in Denton, Texas, is robbed, probably by Machine Gun Kelly, Albert Bates and others.

February 7, 1932 Pretty Boy Floyd and George Birdwell are spotted by police in a car on Admiral Street in Tulsa and escape after a gun battle. Officer W.E. Wilson is wounded.

February 8, 1932 Police Detective O.P. Carpenter is killed by bandits in the attempted robbery of the Mercantile Trust Company in Kansas City, Missouri. Pretty Boy Floyd is named as a suspect.

February 9, 1932 Mad Dog Coll is machine-gunned to death in a drugstore telephone booth at 314 West 23rd Street in Manhattan. Police will later attribute the murder to Leonard Scarnici and Anthony Fabrizzo, freelance hit-men attracted by the large bounties placed on Coll by Dutch Schultz and Owney Madden.

February 10, 1932 Floyd and Birdwell are again spotted by Tulsa police, near Fifth Street and Utica Avenue, but lose their pursuers after a running gun battle.

February 11, 1932 Pretty Boy Floyd and George Birdwell battle police from a house at 513 Young Street in Tulsa but again manage to escape. Floyd's wife and young son are taken into custody.

Kansas City criminal Victor Maddi is cap-

tured in Houston and charged with the Mercantile Trust robbery in Kansas City.

February 15, 1932 Baby Face Nelson, already serving time for robbery, receives an additional one to 20 years for robbing the bank at Wheaton, Illinois.

February 17, 1932 Baby Face Nelson acquires a pistol, slipped to him by a relative, possibly his mother, and escapes while en route by train to the Illinois state prison at Joliet.

March 1, 1932 Charles Augustus Lindbergh, Jr., infant son of the famed aviator, is kidnapped from his home in Hopewell, New Jersey, spurring national outcry against the growing epidemic of kidnappings. Federal agents assist in the investigation but reject offers of assistance from Al Capone, now in prison, who is convinced that the crime was not committed by any organized criminal gang.

March 5, 1932 Margaret Perry, alias Indian Rose Walker, and Marjorie Schwartz, a recent jailmate, are found shot to death in a burning car at Turtle Lake, Wisconsin. The women were killed by Bernard Phillips, bank robber and former policeman, on orders from St. Paul crime boss Harry Sawyer, who received the contract from a St. Paul banker. Margaret Perry was the mistress of Robert Leon Knapp, alias Denver Bobby Walker, yet another suspect in the 1922 Denver Mint robbery.

March 9, 1932 Adam "Eddie" Richetti, L.C. "Blackie" Smalley, W.A. Smalley and Fred Hamner attempt to rob the First National Bank at Mill Creek, Oklahoma. Hamner is killed and the Smalley brothers wounded and captured. Richetti is captured later in the day at Sulphur, Oklahoma, and removed to the state prison at McAlester to await trial.

With a son of his own, a personal loathing for such crimes, and a genuine admiration for Lindbergh, Capone believed that the kidnap-murder of the Lindbergh baby was not the work of any organized gang, and that his nationwide underworld network had a better chance of solving the crime than the authorities. *(Authors' collection)*

March 22, 1932 Clyde Barrow, Bonnie Parker and Ralph Fults steal a car at Mabank, Texas, and are pursued by police. Barrow escapes but Parker and Fults are arrested and held in the Kaufman, Texas, jail.

March 23, 1932 Pretty Boy Floyd and George Birdwell rob Meeker, Oklahoma, bank of $500.

March 25, 1932 Clyde Barrow and Raymond Hamilton rob the Sims Oil Company in Dallas.

March 29, 1932 Alvin Karpis, Fred Barker, Thomas Holden, Bernard Phillips and Lawrence DeVol rob the North American Branch of the Northwestern National Bank in Minneapolis of $266,500 in cash, coins and bonds. This is the first large-scale robbery by the Barker-Karpis gang.

April 6, 1932 Pretty Boy Floyd kills state investigator Erv Kelley near Bixby, Oklahoma, and escapes.

April 19, 1932 Chicago police arrest New York's Charles "Lucky" Luciano and Meyer Lansky with Capone's Rocco Fischetti and Paul "The Waiter" Ricca outside the Congress Hotel, confirming collaboration between the leading mobs in both cities.

April 20, 1932 Pretty Boy Floyd and George Birdwell capture deputies at a funeral parlor in Earlsboro, Oklahoma, in order to pay their last respects to Birdwell's recently deceased father.

April 21, 1932 Floyd and Birdwell rob the First State Bank at Stonewall, Oklahoma, of $600.

April 24, 1932 At Lufkin, Texas, Clyde Barrow and Frank Clause rob a Magnolia service station of $26 and a .38 caliber revolver, and kidnap manager K.R. Bivin. They then rob a Gulf service station of $9 and a revolver and kidnap manager Herman Miller. Both men are released unharmed.

April 25, 1932 Arthur W. Dunlop, Ma Barker's former lover, is found shot to death at Lake Frestead, near Webster, Wisconsin. Police theorize that he was murdered by Alvin Karpis and Fred Barker, as a suspected informer.

April 30, 1932 Clyde Barrow and Raymond Hamilton rob a jewelry store at Hillsboro, Texas, murdering the owner, John N. Bucher.

May 1932 The College Kidnappers, headed by Theodore "Handsome Jack" Klutas, kidnap Blue Island, Illinois, gambler James Hackett, releasing him after payment of $75,000 ransom.

June 7, 1932 Pretty Boy Floyd and George Birdwell escape a police trap near Ada, Oklahoma. Police theorize the outlaws were wearing bulletproof vests, steel sleeves and steel skull-caps.

June 16, 1932 Capone labor racketeer George "Red" Barker is machine-gunned to death in Chicago. The Touhy gang is suspected.

June 17, 1932 The Barker-Karpis gang robs the Citizens National Bank at Fort Scott, Kansas, of $47,000. Frank Sawyer, Jim Clark and Ed Davis, escaped convicts traveling in a stolen car, are arrested the same day at Rich Hill, Missouri, and wrongly charged with the robbery. All three will be convicted.

June 22, 1932 The "Lindbergh Law" is passed, making it a federal crime to transport a kidnapped person across state lines for purpose of ransom.

June 24, 1932 Clyde Barrow and Raymond Hamilton steal 400 money orders from a post office in Port Sullivan, Texas.

June 27, 1932 Bonnie Parker is released from the Kaufman, Texas, jail.

June 29, 1932 Sadie "Mother" Ash, Kansas City underworld character whose sons were murdered by Pretty Boy Floyd and Bill Miller, dies at her home on Holmes Street.

June 30, 1932 Haskell Bohn, son of a refrigerator manufacturer, is kidnapped from his St. Paul home by the Verne Sankey gang, who leave a note demanding $35,000 in ransom. Bohn is released several days later, when the kidnappers settle for only $12,000.

July 1, 1932 The U.S. Justice Department's Bureau of Investigation, headed by J. Edgar Hoover since 1924, officially upgraded to the U.S. Bureau of Investigation, though its jurisdiction is still limited to a few federal crimes, such as interstate transportation of stolen cars, of women "for immoral purposes," and now interstate kidnapping.

Dominic Odierno and Frank Giordano, former members of the Coll mob convicted of murder, are executed at Sing Sing.

July 7, 1932 Thomas Holden, Francis Keating and Harvey Bailey, members of the Barker-Karpis gang, are arrested at the Old Mission Golf Course in Kansas City, Missouri, by agents of the U.S. Bureau of Investigation and Kansas City detectives. Holden and Keating, escaped federal prisoners, will be returned to Leavenworth. Bailey is charged with the Fort Scott bank robbery. Another gang member, Bernard Phillips, an ex-policeman, avoids capture and is later suspected of betraying Holden, Keating and Bailey. Phillips will later disappear, reportedly murdered in New York by Frank Nash and Verne Miller.

July 11, 1932 Edward Popke, alias Fats McCarthy, former henchman of Mad Dog Coll

but a suspect in the murder of both Coll and Legs Diamond, is killed by New York State troopers in a hideout near Albany.

July 16, 1932 In Palestine, Texas, bookkeeper Roy Evans is kidnapped from his office at the Palestine Ice Company, beaten and robbed of $989 by two men he will later identify as Clyde Barrow and Raymond Hamilton.

July 23, 1932 Convicted bank robber Robert "Big Bob" Brady escapes from the McAlester, Oklahoma, state prison.

July 25, 1932 The Barker-Karpis gang robs the Cloud County Bank at Concordia, Kansas, of $250,000 in bonds and cash.

July 27, 1932 Clyde Barrow and Raymond Hamilton rob the First State Bank at Willis, Texas, of $3,000.

July 29, 1932 Clyde Barrow and Raymond Hamilton rob the interurban railroad station at Grand Prairie, Texas.

July 31, 1932 Suspected counterfeiter Robert Sanford found shot to death with his wife in a New York apartment is identified through fingerprints as Bob "Gimpy" Newberry (no relation to Chicago mobster Ted Newberry), a.k.a. Carey or Conroy, another Capone gangster wanted as a suspect in both the St. Valentine's Day Massacre and the Lindbergh kidnapping. "Sanford" allegedly killed his wife and himself in a murder-suicide.

The Ponder, Texas, bank is robbed, probably by Machine Gun Kelly, Eddie Bentz and Albert Bates. Local legend will later attribute the robbery to the Barrow gang.

August 1, 1932 Clyde Barrow and Raymond Hamilton rob the Neuhoff Packing Company in Dallas of several hundred dollars and some diamond rings.

August 3, 1932   Former Tulsa policeman H.W. Nave claims to have been robbed of his car and clothing near Blackwell, Oklahoma, by Pretty Boy Floyd and George Birdwell. Nave will be arrested for fraud when it is discovered he has sold his mortgaged automobile to a used-car dealer in Oklahoma City.

August 5, 1932   Clyde Barrow and Raymond Hamilton murder Deputy Eugene Moore and wound Sheriff C.G. Maxwell outside a dance hall at Stringtown, Oklahoma.

August 8, 1932   Three men rob the Citizens Security Bank at Bixby, Oklahoma, of $1,000. One is identified as Fred Barker, now reported to be associating with Pretty Boy Floyd.

August 14, 1932   Convicted bank robber Aussie Elliott escapes from McAlester, Oklahoma, state prison.

  Clyde Barrow, Bonnie Parker and Raymond Hamilton kidnap Deputy Sheriff Joe Johns near Carlsbad, New Mexico, later releasing him unharmed at San Antonio.

August 17, 1932   Harvey Bailey enters the Kansas state prison at Lansing under a 10-to-50-year sentence for a bank holdup. This is his first imprisonment in 10 years as an armed robber.

August 18, 1932   J. Earl Smith, attorney supposedly hired by the Barker-Karpis gang to defend Harvey Bailey, is found shot to death at the Indian Hills Country Club near Tulsa. Suspects include Fred Barker, Alvin Karpis and Harry Campbell.

  The Second National Bank of Beloit, Wisconsin, is robbed, possibly by the Barker-Karpis gang.

August 25, 1932   Adam Richetti, awaiting trial for bank robbery, is released from the Okla-homa state prison on $15,000 bond, and escapes.

August 30, 1932   Clyde Barrow, Bonnie Parker and Raymond Hamilton shoot their way out of a police trap near Wharton, Texas, wounding one officer.

September 10, 1932   After serving 10 years of a life sentence for murder, Arthur "Dock" Barker, son of Ma Barker, is released from the Oklahoma state prison at McAlester on condition he leave the state. Allegedly, the parole was obtained through bribery of state officials by friends of the Barker-Karpis gang. Similar efforts fail to obtain a parole for Lloyd "Red" Barker, serving 25 years in Leavenworth for mail robbery.

September 21, 1932   Machine Gun Kelly, Albert Bates, Eddie Bentz and others rob the First Trust and Savings Bank at Colfax, Washington, of $77,000 in cash and bonds.

September 23, 1932   The Barker-Karpis gang robs the State Bank and Trust Company at Redwood Falls, Minnesota, of $35,000. Roofing nails dumped on the highway flatten the tires of a pursuing sheriff's car and the gang escapes, despite pursuit also by an airplane. Another gang will be wrongly convicted of this robbery.

September 28, 1932   Claude Chambers of Sapulpa, Oklahoma, a witness in Dock Barker's 1921 murder trial, reports a telephoned death threat from Barker and appeals for police protection. Chambers will later report other threats from Fred Barker and Pretty Boy Floyd.

September 29, 1932   The Eddie Bentz gang robs the Holland State Bank at Holland, Michigan.

September 30, 1932 Sheriff George Cheek sets up an ambush after receiving a tip that Pretty Boy Floyd plans to visit his brother-in-law in Sallisaw, Oklahoma. Floyd escapes.

October 3, 1932 Two fleeing suspects are shot by Deputy Elmer Hutchinson near Enid, Oklahoma. One, never identified, is killed instantly. The other, at first believed to be Floyd, gives his name as Tom Goggin before dying in the Enid Hospital.

October 8, 1932 Raymond Hamilton robs the State Bank at Cedar Hills, Texas, of $1,401, with an accomplice suspected to be Clyde Barrow.

October 11, 1932 Clyde Barrow and Bonnie Parker murder Howard Hall during a grocery store holdup in Sherman, Texas.

November 1, 1932 Pretty Boy Floyd, George Birdwell and Aussie Elliott rob the State Bank at Sallisaw, Oklahoma, of $2,530.

November 3, 1932 Volney Davis, convicted with Dock Barker of a 1921 murder in Tulsa, is granted a two-year leave of absence from the Oklahoma state prison and joins the Barker-Karpis gang in St. Paul.

November 7, 1932 Ford Bradshaw, Newton Clayton and Jim Benge rob the American State Bank at Henryetta, Oklahoma, of $11,252. The robbery is blamed on Pretty Boy Floyd, George Birdwell and Aussie Elliott.

Four unidentified machine gunners rob the State National Bank at Marlow, Oklahoma, of $5,500.

November 9, 1932 Raymond Hamilton and Gene O'Dare rob the Carmine State Bank at LaGrange, Texas, of $1,400.

While meeting with associates in the Hard Tack Social Club at 547 Grand Avenue in New York, Benjamin "Bugsy" Siegel is injured when a bomb is dropped down the chimney.

November 20, 1932 Freelance hitman Tony Fabrizzo is shot to death in New York, allegedly in retribution for the bombing attempt on Bugsy Siegel. Fabrizzo and Leonard Scarnici will later be accused of killing Vincent "Mad Dog" Coll.

November 23, 1932 George Birdwell, Charles Glass and C.C. Patterson attempt to rob the Farmers and Merchants Bank at Boley, Oklahoma. Birdwell, Glass and bank president D.J. Turner are killed in the resulting gun battle, and Patterson is wounded and captured.

November 25, 1932 Raymond Hamilton, Gene O'Dare and Les Stewart rob the State Bank at Cedar Hill, Texas, of $1,800.

November 30, 1932 Machine Gun Kelly, Albert Bates and Eddie Doll rob the Citizens State Bank at Tupelo, Mississippi, of $38,000. Numerous witnesses wrongly identify Pretty Boy Floyd as one of the robbers.

Clyde Barrow, Hollis Hale and Frank Hardy rob the Oronogo Bank at Oronogo, Missouri, of $115.

December 5, 1932 Raymond Hamilton and Gene O'Dare are captured in Bay City, Michigan, and extradited to Texas. Hamilton will be convicted of murder and several robberies and sentenced to 263 years; O'Dare will be convicted of armed robbery and sentenced to 50 years.

December 6, 1932 In a Chicago Loop mail robbery, five bandits armed with pistols and shotguns seize sacks containing $250,000 in bonds and cash.

December 12, 1932 Bank robber Willie "The Actor" Sutton escapes from Sing Sing.

December 13, 1932 Edna "The Kissing Bandit" Murray, girlfriend of Barker-Karpis outlaw Volney Davis, escapes from the women's state prison at Jefferson City, Missouri, where she has been serving a 25-year sentence for armed robbery. It is her third prison break. Irene McCann also escapes.

December 16, 1932 The Barker-Karpis gang robs the Third Northwestern Bank in Minneapolis of $22,000 in cash and $92,000 in bonds, killing two policemen and one bystander.

December 19, 1932 A Chicago police detail, headed by Sergeants Harry Lang and Harry Miller, raids a Capone Syndicate office at 221 North LaSalle Street. Mob boss Frank Nitti is shot, allegedly while resisting arrest, by Sergeant Lang, Nitti survives. Allegations will be made that Chicago Mayor Anton Cermak and former Bugs Moran mobster Ted Newberry plotted to kill Nitti, and that Mayor Cermak also urged Des Plaines bootlegger Roger Touhy to make war on the Capone mob with the assistance of the police department.

December 20, 1932 Big Bob Brady, notorious bank robber and prison escapee, is captured by police at Des Moines, Iowa. He will be later sent to the state prison at Lansing, Kansas, on a life sentence as an habitual criminal.

December 21, 1932 Barker-Karpis gang member Lawrence DeVol is captured in St. Paul. He will be convicted of murder and bank robbery and sentenced to life imprisonment in the state prison at Stillwater, Minnesota, but later transferred to the St. Peter Hospital for the Criminally Insane.

December 25, 1932 Clyde Barrow kills Doyle Johnson during an attempted car theft in Temple, Texas.

December 31, 1932 Odell Chambless, Les Stewart and others, probably Clyde Barrow and Bonnie Parker, rob the Home Bank in Grapevine, Texas, of $2,800.

1933

January 3, 1933 Terrible Tommy Touhy, John "Killer" Schmidt, Gustave "Gloomy Gus" Schafer and others escape following a $74,714 mail robbery at the Minneapolis railroad station.

January 5, 1933 Three men rob the First National Bank at Cleveland, Texas, of $1,200. Pretty Boy Floyd is suspected.

January 6, 1933 Clyde Barrow, Bonnie Parker and W.D. Jones escape a police trap at West Dallas, Texas, home of Lillie McBride (Raymond Hamilton's sister), killing Tarrant County Deputy Malcom Davis.

January 7, 1933 Chicago gangster Ted Newberry is found shot to death near Bailey Town, Indiana.

January 11, 1933 Three men rob Bank of Ash Grove at Ash Grove, Missouri, of $3,000. Pretty Boy Floyd is suspected.

January 18, 1933 Barrow gang associate Odell Chambless, wanted for bank robbery and murder, surrenders to Dallas police. He will be cleared of the murder charge.

January 26, 1933 Highway Patrolman Thomas Persell is kidnapped by Clyde Barrow, Bonnie Parker and W.D. Jones near Springfield, Missouri. He is released unharmed at Poundstone Corner, Missouri.

January 28, 1933 Earl Doyle, Eddie Green, Thomas "Buck" Woulfe and "Dago" Howard Lansdon rob Mrs. Dorothy Jolly, messenger for the National Bank and Trust Company at North

Kansas City, Missouri, of $14,500, wounding Marshal Edgar Nall. Buck Woulfe is also wounded. Near Holt, Missouri, the bandits battle a civilian posse, then steal a car from posse members and flee to Iowa.

January 29, 1933   The North Kansas City bandits steal license plates and two more cars and kidnap policemen John Neuman and Bert Conrey at Knoxville, Iowa, fleeing back to Missouri. The policemen are released unharmed west of Unionville, Missouri.

February 2, 1933   Thomas "Buck" Woulfe, wounded in the North Kansas City robbery on January 28, is captured at the Southeastern Kansas Hospital at Coffeeville, Kansas. Woulfe is transferred to the Clay County Jail at Liberty, Missouri.

February 9, 1933   John "Killer" Schmidt, Gloomy Gus Schafer and others rob a U.S. mail truck of $233,411 at Sacramento, California.

February 12, 1933   Denver millionaire Charles Boettcher II is kidnapped by the Verne Sankey gang and transported to Sankey's ranch near Chamberlain, South Dakota. Charles Boettcher I agrees to pay a $60,000 ransom but not until his son is released.

February 15, 1933   Chicago Mayor Anton Cermak is fatally shot while riding with president-elect Franklin Delano Roosevelt through Miami's Bayfront Park. The assassin, Giuseppe Zangara, claims to be an anarchist attempting to kill Roosevelt, but there has been unconvincing speculation that Cermak was the intended target, and that Zangara, suffering health and possibly mental problems, was hired by the Capone Syndicate.

February 20, 1933   Clyde Barrow, W.D. Jones and Monroe Routon rob Shiro, Texas, bank.

February 24, 1933   Thomas "Buck" Woulfe, captured North Kansas City bank robber, is moved from the Clay County Jail to St. Luke's Hospital in Kansas City, Missouri, suffering from a badly infected groin wound that will prove fatal. He is returned to the Clay County Jail the following day.

March 2, 1933   Charles Boettcher II is released unharmed, and Verne Sankey and Gordon Alcorn collect a $60,000 ransom in Denver, as promised by the victim's father.

March 9, 1933   In a one-day trial in Florida, Giuseppe Zangara is convicted of murdering Mayor Cermak.

March 20, 1933   Zangara is executed.

March 22, 1933   Buck Barrow is released from the Texas state prison at Huntsville, and with his wife, Blanche, joins Clyde Barrow, Bonnie Parker and W.D. Jones in Ft. Smith, Arkansas.

April 4, 1933   The Barker-Karpis gang robs the First National Bank at Fairbury, Nebraska, of $151,350. Gang member Earl Christman is mortally wounded and later secretly buried by the gang in a dry creek bed somewhere near Kansas City.

April 11, 1933   Bank robber Thomas "Buck" Woulfe, suffering from his infected groin wound, dies after surgery in the Clay County Jail infirmary at Liberty, Missouri.

April 12, 1933   Nineteen-year-old Jerome Factor is apparently kidnapped by gangsters outside a Lunt Street apartment building in Chicago, where he lives with his mother. Jerome's father is John "Jake the Barber" Factor, a Capone mob associate and international confidence man, wanted in England for a $7 million stock swindle. Jake Factor turns to the Capone mob for help.

At the Carteret Hotel in Elizabeth, New Jersey, Big Maxey Greenberg and Mandel Hassell, lieutenants of New York's largest bootlegger, Irving Wexler, alias Waxey Gordon, are shot to death by rival gangsters. Gordon, who is under indictment for income tax evasion, escapes death by leaping out the window of an adjoining room. Police attribute the killings to the Dutch Schultz mob.

April 13, 1933   The Barrow gang kills two policemen in escaping from a rented house at 3347 Oakridge Drive in Joplin, Missouri.

April 15, 1933   Chicago police first learn of Jerome Factor's disappearance. Jake Factor releases for publication a letter purported to have come from his son's abductors, demanding payment of $50,000 for Jerome's return.

April 19, 1933   The Chicago Association of Commerce, sponsors of the Chicago Crime Commission, disbands the Secret Six anticrime group, which has been accused of vigilantism for its increasing use of extralegal and sometimes illegal practices.

April 21, 1933   Jerome Factor is unexpectedly released by his kidnappers, who put him out of a car on West Devon Avenue in Chicago. According to his father, no ransom has been paid.

April 27, 1933   H.D. Darby and Sophia Stone are taken hostage and terrorized by the Barrow gang at Ruston, Louisiana, but later are released unharmed at Magnolia, Arkansas.

April 28, 1933   Killer Schmidt, Gloomy Gus Schafer and others rob a U.S. mail car at Salt Lake City, Utah, of $15,500.

The Barrow gang robs a gas station at Broken Bow, Oklahoma, stealing only a few dollars but brutally beating the attendant.

May 1933   Union officials Fred Sass and Morris Goldberg, reputed Capone gangsters, are apparently kidnapped in Chicago. The Touhy gang is suspected.

In the Chicago suburb of Blue Island, gambler James Hackett is kidnapped for the second time by the Handsome Jack Klutas gang and released after payment of $1,500 in ransom.

May 10, 1933   John Herbert Dillinger, who has served nine yeas in Indiana for attempted robbery, is paroled under reformatory supervision by Governor Paul V. McNutt. Dillinger's actual release from the Indiana state prison at Michigan City occurs on May 22.

May 12, 1933   Two women bystanders are wounded by machine-gun fire in an attempted bank robbery at Lucerne, Indiana; the Barrow gang is suspected.

A Paragon, Indiana, bank is robbed. Many will later attribute this crime to John Dillinger, who in fact was still in prison at the time.

May 16, 1933   Buck Barrow is identified as the robber of a filling station in Fort Dodge, Iowa.

May 19, 1933   The Barrow gang suspected of robbing the First State Bank at Okabena, Minnesota, taking $2,500.

May 20, 1933   Convicted train robber Homer Van Meter, a prison friend of John Dillinger, is paroled from the Indiana state prison.

The U.S. Commissioner at Dallas, Texas, files a federal complaint against Clyde Barrow and Bonnie Parker, charging them with interstate transportation of a stolen car. The Barrow gang are now federal fugitives under the Dyer Act.

May 21, 1933   U.S. Marshals arrest Waxey Gordon at a hunting lodge in White Plains, New York.

May 22, 1933   John Dillinger leaves Indiana state prison and arrives at his home in Mooresville, Indiana, resentful that the delay in his release has caused him to miss being with his dying stepmother.

May 27–28, 1933   Mary McElroy, daughter of City Manager Henry McElroy, is kidnapped from her home in Kansas City, Missouri, by a gang who demand $60,000 in ransom. They settle for half that amount and release Mary unharmed.

May 29, 1933   One policeman is killed and another wounded in a $2,000 bank robbery at Rensselaer, New York. The crime is erroneously attributed to Pretty Boy Floyd. Later, Leonard Scarnici, freelance New York hitman, will confess to this murder and 13 others, including that of Mad Dog Coll, and will be convicted and executed.

May 30, 1933   Eleven convicts, including Harvey Bailey, Wilbur Underhill and Big Bob Brady, stage a mass breakout from state prison at Lansing, Kansas, taking hostage the warden and two guards, who are later freed unharmed. The U.S. Bureau of Investigation suspects that the smuggled guns used in the escape were supplied by Bailey's friend Frank Nash.

June 2, 1933   Walter McGee is captured in Amarillo, Texas, and Clarence Click is captured in Kansas City. McGee, his brother George, Clarence Click and, later, Clarence Stevens, will be convicted under Missouri state law of kidnapping Mary McElroy. McGee will be sentenced to death but will die before the sentence can be carried out. The others will receive long terms in the state prison at Jefferson City.

June 4, 1933   Frank Sawyer, one of the Bailey-Underhill escape party, is recaptured near Chickasha, Oklahoma.

John Dillinger, William Shaw and Noble Claycomb rob an Indianapolis supermarket of $100.

June 10, 1933   John Dillinger and two other men rob the National Bank at New Carlisle, Ohio, of $10,600. Later in the day, with William Shaw and Paul "Lefty" Parker, Dillinger robs Haag's Drugstore and a supermarket in Indianapolis.

The Barrow gang wreck their car near Wellington, Texas, and Bonnie Parker is badly burned. The gang take a farm family hostage, accidentally shoot the hand off a woman, and later escape by kidnapping two law officers, who are released at Erick, Oklahoma.

Two more of the Kansas escapees, Cliff Dopson and Billie Woods, are recaptured near Grand Junction, Texas.

June 12, 1933   Three men rob the State Bank of Bussey at Bussey, Iowa, of $8,126. One bandit, Tony Bonacino, wanted for a 1931 Kansas City bank robbery, is slain by a posse five miles west of Bussey, near Marysville, Iowa. Two possemen, Emmet Godfrey of Marysville and Pudd Ballard of Pershing, are wounded. The other two robbers, believed to be Italians, kidnap a coal mine operator about two miles south of Bussey and force him to drive them to the outskirts of Kansas City. Iowa's new police radio network is used for the first time to broadcast descriptions of the Bussey bank robbers.

June 14, 1933   The Farmers and Merchants Bank at Mexico, Missouri, is robbed of $1,628 by two men believed to be Pretty Boy Floyd and Adam Richetti. On same day Sheriff Roger Wilson and highway patrolman Ben Booth are killed near Columbia, Missouri. The double murder will be wrongly attributed to Floyd and Richetti; Barrow gang also wrongly suspected.

June 15–18, 1933   St. Paul brewer William A. Hamm, Jr. is kidnapped by the Barker-Karpis gang and held for $100,000 ransom at the Bensenville, Illinois, home of local postmaster Edmund Bartholmey. He is released unharmed upon payment. Police initially suspect Verne Sankey, the kidnapper of Haskell Bohn and Charles Boettcher II.

June 16, 1933   Pretty Boy Floyd and Adam Richetti kidnap Sheriff William Killingsworth at Bolivar, Missouri. They abandon his car near Clinton, Missouri, and steal another one driven by Walter Griffith, who is also taken hostage. Both men are released that night at Lee's Summit, near Kansas City.

At Hot Springs, Arkansas, agents of the U.S. Bureau of Investigation, accompanied by Chief of Police Orrin "Otto" Reed of McAlester, Oklahoma, arrest notorious bank robber and Leavenworth escapee Frank Nash.

The Bailey-Underhill gang robs a bank at Black Rock, Arkansas.

June 17, 1933   At the Union Station, in Kansas City, Missouri, criminals armed with machine guns attempt to free Frank Nash from federal custody. Special Agent Raymond J. Caffrey, of the U.S. Bureau of Investigation, Chief Orrin Reed, of McAlester, Oklahoma, and Kansas City police detectives William J. Grooms and Frank Hermanson are killed, as is Nash himself. The Bureau of Investigation at first blames the mass murder, known as the Kansas City Massacre, on the Bailey-Underhill gang, but later attributes it to Verne Miller, Adam Richetti and Pretty Boy Floyd, despite recent evidence that the battle was started by a federal agent. Richetti will be captured, tried and executed still protesting his innocence—a claim later supported by others who said Floyd reluctantly took his place because he was too hungover from a night of drinking to participate.

June 21, 1933   On Wheeler Avenue in the Bronx, Lottie Kreisberger Coll and accomplices Joseph Ventre and Alfred Guarino shoot at loanshark Izzy Moroh in an attempted holdup. Moroh escapes but a young woman named Millie Schwartz is fatally wounded by a stray bullet. Lottie Coll is the widow of Vincent "Mad Dog" Coll and is now wanted for several recent holdups.

June 22, 1933   Two men, suspected to be Clyde and Buck Barrow, rob the Commercial Bank in Alma, Arkansas, of $3,600.

June 23, 1933   The Barrow gang robs a Piggly Wiggly store in Fayetteville, Arkansas, and kills Marshal Henry Humphrey of Alma.

Lottie Coll, Joseph Ventre and Alfred Guarino are arrested by New York police at a West 43rd Street hotel.

June 24, 1933   John Dillinger and William Shaw attempt to rob Marshall Field's Thread Mill at Monticello, Indiana. Shaw loses his gun in a wrestling match with manager Fred Fisher, who chases him outside and is wounded in the leg by a richochet bullet fired to scare him by Dillinger who is waiting in the getaway car. After mutual recriminations, the two drive back to Indianapolis and rob a fruit market at 10th and Belfountain.

June 27, 1933   Lottie Coll and her accomplices are indicted for murder and robbery by a Bronx County grand jury. Authorities speculate Lottie has been trying to raise funds and recruit a gang to avenge the killing of her husband, Vincent.

KANSAS CITY MASSACRE

As the temperature rose steadily on the sunny Saturday morning of June 17, 1933, longtime bank bandit and prison escapee Frank Nash was being returned to Leavenworth by several police officers and federal agents after his recapture at Hot Springs, Arkansas. Nash and the others were climbing into two cars in the parking lot of Kansas City's Union Station when two men, possibly three, with submachine guns approached from different directions, one of them shouting "Up! Up! Up!" In the next minute or so, three officers, a federal agent and Nash himself were dead, and at least one or two other gunmen—including Verne Miller, a onetime sheriff turned fulltime outlaw—had escaped. Despite an intensive investigation and books recounting the battle in great and often conflicting detail, little more is known with any certainty about the Kansas City Massacre, which became the crime that launched J. Edgar Hoover's FBI. The Bureau (then the Division of Investigation) laboriously and selectively constructed its own account, which has been largely accepted as gospel. The gist of it is that when word of Nash's arrest reached his friend Miller, and their political sponsor John Lazia declined to put his own hoods at risk in a rescue attempt, Miller recruited Adam Richetti and Pretty Boy Floyd, who were passing through town and conveniently had camped at his house.

This is the official story. Recently uncovered in bits and pieces from thousands of pages of FBI documents by other researchers, but most thoroughly by Robert Unger in his recent book *Union Station Massacre*, is evidence that the FBI account is based more on speculation, perhaps even perjury (survivors could not initially identify Floyd or Richetti), to give the Bureau the excuse it needed to go after Floyd, the first bandit to make national news, killing him in what some accounts describe as a summary execution on Hoover's orders.

Miller's body was found a short time later outside Detroit, killed by fellow criminals never definitely identified and for reasons never definitely established, beyond the fact that he was a loose cannon who had managed to antagonize any number of hoods in a dozen cities. Floyd and Richetti, soon named as suspects in the Massacre, had gone into deep hiding around Buffalo, New York, and managed to elude both federal and state authorities for about a year and a half. Economic necessity eventually forced them to seek "work," possibly with Dillinger in what would prove to be his gang's last bank holdup at South Bend, Indiana, before he himself was betrayed and killed by federal agents on July 22, 1934.

Three months later Richetti and Floyd were spotted by Ohio authorities, who captured Richetti after a gunfight and then called in agents from Chicago. They stumbled onto a desperate Floyd literally by accident, after he had eaten a meal for which a farm family tried to refuse payment. Spotted hiding behind a corn crib, Floyd was wounded in the arm by a policeman's rifle fire as he fled across a field. A few minutes later, after admitting only his identity to Melvin Purvis, he was killed by another federal agent's .45 bullets fired into him as he lay on the ground.

Purvis left and called Hoover, rather than an ambulance, to report Floyd's death. Police ended up loading his body into the back seat of a car. Examined at a mortuary, Floyd's shoulders bore no scars from wounds he reportedly

James Montgomery Flagg's depiction of the Kansas City Massacre, which the *Literary Digest* called the "Machine Gun Challenge to the Nation," introduced the FBI to the American public and was blamed on Pretty Boy Floyd. Eyewitness accounts varied, and only recently have researchers learned that the battle probably was set off not by the rescue party intending to free outlaw Frank Nash but by a panicky federal agent sitting behind him, who apparently killed Nash as well as some fellow officers while trying to operate an unfamiliar shotgun. *(Authors' collection)*

had received in the Kansas City shooting. Worse for the FBI, the captured Nash as well as two officers evidently had been killed by a federal agent sitting behind Nash in the back seat of one of the two cars, and not by the attackers. The agent fumbled, trying desperately to work the action of an unfamiliar 16-gauge shotgun loaded with steel ball bearings, instead of the customary lead buckshot.

Underworld rumors nevertheless said one of the attackers was Floyd, who agreed to join Miller only because Richetti was too hungover from a night of drinking, and because they believed they could rescue Nash without a shot, not reckoning on the panicky G-man with the quirky Model 1897 shotgun, who may have set off the battle inadvertently and done most of the killing himself with shots fired from inside the car.

Two other underworld stories circulated, but without much foundation. One was that Miller did not lead the mission to free Nash but to silence him; the other was that Miller, angry that Nash made no effort to escape, shot him, too. Those stories were circulated second- and third-hand by puzzled underworld characters unaware that Nash may have been dead or dying from steel ball bearings in the back of his head, which are not discussed in the FBI accounts.

The Massacre survivors and several witnesses who originally could not identify the attackers became more certain with time, and Adam Richetti was executed in 1938 insisting to the end he was innocent. Legally that may have been true, but through no fault of his own.

June 29, 1933 John Dillinger and William Shaw rob a sandwich shop on East 28th Street in Indianapolis.

June 30, 1933 Alice Schiffer Diamond, widow of murdered gangster Legs Diamond, is found shot to death in the kitchen of her home at 1641 Ocean Avenue in Brooklyn. Alice reportedly had been claiming that she knew her husband's killers and also had been target shooting in her yard with a pistol.

June 30–July 1, 1933 Jake "The Barber" Factor, whose son was apparently kidnapped in April, is seized by a carload of gunmen outside The Dells roadhouse on Dempster Road, in a township northwest of Chicago, according to his bodyguards. The British consul and others suggest that the kidnapping is a hoax, designed to prevent Factor's extradition to England, where he faces a possible 24-year prison sentence for a massive stock fraud. Captain Daniel "Tubbo" Gilbert, chief investigator for the Cook County State's Attorney's office and secretly on the Capone mob's payroll, says the crime is real and blames Des Plaines gangster Roger Touhy. Touhy is a rival at the Capone Syndicate in bootlegging and labor racketeering and a brother of mail robber Terrible Tommy Touhy. Others attribute the abduction to the College Kidnappers, headed by Theodore "Handsome Jack" Klutas, who specialize in "snatching" underworld figures.

July 3, 1933 The Bailey-Underhill gang robs the First National Bank at Clinton, Oklahoma, of $11,000.

July 5, 1933 Wilbur Underhill robs a Canton, Kansas, bank.

July 6, 1933 Investigating the Kansas City Massacre, Sheriff Thomas Bash, accompanied by deputies and agents of the U.S. Bureau of Investigation, raids the Kansas City home of gangster Frank "Fritz" Mulloy and arrests James "Fur" Sammons. Sammons is a Capone mobster wanted in Chicago, Philadelphia and Baltimore for fur and payroll robberies. He will later receive a life sentence in Indiana as a habitual criminal.

July 8, 1933   The Barrow gang robs a National Guard armory in Enid, Oklahoma, stealing 46 Colt .45-caliber automatics.

July 9, 1933   Willie "The Actor" Sutton, Eddie Wilson and Joe Perlongo rob the Corn Exchange Bank at 100th Street and Broadway in New York of $23,838.

July 12, 1933   Jake Factor reappears in LaGrange, Illinois, and claims to have been released by his kidnappers after payment by his wife of $70,000 ransom.

July 14, 1933   Two of the Kansas state prison escapees, Kenneth Conn and Alva "Sonny" Payton, attempt to rob the Labette County State Bank at Altamont, Kansas. Conn is killed in a resulting gun battle and Payton, shot in the eyes and blinded, is captured.

July 15, 1933   John Dillinger, Harry Copeland and William Shaw rob the Bide-a-Wee tavern in Muncie, Indiana.

July 16, 1933   William Shaw, Paul "Lefty" Parker and Noble Claycomb are captured by police at their Muncie apartment. John Dillinger and Harry Copeland escape. Identified by Claycomb as Dan Dillinger, John finally makes news as "Desperate Dan."

July 17, 1933   John Dillinger and Harry Copeland rob the Commercial Bank in Daleville, Indiana, of $3,500.

July 18, 1933   The Barrow gang robs three gas stations in Fort Dodge, Iowa.

July 19, 1933   John Dillinger is suspected of robbing a Rockville, Indiana, bank.

The Barrow gang is surrounded by police at the Red Crown Cabin Camp, at Ferrelview, near Platte City, Missouri, but shoot their way out, wounding three men. Buck and Blanche Barrow are also wounded but escape with the others to Iowa.

Roger Touhy, Chicago union official Eddie "Chicken" McFadden and bodyguards Gloomy Gus Schafer and Wee Willie Sharkey wreck their car on a road near Elkhorn, Wisconsin. Police find several guns, including a pistol converted to fire fully automatic. (This pistol, and others like it, apparently came from San Antonio gunsmith H.S. Lebman, who also supplied such modified pistols and rifles to Pretty Boy Floyd and the Dillinger gang.) They are arrested and later turned over to Melvin Purvis of the U.S. Bureau of Investigation and Captain Gilbert of the Cook County State's Attorney's office, who charge the Touhy gang with the kidnappings of both William Hamm and Jake "The Barber" Factor.

July 22, 1933   Oklahoma City oilman Charles F. Urschel is kidnapped from the porch of his mansion by Machine Gun Kelly and Albert Bates. Urschel is transported to the Paradise, Texas, ranch of Kelly's stepfather-in-law, Robert "Boss" Shannon. A $200,000 ransom is demanded.

July 24, 1933   The Barrow gang is surrounded by a posse at Dexfield Park, north of Dexter, Iowa. Buck and Blanche Barrow are captured. Clyde Barrow, Bonnie Parker and W.D. Jones escape.

After being arraigned on a bank robbery

GET·DILLINGER!

$15,000 *Reward*

A PROCLAMATION

WHEREAS, One John Dillinger stands charged officially with numerous felonies including murder in several states and his banditry and depredation stamp him as an outlaw, a fugitive from justice and a vicious menace to life and property;

NOW, THEREFORE, We, Paul McNutt, Governor of Indiana; George White, Governor of Ohio; F. B. Olson, Governor of Minnesota; William A. Comstock, Governor of Michigan; and Henry Horner, Governor of Illinois, do hereby proclaim and offer a reward of Five Thousand Dollars ($5,000.00) to be paid to the person or persons who apprehend and deliver the said John Dillinger into the custody of any sheriff of any of the above-mentioned states or his duly authorized agent.

THIS IS IN ADDITION TO THE $10,000.00 OFFERED BY THE FEDERAL GOVERNMENT FOR THE ARREST OF JOHN DILLINGER.

HERE IS HIS FINGERPRINT CLASSIFICATION and DESCRIPTION. ——— FILE THIS FOR IDENTIFICATION PURPOSES.

John Dillinger, (w) age 30 yrs., 5-8½, 160½ lbs., gray eyes, med. chest, hair, med. comp., med. build. Dayton, O., P. D. No. 10587. O. S. B. No. 559-646.

F.P.C. (12)

	M	9	R	O	O	
	S	14	U	OO	8	
13	10	OO	O	O		
u	R	w	w	w		
5	11	15	I	8		
u	U	u	w	u		

FRONT VIEW

Be on the lookout for this desperado. He is heavily armed and usually is protected with bullet-proof vest. Take no unnecessary chances in getting this man. He is thoroughly prepared to shoot his way out of any situation.

GET HIM

DEAD

OR ALIVE

Notify any Sheriff or Chief of Police of Indiana, Ohio, Minnesota, Michigan, Illinois.

or THIS BUREAU

SIDE VIEW

ILLINOIS STATE BUREAU OF CRIMINAL IDENTIFICATION
AND INVESTIGATION
T. P. Sullivan, Supt.   Springfield, Illinois

With its own federal anti-crime laws stalled in Congress on the issue of state's rights, the Justice Department, and Hoover's Division of Investigation, nevertheless persuaded several Midwestern states to collaborate in the hunt for Dillinger and join the U.S. Government in offering $15,000 for his capture "dead or alive," although his only federal crime before March of 1934 was to transport a stolen car across state lines. *(Authors' collection)*

charge at the Chicago Criminal Courts Building, John Scheck breaks free of his guards and fatally shoots policeman John Sevick. Wounded by a bailiff, Scheck is recaptured and his revolver confiscated. Scheck will later claim the gun was smuggled to him in jail by Pretty Boy Floyd.

July 29, 1933   Buck Barrow dies of a head wound in a Perry, Iowa, hospital.

July 30, 1933   E.E. Kirkpatrick, representing the Urschel family, delivers $200,000 to Machine Gun Kelly near the LaSalle Hotel in Kansas City, Missouri.

July 31, 1933   Charles Urschel is released unharmed at Norman, Oklahoma.

August 1933   Using wiretaps, federal agents overhear conversations between Jake "The Barber" Factor and two other men, who threaten to kidnap Factor again unless additional ransom of $50,000 is paid.

August 4, 1933   John Dillinger and Harry Copeland rob the First National Bank at Montpelier, Indiana, of $10,110.

An attractive blond woman and two male accomplices rob James Swock's shoe store at 4050 North Avenue in Chicago. Forty-five minutes later, the same trio rob Gustav Hoeh's haberdashery at 5948 West Division, killing Hoeh. One of the gunmen is also wounded. Newspapers dub the lady bandit "the Blonde Tigress."

August 5, 1933   Wounded gunman Leo Minneci, alias Joe Miller, surrenders to Chicago police in front of the Bell Telephone Company at Madison Street and Homan Boulevard. He confesses to the robberies of the previous day and identifies his accomplices as Eleanor Jarman and her lover, George Dale, alias Kennedy,

and blames the murder of Gustav Hoeh on Kennedy.

August 8, 1933   John Dillinger is suspected of a Gravel Switch, Kentucky, bank robbery.

August 9, 1933   The Bailey-Underhill gang robs the Peoples National Bank at Kingfisher, Oklahoma.

Eleanor Jarman, "the Blonde Tigress," and George Dale are arrested by Chicago police in an apartment at 6323 South Drexel Avenue. Witnesses identify them and Leo Minneci as the perpetrators of at least 37 Chicago robberies. They later confess to 48. Chicago police describe Eleanor Jarman as "the brains of the three" and "a beautiful but vicious animal" who cruelly slugged shopkeepers with a blackjack.

August 10, 1933   The scandal-ridden Prohibition Bureau is transferred from the Treasury Department to the Justice Department despite misgivings of J. Edgar Hoover, who as director of the renamed Division of Investigation seeks a way to popularly distinguish his clean-cut justice agents from the widely detested "revenoors."

The district attorney at Elkhorn, Wisconsin, files a complaint against Roger Touhy, Eddie McFadden, Gus Schafer and Willie Sharkey, charging them with unlawful possession of a machine gun for offensive and aggressive purposes.

August 12, 1933   Roger Touhy, Eddie McFadden, Gus Schafer and Willie Sharkey are indicted in St. Paul for the Hamm kidnapping in June. Though innocent of this crime, committed by the Barker-Karpis gang, Schafer and Sharkey are also wanted for mail and bank robberies.

At Paradise, Texas, police and agents of the Division of Investigation, accompanied by

Charles Urschel, raid the Paradise, Texas, ranch of Kathryn Kelly's stepfather, Robert "Boss" Shannon. The Kellys and Albert Bates have fled but Shannon, his wife, Ora, their son Armon and his wife, and bank robber Harvey Bailey are all arrested and charged with the Urschel kidnapping. Bailey, also wanted for the Kansas City Massacre, is innocent but possesses some of the ransom money, given to him by Machine Gun Kelly to repay a loan as well as the incriminating Thompson purchased by Kathryn for her husband, who had "left his gun at home." Albert Bates, Kelly's partner, is arrested in Denver for passing forged checks.

August 14, 1933   John Dillinger, Harry Copeland and Sam Goldstein rob the Citizens National Bank at Bluffton, Ohio, of $2,100.

Dillinger associates Fred Berman and Clifford "Whitey" Mohler are arrested by Indiana State Police officers at East Chicago.

August 15, 1933   Some 300 police and federal agents stake out Mannheim Road near Chicago to trap two men demanding $50,000 in ransom from Jake "The Barber" Factor. The pair, Basil "The Owl" Banghart and Charles "Ice Wagon" Connors, succeed in retrieving a package containing $500 in marked money and escape after a gun battle. Banghart and Connors deny they are members of the Touhy gang.

August 18, 1933   Eddie Bentz, Baby Face Nelson and others rob the Peoples Savings Bank at Grand Haven, Michigan, of $30,000. One gang member, Earl Doyle, is captured. John Dillinger is routinely suspected of participating in the robbery, but probably did not.

August 22, 1933   Dillinger gang member Sam Goldstein is arrested by Indiana State Police officers in Gary.

August 29, 1933   Pretty Boy Floyd and Adam Richetti are suspected of a $1,000 bank robbery at Galena, Missouri.

August 30, 1933   The Barker-Karpis gang robs Stockyards National Bank messengers of $33,000 at the South St. Paul, Minnesota, post office, killing one policeman and wounding another.

Eleanor "The Blonde Tigress" Jarman, George Dale and Leo Minneci are convicted of murder in Chicago. Dale is sentenced to death, and Jarman and Minneci to 199 years.

September 3, 1933   At Platte City, Missouri, Blanche Barrow is sentenced to 10 years in prison for assaulting police officers.

September 4, 1933   Harvey Bailey escapes from the Dallas County Jail. He is recaptured the same day at Ardmore, Oklahoma.

September 6, 1933   John Dillinger, Harry Copeland and Hilton Crouch (Crough) rob the State Bank of Massachusetts Avenue in Indianapolis of $24,800.

September 12, 1933   John Dillinger is suspected in a $24,000 bank holdup at Farrell, Pennsylvania.

September 21, 1933   Kansas authorities reveal that Peggy Landon, daughter of Governor Alfred Landon, has been placed under police protection when they heard she had been targeted by Oklahoma outlaws. The kidnapping supposedly will be an attempt to force the governor to grant executive clemency to the Harvey Bailey–Wilbur Underhill gang.

September 22, 1933   The Barker-Karpis gang, driving a bulletproofed car equipped with smoke-screen and oilslick devices, robs Federal Reserve Bank messengers on Jackson Boulevard in Chicago, killing Patrolman Miles A.

Cunningham. The crime is wrongly attributed to others, including Machine Gun Kelly, Verne Miller and Pretty Boy Floyd. The loot proves worthless, and the customized car, wrecked in the escape, is traced to 22nd Street auto dealer Joe Bergl whose business is next door to Ralph Capone's Cotton Club. Bergl turns out to be a partner of Gus Winkeler and a major supplier of specially equipped "gangster" cars.

John Dillinger is arrested by police at the Dayton apartment of his girlfriend, Mary Longaker (also Longacre).

Wilbur Underhill and others rob the Peoples National Bank in Stuttgart, Arkansas.

September 24, 1933   Chicago mobster Gus Winkeler is arrested and questioned in connection with the Jackson Boulevard robbery and murder. Police claim that Winkeler, Machine Gun Kelley, Verne Miller, Claude Maddox and James "Fur" Sammons are members of a nationwide robbery and kidnapping syndicate.

September 25, 1933   Clyde Barrow and Bonnie Parker rob a grocery store at McKinney, Texas, taking the grocer as hostage. He is released unharmed the same day.

September 26, 1933   Machine Gun Kelly and his wife, Kathryn, are arrested in Memphis by police and agents of the Division of Investigation.

Harry Pierpont, Charles Makley, John Hamilton, Russell Clark, Ed Shouse, Walter Dietrich, James "Oklahoma Jack" Clark, Joseph Fox, Joseph Burns and James Jenkins escape from the state prison at Michigan City, Indiana, using guns smuggled to them by John Dillinger prior to his arrest in Dayton.

September 28, 1933   Michigan City escapee James Clark is recaptured in Hammond, Indiana.

John Dillinger is transferred to the Allen County Jail at Lima, Ohio, charged with the Bluffton bank robbery.

September 30, 1933   Michigan City escapee James Jenkins is killed by vigilantes near Beanblossom, Indiana.

Harvey Bailey, Albert Bates and the Shannon family are found guilty of participating in the Urschel kidnapping. Minneapolis crime bosses Isidore "Kid Cann" Blumenfeld, Sam Kronick and Sam Kozberg are acquitted of passing the ransom money, but their lieutenants, Clifford Skelly and Edward "Barney" Berman, earn the unwanted distinction of being the first convicted under the new federal Lindbergh Law.

October 3, 1933   Harry Pierpont, Charles Makley, John Hamilton and Russell Clark rob the First National Bank at St. Marys, Ohio, of $14,000.

October 6, 1933   Big Bob Brady and Jim Clark, former members of the Bailey-Underhill gang, rob a Frederick, Oklahoma, bank of $5,000 but are captured the same day near Tucumcari, New Mexico.

Edgar Lebensberger, colleague of Chicago mobster Gus Winkeler and manager of Winkeler's 225 Club, dies of a gunshot wound in the bedroom of his home at 1253 Lake Shore Drive. Despite rumors he was murdered, his death is ruled a suicide.

October 7, 1933   Harvey Bailey, Albert Bates and Robert and Ora Shannon receive life sentences for the Urschel kidnapping. Armon Shannon receives 10 years probation. The money changers, Bermann and Skelly, are each sentenced to five years.

Dallas County Deputy Thomas Manion and Grover C. Bevill are convicted of helping Harvey Bailey escape from the Dallas County Jail. Manion is sentenced to two years in

HOOVER'S "G-MEN"

J. Edgar Hoover's contempt for the Treasury Department's Prohibition Bureau was based both on his antagonism toward all potential rivals and on the fact that its agents were notoriously inept as well as corrupt. His appointment as acting director of the Justice Department's Bureau of Investigation in 1924 did not expand his authority to any great extent, but he had kept his pledge to depoliticize the Bureau, purge it of rotten apples, and impose a degree of discipline that made him both feared and respected. The election of President Roosevelt in 1932 might have cost him his job, for the man FDR had intended to appoint as the new U.S. attorney general had personal objections to Hoover and planned a housecleaning of his own. As Hoover's luck would have it, the prospective appointee died en route to the inauguration, and FDR had to quickly find a replacement. The man he chose was Homer Cummings, an obscure party loyalist but nevertheless an experienced state prosecutor who shared most of Hoover's undeniably progressive ideas about crime control, including the belief that in the age of the automobile crime had become a nationwide problem requiring national solutions. This amounted to a complete reversal of the previous Republican administrations who might have recognized the ineffectuality of localized law enforcement, but feared that new federal criminal laws would sooner or later evolve into a national police force serving the federal government—an American secret police.

Aware of strong states'-rights opposition to federalized crime control, especially in the South, and anxious to make his agency look good, Hoover had to discourage Cummings's overzealous efforts to create a true "national police force," or an "American Scotland Yard," as a New Deal approach to lawlessness, which in 1933 seemed to be reaching epidemic proportions. With desperadoes like Dillinger, Pretty Boy Floyd and Machine Gun Kelly making national headlines (with a little help from the Justice Department), many Americans were advocating just the sort of federal police others greatly feared, so Cummings and Hoover came off as moderates proposing new laws that respected the authority of Congress to regulate only "interstate commerce," and by extension of that doctrine, only crimes interfering with it. This left a good deal of room to maneuver, but officially made most crime control the responsibility of local authorities.

Three problems remained to be resolved. Unaware of Hoover's personal agenda, the Roosevelt administration, gearing up for repeal, took Volstead Act enforcement out of the hands of the Treasury Department and gave it to Justice Department. This dismayed J. Edgar Hoover, who did not want his accountants and law trainees confused in the public mind with the Treasury agents. However, the master bureaucrat deftly sidestepped this threat by engineering his own appointment as director of a new Bureau of Investigation, which would allow him to segregate his Justice agents from the dry agents, keeping them in their respective divisions until the Prohibition amendment could be formally repealed.

This was how an obscure Eliot Ness and his so-called Untouchables ended up working for the Justice Department instead of the Treasury Department, but even more closely with Chicago's "Secret Six" crime fighters, harassing

Eliot Ness was among the Treasury Department Prohibition Agents transferred to the Justice Department over the misgivings of J. Edgar Hoover, who created a special Prohibition enforcement agency to keep his own agents a separate force. Ness and his select group of booze-busters did a commendable job of harassing Capone and other bootleggers to reduce their income from illegal breweries and distilleries, but he owed his notoriety to Oscar Fraley, who coauthored *The Untouchables* around the time of Ness's death. Ness's work was largely ignored by Hoover, technically his superior, and was carried out mostly under the auspices of the Chicago Crime Commission. *(Steve Nickel Collection)*

Capone from the rear while Big Al fought the 11-year tax-conviction sentence already obtained by the Internal Revenue Service. Ness's attacks on Capone breweries earned him little notoriety at the time, and he did not achieve fame until he and writer Oscar Fraley teamed up to give Ness a major role in destroying Capone, a considerable exaggeration. (Ness would later battle organized crime in Cleveland,

with a measure of success, but his failure to solve a series of mutilation murders combined with increasing personal problems to end his law-enforcement career. After his death in 1957, the year his book was published, his ashes remained in a small box in a family member's garage, ignored until a local historian learned of this some 40 years later. He arranged a proper burial ceremony for a man who had become something of an American icon, thanks to a popular if historically inaccurate movie and to never-ending reruns of the original *Untouchables* television series in which he was played by Robert Stack.)

A second problem confronting Hoover was the announcement by an overeager Cummings that the Justice Department would bring its federal muscle to bear on "racketeering," to which Hoover lent lip service while the issue was hot, but in full awareness that the rackets —from gambling to prostitution to union take-overs—were largely consensual crimes that defied traditional police solutions. Nor did the raft of new federal anti-crime statutes that Cummings rammed through Congress in the spring of 1934, at the height of the public-enemy era, give Hoover laws that would deal effectively with racketeering—to Hoover's considerable relief, since he persistently denied the existence of nationally organized crime (as well as to the relief of racketeers who had learned from the Capone example to maintain the lowest possible profile).

Hoover's token response was to create the Bureau's Top Hoodlum Program, which supposedly kept track of the more notorious mobsters for the benefit of local authorities, who probably did little with the information but still were technically responsible for crime control within their jurisdictions.

Another challenge Hoover faced was how to differentiate his men from federal operatives of other government agencies that were less fastidious about their men having the sterling qualities demanded by "the Director," as Hoover was usually called. This problem was largely solved by a freelance Kansas City writer named Courtney Ryley Cooper, whose first article captured the essence of the agency that Hoover was trying to fashion out of an assort-

Courtney Ryley Cooper *(Authors' collection)*

ment of well-educated but inexperienced agents whom local authorities tended to sneer at as "briefcase cops." Some early blunders had not enhanced their reputations as streetwise lawmen.

It was Cooper, a hack writer but a popular one, who combined the kind of purple prose approved by Hoover in describing the enemies of society with a genius for propaganda, and he was virtually drafted by Hoover as his coach in creating an agency whose image combined the best elements of the lone-wolf action detective

Americans expected in their fiction, who was also enlightened and understood the need for teamwork (so much for the lone wolf and personal glory), scientific methods of the modern crime lab, and a soldierly obedience to the country's chief crime-fighter, J. Edgar Hoover, director of what soon would be called the Federal Bureau of Investigation. Homer Cummings had made banner headlines by declaring the nation's first "war on crime" in 1933, but wars are fought by armies led by generals, not politicians, and Cummings soon found himself eclipsed by "general" Hoover whose frontline reports (ghostwritten by Cooper) began appearing in virtually every popular publication.

The formula worked like a charm, especially in combination with the catchy nickname "G-man," to the point where that term had come to mean only one thing to the general public—the FBI—as though that agency alone, under Hoover, invented modern crime control, hunted down and wiped out America's public enemies, set the standards for police professionalism, established the country's first state-of-the-art crime laboratory, served as the clearing house for national crime statistics and so forth.

How this occurred became a staple of FBI lore, and whether it had any basis in fact, or was a myth cooked up by Cooper, Hoover, Rex Collier (another Hoover favorite) or someone else, the invincible G-man instantly caught on—with the public and the entertainment industry, which had been accused of glorifying gangsters until the last scenes in the last reel required their spectacular and moralistic demise. Movie makers simply replaced gangsters with the new G-men, who at first didn't quite fit the Hoover stereotype as formulated by Cooper, but soon learned that FBI cooperation was contingent on getting the message straight.

According to Collier, writing in 1935, the term "G-man" was coined by Machine Gun Kelly who had been captured in an apartment in Memphis on September 26, 1935 (by coincidence, the same day that 10 men of the future Dillinger gang broke out of the Indiana state prison using guns smuggled to them by the recently paroled Dillinger). The FBI version of the Kelly capture has never varied to this day, and states that when confronted by Hoover's heavily armed squad the fugitive threw up his hands and shouted. "Don't shoot, G-men! Don't shoot!" Supposedly the agents had never heard themselves called G-men (although the

Melvin Purvis of the Chicago FBI office is complimented by U.S. Attorney General Homer Cummings, whose "war on crime" was already being waged by J. Edgar Hoover. *(Authors' collection)*

expression crops up in books dating back to the twenties in reference to government agents in general). Thus Kelly earned himself a small measure of immortality when this was reported to Hoover.

But this could be fiction, written by Collier a year after the fact. Local police described the arrest more prosaically: that a rattled and strung-out Kelly simply grinned sheepishly, dropped his gun and said, "Okay, boys, I've been waiting for you all night."

In the middle thirties Hoover and Cooper were the Siamese twins of publishing, both authoring books (written by Cooper), to which one or the other would provide the preface; as well as newspaper features and magazine articles by Cooper, by Hoover with Cooper or as told to Cooper. Then something went wrong, possibly something as minor as Cooper padding out an interminable series of FBI articles for *American* magazine with a couple of pieces done in collaboration with Narcotics Bureau Chief Harry Anslinger, a Hoover nemesis who blamed everything on the Mafia and nationally organized crime, which Hoover insisted did not exist. In any event, the writing team had a falling out in the late 1930s, and in 1940 Cooper hanged himself in a hotel room, driven to suicide, according to his widow, by some wrong done him by Hoover.

A similar fate supposedly overtook Melvin Purvis, the "ace" G-man whose fame threatened to overshadow Hoover at the height of the public-enemy era. Even with so many agents at the scene of Dillinger's shooting, the Bureau had a hard time sorting out events and, under constant pressure from reporters, finally released an "official" diagram of the ambush that put Sam Cowley close to the action and wrote Purvis out of it entirely. This did not escape the press, which put Purvis back in the picture, but not in the right place.

Meanwhile, Hoover sent Purvis on a series of meaningless missions until he resigned from the Bureau in frustration a year later. After that, Hoover always answered Purvis's letters in a manner both disarmingly cheerful and formal, instructing his staff always to tell Purvis he had been unexpectedly called out of town. Meanwhile, he kept track of Purvis, sabotaged his every effort to get back into law enforcement, private security work or even consulting, and had other writers make sarcastic references to former agents who found themselves obliged to endorse commercial products. In 1960, Purvis killed himself at his home in South Carolina —not with the pistol he supposedly carried the night Dillinger was killed, as the story is often told, but with the presentation .45 automatic given him by fellow agents at the time he resigned.

Despite a ruling of accidental death, the FBI and virtually every writer has treated it as a suicide. Recent research, however, indicates that the bullet was a tracer round he was trying to clear from the pistol after some youngsters had gotten into his gun collection.

Refusing even to acknowledge Purvis's death, Hoover later received a terse telegram from his widow: WE ARE HONORED THAT YOU IGNORED MELVIN'S DEATH. YOUR JEALOUSY HURT HIM VERY MUCH BUT UNTIL THE END I THINK HE LOVED YOU.

Leavenworth and fined $10,000. Bevil is sentenced to 14 months.

October 9, 1933   Gus Winkeler, former bank robber and Capone gunman, now a major force in the Chicago Syndicate, is shot to death by unknown killers outside the Charles H. Weber (beer) Distributing Company at 1414 Roscoe Street. Verne Miller is a suspect, for Winkeler had been providing information to federal authorities about him and other federal fugitives; but with Capone now in prison the hit probably was ordered by Frank Nitti to consolidate his position as the mob's new leader.

Wilbur Underhill and others rob the American National Bank at Baxter Springs, Kansas, of $3,000.

Two bandits, armed with a machine gun and a revolver, rob Second National Bank messengers at Warren, Ohio, of $68,000.

October 12, 1933   Harry Pierpont, Charles Makley, Russell Clark, John Hamilton, Ed Shouse and Harry Copeland raid the Lima, Ohio, jail, kill Sheriff Jesse Sarber, and free John Dillinger. This group comprises the first Dillinger gang. Lima authorities request assistance from the U.S. Department of Justice in identifying and apprehending the culprits.

George and Kathryn Kelly are convicted of the Urschel kidnapping and sentenced to life.

October 14, 1933   The Dillinger gang robs a police station in Auburn, Indiana, of machine guns, other weapons and bulletproof vests.

October 17, 1933   Will Casey and Cassey Coleman are convicted of harboring Machine Gun and Kathryn Kelly. Casey is sentenced to two years in a federal penitentiary, Coleman to a year and a day.

October 20, 1933   The Dillinger gang obtains more weapons by robbing the police station in Peru, Indiana.

October 21, 1933   John C. Tichenor and Langford Ramsey are convicted in Memphis of harboring the Kellys. Each is sentenced to two

and a half years in the federal penitentiary at Atlanta, Georgia.

October 22, 1933   Georgette Winkeler, widow of Gus Winkeler, attempts to gas herself to death in her apartment at 3300 Lake Shore Drive in Chicago but is saved by her friend Bernice (Bonnie) Burke, the wife of Fred "Killer" Burke, serving life in Michigan.

October 23, 1933   The Dillinger gang robs the Central National Bank in Greencastle, Indiana, of $74,782.

Baby Face Nelson, Tommy Carroll and others rob the First National Bank at Brainerd, Minnesota, of $32,000.

October 24, 1933   The Dillinger gang is wrongly suspected of a $5,000 bank robbery in South Bend, Indiana. The actual robbers will be apprehended later.

October 26, 1933   Dillinger's daring robberies of banks and police stations prompt Indiana governor Paul V. McNutt to call out the National Guard. The Dillinger gang moves to Chicago.

November 1, 1933   Verne Miller, prime suspect in the Kansas City Massacre, shoots his way out of a trap set by federal agents at the Sherone Apartments, 4423 Sheridan Road in Chicago's Uptown district.

November 2, 1933   Wilbur Underhill, Ford Bradshaw and others rob the Citizens National Bank in Okmulgee, Oklahoma, of $13,000.

November 9, 1933   The trial of the Touhy gang, for the Hamm kidnapping, begins in St. Paul.

November 13, 1933   Russell Hughes, a member of Handsome Jack Klutas's gang (the College Kidnappers), is killed by police in Peoria, Illinois.

November 15, 1933   Police from Indiana join Chicago police in setting a trap for Dillinger outside the office of Dr. Charles Eye, at 4175 West Irving Park Boulevard. Dillinger and girlfriend Evelyn "Billie" Frechette escape after a wild car chase. Officers lose Dillinger but manage to shoot out their own windshield, and allow reporters to assume that they had engaged in a dramatic gun battle with the fleeing desperado.

Clyde Barrow, Bonnie Parker and an unidentified man suspected of robbing Jim McMurray's oil refinery in Overton Township, Texas, of approximately $2,500.

W.D. Jones, former Barrow gang member, is arrested in Houston.

Basil "The Owl" Banghart, Ike Costner, Ludwig "Dutch" Schmidt and Charles "Ice Wagon" Connors rob a U.S. mail truck in Charlotte, North Carolina, of $105,000.

November 17, 1933   Former Dillinger gang member Harry Copeland is arrested by Chicago police after being called to break up an argument in a car between Copeland and his girlfriend.

November 18, 1933   Wilbur Underhill brazenly enters the courthouse at Coalgate, Oklahoma, and purchases a license to marry Hazel Jarrett Hudson. Hazel is the sister of the Jarrett brothers, notorious Oklahoma outlaws.

November 20, 1933   The Dillinger gang robs the American Bank and Trust Company at Racine, Wisconsin, of $27,789.

Albert Silvers (or Silverman), New York/New Jersey mobster who purchased the car Verne Miller used to drive to Chicago, is found stabbed to death at Somers, Connecticut. Miller, already unpopular with Midwest gangsters because of the "heat" caused by the Kansas City Massacre, is rumored to have murdered

a member of the Longy Zwillman mob in New Jersey.

New York mobster Waxey Gordon goes to trial for income tax evasion. The case is prosecuted by Assistant U.S. Attorney Thomas E. Dewey.

November 22, 1933   Clyde Barrow and Bonnie Parker escape police trap near Sowers, Texas.

November 23, 1933   Wilbur Underhill and others rob a bank in Frankfort, Kentucky.

November 24, 1933   Dillinger gang member Leslie Homer is arrested in Chicago. Homer will be sentenced to 28 years in state prison at Waupun, Wisconsin, for the Racine bank holdup.

November 26, 1933   Ed Fletcher and Abe Axler, members of the Detroit Purple Gang, are found murdered near Pontiac, Michigan.

November 28, 1933   Roger Touhy, Gloomy Gus Schafer, Eddie McFadden and Willie Sharkey are acquitted of the Hamm kidnapping but held for Chicago authorities for the alleged kidnapping of Jake "The Barber" Factor.

Gangster Walter Tylczak is found murdered near Detroit.

November 29, 1933   Verne Miller is found murdered near Detroit. The murder is never solved but is believed to be the work of the Zwillman mob.

In Chicago, Vivian Mathias, former mistress of Verne Miller, is sentenced to a year and a day for harboring a federal fugitive.

In New York, Waxey Gordon is convicted of income tax evasion, sentenced to 10 years in prison, and fined $20,000 plus $60,000 in costs.

November 30, 1933 Touhy gangster Willie Sharkey hangs himself in the St. Paul jail.

December 1933 Eight of 10 fugitives on the Chicago Police Department's own "public-enemy" list, including Harry Pierpont's mistress, Mary Kinder, and Kokomo madam Pearl Elliott, are members or associates of the Dillinger gang.

December 5, 1933 Prohibition is repealed by ratification of the 21st Amendment.

Mail robbery at Union Station in Washington, D.C., committed by the Tri-State Gang, headed by Robert Mais and Walter Legurenza, alias Legenza.

December 11, 1933 Police Detective H.C. Perrow is killed in San Antonio by Tommy Carroll of the Baby Face Nelson gang while Nelson is ordering more custom-made guns from H.S. Lebman.

Wilbur Underhill and others attempt to burglarize the First National Bank at Harrah, Oklahoma.

December 13, 1933 Dillinger gang suspected in the looting of safety deposit boxes at Unity Trust and Savings Bank at 2909 West North Avenue in Chicago.

Wilbur Underhill, Jack "Tom" Lloyd and Ralph Roe rob the First National Bank at Coalgate, Oklahoma, of $4,000.

December 14, 1933 Dillinger gang member John Hamilton kills Chicago police officer William Shanley in an auto repair shop at 5320 Broadway.

December 16, 1933 Chicago Police Captain John Stege organizes a 40-man "Dillinger Squad."

Cook County State's Attorney Thomas Courtney declares that the Dillinger, Klutas,

Touhy and Harvey Bailey–Verne Miller gangs have linked up.

December 17, 1933 Arthur "Fish" Johnson (aka Johnston), fence and close Dillinger gang associate, is arrested at 1742 Humbolt in Chicago.

December 20, 1993 Indiana state policeman Eugene Teague is accidentally killed by a fellow officer in the capture of former Dillinger gang member Ed Shouse, at Paris, Illinois.

The Dillinger gang decides to lay low for a while in Daytona Beach.

December 22, 1933 Acting on erroneous tip, Chicago police looking for Dillinger raid a Rogers Park apartment at 1428 Farwell and kill three men, Sam Ginsburg, Lewis Katzewitz and Charles Tattlebaum. The three were small-time bank robbers but not connected with Dillinger.

December 23, 1933 Dillinger associate Hilton Crouch is arrested by Chicago police at 420 Surf Street. He will later be sentenced to 20 years for the Massachusetts Avenue Bank robbery in Indianapolis.

December 30, 1933 Wilbur Underhill is fatally wounded by police and Division of Investigation agents at a honeymoon cottage in Shawnee, Oklahoma. Also fatally wounded is Eva Mae Nichols, girlfriend of Underhill henchman Ralph Roe. Roe and Underhill's recent bride, Hazel Hudson, are captured.

December 31, 1933 Gunmen believed to be the Ford Bradshaw gang terrorize Vian, Oklahoma, driving through town and peppering a hardware store, a restaurant and the town jail with bullets. Authorities believe this to be a gesture of retaliation for the capture of Bradshaw's friend, Wilbur Underhill.

1934

January 1, 1934   A group of machine gunners robs the Beverly Gardens nightclub in Chicago and shoots two policemen. The crime is blamed on the Dillinger gang, then vacationing in Florida.

The former U.S. Army Disciplinary Barracks at Alcatraz Island, in San Francisco Bay, officially becomes a federal penitentiary commonly referred to as The Rock, intended for the gangsters and outlaws considered the most dangerous and incorrigible.

January 2, 1934   Warden James A. Johnston arrives on Alcatraz.

January 6, 1934   Wilbur Underhill dies of wounds in the prison infirmary at McAlester, Oklahoma.

Chicago kidnapper Handsome Jack Klutas is killed by police at a house in the suburb of Bellwood. Earl McMahon, wanted for a $50,000 jewel robbery, and former Dillinger associate Walter Dietrich are captured in the Klutas hideout, Joseph Aiuppa, alias Joey O'Brien, alleged underworld machine-gun supplier, and several other men are also arrested in the vicinity.

January 7, 1934   Oklahoma's Public Enemy Number One, Elmer Inman, is wounded and captured in the town of Bowlegs.

January 11–February 2, 1934   Roger Touhy, Gloomy Gus Schafer and August John Lamarr, alias Albert "Polly Nose" Kator, are tried for the supposed kidnapping of Jake "The Barber" Factor. First trial ends in a hung jury.

January 13, 1934   On Portland Avenue in St. Paul, airline pilot Roy McCord is mistaken for a policeman and machine-gunned by Alvin Karpis and Fred Barker. McCord survives but is crippled for life.

January 15, 1934   John Dillinger, John Hamilton and an unidentified man rob the First National Bank in East Chicago, Indiana, of $20,376, killing Patrolman William O'Malley. This will be the one murder attributed to Dillinger personally.

Willie "The Actor" Sutton, Eddie Wilson and Joe Perlongo rob the Corn Exchange Bank in Philadelphia of $10,980.

January 16, 1934   Clyde Barrow, Bonnie Parker and James Mullen raid the Eastham Prison Farm in Texas, freeing Raymond Hamilton and four other convicts. One guard is killed and another wounded.

January 17–February 7, 1934   The Barker-Karpis gang kidnaps banker Edward George Bremer is St. Paul and transports him to Bensenville, Illinois. Bremer is released unharmed upon payment of $200,000 ransom.

January 19, 1934   Big Bob Brady, Jim Clark and five others escape from the Lansing, Kansas, state prison. Brady and Clark, participants in the May 30 breakout from the same prison, split up. Clark and fellow escapee Frank Delmar kidnap teacher Lewis Dresser and steal his car. Dresser is released in Oklahoma, where the escapees meet Clark's girlfriend, Goldie Johnson, waiting in a car with Texas license plates. Dresser subsequently identifies the woman as Bonnie Parker and the Barrow gang is erroneously suspected of engineering two prison breaks in three days.

January 22, 1934   Big Bob Brady is killed by a posse near Paola, Kansas.

January 23, 1934   Capone gangster William "Three-Fingered Jack" White is murdered in

Oak Park, Illinois, possibly by Fred Goetz. White was believed to be talking to the Justice Department.

January 25, 1934 John Dillinger, Harry Pierpont, Charles Makley and Russell Clark are captured by police in Tucson, Arizona. Dillinger will be extradited to Indiana to face charges of murder and bank robbery. The others will be sent to Ohio, to be tried for the murder of Sheriff Jesse Sarber.

January 30, 1934 On arrival at the Lake County Jail in Crown Point, Indiana, the cocky Dillinger jokes with reporters and poses for chummy pictures with Sheriff Lillian Holley and prosecutor Robert Estill, who are widely criticized for treating him like a celebrity. Estill's political career is ruined.

January 31, 1934 In a Chicago barber shop, police and Division of Investigation agents arrest Verne Sankey for the kidnapping of Charles Boettcher II. Sankey will commit suicide in the Great Falls, South Dakota, prison on February 8.

February 1, 1934 Clyde Barrow and Bonnie Parker are identified in the $270 robbery of the State Savings Bank in Knieram, Iowa.

February 2, 1934 The Needham Trust Company in Needham, Massachusetts, is robbed of $14,500 and two policemen are machine-gunned. Pretty Boy Floyd is wrongly accused. The actual killers, Murton and Irving Millen and Abraham Faber, will later be captured, convicted and executed for this crime.

Four bandits rob the National Bank and Trust Company at Pennsgrove, New Jersey, of $130,000. Local authorities will later speculate, incorrectly, that this bank was robbed to finance Dillinger's escape from the Crown Point jail.

The Barrow gang is suspected of robbing the First National Bank at Coleman, Texas.

February 3–4, 1934 In one particularly violent weekend, eight men are killed in three eastern Oklahoma towns. At Sapulpa, Police Chief Tom Brumley and Patrolman Charles P. Lloyd, and bank robbers Aussie Elliott, Raymond Moore and Eldon Wilson, are slain in a gun battle. At Chelsea, Deputy Sheriff Earl Powell and Ed Newt Clanton, a member of the Ford Bradshaw gang, die in another shootout. At Bokoshe, Dr. H.T. King is shot to death and his son Howard is wounded. Howard King names his father's slayer as City Marshal Calvin Johnson.

February 4, 1934 Ernest Rossi, former Klutas gang associate wanted for a Holland, Michigan, bank robbery, is shot to death by unknown killers at the Chicago home of his brother-in-law, Dago Lawrence Mangano. Rossi is the fifth Chicago mobster slain in recent months for allegedly cooperating with federal authorities. Newspapers speculate that the underworld has a counterinformant working in the Justice Department.

February 5, 1934 Willie "The Actor" Sutton is captured by Philadelphia police. He will be sentenced to 25 years in the Eastern state prison for bank robbery.

John Dillinger's trial date is set for March 12. Indiana officials want Dillinger held in the state prison, but Dillinger's lawyer, Louis Piquett, strongly objects and Judge William Murray leaves him in Sheriff Lillian Holley's heavily guarded Lake County jail at Crown Point.

February 9, 1934 Dock Barker is identified as one of the Bremer kidnappers through a fingerprint found on a gasoline can. Flashlights used by the kidnappers are also found and

DILLINGER'S WOODEN-PISTOL JAILBREAK, MARCH 3, 1934

One stunt more than any other made John Dillinger a legendary outlaw—the classic "trickster" of folklore. It resulted in eternal embarrassment for Crown Point, Indiana, especially the keepers of Lake County's supposedly escape-proof jail. In truth, Dillinger's use of a carved wooden pistol to stage one of the most audacious jailbreaks in history was the culmination of a carefully if desperately orchestrated plan hatched by friends in Chicago, which succeeded largely because at least two key individuals at the jail (and possibly even the warden) were bribed. Collusion was suspected at the time, but even revised accounts include major errors, such as the source of the bribe money and the celebrated "pistol," and what became of it later. This new information was not revealed until 1994, and if it substantially changes the story, it doesn't diminish Dillinger's crowd-pleasing performance.

The standard version is that the ever-resourceful bank robber used a razor blade to whittle a piece of washboard into something crudely resembling a small automatic, which he used to intimidate several guards until he got his hands on the real thing, plus two Thompson submachine guns. Then, with the help of black inmate Herbert Youngblood, arrested for murder, the pair locked up some 26 people in different parts of the building, took two hostages, and motored leisurely in the direction of Peotone, Illinois, Dillinger waving his toy, cracking wise, and singing "Git along, li'l dogie, git along." When he dropped off Deputy Ernest Blunk and mechanic Ed Saager at a country crossroads, shook their hands and gave them a few dollars to get home, it was the slickest breakout the public had ever heard of. No shooting or casualties, except the political career of the prosecutor who had posed for pictures with his arm around Dillinger, the reputation of Sheriff Lillian Holley and the civic image of Crown Point, which became a national laughingstock.

At the time of the escape there was good reason to suspect payoffs, and Blunk and another guard went back on their wooden-gun story only when state authorities brought them up on charges. Both beat the rap for lack of evidence. Later, the FBI, which could now enter the case because Dillinger had driven Sheriff Lillian Holley's stolen car across a state line en route to Chicago (his only federal offense up to that point), officially declared the gun to have been a real one, though Bureau files seem to accept the original version.

G. Russell Girardin, friend of Dillinger attorney Louis Piquett in 1935 and coauthor of *Dillinger: The Untold Story,* believed the G-men decided to accept the "smuggled gun" story mainly to embarrass Indiana State Police Chief Matt Leach, who was becoming ever more critical of their work on the case.

According to Girardin, then a young Chicago ad man who had met Piquett and his assistant, Arthur O'Leary, through a mutual friend, the Crown Point escape was a setup from start to finish. O'Leary was Piquett's connection with the East Chicago mob, headed by Sonny Sheetz, who controlled most of northern Indiana and in 1933 had helped Dillinger and his friends get their start, for a price that included a piece of several prearranged bank robberies,

John Dillinger never seemed fazed by misfortune, delighted the press and the public with his good-natured wisecracks, and was pleased to pose for photographers at the Crown Point jail with his prosecutor, Robert Estill, shortly before breaking out with a wooden pistol. The stunt guaranteed Dillinger a place in the history books, but cost Estill his political career. *(Dennis Hoffman Collection)*

with inflated insurance claims that were shared with him and the bank officials in on the plot.

When Dillinger was arrested in Tucson the following January and extradited to Indiana, his own escape plan was anything but subtle. He wanted his friends on the outside to hit the jail like commandos with dynamite, acetylene torches and plenty of machine-gun fire to intimidate the locals. Piquett, via O'Leary and girlfriend Evelyn Frechette, posing as Mrs. Dillinger, managed to convince him that he could as easily take Cuba, what with all the farmboy National Guardsmen eager to try our their water-cooled Browning machine guns and BARs (Browning Automatic Rifles). Which didn't mean a breakout couldn't be arranged, and without a bloodbath, if he could come up with enough money.

Dillinger complained to Piquett that the Tucson cops had siezed all his loot as evidence. However, his old prison buddy, Homer Van Meter, was then linked up with the Baby Face Nelson gang, and through Piquett managed to cut a deal. Dillinger had no use for the cranky, trigger-happy Nelson, but Van Meter and John Hamilton persuaded the Nelson group that Dillinger would give them some badly needed class. The gang supposedly advanced Piquett more than $11,000, which eventually would lead to some serious quarrelling over who skimmed how much of the bribe money before it reached Crown Point, possibly the jail warden (the FBI later believed) and Dillinger's two ostensible hostages.

Reportedly, $7,500 went to Deputy Blunk, the chief jailer, and $2,500 to garage man Ed Saager, who maintained the county cars—including Sheriff Holley's new V-8 Ford. Dillinger had wanted the money to secure him a real gun, but Blunk rejected that idea from the start. If anything went wrong, he reasoned, he'd be shot first.

O'Leary proposed another plan, or at least took credit for it. As long as Blunk was in on the escape, the gun didn't need to be real, and accordingly he had an elderly German woodworker on Chicago's Northwest Side fashion a crude pistol out of wood and blacken it with shoe polish. The phony pistol had the additional virtue of diverting suspicion from Blunk and one or two others who knew or suspected something. Dillinger would claim he had carved it during the month of February 1934, while pretrial hearings were underway; and to support this he did break up a washboard and whittle a few shavings, which were later found under his bunk.

Even this had proved arduous, and then another problem arose. The wooden-pistol ploy was hatched at the last minute, when Dillinger was fighting transfer to the much more formidable Indiana state prison; and while the woodworker (whom Girardin later met) hurried to complete a credibly crude-looking item, he wasn't in on the scheme or clear on the concept. Believing he was doing O'Leary a favor, he bored out the barrel with 3/8 inch bit and inserted the round metal handle of an old safety razor, to give his product a little added realism.

O'Leary took one look and realized that while Dillinger might plausibly claim he had carved the gun in his cell, he certainly didn't have equipment to do the barrel work. O'Leary could not wait for another carving job and had to invent an additional cover story. Had the breakout failed, it would have been obvious the phoney gun had been made by some outsider with woodworking tools. The best O'Leary could hope for was that nobody would get a close look at the gun, which Dillinger mostly kept in his pocket; and if worse came to worse, O'Leary and Piquett could speculate that gang member Tommy Carroll had smuggled it to

Dillinger's daring deception and escape made national news. *(Authors' collection)*

Dillinger by way of Youngblood, who was not under constant observation.

As it turned out, the jailbreak went down perfectly, and the wooden pistol disappeared with Dillinger, who later sent it to his sister in Mooresville along with a letter. "Pulling that off was worth ten years of my life," he wrote. "Don't part with my wooden gun for any price. For when you feel blue all you will have to do is look at the gun and laugh your blues away. Ha! Ha!"

The gun remained stashed with a few other mementos until after Dillinger's death, when financial hardship forced his father to sign on as "curator" of a Dillinger mini-museum at Emil Wanatka's Little Bohemia Lodge in northern Wisconsin, where the gang had been forced to abandon many weapons and personal belongings when nearly trapped there in April 1934 by the FBI.

Dillinger was killed in Chicago only three months later, on the Sunday night of July 22, outside the Biograph Theatre on North Lincoln Avenue, set up by Anna Sage, a prominent madam with a record, and her boyfriend/partner Martin Zarkovich, a rogue cop from East Chicago. He had cut a deal with the FBI two days earlier on the condition he could participate in

Had Dillinger's wooden-pistol breakout failed, the safety razor handle carefully sleeved into the barrel would have been a tip-off that the phoney gun had been made outside the prison and smuggled in. *(John Dillinger Museum)*

the ambush. Closely linked with the Sheetz mob, presumably his job was to make sure Dillinger didn't survive the trap, learn he'd been betrayed by friends, and spill his guts. For contrary to the popular accounts, Anna already knew attorney Piquett (probably through his representation of local abortion rings), and had sought his help in avoiding deportation to her native Romania as morally undesirable.

Dillinger had been staying at her apartment at 2420 North Halsted, recuperating from his plastic surgery some six weeks earlier, no doubt sent there by Piquett. Whether the lawyer was in on the ambush isn't certain. Dillinger was known to be gunning for the lawyer over money matters and had told O'Leary to take his family on vacation until the matter was settled one way or another. Forewarned, Piquett headed to Platteville, Wisconsin, where he was visiting relatives the night of the shooting. And the nearly two dozen federal agents surrounding the Biograph were so jumpy that when Dillinger walked out with Madam Anna and current girlfriend Polly Hamilton, they simply blew him to immortality, saving "Zark" the effort.

A presumably envious police colleague later described the killing in a newspaper series and stated that in the excitement after the shooting, Zarkovitch had gone through Dillinger's pockets and taken several thousand dollars in cash before the body reached the Cook County Morgue. Anna later confirmed that Dillinger was carrying his "git" money when they left her apartment, and a perfunctory investigation into the robbing of Dillinger's corpse included at least one report by an FBI agent who said that he had noticed what felt like a large roll of bills in one of Dillinger's pockets.

Melvin Purvis got off with Dillinger's ruby ring and diamond stickpin, but the .380 automatic that ended up in an FBI display of Dillinger's belongings turned out to have been manufactured by Colt's some months after the outlaw's death. A story persists that the gun found at the scene went to J. Edgar Hoover, who gave it as a personal gift to his comedian friend Red Skelton, as it was his practice to curry favors with celebrities in the entertainment industry. The morgue inventory of Dillinger's blood-soaked clothing and seven dollars and change was accepted by a gullible press simply as evidence that crime did not pay.

The wooden pistol did not come out of hiding until months after Dillinger's death, and by then apparently no one questioned the bored-and-sleeved barrel. Later it was loaned, along with other Dillinger possessions, to Girardin to be photographed for a series of articles on which he, Piquett and O'Leary were collaborating for the Hearst newspapers. Girardin kept it for some months before sending it back to the Dillinger family. However, the wooden gun they received probably was not the one pictured in the family snapshot of Dillinger holding a machine gun and the fake pistol used in the escape.

Girardin knew for some months that O'Leary craved the "real" wooden gun as a souvenir and wanted to make a duplicate. Figuring that the Dillinger family would end up with O'Leary's copy, Girardin held onto the original and eventually gave it to Piquett, who promised to return it to the Dillingers in person. Sometime later they received a wooden pistol, but it was probably not the one used in the escape, and eventually it disappeared, evidently pocketed by a visitor.

The switch went undetected until after O'Leary's death from a heart attack during a trip to Florida about 1960, and his widow decided to sell their house and move there herself. During renovation, a local workman named Al Kranz opened an air duct and found, along with papers dating back to O'Leary's collaboration with Girardin, a wooden pistol—almost certainly the "real" one—with a handwritten note from Piquett telling O'Leary to be sure he returned it to the Dillingers. This amounted to a receipt to get Piquett off the hook, and means that O'Leary managed to obtain the original after all.

Kranz sold O'Leary's gun to Joe Pinkston, late owner of the John Dillinger Museum in Nashville, Indiana, where it was put on prominent display. Pinkston brought his wooden pistol to Chicago and showed it to Girardin, who seemed to have no doubt it was the original loaned him in 1935 by Dillinger's father, so there should still be somewhere a second, "phoney" wooden pistol—the one later lost by the Dillinger family, and which presumably remains in someone's private collection.

As for the other Dillinger wooden pistols: For years the Chicago Historical Society thought it had the real thing, guaranteed original in an apparently perjured affidavit by Deputy Ernest Blunk (which would not be totally out of character for a jailer who evidently accepted $5,000 in Depression-era dollars to help Dillinger escape). Blunk sold it to the owner of the Walgreens drug chain, who eventually donated it in good faith to the Chicago Historical Society. It shows up in some newsreels of the period, though it obviously was fashioned with a jigsaw and is shaped more like a revolver, with double-edged razor blades tacked on each side to represent the cylinder. One that looks more like an automatic is shown in other films. A British collector bought a "Dillinger" pistol, also shaped like a revolver, from the Melvin Purvis estate. Yet another shaped like a revolver came from the Lake County sheriff's department, and is on display at the American Police Center and Museum in Chicago.

Since Dillinger's escape made Crown Point unhappily famous, the post office knew exactly where to deliver anything addressed simply to Wooden Gun, Indiana; and it probably can be assumed that the sheriff's office there received more than a few homemade wooden pistols from people having fun at the expense of the local authorities.

---

traced to a St. Paul store. From photos, a sales clerk identifies Alvin Karpis as the purchaser.

February 10, 1934 At the request of Lee Simmons, head of the Texas prison system, former Texas Ranger Frank Hamer, who reputedly has killed 53 criminals in his long career as a peace officer, comes out of retirement to track down Clyde Barrow and Bonnie Parker.

February 13–23, 1934 Second trial of the Touhy gang for the Factor kidnapping. Mail robbers Basil "The Owl" Banghart and Ike Costner are captured in Baltimore and rushed to Chicago to testify. Costner swears for the prosecution that he and Banghart participated with Touhy in the kidnapping. Banghart testifies for the defense, stating that he, Costner and Charles "Ice Wagon" Connors, still at large, were hired by Jake Factor to make the kidnapping look real. The jury believes Costner. Roger Touhy, Gus Schafer, Albert Kator and Basil Banghart are sentenced to 99 years in the state prison at Joliet. Costner will later be convicted with Ludwig "Dutch" Schmidt of a mail robbery at Charlotte, North Carolina, and sentenced to 30 years.

February 15, 1934   Eddie Doll, alias Eddie LaRue, formerly an associate of Eddie Bentz, is arrested by federal agents in St. Petersburg, Florida. A reputed burglar, bank robber, professional car thief and freelance hitman, Doll is a suspect in the million-dollar Lincoln bank robbery of 1930 and the kidnappings of Edward Bremer and gambler James Hackett. He will plead guilty to interstate transportation of a stolen car and be sentenced to 10 years in federal prison.

February 17–18, 1934   Searching for Pretty Boy Floyd, the Barrow gang and a host of other outlaws who frequently harbor there, an army of over 1,000 police and National Guardsmen invade the Cookson Hills of eastern Oklahoma. Nineteen other fugitives are arrested.

February 18, 1934   Clifford "Kip" Harback, wanted for murder and bank robbery, is murdered by his mistress, Lillian Tackett, in Hot Springs, Arkansas. Harback was allegedly an associate of Pretty Boy Floyd.

February 19, 1934   The Barrow gang robs a National Guard armory in Ranger, Texas.

February 24, 1934   An unknown gang, including a woman, robs the First National Bank at Galena, Kansas, of $7,100. The Barrow gang is suspected.

February 26, 1934   Alfred Guarino pleads guilty to second-degree murder in Bronx County, New York, for the killing of Millie Schwartz and is sentenced to 20 years to life in Sing Sing. Mrs. Vincent (Lottie) Coll and Joseph Ventre plead guilty to manslaughter in the same case. Lottie receives six to 12 years in Bedford Reformatory and Ventre seven to 15 years in Sing Sing.

February 27, 1934   Clyde Barrow and Raymond Hamilton rob the R.P. Henry & Sons Bank at Lancaster, Texas, of $4,138.

February 28, 1934   Sebron Edward Davis, former Bailey-Underhill outlaw, is arrested in Los Angeles for robbery and kidnapping. He will be sentenced to life in Folsom Prison.

March 2, 1934   The Mais-Legenza gang (the Tri-State Gang) kills a messenger of the State Planters Bank at Richmond, Virginia, during a $60,000 robbery.

March 3, 1934   Using a wooden pistol made in Chicago and reportedly smuggled to him by a bribed guard, John Dillinger escapes from the Crown Point jail, along with accused "Negro" murderer Herbert Youngblood. They arm themselves with machine guns and pistols from the sheriff's office, take two hostages who were probably in on the plot, release them near Peotone, Illinois, and flee to Chicago in Sheriff Holley's car. Crossing a state line in a stolen car makes Dillinger at last a federal fugitive and the object of a nationwide manhunt by J. Edgar Hoover's G-men.

Bank robber Ford Bradshaw is killed by Deputy William Harper at Ardmore, Oklahoma.

The Barrow gang is suspected of robbing a bank at Mesquite, Texas.

March 4, 1934   In St. Paul, Baby Face Nelson kills Theodore H. Kidder, supposedly over a minor auto accident.

In fact, there wasn't any accident. A car carrying several men followed Kidder to his home, the driver called him by name and a passenger—presumably Nelson—shot him as he approached. It would turn out that Kidder worked for a sporting goods store and sold guns and ammunition on the side, so his murder likely stemmed from some dispute over an arms transaction.

March 6, 1934   Dillinger joins Baby Face Nelson, John Hamilton, Homer Van Meter, Tommy Carroll and Eddie Green in robbing the Security National Bank at Sioux Falls, South Dakota, of $49,500 and wounding a policeman. Though the group had been assembled by Nelson and Van Meter, who reportedly fronted the bribe money for the Crown Point escape, it becomes known as the "second" Dillinger gang.

March 7, 1934   Four men rob the Whitesboro National Bank at Whitesboro, Texas, of $13,000, taking three bank employees hostage.

Bonnie Parker's husband, Roy Thornton, serving a 55-year sentence for robbery, and four others attempt to scale the wall of the Texas state prison at Huntsville. Three of the escapees are wounded by guards and recaptured. Thornton and Robert Hill, convicted of the 1927 "Santa Claus" bank robbery at Cisco, Texas, surrender. Prison authorities attribute leadership of the break to Thornton, citing his continuing love for Bonnie as the motive for the break.

March 8, 1934   A federal complaint is filed in Chicago against John Dillinger for interstate transportation of a stolen car, confirming his status as a federal fugitive.

March 10, 1934   John Dillinger is suspected in a gun battle with police at Schiller Park, Illinois.

March 10, 1934 (approx.)   In Chicago, Dr. Joseph Moran performs plastic surgery on the faces of Alvin Karpis and Fred Barker and attempts to remove their fingerprints. With Karpis, and contrary to general beliefs of the day, the print removal was successful, and would cause him problems after his eventual release

from prison when he needed prints for such routine matters as obtaining a passport.

March–April 1934   Dr. Moran conspires with Chicago politician John "Boss" McLaughlin, Sr., to pass ransom money from the Bremer kidnapping.

March 12, 1934   Bandits rob the Exchange National and Exchange State Banks, associated in the same building, at Atchinson, Kansas, of $21,000, wounding Police Chief Willard Linville with machine-gun fire. Witnesses erroneously identify Clyde Barrow as the gang's leader.

March 13, 1934   The Dillinger gang robs the First National Bank at Mason City, Iowa, of $52,344.

March 14, 1934   Charles "Ice Wagon" Connors, alleged Touhy gangster wanted for mail robbery and the Factor kidnapping, is found murdered near Chicago.

Six men and two women, including Bremer kidnapping suspects Glen Leroy Wright and Charles "Cotton" Cotner, are arrested in a raid by federal agents and police on a farmhouse near Mannford, Oklahoma. Cotner is wanted for two murders and the attempted kidnapping of Peggy Landon, daughter of Kansas governor Alfred Landon.

March 16, 1934   Herbert Youngblood, who escaped with Dillinger from the Crown Point jail, kills Deputy Charles Cavanaugh in Port Huron, Michigan, but is mortally wounded by other officers on the scene.

March 19, 1934   Raymond and Floyd Hamilton and John Basden rob the State Bank at Grand Prairie, Texas, of $1,500.

March 21, 1934   Fred Goetz, alias "Shotgun" George Ziegler, Capone gunman also connected with the Barker-Karpis gang, is shotgunned to death by unknown assailants in Cicero, Illinois. Goetz likely participated in the St. Valentine's Day Massacre of 1929.

March 22, 1934 Roy Frisch, witness in a U.S. mail fraud case against Reno gamblers William Graham and James McKay, disappears, probably murdered by Baby Face Nelson and John Paul Chase, on a contract from Graham and McKay.

March 24, 1934 Dillinger gang members Harry Pierpont and Charles Makley are sentenced to death for the murder of Sheriff Jesse Sarber at Lima, Ohio; Russell Clark receives life.

March 31, 1934 John Dillinger and Homer Van Meter, located unexpectedly in a St. Paul apartment by federal agents, shoot their way out.

A special grand jury finds little evidence of political or police corruption in St. Paul and ridicules charges that the city is a haven for outlaws.

Raymond Hamilton and Mary O'Dare rob the State National Bank at West, Texas, of $1,862.

April 1, 1934 The Barrow gang kills two highway patrolmen near Grapevine, Texas. Although Raymond Hamilton probably did the shooting, Clyde Barrow is named Texas's Public Enemy Number One.

April 3, 1934 Dillinger gang member Eddie Green, though unarmed, is shot by Division of Investigation agents in St. Paul. Before he dies, the delerious Green and his wife, Bessie, provide much new information about the Dillinger and Barker-Karpis gangs and the St. Paul underworld. Until then, the G-men had no clear picture of the Barker-Karpis gang and learn they often travel with a woman they call "Ma."

April 5, 1934 The Tri-State Gang, headed by Robert Mais and Walter Legenza, hijacks a truckload of Camel cigarettes and Prince Albert tobacco, valued at approximately $17,000, near Norlina, North Carolina. The drivers are kidnapped and left handcuffed to trees at Bowling Green, Virginia.

April 5–8, 1934 John Dillinger, now the country's most hunted criminal, decides no one would expect him to go to Mooresville, Indiana, and spends a weekend at his father's farm with relatives and friends. Federal agents observe the homecoming through binoculars but respond too late. Many of Mooresville's residents will sign a petition asking Governor Paul McNutt to pardon Dillinger if he surrenders.

April 6, 1934 The Barrow gang kills Constable Cal Campbell and wounds and kidnaps Chief of Police Percy Boyd, near Commerce, Oklahoma. Boyd is released near Fort Scott, Kansas. Thirty officers, led by federal agent Herman Hollis, Ottawa County Sheriff Dee Watters and Craig County Sheriff John York, raid the Welch, Oklahoma, farmhouse of Ab Clark, searching for the Barrow gang. Clark is the uncle of Oklahoma bank robber Jim Clark.

April 9, 1934 Acting on a tip, Melvin Purvis, special agent in charge of the FBI's Chicago office, arrests Dillinger's girlfriend, Evelyn "Billie" Frechette, at Larry Strong's State & Austin Tavern, 416 North State Street, but misses Dillinger, who is parked outside.

April 11, 1934 Eddie Green dies in a St. Paul hospital.

April 12, 1934 William Benjamin "Big Bill" Phillips, a member of the Tri-State Gang, is slain by federal agents and police at Adams Mill Road and Ontario Place in Washington, D.C.

April 13, 1934 John Dillinger and Homer Van Meter rob the police station at Warsaw, Indiana, but get only two revolvers and three bulletproof vests.

April 16, 1934 The Barrow gang robs the First National Bank at Stuart, Iowa, of $2,000.

April 17, 1934 A federal trap being set for Dillinger in Louisville is reported by a newspaper, so Dillinger, Hamilton and girlfriend Pat Cherrington instead visit Hamilton's sister in Sault Sainte Marie, Michigan, which leads to her arrest for harboring.

April 19, 1934 The Dillinger gang is suspected in a $27,000 bank robbery at Pana, Illinios.

In Chicago, George Dale, accomplice of "Blonde Tigress" Eleanor Jarman, is executed at the Cook County Jail for the murder of Gustav Hoeh. Before walking to the electric chair, Dale reportedly writes a love letter to Jarman, serving a 199-year sentence in the women's prison at Dwight, Illinois.

April 20, 1934 A lone bandit robs the Iredell State Bank at Iredell, Texas. Clyde Barrow is a suspect.

April 22, 1934 The Dillinger gang shoots its way out of a federal trap at the Little Bohemia Lodge near Rhinelander, Wisconsin. Agents, led by Melvin Purvis, prematurely start the battle by mistakenly shooting three innocent customers, killing one. Later agent W. Carter Baum is slain and two other lawmen wounded by Baby Face Nelson during his escape. Three of the gang's women are left behind and captured.

April 23, 1934 John Dillinger, John Hamilton and Homer Van Meter battle deputies near South St. Paul. Hamilton is described as mortally wounded but is refused treatment by a Chicago underworld doctor and taken to the Aurora, Illinois, hideout of Barker-Karpis gang member Volney Davis and his girlfriend, Edna "The Kissing Bandit" Murray.

April 25, 1934 Raymond Hamilton and Ted Brooks rob the First National Bank at Lewisville, Texas, of $2,300 but are captured later in the day near Howe, Texas.

April 26, 1934 Bookie William Edward Vidler is arrested by federal agents in Chicago for passing Bremer ransom money.

Elizabeth Fontaine, formerly the moll of Big Bill Phillips, is shot and seriously wounded by gang leader Robert Mais in an apartment at Upper Darby, Pennsylvania. She survives and provides federal agents with much information on the Tri-State Gang.

April 28, 1934 Chicago politician Boss McLaughlin is arrested by federal agents for passing Bremer ransom money.

April 30, 1934 Federal agents in San Antonio arrest gunsmith H.S. Lebman on suspicion of supplying machine guns and specially modified machine pistols to the Dillinger gang.

In federal court in San Angelo, Texas, Louise Magness is convicted of harboring Kathryn and George "Machine Gun" Kelly, and sentenced to a year and a day in the Women's Federal Prison at Alderson, West Virginia.

April 30, 1934 (approx.) John Hamilton reportedly dies at Aurora, Illinois, and is secretly buried near the town of Oswego by Dillinger, Van Meter and members of the Barker-Karpis gang.

May 1, 1934   Three policemen are slugged and disarmed at Bellwood, Indiana. Dillinger is suspected.

May 3, 1934   The Division of Investigation notifies Scottish authorities that Dillinger may be aboard the S.S. *Duchess of York*, bound for Glasgow. Though Dillinger is not on the ship, the tip will lead to the arrest of another fugitive, Trebilsch Lincoln, alias Abbot Chao Kung, a German spy during the First World War, wanted for fomenting rebellion in India. The false tip comes from Dillinger attorney Louis Piquett, having sport with a bothersome reporter.

The Barrow gang robs a bank in Everly, Iowa, of $700.

May 4, 1934   Three men rob the First National Bank at Fostoria, Ohio, of $17,000, killing Chief of Police Frank Culp and wounding others. Two of the robbers are identified by witnesses as John Dillinger and Homer Van Meter.

A federal grand jury in St. Paul indict Dock Barker, Alvin Karpis, John J. "Boss" McLaughlin, Sr., John J. McLaughlin, Jr., William Edward Vidler, Philip J. Delaney, Slim, Izzy, Frankie Wright, John Doe, and Richard Roe for conspiracy to kidnap Edward George Bremer and transport him from Minnesota to the State of Illinois.

A federal complaint filed at Wilmington, North Carolina, charges Tri-State Gang members Walter Legurenza, Morris Kauffman and John Kendrick with theft from a shipment in interstate commerce.

May 18, 1934   Three men rob the Citizens Commercial Savings Bank at Flint, Michigan, of $25,000. Dillinger is suspected.

Clyde Barrow, Raymond Hamilton, Henry Methvin and Joe Palmer are indicted by a federal grand jury in Dallas for theft of U.S. Government property in their raids on armories.

May 19, 1934   A federal grand jury at Madison, Wisconsin, indicts John Dillinger for conspiracy to harbor Tommy Carroll, wanted for post office robbery. Tommy Carroll is indicted for conspiracy to harbor John Dillinger. Homer Van Meter, John Hamilton and Lester Gillis, alias Baby Face Nelson, are indicted for conspiracy to harbor John Dillinger, Tommy Carroll and each other.

Billie Jean Mace, Bonnie Parker's sister, is arrested in Gladewater, Texas, on suspicion of murder.

May 20, 1934   Barrow gang associate Jack Nichols is arrested in Longview, Texas.

May 23, 1934   Clyde Barrow and Bonnie Parker are ambushed and killed on the road between Gibsland and Sailes, Louisiana, by Texas and Louisiana peace officers, led by Captain Frank Hamer.

In St. Paul, Evelyn Frechette and Dr. Clayton E. May are convicted of harboring Dillinger. Both are sentenced to two years and fined $10,000.

Morris Kauffman, member of the Tri-State Gang, is found murdered in Pittsburgh.

May 24, 1934   Two policemen are machine-gunned near East Chicago, Indiana, after encountering a panel truck driven by Homer Van Meter and John Dillinger. Two stories circulate: that Sergeant Martin Zarkovich sent them to investigate the truck without telling them who was in it, or they knew and their intention was a shakedown.

Five state governors enter into a "Five-State Pact" at the urging of the FBI and collectively post a $5,000 reward for Dillinger's capture,

"I HATE TO BUST A CAP ON A LADY, ESPECIALLY WHEN SHE'S SITTING DOWN."

—FRANK HAMER, LEADER OF THE BONNIE AND CLYDE AMBUSH PARTY

To the extent that Depression-era Texans were at all class-conscious, Clyde Barrow and Bonnie Parker probably would have been looked upon as "white trash." They distinguished themselves from the state's sizable population of lawbreakers by being impulsive, deadly and thoroughly unprofessional. They mostly hit grocery stores and filling stations, killing without qualms, provoking John Dillinger to gripe that these were the kind of punks who gave armed robbery a bad name. What earned them a place in criminal history was their elusiveness, and the public's fascination with a boy-and-girl bandit team who had a flair for the dramatic and enjoyed their publicity. They took pictures of each other engaging in horseplay with guns, and mailed bad poetry to newspapers. Bonnie's main beef with the press was the frequent publishing of a captured photo of her smoking a cigar, which she claimed was taken strictly as a joke.

Despite their small stature and underage looks, they were armed to the teeth, Clyde favoring the heavy Browning Automatic Rifle

Bonnie and Clyde took their place among the ranks of dead outlaws in 1934. *(Lorraine Joyner Collection)*

(the BAR, usually stolen from National Guard armories and shortened) designed for muscular soldiers. Their narrow escapes in shootouts became front-page news, and taught their pursuers that the Thompson gun would not always penetrate the tough skin of the V-8 Fords Bonnie and Clyde generally used. So when police finally ambushed the outlaws in Louisiana with a posse led by Frank Hamer, a legendary former Texas Ranger hired specifically to bring them down, the lawmen shredded their car and its two notorious passengers with 167 bullets mainly from high-powered rifles.

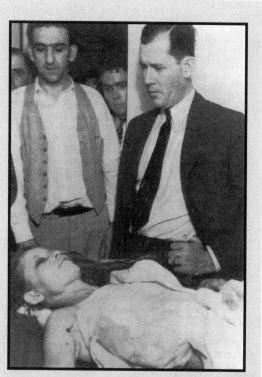

(Author's collection)

After ambushing and killing Clyde Barrow and Bonnie Parker with 167 rifle bullets, officers left their bodies in the duo's signature V-8 Ford while they towed it to Arcadia, Louisiana. *(Authors' collection)*

Bonnie and Clyde's deaths made national headlines at the height of the public-enemy era, and the morbidly curious had a field day. The Barrow car was towed to the town of Arcadia with the bodies still inside, and the battered corpses were laid out in gory splendor for the benefit of sightseers, one of whom had to be constrained from cutting off Clyde's trigger finger for a souvenir. Others were content to pose for pictures with the riddled and blood-soaked Ford, which has remained a popular tourist attraction wherever displayed.

Despite a minimum of redeeming personal qualities, Bonnie and Clyde still have a large following, and left a legacy of questions still argued in books on their career. Their betrayal is part of the mystery; the members of the ambush party later gave conflicting versions of the killing; Clyde's sexual character is still debated; and the story persists that authorities covered up the fact Bonnie died pregnant. It's true that Clyde wrote a letter to Henry Ford complimenting his automobile; but a similar letter to Ford from John Dillinger has been studied by handwriting experts and declared a fake.

The two were not buried side by side, as Bonnie had predicted in one of her poems, but their respective gravestones bear memorable epitaphs. Bonnie's reads, ingenuously,

AS THE FLOWERS ARE ALL MADE SWEETER BY THE SUNSHINE AND THE DEW, SO THIS OLD WORLD IS MADE BRIGHTER BY THE LIVES OF FOLKS LIKE YOU

Clyde's is a bit more fitting:

GONE BUT NOT FORGOTTEN.

dead or alive. *Liberty* magazine offers a $1,000 reward.

May 25, 1934 Raymond Hamilton, already serving a 263-year prison sentence, is convicted of another bank robbery and sentenced to an additional 99 years.

May 27, 1934 Drs. Wilhelm Loeser and Harold Cassidy perform plastic surgery on the faces and fingerprints of John Dillinger and Homer Van Meter at the Chicago home of hoodlum James Probasco, 2509 N. Caldwell (now Pulaski).

May–June 1934 Congress passes a series of federal anti-crime bills, granting the U.S. Attorney General authority to offer rewards of up to $25,000 for the capture of federal fugitives, arming Division of Investigation agents at all times, amending the Lindbergh Law to include interstate kidnappings with or without ransom demands, making it a federal crime to transport stolen property valued at $5,000 or more across state lines, rob a federal bank, assault or kill a federal agent, bribe a federal prison employee, possess an unregistered machine gun or flee

across state lines to avoid prosecution or giving testimony.

June 2, 1934 Dillinger gang molls sisters Opal Long and Patricia Cherrington are arrested by federal agents at the Chateau Hotel, 3838 North Broadway, in Chicago. Jean Helen Burke, girlfriend of Dillinger contact Arthur "Fish" Johnson, is also picked up.

The Tri-State Gang robs a National Guard armory at Hyattsville, Maryland.

June 4, 1934 Joseph Fox, one of the 10 escapees from the Indiana State Prison in 1933, is recaptured in Chicago.

Eddie Bentz and others rob the Caledonia National Bank at Danville, Vermont, of $8,500. Like Harvey Bailey, Bentz has successfully robbed banks for years, and is a suspect in the million-dollar bank job at Lincoln, Nebraska, in 1930.

Tri-State Gang members Robert Mais, Walter Legenza and Marie McKeever are captured by police after a gun battle near the local fairgrounds in Baltimore, Maryland. Mais and Legenza will be convicted of murder in Virginia and sentenced to death.

June 7, 1934 Dillinger outlaw Tommy Carroll is killed by police in Waterloo, Iowa. His mistress, Jean Delaney, is captured (Jean is the sister of Dolores Delaney, Alvin Karpis's mistress, and of Helen "Babe" Delaney Reilly, wife of Dillinger associate Albert "Pat" Reilly).

June 8, 1934 Dillinger is formally indicted by a federal grand jury at South Bend, Indiana, for interstate transportation of a car stolen in the Crown Point jailbreak.

June 11, 1934 Raymond Hamilton and Joe Palmer, former Barrow gang members, are tried for the murder of a prison guard at Huntsville, Texas. Both will be convicted and sentenced to death.

June 14, 1934 A Ramsey County grand jury indicts John Dillinger and Homer Van Meter for assault in connection with their March 31 gun battle in St. Paul.

June 22, 1934 Although J. Edgar Hoover refuses to rank "public enemies," John Dillinger is informally declared the first national Public Enemy Number One in a speech by U.S. Attorney General Homer S. Cummings.

In Chicago, Dillinger celebrates his 31st birthday with new girlfriend Polly Hamilton at the French Casino nightclub, 4812 North Clark Street.

June 23, 1934 U.S. Department of Justice offers a reward of $10,000 for the capture of John Dillinger, or $5,000 for information leading to his capture. Half that amount is offered for Baby Face Nelson, to his considerable annoyance. Dillinger and Polly Hamilton again visit the French Casino, to celebrate Polly's birthday.

June 24, 1934 Some 60 state and federal officers raid a ranch near Branson, Missouri, on a tip that both Dillinger and Pretty Boy Floyd are there recovering from wounds.

June 27, 1934 Albert "Pat" Reilly is arrested by federal agents in St. Paul on a charge of harboring Dillinger. Reilly claims to have heard that Dillinger is dead.

June 30, 1934 John Dillinger, Baby Face Nelson, Homer Van Meter, John Paul Chase and two other men rob the Merchants National Bank at South Bend of $29,890, killing Patrolman Howard Wagner. Evidence from several sources suggests that one unidentified robber was Pretty Boy Floyd, which would mark probably the only occasion that Floyd and Dillinger worked together. The other was Jack Perkins, boyhood friend of Baby Face Nelson, who was tried but acquitted.

July 6, 1934 Patricia Cherrington is convicted at Madison, Wisconsin, of harboring Dillinger and sentenced to two years.

July 10, 1934 Mob boss John Lazia, prominent in the Kansas City Massacre case, is machine-gunned by rival gangsters in Kansas City.

July 14, 1934 A Dillinger gang meeting at a rural schoolyard northwest of Chicago is interrupted by the arrival of two police officers, who are shot and wounded by Baby Face Nelson.

July 22, 1934 John Dillinger is killed by federal agents and policemen from East Chicago, Indiana, led by Melvin Purvis and Sam Cowley, outside Chicago's Biograph Theater at 2433 North Lincoln Avenue, after being set up by Polly Hamilton's friend Anna Sage, the "Lady in Red," and her friend, Sergeant Martin Zarkovich.

Using smuggled guns, Raymond Hamilton, Joe Palmer and Irwin "Blackie" Thompson shoot their way out of the Texas state prison

JOHN DILLINGER'S SUPPOSEDLY MISSING PARTS

Some credit for the outlaw's enduring popularity must go to two Chicago writers who in the early 1970s breathed life back into speculation that the man killed by federal agents outside the Biograph Theater was not, in fact, John Dillinger. That idea has been around since

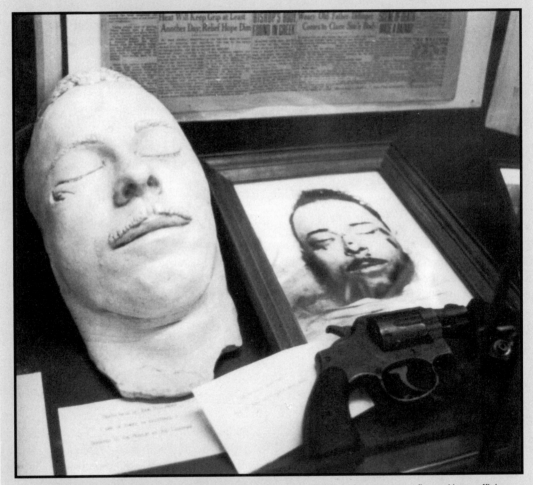

A Dillinger death-mask, being made by a group of embalming students and their professor, was confiscated by an officious police sergeant named Mulvaney. While one of the female students, Marjorie Eker, kept Mulvaney distracted, the group managed to make another and slip it out undetected. At least two other persons succeeded in making masks either by talking or bribing their way past officers or morgue officials. *(American Police Museum, Chicago)*

Dillinger's death in 1934, when people who claimed to have known the outlaw saw his body on the slab in the Cook County Morgue and discovered they could get an inch or two of newspaper coverage by insisting *it didn't look like him.* In the late 1930s a letter ostensibly written by Dillinger reached his family in Indiana and convinced some members that John was still alive. In 1938, an FBI agent, passing through Dillinger's home town of Mooresville, reported that a substantial number of citizens remained convinced that "Johnnie" had somehow pulled a fast one on the feds. *Dillinger: Dead or Alive?,* published in 1970, attempted to build a convoluted conspiracy theory—or theories, since none seemed complete or plausible—on the many discrepancies in official records, and if it had to overlook some convincing evidence of Dillinger's demise, it at least yielded much new information overlooked by other researchers. It also proved that, even if dead and buried, Dillinger still lived in the hearts and minds of a great many Americans for whom he was the last of the great antiheroes who became a legend in his own time.

Part of the legend holds that Dillinger's brain was "stolen" during his autopsy, and that belief contains at least some element of truth. The young medical intern and resident who were buttonholed by police the night of the killing and found themselves performing the postmortem in the absence of the Cook County medical examiner, who signed the report for posterity, did in fact remove Dillinger's brain and send it to the pathology department. They did so because it seemed like the thing to do, as some in the medical community still expected to discover obvious abnormalities in the brains of arch criminals. And that was the last they saw of it. When an undertaker reported the brain was missing, and no one claimed to have it, the word

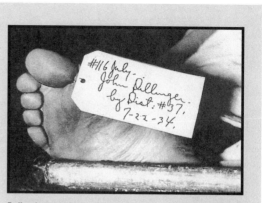

Police kept replacing Dillinger's toe tags, which were being removed as souvenirs. *(Authors' collection)*

"stolen" found its way into newspaper headlines, leading the Dillinger family to threaten a lawsuit against Cook County out of fear it would end up as a carnival attraction (offers for Dillinger's body had been angrily turned down), or be otherwise displayed. In the chaos that prevailed at the morgue that night and all the next day, at least three different parties had bullied or bribed their way past the police and through the crowds to make unauthorized death masks of the infamous Dillinger's face, so the family had reason to believe the worst.

Already criticized for the death-mask making and general treatment of the corpse, Cook County authorities scrambled to solve the mystery of the missing brain without communicating well enough to get their stories straight. Coroner Frank Walsh first denied that the brain was missing, only to learn that Medical Examiner Kearns had acknowledged the removal of an ounce or two of gray matter for scientific testing. Unaware of Kearns's announcement, a coroner's toxicologist contradicted both by reporting that he had half the brain in a jar of preservative, and thought the other half had been put in the corpse's stomach cavity, to avoid reopening the skull. Before that information

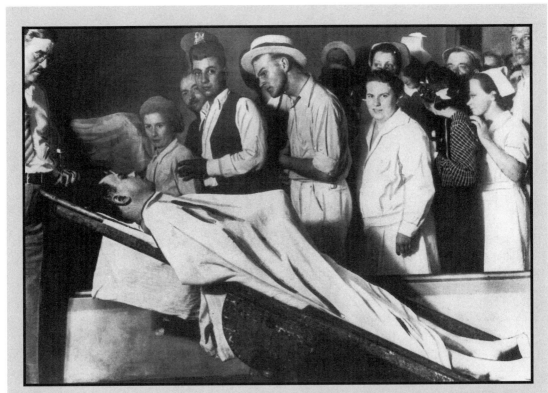

Dillinger's body on display at the Cook County Morgue in Chicago. The position of Dillinger's arm in this unfortunately posed photograph sparked many rumors about the outlaw's sexual endowment. Police could not control the crowds gathered to view the body despite a July heat wave. Newspapers estimated about 15,000 people visited the Cook County Morgue, where Dillinger's corpse was held an extra day before being released to a local mortuary. *(Sandy Jones Collection)*

death house and escape at Huntsville. All are bank robbers and killers, and are described in press releases as "embryonic Dillingers."

July 24, 1934 Dr. Wilhelm Loeser, who performed the plastic surgery on Dillinger, is arrested by federal agents at 1127 South Harvey in Oak Park, Illinois.

Billie Mace, sister of Bonnie Parker, and Floyd Hamilton, brother of Raymond Hamilton, are acquitted of the Easter Sunday murders of two highway patrolmen near Grapevine, Texas.

July 25, 1934 Salvatore Serpa, a reputed member of the Tri-State Gang, wanted in New Jersey for the murders of Edward "Cowboy" Wallace and gang molls Florence Miller and Ethel Greentree, is found murdered in Chicago.

July 26, 1934 Four men in overalls, carrying pistols and sawed-off shotguns, rob the Farmers Bank and Trust Company in Henderson, Kentucky, of $34,237. Baby Face Nelson is wrongly named as a suspect.

July 27, 1934 James Probasco, owner of the house in which Dillinger underwent plastic sur-

reached Dr. Kearns, he suddenly remembered having sent the toxicologist two-thirds of the brain and keeping one-third in his lab. On August 3, a waggish reporter for the Chicago *Daily Times* totaled up the fractions located in different departments and complimented the coroner's office on finally accounting for more of Dillinger's brain than he had to begin with.

Persuaded that the brain had not been removed for malicious or commercial purposes, the Dillingers dropped their suit, and with what must have been a sigh of relief heard all over Cook County, Coroner Walsh advised that whatever portions had been removed were destroyed in various tests, none of which revealed any abnormalities.

Which does not quite end the matter. Years later someone connected with Northwestern University's Medical School is supposed to have discovered Dillinger's brain, more or less intact, hidden in a laboratory that underwent remodeling after World War II. Supposedly, one of the professors kept it for a time as a souvenir, then gave it to a physician friend in another state, who eventually sold it to a Chicago optometrist named, the story goes, Dr. Brayne.

Which leaves only the matter of Dillinger's sexual endowment. That he easily charmed women with his cryptic smile, romantic style and display of confidence cannot be questioned. But how that translated into a penis of heroic proportions may forever remain a mystery, since his autopsy revealed an organ of average size. The tendency to endow famous men with great sexual prowess is well known to students of folklore, and in Dillinger's case this may have been enchanced by a front-page photo in *The Chicago Daily News,* which appeared to give his sheet-covered body an impressive erection. Most other papers publishing that picture had a retoucher flatten the sheet, whose effect was actually caused by the position of his arm. But soon after his death the story began to circulate that the size of Dillinger's organ qualified it for display at the Smithsonian Institution, or alternatively at the National Medical Museum long located on the Institution's grounds. So widespread is the rumor, at least in certain circles, that both organizations had to print form letters politely and euphemistically denying they have ever possessed, much less displayed, any part of Dillinger's anatomy, that part especially.

gery, allegedly commits suicide by leaping from a 19th-floor window of the Division of Investigation offices in Chicago's Bankers' Building. The rumor circulates that he fell to his death while being held out the window during interrogation.

Late July 1934 Dr. Joseph Moran, Barker-Karpis associate, disappears in Toledo. No body is found, but the Division of Investigation will conclude that Moran was murdered by the gang.

August 1, 1934 Bank robber and Kansas prison escapee Jim Clark is recaptured in Tulsa.

August 11, 1934 Joe Palmer, Texas prison escapee and former Barrow gang member, is recaptured in Paducah, Kentucky. Palmer brags that he planned the recent Henderson, Kentucky, bank robbery.

August 21, 1934 A United States Trucking Corporation armored car is robbed of $427,950 at the Rubel Ice Plant in Brooklyn by the John Manning gang. It is Brooklyn's first armored car robbery. Gang member Benny "The Bum" McMahon accidentally shoots himself during the getaway and later dies of blood poisoning.

THE BATTLE OF BARRINGTON AND THE MYSTERY OF BABY FACE NELSON'S DEATH

Of the many headline gun battles that marked the Public Enemy Era, the most bizarre and least logical was the machine-gun shootout near Barrington, Illinois, that cost two federal agents their lives and enabled Baby Face Nelson to escape in spite of 17 wounds. He died later that same evening, but in a house somehow connected with the FBI, and in the care of persons whom the Bureau, for reasons unknown, decided not to prosecute.

Nelson, born Lester Joseph Gillis, had grown up in a neighborhood on Chicago's Near West Side known as the Patch, had graduated from stealing car parts to robbing banks in the early 1930s, knew several ascending members of the Chicago mob, escaped from a guard en route to prison, but had not attracted much attention until Dillinger escaped from the Crown Point jail and joined his fledgling gang. That Nelson suddenly found himself described as a member of the famous Dillinger gang, instead of the other way around, seriously bruised his ego, leaving Dillinger obliged to flatter "Jimmie Williams," Nelson's favorite alias, and defer to his sense of personal importance. Most difficult was keeping peace among the members of this "second" Dillinger gang, due to the irascible Nelson's willingness to shoot police and civilians unnecessarily; he had even threatened to shoot colleagues, who could easily incur his wrath. On the other hand, he was cool in a crisis, and utterly fearless.

Following Dillinger's death in July 1934, Nelson packed up his wife, Helen, his son Ronald, two friends and their child, and fled to California. That November he and Helen left

This editorial cartoon summed up the general tenor of the government's solution to the problem of outlaws.
(Jeffery King Collection)

Ronald with relatives and returned to the Chicago area with a starstruck young bootlegger named John Paul Chase, intending to hole up at the Lake Como Hotel (now the French Country Inn), near Lake Geneva, Wisconsin, just north of the Illinois state line. The Lake Como was a pleasant, no-questions-asked waterfront resort operated by Hobart Hermanson, a former bootlegger living on the grounds and courting the estranged wife of Bugs Moran, who had his summer place a little farther down the same dirt road.

Tipped off that the Nelsons intended to winter at the hotel, FBI agents prevailed on Hermanson to loan them his house, but were caught totally off guard on the day a Ford they mistook for Hermanson's pulled up in front with three passengers. Nelson realized he'd driven into an unset trap, about the same time the agents recognized their visitor. Nelson exchanged a few words and sped off unhindered, for one agent had driven the FBI car to the nearby town of Lake Geneva to pick up groceries.

A frantic phone call to the Chicago office sent three carloads of federal agents rushing to Wisconsin in hopes of intercepting Nelson on what still is called the Northwest Highway but now paralled by a modern tollway. The first team of G-men encountered Nelson's car near the town of Fox River Grove and turned around to give chase, only to discover that Nelson had done the same. As the two vehicles passed a second time, Nelson, instead of running, again spun his car around and began pursuing his pursuers. The surprised agents floored their

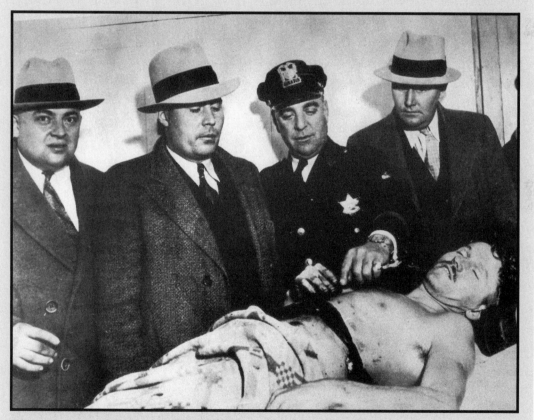

Baby Face Nelson took 17 bullets after killing two FBI agents in a machine-gun battle near Barrington, Illinois. With the help of his wife, Helen, and John Paul Chase, he managed to live a few more hours until succumbing to blood loss at a house in the Chicago suburb of Niles Center, now Skokie. *(Chuck Webb Collection)*

coupe and began firing out its back window as Nelson's faster machine closed the gap. With Helen Nelson crouching on the front floorboards, Chase, in the back seat, let go with a burst of fire from a .30–'06 Monitor, the commercial version of the military Browning Automatic Rifle. However, a lucky shot from the FBI car had punched through Nelson's radiator and disabled the fuel pump, allowing the agents to escape.

Meanwhile, an FBI Hudson, carrying Inspector Sam Cowley and Agent Herman Hollis, had encountered the running gun battle, wondered why it was going in the wrong direction with the wrong car in pursuit, and turned around to catch Nelson from behind. But Nelson's Ford already was losing speed, and the agents' Hudson skidded past when Nelson ditched his car at the dirt road entrance to Barrington's city park on the northwest edge of town. Hollis died with a bullet in his head when he ran for cover behind a telephone pole. Nelson, already hit by a Thompson slug, let out a curse and marched straight into the blasts from Cowley's shotgun, killing the second agent as well.

Though mortally wounded, Nelson managed to back the FBI Hudson up to his own disabled car, help load it with guns and ammunition, and with Chase driving made it into the Chicago suburb of Wilmette. He died a short time later in a cottage at 1627 Walnut Street in the neighboring town of Niles Center [now Skokie], and

was found late the next morning, wrapped in a blanket next to St. Paul's cemetery.

Few details of his death were reported in the usually inquisitive press, nor did the FBI reveal where Nelson died or charge those who had tried to save his life. Although agents found the house and placed it under close surveillance, Bureau files are strangely silent concerning the investigation, despite its vigorous prosecution of a dozen or more other people whose contact with Nelson was sometimes minimal or even innocent.

The only clue to this seemingly odd decision not to prosecute was found in a document filed some four years later containing the statement of a neighbor. He told the Bureau that the woman still living in the house said it belonged to someone closely connected with the FBI, probably as an informant, who had also been supplying Nelson with inside information from the Bureau. Nelson, she said, had decided the Walnut Street cottage would be the last place the G-men would think to look for him, adding that as far as she knew, Nelson's guns were still somewhere in the city, looking for a buyer.

Despite the limited information, it permits speculation that the Bureau, upon discovering where Nelson died, decided to let the matter go rather than reveal that the most notorious public enemy of the day had spent his last hours in the care of someone the FBI thought was working for it.

August 22, 1934   Al Capone and 52 other prisoners arrive at Alcatraz, transferred from the federal penitentiary in Atlanta.

Oliver "Izzy" Berg, friend of "Doc" Moran, and a Barker-Karpis associate, is arrested by federal agents at his sister's home in Chicago for passing Bremer ransom money.

August 23, 1934   Homer Van Meter is killed by police in St. Paul.

September 4, 1934   James Wilson, nephew of Doc Moran and former Barker-Karpis gang associate, fearing for his life, surrenders to federal agents in Denver.

September 5, 1934 Paula "Fat-Witted" Harmon, Wynona Burdette and Gladys Sawyer, Barker-Karpis gang molls, are arrested by police after a drunken disturbance at a Cleveland hotel. The Division of Investigation is notified but fails to trap the men of the gang.

September 22, 1934 Former Dillinger outlaws Harry Pierpont and Charles Makley fail in their attempt to escape from the death house of the state prison at Columbus, Ohio, using fake pistols carved from soap. Makley is killed and Pierpont wounded.

Richard Tallman Galatas, former Hot Springs bookie and conspiracy suspect in the Kansas City Massacre case, is arrested with his wife Elizabeth by federal agents in New Orleans.

September 26, 1934 Gambler Cassius McDonald is arrested by federal agents in Detroit for passing ransom money from the Bremer kidnapping.

September 29, 1934 Robert Mais and Walter Legenza, Tri-State Gang leaders sentenced to death, shoot their way out of the Richmond, Virginia, jail, killing a policeman.

October 11, 1934 Three men escape after a gun battle with police near Cresco, Iowa. Two are erroneously reported to be Pretty Boy Floyd and Adam Richetti.

October 17, 1934 Harry Pierpont is executed for murder in the Ohio State Prison.

October 19, 1934 Pretty Boy Floyd and Adam Richetti are suspected in a $500 bank robbery at Tiltonsville, Ohio.

October 21, 1934 Adam Richetti is captured by police near Wellsville, Ohio. Pretty Boy Floyd escapes.

October 22, 1934 Pretty Boy Floyd is killed by police and federal agents led by Melvin Purvis near Clarkson, Ohio.

October 26, 1934 The Tri-State Gang kidnaps Philadelphia racketeer William Weiss, demanding $100,000. After much haggling, they settle for $12,000. The kidnapping is not reported to police.

November 5, 1934 Albert Mayor, a friend of William Weiss, delivers a package containing $8,000 to a contact for the Tri-State Gang. A second package, containing the remaining $4,000, is apparently overlooked.

November 6, 1934 William Weiss is killed by his kidnappers and dumped in Neshominy Creek near Doylestown, Pennsylvania.

November 19, 1934 The Philadelphia office of the Division of Investigation receives an underworld tip reporting the Weiss abduction.

November 26, 1934 Matt Kimes, longtime bank robber and convicted murderer of two lawmen, is granted a six-day leave of absence from the state prison at McAlester, Oklahoma, to go quail hunting with his lawyer.

November 27, 1934 Baby Face Nelson and John Paul Chase battle federal agents near Barrington, Illinois, killing Inspector Samuel Cowley and Special Agent Herman Hollis. Despite 17 wounds, Nelson escapes in the federal car with his wife Helen and Chase, but dies that evening in a hideout at 1627 Walnut in the Chicago suburb of Skokie, then called Niles Center.

November 28, 1934 Nelson's body is found beside Skokie's St. Peter's cemetery. His wife, Helen Gillis, is headlined as the first female Public Enemy Number One.

New York mobster Arthur Flegenheimer,

alias Dutch Schultz, wanted on federal charges of income tax evasion, surrenders to the U.S. Commissioner at Albany, New York. After two trials Schultz will be acquitted.

November 29, 1934   In Chicago, Helen Gillis surrenders to federal agents who conceal this from the press and later insist she was "captured."

Big Homer Wilson, alleged Barker-Karpis gang member, dies at his Chicago home, apparently of natural causes. Wilson had robbed banks for years without being arrested.

December 1, 1934   Denver Police Chief A.T. Clark announces that the Denver Mint robbery (actually the $200,000 robbery of a Federal Reserve Bank truck outside the Mint) of December 18, 1922, has finally been solved. The crime supposedly was carried out by five men and two women, the only survivors of the gang being Harvey Bailey and James "Oklahoma Jack" Clark, both serving life sentences for other crimes.

December 4, 1934   Joseph Burns, last survivor of the Michigan City prison break, is recaptured in Chicago. The search continues for John Hamilton by authorities not yet convinced he is dead.

December 6, 1934   Irwin "Blackie" Thompson, Huntsville death house escapee, is slain by police in Amarillo, Texas.

December 11, 1934   The Tri-State Gang robs a National Guard armory at Morristown, Pennsylvania, taking 13 pistols, five automatic rifles and a thousand rounds of ammunition.

December 13, 1934   Philadelphia police raid a North Sixth Street house and arrest Tri-State Gang members Beatrice Wilkerson, Roy Willey, Joseph Darrow, Charles Zeid and Robert Eckert. Walter Legenza escapes after leaping from an elevated platform at the Wayne Street railroad station. He fractures both feet but eludes capture and flees to New York with Robert Mais and Marie McKeever.

December 17, 1934   A federal complaint is filed at Baltimore, charging Robert Mais, Walter Legenza and Marie McKeever with theft of government property.

December 27, 1934   John Paul Chase, last of the Nelson-Dillinger gang, is captured by police in Mount Shasta, California.

1935

January 2, 1935   Michael James "Jimmy the Needle" LaCapra, gangster-turned-informer in the Kansas City Massacre case, is released from Sumner County Jail in Wellington, Kansas.

Terrible Tommy Touhy, a semi-invalid drug addict suffering from palsy, is captured by police at an apartment in Chicago's Logan Square district. He will be convicted of mail robbery and sentenced to 23 years in Leavenworth.

January 4, 1935   Richard Galatas, Herbert "Deafy" Farmer, Frank "Fritz" Mulloy and Louis "Doc" Stacci, who supplied information for the Nash rescue attempt, are convicted of conspiracy to obstruct justice in the Kansas City Massacre case. Each is sentenced to two years in a federal penitentiary and fined $10,000.

January 5, 1935   Willie Harrison, a Barker-Karpis gang member considered unreliable by the others, is shot to death by Arthur "Dock" Barker, thrown into a barn at Ontarioville, Illinois, and burned.

January 8, 1935   Dock Barker and girlfriend Mildred Kuhlman are arrested by Melvin Purvis at 432 Surf Street in Chicago. Other federal agents raid a Barker-Karpis apartment at 3920

North Pine Grove and capture Byron [Bryan] "Monty" Bolton, Ruth Heidt and Clara Fisher in a night of commotion, shooting and tear gas. Russell Gibson, alias Roy "Slim" Gray, chooses to fight it out and is killed. Chicago police, responding to frantic phone calls from other residents, nearly shoot the G-men and protest not being informed in advance.

January 16, 1935 Ma and Fred Barker are killed by federal agents in a house on Lake Weir, at Oklawaha, Florida, after a four-and-a-half-hour gun battle. This is the first the public learns of Ma, who is made out to be a criminal mastermind.

Elmer Farmer, Barker-Karpis gang associate, is arrested in Bensenville, Illinois, and admits his part in the Edward Bremer kidnapping.

Using guns smuggled into the prison by bank robber Clyde Stevens, four convicts pistol-whip San Quentin Warden James R. Holohan, take four visiting prison and parole board members hostage and escape. A short time later, the escapees' stolen car is disabled by police bullets, and Rudolph "Bad Boy" Straight resists and is killed. The others surrender. Clyde Stevens, outside organizer of the break, and his partner, Albert Kissell, are captured on Sherman Island, California.

An attempted robbery of the State Bank of Leonore, Illinois, results in a three-country pursuit and a series of gun battles in which Marshall County Sheriff Glen Axline, cashier Charles Bundy and robber Melvin Liest are killed and four persons wounded. The other bandits, Arthur Thielen, Fred Gerner and John H. Hauff, are captured.

January 17, 1935 Harold Alderton, former owner of the Bensenville, Illinois, house where Edward Bremer was held by the Barker-Karpis gang, is arrested by federal agents in Marion, Indiana, and confesses his involvement.

Federal agents arrest Walter Legenza at Presbyterian Hospital in New York City. Two other Tri-State Gang members, Martin Farrell and Edwin Cale, are arrested in New York the same day.

January 18, 1935 Federal agents and police arrest Robert Mais and Marie McKeever at their Manhattan Avenue apartment in New York.

January 19, 1935 Edward Bremer identifies Harold Alderton's in Bensenville, Illinois, as the place of his confinement.

Two gunmen, one identified as Raymond Hamilton, rob the First National Bank at Handley, Texas, of $500.

January 20, 1935 Alvin Karpis and Harry Campbell battle police and escape from the Dan Mor Hotel in Atlantic City. Their girlfriends, Dolores Delaney and Wynona Burdette, are captured.

January 20–21, 1935 Alvin Karpis and Harry Campbell take Dr. Horace Hunsicker hostage and commandeer his car near Allentown, Pennsylvania. Dr. Hunsicker is left bound and gagged in Ohio and his car is later located in Monroe, Michigan.

January 22, 1935 A federal grand Jury at St. Paul returns new Bremer kidnapping indictments, superseding the indictments of May 4, 1934. Arthur "Dock" Barker, Alvin Karpis, Volney Davis, Harry Campbell, Elmer Farmer, Harold Alderton, William Weaver, Harry Sawyer, William J. Harrison, Bryan [Byron, Monty] Bolton, "John Doe," and "Richard Roe" are indicted for kidnapping Bremer and transporting him from St. Paul, Minnesota, to Bensenville, Illinois. These individuals and Dr. Joseph P. Moran, Oliver A. Berg, John J. "Boss"

McLauglin, Edna Murray, Myrtle Eaton, James J. Wilson, Jess Doyle, William E. Vidler, Philip J. Delaney and one "Whitey," are also indicted for conspiring with one another and with deceased conspirators Fred Goetz ("Shotgun George" Ziegler), Fred Barker, Russell Gibson and Ma Barker to kidnap Bremer.

The weighted body of William Weiss is recovered from Neshominy Creek, near Doylestown, Pennsylvania.

January 31, 1935   Joseph "Dutch" Cretzer, Arnold Kyle and Milton Hartman rob the Union Avenue Branch of the United States National Bank at Portland, Oregon, of $3,396.

February 2, 1935   Robert Mais and Walter Legenza die in the electric chair at Richmond, Virginia.

February 4, 1935   Raymond and Floyd Hamilton rob a Carthage, Texas, bank of $1,000. That night they reach their apartment in Dallas and are surprised by a posse, but manage to escape.

February 6, 1935   Barker-Karpis gang member Volney Davis is captured by federal agents in St. Louis.

In a Philadelphia hospital, Dolores Delaney gives birth to Alvin Karpis's son. The boy, named Raymond Alvin Karpaviecz, is given to Karpis's parents in Chicago.

February 7, 1935   Volney Davis escapes federal custody at Yorkville, Illinois.

Edna "The Kissing Bandit" Murray and Jess Doyle of the Barker-Karpis gang are captured in Kansas.

February 17, 1935   Raymond Hamilton and Ralph Fults steal eight Browning Automatic Rifles from a National Guard armory at Beaumont, Texas.

February 22, 1935   Some 23 relatives and friends of Clyde Barrow, Bonnie Parker and Raymond Hamilton are tried in Dallas for conspiracy to harbor federal fugitives. Hamilton's sister, Lillie McBride, is acquitted, but the others are convicted and sentenced to prison or jail terms of varying lengths.

February 28, 1935   Alva Dewey Hunt, Hugh Gant and others rob the State Bank at Haines City, Florida, of $4,000.

March 12, 1935   In a Kansas federal court, Harry C. Stanley is convicted of harboring his sister, Edna "The Kissing Bandit" Murray, sentenced to six months in the Sedgewick County Jail at Wichita, and fined $1,000. His wife, Mary, is also convicted and given a five-year suspended sentence.

March 18, 1935   John Paul Chase, associate of the late Baby Face Nelson, becomes the first man tried under one of the new laws that make killing a government agent a federal crime. He will be convicted and sentenced to life in Alcatraz.

March 19, 1935   Raymond Hamilton allegedly kidnaps Houston newspaperman Harry McCormick, dictates his version of his criminal career for publication, then releases him. Years later, the newspaperman will write that he contacted Hamilton and arranged the interview, then concocted the kidnapping story to avoid a harboring charge.

March 25, 1935   In federal court at Miami, Florida, Dolores Delaney and Wynona Burdette plead guilty to harboring Alvin Karpis and Harry Campbell. Both are sentenced to five years at the U.S. Detention Farm in Milan, Michigan.

March 28, 1935   Raymond Hamilton and Ralph Fults rob the Bank of Blountville at Prentiss, Mississippi, of $933, then capture 15 members of a pursuing posse, who are later released unharmed.

April 5, 1935 In San Francisco, Thomas "Tobe" Williams, Harry "Tex" Hall, Anthony "Soap" Moreno and Frank Cochran receive federal prison terms for harboring Baby Face Nelson. Louis "Doc Bones" Tambini and others are acquitted.

April 6, 1935 Raymond Hamilton is captured by Dallas County deputies in Grapevine, Texas.

April 15–May 6, 1935 Dock Barker and other members of the Barker-Karpis gang are tried and convicted in St. Paul of kidnapping Edward Bremer. Barker and others are sentenced to life.

April 24, 1935 Alvin Karpis, Harry Campbell and Joe Rich rob a U.S. mail truck at Warren, Ohio, of $72,000.

May 3, 1935 Harry and Gladys Sawyer, Barker-Karpis gang associates, are arrested by federal agents in Pass Christian, Mississippi.

May 10, 1935 Raymond Hamilton and Joe Palmer are electrocuted at the Texas state prison at Huntsville.

June 1, 1935 Volney Davis is recaptured in Chicago by Melvin Purvis.

June 10, 1935 Adam Richetti is tried as a participant in the Kansas City Massacre and sentenced to death.

June 25, 1935 Louis Piquett, former attorney of John Dillinger, is sentenced to two years in Leavenworth and fined $10,000 for harboring Homer Van Meter, who did not legally qualify as his client.

June 27, 1935 Leonard Scarnici, bank robber and confessed slayer of Vincent "Mad Dog" Coll and 13 others, dies in the Sing Sing electric chair for the 1933 murder of Rensselaer, New York, police detective Charles A. Stevens.

July 1, 1935 Congress authorizes changing the Division of Investigation to the Federal Bureau of Investigation (FBI).

July 10, 1935 Melvin Purvis submits his resignation to J. Edgar Hoover.

July 18, 1935 Leland Varain, alias "Two-Gun" Louie Alterie, one of the last survivors of the Bugs Moran gang, is shot to death by unidentified gunmen outside his apartment at 926 Eastwood Terrace in Chicago.

August 1, 1935 Alva Dewey Hunt, Hugh Gant and others rob the State Bank at Mulberry, Florida.

August 21, 1935 Michael James "Jimmy the Needle" LaCapra, who testified in the Kansas City Massacre case, is murdered at New Paltz, New York.

August 28, 1935 Acting on information from Volney Davis and Edna Murray, FBI agents recover a badly decomposed body from shallow grave near a gravel pit outside of Oswego, Illinois. The body is identified as John Hamilton's only through prison dental records, despite recurring reports that Hamilton is still alive.

September 1, 1935 Bill "Lapland Willie" Weaver and Myrtle Eaton, former Barker-Karpis gang members, are captured by the FBI at Allandale, Florida.

September 3, 1935 Bank robber Sam Coker is paroled from Oklahoma State Prison, allegedly as the result of bribery by persons connected with Alvin Karpis.

THE BODY IDENTIFIED AS JOHN HAMILTON'S

The possibility that some archvillain (in modern times, Hitler and Martin Bormann) successfully eluded justice, or tricked history into believing him dead, is a staple of folklore that has included a number of celebrity criminals from Jesse James to Butch Cassidy and Harry Longbaugh (the "Sundance Kid"). Of the criminals in the Public Enemy era, some still believe that the man killed outside the Biograph was not John Dillinger, despite convincing evidence otherwise. In 1938 a federal agent reported that many citizens in his hometown of

The body of Dillinger gang member John Hamilton was found in a shallow grave, so badly decomposed it could only be identified by dental records. Supposedly Hamilton was fatally wounded in a gunfight in near St. Paul, but some evidence suggests that he may have survived and escaped to Canada. *(Bruce Hamilton Collection)*

September 8, 1935   Philadelphia's Public Enemy Number One, Anthony "The Stinger" Cugino, is captured in New York City. After 15 hours of questioning, Cugino confesses to eight murders, then hangs himself in his cell. Cugino was allegedly affiliated with the Tri-State Gang.

October 12, 1935   Al Brady and Jim Dalhover rob a movie theater in Crothersville, Indiana, of $18.

October 23, 1935   Mobster Dutch Schultz and three henchmen are fatally shot by rival gangsters at the Palace Chop House in Newark, New Jersey. Police attribute the murders to a rising New York/New Jersey crime syndicate, which seeks control of the Schultz rackets. Leaders of the syndicate are named as Charles "Lucky" Luciano, Louis "Lepke" Buchalter, Jacob "Gurrah" Shapiro, Frank Costello, Joe Adonis, Benjamin "Bugsy" Siegel, Meyer Lansky, Abner "Longy" Zwillman and Johnny Torrio. Mob informers will later reveal that the syndicate murdered Schultz primarily to prevent him from assassinating Manhattan Special Prosecutor Thomas E. Dewey.

October–December 1935   The Brady gang (Al Brady, Clarence Shaffer, Jim Dalhover and Charles Geiseking) rob an estimated 150 grocery stores, drugstores and gas stations in Indiana and Ohio.

Mooresville, Indiana, including some family members, believed he took advantage of an FBI mistake and went into hiding, a notion that inspired a book (*Dillinger: Dead or Alive?*) as recently as 1970.

But the only prominent fugitive of the period who even possibly survived his own widely reported death was Dillinger gang member John Hamilton, believed mortally wounded in the spring of 1934, but whose gravesite remained a mystery for another 16 months. When eventually located by the FBI outside Oswego, Illinois, the body could not be identified except by prison dental records, which the Bureau declined to release. There were witnesses and other circumstantial evidence confirming his death, but also evidence to the contrary.

Those insisting he had died at a house in Aurora, Illinois, were friends and accomplices whose stories seemed convincing at the time. However, conflicting accounts from other gang associates had his body weighted and buried in an abandoned mineshaft in Wisconsin, or in the sand dune area of northern Indiana. The FBI itself received more than one confidential letter or statement claiming Hamilton had in fact survived, some inquiring about reward offers.

More significant are the childhood recollections of a nephew, Bruce Hamilton, Jr., who describes a mysterious family odyssey through several parts of the U.S., during which substantial sums of cash were obtained. The journey concluded with a visit to a small town in Canada (Hamilton's home country) and a secret family reunion, where he later was told that he had met his fugitive uncle, very much alive.

The death of Bruce Hamilton's father, who would never discuss the trip, and Hamilton's lack of success in locating another relative who could shed light on the subject, leaves the mystery unsolved. But as mysteries of this kind go, it's the only one in town.

November 3, 1935   Vivian Chase, wanted for bank robbery, jailbreaking and kidnapping, is found shot to death in a parked car outside St. Luke's Hospital in Kansas City, Missouri. Alvin Karpis is mentioned as a suspect.

November 7, 1935   Alvin Karpis leads his new gang in robbing a U.S. mail train of $34,000 at Garrettsville, Ohio. They make their getaway in an airplane.

November 29, 1935   Dutch Cretzer, Arnold Kyle and Milton Hartman rob the Ambassador Hotel Branch of the Security National Bank in Los Angeles of $2,765.

November 30, 1935   The Brady gang robs a grocery store at Crawfordsville, Indiana, and wounds two policemen in a gun battle.

December 30, 1935   Former Chicago politician John "Boss" McLaughlin, serving a five-year sentence for passing Bremer ransom money, dies in Leavenworth.

1936

January 6–24, 1936   Harry Sawyer, Bill Weaver and Cassius McDonald are tried and convicted in St. Paul for their involvement in the Bremer kidnapping. Sawyer and Weaver are sentenced to life, McDonald to 15 years.

January 11, 1936   Cleveland Public Safety Director Eliot Ness leads a raid on the Harvard Club, a casino in Newburgh Heights, Ohio, whose owners have often harbored the Barker-Karpis gang.

January 14, 1936 The Hunt-Gant gang robs the Dixie County State Bank at Cross City, Florida, of $4,000.

January 23, 1936 Dutch Cretzer, Arnold Kyle and Milton Hartman rob a branch of the American Trust Company of Oakland, California, of $6,000.

January 24, 1936 Cretzer, Kyle and Hartman rob the Vineyard and Washington Branch of the Bank of America in Los Angeles of $1,475.

February 15, 1936 Capone gunman Vincent Gebardi, alias DeMora, alias Machine Gun Jack McGurn, is shot to death by unknown killers in a bowling alley at 805 Milwaukee in Chicago. Years later, FBI tapes reveal one of the killers was McGurn's former associate John ("Screwy") Moore, better known as Claude Maddox.

March 2, 1936 Cretzer, Kyle and Hartman rob the Melrose and Bronson Branch of the Bank of America in Los Angeles of $6,100.

March 3, 1936 The Hunt-Gant gang robs the Columbia Bank in Ybor City, Florida, of $30,459.

Anthony DeMora, who has sworn to avenge his half-brother "Machine Gun" Jack McGurn, is murdered by gunmen outside a poolroom in Chicago's "Little Italy."

March 4, 1936 The Brady gang steals $8,000 worth of gems from a jewelry store in Greenville, Ohio.

March 13, 1936 Edward Wilhelm "Eddie" Bentz, longtime bank robber, is arrested by the FBI in New York City. He will be sentenced to 20 years in federal prison for a Danville, Vermont, bank robbery. Bentz boasts of having hidden millions of dollars in stolen bank bonds, which are never found.

March 19, 1936 The Brady gang steals $6,800 in gems from a jewelry store in Lima, Ohio.

March 26, 1936 The FBI fails to capture Alvin Karpis in Hot Springs, Arkansas. It is later alleged that Karpis contributed $6,500 to the mayor's election campaign.

New York Mafia boss Charles "Lucky" Luciano, under indictment as head of a vice ring, is also living in Hot Springs.

March 30, 1936 Preston Patton, son of Edna "The Kissing Bandit" Murray, and other young delinquents murder Night Marshal Ben Wiggins when he catches them cracking a safe at the Booker Williamson furniture store in Lyons, Kansas. Patton and the others will be captured, convicted and sentenced to life imprisonment.

April 9, 1936 The Brady gang commits a $27,000 jewelry store robbery in Dayton.

Charles J. Fitzgerald, former Barker-Karpis outlaw, is arrested by the FBI in Los Angeles and charged with the William Hamm kidnapping.

April 17, 1936 Hamm identifies the Bensenville, Illinois, home of Postmaster Edmund Bartholmey as the place of his confinement in June 1933. Bartholmey is arrested by the FBI and confesses his involvement in the kidnapping.

April 18, 1936 St. Paul gangster Jack Peifer (or Peiffer) is arrested by the FBI for the Hamm kidnapping.

April 22, 1936 Alvin Karpis, Dock Barker, Charles J. Fitzgerald, Edmund Bartholmey, Bryan (or Byron) Bolton, Jack Peifer and Elmer Farmer are indicted for the kidnapping of William Hamm.

The U.S. Department of Justice offers a

$5,000 reward for the capture of Alvin Karpis or Harry Campbell.

The Brady gang murders clerk Edward Linsey in a grocery store holdup in Piqua, Ohio.

April 27, 1936 U.S. postal officials offer a $2,000 reward for the capture of Alvin Karpis.

The Brady gang robs the same Lima, Ohio, jewelry store they held up on March 19. Later in the day, they murder police sergeant Richard Rivers in Indianapolis.

April 29, 1936 Al Brady is arrested by Chicago police.

May 1, 1936 Alvin Karpis, Fred Hunter and Ruth Hamm Robison, alias Connie Morris, are arrested in New Orleans by FBI agents, led "personally" by Director J. Edgar Hoover; Karpis disputes Hoover's account, claiming he was siezed by agents and held at gunpoint while Hoover was summoned from a nearby alley to proclaim him arrested.

May 7, 1936 Harry Campbell and Sam Coker, Karpis gang members, are arrested by the FBI in Toledo. J. Edgar Hoover again leads the raiding party.

Alvin Karpis is arraigned in St. Paul for the kidnappings of William A. Hamm, Jr. and Edward George Bremer and held under $500,000 bond.

May 9, 1936 Sam Coker is returned to Oklahoma state prison to complete a 30-year sentence for bank robbery.

May 11, 1936 Clarence Shaffer of the Brady gang is arrested at his home near Indianapolis.

In Manhattan, crime boss Charles "Lucky" Luciano goes to trial on charges of compulsory prostitution. The prosecutor is Thomas E. Dewey.

May 14, 1936 Avery Simons, alias Dan or Jim Ripley, wanted for the $2 million bank robbery at Lincoln, Nebraska, in 1930, is arrested by the FBI in Los Angeles while attempting to again flee to South America. Formerly a partner of Eddie Bentz and Eddie Doll, he will shortly rejoin them at Alcatraz, under two consecutive 12-year sentences for bank robbery.

May 15, 1936 Brady gang member Jim Dalhover is arrested in Chicago.

May 27, 1936 Fred Hunter pleads guilty to harboring Alvin Karpis and is sentenced to two years in federal prison. He will later be convicted of mail robbery.

June 2, 1936 The Hunt-Gant gang robs the Farmers and Merchants Bank at Foley, Alabama, of $7,242.

June 6, 1936 Former Barker-Karpis outlaw Lawrence DeVol and 15 other inmates escape from the St. Peter Hospital for the Criminally Insane in Minnesota.

Lucky Luciano is convicted of compulsory prostitution.

June 8, 1936 John Callahan, formerly a bootlegger, narcotics trafficker and the biggest receiver of stolen goods in the Southwest, dies at the age of 70 at his home in Wichita, Kansas. For years Callahan had served as a Fagin figure, training such criminal apprentices as Pretty Boy Floyd.

June 18, 1936 Lucky Luciano is sentenced to 30 to 50 years in Dannamora Prison in New York. His sentence will be commuted in 1945 by his former prosecutor, now Governor Thomas E. Dewey, for using his influence among dock workers to prevent wartime sabotage, and he will be deported to Italy.

June 19, 1936 Outlaw Arthur Gooch is hanged at McAlester, Oklahoma, for the kidnapping of two Texas policemen. He is the first man to be executed under the federal Lindbergh Law.

July 1, 1936 Dutch Cretzer, Arnold Kyle and Milton Hartman rob the Wilshire and Vermont Branch of the Seaboard National Bank in Los Angeles of $1,996.

July 5, 1936 John Manning, planner of the Rubel Ice company armored car robbery, is found murdered in Manhattan. Other members of the gang will later be imprisoned for the robbery.

July 8, 1936 After robbing a bank at Turon, Kansas, Lawrence DeVol is surrounded by police at the German Village Tavern in Enid, Oklahoma. In the ensuing gun battle, DeVol and Officer Cal Palmer are killed.

July 27, 1936 Dutch Cretzer, Arnold Kyle and Milton Hartman rob the Broadway Branch of the First National Bank in Seattle of $14,581.

Alvin Karpis pleads guilty to the Hamm kidnapping and is sentenced to life.

July 31, 1936 Charles Fitzgerald is sentenced to life for the Hamm kidnapping. Jack Peifer is sentenced to 30 years for the same crime but commits suicide by chewing poisoned gum in the St. Paul jail. Edmund Bartholmey, in whose house Hamm was held, receives a six-year sentence. Byron (also Bryan or Monty) Bolton, who testified against the others, is sentenced to three to five years, to be served concurrently with a similar term for the Edward Bremer kidnapping.

August 7, 1936 Alvin Karpis enters Alcatraz.

September 12, 1936 Brady gang member Charles Geiseking is arrested in Henderson, Kentucky.

October 11, 1936 Al Brady, Clarence Shaffer and Jim Dalhover escape from the Hancock County Jail at Greenfield, Indiana.

October 13, 1936 A complaint is filed before the U.S. Commissioner at Cleveland charging Brady, Shaffer and Dalhover with interstate transportation of stolen property valued in excess of $5,000. The Brady gang are now federal fugitives, wanted by the FBI.

November 23, 1936 The Brady gang robs a bank at North Madison, Indiana, of $1,630.

November 27, 1936 Arnold Kyle and Milton Hartman rob the Greenwood Branch of the First National Bank in Seattle of $8,000.

December 14, 1936 FBI agents, again led by J. Edgar Hoover, lay siege to an apartment building on West 102nd Street in New York, accidentally setting it afire with a tear-gas bomb, and capture bank robber Harry Brunette and his wife.

December 16, 1936 The Brady gang robs a Carthage, Indiana, bank of $2,158.

December 27, 1936 Mistaken for another fugitive, Oklahoma outlaw Carl Janaway shoots a St. Louis policeman in the legs and attempts to flee, but is struck by a taxi and captured.

1937

January 28, 1937 Milton Hartman robs the Sunset and Clark Branch of the Bank of America in Los Angeles of $2,870.

March 29, 1937 Arnold Kyle, Milton Hartman and John Oscar Hetzer rob the Rose City Branch of the First National Bank in Portland of $18,195.

April 6, 1937   John Oscar Hetzer is arrested by the FBI at a Los Angeles garage.

April 7, 1937   Cornered by the FBI, Milton Hartman commits suicide in his room at the Stuart Hotel in Los Angeles.

April 27, 1937   The Brady gang robs the Winchester Peoples Loan and Trust Company branch at Farmland, Indiana, of $1,427.

May 25, 1937   The Brady gang robs the Goodland, Indiana, bank of $2,528. Fifteen miles outside of town, they shoot up a police car, killing Indiana state policeman Paul Minneman and wounding Deputy Elmer Craig.

June 30, 1937   At the U.S. District Court in Cleveland, Arthur Hebebrand and John Francis "Sharkey" Gorman plead guilty to harboring Alvin Karpis and Harry Campbell. Hebebrand is sentenced to two years in federal prison and fined $1,000. Gorman is sentenced to three years and fined $1,000.

August 7, 1937   The Brady gang escapes from police in a gun battle in Baltimore, leaving behind an arsenal of weapons and ammunition.

August 23, 1937   The Brady gang robs the Peoples Exchange Bank at Thorp, Wisconsin, of $7,000.

September 19, 1937   At California's Folsom Prison, a bloody escape attempt results in the deaths of guard H.D. Martin and inmate Clyde Stevens. Warden James Larkin and inmate Ben Kucharski will die several days later. The five surviving participants in the attempted breakout will be sentenced to the gas chamber at San Quentin.

September 28, 1937   The Brady gang is suspected in the murder of Highway Patrolman George Conn near Freeport, Ohio.

October 3, 1937   Roy Thornton and Austin Avers are killed attempting to escape from the "Little Alcatraz" unit at Eastham Prison Farm in Texas. Thornton had been Bonnie Parker's husband who was serving time when she met Clyde Barrow.

October 12, 1937   The Brady gang is surrounded by FBI agents and police at a sporting goods store in Bangor, Maine. Al Brady and Clarence Shaffer are killed and Jim Dalhover is captured.

1938

January 11, 1938   Alva Dewey Hunt and Hugh Gant are captured by the FBI in Houston.

January 25, 1938   Under the alias of Kay Wallace, Edna Kyle Cretzer is arrested for operating a house of prostitution in Pittsburgh, California, and released on bond. Edna is the wife of fugitive bank robber Joseph "Dutch" Cretzer.

June 7, 1938   Floyd Hamilton and Ted Walters rob a Bradley, Arkansas, bank of $685.

June 23, 1938   Ruth Hamm Robison, alias Connie Morris, pleads guilty in federal court at Little Rock, Arkansas, to harboring Alvin Karpis and is sentenced to a year and a day.

July 21, 1938   Three suspected bandits, one identified as Floyd Hamilton, escape a police trap after battling highway patrolmen at Wills Point, Texas.

July 31, 1938   Missouri Highway Patrol officers unsuccessfully pursue three bandits, two identified as Floyd Hamilton and Ted Walters.

August 3, 1938   Bank robber Bennie Dickson marries 15-year-old Stella Mae Irwin at Pipestone, Minnesota.

August 5, 1938   Three men rob a messenger of the First National Bank at Wood River, Illinois, of $34,000. Floyd Hamilton and Ted Walters are suspects.

August 8, 1938   Two heavily armed men, believed to be Floyd Hamilton and Ted Walters, escape police in a running gun battle near Fort Worth.

August 21, 1938   Floyd Hamilton and Ted Walters are captured in Dallas. Both will be sentenced to long terms at Alcatraz.

August 25, 1938   Bennie and Stella Dickson rob the Corn Exchange Bank at Elkton, South Dakota, of $2,174. It is the eve of Stella's 16th birthday.

October 7, 1938   Adam Richetti, still claiming innocence in the Kansas City Massacre, dies in the Missouri state prison gas chamber at Jefferson City.

October 14, 1938   James Murray, George Slade and John Dorsch rob the Peoples National Bank at Clintonville, Pennsylvania, of $85,000 in cash, securities and jewelry. Murray, a former Chicago politician and bootlegger, had served time for the $2 million train robbery at Rondout, Illinois, in 1924, harbored members of the Dillinger gang, used the house where Baby Face Nelson died and evidently helped move his body to the cemetery where it was found the next day.

October 29, 1938   In a Little Rock, Arkansas, federal court, Jewell LaVerne Grayson, alias Grace Goldstein, former girlfriend of Alvin Karpis, along with Hot Springs Police Chief Joseph Wakelin, Chief of Detectives Herbert "Dutch" Akers and Lieutenant Cecil Brock, are convicted of harboring Karpis. Each is sentenced to two years in a federal penitentiary.

October 31, 1938   Bennie and Stella Dickson rob the Brookings, South Dakota, branch of the Northwest Security National Bank of Sioux Falls of $47,233 in cash and bonds.

November 18, 1938   Brady gang member James Dalhover is electrocuted at the Indiana state prison in Michigan City.

November 24, 1938   Bennie and Stella Dickson separately escape police at a tourist camp in Topeka, Kansas. Stella spends the night under a bridge. Bennie drives to South Clinton, Iowa, hijacks another car, and meets Stella again the next day near Topeka. Over the next few days, they will battle police in Michigan, with Stella shooting out the tires of a patrol car, then take three men hostage and steal two more cars in Michigan and Indiana.

December 6, 1938   Former Hot Springs Chief of Detectives Herbert "Dutch" Akers is convicted of harboring bank robber Thomas Nathan Norris and sentenced to an additional two years.

December 16, 1938   Albert Kessel, Robert Cannon, Fred Barnes, Wesley Eudy and Sebron Edward Davis, participants in an attempted breakout from Folsom Prison, are executed at San Quentin.

1939

January 13, 1939   Arthur "Dock" Barker is fatally wounded while attempting to escape from Alcatraz.

February 8, 1939   Arnold Kyle robs the Kansas State Bank in Wichita of $9,115.

April 6, 1939   Bennie Dickson is killed by FBI agents at a hamburger stand in St. Louis. Stella Dickson escapes.

April 7, 1939   Stella Dickson, now known as Sure Shot Stella, is arrested by the FBI in Kansas City. She will be convicted of bank robbery in South Dakota and sentenced to 10 years.

April 16, 1939   FBI agents arrest former Dillinger associate James Murray at his Chicago home for the bank robbery at Clintonville, Pennsylvania. Murray will be convicted and sentenced to 25 years in Alcatraz.

May 18, 1939   Under the alias of Raymond J. Palmer, Arnold Kyle is arrested for drunken driving in Minneapolis and turned over to the FBI.

June 7, 1939   Arnold Kyle pleads guilty to bank robbery and is sentenced to 25 years in the federal penitentiary at McNeil Island, Washington.

August 24, 1939   At Fifth Avenue and 28th Street in New York, mob boss Louis "Lepke" Buchalter, wanted for murder, narcotics conspiracy, extortion and antitrust violations, arranges with celebrity newsman Walter Winchell to surrender in person to FBI Director J. Edgar Hoover. Buchalter will be executed by the state of New York in 1944.

August 27, 1939   Joseph "Dutch" Cretzer is arrested by the FBI in Chicago.

November 6, 1939   Edna Kyle Cretzer pleads guilty to harboring her husband and is sentenced to 85 days in jail.

November 8, 1939   Edward J. O'Hare, dogtrack owner, who popularized the mechanical rabbit and informer in the Capone tax case, is shotgunned to death in his car on Ogden Avenue in Chicago. The city's new airport will be named after his son, the first Chicago naval aviator to die a war hero soon after the bombing of Pearl Harbor.

November 16, 1939   Al Capone is released from prison; retires in failing health to his Palm Island estate in Florida.

POSTSCRIPT:

January 24, 1940   Joseph "Dutch" Cretzer pleads guilty to bank robbery in Los Angeles and is sentenced to 25 years in the federal penitentiary at McNeil Island, Washington.

April 11, 1940   Cretzer and Arnold Kyle escape from the prison but not McNeil Island and will be recaptured on April 14.

July 10, 1940   Fred "Killer" Burke, serving a life sentence for murder, dies of natural causes at the Michigan state prison.

August 8, 1940   Eleanor "The Blonde Tigress" Jarman, Depression bandit and convicted murderess, escapes from the women's prison at Dwight, Illinois. She is never recaptured.

August 22, 1940   Joseph "Dutch" Cretzer and Arnold Kyle are sentenced to five more years for their escape attempt and in the courtroom assault U.S. Marshal A.J. Chitty in another attempt. Chitty dies of a heart attack, and both are sentenced to life on Alcatraz.

February 28, 1941   George Elias Barker, husband of Kate "Ma" Barker, dies at his home in Webb City, Missouri, near Joplin.

October 9, 1942   Roger Touhy, Basil "The Owl" Banghart, Edward Darlak, William Stewart, Martlick Nelson, James O'Connor and St. Clair McInerney escape from Joliet, Illinois, prison. The FBI enters the case on the novel legal point that the escapees have changed addresses without notifying Selective Service, thereby violating the draft law.

LOUIS PIQUETT

Dillinger attorney Louis Piquett practiced law the way most Chicago aldermen practiced politics—without fear, favor (except at a price) or anything resembling scruples. He'd "read" for his license while working as a bartender and stuffing ballot boxes for Mayor Big Bill Thompson, which earned him a job as city prosecutor, which he kept until he had met enough crooks to support him in private practice. He represented local abortion rings and was the designated "fixer" for one or more police districts. When the wife of Russell Gibson (later of the Barker-Karpis gang) tried to bail out her husband on a jewel-theft charge, the cops told her to keep her cash and go see Piquett, who had streamlined the municipal justice system to the point where $500 resolved the matter to everyone's satisfaction without any burdensome paperwork. His clients included the renowned con man William Elmer Meade and St. Louis gunman Leo Brothers, whose paid shooting of *Chicago Tribune* reporter Jake Lingle in a crowded downtown underpass caused the greatest uproar since the St. Valentine's Day Massacre. Brothers made local history as the first "gangster" convicted of murder in five years of beer wars, but Piquett negotiated a sentence of only 14 years.

The FBI was not especially surprised when Dillinger, facing an Indiana murder charge, became Piquett's next notorious client, but they never learned the ruse the lawyer used to accomplish this. Piquett knew plenty of Michigan City prisoners who would have known Dillinger, and after a few inquiries he had his business card smuggled to the Crown Point jail's celebrity inmate, who found written on the back, "Hire no lawyer but this one. Gang raising funds.

Dillinger's lawyer, Louis Piquett, was already in contact with Anna Sage, "the woman in red," who later set the outlaw up for a fatal ambush outside Chicago's Biograph Theater. Apparently, Piquett sent Dillinger to stay with her. *(Authors' collection)*

—*Happy.*" That was a name Dillinger apparently knew, and he found in Piquett a legal counselor in many ways less principled than himself. Piquett's services stretched the bounds of attorney-client privilege—from engineering Dillinger's wooden-pistol jailbreak to providing him and Homer Van Meter with plastic surgeons, an act which ultimately cost him his license and a stretch in prison, when a trial established that Van Meter was not legally his client. He ended up financially ruined, and avoiding his former friends. The bar he eventually returned to was in a tavern instead a courthouse.

December 18, 1942 Touhy and Banghart are suspected of a $20,000 truck robbery in Melrose Park, Illinois.

December 28, 1942 James O'Connor and St. Clair McInerney are killed by FBI agents at 1254 Leland Avenue in Chicago.

December 29, 1942 Roger Touhy, Basil Banghart and Edward Darlak are captured by FBI agents, led by J. Edgar Hoover, in a nearby apartment at 5116 Kenmore Avenue in Chicago. It is Hoover's last "personal arrest."

June 20, 1944 William Weaver, serving a life sentence for the Bremer kidnapping, dies on Alcatraz.

January 9, 1945 Charles J. Fitzgerald, serving a life sentence for the Hamm kidnapping, dies at Leavenworth.

December 1, 1945 Twenties bank robber Matt Kimes, on leave of absence from the McAlester, Oklahoma, state prison and wanted for a recent bank robbery at Merton, Texas, dies from injuries when he is run over by a poultry truck in North Little Rock, Arkansas.

May 24, 1946 An escape attempt from Alcatraz erupts into a bloody riot as convicts raid the prison arsenal and take guards hostage. U.S. Marines and prison guards lay siege to the convicts' cellblocks stronghold. Inmates Bernard Paul Coy, Joseph "Dutch" Cretzer and Marvin Hubbard, and guards William A. Miller and Harold P. Stites, are killed. Several other guards are wounded.

July 30, 1946 Dr. Harold Cassidy, who assisted in Dillinger's plastic surgery, commits suicide at his sister's home in Chicago.

November 20–December 22, 1946 Miran Edgar "Buddy" Thompson, Sam Shockley and Clarence Carnes, survivors of the Alcatraz riot, are tried and convicted of the murder of guard Miller. Thompson and Shockley are sentenced to death, Carnes to life imprisonment.

January 25, 1947 Al Capone dies at his estate on Palm Island, Florida.

February 10, 1947 Willie "The Actor" Sutton and others escape from Holmesburg prison in Philadelphia

April 25, 1947 Anna Sage, the notorious "Lady in Red" who betrayed Dillinger, dies of liver failure in Romania.

November 28, 1947 Former Barker-Karpis gang member Thomas James Holden is paroled from a 25-year sentence for mail train robbery.

April 19, 1948 Former Barrow gang member Henry Methvin is hit by a train and killed at Sulphur, Louisiana. Rumors persist in the area that Methvin, suspected of betraying Bonnie and Clyde in 1934, was actually murdered.

July 2, 1948 Twenties outlaw George Kimes, serving a 50-year sentence for bank robbery, escapes from the Oklahoma state prison.

July 4, 1948 Albert Bates, serving a life sentence for the Urschel kidnapping, dies on Alcatraz.

September 14, 1948 Depression bank robber Glen LeRoy Wright, serving a life sentence for robbery, shoots his way out of the Oklahoma state prison with a smuggled pistol.

December 2, 1948 Buddy Thompson and Sam Shockley are executed in the San Quentin gas chamber.

March 18, 1949 Lloyd "Red" Barker, last surviving son of Ma Barker, is killed by his wife Jennie at their home in Westminister, Colorado, near Denver.

"SHOOT INTO HIM!"

The Execution of Pretty Boy Floyd

The first of the Depression outlaws to attract national attention was Pretty Boy Floyd, whom the *Literary Digest* described as "Oklahoma's Bandit King" for his audacity, cockiness, use of a submachine gun and the fact that his identity was known. Armed robbery of banks, trains and payroll guards had flourished in the Midwest after the Civil War until suppressed by private police agencies such as the Pinkertons, who functioned as an extralegal version of the FBI in their interstate pursuit of the James boys, Dalton brothers and other "Old West" outlaws of the horseback era.

With the improvements in automobiles, that type of outlawry returned in the 1920s, and some of the new "motorized bandits," as they were called, thrived for years on a combination of mobility and anonymity that also kept their names out of the history books. Floyd was among the first to acquire personal notoriety, and if his lawbreaking never came close to that of Baron H.K. Lamm, Harvey Bailey, Eddie Bentz or the Newton Brothers, he did commit (or maybe bungle) the spectacular crime the press proclaimed "A Machine-Gun Challenge to a Nation," and which helped launch the modern FBI.

Legend as well as fact have turned Floyd into something of a Robin Hood character, thanks partly to the Depression, his absence of gratuitous cruelty, and his admired if self-serving stunt of destroying bank-loan records, which made farm foreclosures more difficult. Other aspects of his life and death raise questions that do not have the tidy answers found in standard accounts of his career.

The crime that gained Floyd the greatest notoriety was his presumed involvement in the Kansas City Massacre of June 17, 1933. Several lawmen, including federal agent Raymond Caffrey, were transporting escaped bank robber Frank "Jelly" Nash back to Leavenworth that morning when the group found themselves confronted in the Union Station parking lot by two or more gunmen. Moments later, four of the officers and Nash himself died in a barrage of bullets, and evidence found at the house of one of the suspects led the Bureau to believe that the shooters were Verne Miller, a onetime sheriff turned fulltime hoodlum; Adam Richetti, whose fingerprints were found on a beer bottle; and Richetti's main partner in crime, Pretty Boy Floyd.

Whether the killing of Nash was accidental, because he was sitting behind the wheel of one of the police cars, or whether it was intended to silence an inside member of the Kansas City crime organization, remains unresolved in FBI accounts, which fail to mention that he apparently was killed inadvertently by one of its own agents sitting behind him and trying to work the action of an unfamiliar shotgun. Moreover, some biographers have found the evidence against Floyd suppositional, and such wanton killing to be out of character. But the FBI made his capture top priority because it involved the death of a federal officer, and he was gunned down on an Ohio farm on October 22, 1934, under circumstances that now appear tantamount to summary execution.

In her unpublished manuscript, Gus Winkeler's widow, Georgette, gives an interesting version that has a ring of truth supported later by outlaw Harvey Bailey. Well-acquainted

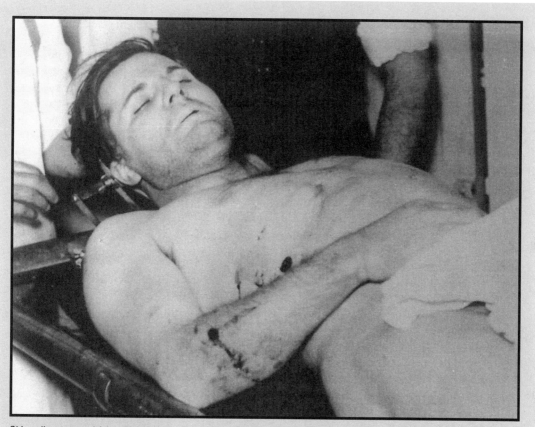

Ohio police captured Adam Richetti after a gunfight, but Pretty Boy Floyd escaped. The officers notified the Chicago FBI, whose agents soon became lost on back country roads; the FBI, in turn, had to call in the locals, who found the G-men and also Floyd. Wounded as he fled across an open field, Floyd later ignored Purvis's questions about the Kansas City Massacre, giving only his proper name and a string of profanities. According to the last surviving Ohio officer, but previously confirmed by others, Purvis then ordered an agent with a Thompson submachine gun to finish Floyd off.   *(Goddard Collection)*

with Verne Miller from her husband's days in and around St. Louis, she says the shooting occurred in a rescue attempt by Miller and Floyd, with no mention of Richetti. (According to Bailey, the second man was supposed to be Richetti, but a night of drinking had left him totally incapacitated, and Floyd reluctantly agreed to take his place.) Georgette's information came from her husband, who said that Miller, a borderline psychopath at best, approached the cars yelling "Up! Up! Up!" and

when Nash only sat there looking puzzled, Miller lost his temper and loosed his machine gun on the entire group. With one or more officers firing back, Floyd joined the firefight before escaping in a getaway car.

The killings made headlines nationwide, and Floyd and Richetti went into hiding around Buffalo, New York. Only when their funds ran low did they venture back to the Midwest in search of a gang to work with. Though more a loner than a joiner, Floyd probably used mutual connections to participate in the Dillinger gang's last holdup on June 30, 1934, when the Merchant's National Bank of South Bend, Indiana, lost $30,000, with one policeman killed and four civilians wounded. One of the gunmen was identified as Floyd at the time, though witnesses tended to want their banks robbed only by the famous. Fatso Negri, when later grilled as a pal of gang member Baby Face Nelson, said the group did include a notorious but unnamed "guest" robber who somehow had antagonized the hot-headed Nelson to the point where Nelson threatened to kill him. The ever diplomatic Dillinger told Nelson that killing their new man was a fine idea, if he was also prepared to take on Adam Richetti, whom everyone knew to be Floyd's partner.

Interrogations of other suspects also pointed to Floyd, but Negri best remembered Baby Face throwing a minor tantrum when agents killed Floyd in October. Nelson's complaint was that Hoover's meddlesome G-men had deprived him of the pleasure of killing Floyd personally.

Floyd's efforts to find "work" had already led him to contact Clyde Barrow, but Bonnie and Clyde were killed in a Louisiana ambush on May 23, before any jobs could be planned; and if he indeed teamed up with Dillinger on the South Bend job, Dillinger's death on July 22 ended any further collaboration. He and Richetti were in Ohio when a fight with local authorities led police to call the FBI.

Richetti had already been wounded and captured when Melvin Purvis and several other agents joined local officers to search for Floyd in the vicinity of East Liverpool. In fact, the only reason the Ohio lawmen remained involved is that the G-men managed to get themselves lost on unmarked country roads and had called the East Liverpool police asking for directions. Local officers met the agents at the farm of widow Ellen Conkle, and while leading them back to town policeman Chester Smith spotted a suspicious man in a suit dashing behind a corn crib. The FBI's official version of what happened is typically tidy, with no loose ends: Floyd took off running across a field, and the G-men, after

During the "public enemy" era, Melvin Purvis began upstaging his supervisor, J. Edgar Hoover, who then gave Purvis nuisance assignments that eventually forced him to resign. *(Authors' collection)*

May 3, 1949 Patricia Cherrington, former Dillinger gang moll, is found dead, apparently of natural causes, in her room at the Burton Hotel, 1424 North Clark Street, Chicago. She was 45.

ordering him to halt, wounded him mortally with gunfire. He lived only long enough for Purvis to ask him if he was Pretty Boy Floyd, involved in the Kansas City Massacre. He supposedly snarled back, "My name is Charles Arthur Floyd" and died.

Forty years later a much different version of Floyd's death was described by Chester Smith, the last surviving local lawman who had seen Floyd duck behind the corn crib. According to Smith, he was the first to approach the crib and saw Floyd take off running across an open field with a .45 automatic in each hand. When Floyd continued toward a wooded area, Smith fired a shot from his Wincester rifle, hitting Floyd in one arm and knocking him down. Floyd struggled back to his feet, again tried to run and was shot a second time by Smith. He had picked up both of Floyd's pistols and was starting to talk to him when Purvis arrived and ordered Smith to stand back. Soon, the other federal agents and local lawmen were standing around, with Floyd propped up in a sitting position against the trunk of a tree.

Smith, who made news with his story in 1974, says that Purvis exchanged only a few words with Floyd, mainly asking him if he had been involved in the Kansas City Massacre. When Floyd snapped back, "I woudn't tell you son of bitch nothing!" Purvis turned to a G-man holding a Thompson and said simply, "Shoot into him." The agent fired some single shots from the Thompson, knocking Floyd over, and Purvis left to make a telephone call. Smith assumed that call was for an ambulance, and meanwhile helped carry Floyd back to the roadside, where he died.

Purvis returned a short time later. He hadn't called an ambulance, but rather J. Edgar Hoover in Washington, D.C., to inform him that "we've killed Floyd." The officers put the body in the back seat of a car and drove it to an East Liverpool funeral home, where a cursory postmortem examination stated merely that Floyd had died from multiple gunshot wounds while resisting arrest.

Asked why he had waited so many years to tell his story, which had long been rumored, Smith said he had not been asked to file a report, was reluctant to challenge the FBI account, but now that his colleagues were all dead, he felt obliged to reveal what had really happened. He still had a .45 caliber slug from Floyd's body whose rifling marks indicated it had come from a Thompson, which one of the G-men possessed. Despite its outwardly clean appearance and the passage of many years, the bullet recently tested positive for blood, which evidently had dried in the grooves and lead-filled base of the metal-jacketed round.

A subject of continuing curiosity is how Pretty Boy got his nickname. The account most widely accepted is that it was bestowed on him by good-natured prostitute Beulah Baird, who liked his fancy clothes and careful grooming. However, policeman/researcher Michael Webb in the St. Louis area has found reason to believe Floyd acquired it through a simple case of mistaken identity. One of Floyd's early partners in crime had also worked with a young hood known as Pretty Boy Smith, and police later assumed that Floyd and Smith were the same person. A newspaper account of Floyd's arrest stated simply that the two turned out to be different men, but the name "Pretty Boy" apparently stuck.

June 5, 1949   Thomas James Holden escapes police after murdering his wife Lillian and her two brothers in a drunken argument at their Chicago apartment.

June 8, 1949   George Kimes, employed at a lumber camp, is recaptured by deputies at Burns, Oregon.

March 9, 1950   Willie "The Actor" Sutton leads new gang in robbing the Manufacturers Trust Company at 4711 Queens Boulevard, Long Island, of $63,942.

March 14, 1950   Thirties outlaw Thomas Holden becomes the first fugitive named to the FBI's "Ten Most Wanted" list—the Bureau's official concession to the mistaken but widespread notion it designated "public enemies."

March 20, 1950   Willie "The Actor" Sutton is named to the FBI's "Ten Most Wanted List."

March 22, 1950   Glen LeRoy Wright is named to the FBI's "Ten Most Wanted" list.

December 13, 1950   Glen LeRoy Wright is recaptured by the FBI at Salina, Kansas.

June 23, 1951   Thomas Holden is captured by the FBI at Beaverton, Oregon.

December 12, 1951   Louis Piquett, John Dillinger's disbarred attorney, dies of a heart attack while living at 661 Sheridan Road in Chicago.

February 18, 1952   Willie Sutton is recaptured by Brooklyn police on a tip from clothing salesman Arnold Schuster.

March 8, 1952   Schuster is shot to death near his Brooklyn home, apparently by a Willie Sutton fan acting on his own.

December 18, 1953   Thomas Holden dies in prison in Illinois while serving a life sentence for murder.

July 18, 1954   George "Machine Gun" Kelly dies of a heart attack in Leavenworth, soon after turning 54.

July 10, 1955   Retired Texas Ranger Frank Hamer, who led the ambush of Bonnie and Clyde, dies at his home in Austin.

November 18, 1955   Ted Bentz, brother of notorious bank robber Eddie Bentz, is paroled after serving 21 years for the 1933 Grand Haven, Michigan, bank robbery actually committed by his brother and Baby Face Nelson.

December 25, 1956   Robert "Boss" Shannon, pardoned in 1944 from his life sentence for the Urschel kidnapping, dies in a hospital at Bridgeport, Texas.

February 25, 1957   Former Capone rival George "Bugs" Moran dies of lung cancer in Leavenworth while serving time for bank robbery.

June 9, 1959   Kathryn Kelly and her mother, Ora Shannon, convicted of the Urschel kidnapping in 1933, are released on bond pending appeal. They remain free when the FBI lets the case lapse by refusing to release records, including a document that might have embarrassed the Bureau by diminishing her role in the crime.

November 24, 1959   After serving 25 years for the supposed kidnapping of Jake "The Barber" Factor, former bootlegger Roger Touhy is paroled after courts decide the snatch was a hoax probably perpetrated by the Chicago syndicate to eliminate an important competitor.

December 16, 1959   Touhy is murdered on the front porch of his sister's home at 125 North Lotus in Chicago.

February 29, 1960   Melvin Purvis killed at his home in Florence, South Carolina—not with the gun he carried at the Biograph, as often claimed, but with a .45 automatic given him as a present by fellow agents when he resigned from the FBI. Though called a suicide by the FBI, his death was ruled accidental and may have occured when he was trying to clear a tracer bullet lodged in the pistol.

July 24, 1961 Harvey Bailey, wrongly convicted of the Urschel kidnapping in 1933, is released from the Federal Correctional Institute at Seagoville, Texas, only to be immediately rearrested by Kansas authorities who still want him for his 1933 prison escape.

May 15, 1963 The federal penitentiary on Alcatraz is closed.

June 8, 1963 Roy Kimes, career criminal and jailbreaker since the 1930s, is shot and killed by storeowner Bill Cason during a burglary in Kiowa, Oklahoma. Kimes was the cousin of 1920s outlaws Matt and George Kimes.

March 31, 1965 Harvey Bailey is released on parole from the state prison at Lansing, Kansas.

October 31, 1966 John Paul Chase, Baby Face Nelson's accomplice convicted in 1935 of murdering an FBI agent in the Barrington, Illinois, gun battle, is released on parole from Leavenworth over protests by J. Edgar Hoover.

August 14, 1968 Former Dillinger gang member Russell Clark, dying of cancer, is released from the state prison at Columbus, Ohio, after serving 35 years of a life sentence for the murder of Sheriff Jesse Sarber.

December 24, 1968 Russell Clark dies in Detroit.

January 13, 1969 Evelyn Tic, formerly Evelyn "Billie" Frechette, dies at the age of 61 at Shawano, Wisconsin.

January 14, 1969 Alvin Karpis is released on parole from the federal prison at McNeil Island, Washington, and deported to Canada. Karpis tells reporters he plans to see the movie *Bonnie and Clyde.*

February 19, 1969 Edythe Black, formerly Rita "Polly" Hamilton Keele, John Dillinger's last girlfriend, dies in Chicago after a quiet 30 years as the wife of a salesman.

September 18, 1969 Kansas Governor Robert Docking pardons Frank Sawyer after receiving an affidavit from Alvin Karpis admitting that he committed the bank robbery for which Sawyer was convicted. Sawyer was wanted in Oklahoma also for kidnapping and jailbreaking.

October 30, 1969 Former East Chicago, Indiana, policeman Martin Zarkovich, friend of Anna Sage and participant in the killing of John Dillinger, dies at St. Catherine's Hospital in East Chicago, Indiana.

December 24, 1969 Willie Sutton is released from Attica prison in New York.

October 14, 1971 Thirties bank robber Terrible Ted Walters, once the partner of Floyd Hamilton, is shot to death by Texas Rangers while holding a farm family hostage near Fort Worth.

May 1, 1972 J. Edgar Hoover dies in his sleep, after 48 years as director of the FBI. It is the 36th anniversary of Hoover's highly publicized arrest of Alvin Karpis in New Orleans.

August 3, 1973 Retired FBI agent Charles B. Winstead, credited by Hoover with killing John Dillinger in 1934, dies at the age of 82 in Albuquerque, New Mexico.

A map of the ambush finally released to the press differs from the official FBI diagram, removing Purvis and adding Agent Cowley, now shown running across the street at Dillinger from a point near where East Chicago policeman Zarkovitch had been standing.

October 5, 1973   John Paul Chase dies of cancer at Palo Alto, California.

August 20, 1974   Former Barrow gang member W.D. Jones is shot to death in a brawl in Houston.

October 22, 1974   On the 40th anniversary of Pretty Boy Floyd's death, Chester Smith, former East Liverpool, Ohio, police officer and one of the last surviving members of the posse that killed Floyd, claims the wounded outlaw was in fact executed by an FBI agent on orders from Melvin Purvis. Smith will repeat the allegation in 1979, with slight variations. His account predictably is denied by the only other survivor of the party, former FBI agent W.E. "Bud" Hopton.

March 1, 1979   Harvey Bailey dies at the age of 91 in Joplin, Missouri.

August 26, 1979   Alvin Karpis dies in Torremolinos, Spain, of an apparent (and possibly accidental) overdose of sleeping pills.

November 2, 1980   Willie Sutton dies at Spring Hill, Florida.

July 24, 1984   Thirties bank robber Floyd Hamilton dies in Grand Prairie, Texas.

October 23, 1984   Former East Liverpool, Ohio, policeman Chester Smith dies one day after the 50th anniversary of the death of Pretty Boy Floyd.

January 1, 1991   Former FBI agent G.C. Campbell, who took part in the ambush of Dillinger, dies of a heart attack at Palo Alto, California.

March 17, 1993   Ralph Fults, last known survivor of the Barrow gang, dies in Dallas, Texas.

June 12, 1994   Lillian Holley, sheriff at the time of Dillinger's "wooden gun" jailbreak, dies at age 103 in her Crown Point, Indiana, home. She has never discussed the escape, and implacably fought periodic efforts of the city and local businesses to promote the event as a tourist attraction. After her death and that of Dillinger museum owner Joe Pinkston, the museum is eventually purchased by the Lake County tourist bureau.

7

The American legal system had its roots in British common law, but in an underpopulated, rapidly expanding nation that rejected a strong central government, lawmaking and law enforcement were specifically relegated to state and local authorities who put together an amazing patchwork of statutes reflecting regional conditions and priorities. Thus law enforcement was highly politicized from the start, and crime control largely a do-it-yourself proposition. Sheriffs, marshals, posses, vigilance committees and private detective agencies like the Pinkertons were "the law" in the western states, where most individual disputes were handled out of court one way or another, or adjudicted by a peace justice with a minimum of legal formalities.

Despite its reputation for lawlessness, the sparsely settled West, where citizens felt a moral duty to protect one another, was in most ways safer than the nation's cities. Even when municipal governments began establishing official police departments in the mid-19th century, in places like Chicago and New York no

sensible person ventured out at night without a sword cane or pocket pistol; and it was not until 1911 that New York City passed the Sullivan

Auto-Salesman (to prospective customer): ANY SPEED?
MY DEAR SIR—THIS IS THE SORT OF CAR THAT BANDITS GET AWAY IN.

Outlaws often used their ill-gotten wealth to purchase faster, better automobiles to keep well ahead of the police. *(Authors' collection)*

247

The increasing number of armed robberies by "motorized bandits" led local police to try various "control of the road" strategies such as the ones seen here. *(Authors' collection)*

Act, which prohibited the routine carrying of guns. Increased demands for "police professionalism" included departments that, at least in theory, were responsible to the mayor or his personal representative, such as a chief or a superintendent.

Despite civil service formalities and fledgling efforts to institute training, the typical metropolitan police district remained nearly autonomous, ruled by a captain who had more practical authority than his superiors, was the instrument of his ward boss's own law-enforcement policies and employed politically loyal patrolmen who kept the peace with as much brutality as public opinion would tolerate. Municipal codes were enforced (or ignored) differently from one ethnic neighborhood to another, accommodating whichever vice operations paid for protection and were acceptable to local residents. Citizens correctly regarded city police as the private army of whichever party was in power. Justice, at least at the neighborhood level, was commonly dispensed by a ward boss who held his own form of court without legal authority, but with enough impartiality to gain a reputation for fairness and commonsense decisions that avoided legal wrangling in an often fixed, formal trial.

The Progressive Movement had included public safety among its campaigns for civic reform, but it was not until the 1920s that reform efforts produced substantial changes in law-enforcement organization, strategies or performance. These occurred largely in response to the dramatic increase in crime that followed the World War and coincided with Prohibition. Previously, holdups by gangs of armed men had been so rare that such crimes were still called "highway robberies," an expression left over from the days when desperadoes on horseback waylaid stagecoaches. Now the country was confronted with a revival of outlawry in the form of "motorized bandits" who had discovered the automobile. They were striking it rich robbing jewelry stores, saloons, payroll messengers and banks, creating turmoil in cities whose police had limited means of pursuit or effective communication.

Many foreign countries were far ahead of the U.S. in every phase of police work, from organization and administration to the forensic sciences. In the U.S., police departments spent the 1920s acquiring automobiles and motorcycles and better weapons, compiling statistics, setting up identification bureaus, and discovering radio and teletype and fingerprinting, a long overdue replacement for the complicated Bertillon system of physical measurements imported 30 years earlier from France. But even ballistics testing did not find wide use or legal acceptance until 1929, when the St. Valentine's Day Massacre inspired several wealthy Chicagoans personally to fund the establishment of this country's first Scientific Crime Detection Laboratory—one like those used in other countries for many years. The progress of police professionalism in America during this period can be crudely measured by the ongoing debate over use of the "third degree" on criminal suspects, and testimonials promoting the whipping post.

A revolution in crime control and the triumph of the professionalism movement occurred by political happenstance. In 1933, President Franklin D. Roosevelt all but reversed the country's antiquated law-enforcement philosophy, policies and practices. In response to a heavily promoted crime wave featuring a new crop of Public Enemies, the Depression outlaws, Congress reluctantly passed a series of unprecedented federal laws that would ultimately make J. Edgar Hoover the world's most celebrated crime fighter. Hoover used every trick in the book to promote the image of his special agents as a new breed of incorruptible scientific investigator (with a few experienced gunfighters quietly thrown in) and to professionalize the nation's state and municipal police agencies, whether they liked it or not.

Once Justice Department publicity made the G-man a national hero and a role model, local departments had to swallow their resentment of FBI grandstanding and join the program, or appear as backward and corrupt as many actually were. Some still are both, but no longer have the luxury of near autonomy and selective enforcement policies that existed openly during the public enemy era.

The most widely (and sometimes wildly) varying efforts to "fight crime" took place during the 1920s and 1930s.

Chronology of Crime Control in the United States, 1919–1940

1919

January 1 Chicago Association of Commerce establishes independently funded Chicago Crime Commissioon as a watchdog and advisory group of prominent private citizens to improve police department efficiency and administration. This begins a national movement in which nearly every state and many cities establish similar commissions.

January 16 Thirty-six states ratify the Eighteenth Amendment establishing National Prohibition, which will begin in one year and ban the manufacture, transportation and sale of alcoholic beverages; wartime Prohibition goes into effect.

February 28 New York police commissioner Enright advances theory that recent crime wave is the work of "demented soldiers."

April 4 New York regular and special grand juries recommend more severe punishment for robberies and crimes of violence.

April 7 Eleven robberies reported in New York in 24 hours.

April 12 New York mayor denies existence of any crime wave.

July 1 William J. Flynn named director of Justice Department's Bureau of Investigation (BOI).

September 9 Boston police strike of 1,117 patrolmen over long hours and low pay is first to leave a major U.S. city without police protection; mayor calls on the militia to put down crime and rioting that kills two and wounds many more; Governor Calvin Coolidge re-

places strikers with new men, including war veterans, and virtually guarantees his later election as U.S. president by declaring, "There is no right to strike against the public safety by anybody, anywhere, any time."

November 15 California's Alameda County reveals plan to frighten confessions from suspects by having stunt pilots take them on perilous airplane rides.

1920

January 1 Chicago merchants reveal plans to install electric sirens outside their stores and arm themselves with shotguns.

January 13 Chicago police announce the roundup of 600 suspects in the previous week.

January 16 The Volstead Act goes into effect, providing for enforcement of the 18th Amendment establishing National Prohibition.

November 10 Investigation discloses that in New York, the first major city to pass a restrictive firearm law (the Sullivan Act, 1911), justices of the peace are selling pistol permits indiscriminately for as little as $2 each.

December 3 New York City appropriates funds for a fleet of police motorcycles for night patrols.

December 8 Philadelphia judge approves carrying of revolvers during outbreak of lawlessness.

December 9 Chicago police, after a campaign against gambling houses, announce they will use gas grenades against barricaded criminals.

December 16   Sterling Silver Manufacturers' Association of New York responds to the murder of a member with a resolution protesting lack of police protection and proposing formation of a vigilante group.

December 17   Fifth Avenue jewelers' organization forms vigilance committee over objections of New York police commissioner Enright, who sees no need for vigilantes or possess and assigns 50 detectives to patrol the city day and night, using automobiles.

National Jewelers Board of Trade reports $359,000 in robberies in six weeks.

President of Women's Republican Club asks mayor and police commissioner to declare martial law.

December 17   In Baltimore, 100 holdups and burglaries reported in two months; police will be ordered to watch for influx of New York crooks.

December 20   American Legion and Military Order of the World War offers New York 500 to 5,000 ex-servicemen to back up police; Commissioner Enright calls crime wave a little "flurry" but abolishes patrolmen's 30-minute lunch hour and orders them to question citizens on the street at late hours.

December 20–31   Assistant U.S. Attorney calls on New Yorkers to form Citizens Protective League to fight crime.

New York grants and then rejects Enright's request for 769 additional patrolmen, but he adds 700 police reserves, tranfers 600 men from desk jobs to patrol duty, assigns 20 handpicked sharpshooters with rifles and patrol cars to seek out robbers, organizes special squads to guard all entrances to the city and assigns sidecar motorcycles to patrol the Bronx, Queens and Staten Island; he also assails newspaper scare headlines that he thinks attract crooks from other places.

Chief Fitzmorris of Chicago denies criticizing New York Police.

December 22   Missouri legislature will consider making robbery punishable by death, while a New Jersey bill would subject "highwaymen" to life imprisonment.

Chicago aldermen endorse promotion for patrolmen who kill robbers; police arrest 100 in 24 hours.

December 27   Tulsa, Oklahoma, police commissioner urges stores to employ armed guards.

December 28   Toledo, Ohio, police are ordered to combat local crime wave by arresting every "suspicious character" and shooting to kill if necessary.

Citizens of Wappinger Falls, New York, form vigilante group to guard village; Westchester County citizens will also organize patrols.

1921

January 3   After two fatal holdups, Cleveland police receive orders to shoot to kill.

January 4   Chicago police forbid films showing criminals at work.

January 6   New York relents and grants Commissioner Enright funds for 600 police recruits.

January 8   Press reports that several Long Island towns have organized citizen posses to check crime.

January 18   New York City Board of Aldermen resolution calls for life imprisonment for gunmen.

January 22   New York police commissioner Enright proposes life imprisonment for burglars.

CRIMINAL ANTHROPOLOGY

Long after phrenology had lost the support of the scientific community, the belief persisted that there still must be some correlation between criminal behavior and physical abnormality. This seemed obvious to the general public, accustomed to seeing newspaper pictures of thugs captured by police and not looking their best, and cartoon caricatures of hoodlums with low foreheads and big chins. But if scientists had rejected the original theories of the Italian Cesare Lombroso, who later doubted them himself and still qualifies as criminology's pioneer, they were on the right track in suspecting that some criminal behavior might be associated with brain abnormalities. Thus the brains of John Dillinger and other notorious criminals were sometimes removed for study, without yielding any useful information. The technol-

Drawings from Professor Van Hooton's book, *Crime and the Man*, published by Harvard University in 1938 as one of the last misguided efforts of a so-called criminal anthropologist to associate lawbreaking with physical features and nationality. *(Author's collection)*

ogy of the times was not sufficiently advanced to detect inconspicuous defects, giving support to the "nurture" school of criminology before researchers developed more sophisticated tests that found many criminals to have brain damage of one kind or another.

The inability of pathologists to find obvious abnormalities led to a brief revival of Lombrosian theories under the more scientific-sounding nomenclature of "criminal anthropology." A leading proponent of this new version of phrenology was an American anthropologist named E.A. Hooten, who somehow persuaded Harvard University Press to publish his hefty volume titled *Crime and the Man* as late as 1939. Hooten took body measurements of thousands of inmates in prisons

around the country and came up with some of the most bizarre findings ever to see print, especially in the academic community. Concluding flatly that "the primary cause of crime is biological inferiority," he did not stop with obvious physical characteristics but went on to attribute different criminal propensities to different nationalities in what now would be a monument to political incorrectness, especially concerning race. Today the book reads like pseudoscientific gibberish, and its illustrations would cause professorial heart failure, but there probably exists no better reflection of attitudes, prejudices and preconceptions that were widely accepted by the American public and lawmakers of the times.

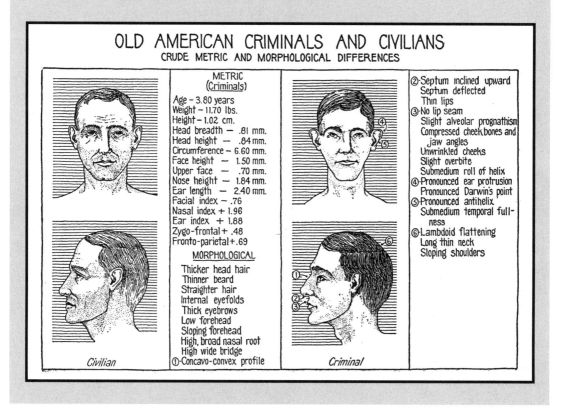

OLD AMERICAN CRIMINALS AND CIVILIANS
CRUDE METRIC AND MORPHOLOGICAL DIFFERENCES

In the 1920s, gangsters and outlaws often took advantage of new technology well before law enforcement agents could, making them harder to find and bring to justice. *(Authors' collection)*

January 31 Delaware law passed making robbers subject to 40 lashes, 20 years in prison and $500 fine.

February 1 Arkansas senate passes bill providing death penalty for bank robbery.

February 7 Vigilantes are now patroling highways in Union County, New Jersey.

March 7 National Surety Company declares that the automobile is responsible for much of the country's crime.

April 12–28 Chicago police experiment with "wireless telephone" communications, new police auto patrol, and "bulletproof" screen in war on criminals.

April 23 Detroit announces first "one-way" police radio system to broadcast descriptions of escaped criminals.

July 28 Detroit Clearing House Association offers $5,000 for each bank robber slain.

August 21 William J. Burns replaces William J. Flynn as director of Justice Department's BOI.

August 25 Brooklyn district attorney begins investigation into organized traffic in pistol permits.

September 7 Chicago banks announce tunnel plan to protect messengers from holdups.

September 28 New York's Nassau County sheriff equips deputies and policemen with riot shotguns for use against bandits.

October 14 Cedar Grove, New Jersey, will ring fire bell in case of attacks on women.

October 22 U.S. judges, district attorneys and state governors propose confiscation of all firearms under three feet in length, heavier punishment for robbers and less prison reform as a means of checking daylight holdups.

November 14   Judge Scanlan calls Chicago the most lawless community in the world.

November 17   Comments in a *New York Times* editorial compare current crime wave with that of 1864.

1922

January 1   Bronx announces plan to organize vigilance committee.

January 9   New York magistrate advocates amendment to the Sullivan law making carrying of firearms a felony.

January 12   New York State senator introduces bill requiring ammunition purchasers to have license.

January 13   New York district attorney J.E. Rustan advocates the branding of criminals.

January 26   Six Chicago policemen suspended for substituting six strangers for suspects being held in a cell.

February 6   New York police commissioner Enright blames crime on too much leniency toward criminals and too much prison reform.

February 8   Rochester, New York, bank employees will be trained to shoot robbers.

February 13   Pennsylvania Bankers' Association advocates making bank robbery a capital crime.

March 6   Woodlynne, New Jersey, announces it will tar and feather highway robbers.

March 14   Armed robber interrogated by New York City police states that most criminals purchase their guns from mail-order houses.

March 27–28   New York police will begin patrolling the city with 10 Ford motor cars, one assigned to each precinct.

April 6   *New York Times* editorial reports on citizens arming in self-defense.

April 7   New Jersey state law, possibly signed by mistake, will permit vehicle owners to be armed.

April 14   Following seven safe crackings, New York police commissioner Enright cancels all vacations and orders captains to sleep in their stations.

May 21   Wealthy Chicagoans are reported hiring private policemen to guard their homes.

July 26   Long Island residents plan vigilance committee.

August 11   Commission on Law Enforcement of the American Bar Association advocates banning private ownership of handguns.

December 15   Crestwood, New York, announces vigilance committee to halt robberies.

December 23   New York police commissioner Enright mobilizes all police forces with extra automobile squad to repel influx of western outlaws.

December 30   Five prisoners flogged in Wilmington, Delaware.

1923

January 2   New York district attorney Banton declares crime wave has been ended by speedy trials.

February 13   President of U.S. Revolver Association supports passage of law regulating sale of firearms.

April 1   Scores of automobiles added to New York police fleet, and entire department,

BULLETPROOFING CARS

Payroll messengers and unprotected money trucks were easy prey for the new "auto bandits," who found them easier to stop than trains. (The largest and one of the last train robberies occurred in 1924 near Rondout some 30 miles north of Chicago, and despite a successful escape with nearly $2 million, it quickly unravelled because one of the bandits had accidentally shot a fellow robber whose hideout became known to the police.) The attacks on money messengers gave rise to an armoring industry that borrowed ideas from early military vehicles and by the 1930s was building armored cars and trucks specially designed to stand off the most aggressive bandit attacks. Soon big-league gangsters and outlaws were also having their machines bulletproofed, sometimes adding sirens and smoke-screen devices to facilitate escape from the scene of a shooting or robbery.

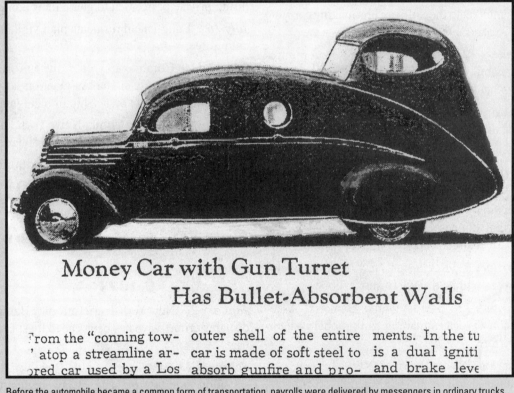

Money Car with Gun Turret Has Bullet-Absorbent Walls

From the "conning tow- ' atop a streamline ar- ored car used by a Los

outer shell of the entire car is made of soft steel to absorb gunfire and pro-

ments. In the tu is a dual igniti and brake leve

Before the automobile became a common form of transportation, payrolls were delivered by messengers in ordinary trucks. This method proved highly vulnerable, giving rise to an armored car industry that by the late 1930s was producing vehicles prepared to withstand virtually any kind of attack. *(Authors' collection)*

After an otherwise well-planned bank-messenger holdup in downtown Chicago netted them only bags full of canceled checks, the Barker-Karpis Gang made their getaway in a professionally armored sedan, only to wreck it a few blocks away. They piled out, guns blazing, and escaped in a car taken from a passing motorist. Police traced the bandit car to Joe Bergl, whose garage just happened to adjoin Ralph Capone's Cotton Club, barely outside Chicago's western city limits on the main street (22nd St., later Cermack) of Cicero. They deduced that Bergl had provided similar cars for Capone gunmen, including the one that had escaped behind a smoke screen after shooting up a police car carrying a Moran gangster who had made bail only to find the police station itself surrounded by Capone gunmen waiting for him to step outside. Bergl also had armored a car for Machine Gun Kelly, and probably others. The police investigation of his business uncovered the fact that a partner in Bergl Auto Sales was former East St. Louis gunman Gus Winkeler, related to Bergl by marriage and close friend of Fred "Killer" Burke, whose successful hit on New York's Frankie Yale in 1928 supposedly had qualified him, Burke and some of Capone's other "American boys" to participate in the St. Valentine's Day Massacre a few months later.

Bergl's chief competitor in the car-armoring business was Clarence Lieder, owner of Oakley Auto Construction Co. at Division St. and Oakley on Chicago's Near Northwest Side. He was a long-time friend of Baby Face Nelson and also supplied cars to crooks, adding smoke-screen devices of his own design upon request. John Dillinger and Homer Van Meter had used his garage as a hideout in the late spring of 1934, when they were too hot to find a safe haven with anyone they could trust. They spent some weeks living out of a panel truck, driving the backroads

THEY WILL GET THOSE BANDITS!

Because

THEY ARE SAFE BEHIND INDESTRUCTO BULLET RESISTING GLASS

Bulletproof glass seemed sensible to its inventor, but Model T police cars were no match for the expensive machines used by armed robbers. *(Goddard Collection)*

around East Chicago, Indiana; and if business with attorney Louis Piquett or his assistant Art O'Leary required a visit to Chicago, they would use Lieder's garage, parking at night in his vehicle elevator, which they would raise to a position between the first and second floors. When Dillinger was killed and Nelson had fled to California, Lieder, figuring the end was near, put a Closed sign on his shop and took off.

including inspectors, ordered on patrol duty as holdups and burglaries continue.

July 25 Muskegon, Michigan, judge advises he will begin jailing wives also in home brew cases.

August 2 Bronx jewelers organize to train in use of firearms.

November 16 New York police commissioner Enright abolishes lunch hour, suspends all vacations and time off, and orders extra duty for every policeman in effort to check crime wave.

1924

January 8–13 New York police commissioner Enright plans drive against "undesirables" from Philadelphia; city declared clear of known criminals following arrest of 250 (none, however, from Philadelphia); magistrate denounces spectacular raids that result in few prosecutions.

March 13 Commissioner Enright urges Civitan Club to support federal bill to tax handguns out of existence.

March 19 New York Kiwanis Club luncheon told that half of Sing Sing's inmates are under 25.

April 20 Responding to crime wave, Chicago's Chief Collins orders all policemen to carry their pistols in a position for quick use.

April 13–21 Long Island firemen will aid police by blocking roads following holdups; Suffolk and Nassau County firemen will organize as emergency police and carry arms.

May 7 Prudential Life Insurance Company releases statistics indicating 10,000 murders in U.S. in 1923.

May 10 Attorney General Harlan Fiske Stone promotes J. Edgar Hoover to acting director of the Justice Department's Bureau of Investigation (BOI).

July 1 At the urging of the International Association of Chiefs of Police (IACP), Congress authorizes the Justice Department to establish a special Indentification Division within the BOI as a national fingerprint repository.

July 13 Indianapolis police announce 261 arrests in campaign to check local crime wave.

August 16 U.S. Post Office Department plans to order 3,000 armored cars to protect against mail robberies.

November 2 The *New York Times* publishes special feature on the U.S. as the most lawless nation.

November 29 St. Louis police mobilize against new crime wave.

December 10 Meeting of Illinois Federation of Women's Clubs in Chicago is told that the city needs to hang criminals to discourage crime.

J. Edgar Hoover named permanent director of Bureau of Investigation (BOI).

December 21 Press reports that the U.S. Supreme Court has overturned murder conviction of Chinese student subjected to police "third degree."

1925

January 6 At New York City dinner for Committee of 1000 for Law Enforcement, Chicago's Mayor Dever declares that strict enforcement of Prohibition has remedied the city's crime wave.

January 8   Chicago and Cook County Bankers' Association plans burglar-alarm system and armed motorcycle patrols.

January 10   Chicago Crime Commission cites crime figures for 1924 to support charges of police demoralization.

January 16   Chicago's Chief Collins orders his policemen to put a stop to crime or quit the force.

January 17   Group of Brooklyn judges blames crime and violence on the evil influence of improper films.

January 19   St. Louis businessman personally offers rewards to policemen who capture or kill robbers.

February 10   New York State senator introduces bill extending maximum armed robbery term from 20 to 40 years.

March 10   Vermont restricts police use of "third degree."

March 24   New York police, ordered to arrest all known crooks, jail 98 during first day of round-up.

March 25   Delaware legislature votes to retain whipping post.

April 3   New York, Chicago and San Francisco experiment with system for wiring criminals' pictures between cities.

April 16   Michigan state senate discusses establishment of whipping posts.

April 28   Illinois senate passes bill providing for hanging armed burglars.

May 10   Illinois senator C.R. McNay plans bill to disinherit murderers.

May 27   New York chief magistrate McAdoo blames crime on pistols, narcotics and automobiles.

June 15   Chicago police arrest 400 in roundup of suspected gangsters.

June 23   Retired General Smedley Butler, as new public safety director, declares "war to the finish" on crime in Philadelphia.

July 5   Chicago and Cook County Bankers' Association offers $2,500 for each bandit killed.

July 27   Chicago Crime Commission director H.B. Chamberlin declares crime conditions beyond control.

August 5   Chicago mayor W.E. Dever appeals to residents to correct impression of city's criminality and general lawlessness.

August 12   National Crime Commission privately organized in New York City to promote police professionalism and crime laboratories, gather uniform crime statistics and study punitive measures in various states; includes future president Franklin D. Roosevelt, Supreme Court Chief Justice Charles Evans Hughes, former Illinois governor Frank Lowden, and former Secretary of War Newton Baker.

September 13   New York State Supreme Court justice Smith supports repeal of law that juries may not infer guilt from refusal of defendants to testify.

September 23   Milwaukee Clearing House offers $2,500 reward each for dead bank robbers and $1,000 each for live ones.

October 6   Boston post office fortified in response to citywide crime wave.

October 25   New York City judge Taylor urges alarm sirens in stores and arming of employees.

November 4   Commissioner Enright announces new antibandit patrols using nine radio-

BULLETPROOFING PEOPLE

The willingness of criminals to do battle with the police partly reflected their sense that most cops also were crooked, and if they could be bought they could also be shot. This view was not shared by the police or the public, and paralleling the armored car industry were efforts to develop bullet-resistant glass, portable shields and garments. Around the turn of the century a Chicagoan named Peter Zeglen, impressed by stage stunts here and in Europe in which performers wearing supposedly bulletproof vests let assistants shoot them with no apparent harm (usually with trick bullets, or real bullets but very light loads), made a serious effort to develop "soft" body armor, the forerunner of modern Kevlar. Zeglen was a Catholic Church brother and sacristan who took care of priestly raiments made of heavy silk that was nearly impenetrable. He persuaded his superiors to let him work on developing a truly bulletproof vest, which could be manufactured under license for sale to armies, which presumably had God on their side. After much research he developed a silk-based fabric that would stop most bullets of the day, and managed to sell a substantial number to the Russian Imperial Army. But in the absence of any major wars, no profitable market developed, and his vest proved to be an invention whose time had not yet come.

Nothing comparable emerged from the First World War, probably because smokeless powder and advances in projectile design led to rifle bullets with much greater penetrating power. However, the sharp increase in violence that accompanied Prohibition involved mostly handguns and shotguns and revived interest in bulletproofing people, especially police. It also

resulted in fierce competition between two other Chicago inventors to develop "hard" body armor—overlapping steel plates sewn into garments clearly intended to stop bullets, or concealed in vests tailored to look as much as possible like ordinary clothing.

Al Dunlap, publisher of a police trade magazine called *The Detective*, and Elliot T. Wisbrod, a metallurgist allied with gun dealer Peter von Frantzius, both developed "hard" body armor similar enough in design and appearance that each accused the other of patent infringements; and to promote their vests, each had police constantly staging demonstrations, shooting at the respective inventors or each other at recklessly close range, with both pistols and machine

HERR DOWE SUBMITTING TO THE TEST.

Bulletproof vests made their first appearance on stages in the 19th century, and in most cases were capable of protecting the "magician" only from lightly loaded rounds. *(Authors' collection)*

Efforts to armor-plate police officers reached fairly ridiculous proportions.   *(Authors' collection)*

guns, while other cops crowded around approvingly, oblivious to ricochets. Predictably, gangsters also bought the vests and outlaws stole them in raids on police stations. An investigation following the St. Valentine's Day Massacre determined that Dunlap and von Frantzius both were selling not only vests but also submachine guns to nearly everyone on any pretext.

The two Thompsons used in the St. Valentine's Day Massacre had come from von Frantzius, as had the revolver of victim Frank Gusenberg, found on the floor of the garage. Under grand jury questioning von Frantzius admitted that he rarely, if ever, turned away a potential customer; and that for an additional two dollars he would obligingly grind off firearm serial numbers, unaware that the crime lab established since the Massacre usually could restore them with acid. Removing a gun's serial number later became a federal offense, but was perfectly legal at the time.

dispatched cars specially equipped with machine guns, rifles, bombs and shotguns.

November 18   Former U.S. attorney general George W. Wickersham calls for central crime records bureau.

December 4   Kings County grand jury recommends life sentences for burglars.

December 30   New York chief magistrate McAdoo urges ban on toy pistols.

1926

February 3   New York state assemblyman Cuvillier calls for use of whipping posts.

February 5   New Jersey legislature passes bill restricting sale of machine guns; subcommittee of National Crime Commission meets in New York to draft law banning private ownership of machine guns.

February 6   New York's Citizens' Crime Conference adopts plan to wear silver buttons supporting the Marshall Stillman Movement, an organization for helping and rehabilitating criminals, to ward off holdup men.

February 7   New York officials call Marshall Stillman button plan ridiculous and no deterrent to robbers.

March 1   New York fire chief submits plan to mayor for police telegraphic intercommunication system like fire department's.

March 2   Chicago newspapers publish photographs of State's Attorney Crowe and other prominent officials attending banquet for the notorious Genna brothers.

March 4   New York police commissioner McLaughlin urges parole boards be suspended during crime-wave emergencies.

March 18   McLaughlin vetoes New York's annual police parade, declaring policemen need to fight crime.

April 2   Milwaukee sets example for speedy justice by catching, convicting and sentencing four robbers in one day.

April 6   U.S. authorities report that 35 percent of federal prisoners are drug-law violators.

April 9   Banker's associations of Illinois, Indiana, Wisconsin, Minnesota and Iowa claim their concerted drive against bandits reduced robberies by 80 percent in 1925.

April 15   Civitan Club Crime Committee reports declares that comfortable prison life is alluring to criminals.

April 16   Chicago trial judge Marcus Kavanagh claims there are 118,000 unpunished murderers at large in the U.S.

April 24   New York state legislature ends session after passing 25 bills proposed by the Baumes Legislative Crime Commission to introduce new laws and law-enforcement policies, tighten parole practices, and drastically increase existing criminal penalties, including life prison sentences for fourth offenders who commit even nonviolent crimes.

May 8   President of New York's Holmes Electric Protective Co. suggests crime would be reduced by jailing crime victims who tempt thieves with displays of goods.

May 20   Supreme Court justice Black proposes death penalty for perjury in murder cases.

June 19   Representative J.F. Miller introduces bill to ban interstate transportation of crime movies on grounds they breed criminality; Cincinnati police will be equipped with cameras.

July 20   International Secret Service Association condemns police use of "third degree" methods to gain confessions.

July 29   Average age of Sing Sing prison inmates drops to 22.

August 29   Newspapers report invention of a "camera gun" which takes a picture of whatever it shoots.

August 30   Newspapers report invention of a "hidden camera" which takes pictures of thieves at work.

August 31   Governor Ferguson of Texas discovered to have issued 2,333 clemency proclamations in past 20 months.

September 1   New York police will require each man on force to carry copy of monthly bulletin to help identify suspects.

September 16   State penitentiary at Trenton, New Jersey, erecting siren to warn city of prison breaks.

October 20   New Jersey official advocates use of machine guns and radio to combat crime wave.

November 2   Former Alabama prison warden charged with murder of inmate who apparently died from being plunged into hot and cold water as punishment.

December 25   Cleveland issues police "shoot to kill" orders to combat new crime wave.

December 27   Chicago Police Department plans to acquire 34 Thompson submachine guns to quell gangland violence.

December 30   Sing Sing officials quoted as claiming judges are reducing felony charges to misdemeanors to circumvent harsh Baumes Laws.

1927

January 5   American Railway Express advises it will cooperate with authorities in stopping firearm shipments to New York City.

February 22   National Crime Commission proposes uniform state law drastically restricting pistols.

April 6   Michigan House of Representatives passes bill on whipping post for bank robbers.

May 10   New federal law bars sending firearms through U.S. mails.

August 16–28   Chicago subjects gunmen to "sanity tests." Machine Gun Jack McGurn among first tested; Frank and Vincent McErlane seek release from psychiatric ward on habeas corpus writs; Polack Joe Saltis and Dingbat Oberta attempt to avoid tests.

November 19   Though the term *racket* probably originated in New York, Cook County prosecutor credited with coining the word *racketeers* to describe Chicago criminals who prey on businessmen.

1928

January 8   Chicago police plan to take motion pictures of crooks at line ups for identification purposes.

January 31   Increasing criticism of Baumes Laws in recent months leads New York City assemblyman to introduce a bill to modify "fourth felony" section.

March 27   Michigan convict serving life for illegal possession of one pint of gin wins right to appeal his sentence.

March 30   Lake County, Indiana, sheriff acquires airplane for pursuit of bandits.

March 31   Supporters of Chicago mayor William Hale Thompson protest efforts of federal agents to help track down bombers during so-called Pineapple Primary.

April 3   Federal agents ignore Chicago officials and investigate bombings of homes of Senator Deneen and Judge Swanson.

May 8   New York City Bar Association asks New York State Crime Commission to investigate police brutality in use of "third degree."

May 9   Chicago Bar Association files criminal court petition charging State's Attorney Crowe's faction with murder, kidnapping, assault, bombing and vote thievery.

July 27   American Bar Association formally opposes Baumes Law "fourth offense" provision.

August 14   Bronx County Jail report reveals majority of prisoners held for violent crimes are between 16 and 21 years old.

September 1   National Probation Association survey reveals that delinquency increases with summer temperatures.

September 4–28   Philadelphia mayor H.A. Mackey gives police department 24 hours to "clean up" the city, but speakeasies merely suspend business until after raids; District Attorney Monaghan reports bootlegger bribes to police reach $2 million yearly; 23 policemen at one station jailed, more arrests predicted.

September 23   New York police plan special arson bureau.

October 1–31   In Philadelphia, former police captain and two detectives indicted on charges of extorting saloon keepers; more police indicted, 4,800 transferred; entire police force ordered to fill out wealth questionnaires; Mayor Mackey suspends 21 police heads.

November 3   Chicago grand jury recommends that polling places be guarded by armed volunteers.

November 8   Philadelphia police "bandit division" formed; prevention squad of 200 motorcycly policemen planned.

December 2   After two burglaries, owner of Haverstrow, New York, garage installs guard bears.

December 26   New York police commissioner Whalen revives "strong-arm" squad and employs vagrancy law to rid city of thugs; courts become jammed.

1929

January 3   New York police "strong-arm" squads raid 60 dens with orders to rough up gangsters; criminals reported leaving city for Chicago; Chicago promises to return them "in boxes."

January 5   To discourage influx of New York and Chicago gangsters, Detroit Police Commissioner announces $10 bounty for each dead criminal.

January 6   Federal and state raiding party of 150 siezes control of Chicago Heights and arrests entire city police force for corruption.

January 9   White Plains, New York, directs that bandits be shot on sight.

January 10   Bill introduced in Missouri legislature providing death penalty for bombers.

January 13   Hammonton, New Jersey, begins drive against gangsters; nets 34 traffic offenders.

January 17   Indianapolis bill would make gun carrying punishable by whipping.

January 20–21   One hundred Chicago police squads arrest 2,600 in record raid; 3,994 total in round-up.

January 21   New York commissioner Whalen plans to close 996 crime nests by naming owners.

January 30   Michigan state senator drafts bill to curb publication of crime news.

January 31   Memphis police chief issues "shoot to kill" orders to check local crime wave.

February 3   Commissioner Whalen claims New York gunmen have been dispersed.

What first strikes the stranger on arriving in New York.

Crime was as common in New York City as in Chicago, but New York officials tried to convey an image of control and order. *(Authors' collection)*

February 18   Chicago authorities make 255 detectives account for their activities at time of St. Valentine's Day Massacre.

February 23   New York City resident charged under Sullivan Law after showing pistol he had wrested from would-be robber.

February 25   Commissioner Whalen declares that strong-arm methods will prevent New York from becoming a second Chicago.

February 28   New York plans alarm signals combined with traffic lights.

March 2   New York commissioner Whalen asks for legislation enabling police to arrest, fingerprint and arraign young "loafers" and "potential" criminals.

March 12   Major F.D. Silloway transferred from Prohibition Bureau in Chicago for charging that Massacre may have been committed by local police.

March 25   New York City governing boards approve $277,000 for new, fast cars to help police catch escaping criminals.

April 19　Thief receives life sentence under New York's Baumes Laws for fourth offense of stealing one dollar.

April 24　After suspending days-off for police, Philadelphia Public Safety Director issues "shoot to kill" orders to end crime outbreak.

May 1　For the first time in recent years, New York newspapers report no homicides during the week ended April 27.

May 3　Grand jury in Chicago indicts 124 in one week, including city officials, six police captains and numerous gangsters in connection with slot machine racket said to yield $10 million a year.

May 20　President Hoover creates National Commission on Law Observance and Enforcement under chairmanship of former attorney general George W. Wickersham. Known as the Wickersham Commission, the group is the first to hold hearings throughout the country and develop voluminous statistics on Prohibition-era crime and corruption, but without concluding that Prohibition should be repealed.

June 2　Detroit announces that its new radio-equipped police cars, part of the country's first full-scale police radio system, enabled 96 captures during the month of May.

August 17　New York City Pistol License Bureau reports issuing 32,400 gun permits.

September 5　Police commissioner Whalen tells New York governor Franklin Roosevelt that Baumes Laws are too harsh.

September 21　Philadelphia police seek to establish radio station and use machine guns to combat banditry.

September 22　Governor Roosevelt requests change in Baumes Law that mandates life terms for fourth offenders.

October 13　Uniform plan for recording crime statistics outlined by Committee of National Commission on Law Observance and Enforcement (Wickersham Commission).

November 1　Philadelphia police will make "talking motion picture" of criminal's confession.

November 22　Arkansas judge orders destruction of "electric chair" used by sheriff to force confessions.

November 24　Distrust of city's police lead sponsors of the new Goddard "crime laboratory" to affiliate it with Chicago's Northwestern University Law School, which will work on crime cases and offer classes in the forensic sciences.

December 4　Sing Sing warden Lewis Lawes reports average age of bandits is 19.

December 9　Wife of Alabama inmate discloses use of "electric chair" by Kilby prison officials to force her husband's murder confession.

1930

January 11　New York and Chicago police departments agree to share ballistics information.

February 9　New York City police launch drive against crime that nets 3,000 arrests in a week, including 1,017 arrested in one night; few held.

　Pennsylvania authorities announce that state's new teletype system has resulted in 234 arrests.

February 15　Detroit police blame upsurge in crime on gangster exodus from Chicago.

February 27　Chicago's Association of Commerce, sponsors of the Chicago Crime Commission, announces organization of a secret committee employing its own "detectives" who will seek to end the city's crime problem within six months. Dubbed the "Secret Six" by the press, the group will consist of prominent but anonymous business leaders and their hired guns who will not be known to the Chicago underworld.

March 22 Newark forms "Committee of 1000" to fight crime.

April 23 Chicago Crime Commission creates first official "Public Enemy" list of 28 notorious hoodlums, which generates national publicity. Al Capone declared "Public Enemy Number One." Chicago police plan "hoodlum" squad to harass gangsters.

May 7 Maxim Company announces it will discontinue the manufacture of firearm silencers.

June 16 Chicago's police commissioner Russell and Captain John Stege forced by city administration to resign in wake of murder of *Chicago Tribune* crime reporter Jake Lingle, who will turn out to have close ties with the Chicago mob. City Council will investigate police department corruption.

June 24 Chicago City Council drops police department investigation after appointing J.H. Alcock as new police commissioner.

July 23 Michigan governor threatens to call in troops after crusading Detroit radio announcer becomes 11th murder victim in 10 days.

August 9 Chicago police establish police radio communications similar to the system pioneered by Detroit.

August–September New York gangster Legs Diamond attempts to vacation in Europe, only to be constantly denied entry, arrested, driven from one country to another and finally deported back to U.S. by Germans on New York–bound freighter; he sues Prussian authorities for illegal detention.

October 18 Success of police radio in Detroit and Chicago leads 51 cities to plan similar systems.

October 19 Chicago suburb of Evanston encourages arming of citizens to combat anticipated crime wave.

November 3 Al Capone supposedly offers to quit "racketeering" in exchange for a monopoly on supplying beer; his offer is rejected by Chief Justice McGoorty.

November 26 President Herbert Hoover calls for nationwide war on gangsters, but opposes extension of federals laws, holding that crime control is the responsibility of the states.

December 26 City of Philadelphia declares itself rid of "racketeers."

1931

February 28 Federal government reports intentions to prosecute gangsters under income tax laws.

March 22 Oklahoma governor Murray exiles three paroled convicts; three days later he states that use of the whipping post has substantially reduced crime in his state.

April 16 Michigan legislature considers bill to establish whipping posts.

May 8 American Law Institute opposes limitations on the right of the police to kill or wound criminals.

June 27 In Colorado, some 30 individuals file claims for the reward money offered for capture of the Fleagle gang.

CRIMINAL IDENTIFICATION

Fingerprints

With evidence as arcane as DNA routinely used in present-day trials, it may seem strange that an identification technique as generally simple and as nearly infallible as fingerprints should have taken so long to find acceptance in the American legal community. But well into the 1920s both the police and the public considered crook-catching one of the manly arts, like shooting—more a craft than a science—and the average juror found it hard to accept that something so trifling as the swirls on a fingertip could be enough to identify an entire human being. Fingerprints had long been used as a kind of signature, though it isn't clear whether the patterns were understood to be unique to an individual or mainly symbolic. In any case, they apparently lacked forensic significance until the middle of the 19th century, and then the absence of any system of classification limited their value in police work.

Instead, police and penal authorities made do with the laborious and imperfect Bertillon method, developed in the 1870s by a French anthropologists who sought to indentify adult individuals by means of photographs and a dozen or more body measurements. At best, the system served no investigative purpose, but only provided an improvement over name and general physical description for identifying people already in custody.

Even when recognized as individually unique, fingerprints still were employed mainly for identification, and thus made their way into the U.S. legal system first by way of prisons as an improvement on the Bertillon system. The shortcomings of that method became glaringly apparent in 1903 when officials at Leavenworth refused to believe a newly arrived inmate named Will West, who insisted he was not a veteran of their pen. Records showed the previous incarceration of a William West, whose photograph and Bertillon measurements seemed to identify him as the same man. When officials bothered to check, they discovered that William West was still in their prison.

July 30   Recent killing of child and wounding of four others by Mad Dog Coll gunmen prompts New York mayor Walker to sanction police instructions to "shoot to kill" gangsters; Patrolmen's Benevolent Association offers $10,000 reward for child's killers; *New York Daily News* planning offer of $5,000.

July 31   Chicago Crime Commission designates an additional 28 criminals as "public enemies."

August 4   U.S. Attorney General Mitchell repeats President Hoover's contention that the war against racketeering is the responsibility of the states, not the federal government.

August 14   American Legion announces plans to "mobilize" 30,000 members on August 24th as a warning to gangsters.

August 22   Boston police superintendent Crowley declares a "war on crime" and instructs his men to "shoot to kill."

August 24   Twenty thousand New Yorkers attend an anti-gang rally; radio equipment voted for police cars.

The seemingly impossible coincidence of two criminals nearly identical in age, appearance, body measurements and names, but with conspicuously different fingerprints, blew a hole in the Bertillon system that its defenders could not patch. Only habit and technological inertia had American police departments still measuring culprits with calipers for another quarter century, resisting adoption of a relatively simple fingerprint classification system devised some years earlier by Britain's Sir Edward Richard Henry, by then commissioner of London's metropolitan police. His was an improvement on even earlier systems developed by criminalists in several countries more scientifically inclined than the U.S. It was not until 1911 that an appellate court in Illinois deemed fingerprints admissible as evidence, leaving the credibility of expert witnesses up to the jury.

When science finally took this country by storm in the 1920s, the Henry system, with refinements, was adopted and promoted by J. Edgar Hoover's Division of Investigation, which flogged Congress into authorizing a national fingerprint respository in 1924. By the 1930s, "scientific crime detection" had taken on the proportions of a fad, aided and abetted by Hoover's new G-men, who soon were fighting the country's first "war on crime" with microscopes as well as machine guns. Local authorities, whose virtual autonomy had allowed them to combine a modest amount of crime control with consummate corruption, had no choice but to go along. How much the public's sudden enthusiasm for "crime labs" was influenced by Mark Twain's fictional promotion of fingerprinting and the test-tube performances of Sherlock Holmes is anybody's guess.

In 1933, the Bureau of Investigation creates a special Latent Fingerprint Section for the examination of both inked prints from the records divisions of prisons and police departments and of latent prints obtained from objects and crime scenes. A Civil Identification Section is added on November 10 of that year, and by 1939 the number of fingerprint cards is approaching 10 million. During World War II, the civil fingerprint records of aliens, military personnel and defense industry employees greatly exceeds the number of arrest prints, and on January 31, 1946, the Bureau announces, with considerable fanfare, that its grand total has reached 100 million.

August 29   Following major robbery and gun battle in which taxi drivers aided in bandit chase, New Yorker writes to suggest deputizing cabbies to aid in war on crime.

August 30   Two woodsmen from Maine declare they will come to New York to show police how to stalk gangsters.

September 11   New York judge advocates whipping post to deal with second offenders.

September 15   Newspapers report that New York mayor Jimmy Walker, visiting England, advises Londoners that gangsters should be beaten by police.

September 18   Government reports racketeers and hoodlums rushing to pay income taxes following first convictions.

New York State probation authorities back Wickersham Commission's report condemning police use of "third degree."

October 21   New York State "public enemy" law permitting arrest of anyone who associates with persons of bad repute will face constitutional challenge. Nine will later be freed on grounds that prosecution failed to prove unlawful intent.

December 20 Chicago Crime Commission optimistically declares that its year's work has resulted in the crushing of organized crime.

December 26 Chicago police report the slaying of 70 "outlaws" during the past year.

1932

March 25 Frank J. Loesch of Chicago Crime Commission reports secret meeting with Al Capone who offered to police the city in return for retaining control of unions, beer, liquor and gambling.

April 5 Increasing opposition to the harshness of New York State Baumes Laws leads Governor Franklin Roosevelt to sign bill reducing the mandatory life sentence for fourth offenders to a minimum of 15 years.

April 9 New York City Boy Scouts declare war on crime.

June 22 Kidnap-murder of the Lindbergh baby compels Congress to pass first federal kidnapping law, despite reservations of President Hoover and his attorney general about involving the federal government in crime control.

July 1 Justice Department's "BOI" renamed United States Bureau of Investigation, which will take over Prohibition enforcement duties of the Treasury Department. Director Hoover seeks separate division for that purpose, to avoid combining Prohibition and Justice Department agents.

October 10 Members of Philadelphia's Presbyterian Ministers' Social Union call for whipping post as "cure for crime."

November 8 Atlanta vigilantes organizing in response to a series of major crimes.

November 24 Borrowing techniques from the country's first Scientific Crime Detection Laboratory directed by Major Calvin Goddard in Chicago, Bureau of Investigation establishes the first national crime lab, which will serve both federal and local law enforcement agencies. Hoover predictably fails to mention the source of FBI's sudden crime lab expertise.

December 2 Atlantic City follows Chicago's lead in listing 60 "public enemies."

December 7 The New Jersey Grange association recommends return of whipping posts.

1933

January 10 Murray "The Camel" Humphreys replaces Al Capone as Chicago's Public Enemy Number One.

January 17 Chicago's mayor Cermak orders city policemen to stop working with the Citizens' Committee for the Prevention and Punishment of Crime (The "Secret Six"), whose vigilante practices were getting out of hand.

March 10 North Carolina bill would permit lashing in petty crimes to relieve jail overcrowding.

April 16 Group of six self-appointed crime fighters indicted under state law against "night riders."

June 10 U.S. Attorney General Homer Cummings, reversing policies of his predecessors, and to Hoover's personal dismay, declares that the Justice Department will fight racketeering.

July 13 Cummings announces plans for new federal legislation to combat racketeers.

July 27 President Roosevelt confers with Cummings, proposes a "super-police force" to combat interstate crime; will use Justice Department's Bureau of Investigation as nucleus of federal campaign against racketeering, a plan quietly opposed by J. Edgar Hoover.

July 29 J. Edgar Hoover, Bureau of Investigation director since 1924, named director of expanded agency to be called Division of Investigation.

Increasing interest in police crime laboratories leads New York University and the Bellevue Hospital Medical College to form departments of forensic medicine.

July 15 Bronx police sieze three armored gang cars, but their drivers escape.

July 26 Citizen "Minute Men" reported organized in Indiana to fight crime and gangsters.

August 6 Federal Bar Association proposes national police force.

August 10 United States Bureau of Investigation renamed Division of Investigation, incorporating the Bureau of Prohibition as a separate agency under Hoover's direction.

August 13–14 Warden Lewis E. Lawes urges U.S. Senate subcommittee to make all major crimes federal offenses, and recommends president declare modified martial law pending adoption of a constitutional amendment eliminating state lines.

August 31 Kings County, New York, grand jury proposes flogging for youthful offenders.

September 10 Four Chicagoans jailed under new municipal law that permits arrests on criminal reputations alone.

September 12 Los Angeles begins anti-crime campaign by requiring the registration of all felons.

September 15 American Society of Composers, Authors and Publishers opposes the sale of popular song sheets on the streets by youths, declaring this breeds criminals.

September 27 U.S. announces its war on racketeering will include prosecution of lawyers who aid and abet crimes of their gangster clients.

October 1 U.S. Flag Association awards first-place prize in its anti-crime contest to entrant advocating censorship of crime news.

October 7 Chicago Crime Commission head Frank Loesch urges U.S. Justice Department to establish a national "public enemy" list.

October 19 Supreme Court declares Michigan's "public enemy" law against associating with suspected criminals to be unconstitutional.

December 16 New York City supports plan to require visitors with criminal records to register with police.

1934

January 29 New York State Chamber of Commerce issues report suggesting registration of both U.S. citizens and aliens and the fingerprinting of all aliens.

February 10 New York County Lawyers' Association proposes law to require persons ever convicted of any or of certain misdemeanors to register with police and file their fingerprints with the Bureau of Identification.

February 15 New York judge J.E. Corrigan proposes electrically powered whipping post for lashing racketeers.

February 19 U.S. Attorney General Homer Cummings unveils his "Twelve Point Program" of federalized crime control.

March 12   New York City proposes official ostracism of persons with criminal records, barring them from the country's major cities; decides afterward that such ostracism could be limited to habitual criminals.

April 14   New York State legislature will consider series of bills intended to eliminate the "technicalities" presently protecting criminals.

April 21   Illinois Supreme Court voids law that permitted jailing of individuals on the basis of their criminal reputations.

April 26   U.S. House Judiciary Committee rushes action on new federal anti-crime bills; Cummings reports offer from U.S. War Department to supply airplanes in war on crime.

April 28   Pittsburgh repeals its ordinance permitting the arrest of "suspicious" persons.

May 7   New York City commissioner Ryan advocates banishment of 10,000 criminals.

May 18   President Roosevelt signs six federal anti-crime bills.

June 6   Roosevelt authorizes Justice Department to offer reward money.

June 18   Congress grants BOI agents full arrest powers in federal cases and authorizes their carrying of firearms without obtaining special permission.

June 30   Assistant Attorney General J.B. Keenan warns that unless law enforcement improves, police power will be taken over by the federal government.

October 7   Cummings calls for national conference on crime.

November 1   New York State Chamber of Commerce adopts resolution promoting a system for registering all U.S. citizens.

November 27   New York police commissioner Valentine orders his force to "terrorize" known criminals.

November 31   U.S. Justice Department orders strict enforcement of laws against harboring criminals.

December 10   National Conference on Crime opens in Washington, D.C.

1935

January 26   New York mayor LaGuardia supports Police Commissioner Valentine's order to "terrorize" criminals.

February 6–12   Hundreds arrested under Section 722 of New York municipal code which forbids consorting with known criminals; most freed on "loopholes."

April 1   New York state assembly passes temporary "public enemy" bill, similar to New York City's law, making it illegal for persons engaged in unlawful occupations or bearing "evil reputations" to consort with known criminals.

April 11   J. Edgar Hoover warns doctors against altering faces and fingerprints of criminals.

July 1   Thomas E. Dewey appointed special New York rackets prosecutor over objections of mob-influenced politicians; major investigations will bring him national prominence as country's most effective and colorful crime buster. Publicizes and campaigns against established criminals like Schultz, but also new crop of gang leaders that includes Luciano, Siegel, Lansky, Buchalter, Shapiro and Zwillman. Torrio still regarded as power behind the scenes.

   U.S. Division of Investigation renamed Federal Bureau of Investigation (FBI). National FBI Academy established.

July 3 Birmingham, Alabama, will register all ex-felons living in city.

August 10 Oklahoma announces establishment of state Bureau of Identification and Investigation.

October 30 New York police to revive strong-arm "gangster squad."

November 10 Miami police ordered to arrest "undesirables" on sight.

November 25 Chicago Crime Commission's Frank Loesch says New York is now nation's crime capital.

November 26 New York police commissioner Valentine says it isn't.

December 24 Delaware and other state assemblies will consider legislation to remove state-line obstacles to law enforcement.

1936

January 7 New York State appeals court voids convictions under existing "public enemy" law.

January 10 Sheriff P.J. McGuinness will swear in 5,000 special deputies to help in New York anti-crime drive.

February 3 New York County Lawyers Association opposes bill allowing police to make arrests across state lines.

February 13 Philadelphia city council passes ordinance requiring all criminals in the city to be registered by police.

February 26 New York governor Lehman signs bill providing additional penalties for crimes committed with weapons.

March 2 New St. Paul law will require residents convicted of felonies in past 10 years to register with police.

March 14 Minneapolis mayor Latimer orders special police drive against vice and gambling.

May 6 New York legislature passes bill to make "public enemy" law permanent.

June 16 Philadelphia police assemble photos of 10,000 criminals prior to Democratic National Convention.

August 19 Authorities report racketeers rushing to pay New York State income and corporation taxes to avoid Dewey investigation.

October 5 FBI official H.H. Clegg credits favorable G-men publicity with reducing juvenile delinquency.

October 21 Citizens Committee on the Control of Crime formally organized in New York.

1937

January 2 Philadelphia mayor Wilson orders police to drive all known gangsters and racketeers from city.

March 4 Thomas E. Dewey's rackets war continues unabated, earns him medal from the Hundred Year Association; police helping Dewey will be cited and promoted.

April 22 New York Senate kills bill that would have banned use of "third-degree" methods by police.

June 10 Dewey credited with 61 racketeering convictions without an acquittal.

October 23 FBI announces compilation of file on criminals' nicknames.

December 20 U.S. Supreme Court declares wiretapping violates Federal Communications Act, but U.S. Circuit Court of Appeals will rule intrastate wiretapping legal; decisions debated in Washington.

THE "FOUR-STATE PACT"

The First Experiment in Cooperative Crime Control

Just as the Constitution favored state militias over a strong peacetime army, it also made crime control almost entirely the responsibility of state and local authorities, and for essentially the same reason: fear that a national police or military force could become an instrument of political tyranny. The Palmer "Red Raids" following World War I and the excesses of federal Prohibition agents in the 1920s were reminders of this possibility. Even when the 1932 kidnap-murder of the Lindbergh baby forced Congress to pass a federal kidnapping law, President Herbert Hoover's attorney general warned an outraged public that "you are never going to end the crime problem in this country by having the federal government step in."

The Roosevelt Administration took the opposite position, declaring violent crime to be a nationwide problem beyond the capabilities of localized law enforcement, and one requiring, at the very least, federal coordination of local efforts. Mindful of fears over too much centralized authority, President Roosevelt, U.S. Attorney General Homer Cummings and the director of the Justice Department's Division of Investigation, J. Edgar Hoover, soon rejected the idea of an "American Scotland Yard" as too radical and probably unconstitutional, but nevertheless created a modified version of it in what would become the Federal Bureau of Investigation.

As part of Roosevelt's New Deal in law enforcement, the Justice Department quickly demonstrated the effectiveness of interstate crime control by cracking the sensational Urschel kidnapping case in about a month with a well-orchestrated investigation that covered some 26 states and immortalized Machine Gun Kelly, a bootlegger whose machine gun was a gift from his wife. The hoopla over this success sold most Americans on the idea of a federal police force, but Hoover wisely (and politically) agreed that the role of the Bureau of Investigation should be limited to establishing national fingerprint files, a crime records repository, a state-of-the-art crime lab such as then existed only in Chicago, a police training academy, and otherwise helping the state and local authorities coordinate their crime-control efforts.

In the absence of formal police powers, Hoover's Bureau contented itself with promoting interstate cooperation and offering its services as a central clearinghouse for information on interstate fugitives. This included reprinting and distributing "wanted" posters issued by the individual states, but listing on the reverse side the federal offices which could be contacted by any state that nabbed a fugitive wanted in another. This was both a calculated courtesy and a nod to the idea of state sovereignty in matters of criminal-law enforcement, for Justice Department agents at the time could neither make arrests nor carry guns unless deputized by state or local authorities.

However, the violent crime that seemed to increase during the Depression (thanks partly to the FBI's inauguration of centralized record keeping) led several midwestern states to heed Justice Department admonitions and begin cooperating with one another. In 1934 Governors Horner of Illinois and Townsend of Indiana proposed a five-state "pact," inviting Michigan, Ohio and Minnesota to join them in offering a $5,000 reward for the capture of the country's most notorious criminals, starting with John Dillinger, whose only federal offense to date was interstate car theft following his escape from Indiana's Crown Point jail.

Dillinger's subsequent "rampage" through the Midwest compelled a reluctant Congress to pass a series of national criminal laws that greatly expanded federal police powers, just as J. Edgar Hoover had hoped; and thereafter the "wanted" posters most widely distributed were eight-by-eight-inch "Identification Orders" resembling those of the states but issued nationally by the U.S. Department of Justice.

The proposed "five-state pact" became a four-state pact when Minnesota and Ohio opted out and Wisconsin opted in, but it represented the first time regional law-enforcement officials relaxed their jurisdictional jealousies and began working together, granting each other's police the authority to cross state lines in pursuit of fugitives. While the FBI made most of the headlines chasing bank robbers, kidnappers and assorted public enemies, the midwestern states in the mutual-assistance pact found their combined resources did in fact help in capturing other criminals, especially those who feared the newly empowered G-men enough to avoid deliberately breaking federal laws.

The FBI still describes itself as a primarily investigative agency and at least technically defers to local authorities unless a crime is clearly a federal violation, or local authorities (usually to satisfy a popular demand, and often with reluctance) may formally ask for FBI assistance in a particularly sensational or difficult case.

Roosevelt had not made crime control a major plank of his campaign in 1932; however, the fall of Al Capone seemed to signal the end of the "gangster" era, Roosevelt's inauguration doomed Prohibition and his first few months in

office coincided with a shift in public attention from the big-city booze wars to old-fashioned outlawry, particularly in the Middle West. The Kansas City Massacre, two major kidnappings, and the "arrival" of Pretty Boy Floyd, Bonnie and Clyde and the Dillinger gang took headlines away from the gangland murders which had long since become routine, and coincided nicely with the new attorney general's declaration of a national "war on crime" to be waged by J. Edgar Hoover and his newly minted G-men.

J. Edgar Hoover grudgingly congratulates Melvin Purvis following the killing of John Dillinger. *(Authors' collection)*

Hoover's exposé of a nationwide "criminal army" impressed the public more than the police, who in many places were part of it. Because alliances were mainly local and limited to payoffs, crooked cops were probably like field soldiers satisfied to operate on a "need to know" basis. And of course there was no criminal army in terms of a single organization. Federal authorities correctly assumed that every city had its cop-and-crook alliances, but with Hoover's own men now girding to fight crime throughout the country, the director may well have been surprised to discover that his military metaphor had some basis in fact. The criminal community might lack a supreme commander, but it had the equivalent of many generals in form of corrupt mayors, sheriffs and police chiefs; and Hoover would learn from comparing field office reports that if the country's hoodlums were not incorporated, they at least asso-

ciated, and sometimes cooperated, to a far greater extent than previously imagined.

In short, the majority of professional crooks knew each other, personally, by reputation, or through mutual friends in the nationwide network of lawyers, bail bondsmen, doctors, tavern owners, fences, car dealers, gun sellers, even policemen who functioned as a support group in much the same way pirates in their day were kept provisioned by ostensibly legitimate businessmen. This growing awareness led to a field office memo advising Hoover of the mutual connections between the Chicago crime syndicate and various outlaws who up to then had been regarded as small bands of predatory, independent and usually unidentified gunmen. The memo, indicated much closer connections than previously realized, particularly between Chicago mobsters and the Dillinger and Barker-Karpis gangs.

1938

January 30   Two New York City magistrates criticize police policy of wholesale arrests and discharge most of 600 cases.

February 5   Special grand jury empaneled in Philadelphia to investigate links between gangsters in that city and New York.

June 1   New York's Mayor LaGuardia announces special "rules" for gangsters during the coming World's Fair.

July 13   Chicago police department announces purchase of Northwestern University's Scientific Crime Detection Laboratory, the country's first full-scale "crime lab" established with private funds and originally directed by firearm-identification expert Major Calvin Goddard following the St. Valentine's Day Massacre. Goddard had linked the machine

guns seized at the Michigan home of Fred "Killer" Burke with both the Massacre and the New York murder of Frankie Yale.

August 17–19   Philadelphia grand jury finds connections between city officials, police and crime ring, recommends firing 11 policemen. Civil Service Commission will hear charges against 41 in September.

August 27   *Chicago Tribune* publisher Col. Robert McCormick attacks the continuing alliance between politicians and criminals in northern Indiana.

September 3   Delta Theta Phi law fraternity favors denying legal services to habitual criminals.

October 18   Records of 7,200 prisoners discovered stolen from Brooklyn's Bergen Street police station.

October 31–November 3 Tom Dewey condemns conditions in Brooklyn as well as Tammany Hall protection of racketeers, citing onetime appointment of Dutch Schultz as Bronx deputy sheriff by Democratic leader E. J. Flynn.

1939

March 27 U.S. Supreme Court holds New Jersey's Gangster Act of 1934 unconstitutional.

April 10 Antiquated Bertillon method of criminal identification eliminated by law in New York.

April 19 Philadelphia police receive demonstration of equipment to transmit photos of criminals by radio.

August 5 President Roosevelt signs national bill ending statute of limitations for crimes involving the death penalty.

The New Deal Justice Department needed something truly impressive to symbolize the first nationwide "war on crime." One newspaper proposed an American version of Devil's Island and mapped out possibilities alongside a composite photo of Al Capone, convicted of paying no taxes on illegal income, which the Supreme Court only then ruled was still a violation of tax law. The government chose Alcatraz as closer to home and a better showcase for celebrity lawbreakers. *(Authors' collection)*

ALCATRAZ, 1868–1963

New Deal attorney general Homer Cummings needed something more impressive and tangible than a package of federal laws to symbolize the country's first nationwide "war on crime," and he found it in the middle of San Francisco Bay. Alcatraz Island had been a military fortification and then an army prison, but by the 1930s it had little strategic value. It was isolated by a mile or more of cold, swift-flowing and ostensibly shark-infested waters, however, and large enough to serve as a highly and ominously visible monument to the federal government's determination to end what seemed like an era of uncontrolled lawlessness. With little discussion, the War Department turned its facility over to the Justice Department, which transformed it into a maximum-security federal penitentiary that amounted to an American Devil's Island. In fact, other federal prisons were probably as secure, but well-publicized policies and practices verging on simple brutality made "The Rock" an incarceration experience to be dreaded as truly the end of the line for incorrigible criminals—or at least celebrity criminals, for which it became a showcase.

On October 12, 1933, the War Department transfers Alcatraz to the Justice Department for use as a federal penitentiary. On March 21, 1963, after an increasing number of escape attempts due to the deteriorating buildings, the last 27 prisoners are removed from "the Rock" and sent to other federal prisons. Two months later Alcatraz is officially closed by Attorney General Robert Kennedy. After a tedious cleanup it is reopened in 1973 to the sight-seeing public.

September 3   Federal grand jury finds New York City racketeering dominated by Bugsy Siegel and Meyer Lansky crime ring.

1940

January 8   Women of Forest Hills and Kew Gardens, in Queens, New York, threaten to form own vigilante committee unless they receive more police protection.

March 17   Evidence of murder-for-hire ring emerges during investigation by Brooklyn District Attorney William O'Dwyer; press will dub killers "Murder, Incorporated."

April 19   Topeka, Kansas, *State Journal* editor fined for refusal to reveal sources of his information on local political corruption.

May 1   J. Edgar Hoover reports most arrests are occurring among 19-year-olds.

May 15   Abe Reles, as state's witness, describes his involvement in six murders.

June 3   O'Dwyer claims 56 murders solved by his investigation.

July 31   Vieux Carré Property Owners Association calls mass citizen rally to demand cleanup of crime conditions in New Orleans.

August 29   Army announces ban on recruiting of persons convicted of crimes.

September 16   Abe Reles admits involvement in five more murders. He dies the following year in a fall from a window of a Coney Island hotel where he is being held in protective custody. Rumors persist that his fall was not accidental.

HOMICIDE, GUN CONTROL AND TEENAGE CRIME

Just as earlier reformers blamed the saloon and the liquor interests for the country's extravagant drinking, their modern counterparts blame its impressive murder rate on the abundance of firearms and the national gun lobby. The connection seems too obvious to argue. The unregulated saloon appeared to foster public drunkenness, indirectly; the drinking itself was voluntary. And most killings are committed with guns, especially handguns; but deciding when to use them is as hard to legislate as temperance. If the problems associated with booze and bullets have many similarities, they also defy any simple solutions.

When Sunday-closing laws and other legal measures failed to remedy drunkenness, the word "temperance" became a euphemism for prohibition. Today, laws restricting or banning gun sales have likewise failed to reduce violence, so that the expression "gun control," which sounds perfectly reasonable, is now understood by the militants on both sides to be a euphemism for firearm prohibition. This was a major semantic victory for the anti-gun movement, which can accuse those who fail to support even some totally impractical measure as being "against gun control."

This confuses most Americans who support controls short of prohibition, and it fuels the ongoing debate between highly vocal pro-gun and anti-gun minorities for whom it masks quite different life experiences, attitudes and political agendas.

The fact that there are about as many privately owned firearms in the U.S. as automobiles, and that they can be found in more than half the country's households, can be translated two ways: Americans are dangerously gun-happy, armed far beyond the limits of any other modern, Western, industrialized nation (such qualifiers greatly limit the comparisons); or Americans, although armed to the teeth, have proved themselves the safest and most responsible gun owners in the world. Firearm opponents can shock the average citizen with posters revealing that U.S. firearm deaths exceed those in selected foreign countries by 10 or 100 to one, and having an inside track to a media largely controlled by educated urban professionals to whom guns equate almost entirely with crime and violence, their message is widely promulgated. The gun community, less sophisticated or media-wise, challenges this idea with generally valid but tedious research that does not lend itself to simple sound bites or news items, or penetrate the unconscious prejudices of an "eastern liberal establishment" that delights in portraying the National Rifle Association and gun dealers the way prohibitionists once caricatured brewers and bartenders.

Neither side has qualms about misrepresenting its position on anything from "cop-killer bullets" (which have yet to kill a cop) to the merits of privately owned firearms as a major deterrent to crime. What vexes both sides is the fact that murder in America seems not to reflect gun laws one way or the other.

Prohibition led to a decline in so-called social drinking, which no doubt saved some individuals from themselves, but at a terrible cost in corruption, crime and literally thousands killed or maimed by trigger-happy Prohibition agents and poisonous industrial alcohol. It also transformed drunkenness from a working-class vice into a fashionable form of middle-class rebellion that coincided disastrously with the proliferation of automobiles, creating yet a new national problem.

Increasingly restrictive gun laws seem essential to reduce a murder rate that has doubled since the relatively peaceful fifties and early sixties, but both per capita and in total number, the firearm murders that reached shocking levels in recent years only matched the record levels of violence that distressed the country for periods in the "Roaring Twenties" and early 1930s, when the U.S. population was half what is today and gun laws were virtually nonexistent. Nor did the laws in places like New York and Chicago regulate thousands of private dealers, pawn shops and magazine advertisers, from whom both cheap and expensive handguns could be purchased for cash or ordered by mail with no papers to fill out and no questions asked. Certain periods of the 19th century were so murderous that virtually no one went out, especially at night, unarmed or unescorted; and one of the objections municipal police at that time had to wearing uniforms or even visible badges was that these invited attack by neighborhood gangs.

Killing, with or without firearms, seems to reflect a number of social conditions, the most important of which is the population of young people in their crime-prone years. Booze wars and drug wars always aggravate violence, but a study of newspapers from the twenties and thirties finds them filled with alarmist articles on recurring murder "epidemics" and full-page features on the homicidal tendencies of children in their teens.

So it hardly serves the gun-control community to report that the 10,000 or so increasingly restrictive laws it has managed to pass locally and nationally since the twenties have done little more than make it harder to purchase firearms legally. Nor does it serve the pro-gun people to cheerfully remind Americans that they are not shooting one another any more often today than in the 1930s, despite a virtual doubling of the national firearms population in the past 40 years. They try to get across the fact that the firearm accident rate actually has plummeted despite this vast increase in weaponry (which has been an unintended byproduct of anti-gun campaigns); and that the suicide rate has not significantly changed in the past 90 years. But even the gun buffs recognize this as negative advertising, hardly reassuring to residents of a crime-ravaged city, or to the "gun grabbers," as they call their adversaries.

Two things make statistics on legal firearm ownership nearly meaningless in connection with the amount of violent crime. One is that nearly all gun violence involves a tiny fraction of 1 percent of the total gun population, and these already are in criminal or otherwise irresponsible hands, outside the gun-control loop. The second is that while robbing or shooting somebody is definitely a reason to call the cops, unlawful firearm sales and possession are "consensual crimes," like gambling or prostitution, or drugs, prohibited by laws that are on the books and nearly impossible to enforce. A small irony here is that a convicted felon, who cannot legally possess a firearm, also cannot be prosecuted for failing to register one, for registering would be self-incrimination under the Fifth Amendment.

A third factor undermines practical efforts at "gun control." Police in cities like New York and Chicago routinely confiscate over 20,000 guns a year, despite the fact that handgun sales and possession are virtually prohibited (in New York since 1911, and in Chicago since 1982). These guns are taken from individuals who have done something to attract police attention. Several years ago a Chicago study of gun-law violators found that out of 100 persons charged with UUW (Unlawful Use or a Weapon, the city's catch-all for having a gun), only one in 10 was convicted, and only one in 10 of those received a jail sentence. The police kept the guns, but most of those convicted got off with fines averaging $47. Hence Chicago's ban on guns strikes little fear in the hearts of youths who tangle with cops so often that the district station is like a second home.

Partly in response to the notion that criminals are the last to comply with gun laws, more and more states have been licensing ordinary citizens to carry weapons. A few states already allowed this with few or no restrictions. The surprise occurred when Florida and several other states created official "carry licenses" requiring training courses and considerable red tape, and still were inundated with applications. Thousands of such licenses have now been issued, but instead of the bloodbath predicted by some, crime rates generally declined, presumably because second thoughts began to cross the minds of predatory criminals who now must weigh the possibility that a prospective victim might have a pistol. In this case, the unintended consequence is that the armed or unarmed robber may pass up a prosperous-looking businessman in favor of little old ladies cashing their Social Security checks.

Urban geographics, unequal police protection and the new concept of "victimology" make personal risk factors hard to establish. No doubt with good intentions, the FBI early defined a "friends, family and acquaintances" category of murder, as distinct from the felony murder committed during a holdup or some other crime. Such polite terminology implies that these killings are bedroom and barroom crimes of passion that proved fatal mainly because a gun was within easy reach. This remains

an article of faith in the anti-gun community (along with a simplistic and misleading "dead burglar" statistic which shows the relatively few professional burglars killed by armed homeowners and remains a staple in arguments against household guns). A closer examination finds that police use this friends-and-family category as dumping ground for most homicides where the victim was simply known to his assailant, who might be a rival drug dealer, a street-gang member, or acquaintances who never did like each other. It often includes so-called victim-precipitated murders, when a threatened individual pulls a gun to avert a beating, and his opponent proclaims that he hasn't got the guts to use it. [Police usually find that both parties were influenced by drugs or alcohol, and that both had a history of arrests.]

Even so, the murder rate for handguns is around five per 100,000, but it put the peril in perspective. Especially when it's understood that the vast majority of U.S. murders occur in a few of our largest cities (most of which, incidentally, prohibit handguns), and in certain high-crime neighborhoods where danger and risk-taking are antidotes to boredom. And in these neighborhoods guns circulate as freely as drugs, with no paperwork or waiting periods.

Such social realities have no meaning in the gun-control debate, which represents a clash of cultures, lifestyles and prejudices as much as did Prohibition. The "gun control" advocates, who tend to be educated and insulated urban professionals, harbor a gut-level conviction that in the city most gun people are criminals and elsewhere are rednecks and country bumpkins who would shoot Bambi's mother; that firearms serve no good purpose in modern society; and that somehow, some way, fewer guns simply have to mean fewer killings. With equal sincerity and simplicity, their gun-buff adversaries, insulated from daily urban concerns, regard the possession of the means of self-defense as the Eleventh Commandment and the one thing still right with America. These positions are as deeply felt and nonnegotiable as the Right to Life or the Right to Choose.

The magnitude of the problem—and the practice of comparing the U.S. murder rate to those in other countries—is a perennial theme in newspaper reporting, which has always treated violence as the peril of the day. Both concerns were woven into a typical article published in the *Chicago Tribune* for April 9, 1931, headlined: HOMICIDE RATE LEAPS FROM 9.9 TO 10.9 IN YEAR.

The story quoted a reformer who was arguing against the death penalty, but the writer found his statistics to be more newsworthy than his ideas and used those to deplore the willingness of Americans to murder one another.

"... The homicide rate for the country leaped from 9.9 in 1929 to 10.9 last year. It has been higher only twice since 1900—in 1924 it was 11.2, and in 1923 it was 11.3.

"The 1929 figure for England and Wales was 0.5 [while] Germany, in 1927, had a rate of only 2.0."

Until the FBI started keeping national crime statistics in the 1930s, newspapers pulled numbers together from insurance companies, the Census Bureau and other government agencies, and had to assume that some homicides were never reported or properly recorded, so their figures varied considerably. What was apparent, however, and hard to explain, was absence of obvious correlations with guns, gun laws or even the size of the population. The only thing

truly predictable was that the U.S. murder rate per 100,000 usually involved firearms and tracked closely with the percentage of Americans in their "crime-prone" years, a relationship that has tended to decline depending on other factors like immigration, mandatory public education and marriage age.

The following statistics are from three similar periods. The data are from books on homicide in the United States, almanacs and contemporary *Uniform Crime Reports*, so while accurate comparisons are impossible, the trends are apparent.

1889.....5.8	1919....7.2	1969....7.7
1890.....6.9	1920....6.8	1970....8.3
1891.....9.2	1921....8.1	1971....8.6
1892....10.4	1922....8.0	1972....9.0
1893.....9.6	1923....7.8	1973....9.4
1894....14.5	1924....8.1	1974....9.8
1895....15.2	1925....8.3	1975....9.6
1896....15.1	1926....8.4	1976....8.8
1897....13.3	1927....8.4	1977....8.8
1898....10.7	1928....8.6	1978....9.0
1899.....8.4	1929....8.4	1979....9.7
1900....10.9	1930....8.8	1980...10.2
1901....10.1	1931....9.2	1981....9.8
1902....11.2	1932....9.0	1982....9.1
1903....11.2	1933....9.7	1983....8.3
1904....N/A	1934....9.5	1984....7.9
1905....N/A	1935....8.3	1985....7.9
1906....N/A	1936....8.0	1986....8.6
1907....N/A	1937....7.6	1987....8.3
1908....N/A	1938....6.8	1988....8.4
1909....N/A	1939....6.4	1989....8.7
1910.....9.6	1940....6.3	1990....9.4

Different sources had different figures for the same years, and the older data seem especially unreliable, probably erring on the low side. But earlier periods had murder rates that would either decline or increase greatly for several years in a row, reflecting westward migration, frontier conditions, war, urbanization and other variables. In recent years professionalized policing has tamed the towns but not the cities, about five or six of which presently account for nearly 80 percent of the nation's murders, with homicide approaching 90 per 100,000 in their high-crime neighborhoods. So the only thing such figures definitely establish is that violence, as the man said, is as American as apple pie—a remark that caused great moral indignation in the press despite statistics to substantiate it.

A situation puzzling enough to rarely see print is that the tremendous proliferation of firearms since the 1960s has had no apparent effect on the national suicide rate, which has ranged between 10 and 15 per 100,000 since 1900. And while every child killed accidentally with a gun receives the coverage of an airplane crash, the press has faithfully ignored the 50 percent decline in fatal accidents during the same years the national firearm population doubled. Gun buffs, unwise in the ways of journalism, see this as a conspiracy of silence rather than a matter of perspective on the part of an urban intelligentsia that associates guns more with crime than with sport.

Another journalistic hypocrisy, conscious or otherwise, is the steady diet of reports on the criminality of youth. The most conspicuous difference between teenage violence now and in the public-enemy era is that the perpetrators then were white, at least as portrayed in newspapers so comfortably racist they ignored any mayhem that confined itself to the black community. In 1933 the *Chicago Herald & Examiner* devoted a full page to the problem of "THE NATIONS'S BIGGEST CRIMINAL GROUP—AGED 20!" Two years later, the *Chicago Daily News* published a similar page headlined, "YOUTH PREDOMINATES IN CRIME—60,000 JAILED EACH YEAR."

By then the offenders' average age had started its slow if steady decline but had only reached 19, which included Francis "Two-Gun" Crowley, who concluded a short but impressive crime spree in New York by killing a policeman before barricading himself in a room on a high floor of an Upper West Side apartment building. From there, he and his partner, Rudolf Duringer, with a girlfriend loading their guns, battled over 200 cops in the street below, in other buildings and on rooftops, while thousands of spectators subwayed to the scene to watch. Crowley made nationwide headlines with his spectacular last stand until he was exhausted, wounded and captured; and his case remained front-page news until he was executed at Sing Sing.

The battle involved one quirky incident that illustrated the inability of most people (at least in the days before answering machines) to ignore a ringing telephone. Some enterprising reporter obtained the number of the apartment where Crowley was bunkered and dialed it to see what, if anything, would happen. Despite the fact that the police were shooting the place to pieces, the embattled "Two-Gun" stopped his own firing to answer the phone. When the caller identified himself as a newsman, all Crowley could think of to say was that he was too busy to talk to him.

HOOVER AND LA COSA NOSTRA

Why the nation's premier lawman, J. Edgar Hoover, so long denied the existence of a "Mafia" or even nationally organized crime mystified his friends and enemies alike. Even though New York racket-buster Thomas Dewey had taken on Murder, Incorporated in the late '30s and exposed the operations of powerful crime families with affiliates around the country, Hoover continued to regard racketeering as a local phenomenon to be prosecuted by local authorities, once they availed themselves of FBI training, identification and crime laboratory services.

The Bureau routinely collected data on "top hoodlums," but the fall of Al Capone and the repeal of Prohibition ended popular concern over modern organized crime before it was recognized as such and before the FBI had acquired much jurisdictional authority to deal with it. The New Deal Justice Department's "war" against interstate banditry had been so successfully conducted by the Bureau's new breed of scientific detectives called G-men that Hoover could declare victory over America's "public enemies" with the capture of Alvin Karpis in 1936, leaving only a few stragglers to be mopped up as time permitted.

However, the public enemies vanquished by the FBI were fugitive outlaws, not racketeers. The powerful urban criminal organizations spawned by Prohibition had only sighed with relief when the flamboyant Al Capone, the Chicago Crime Commission's first Public Enemy Number One, tripped over the federal tax laws and could be ceremoniously locked up in the new maximum-security fortress of Alcatraz, as though it had been built especially for him.

Repeal spelled the end of organized crime as the average citizen understood it.

With the election of Franklin D. Roosevelt as president, the Justice Department reversed course completely and national attention shifted to the peril represented by bank robbers and kidnappers, partly in response to the kidnap-murder of the Lindbergh baby and a raft of robberies that attracted more than the usual attention. After 1933 the country's Public Enemies were outlaws like John Dillinger and Pretty Boy Floyd, who now served the Justice Department's purposes far better than any out-of-work bootleggers. As Americans excitedly followed the new national game of cops 'n' robbers, the Frank Nittis and Jake Guziks and Lucky Lucianos quietly transformed their racketeering and other criminal enterprises into a cartel that by the end of the decade finally qualified as nationally organized crime.

The systematic takeovers of unions and shakedowns of industries were largely ignored by Hoover's FBI in favor of sexier targets like Nazi saboteurs, black-marketeers and postwar Communists. But by 1950 enough "organized" criminal activity could be observed in action that Senator Estes Kefauver launched the first of several investigations into racketeering. The Kefauver Committee held hearings in 14 cities, heard testimony from more than 600 witnesses and announced proof of the existence of the "Mafia": a sinister, nationwide criminal conspiracy, transplanted and transformed from its origins in Sicily and now the glue that bound the successors of the old Capone "Outfit" (Accardo, Guzik and Fischetti), the Lansky-Costello Syndicate that controlled New York and the criminal organizations in dozens of other cities. After the "Americanization" of the Mafia under Luciano in the early 1930s, the mob was still dominated by foreign-sounding names but as a practical matter it had become an equal-opportunity conspiracy.

The Kefauver Committee largely reflected the beliefs already held by local crime commissions, the Bureau of Narcotics and journalists, and it perpetuated every misconception, exaggeration and myth voiced by law enforcers and law-breakers alike. More important, it did so through the exciting new medium of television, which kept millions of Americans glued to their black-and-white sets, and the resulting Mafia madness inspired countless books containing some of the most naive and crackpot descriptions of organized crime ever to thrill and chill a nation.

Probably the commission's most significant contribution was to give names to the mobsters who had managed to infiltrate the American labor movement and business community at nearly every level while Hoover's G-men were ridding the land of bank robbers. It seemed not to have occurred to the media that the Giancanas, Accardos, Costellos, Anastasias, Genoveses, Lanskys and Siegels, who now stood exposed as the leaders of organized crime, were not the colorful young gangsters of the Prohibition era who usually died by gunfire while still in their twenties, but middle-aged or even elderly mob bosses who had been growing wealthy in the rackets all their adult lives with welcome anonymity.

The Kefauver investigations segued into others that took similar delight in parading mobsters great and small before the TV cameras, much to the aggravation of Hoover, who still maintained that a large agglomeration of hoodlums did not a Mafia make.

The first major event to shake Hoover's stance was the accidental discovery in November 1957 of a mobster summit meeting near Apalachin, New York. A nosy state trooper observed an unusually large number of expensive cars with out-of-state licenses congregated at the rural estate of reputed organized-crime figure Joseph M. Barbara, and a hasty police raid sent nearly a hundred guests fleeing in all directions. The 60 or so who were arrested had Italian names that dispelled any public doubt of a nationwide Mafia such as the Bureau of Narcotics had been clamoring about for years, and provided fodder for both the journalistic community and the McClellan Committee, which had already accepted racketeering as a national phenomenon and decided to investigate mob control of the Teamsters Union.

If the Kefauver Committee witnesses had confirmed the existence of organized crime merely by "taking the Fifth" in response to every question, the McClellan Committee struck gold in one Joseph Valachi, a low-ranking member of the Genovese crime family serving time on a narcotics conviction who believed he was marked for death anyway. When put on the stand in 1963, he enthralled the senators and the nation with graphic descriptions of life (and death) in an organized-crime family, confirming every suspicion, myth and rumor about the Mafia. Much of his testimony was hearsay, shoptalk and legend, but it painted a thrilling picture of *capos, caporegimes* and *capo de tutti capis* and secret ceremonies with daggers and blood oaths of what one author called a "Brotherhood of Evil." What Valachi called it was not the Mafia, however, but "La Cosa Nostra."

La Cosa Nostra translated as "our thing," or "this thing of ours," and was no more a monolithic organization than the Mafia; both terms were insider or outsider references to that substantial segment of organized crime still dominated by Italians, native or otherwise; but giving it a new name saved Hoover the embarrassment of admitting he had been fooled. The men Valachi named were more or less the "Top Hoodlums" the Bureau had been keeping tabs on for years; thanks to Valachi they now had a name that the FBI could adopt as shorthand for the "national crime syndicate" whose existence as "the Mafia" it had long denied.

One explanation for Hoover's denials held that he had a tacit agreement to lay off organized crime because he was personally corrupt and accepted favors from racketeers (especially their hospitality and their willingness to write off his gambling losses). Another was that Hoover had no wish to turn over rocks that might reveal ties between organized crime and U.S. senators or congressmen, especially any who might hold the Bureau's purse strings. A more ominous explanation to surface later contended that Hoover was an active but homophobic homosexual, living in sin with his faithful Clyde Tolson, and that the mob had photographic or other incriminating evidence it was holding over his head.

But there were several practical reasons the FBI had seemed to ignore organized crime, or OC as it was now becoming known, and Hoover's refusal to acknowledge it may have been more a personal idiosyncracy and public-relations preference than a Bureau blindspot. While the New Deal Justice Department's "war on crime" supposedly included racketeers, the fact was that Attorney General Homer Cummings' celebrated Twelve-Point Program of federalized crime control did not include laws that gave the FBI effective jurisdiction over some of the new and increasingly sophisticated forms of crime emerging in the post-outlaw era. Moreover, Hoover was a strong advocate of

police professionalism who honestly wanted to depoliticize law enforcement, offer advanced training at an academy staffed by experts, provide centralized record keeping and criminal identification facilities and maintain a state-of-the-art crime laboratory that could serve the scientific needs of law enforcers from the largest metropolitan police agencies down to one-man departments in the smallest towns.

That was Hoover's personal mission, but there were other considerations. Hoover was a master publicist who had honed his agency into a highly independent, squeaky-clean parody of itself (as delightfully satirized in the James Coburn movie, *The President's Analyst*). He did not relish a campaign against anything as amorphous as organized crime, which would require collaboration with other state and federal agencies, weaken his voice in policy matters and loosen his control of his own men. When Repeal was pending prior to 1933 and Prohibition enforcement was transferred to the Justice Department, he had barely avoided contaminating his Division of Investigation with an army of notoriously inept and corrupt Prohibition Bureau agents from the Treasury Department. Hoover created an enforcement agency, which included Eliot Ness, but persuaded Attorney General Cummings to keep it separate from his G-men, who had won the public's hearts and minds and would henceforth be members of the Federal Bureau of Investigation.

Also, Hoover's Bureau had created for itself an image of invincibility based on tidy statistics of ever greater numbers of fugitives captured and convicted. This was no great feat given the Bureau's selection of targets and increasingly effective investigative tools, but the success of the FBI in the eyes of the public probably did more than anything else to restore faith in the national government, whose other reforms were less tangible and certainly less interesting.

Another consideration was the rivalry between Hoover and Harry Anslinger, director of the Bureau of Narcotics, whose "reefer madness" mentality had been trying to make the Mafia a bogeyman since the 1930s. Indeed, Hoover's counterparts in other federal agencies virtually conspired to embarrass him at every opportunity, partly out of resentment of Hoover's self-promotion and partly out of plain jealousy, making cooperation all but impossible.

So while the Bureau could have gotten into the game by way of several federal laws that might have inconvenienced organized mobsters, these were riddled with loopholes that made serious prosecution efforts difficult if not impossible. Finally, however, the Kefauver hearings, the Apalachin meeting and the melodramatic revelations of Valachi before the McClennan committee, plus the marching orders issued by Attorney General Robert Kennedy, put Hoover on the spot. He had no choice but to acknowledge that his Top Hoodlums had a closer working relationship than previously realized, and that this now looked like a job for the FBI.

At the same time, Congress armed the Justice Department with new wiretap authority and a new law specifically tailored to deal with the problem—the Interstate Transportation in Aid of Racketeering Act (ITAR). Probably for reasons of ego, Hoover still shunned the word "Mafia" and went instead with the term used by Valachi, *La Cosa Nostra,* which was not inconsistent with Hoover's Top Hoodlum program. So the FBI's version of the Mafia became the LCN, the top hoodlums of which had been tracked by the Bureau for years, he could say, as a service to local authorities.

Once the Bureau was in the business, its investigations increased steadily from 131 in 1965 to 813 in 1972, the year of Hoover's death. Two years previously, Congress had passed a new piece of legislation that, when its important provisions survived the usual Supreme Court challenges and a newly motivated Bureau learned the tricks of using it, doomed the organized crime families that were still controlled by their aging leaders. After 1970, confronted by the Racketeer-Influenced and Corrupt Organizations Act (the RICO law) combined with other successful prosecutions and a general disintegration of gang discipline, the underworld machinery that had operated smoothly for over 20 years began to fall apart. Even before the federal organized crime task forces demonstrated the full power of RICO, the Bureau could point to some prosecutions that had symbolic importance, if not much jail time:

June 1, 1965   Chicago's Sam Giancana, one year for contempt of court;

November 10, 1967   Johnny Dioguardo, five years for federal bankruptcy fraud;

March 8, 1968   New England crime boss Ray Patriarca, racketeering;

March 21, 1968   New Jersey boss Sam DeCavalcante, arrested for extortion;

August 8, 1968   Buffalo's Stefano Magaddino, federal gambling law conviction;

July 9, 1969   Los Angeles crime boss Nicolo Licata, jailed for contempt;

May 9, 1970   Chicago's John Cerone, five years for violation of federal gambling laws;

April 26, 1972   St. Louis crime boss Anthony Giardano convicted for interstate gambling.

Perhaps the best explanation for Hoover's slow response to organized crime was that he had become less a crook catcher than an image maker and an empire builder. A top-ranking Bureau official later revealed that when the Apalachin meeting left the FBI open to criticism and embarrassment, Hoover called on him with naive questions about the Mafia, and accepted his offer to conduct a major study of organized crime. His impression was that Hoover truly didn't understand the nature or extent of the problem. Others attempting to discuss policy issues found Hoover frozen in time, still stalking the ghosts of Dillinger and Nelson and Machine Gun Kelly, and in his dotage would exhaust the patience of guests by revisiting the glory days of yesteryear with accounts of the Bureau's triumphs over the outlaws who made the G-men famous, and vice versa.

With Hoover finally in his grave, the FBI waged full-scale war on organized crime, even creating a chronology, or perhaps a genealogy, in 1987 of the rise and fall of America's top crime bosses since 1920. It still did not use the term Mafia, except in an introductory reference, perhaps out of deference to Hoover's sensibilities, and steadfastly referred to the crime families of the U.S. as the LCN. Its introduction provides interesting insight into the Bureau's conception of the history and structure of organized crime, including its misconceptions. Whether the 1890 murder of New Orleans police chief Hennessey was a "Mafia" crime, as the chronolgy asserted, is open to debate, but it introduced Americans to the term, which later flourished as code for all organized crime until the increasing awareness of Jewish and other non-Italian or Sicilian gangsters brought "OC" into vogue—except with the FBI and its LCN, at least until recently. The chronology also buys the Valachi account of the 1931 purge known as the Night of the Sicilian Vespers, which has become an indelible item of Mafia lore despite the discovery by some nit-picking historians that it never happened.

8

THE CHICAGO CRIME COMMISSION AND ITS GANGLAND BODY COUNT

After 1918, the period of lawlessness that typically follows major wars began in the U.S. even before the armistice was signed and was aggravated by several factors. Besides inflation and unemployment for returning veterans, the country had to deal with race riots and increasing labor unrest. The best new career opportunity was created by Prohibition. Technically, bootlegging was a consensual crime, but the automobile had put all crime on wheels instead of horses, and Chicagoans were still in an uproar over the city's first-ever daylight payroll robbery in 1917 in which two messengers were killed. Soon enough, the otherwise harmless bootlegger would find himself drawn into the established criminal community and one day start carrying a gun, *just in case.*

Meanwhile, most urban political leadership remained a monument to bad government. New York had long been ruled by the Tammany Hall politicians who carried on the corruption of Boss Tweed after the Tweed Ring's flagrant lawbreaking landed him in jail. They remained impervious to reform during the city's adolescence in the 19th century, controlling street crime with gang muscle during elections, grant-

ing or denying immunity from the law and from their goon squads credentialed as police. Even the goons did not venture into certain neighborhoods such as the notorious "Five-Points" intersection in lower Manhattan where vice and violence could flourish without civic interference. Bodies were dumped in the East River, or carted to neutral territory bordering the district, where they could be conveniently collected without a lot of aggravating paperwork. Official police did not trespass there except when a respectable or prominent citizen had been mistaken for an ordinary drunk and protested a beating and robbery, if he survived, or when influential family members identified a body that made waves at City Hall. If a "copper" investigated, he would take several colleagues, and in some cases a small army of New York's "finest."

The era of New York's fighting gangs predated the revolution in transportation, communications and journalism that took place around the turn of the century, by which time the Tammany political machine had become powerful enough to impose controls and polish the city's image.

Meanwhile Chicago was still a growing trade center, starting to clean house since the days of wide-open prostitution and gambling in its Levee vice districts bordering what would become the "Loop" (so-called for the rectangle of elevated tracks around the central business district). But it remained controlled by ward politicians more responsive to their ethnic constituents than to City Hall, who maintained order mainly by subsidizing the larger gangs in their social activities (ranging from baseball to burglary). Except for occasional brawling, they functioned as a kind of underworld police, providing neighborhood businessmen with affordably priced protection against outsiders, or themselves.

For years the hard-core vice district even had its own newspapers, which thrived on gossip, criticized "unethical" conduct by named prostitutes and implicitly warned citizens which brothels were hazardous to patronize. Such peer pressure was usually more effective than any half-hearted law enforcement. When do-gooders tried to close down the increasingly notorious Levee district, lavish and well-regulated whorehouses like one operated by the Everleigh sisters simply instructed their inmates to don their Sunday best, and either march in protest or go door to door in respectable neighborhoods asking to rent rooms.

These stunts were often inspired by such prominent Chicago aldermen as Hinky Dink Kenna and Bathhouse John Coughlin, who rivaled or exceeded New York officials in their unabashed venality and who controlled local politics for decades. Their boldness prompted one disgruntled reform candidate to grump that "Chicago is unique; it is the only totally corrupt city in America."

Because of primitive communications and parochial journalism, New York had weathered its own worst years in the middle and late 19th century without attracting national publicity. Chicago acquired its reputation as the country's capital of crime and corruption only after it, too, became a major metropolis, which coincided with such other early-20th-century developments as newspaper chains connected by telegraphic wire services, and the novel forms of crime and violence that accompanied Prohibition.

Despite a fledgling movement to professionalize, most police departments remained relics of the past in their organization, administration, enforcement practices and allegiance to ward bosses who easily circumvented civil-service rules. But the corruption and incompetence that citizens were helpless to correct at the polls could at least be mitigated by commercial interests, the traditional source of a city's prosperity. Crime, especially murder and other violent crime, was bad for business, which gave prominent businessmen enough leverage to demand reforms. In Chicago, the device created to accomplish this was an independently organized, privately funded crime commission sponsored by the Chicago Association of Commerce.

The Chicago Crime Commission was the first of its kind in the U.S.—a watchdog group formed in 1919 to investigate and report "upon the prevalence and prevention of crime," monitor police performance and work to improve police services through better administration. It had no law-enforcement authority, and in fact was barred by its charter from engaging in crime fighting directly. But through its sponsoring association it could initiate and influence legislation, and it could make life uncomfortable for city politicians and their personally appointed police officials, who had little if any aptitude, experience, training or administrative ability. The Commission aimed to coax and/or threaten city government into professionalizing the police department, the way stockholders might force changes in a badly run corporation. Since the same conditions prevailed in nearly every city, the Chicago Crime Commission became the prototype for dozens of similar organizations at municipal and state levels throughout the country, all sponsored by associations of businessmen.

By 1925 the idea was so popular, and the crime problem so pressing, that a National Crime Commission was formed in New York City at the behest of Elbert H. Gary, chief of the United States Steel Corporation, who then pressured such prominent men as Chief Justice Charles Evans Hughes, future president Franklin Roosevelt, former Illinois governor Newton Baker and a former U.S. secretary of war to serve as its executive committee. American police agencies everywhere found themselves operating in a spotlight of publicity, and being pressed to organize more efficiently, modernize their procedures, set up centralized fingerprint files and criminal identification bureaus, adopt radio and other new technology and network with each other to exchange information.

The Chicago Crime Commission not only pioneered the movement but formalized the concept of "public enemies." Its first such list, issued in 1930, named Al Capone as "Public Enemy Number One," much to Capone's annoyance. The Big Fellow had emerged as the city's leading bootlegger, but had gone to some pains to portray himself as a businessman and public benefactor who made sure the booze got through. When the Depression struck, he opened soup kitchens, to which merchants donated cheerfully when visited by young men whose suits were specially tailored to accommodate shoulder holsters. Most Chicagoans had no beef with Big Al, and some considered him a true Horatio Alger character to have done so much with so little.

Declaring Capone the city's top Public Enemy was a public-relations triumph for the Commission, just as the recent St. Valentine's Day Massacre had been a public-relations disaster for Capone. Newspapers everywhere bannered this new publicity gimmick, and the "public enemy" concept captured the nation's imagination. It helped transform him from the Babe Ruth of American gangsters, as someone put it, back into "Scarface" and confirmed Chicago as the gangster capital of the world.

A few years earlier the Chicago Crime Commission, its novelty diminishing, had saved itself from extinction by subordinating its police advisory function to full-scale gangster-bashing. The machine-gun murder of State's Attorney William McSwiggin in 1926 appeared to violate the understanding that gangsters only killed each other, and though McSwiggin's death was probably a fluke (a case of his visiting a speakeasy in the company of bootleggers, for reasons never satisfactorily explained), the Commission launched a major investigation, which revived public alarm over gangland violence. It also worked with a special squad of anonymous crime fighters nicknamed the Secret Six. Limited by its own charter to improving police administration, it supported the Commerce Association's plan to grow an "action arm" of unidentified men who organized a private, extralegal police force, composed mainly of off-duty cops.

The Association of Commerce eventually had to disband the Secret Six for using vigilante tactics, but the Crime Commission survived by becoming professional mob-watchers—pestering the gangs with publicity and creating voluminous files on every hoodlum in town.

The most remarkable project of the Chicago Crime Commission was to start and keep a running body count of every "gangland-style" (to use its own terminology) slaying since 1919, which provided statistics of a sort, and always good newspaper copy, by documenting the shortage of suspects and the nearly total absence of prosecutions, much less convictions, in Chicago's gangland murders. For the victims, it served no worthwhile purpose, except to give each at least some small measure of immortality.

GANGLAND-STYLE MURDERS

1919

January 4	Frank Poroino
January 12	Joseph Introviaia, alias Giuseppe Latravara
January 19	Charles Stillwell, alias Chancelor Stillwell
January 21	Tony DeBrouse
January 21	Hanes Cheren
February 20	Luigi Cascio
February 28	Garnetta Ellis
March 5	Frank Gento
March 6	Guitano Lopresti
April 5	Fred Woeifel
April 25	John Altobelli
May 11	William Marshan, alias Marchand
May 12	Moses Flanigan, alias Thomas Mulroney alias Moroney
May 22	Vincenzo Rieno, alias Jim Arine
May 22	Giacano Rieno, alias John Russo
June 5	Joseph L. Doyle
July 15	Giuseppe A. Saliani
August 1	Frank A. Surianello
September 7	Rosario Cacciatore
September 8	John Gagliardo
September 8	Charles Ramondi
November 17	Joseph McArdle
November 19	Balasario Aborino
December 10	Rocco Mossow

1920

February 2	Maurice Enright
February 13	Bernard J. Reilly
March 17	Jeseph Hurley
April 23	Edward J. Coleman
May 5	Robert J. Hopkins
May 10	Joseph Beneditto
May 11	James Colosimo
May 17	John Kikulski
June 13	Paul G. Torina
June 17	Patrick Ryan
June 21	Nick Valente
June 24	Ethel O. Roberts
August 13	Frank Gebbia
August 29	Joseph Gallido
September 1	Fred Russo
November 1	Louis Porrovicchio
November 2	George Stevenson
November 9	Anthony Bentivegna
November 10	Eugene McSweeney
November 12	John W. Harris
November 28	William J. Tynan
December 14	Vincent Salano
December 15	Fred DeVita (tentative)

1921

January 17	Mike DeRosa
January 18	Lenardo DiMarco
January 18	Armond Boquist
February 26	Guy Esposito
March 6	Dinutris Marabito
March 8	Harry Raimondi
March 8	Paul A. Labriola
March 10	William Weltenstein
April 8	Sam Caruso
April 10	Michael Danoras
April 18	Pasquale Bavagonti
April 20	Antonio Salfornis
April 30	John J. Mahoney
May 12	Anthony DeAndrea
May 26	Mike Lucari
June 9	Thomas A. Skriven
June 22	Carmente Basile
June 23	Antonio Marschese
June 26	Joseph Lastasia
July 19	Nick Torino
July 22	Andrea Ortolano
July 23	John Gaudino, alias Two Gun Johnny
August 14	Vincenzo Sinacola
August 26	Dominick Guttilo
September 7	Michael Henry
October 6	Joseph Marino
November 24	Nicholas Adams
November 29	Malate Milici
December 31	Giuseppe Gangidno

1922

February 5	Mike Maro
February 14	Peter Cannella
February 17	John Gurrieri
February 18	Antonio Vaccorilla
February 20	Dominick Coffaro

March 11	Nicolo Maggio
March 16	Paul Notte
March 28	Steve Moggio
April 3	Louis Cutia
April 9	Abe Rubin
April 10	David Friedman
April 16	Samuel Bianco
April 27	Peter Tomasello
April 29	Pasquale Parcelli
May 2	Ignatzio Landando
May 10	Thomas J. Clark
May 10	Terrence Lyons
May 13	Vito DeGeorgio
May 13	James Locasio
June 6	Antonio Albinanti
July 2	T. R. Petrotla
August 1	Angelo Damco
August 5	John Patti
August 21	James Colabria
August 30	Albert Schulz
October 7	George W. Heller
October 9	Vito Amaro
October 26	Vito Delise
November 4	Vito Fondanette
November 5	Giovani Scalzetti
November 6	Charles P. Brennan
Unknown	Unknown white man about 30 years old.
December 1	Fred J. Ragan (Waiters Union, Local #71)
December 6	Giuseppe Albergo
December 8	Giuseppe Maggio
December 18	Rosario DeMarco

1923

January 8	Angelo DeMora
January 14	Joseph Cichy
January 27	Peter Sciangula
January 28	John Granita
February 28	William J. "Red" Kinsella
February 28	Paul Radin
March 23	Frederico Amadio
April 9	Stanley O. King
April 10	Cassino Polumbo
April 21	Luigi Rocchette
May 20	Guiseppe Tropea
May 29	Charles Gullo

June 6	Francis Sexton
June 29	George Charkus
June 29	Thomas Visvardis
July 1	Lucia Tricla
July 2	Alvin Jones
July 4	John Czarnik
July 5	Procopis Palazzallo
July 9	Joseph Costello
July 18	Gerome Gambino
July 25	Joseph Costello
August 4	Unknown white man
August 10	Mike Lorchar
August 21	Bias Jefferson
August 25	Sam Geroci
August 29	Nicola Mastro
September 3	Vincenzo Vitale
September 5	Thomas Raymond, alias John Gall
September 7	Jeremiah O'Connor
September 10	Ernest Yearh
September 13	Sam Algozeno
September 17	George Bucher
September 17	George Meegan
September 28	Anthony Forti
October 11	Anastasia Plaznetia
October 27	Lawrence Hartnett, Jr.
November 3	Vincenzo Albanese
November 5	Mike Izzo
November 10	Frank DiMarco
November 10	Robert Menga
November 13	Martin DeVries
November 25	Freeman L. Tracy
December 2	Mike Diovardi
December 3	Adolph Skoff
December 6	Dominick Armato
December 7	Henry Bing
December 7	Leopold P. Guth
December 7	John Sheey
December 15	Sam Belcastro
December 26	Fred Guerrieri

1924

January 7	John A. Gilmore
January 9	Vito Partipilo
January 10	Ferdinand Tatge
January 11	Edward J. Quinn
January 20	John Puccio
February 3	William Newman
February 9	Israel Rappaport

March 2	Joseph Rito
March 5	William P. Calagham
March 6	Joseph Tuleo
March 22	Philip Mazzio
April 2	Philip Smith
April 17	Anotonine Sanfilippo
April 21	John H. Rose
April 28	Samuel S. Bills
April 28	Robert Devere
May 4	William Sedlacek
June 5	Joseph Roberts
June 7	Attillio Mancini
June 24	Peter Chiarelli
July 4	Alfred D. Deckman
July 5	Charles Saloman
July 26	Fred Ziegler
July 30	Samuel Riccardo
August 8	George Mustakis
August 10	Vincenzo DeCaro
August 13	Michael Laricchia
August 19	George T. Swan
August 28	Salvatore Falzone
August 29	Frank Marotta
September 8	Jack Graziana

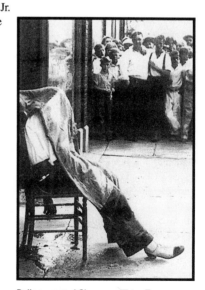

Police granted Cicero gangster Tony Marino the small courtesy of covering his body until they completed their investigation. *(Goddard Collection)*

September 12	Unknown white man about 35 years old
September 22	Samuel Goldfarb
September 25	Davil L. Boitano
September 30	Dominick Busta
October 3	Carmela G. Bartucci
October 5	Philip Corrigan
October 19	Bruno Martine, alias Mike Searfi
November 4	John Mackey
November 7	Angelo Barbas
November 10	Salvatore DeLaurentis
November 10	Charles Dean O'Banion
November 20	Tony Mancuso
November 23	Edward Tancl
November 23	Leo Klimas
November 29	Walter Langille
December 6	Michaele Pernice
December 11	Omar Finch
December 16	Harry D. Johnson
December 19	Nick Ranieri
December 20	Unknown white man
December 21	John Pusateri

1925

January 26	Raffela Amores
February 2	Mike DeMilio
February 2	Gabriel Serpio
February 9	Harry Filice
February 9	Anthony Dominick
February 10	Lozzero Clemente
February 21	Leah Belle Exley
February 22	John Dougherty
March 3	Thomas J. Gaughan
March 3	Peter Hayden
March 9	Favo Randazzo
March 15	Louis A. Cella, Jr.
April 4	Joseph Montana
April 7	Joseph Larson
April 15	Giuseppe Giordano
April 17	Joseph Tuminello
April 29	Louis Cama
May 12	Joseph Saitta
May 19	George Garines
May 25	Frank DeAngelo
May 25	John Ciapetta
May 26	Angelo Genna
June 13	Charles B. Walsh

June 13	Harold P. Olson
June 27	Otto Corra
July 6	Joseph Lasorelli
July 8	Anthony Genna
July 9	Walter A. O'Donnell
July 14	Vincenzo Russo
July 15	Savario Lavenuto
July 15	Anthony Campagna
July 16	Louis I. Sniderman
July 18	Joseph Granata
July 18	James Vinci
July 23	George Karl, Jr.
August 17	Felix Scalto
August 23	Frank Spino
August 23	Joseph Vecchio
August 24	Joseph Reiti
August 28	Harry Berman
August 29	Irving Schlig
September 3	William Dickman
September 7	Joseph Agate
September 10	Nick Malella
September 14	Frank Izarella
September 15	Manuel Lozano
September 27	Aniello Taddeo
October 3	Charles Kelly
October 12	Edward Lottjak
October 13	John Russo
October 18	Christopher Murray
October 20	Rosario Giorvano
October 21	Pasquale Polizzetto
November 2	Frank Canale
November 13	Salvatore Amatuna
November 13	Marco Inburgia
November 15	Placide Divarco
November 18	Edward C. Zine
November 20	Mariano Muscarello
November 20	Michael Vinci
November 21	Abraham Goldstine
November 21	John Minetti
December 13	Charles Williams
December 13	Frank Alonzi
December 22	Edwin A. Harmening
December 22	Joseph B. Brook

1926

January 7	James Campanile
January 7	James O'Brien
January 10	Henry Spingola
January 16	Harry Schneider

January 19	Edward Ryan
January 27	Augustino Morici
January 29	Antonio Morici
January 31	Isaac Stein
February 6	Charles Pope
February 14	Clarence W. Glynn
February 15	Orazio Tropie
February 20	Vito Basccno
February 23	Edward Baldelli
March 2	David P. Feeley
March 6	Joseph Calabrise
March 6	Francis P. Lawrence
March 11	Harold Flynn
March 15	Daniel Cerone
March 17	Joseph Staliga
March 17	Effrey Marks
March 23	George J. Dietrich
April 1	Fred Boeseneiler, alias Andre Anderson
April 3	Walter Quinlan
April 10	Walter Johnson
April 10	Francisco DeLamentis
April 10	Jacomino Tuccillo
April 14	Santo Ilacqua, alias Calabresi
April 16	Gioachino Cuilla
April 19	William Byrne
April 24	Lena Chepulis
April 27	Salvatore Policano
April 27	James J. Doherty
April 27	Thomas Duffy
May 7	Antonia V. DeFrank
May 17	Thomas Dire
May 21	Frank Cremaldi
June 2	Geralanes Lamberto
June 2	Crystal W. Barrier
June 7	James E. Sexton
June 23	Charles Carrao
July 4	Carl Cafforello
July 7	Louis Barbogallo
July 13	Joseph Cicore or Bicone
July 14	Jules Portugene
July 21	Ben Russo
July 22	Philip Piazza
July 23	John Conlon
August 3	Tony Cuiringione, alias Tommy Rosa

August 3	Giuseppe (Joseph) Salvo	June 8	Joseph Agnello
August 6	John "Mitters" Foley	June 19	George Joseph Lauer
August 8	Joseph Catanda	June 26	Ignatius Gungliardo
August 10	Louis "Big" Smith	June 29	Lawrence Alagna
August 10	Joan Andreadis	June 29	Diego Altomonto
August 20	Joseph Nerona, alias Caviliero	June 29	Gaspera Alagna
		June 30	Nunio Jamnerze
August 23	Joe Delbuors, alias Michael Blando	July 7	Peter Sansone
		July 8	Sam Salerno
August 29	Frank Cappello	July 9	Frank Albaniese
September 2	Tony DiStefano	July 10	Joseph Montana
September 22	Ignazio Mingare	July 11	Giovanni Blandini
September 27	Joseph Chivetta	July 12	Simoni Galioto
October 11	Earl J. Weiss	July 13	Dominick Cinderello
October 17	John D'Anna	July 14	Adam Brzezinski
October 21	James C. Williams	July 20	Michael Stopec
November 16	Edward Dunn	July 25	Angelo Corona
November 18	George Martini	July 27	Frank P. Hitchcock
November 20	William Raggio	August 9	Tony Russo
November 26	James Gusdagno	August 9	Vincent Sipicuzza
November 28	Theodore J. Anton	September 17	John Walsh
December 9	Joseph Albergo	September 22	Salvatori Mozzapelle
December 11	Charles Tremblay, alias Chuck Moran	September 28	Samuel Guzzardo
		October 12	Frank C. Passani
December 12	Joseph Wokrol	October 12	Katherine Jones
December 16	Hilary Clements	November 7	Max Willner
December 19	John Wolwark	November 8	Frank Scallo
December 21	Samuel Cohen	November 8	Paul Scallo
		November 14	Joe Vanela
		November 24	Argyle G. Hartz
1927		November 27	Roy H. Flynn
January 7	John Castenaro	December 1	Fred A. Dullard
February 6	John Petrack	December 6	George Clemens
February 19	Vinerella Guadagni	December 18	Peter Buffalo
March 11	Francis Hubacek	December 21	Michael J. Loftus
March 11	Benjamin Schneider	December 28	Charles E. Miller
March 23	Chin Poch	December 28	John Touhy
March 24	Moy Sing	December 31	Harry Portugias
March 24	Moy Yuk Hong		
March 29	Frank Palumbo	**1928**	
April 8	Alex Burba	January 1	Frank E. Carpenter
April 10	Anthony Sicoli	January 18	Joe Concialdi
May 20	Frank Gremaldi	January 18	Joseph Faso
May 25	Tony Tochie	January 18	Harry Fuller
May 31	Herman Carcelli	January 30	Jack Mallardi
May ?	Paul Grandolfo	February 1	Andrew DeLuca
June 1	Lawrence Lopresti	February 17	Isadore Goldberg
June 4	Jasper DiGiovanni	February 23	Phillip Leonetti
June 6	Salvatore Vito Emma	February 26	Robert J. Rutshaw

March 8	Joseph Cicala
March 8	Frank C. Siciliano
March 21	Joseph Esposito
March 22	John Infantino
March 27	John Zocoalo
March 28	Jasper Montalbano
March 29	Joseph Sakalanskas
March 29	Charles Abrago
March 31	Thomas J. Johnson
April 11	Thomas A. Johnson
April 13	Unknown white man
April 15	Joseph Roberti
April 23	Benjamin Newmark
May 8	William Jackson
May 14	Giuseppe Cavarette
June 12	James Lupino
June 16	Frank Barnes
June 19	John Oliveri
June 19	Joseph Salomone
June 19	Jimmie Raggio
June 26	Timothy D. Murphy
June 27	Willie Irving
July 13	John Joseph Paul
July 19	Dominick Aiello
July 24	Joseph Catironotta
July 26	Sam Canalo
July 31	Benjamin Zion
August 2	Lawerence Canda
August 3	John Vella
August 5	Dominico Calandrino
August 7	Edward Divis
August 9	Virgilio Aleotto
August 9	Tony Buttita
August 13	One "Michlevich"
August 19	Frank Scarpinato
August 19	Frank Alista
August 22	Louis DiBirnardo
August 29	Tony Soverino
September 7	Antonio Lombardo
September 9	Giuseppe Ferraro Morici
September 22	Eugene G. Thivierge
October 14	Eng Pake
October 16	Jung Bu Ging
October 17	Ralph J. Murphy
October 27	Peter Rizzuto
October 30	Vincent P. Signorelli
November 5	Alfie Fricano

The body of Dominic Aiello, uncle of Chicago's Aiello brothers, provides block-party amusement for local children who routinely turned out to ogle gangland killings during the Prohibition period. *(Goddard Collection)*

1929

January 8	Pasqualino Lolordo
January 31	Steve Kuczynski
February 4	William M. Cantwell
February 9	James A. Fee
February 14	Al R. Weinshank; Peter Gusenberg; Frank Gusenberg; Albert Kachallek, alias James Clark; John May; Dr. Reinhart Schwimmer; Adam Heyer; Alfred Weinshank

February 22	Pete Locasto
March 19	William J. Vercoe
March 22	Raymond Cassidy
March 29	Settimio Conti
April 5	Frank Louis "Red" Krueger
April 12	William F. Clifford
April 12	Michael F. Reilley, Jr.
April 24	Frank Raday, alias Frank Lee Brady
April 28	Enrico Arduini
May 3	Charles Folisi
May 15	Raymond E. Martin
May 21	John D. Hand

May 22	Joseph J. Sullivan
May 26	Bruno Borrelli
May 28	Charles Levy
May 30	Thomas McElligott
May 31	Ettore Quaterri
June 2	Herman Bloom
June 5	Patrick Maloney
June 15	Louis Sevcik
June 16	Ralph Cerra
June 26	Sam Muschia
July 3	Ernest Hoffman
July 10	Nathan Rossman, alias Joseph Resnikoff
July 31	Thomas A. McNichols
July 31	James Shupe
August 4	Yee Sun
August 9	Louis F. Heisler
August 15	John Woytko
August 28	John F. Bowman
August 29	Tony Domingo
September 2	Henry Connors
September 5	Edward Wescott
September 5	Frank Cawley
September 11	Charles Brown
September 16	"Pullizzi"
October 13	Casmir Holzwork, alias Riggins
October 30	H. Myles Cannaven
October 31	Rocco Maggio
November 9	Charles R. Rice
November 10	Joseph Lopiccolo
November 16	John G. Clay
November 24	Edward J. Tracy
November 30	Joseph Martino
December 1	Edward Baron
December 3	John Voegtle, alias Paddy King
December 6	Leroy Gilbert
December 6	Salvatore Lima
December 8	John LaPrizza
December 10	Dominick Sposato
December 11	Tomaso Tiritilli
December 12	Frank Basile
December 18	Ole Soully
December 19	Thomas Clyde Healy
December 20	Fillippo La Paglia
December 22	Roy F. Savery

December 27	Louis Nelson	February 4	Phillip Marchese	April 16	Joseph M. Cameron,
December 30	William J. Davern	February 4	Giuseppe Bucheri		alias Blue
December 31	William McPadden	February 5	William Healy	April 20	Frank Dire,
	George Maloney	February 14	Tony Lombardo		alias Del Re
December 31	Hugh McGovern	February 23	Lorenzo Pizziferri	April 20	Walter L. Wakefield
		March 4	Joe Cerrito	May 7	Harry Anthony
1930		March 6	John "Dingbat"	May 9	Dominico Sciortino
January 5	James Strangis		Oberta	May 25	Peter Plescia
January 7	Louis Antonucci	March 6	Sam Malaga	May 31	Filippo Ignolfo,
January 8	James H. McManus	March 16	John Rito		alias Abati
January 11	Leo DeLorenzo	March 17	Peter Bica		
January 30	Barney J. Mitchell	March 20	Cisaro Basile	June 1	Joseph Ferrara
January 30	Glenn Jackson	March 22	Andrew Racine	June 1	Sam Monastero
February 1	Julius Rosenhein	April 1	Martin "Babe"	June 3	Thomas Somnerio
February 2	Joseph Cada, Jr.		Mullaney	June 3	Santo Mascellino

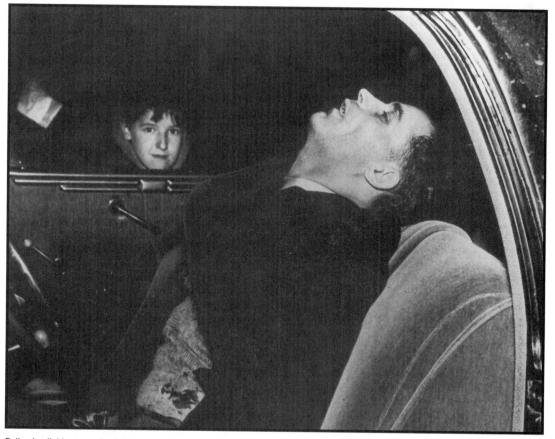

Police implicitly recognized the entertainment value of letting spectators of any age gawk at stiffs, unless they were too gruesomely splattered by shotgun blasts. *(Goddard Collection)*

CHICAGO'S "PUBLIC ENEMY" CAMPAIGN

The expression "public enemy" had cropped up occasionally in print and speeches prior to 1930 without acquiring any degree of formality, much less the status of a campaign, until the Chicago Crime Commission decided it should be applied to that city's ranking hoodlums whose disdain for the law was making them the criminal equivalent of tough-guy movie stars. The St. Valentine's Day Massacre of 1929 had forced Chicagoans, jaded by routine killings, to take gangland murder more seriously—seven unarmed men lined up and machine-gunned in cold blood far exceeded the limit people would tolerate, which was about two or at most three in an honest gun battle. Whether such a bloodbath had been planned, or was simply bad judgment on the part of subordinates gunning mainly for Bugs Moran, who (legend has it) saw the phoney police car and decided to have his coffee at a corner cafe instead, the city convulsed in horror at the "gangland crime of the century."

Chicago "closed down" for several weeks while police laid siege to speakeasies and ignored every rule of law to "round up the usual suspects," none of whom was ever tried. But Capone could no longer return from Miami to cheering crowds at baseball games. Despite having opened a large soup kitchen for Depression victims near the police station at 11th and State Street, he still found himself at the top of the list of "Public Enemies" released with great fanfare by the Crime Commission in April 1930. A newly-righteous press promoted the campaign with such enthusiasm that soon the police in Chicago and other cities and states were transforming it into a national if uncoordinated effort, with newspapers taking up the slack by naming public enemies of their own if the authorities were not keeping up with the headlines.

But the FBI would soon be credited with creating the public enemies campaign, and did in fact capitalize on it in the outlaw era to follow. Hoover ostensibly objected to ranking criminals by number, but finally bowed to a long-standing public misconception that the Bureau did so and created a "Ten Most Wanted" list many years later.

The Chicago Crime Commission had generously proposed a similar list to the Justice Department, only to be turned down, but in June 1930, Commission president Frank J. Loesch was pleased to issue a report on the success of

June 7		July 8	Vincenzo Phillipes	August 24	Joseph Terravicchia
(Found)	Eugene "Red"	July 12	Leonard A. Perdenza	September 9	Peter Nicastro,
	McLaughlin	July 15	Elsworth Moss		alias "The Ape"
June 7	Gasper Rokette	July 21	Pete Inserra,	September 14	Angelo Spano,
June 9	Alfred "Jake" Lingle		alias "Ash Can Pete"		alias Jack Costo
June 9	Aloysius Kearney	July 30	August Pusateri	September 18	John Roscoe
June 20	Lorenzo J. Juliano	August 10	Samuel Siciliano	September 19	George Peters
June 30	Frank Petita,	August 14	Daniel Vallo	September 19	Mike Lafakis
	alias Mike Gallichia	August 20	Charles Robert	October 13	David W. Emmett
July 1	Anthony Amato		Mulcahy	October 23	Joseph Aiello
July 2	Elbert Lusader	August 21	Bernard M. Ruberry	October 24	John Guida

its campaign during the two months since the original list naming the first 28 public enemies had been so enthusiastically received by the press.

1. ALPHONSE CAPONE ("Scarface")

2. ANTHONY VOLPE ("Mops")

3. RALPH CAPONE

4. FRANK RIO ("Frank Kline," "Frank Cline" and "James Costa")

5. JACK McGURN ("Machine Gun," "Jack DeMore" [among other spellings])

6. JAMES BELCASTRO

7. ROCCO FANELLI

8. LAWRENCE MANGANO

9. JACK ZUTA

10. JACK GUSICK

11. FRANK DIAMOND ("Frank Permaratta")

12. GEORGE ("Bugs") MORAN

13. JOE AIELLO

14. EDWARD ("Spike") O'DONNELL

15. JOE SALTIS ("Polack Joe")

16. FRANK McERLANE

17. VINCENT McERLANE

18. WILLIAM NEIMOTH

19. DANNY STANTON

20. MYLES O'DONNELL

21. FRANK LAKE

23. WILLIAM O'DONNELL ("Klondike")

24. GEORGE BARKER ("Red")

25. WILLIAM WHITE ("Three Finger Jack")

26. JOSEPH GENERO ("Peppy")

27. LEO MONGOVEN

28. JAMES ("Fur") SAMMONS

November 1	Peter Zubulikis, alias Jappas	January 6	Frank Candela	March 21	John Annerino, alias Genero
December 8	Tony May	January 9	Petro Porto, alias Pasquale Caruso	March 30	Max Tender
December 11	Marco Magnabosco	January 10	Elmer Gasparino	April 7	Anton Bagdon
December 12	Rudolph Marino, alias Tommasello	January 14	Enrico Bartocchi	April 17	Walter Van DeWerken
December 12	Samuel Marino	January 28	Morris Berkowitz	April 21	Edward Fitzgerald
		February 7	Joseph Tanzillo	April 29	Mike "The Pike" Heitler
	1931	February 18	Albert B. Courchene		
		February 24	Francis J. Carr, Jr.	May 12	Harry Hyter
January 4	August Battaglia	March 3	William J. Mayer	May 24	Joseph Sobotka
January 6	Pasquali Tardi	March 19	William J. Rooney		

KILLED IN THE LINE OF DUTY

It's probably safe to say that "the policeman's lot" is no happier today than it was during many early periods of law-enforcement history, though often for different reasons. The first efforts to organize urban police departments encountered resistance to the use of uniforms, sometimes even the display of badges, which invited physical attacks by organized and often politically protected street gangs (especially in New York) long accustomed to imposing their own rules of behavior in neighborhoods they controlled.

The general public was ambivalent, sometimes heroizing the "men in blue" or "New York's Finest," sometimes regarding them as little more than goons on the city payroll hired to oppress minorities, immigrants and "radicals," or otherwise do the bidding of the corrupt politicians to whom they owed their jobs. The role of the "detective" often was not the prevention of crime or the arrest of criminals, but negotiating (for a price) the return of stolen property to its rightful owners.

The Boston police strike of 1919 threw a scare into the entire country when a major city found itself unprotected against both violent and property crime. In the end, order was restored by military forces, the strike fizzled, and both citizens and civil authorities had to acknowledge that even a poorly trained or crooked cop was better than no cop at all.

A snail-paced movement toward police professionalism found increasing public support, but suffered a setback under Prohibition. Not many police could resist the bribery of bootleggers and speakeasy operators who didn't blink at weekly cash payoffs that might exceed an officer's annual salary. Paradoxi-cally, such graft, while again diminishing the public's respect for the law and its ostensible enforcers, did not necessarily lessen a police-man's personal commitment to protecting the public and keeping the peace; many used their ill-gotten gains to finance children's college educations that they could never have afforded on a policeman's salary. More than a few boot-leggers did the same, using part of their illicit profits to move their families out of the slums where they had grown up and into good neigh-borhoods, schools and legitimate businesses. How many law and medical degrees were directly financed by Prohibition is anybody's guess, but even sociologists of the day discovered that the Volstead Act served as a kind of G.I. bill for the children of families on both sides of the law.

The downside to this twisted form of altruism was a renewed contempt for both local and federal law enforcers and officers of the court, whose collusion with hoodlums and crooked politicians did not always stop with "honest graft." The protection purchased by the criminal community had no finely drawn line, which crippled efforts of the justice system to deal with far more serious crime: It delivered virtually no gangland murder convictions over more than a decade. The guilty verdict returned against Leo Brothers in the killing of Chicago journalist Jake Lingle, himself a mob insider, was hailed as a milestone of justice in a front-page editorial cartoon published by the *Chicago Tribune* (which had been his employer). Even that was a farce. For stalking and shooting Lingle in the back of the head, Brothers, a professional gun-man with an impressive record, received only 14 years.

Following a minor auto accident in St. Joseph, Michigan, Patrolman Charles Skelly was shot to death by one of the drivers, who then wrecked his car in making good his escape. With Berrien County sheriff's deputies, the police raided the nicely furnished bungalow of a "Frederick Dane," to whom the car was registered, and discovered an arsenal of guns, ammunition and bulletproof vests. Dane turned out to be Fred "Killer" Burke, formerly of St. Louis, and the most wanted man in the United States, suspected of participating in the St. Valentine's Day Massacre. *(Authors' collection)*

Such conditions made crime control in Chicago, New York and other cities less a campaign of reform than a grudge match between cops and crooks who had personally crossed each other, or who tangled in public in ways that made a gun battle mandatory. Even in clear-cut murder cases

with plenty of eyewitnesses, securing truthful testimony was as difficult as impaneling an honest jury, because of high mortality rates or bribe offers that might be fatal to turn down.

One vivid example of such quirky justice involved three trials and ultimately the acquittal of two of Chicago's most vicious hoodlums. Albert Anselmi and John Scalise, known as the "homicide squad," killed not only two policemen following a high-speed car chase, but in all likelihood members of their own "Little Italy" community who failed to contribute to their defense fund. After a hung jury necessitated a second trial, their attorney, the dashing Michael J. Ahern (who specialized in defending top mobsters), got them a verdict of manslaughter on the remarkable grounds that their pursuers lacked probable cause to arrest even such notorious criminals: "If a policeman detains you,

even for a moment, against your will, you are not guilty of murder, but only of manslaughter. If the policeman uses force of arms, you may kill him in self-defense and emerge from the law unscathed." During yet a third trial, both were simply acquitted by jurors bombarded by threats on their lives.

Thus death in the line of duty was a far greater occupational hazard for police officers then than now, when killing a cop guarantees relentless pursuit by a far better organized and far less corrupt law-enforcement community.

June 11	Dominick Latronica		**1932**		October 21	Tony Jerfita
June 13	Lorenzo Bua	January 11	Benjamin Rosenberg		October 26	Frank Amato, alias
June 19	James Janis	January 22	Michael J. Gallo			Joseph Farinella
June 20	Jack Kaufman	January 22	Carmello Luchesi		October 29	Harry Lefkovitz
June 23	Sam Pullano	January 28	Philip Flavin		November 5	Joseph Baron, Sr.
June 28	Frank Scavo	February 20	Joseph Morriss		December 1	Joseph Brovengano
July 2	John P. Carr	February 27	Joseph Dubett		December 6	John Liberto
July 10	Frank Caliendo	March 17	Joseph L. Lacheta		December 7	Anthony Persico
July 15	Edgar Smith	March 20	Frank Battaglia		December 7	Nicholas Maggio
July 16	Bernard McCone	March 23	Otto Froneck		December 16	Nohn Rinella
July 16	Herman Diehm	March 27	Carmino Spinelli		December 25	Ralph Pisano
July 26	Elija H. Orr	April 4	Charles O'Donnell			
August 11	Adolph J. Dumont	April 5	Herman Gleck		**1933**	
September 16	Carlo Piazza	April 7	Benjamin Applequist		January 19	Edward J. Fitzsimmins
September 16	Joseph Pelligrino	April 7	Ernest Applequist		February 7	Fred Petitti
October 8	Elfrieda Rigas	April 9	Michael Carmen		February 8	William J. O'Brien
	McErlane	April 20	Sam Mule, alias		February 24	Dennis Bruce Ziegler
	[alias Marion Miller]		Morley		March 1	Dan Lynch
October 11	George Wilson	June 16	George "Red" Barker		March 10	Samuel LaRocca
October 18	Mathias Kolb	June 29	George Brooks		March 12	Fred Russo
October 23	Michael J. Brannigan	July 22	Jack A. Werner		March 21	Joe Hanley
November 5	Salvatore Loverde	August 10	Joseph F. Connell		April 5	Joseph Zurek
November 7	Richard Fishman	August 16	Edward Hiller		May 15	Rocco Belcastro
November 9	Timothy Joseph	August 23	Herman Brin		May 24	Edward Gambino
	Lynch	August 24	Nello Pellegrini		June 3	Carl Verdoni
November 30	John Alerri	August 31	Charles Argento		June 11	George Navigato
December 1	Vincent Petrikos	September 2	Walter Zwolinski		June 16	Joseph Petitte
December 17	Joseph M. Barrie	September 25	Michael Tamburrino		June 18	Joseph Marzullo
December 22	Daniel Fognotti	September 29	Iron Barger		July 18	Emil Onesto
December 22	Walter Schreffer	October 11	Richard J. Roberts		July 20	Aloysius Strook
December 30	Abraham Schnieder	October 14	Thomas P. Kane		July 26	William E. Carr

July 28   Thomas Fredinordo
August 1   Tony Marino
August 12   John Perillo
August 21   Loreto Mule
August 29   John Pippan
September 9   Nicholas Museato
September 16 Sam Incandella
October 5   Joseph Pawlowski
October 9   August Winkler
October 10   Antonio Belmonte
October 23   John Paplinski, alias
              Plynn
October 27   Louis B. Cowen
October 27   Patsy Damato
November 5   Joseph Spinnato

1934

January 1   Michael W. Reagan
January 13   Walter Stifaniak
January 24   William "Three
              Finger Jack" White
January 31   William Evans
February 4   Ernest Rossi
February 19   Grover Cline
February 27   Joseph Smith

March 7   Daniel Losec
March 7   Frank Pope
March 14   Charles Connors
March 17   Kay A. Jespersen
March 21   Frederick S. Goetz,
              alias George Ziegler
April 26   Edward Dudeck
April 27   Tony Canzoneri
May 5   Chester Geisler
June 1   Clarence W. Haggerty
June 12   Peter Easer
June 21   Zigmund Masiong
June 28   Robert Millay
July 3   Fred Zehrol
July 19   Michael H. Quinlan
July 25   Sullivano Serpa
August 12   John Imperato
August 13   Robert Stamm
August 19   Ray James
              Thompson
September 10 Michael Lamperelli
September 10 John J. Sandrik
September 15 Joseph Adduci
September 29 Edward J. Meehan
October 26   James Canzoneri

October 31   William Franceschi,
              alias Willie Francis
November 3   Joseph Carracio
November 25   Anthony Dicaro
November 25   John Wells
November 27   Herman E. Hollis
November 27   Samuel Cowby
December 16   Christ Peter Soupos

1935

January 13   Frank Panio
January 14   Frank Abrignani
February 1   Joseph Catrino
February 4   Thomas Maloy
April 16   John Donahue
May 4   Frank A. Young, alias
              Anthony Calatorius
May 25   Clyde Osterberg
June 3   Jack Magliola,
              alias Magleo
July 18   Leland Varain, alias
              Louis Alterie
September 24 Edward J. Arendt
November 14   Frank Stypulkowski
November 15   Angelo Kleronomos
November 15   Joseph Scaffidi
November 19   Sam Incandella
December 19   Joseph Genero
December 26   Sam Latella
December 29   Albert J. Prignano

1936

January 3   Elsie Kenneman
January 13   Eugenio Belmonte
February 15   Vincent Gebardi,
              alias De Mora, De-
              Mory, and
              "Machine Gun" Jack
              McGurn
March 2   Anthony DeMory
March 29   Claude Cooley
July 9   John M. Bolton
September 2   Joseph Campisciano
September 9   Paul Phemister
October 28   Adolph Anzona
November 15   John Benedetto
November 23   Michael Galvin
December 17   Dominick Scaduto

The victim of a "speakeasy" or "beer flat" killing was usually written off as simply another casualty of Chicago's beer wars and went into the record books as such. *(Goddard Collection)*

1937

January 8	Benjamin Greco
October 3	Patsy Trotti
October 20	Joseph Locascio

1938

February 12	Lloyd B. Rourke
May 16	Henry G. Schneider
June 11	Eugene Dalassandro
June 29	Harry L. Minor

July 24	Nicholas Chiara-monte
August 6	Bruno Switaj
August 6	Leo Mosinski
August 8	James G. Dungan
August 9	Sam Picciotto
August 12	Joseph Laporte
August 24	Paul Battaglia
October 21	Bert Delaney
November 24	Joseph Bolton

December 23	John Minoque

1939

April 12	James Lawrence
May 1	Matthew R. Hyland
July 5	Louis Schiavone
October 9	Amerigo Bertolini
October 31	Paul Peters
November 8	Edward J. O'Hare

BIBLIOGRAPHY

A comprehensive list of works on twenties and thirties crime and crime control would require a separate volume and still not include many self-published books and booklets; journal and magazine articles; accounts of notorious individual crimes; city histories; and books of a professional or technical nature on police work, political corruption, criminology, sociology, forensic science and law.

A few of these are included here as especially relevant in establishing historical context (especially concerning New York and Chicago, contemporary journalism, political leaders and two crime surveys of lasting importance), along with bibliographies on such related subjects as Mafia that are themselves extensive. But its emphasis is on books discussing what the general public perceived as "national lawlessness" during the two decades when both crime and crime control underwent their most dramatic changes.

Given that focus, the following bibliography (on what we'll call "professional crime" from 1920 to 1940) covers the increasingly organized lawlessness and racketeering fostered by Prohibition, the revival of banditry and efforts to combat both, which will serve the social histo-

rian, writer, researcher and book collector who might value or disregard a particular entry for entirely different reasons. It pays special attention to the accounts and biographies of the gangsters and outlaws of the Prohibition and Depression eras—the so-called public enemies who, accurately or not, symbolized the crime conditions of the day—and the confusion among reformers, journalists, law makers and law enforcers in distinguishing between the violence committed by gangs warring with one another for control of territory, organizations and businesses (racketeering); and that committed by bandits against banks and payroll messengers (armed robbery). This confusion is reflected in the fact that the terms "gangster" and "public enemy" first described urban bootleggers and racketeers like Al Capone, but soon came to mean outlaws like John Dillinger, an entirely different kind of criminal.

Most listed here represent the efforts of writers and public officials to understand the country's rapidly changing crime conditions with little hindsight or historical perspective. Some reveal basic misconceptions that still persist, especially among reformers and politicians who habitually search for either scapegoats or panaceas with more popular appeal than legal practicality. Others that view prominent criminals as contemporaries rather than celebrities provide insight into popular views and attitudes of the times.

Many of the entries are annotated in the hope of providing at least some indication of their relative worth, accuracy and attention to historical detail. The early books tended to be little more than potboilers rushed out by newspaper reporters writing from memory and morgue files, and whose many factual errors have been perpetuated by nearly every popular writer who later relied on them as original sources. Some crime reporters-turned-authors were pleased to spread both the police and underworld rumors of the day, while others had no qualms about creating legends that have since been accepted as fact. Accounts of the St. Valentine's Day Massacre, for instance, generally recite the version settled on by Chicago police and newspapers in 1929 and by movie makers ever since, but which no longer stands close scrutiny. Similarly, descriptions of John Dillinger's historic escape from the Crown Point jail either repeat the popular notion that he whittled the wooden pistol from a washboard in his jail cell, or contend that the wooden gun was only camouflage to protect the smuggler of a real one. Recent research finds neither version true.

Thus many of these books are unreliable for serious research, but still are encountered so often in libraries, new and used bookstores and private collections that some comment on them is appropriate. Even highly inaccurate works often are interesting or entertaining, and for collectors may be worth acquiring merely for the sake of completeness. Likewise, a few are carefully researched and very useful, but hard to find and rarely listed in other bibliographies.

Books listed without comment usually are those offering more opinion and commentary than historical detail, and may display what now represents either progressive thinking or dismal ignorance of the subject, which also can be instructional.

Some pictorial histories and coffee-table books are listed because of their production quality or rare photographs, although their texts usually are superficial and derived almost entirely from the most commonly available sources.

The criteria for inclusion here are largely subjective, based on an estimation of the usefulness of the works, their uniqueness or interest or simply their value to the library of anyone desiring to cover the "public enemy" era as thoroughly as possible.

Abadinski, Howard. *Organized Crime.* Boston: Allyn and Bacon, 1981 4th ed., Chicago: Nelson-Hall, 1994. Academic but highly readable study of the origins, rise and operations of modern organized crime by an established authority, who also debunks many of the commonly associated myths and misconceptions. Excellent works also on the Gambino and Genovese crime families include *The Mafia in America* (1981) and *The Criminal Elite* (1983).

Abernathy, Francis Edward, ed. *Legendary Ladies of Texas.* Dallas: E-Hearst Press, 1981. Includes a good chapter, by John Neal Phillips and Andre L. Gorzell, on Bonnie Parker, disputing the rumor that Bonnie was pregnant at the time of her death.

Adamic, Louis. *Dynamite: The Story of Class Violence in America.* New York: Viking, 1931. Attack on racketeering as a byproduct of capitalism comes off as a lively polemic virtually promoting class warfare.

Adams, Verdon R. *Tom White, The Life of a Lawman.* El Paso: Texas Western Press, 1972. White was a

Texas Ranger, an FBI agent in the 1920s and later warden at Leavenworth. He was taken hostage by former members of the Al Spencer gang during their 1931 prison break, engineered from the outside by Frank Nash. White's father and brothers were also lawmen. One brother, James "Doc" White, an FBI agent, participated in the capture of Machine Gun Kelly, the Dillinger investigation and the killings of Ma and Fred Barker and Russell Gibson, of the Barker-Karpis gang. Goes well with *The Gonif,* memoirs of White's friend Morris "Red" Rudensky (former burglar and expert jailbreaker), which also includes a good account of the Leavenworth prison escape.

Addy, Ted. *The "Dutch" Schultz Story.* Derby, Conn.: Monarch Books, 1962. Reprint with photos, New York: Tower Books, 1968. Largely fictional paperback "biography." Reprint is part of a series on "Public Enemies of the 1930s."

Adler, Polly. *A House Is Not a Home.* New York: Rinehart, 1953. Popular autobiography of America's most notorious madam of the 1920s and '30s, with much material on her gangster friends, especially Arthur "Dutch Schultz" Flegenheimer and Charles "Lucky" Luciano, but also Al Capone, Frank Costello, Bugsy Siegel, others.

Ahearn, Danny. *The Confessions of a Gunman.* London: Routledge, 1930; U.S. ed. *How to Commit Murder.* New York: Ives Washburn, 1930. Unsubstantiated mobster melodrama.

Albini, Joseph L. *The American Mafia, Genesis of a Legend.* New York: Appleton-Century-Crofts, 1971. Considers the term "Mafia" more a "synonym for syndicated crime" than an actual organization.

Alcorn, Robert Hayden. *The Count of Gramercy Park.* London: Hurst & Blackett, 1955. Biography of Gerald Chapman.

Alix, Ernest Kahlar. *Ransom Kidnapping in America, 1874–1974: The Creation of a Capital Crime.* Carbondale: Southern Illinois University, 1978. Scholarly work on the history of kidnapping in America. Good source on the passage of the Lindbergh Law and gangster era in general.

Allen, Edward J. *Merchants of Menace—The Mafia.* Springfield, Ill.: Charles C. Thomas, 1962. By a police chief who views the Mafia as highly structured.

Allen, Robert S., ed. *Our Fair City.* New York: Vanguard, 1947. Survey of American cities and their political and police corruption.

Allen, Troy. *Gang Wars of the Twenties.* Chatsworth, Calif.: Barclay House, 1974. Undistinguished paperpack containing some photos not commonly seen.

Allsop, Kenneth. *The Bootleggers and Their Era.* London: Hutchinson, 1961. Reprint, *The Bootleggers: The Story of Chicago's Prohibition Era,* New Rochelle, N.Y.: Arlington House, 1968. Detailed if not always accurate account of Chicago gangs and beer wars in 1920s. Reprint has a new introduction by Allsop and this time a useful index.

Andrews, Wayne. *Battle for Chicago.* New York: Harcourt Brace, 1946.

Angle, Paul M. *Bloody Williamson.* New York: Knopf, 1952. Well-researched work on the violent history of Williamson County, Illinois, through the bloody Birger-Shelton gang war of the 1920s that included airplanes, homemade armored cars and fortified roadhouses in some epic battles, and culminated in Illinois's last public hanging of Charlie Birger, who delivered wisecracks from the gallows.

Anon. *Alcatraz.* San Francisco: E. Crowell Mensch, 1937.

Anon. *Bonnie Parker: The Story of Suicide Sal.* Ill-Vis Rules Publications, 1987. Miniature "kitchen-table" art booklet containing one of Bonnie's poems, illustrated with newspaper clippings, drawings and photos of Bonnie and Clyde. Only 400 copies printed, so may be of some remote interest to collectors. "Sal" and Parker's other doggeral, "The Story of Bonnie and Clyde," have appeared many times in books, newspapers, etc. Back cover illustration is nude morgue photo of Bonnie.

Anon. *The Inside Story of Chicago's Master Criminal.* Minneapolis: Graphic Arts/Fawcett, 1929. One of the first Capone books, in magazine format.

Anon. *I Worked for Lucky Luciano.* New York: Avon (paperback), 1954. Purports to be a first-person narrative by a former Luciano prostitute, but if anything a composite of several women by a male reporter who wisely declined a byline. Later retitled *I Am a Marked Woman.*

Anon. *Life and Exploits of S. Glenn Young.* Herrin, Ill.: Mrs. S. Glenn Young, 1925. Reprint, Herrin, Ill.: Crossfire Press, 1989. S. Glenn Young was a colorful character in southern Illinois during the 1920s, both as Prohibition agent and as Ku Klux Klan vigilante, who fought the Birger and Shelton gangs but also lined his pockets by ransacking the homes of honest citizens, as well as bootleggers. Murdered in 1925, apparently by the Shelton gang, and his devoted wife, blinded in an assassination attempt, produced this less than objective biography.

Anon. *The Life Story of Charlie Birger.* Marion: Illinois Book Co., 1927.

Anon. *The Morgue: The Gangster's Final Resting Place.* Chicago: 1933. Magazine-format collection of perfectly gruesome morgue photos with short biographies of the better-known Chicago gangsters.

Anon. *X Marks the Spot: Chicago Gang Wars in Pictures.* Chicago: Spot Publishing, 1930. Good contemporary account of Prohibition gang violence, published in magazine format. The author eventually revealed himself to be a Chicago journalist named Hal Andrews, who in *Real Detective* magazine complained at the way moralists (including civic leaders, and possibly gangsters themselves) obstructed distribution because of the gruesome photos, forcing him to sell it by mail order. Very scarce in the original, but some later reprints still in circulation.

Anslinger, Harry J. *The Murderers.* New York: Farrar, Straus & Cudahy, 1961. J. Edgar Hoover's chief rival and personal nemesis in national crime fighting melodramatically describes America's "war" on narcotics, popularizing the term "Mafia" that Hoover rejected. Almost singlehandedly replaced the alcohol peril with the "Reefer Madness" menace to get marijuana outlawed once Repeal left thousands of Prohibition agents looking for work.

———. *The Protectors.* New York: Farrar, Straus, 1964.

Anslinger, H.J., and William F. Tompkins. *The Traffic in Narcotics.* New York: Funk & Wagnals, 1953. Anslinger was U.S. Commissioner of Narcotics and Tompkins was U.S. Attorney, New Jersey.

Arm, Walter. *Pay-Off: The Inside Story of Big City Corruption.* New York: Appleton-Century-Crofts, 1951.

Asbury, Herbert. *The Gangs of New York: An Informal History of the New York Underworld.* New York: Knopf, 1927. Deals mainly with such 19th and early 20th century fighting gangs as the Bowery Boys, Dead Rabbits, etc., headed by the likes of Monk Eastman, Big Jack Zelig, and Gyp the Blood, ironically declaring the "gangster" era ended thanks to new and enlightened civic policies that were striking at the roots of urban crime. By the time the book appeared, the term gangster had been redefined to describe the increasingly organized bootleggers, racketeers and professional criminals spawned by Prohibition, and the bank robbers of the Depression.

———. *Gem of the Prairie: An Informal History of the Chicago Underworld.* New York: Knopf, 1940. Asbury catches up with the times, and provides a highly entertaining description of the city's crime and vice lords from the 18th century through the gangsters of the Roaring Twenties.

———. *The Great Illusion: An Informal History of Prohibition.* Garden City, N.Y.: Doubleday, 1950. Asbury's other books include *The Barbary Coast: An Informal History of the San Francisco*

Underworld, 1933; and *The French Quarter: An Informal History of the New Orleans Underworld,* 1936. These also were published by Knopf and deal mainly with 19th-century crime and vice in those cities.

Asinof, Eliot. *Eight Men Out.* New York: Holt, Rinehart & Winston, 1963. Good detailed account of the "Black Sox" scandal, the 1919 World Series fix allegedly masterminded by Arnold Rothstein. No index or bibliography, as typical of older crime books and many recent ones.

Askins, Colonel Charles. *Texans, Guns & History.* New York: Bonanza, 1970. Includes distorted chapter on Bonnie and Clyde, and Frank Hamer's account of their ambush (originally published in Walter Prescott Webb's *The Texas Rangers*).

Aswell, Thomas E. *The Story of Bonnie and Clyde.* Ruston, La.: H.M.G., Inc., 1968.

Audett, James Henry "Blackie." *Rap Sheet.* New York: Sloane, 1954. Widely sold "autobiography" of a 1930s bank robber who claimed personal involvement with nearly every crime and gang from the Kansas City Massacre to John Dillinger. Largely imaginary.

Bain, Donald. *War in Illinois.* Englewood Cliffs, N.J.: Prentice-Hall, 1978. Respectable account of Birger-Shelton gang war of 1920s, with good photos and contemporary sketches by Birger gangster Harvey Dungey. Well-researched, but contain much invented dialogue that diminishes its historical value.

Bain, George F. *The Barrow Gang: Clyde Barrow and Bonnie Parker: The Real Story.* 1968. Booklet, mainly fiction, though in places it reads like somebody's confused recollections.

Balsamo, William, with George Carpozi, Jr. *Always Kill a Brother: The Bloody Saga of the Irish-Italian Crime War That Put the Mafia in Power!* New York: Dell, 1977. Twenties gang war between Brooklyn Mafia group run by Frankie Yale (Francesco Uale) and the Irish "White Hand" gang, headed by Peg Leg Lonergan, allegedly killed by Al Capone.

———. *Under the Clock: The Inside Story of the Mafia's First Hundred Years.* Far Hills, N.J.: New Horizon, 1988. Bill Balsamo, retired New York longshoreman turned crime historian, makes good use of friend-and-family ties with old mobsters, including an original Brooklyn "godfather." Reprinted in 1991 as *Crime Incorporated.*

Barbican, James. *The Confessions of a Rum-Runner.* New York: Ives Washburn, 1928. Highly personalized and dramatized, but undocumented and undetailed account of a self-described rum-runner, apparently an Englishman using a pseudonym, who blundered into the business somewhere along the upper East Coast.

Barnes, Bruce. *Machine Gun Kelly: To Right a Wrong.* Perris, Calif.: Tipper, 1991. Life story of George Barnes, alias Machine Gun Kelly, at least as he related it to his son Bruce. Bruce Barnes also corresponded extensively with his stepmother, Kathryn Kelly, for a time. Less than detailed and somewhat overblown, but corrects many common errors about Kelly's family background and personal history. First book to give Kelly's correct birthplace, birthdate and name.

Barnes, Harry Elmer. *Battling the Crime Wave: Applying Sense and Science to the Repression of Crime.* Boston: Stratford, 1931. Prominent prison-reform advocate's excursion into contemporary crime control, treating it as a quasi-military campaign with crooks as the enemy.

———. *The Repression of Crime: Studies in Historical Penology.* 1926. Reprint. Montclair, N.J.: Patterson Smith, 1969.

Barrett, Paul W., and Mary H. Barrett. *Young Brothers Massacre.* Columbia: University of Missouri, 1988. Well-documented account of the killing of six law officers by Harry and Jennings Young at their mother's farm near Springfield, Mo., in January 1932. Speculation that Fred Barker may have been involved, and some new material on Pretty Boy Floyd, who apparently knew the Youngs and was erroneously suspected.

Beeley, Arthur L. *The Bail System in Chicago.* 1927. Reprint. Chicago: University of Chicago Press, 1966.

Bennett, James O'Donnell. *Chicago Gangland.* Chicago: Tribune Publishing, 1929. Scarce but distinctive softcover collection of Bennett's crime reporting for the *Chicago Tribune,* probably as accurate as other contemporary accounts, and includes many small, hard-to-find photos. Similar to *X Marks the Spot,* but smaller (6-inch by 9-inch) format.

Berman, Susan. *Easy Street.* New York: Dial, 1981. Memoirs of the daughter of lesser gangster Dave Berman, whose criminal career extended from robbing Midwest banks in the twenties to operating mob-controlled hotel-casinos in Las Vegas in the 1950s.

Best, Harry. *Crime and the Criminal Law in the United States.* New York: Macmillan, 1931. Exhaustive and exhausting (615 pages) study of law enforcement and the criminal justice system.

Biffle, Kent. *A Month of Sundays.* Denton: University of North Texas Press, 1993. Collection of Biffle's columns from the *Dallas Morning News* includes much Texas history, with interesting coverage of such celebrity outlaws as Bonnie and Clyde; Bonnie's husband, Roy Thornton; Raymond Hamilton; the Newton brothers (who took part in the famous $2 million train robbery near Rondout, Illinois, in 1924); the 1927 "Santa Claus bank robbery" in Cisco, Texas; plus Machine Gun Kelly and Harvey Bailey. Also a section on Bailey's biographer, J. Evetts Haley.

Bilbo, Jack [Hugo C.K. Baruch]. *Carrying a Gun for Al Capone.* New York: Putnam's, 1932. Bogus "autobiography" of an English artist claiming to be a former Capone bodyguard. Published in England and Germany during the thirties and forties, illustrating mainly the continuing worldwide fascination with American gangsters in general and Capone in particular.

Block, Alan. *East Side–West Side: Organizing Crime in New York 1930–1950.* Cardiff, U.K.: University of Cardiff Press, 1980. Excellent and revisionist account (with many mug shots) of the interconnection between gangland violence and political life during a 20-year period in New York City. Includes what is probably the best critical account of "Murder, Inc."

Blumenthal, Ralph. *Last Days of the Sicilians: The FBI's War against the Mafia,* New York: Times Books, 1988. Contemporary; historically superficial.

Boar, Roger, and Nigel Blundell. *Crooks, Crime and Corruption.* London: Octopus, 1987; New York: Dorset, 1991. Vast, superficial, unfocused, with obligatory nods to famous American mobsters. Also published as *The World's Most Infamous Crimes and Criminals.* London: Octopus, 1987. Over 700 pages on murderers, murderesses, tyrants, war criminals, swindlers and lawbreakers of all sorts from all ages. Most relevant gangster material consists of short and unoriginal accounts in a chapter called "Thieves and Villains," which includes Bonnie and Clyde, the Mafia, Lansky, Luciano and Genovese, Al Capone, Bugsy Siegel, Legs Diamond and Dutch Schultz. Strangely absent is John Dillinger. Reprinted as *Crooks, Crime and Corruption,* New York: Dorset, 1991.

Boettiger, John. *Jake Lingle: Or Chicago on the Spot.* New York: E. P. Dutton, 1931. Detailed account of local crime conditions and the murder of *Chicago Tribune* reporter Jake Lingle, seen as a martyr to investigative journalism until a closer look discovered his involvement in the rackets. *Tribune* writer Boettiger tends to soft-peddle Lingle's mob connections and agree with the jury that the killer was a young, transplanted St. Louis gunman named Leo Brothers, who distinguished himself mainly as Chicago gangland's only convicted murderer of any importance during the Prohibition era. Represented by future Dillinger attorney Louis Piquett, Brothers was found guilty despite questionable evidence, and his unusually light sentence of 14 years may have been part of an underworld deal.

Bonanno, Joseph, with Sergio Lalli. *A Man of Honor: The Autobiography of the Boss of Bosses.* New York: Simon & Schuster, 1983. Interesting and informative insider's view of life within Italian crime families in the United States. Bonanno considers what outsiders call Mafia to be a "Sicilian tradition" rather than an actual organization, once represented by "Men of Honor" (as he regards himself) but gradually corrupted by young "Americanized" gangsters and such non-Sicilians as Al Capone (whose last name, says Bonanno, means "castrated male chicken"). Valachi's testimony made "Joe Bananas" a celebrity at hearings in the 1960s, but Bonanno had headed a Brooklyn crime family since 1931. Has much on New York's Castellammarese War, Luciano, Capone, Aiello and others. The book supposedly landed Bonanno his first jail sentence, when he refused to testify before a mafia commission. Bonanno also sued his publisher for a cover illustration he thought made him look like a "cheap gangster."

Booker, Anton S. *Wildcats in Petticoats: A Garland of Female Desperadoes—Lizzie Merton, Zoe Wilkins, Flora Quick Mundis, Bonnie Parker, Katie Bender and Belle Starr.* Girard, Kans.: Haldeman-Julius, 1945. Trivial but collectible 24-page booklet.

Boynton, Captain Tom. *The Gang Wars of Chicago and the Rise of the Super Chiefs.* Chicago: Prohibition Research Association, 1930. Magazine format booklet similar to *X Marks the Spot;* more chronological and biographical, but by comparison poorly written, proofread and produced.

Brearley, H.C. *Homicide in the United States.* Chapel Hill: University of North Carolina, 1932. Reprint. Montclair, N.J.: Patterson Smith, 1969. One of several academic efforts to examine Americans' penchant for killing each other; includes some good data and insights but sometimes misses the obvious.

Brennan, Bill. *The Frank Costello Story.* Derby, Conn.: Monarch, 1962. Monarch paperback series of "gangster biographies" are collectibles, at best.

Browning, Frank, and John Gerassi. *The American Way of Crime: From Salem to Watergate, A Stunning New Perspective on American History.* New York: Putnam, 1980.

Breuer, William B. *J. Edgar Hoover and His G-Men.* Westport, Conn.: Praeger, 1995. Pure party line homage to Hoover, with many errors.

Burns, Walter Noble. *The One-Way Ride.* Garden City, N.Y.: Doubleday, Doran, 1931. An exciting and melodramatic if historically dubious account of the Capone era in Chicago. Burns also wrote *The Saga of Billy the Kid,* lurid fiction masquerading as fact.

Burroughs, William S. *The Last Words of Dutch Schultz.* New York: Viking, 1975. Written as a play, but contains many photos and the deliriously poetic deathbed babbling of the mortally wounded Schultz.

Busch, Francis X. *Enemies of the State.* New York: Bobbs-Merrill, 1954. Includes an interesting if inaccurate chapter on Capone.

Bruns, Roger A. *The Bandit Kings: From Jesse James to Pretty Boy Floyd.* New York: Crown, 1995. Superficial treatment of all the big-name outlaws from the frontier period through the public-enemy era, interesting mainly for its design, superior production and good collection of photos.

Calhoun, Frederick S. *The Lawmen: United States Marshals and Their Deputies, 1789–1989.* Washington, D.C.: Smithsonian Institution Press, 1989. Two-hundred year history of the U.S. Marshals Service includes a chapter on Prohibition describing its members busting bootleggers on evidence gathered by Prohibition agents, and the arrest of Capone on tax charges by Treasury agents specially deputized as U.S. Marshals by the Justice Department. Touches briefly on the rivalry between the Marshals Service and the FBI.

Callahan, Clyde C., and Byron B. Jones. *Heritage of an Outlaw—The Story of Frank Nash.* Hobart, Okla.: Schoonmaker, 1979. Biography of hoodlum Frank "Jelly" Nash, killed in the "Kansas City Massacre" of 1933. Contains gangster genealogy similar to that in Paul Wellman's *A Dynasty of Western Outlaws.* Published in Nash's hometown both as individual book and as part of a regional series (Volume 5, *Pioneering in Kiowa County,* sold by the county historical society).

Callow, Alexander B., Jr. *The Tweed Ring.* New York: Oxford University Press, 1965. Good background study of origins of civic corruption that served as a prototype for political-machine bossism and graft that survived sporadic reform efforts to flourish in most large U.S. cities, especially in the twenties and thirties.

Campbell, Rodney. *The Luciano Project.* New York: McGraw-Hill, 1977. Details Lucky Luciano's contribution to the war effort, which some question. While in prison, Luciano supposedly collaborated with Naval Intelligence in suppressing espionage and sabotage on the New York waterfront and later worked with the OSS (forerunner of the CIA) in setting up a Mafia resistance movement to aid the Allied invasion of Sicily. Well researched.

Carey, Arthur A. *On the Track of Murder.* London: Jarrolds, 1930. Adventures and recollections of longtime New York Homicide Bureau deputy inspector, with extensive coverage of local hoodlums before and during Prohibition.

Carey, Arthur, with Howard McLellan. *Memoirs of a Murder Man.* Garden City, N.Y.: Doubleday, Doran, 1930. A retitled and abbreviated version of the British edition.

Carlson, Oliver, and Earnest Sutherland Bates. *Hearst, Lord of Sam Simeon.* New York: Viking, 1936. Study of the powerful, eccentric newspaper magnate whose intense rivalry with other press lords helped make his name synonymous with sensational journalism of the period.

Carpozi, George, Jr. *Bugsy: The High-Rolling, Bullet-Riddled Story of Benjamin "Bugsy" Siegel.* New York: Pinnacle, 1973. Superficial "biography" compares poorly with Dean Jennings's *We Only Kill Each Other.*

———. *Gangland Killers.* New York: Manor, 1979. Includes chapters on the St. Valentine's Day Massacre, Legs Diamond, Raymond Hamilton, Bonnie and Clyde, Al Capone, Dutch Schultz, the Kansas City Massacre, Pretty Boy Floyd, Mad Dog Coll, the Barker-Karpis gang, Baby Face Nelson, Machine Gun Kelly and John Dillinger. Grossly inaccurate with invented dialogue.

Carse, Robert. *Rum Row.* New York: Holt, Rinehart & Winston, 1959.

Casey, Robert J., and W.A.S. Douglas. *The Midwesterner.* Chicago: Wilcox & Follett, 1948. A cryptically titled but well-written biography of Illinois's slightly quirky Governor Dwight Green that includes an absorbing account of Chicago's underworld warfare, the fall of Capone and battles with other colorful scoundrels of the period.

Chamberlain, John. *Farewell to Reform.* New York: Liveright, 1932.

Chandler, David Leon. *Brothers in Blood: The Rise of the Criminal Brotherhoods.* New York: E.P. Dutton, 1975. Supposed genealogy of Mediterranean criminal fraternities (the Spanish Garduna, the Camorra, Mafia, "Cosa Nostra" and Unione Corse) and their transplantation to North America and Australia.

Charbonneau, Jean-Paul. *The Canadian Connection.* Montreal: Optimum, 1976. (See also Dubro and Rowland, *King of the Mob.*)

Cherrington, Ernest H. *The Evolution of Prohibition in the United States of America.* Westerville, Ohio: American Issue Press, 1920. Reprint. Montclair, N.J.: Patterson Smith, 1969. Thoroughly biased but still useful mainly for its extensive and detailed description of America's

Prohibition movement going back to the colonial period.

Churchill, Allen. *A Pictorial History of American Crime.* New York: Holt, Rinehart & Winston, 1964. Coffee-table format, superficial text and presenting the most commonly published crime photos.

Cipes, Robert M. *The Crime War, the Manufactured Crusade.* New York: New American Library, 1968. Includes published material from other sources, tending to discredit the "war on crime" campaigns as more political than practical.

Citizens' Police Committee, *Chicago Police Problems.* Chicago: University of Chicago, 1931. Reprint. Montclair, N.J.: Patterson Smith, 1969. A critical examination of how police administrative and organizational policies were crippling law-enforcement in most large cities where policing efforts were fragmented, poorly coordinated and sometimes competitive due to district political influence.

Claitor, Diana. *Outlaws, Mobsters and Murderers.* New York: M & M Books, 1991. Nicely produced and profusely illustrated coffee-table book covering nearly all the famous gangsters and outlaws, serial killers, spectacular crimes, etc. Nothing new, but fairly accurate.

Clarke, Donald Henderson. *In the Reign of Rothstein.* New York: Vanguard, 1929. Biography of Arnold Rothstein, rushed into print shortly after his murder.

Clayton, Merle. *Union Station Massacre.* New York: Bobbs-Merrill, 1975. Extensive account of Pretty Boy Floyd and Kansas City Massacre derived mainly from newspaper clippings, although the writer apparently had access to FBI files. Falls far short of Robert Unger's 1997 book with the same title.

Coffee, Thomas M. *The Long Thirst: Prohibition in America: 1920–1933.* New York: W.W. Norton, 1975. A worthwhile social history of Prohibition.

Cohen, Daniel. *The Encyclopedia of Unsolved Crimes.* New York: Dorset Press, 1988. Gangster material includes the murders of Arnold Rothstein, Abe "Kid Twist" Reles and Roger Touhy, possible mob involvement in the disappearance of Judge Crater and the death of Thelma Todd; the escape of Terrible Tommy O'Connor and Jay Robert Nash's conspiracy theory of Dillinger's survival, which Cohen quickly dismisses.

Cohen, Mickey, with John Peer Nugent. *Mickey Cohen: In My Own Words.* Englewood Cliffs, N.J.: Prentice-Hall, 1975. Cohen worked for Al Capone and Bugsy Siegel, was a Los Angeles bookmaking boss, survived assassination attempts, and served time at Alcatraz with Alvin Karpis, but his "own words" make for dull reading with little original information.

Cohen, Rich. *Tough Jews: Fathers, Sons and Gangster Dreams.* New York: Simon & Schuster, 1998. Carefully researched but stylishly written account of New York's Jewish gangsters.

Cohen, Sam D. *100 True Crime Stories.* Cleveland/New York: World, 1946. Short accounts of miscellaneous and unmemorable murders and robberies, mostly in the U.S., mostly from the 1930s.

Cohn, Art. *The Joker Is Wild.* New York: Random House, 1955. Overblown biography of comedian Joe E. Lewis, who survived a throat-slashing after quitting a Capone-affiliated nightclub, The Green Mill (still in operation, under new management). Much on Capone, Machine Gun Jack McGurn, other Chicago gangsters, plus a chapter on Dutch Schultz.

Collins, Frederick Lewis. *The FBI in Peace and War.* New York: G.P. Putnam's Sons, 1943. Like other FBI-approved books, this one has an introduction by J. Edgar Hoover, lauds the Bureau's war on crime and saboteurs and has much on the Depression outlaws, who were then recent history.

Cook, Fred J. *The FBI Nobody Knows.* New York: Macmillan, 1964. Former agent created a stir criticizing the FBI. Tossed in Dillinger, the Urschel kidnapping, the Kansas City Massacre, the Barker-Karpis gang, Bonnie and Clyde, Capone and Louis "Lepke" Buchalter, errors and all.

————. *A Two-Dollar Bet Means Murder.* New York: Dial, 1961. Some superficial history, but mainly argues that gambling is the steadiest source of income for the modern-day mob.

————. *The Secret Rulers: Criminal Syndicates and How They Control the U.S.* New York: Duell, Sloan & Pierce, 1966.

————. *Mafia.* Greenwich, Conn.: Fawcett, 1973.

Cooper, Courtney Ryley. *Ten Thousand Public Enemies.* Boston: Little, Brown, 1935. Mainly about Depression outlaws, including Dillinger, Floyd, Nelson, Barker-Karpis gang, Machine Gun Kelly, the Barrows, Wilbur Underhill, Jake Fleagle, the Tri-State Gang, and many lesser-known criminals, with some references to Capone, partly derived from his own series of articles in *American* magazine. Glorifies Hoover and the FBI (then called the Division of Investigation) in the most purple of period prose, but as Hoover's favorite crime writer, ghost writer and personal crony Cooper had access to the Bureau's files. Flowery forward by Hoover, who reportedly followed Cooper's advice in popularizing the term "G-man" and fostering the Bureau's image as a dedicated team of selfless, incorruptible, invincible, scientific crime fighters. Cooper later committed suicide, supposedly after a falling out with Hoover, possibly over his unwitting "infidelity" of collaborating with Hoover's archrival, Harry Anslinger, on drug stories that promoted the Federal Bureau of Narcotics.

————. *Here's to Crime.* Boston: Little, Brown, 1937. Largely a rehash of *Ten Thousand Public Enemies,* with added material on rackets, miscellaneous crime, police, prisons, courts, and other federal agencies. In 1939 he published a lurid exposé of prostitution, *Designs in Scarlet.*

Cordry, H.D., Jr. *Oklahoma Outlaw and Lawman Map, 1865–1935.* Oklahoma City: Oklahoma Heritage Association, 1990. Compiled with an agent of Oklahoma's State Crime Bureau, poster-size map includes dozens of sites connected with southwestern outlaws of the twenties and thirties, including Al Spencer, Frank Nash, the Kimes-Terrill gang, the Barkers, Pretty Boy Floyd, Bonnie and Clyde, Machine Gun Kelly, Harvey Bailey and Wilbur Underhill, as well as earlier criminals from the horseback era. Photos and text on Oklahoma's outlaw and lawman history. Carefully researched.

Corey, Herbert. *Farewell, Mr. Gangster!* New York: D. Appleton-Century, 1936. Another detailed, complimentary but well-researched account (far less lurid than Cooper's) of the FBI's extermination of the Depression outlaw gangs. Forward by Hoover suggests Corey also had access to FBI files.

Courtney, Thomas J., Wilbert F. Crowley and Marshall B. Kearney. *Statement in Opposition to the Release of Banghart: "The Factor Kidnapping Was Not a Hoax, Touhy Was Not Framed."* Printed by Champlin-Shealy Co., Chicago. Privately published, c.1960. Prosecutors of Capone-era gangsters Roger Touhy [*The Stolen Years*] and Basil Banghart defend their case against Touhy in a thick, rare, detailed document-like paperback after Touhy's conviction was finally reversed (to their embarrassment).

Cox, Bill G., et al. *Crimes of the 20th Century.* New York: Crescent Books, 1991. Contributors include Bill G. Cox, Bill Francis, William J. Helmer, Gary C. King, Julie Malear, Darrell Moore, David Nemec, Samuel Roen and Billie Francis Taylor. Some personal reports, but mostly from published sources, some accurate, some not.

Cox, Roger A. *The Thompson Submachine Gun.* Athens, Ga.: Law Enforcement Ordnance Co., 1982. Mainly a less-than-comprehensive (or accurate) collection of tommy-gun serial numbers for the collector community, but with some coverage of its use by police and criminals. Includes longish introduction by William Helmer, whose *Gun That Made the Twenties Roar* (1969) was until recently (see Hill, Tracie) the only comprehensive history of the weapon.

Craig, Jonathan, and Richard Posner. *The New York Crime Book.* New York: Pyramid, 1972. Extended history of Gotham lawlessness with nothing new, but a readable rehash of oft-told tales.

Crain, Milton, ed. *Sins of New York.* New York: Boni & Gaer, 1947.

Cressey, Donald R. *Theft of the Nation: The Structure and Operations of Organized Crime in America.* New York: Harper & Row, 1969. Academic study of the Italian crime families mostly in the sixties, probably inspired by the Senate revelations of mob turncoat Joe Valachi. Some historical background on the twenties and thirties.

Cressey, Paul G. *The Taxi-Dance Hall: A Sociological Study of Commercial Recreation in City Life.* Chicago: University of Chicago, 1932. Reprint, Montclair, N.J.: Patterson Smith, 1969. Interesting study of the once ubiquitous public dancehall phenomenon and its relation to urban vice conditions.

Cromie, Robert, and Joseph Pinkston. *Dillinger: A Short and Violent Life.* New York: McGraw-Hill, 1962. Reprint, Evanston, Ill.: Chicago Historical Bookworks, 1990. The first carefully researched and heavily detailed Dillinger biography. Pinkston remained the country's leading Dillinger authority and operated the John Dillinger Historical Museum in Nashville, Ind., until his death in 1996.

Crouse, Russel. *Murder Won't Out.* Garden City, New York: Doubleday, Doran, 1932. Odd but interesting mix of police work and unsolved murders, including Arnold Rothstein's.

Crowell, Chester Theodore. *Liquor, Loot and Ladies.* New York: Knopf, 1930.

Crump, Irving, and John W. Newton. *Our G-Men.* New York: Dodd, Mead, 1937.

Culver, Dorothy Campbell, comp. *Bibliography of Crime and Criminal Justice, 1927–1931.* New York: H.W. Wilson, 1934. Reprint, Montclair, N.J.: Patterson Smith, 1969. Literally thousands of entries, including scholarly and popular books, pamphlets, reports and documents, as well as articles from hundreds of journals and magazines, in English and other languages, under dozens of categories related to crime and the criminal justice system. Essential to serious research on the subject in its broadest sense.

———. *Bibliography of Crime and Criminal Justice, 1932–1937.* [1939] Similar to the author's earlier work, but focused more on professional and technical materials. Also reprinted by Patterson Smith, 1969.

Cummings, Homer S. *Selected Papers.* New York: Charles Scribner's Sons, 1939. A presentation of Cummings' crime-fighting proposals that were considered progressive, even revolutionary at the time.

———. *We Can Prevent Crime.* Slender and elegantly self-published (bound in red leather with gold lettering) 34-page collection of four articles from *Liberty* magazine by the first U.S. Attorney General under President Roosevelt, brimming with New Deal optimism and naïveté.

Cummings, Homer S., and Carl McFarland. *Federal Justice*: *Chapters in the History of Justice in the Federal Executive.* New York: Macmillan, 1937. Appointed attorney general by President Roosevelt in 1933, Cummings launched the first national "war on crime" that used celebrity fugitives like Dillinger to obtain passage of unprecedented federal anti-crime laws that unleashed the FBI. Reprinted by New York: Da Capo, 1970.

Cummings, John, and Ernest Volkman. *Goombata: The Improbable Rise of John Gotti and His Gang.* Boston: Little, Brown, 1990.

Curzon, Sam. *Legs Diamond.* Derby, Conn.: Monarch Books, 1961. Reprint with photos. New York: Tower Books, 1969. Mainly of interest to collectors of obscure crime paperbacks. Inaccurate but interesting for some trivia about twenties gangsters and Prohibition.

Danforth, Harold, and James D. Horan. *The D.A.'s Man.* New York: Crown, 1957. By an investigator for the New York District Attorney's office under

Thomas E. Dewey and Frank Hogan, who worked on the Dutch Schultz, Luciano and Jimmy Hines cases. Also authored *The Mob's Man.*

Davis, John H. *Mafia Dynasty: The Rise and Fall of the Gambino Crime Family.* New York: Harper-Collins, 1993. Traces history of the Gambinos from the Castellammarese War of 1931 to the fall of John Gotti in 1992.

Day, James M. *Captain Clint Peoples, Texas Ranger: Fifty Years a Lawman.* Waco, Tex.: Texian Press, 1980. Among the miscreants pursued by Captain Peoples were Bonnie and Clyde.

De Nevi, Don. *Western Train Robberies.* Millbrae, Calif.: Celestial Arts, 1976. Includes chapters on train robberies in the 1920s.

deFord, Miriam Allen. *The Real Bonnie & Clyde.* New York: Ace, 1968. Superficially derived from the 1934 book *Fugitives* by Bonnie's mother and Clyde's sister, Toland's *Dillinger Days,* and a few newspaper stories. Slim paperback cashing in on the movie *Bonnie and Clyde.*

————. *The Real Ma Barker.* New York: Ace, 1970. Worst yet tale of the Barker-Karpis gang uses other inaccurate published sources and takes up only half the book. Filler material includes equally spurious biographies of other gangsters of the period, both bank robbers and racketeers. A cash-in on the movie *Bloody Mama.*

Demaris, Ovid. *Captive City.* Secaucus, N.J.: Lyle Stuart, 1969. Exceptionally good description of organized crime and political corruption in Chicago, especially considering Demaris's previous paperback potboilers. Focus is on latter-day Syndicate activities and personalities, but has much on Capone era, a biographical section and extensive index. Accurate enough to dismay the city's working mobsters.

————. *America the Violent.* New York: Cowles, 1970; Baltimore: Penguin, 1971. Interesting but unselective review of U.S. violence as a national pastime.

————. *The Dillinger Story.* Derby, Conn.: Monarch, 1961. Reprint, New York: Tower, 1968. Low-grade but collectible Monarchia. Reprinted by Belmont Tower, as *Dillinger,* in 1973.

————. *The Director: An Oral Biography of J. Edgar Hoover.* New York: Harper & Row, 1975; Reprint, *J. Edgar Hoover: As They Knew Him, an Oral Biography,* New York: Carroll & Graf/Richard Gallen, 1994. Slight gangster material (mostly on Dillinger) but interesting insider views of Hoover as a tarnished American legend.

————. *Lucky Luciano Story.* Derby, Conn.: Monarch, 1960. Reprinted with photos, New York: Tower, 1969. Another superficial paperback biography. Reprinted in Tower's "Public Enemies of the 1930s" series, and again in 1973 by Belmont Tower as *The Lucky Luciano Story: The Mafioso and the Violent '30s,* as part of a "Godfather" series.

DeNeal, Gary. *A Knight of Another Sort: Prohibition Days and Charlie Birger.* Danville, Ill.: Interstate Printers & Publishers, 1981. Biography of Birger from close up, with good collection of photos. Well-researched and probably the most detailed account yet of the Birger and Shelton gangs.

DeSimone, Donald. *"I Rob Banks: That's Where the Money Is!": The Story of Bank Robber Willie "The Actor" Sutton and the Killing of Arnold Schuster.* New York: Shapolsky, 1991. Poor repeat on Willie Sutton, including his bogus quotation, but purports to describe the revenge murder of the man who turned him in.

DeSola, Ralph. *Crime Dictionary.* New York: Facts on File, 1982.

de Toledano, Ralph. *J. Edgar Hoover, the Man in His Time.* New Rochelle, N.Y.: Arlington House, 1973. Tribute to Hoover, written soon after his death. Gangster cases, inaccurately reported, include Dillinger, Machine Gun Kelly, Barker-Karpis gang, Bonnie and Clyde and Lepke Buchalter.

Dewey, Thomas E. *Twenty against the Underworld.* Garden City, N.Y.: Doubleday, 1974. Dewey's "racket busting" as a prosecutor launched his failed career in national politics. But he convicted, among others, Waxey Gordon and Lucky Luciano (whom he later paroled). Couldn't get Dutch Schultz, but Schultz died trying to get him.

Dillon, Richard H. *The Hatchet Men.* New York: Coward-McCann, 1962. History of the tong wars of San Francisco's Chinatown. Mainly 19th century, but last chapter includes 1920s and mentions what is likely the first use of a machine gun by criminals (a .30-caliber water-cooled Browning mounted on an automobile in 1914).

Dingler, Jerry, comp. *Historical Collector Edition: Bonnie and Clyde Ambush.* Privately printed, Arcadia, La., 1984. 50th anniversary commemorative newspaper includes contemporary articles of the famous ambush, which occurred near Arcadia.

Dinneen, Joseph F. *Underworld U.S.A.* New York: Farrar, Straus & Cudahy, 1955.

Dobyns, Fletcher. *The Underworld of American Politics.* New York: Fletcher Dobyns, 1932. Good contemporary description of political corruption during Prohibition.

Dorigo, Joe. *Mafia: A Chilling Illustrated History of the Underworld.* Secaucus, N.J.: Chartwell, 1992. Slim, poorly researched coffee-table book of interest chiefly for its photos.

Dorman, Michael. *Pay-off.* New York: David McKay, 1972. Nationwide organized crime and political corruption. Chapter entitled "The Big Fix" describes the career of Jack Halfen, a minor southwestern crook who abandoned banditry in the thirties to become a major gambling boss and bagman for organized crime in Texas. Includes interesting anecdotes from his alleged associations with Pretty Boy Floyd, Clyde Barrow and Bonnie Parker, before he moved up in the world.

Dornfeld, A.A. *Behind the Front Page: The Story of the City News Bureau of Chicago.* Chicago: Academy, 1983. Reprinted in softcover as *Hello, Sweetheart, Get Me Rewrite!* Chicago: Academy, 1988. Illuminates some interesting features of the "Chicago school of journalism" and includes an-

ecdotal material on press coverage of such historic crimes as the St. Valentine's Day Massacre.

Draper, W.R., and Mabel Draper. *The Blood-Soaked Career of Bonnie Parker: How Bandit Clyde Barrow and His Cigar-Smoking Moll Fought It Out with the Law.* Girard, Kans.: Haldemann-Julius, 1945. A wild 24-pager in larger format from the longtime publisher of the quirky "Little Blue Books" on every subject imaginable.

Draper, W.R. *On the Trail of "Pretty Boy" Floyd.* Girard, Kans.: Haldemann-Julius, 1946. Similar booklet consisting mainly of articles Draper wrote for a Kansas City newspaper in 1934. Fairly accurate account of Floyd's career, with minor errors. Includes chronology of Floyd's crimes and interviews with his wife and mother.

Dubro, James, and Robin F. Rowland. *King of the Mob: Rocco Perri and the Women Who Ran His Rackets.* Ontario: Penguin, 1988. Perri was Canada's equivalent of Chicago's Al Capone, without the national publicity. (See also Charbonneau, *The Canadian Connection.*)

Edge, L.L. *Run the Cat Roads.* New York: Dembner Books, 1981. Mainly about the Memorial Day 1933 escape of 11 convicts, led by Harvey Bailey and Wilbur Underhill, from the Kansas state prison in Lansing; the crimes and recapture of the Bailey-Underhill gang; and related events, such as the Urschel kidnapping and the Kansas City Massacre. Contains new information from some surviving participants, including Harvey Bailey, but appears to draw heavily on Bailey's fairly obscure biography by J. Evetts Haley (*Robbing Banks Was My Business*). Discussion of other outlaws, especially Dillinger and Barker-Karpis gangs, includes many errors.

Edmonds, Andy. *Hot Toddy.* New York: William Morrow, 1989. Contends that Lucky Luciano ordered the murder of film star Thelma Todd. Includes highly inaccurate biographical sketches of Luciano and Al Capone.

———. *Bugsy's Baby: The Secret Life of Mob Queen Virginia Hill.* New York: Birch Lane,

1993. Repeats the errors found in *Hot Toddy* but otherwise a fairly good biography of Hill. Ed Reid's *The Mistress and the Mafia* and Dean Jennings's *We Only Kill Each Other* are better, but Edmonds's book includes an interesting account of Hill's death.

Einstein, Izzy. *Prohibition Agent No. 1.* New York: Frederick A. Stokes, 1932. Izzy Einstein and Moe Smith, with their comical disguises and subterfuges, were the Abbott and Costello of Prohibition agents, who claim they arrested over 4,000 New York bootleggers and confiscated some 5 million bottles of booze before their notoriety got them sidelined. A lot more fun than Eliot Ness. Another writer who gives no source says Izzy's memoirs sold only 575 copies.

Eisenberg, Dennis, Uri Dan, and Eli Landau. *Meyer Lansky: Mogul of the Mob.* New York: Paddington, 1979. Meyer Lansky's version of his life story, as told by the Israeli journalists who interviewed him. Supplemented from FBI and Narcotics Bureau files. Corroborates some aspects of the controversial Luciano memoirs (Gosch and Hammer), or may have borrowed from them.

Elliott, Neal. *My Years with Capone: Jack Woodford-Al Capone, 1924–1932.* Seattle, Wash.: Woodford Memorial Editions, 1985. Ostensibly a long interview with thirties' writer/pornographer Woodford on his association with Big Al, but virtually a hoax. The interview subject actually was a Chicago lawyer named Louis Kutner, who probably never knew Big Al, according to one Capone biographer.

Ellis, John. *The Social History of the Machine Gun.* New York: Random House, 1975. Discusses machine-gun use by real and movie gangsters.

Elman, Robert. *Fired in Anger: The Personal Handguns of American Heroes and Villains.* Garden City, N.Y.: Doubleday, 1968. Includes chapters on Dillinger and Baby Face Nelson, Pretty Boy Floyd. Inaccurate regarding their criminal careers, but interesting details on the gangsters' guns.

Enright, Richard T. *Al Capone on the Spot.* Minneapolis, Minn.: Graphic Arts Corporation, 1931. Reprint, with introduction and supplementary materials by Ray R. Cowdery, as *Capone's Chicago,* Lakeville, Minn.: Northstar Maschek, 1987.

Eshelman, Byron E., with Frank Riley. *Death Row Chaplain.* Englewood Cliffs, N.J.: Prentice-Hall, 1962. Rev. Eshelman's career as prison chaplain included tours of duty at the Federal Detention Headquarters in New York, Alcatraz and San Quentin. Includes recollections of Louis "Lepke" Buchalter, George "Machine Gun" Kelly and Alvin Karpis.

Ettinger, Clayton J. *The Problem of Crime.* New York: Long & Smith, 1932. Weighty examination (538 pages) of nearly every aspect of criminality, criminology, penology and the criminal justice system.

Faber, Elmer, ed. *Behind the Law: True Stories Compiled from the Archives of the Pennsylvania State Police.* Greenburg, Pa.: Chas H. Henry Printing, 1933. Reflects Justice Department support of greater police professionalism.

Farr, Finis. *Chicago: A Personal History of America's Most American City.* New Rochelle, N.Y.: Arlington House, 1973.

Feder, Sid, and Joachim Joesten. *The Luciano Story.* New York: David McKay, 1954. One of the first biographies of Charles "Lucky" Luciano, written while the mob boss was living in exile in Naples; one of the better Mafia books of the 1950s, considering how little was known about organized crime at that time. Award Books, in New York, published a revised and updated paperback version in 1972. Sid Feder co-authored the best-selling *Murder, Inc.*

Federal Bureau of Investigation. *FBI: Facts and History.* rev. ed., with foreword by director William S. Sessions, Washington, D.C.: U.S. Government Printing Office, n.d. Updated version of earlier materials. Interesting summary of the public enemy era with some good photos.

Ferber, Nat. *I Found Out!: A Confidential Chronicle of the Twenties.* New York: Dial, 1939. Entertaining but regrettably rare memoirs of what today would be called an investigative reporter who worked for several New York papers and hassled name-brand hoodlums and politicians with journalistic exposés.

Ferrier, J. Kenneth. *Crooks and Crime.* Philadelphia: Lippincott, 1927.

Fiaschetti, Michael, with Prosper Buranelli. *You Gotta Be Rough: The Adventures of Detective Fiaschetti of the Italian Squad.* New York: Doubleday, 1930. Personal experiences of a old-school New York cop with a flamboyant streak, who became a minor celebrity during Prohibition. British edition same year titled *The Man They Couldn't Escape.*

Fido, Martin. *The Chronicle of Crime: The Infamous Felons of Modern History and Their Hideous Crimes.* New York: Carroll & Graf, 1993. Attempts to cover the world's headline crimes and criminals from 1800–1993 in 320 pages (including index). Many photos but hardly comprehensive, with many errors (places the famous Boston Brink's robbery of 1950 in Chicago). Fido, who also authored *Murder Guide to London* and *The Crimes, Detection and Death of Jack the Ripper,* may be on firmer ground with British crime.

First National Bank of Cisco, Texas. *The Santa Claus Bank Robbery.* Cisco: Longhorn Press, 1958. Commemorative booklet put out by the bank involved in a famously bloody holdup during Christmas week of 1927 by bandits whose leader wore a Santa outfit. Well-researched with good collection of contemporary photos.

Fosdick, Raymond B. *American Police Systems.* New York: Century, 1920. Early effort to promote greater professionalism in police work.

Fowler, Gene. *The Great Mouthpiece: A Life Story of William J. Fallon.* New York: Blue Ribbon, 1931. New York criminal lawyer (emphasis on criminal), rivaled only by Dixie Davis in his talent for outwitting the system in behalf of leading mobsters.

Fox, Stephen. *Blood and Power: Organized Crime in Twentieth Century America.* New York: William Morrow, 1989. Generally excellent, well-documented history of organized crime, covering all aspects and then some, such as the theory that the mob assassinated JFK.

Fraley, Oscar. *4 against the Mob.* New York: Popular Library, 1961. Lightweight effort to revive former "Untouchable" Eliot Ness, stranded by Repeal and recruited by Cleveland as public safety director, where his "Unknowns" battled Moe Dalitz with some success but little publicity.

Fraley, Oscar, with Paul Robsky. *The Last of the Untouchables.* New York: Universal, 1962. Paperback reprint, New York: Award, 1976. "Personal" sequel to *The Untouchables* about another aging Untouchable.

Frank, Martin M. *Diary of a D.A.* New York: Holt, Rinehart & Winston, 1960. Memoirs of a former Bronx County District Attorney, with a good chapter on Vincent "Mad Dog" Coll.

Frasca, Dom. *King of Crime: The Story of Vito Genovese, Mafia Czar.* New York: Crown, 1959. Little documentation, and the usual effort to overstate the subject's importance.

Fredericks, Dean. *John Dillinger.* New York: Pyramid, 1963. Thrill-packed nonsense, similar to the Monarch gangster series.

Fried, Albert. *The Rise and Fall of the Jewish Gangster in America.* New York: Holt, Rinehart & Winston, 1980. Well-researched history of Jewish organized crime from the days of city street gangs, and the gradual displacement of top Jewish gang leaders by Italian-American crime families. Chapters on Irving "Waxey Gordon" Wexler, Arthur "Dutch Schultz" Flegenheimer, Louis "Lepke" Buchalter, and Meyer Lansky.

Friedman, Lawrence M. *Crime and Punishment in American History.* New York: Basic Books, 1993. Major effort to touch every base results in more scope than depth.

Gage, Nicholas. *The Mafia Is Not an Equal Opportunity Employer.* New York: McGraw-Hill, 1971. One of a rash of Mafia books that followed the success of Mario Puzo's *The Godfather* and the much publicized Gallo-Colombo gang war in New York. Includes a biographical chapter on Meyer Lansky and much other historical information.

———, ed. *Mafia, U.S.A.* Chicago: Playboy Press, 1972. Collection of Mafia stories from various books and periodicals.

Gallagaer, Basil. *The Life of John Dillinger, Public Enemy #1.* Indianapolis, Ind.: Stephens, 1934. One of the early (and of course rare) Dillinger books, in magazine format.

Galligan, George, and Jack Wilkinson. *In Bloody Williamson.* 1927. Reprint. Williamson County (Ill.) Historical Society, 1985. Galligan was sheriff of Williamson County and Wilkinson was his deputy in the 1920s. Deals mainly with battles against S. Glenn Young and the Ku Klux Klan, but mentions the Birger and Shelton gangs, who were briefly allied with Galligan against the Klan. Includes brief section on the later feud between Charlie Birger and the Shelton brothers.

Gardner, Arthur R.L. *The Art of Crime.* London: Philip Allan, 1931. British writer's somewhat genteel view of criminal enterprise in general.

Gaute, J.H.H., and Robin Odell. *The Murderers' Who's Who.* Montreal: Optimum, London: Harrap, 1979. An encyclopedia of notorious murderers and murder cases from around the world. Mostly serial killers and such, but with entries on the Barkers, Bonnie and Clyde and Louis "Lepke" Buchalter. Gangster material comes mainly from Nash's *Bloodletters and Badmen,* complete with inaccuracies. Subject titles indexed to bibliographies, plus an address list of booksellers specializing in true crime. Revised and updated version, *The New Murderers' Who's Who,* published by Dorset, in New York, 1989.

Gelman, B., and R. Lackmann. *The Bonnie and Clyde Scrapbook.* New York: Nostalgia Press, c.1970. Softcover picture book, with slight text largely culled from *Fugitives,* by Parker and Cowan. Good collection of Barrow gang photos, news clippings, etc., with brief references to other gangs; section of stills from the movie *Bonnie and Clyde.* More collectible than informative.

Gentry, Curt. *J. Edgar Hoover: The Man and the Secrets.* New York: W.W. Norton, 1991. Massive and seemingly well-documented critical biography of J. Edgar Hoover's political blackmailing. Much gangster material, including previously unpublished photos of Ma and Fred Barker dead in the house at Oklawaha, Florida, following their shootout with the FBI.

Giancana, Sam, and Chuck Giancana. *Doublecross: The Explosive, Inside Story of the Mobster Who Controlled America.* New York: Warner, 1992. Generally dismissed as unsubstantiated yarns.

Gibson, Walter B., ed. *The Fine Art of Robbery.* New York: Grosset & Dunlap, 1966. Includes reprinted accounts of the Rondout train robbery and Brooklyn armored car holdup.

Girardin, G. Russell, with William J. Helmer. *Dillinger: The Untold Story.* Bloomington: Indiana University, 1994. Based on an unpublished manuscript written in the thirties by Girardin in collaboration with Dillinger's lawyer, Louis Piquett, and his assistant, Arthur O'Leary; updated in footnotes by Girardin just before his death in 1990 to reveal previously concealed information on the Dillinger gang and the wooden-pistol escape; edited and expanded by Helmer with new introductory material and copious endnotes elaborating on Girardin's manuscript, which revises some major elements of the Dillinger story.

Gish, Anthony. *American Bandits.* Girard, Kans.: Haldemann-Julius, 1938. Long booklet containing brief biographical sketches of outlaws from the colonial period through the 1930s. Gish cites J. Edgar Hoover as his source of information on modern bandits, who include Al Spencer, Frank Nash, Verne Miller, the Barkers, Alvin Karpis,

Machine Gun Kelly, Jake and Ralph Fleagle, Wilbur Underhill, Pretty Boy Floyd, Eddie Bentz, Harvey Bailey, Fred "Killer" Burke, John Dillinger, Baby Face Nelson, Bonnie and Clyde and others, including some who were still fugitives at the time of publication. Many errors.

Godwin, John. *Alcatraz: 1868–1963.* Garden City, N.Y.: Doubleday, 1963. For Alcatraz collectors; many mistakes, including some serious ones (such as claiming Karpis and John Paul Chase died in the prison).

————. *Murder U.S.A.* New York: Ballantine, 1978. More information but nothing original.

Goldin, Hyman E., Frank O'Leary, and Morris Lipsius. *Dictionary of American Underworld Lingo.* New York: Twayne, 1950. O'Leary and Lipsius were Sing Sing inmates, and Lipsius gained notoriety as the stool pigeon who set up Waxey Gordon's narcotics bust.

Gollomb, Joseph. *Crimes of the Year.* New York: Liveright, 1931 [U.S. Edition]. Popular crime writer includes interesting chapter on Chicago mobsters ("Chicago Contributes") and on the Birger-Shelton gang war in southern Illinois ("County of Crime").

Gong, Eng Ying (Eddie), with Bruce Grant. *Tong War!* New York: Nicholas L. Brown, 1930. Former leader of the Hip Sing tong gives his version of the early years of Chinese organized crime in America. Gong's stories are accepted by many popular crime writers, but debunked in some more carefully researched accounts, such as Dillon's *The Hatchet Men.*

Goodman, Avery. *Why Gun Girls?* Minneapolis, Minn.: Fairway, c. 1932. A "noted sociologist" ostensibly studies gang molls and female felons in a heavily illustrated, interestingly written but unfortunately rare magazine-format booklet similar to *The Morgue* and *X Marks the Spot,* with plenty of gangland stiffs included as photographic filler.

Goodman, Jonathan, ed. *Masterpieces of Murder,* New York: Carroll & Graf, 1992.

Gosch, Martin A., and Richard Hammer. *The Last Testament of Lucky Luciano.* Boston: Little, Brown, 1975. Supposedly based on Gosch's taped interviews with the mobster in Italy before his death, but doesn't square with many known facts, due either to Luciano's failing memory or Gosch's creativity.

Gosnell, Harold F. *Machine Politics, Chicago Model.* Chicago: University of Chicago, 1937; reprint, 1968.

Gottfried, Alex. *Boss Cermak of Chicago: A Study of Political Leadership.* Seattle: University of Washington, 1962. Conventionally crooked but crafty mayor killed during a New Orleans political tour by an assassin's bullet fired at Franklin Roosevelt; rumors persist that Cermak was the intended target of a demented anarchist paid by Chicago mobsters.

Goulart, Ron. *Lineup, Tough Guys.* Los Angeles: Sherbourne, 1966. Has biographical chapters on Capone, Dutch Schultz, Owney Madden, Legs Diamond, other Chicago and New York mobsters; also John Dillinger, Alvin Karpis and Machine Gun Kelly. All from published sources but reasonably accurate, even if it perpetuates Godwin's error of Karpis dying in prison. Brief commentary on gangster movies, comics, etc.

Graham, Hugh Davis, and Ted Robert Gurr, eds. *Violence in America: Historical and Comparative Perspectives, A Report to the National Commission on the Causes and Prevention of Violence.* Cover title of commercial paperback edition of government report, *The History of Violence in America.* New York: New York Times/Bantam Books, 1969.

Granlund, Nils T., with Sid Feder. *Blondes, Brunettes and Bullets.* New York: David McKay, 1957. A New York radio celebrity in the twenties, Granlund knew such mobsters as Dutch Schultz, Jack "Legs" Diamond, Larry Fay, Arnold Rothstein, Nicky Arnstein, Lucky Luciano and Anthony Carfano, alias Little Augie Pisano.

Grant, Bruce, *Fight for a City: The Story of the Union League Club of Chicago and Its Times, 1880–1955.* Chicago: Rand McNally, 1955. Includes less-than-thrilling discussion of a civic group's battle against political corruption.

Green, Jonathon. *The Directory of Infamy.* London: Mills & Boon, 1980. Reprint. *The Greatest Criminals of All Time.* New York: Stein & Day, 1982. Biographical sketches of over 600 criminals from around the world, including most of the major twenties and thirties mobsters and outlaws. Many errors. Green's unreliable sources include Demaris's *The Dillinger Story* and Nash's *Bloodletters and Badmen.*

Greene, A.C. *The Santa Claus Bank Robbery.* New York: Knopf, 1972. Violent 1927 bank robbery at Cisco, Texas, committed by a gang whose leader wore a Santa Claus suit. Invented dialogue detracts from the author's otherwise good research.

Gregg, Leah. *Scarface Al: The Story of "Scarface Al" Capone, Professional Gangster; His Ruthless Machine-Gun Massacres Shocked the Nation.* Girard, Kans.: Haldeman-Julius "Little Blue Book," c.1930. Surprisingly accurate, for what it is—a collectible mini-paperback.

Gruber, Frank. *The Dillinger Book.* Mt. Morris, Ill.: R.C. Remington, 1934. Early Dillinger book, allegedly suppressed in its first printing by FBI. Cover type in red ink and extremely rare. Second printing (1934) slightly smaller in page size with new cover and new title, *The Life and Exploits of John Dillinger.* Also rare.

Guerin, Eddie. *Crime: The Autobiography of a Crook.* London: Murray, 1928.

———. *I Was a Bandit.* New York: Doubleday, 1929. Memoirs of a Chicago gunman remembered (barely) for his escape from Devil's Island; his brother Paddy made more news.

Guns & Ammo magazine staff, eds. *Guns & Ammo Guide to Guns of the Gunfighters.* Los Angeles: Petersen, 1975. Reprint, *Guns and the Gunfighters,* New York: Bonanza Books, 1982. Collection originally published as articles in *Guns & Ammo* magazine on various outlaws, lawmen, soldiers and "gunfighters" of 19th and 20th centuries, and the hardware they used. Includes Dillinger, Bonnie and Clyde, and Melvin Purvis. Discusses Thompson submachine gun and other weapons of notable gangsters.

Hagerty, James E. *Twentieth Century Crime: Eighteenth Century Methods of Control.* Boston: Stratford, 1934. The failure of traditional, localized law-enforcement strategies to combat lawlessness in the age of the automobile, machine guns and interstate crime.

Haley, J. Evetts. *Robbing Banks Was My Business.* Canyon, Tex.: Palo Duro Press, 1973. Superior biography of Harvey Bailey, an uncrowned king of midwestern bank robbers whose bad luck was to be a friend of Machine Gun Kelly when the FBI closed in on the Urschel kidnappers. Extensively interviewed by the author. Rare in both hardcover and paperback.

Hall, Angus, ed. *The Gangsters.* New York: Paradise, 1975. Magazine-format book consisting of articles originally published in the 20-volume set *Crimes and Punishment.* Includes Capone, Dillinger, Bonnie and Clyde, the 1934 Rubel Ice Company robbery (Brooklyn's first armored car job), along with the Brink's robbery and various English and European gangsters.

Halper, Albert, ed. *This Is Chicago: An Anthology.* New York: Henry Holt, 1952. Reprint, *The Chicago Crime Book.* New York: World, 1967. Collection of stories on Chicago crime from various publications. First section of book deals with Chicago gangsters of the twenties and thirties, with much on Capone and Prohibition gang wars, St. Valentine's Day Massacre, Roger Touhy case and Lingle murder, plus Toland's account of the killing of Dillinger.

Hamilton, Floyd. *Public Enemy No. 1.* Dallas, Tex.: Acclaimed Books/International Prison Ministry, 1978. Former bank robber and Alcatraz inmate Floyd Hamilton had been friends with Clyde Barrow and Bonnie Parker. His brother Raymond, a member of the Barrow gang, was electrocuted in Texas in 1935.

Hamilton, Floyd, with Chaplain Ray. *Floyd Hamilton, Public Enemy No. 1, and Other True Stories.* Dallas, Tex.: Acclaimed Books/International Prison Ministry, [1983?]. Magazine-format book contains transcript of radio interview with Floyd Hamilton, "last of the Bonnie and Clyde gang," by Chaplain Ray, prison evangelist, followed by moralistic stories of other convicts.

Hamilton, Sue L. Produced a "Public Enemy" series of 32-page children's books on the Depression outlaws (*Bonnie & Clyde, John Dillinger, Ma Barker, Machine Gun Kelly, Pretty Boy Floyd*). Minneapolis, Minn.: Abdo & Daughters/Rock Bottom Press, 1989. Strictly a novelty. The book on Floyd mistakenly uses pictures of Floyd's crime partner, Adam Richetti.

Hammer, Richard. *Playboy's Illustrated History of Organized Crime.* Chicago: Playboy Press, 1975. Large, well-researched, profusely illustrated coffee-table collection of articles by Hammer and edited by Helmer for publication in *Playboy,* August 1973 through July 1974.

Hanna, David. *Bugsy Siegel: The Man Who Invented Murder, Inc.* New York: Belmont Tower, 1974.

———. *Frank Costello: The Gangster of a Thousand Faces.* New York: Belmont Tower, 1974.

———. *Vito Genovese.* New York: Belmont Tower, 1974.

———. *The Killers of Murder, Inc.* New York: Nordon Publications, 1974.

———. *The Lucky Luciano Inheritance.* New York: Belmont Tower, 1975.

———. *Virginia Hill: Queen of the Underworld.* New York: Belmont Tower, 1975. Hanna's paperbacks are mainly of interest to collectors of gangster kitsch.

Harland, Robert O. *The Vice Bondage of a Great City: Or, The Wickedest City in the World; The Reign of Vice, Graft and Political Corruption.* Chicago: Young People's Civic League, 1912. Exposé of Chicago's "monstrous Vice Trust" in the same vein as the earlier William Stead classic, *If Christ Came to Chicago!*

Harris, Louis. *The Story of Crime.* Boston: Stratford, 1929.

Heimel, Paul W. *Eliot Ness: The Real Story.* Condersport, Pa.: Knox Books, 1997. Little known but far superior version of *The Untouchables,* tracking Ness's sometimes rocky career in both Chicago and Cleveland.

Helmer, William J. *The Gun That Made the Twenties Roar.* New York: Macmillan, 1969; reprint, Highland Park, N.J.: Gun Room Press. Technical, social, criminal, military and business history of the Thompson submachine gun and General Thompson's Auto-Ordnance Corporation, based partly on correspondence and interviews with the men who once worked for the company and actually designed the gun. Much gangster stuff. [See Hill, Tracie L.]

Hershkowitz, Leo. *Tweed's New York: Another Look.* New York: Anchor/Doubleday, 1977.

Herzog, Asa S., and A.J. Erickson, *Camera, Take the Stand!* New York: Prentice-Hall, 1940. Contemporary study of the expanding role of forensic photography in criminal cases of the times, including Dillinger and Jake Fleagle.

Hibbert, Christopher. *The Roots of Evil: A Social History of Crime and Punishment.* London: Weidenfeld and Nicholson; Boston: Little, Brown, 1963. Interesting, copious, encyclopedic treatment of crime and criminals, U.S. and foreign, with material on Capone, Dutch Schultz and others.

Hill, E. Bishop. *Complete History of the Southern Illinois Gang War.* Harrisburg, Ill.: Hill Publishing, 1927. Early and scarce book on the Birger and Shelton gangs.

Hill, Tracie L, et al. *Thompson: The American Legend: The First Submachine Gun.* Cobourg, Ontario: Collector Grade Publications, 1996. Well-illustrated coffeetable epic on all aspects of the tommy gun.

Hinton, Ted, with Larry Grove. *Ambush: The Real Story of Bonnie and Clyde.* Bryan, Tex.: Shoal Creek, 1979. Hinton (with five other officers, including Frank Hamer) ambushed and killed Bonnie and Clyde, but his personal friendship with Barrow and Parker families gives this book a uniquely personal viewpoint. Unfortunately, the account of the Stringtown, Oklahoma, shooting is taken almost word for word from the Drapers' lurid *The Blood-Soaked Career of Bonnie Parker* and has Bonnie present (she wasn't); the chapter on Harvey Bailey and Machine Gun Kelly is badly flawed; and even Hinton's version of the ambush has been questioned.

Hirsch, Phil, ed. *The Racketeers.* New York: Pyramid, 1970. Collection of gangster stories by various writers dealing mostly with modern organized crime, but also covers Al Capone, Hymie Weiss, Pretty Boy Floyd and the wipeout of the Shelton gang, by Frank "Buster" Wortman. Later reprinted in magazine format by Peacock, Franklin Park, Ill., as *The Underworld.*

Hoffman, Dennis E. *Business Vs. Organized Crime: Chicago's Private War on Al Capone.* Chicago: Chicago Crime Commission, 1989. Booklet describing the downfall of Capone through the combined efforts of the Chicago Crime Commission, the "Secret Six" and the IRS. Gently discredits Eliot Ness, who harassed Capone operations but had little to do with sending him to prison.

———. *Scarface Al and the Crime Crusaders: Chicago's Private War Against Al Capone.* Carbondale, Ill.: Southern Illinois University, 1993. Hoffman's earlier work greatly expanded into hardcover. Well researched and documented.

Hollatz, Tom. *Gangster Holidays: The Lore and Legends of the Bad Guys.* St. Cloud, Minn.: North Star Press, 1989. Well-illustrated magazine-format softcover book covers gangsters who vacationed in Wisconsin: Al and Ralph Capone, Polack Joe Saltis, Roger Touhy, other Chicago mobsters, with sidetrips on John Dillinger, Baby Face Nelson and the Little Bohemia gun battle.

Homer, Frederic D. *Guns and Garlic: Myths and Realities of Organized Crime.* West Lafayette, Ind.: Purdue University, 1974. A persuasive reappraisal of the history and nature of organized crime that debunks the popular concepts with a carefully reasoned approach comparable to Abadinski's.

Hooton, Ernest Albert. *Crime and the Man.* Cambridge: Harvard University, 1939. Last-gasp, almost comical effort to salvage notions of pioneer criminologist Cesare Lombroso that criminals are anthropologically inferior and physically distinguishable from law-abiding citizens. Combines immigrant stereotypes and predictable criminal traits to make this about the most politically incorrect book ever issued by an academic press, reputable or otherwise. Incredible illustrations.

Hoover, J. Edgar. *Persons in Hiding.* Boston: Little, Brown, 1938. Hoover's revenge for Melvin's Purvis's *American Agent,* ghostwritten in purple prose by his "kept" crime writer Courtney Ryley Cooper. This account of the public-enemy era minimizes cases involving Purvis, who is never mentioned by name, or credits them to others, especially Sam Cowley, who died in battle with Baby Face Nelson. Includes informative chapters on such underappreciated outlaws as Eddie Bentz and Eddie Doll, with plenty of attention to the director's other "human vermin" in form of molls, associates and harborers. Fosters many Bureau legends since disputed by more objective researchers.

Horan, James D. *The Desperate Years: A Pictorial History of the Thirties.* New York: Crown, 1962. Interesting if superficial; includes the Depression gangsters.

———. *The Mob's Man.* New York: Crown, 1959.

Hostetter, Gordon L., and Thomas Quinn Beesley. *It's a Racket!* Chicago: Les Quin, 1929. Declares Chicago the birthplace of modern rackets and racketeering, defined as the systematic takeover or exploitation of legitimate businesses and unions by professional criminals; good contemporary account of the problem in Chicago, with a list of 157 bombings between October 1927 and January 1929 plus glossary of hoodlum lingo.

Hounschell, Jim. *Lawmen and Outlaws: 116 Years in Joplin's History.* Joplin, Mo.: Walsworth/Fraternal Order of Police Lodge #27, 1989. Good history of the local police, written by a Joplin cop. Includes many photos and some original material in chapters on Bonnie and Clyde, the Kansas City Massacre, the Barker-Karpis gang, and Machine Gun Kelly.

Hyde, Montgomery H. *United in Crime.* New York: Roy, 1955 (U.S. edition). By British lawyer and Member of Parliament who generalizes about crime, detection and punishment in England and other countries with interesting commentary and case histories, providing international perspective on the subject but only brief discussion of conditions in the U.S.

Hynd, Alan. *We Are the Public Enemies.* New York: Gold Medal, 1949. Error-filled paperback, with chapters on Dillinger, Pretty Boy Floyd and the Barrow and Barker-Karpis gangs (Lloyd Barker is called "Floyd"). Of interest mainly to collectors.

———. *Murder, Mayhem and Mystery.* New York: A.S. Barnes, 1958. Includes chapter on the Urschel kidnapping.

———. *Brutes, Beasts and Human Fiends.* New York: Paperback Library, 1964. Includes a chapter on 1930s New York gangster Louis "Pretty" Amberg.

———. *Great True Detective Mysteries.* New York: Grosset & Dunlap, 1969. Includes fair chapter on the Urschel kidnapping.

Ianni, Francis A.J., and Elizabeth Reuss-Ianni, eds. *The Crime Society: Organized Crime and Corruption in America.* New York: New American Library, 1976.

Ianni, Francis A.J., with Elizabeth Reuss-Ianni. *A Family Business: Kinship and Social Control in Organized Crime.* New York: Russell Sage Foundation, 1972. Rejects the notion of a monolithic Mafia or Cosa Nostra in studying a pseudonymous "Lupollo Family," which they consider part of a nationwide but informal network of relatively autonomous crime organizations.

Illinois Association for Criminal Justice. *The Illinois Crime Survey.* Chicago, 1929. Reprint, Montclair, N.J.: Patterson Smith, 1968. Part III consists of John Landesco's justly famous "Organized Crime in Chicago." [See Landesco, John.]

Illman, Harry R. *Unholy Toledo: The True Story of Detroit's Purple-Licavoli Gang's Take-Over of an Ohio City.* San Francisco: Polemic Press, 1985. Obscure, heavy on detail, with inside blurb that reads: "An informal history of a typical American city which was not muckraked by Lincoln Steffins [sic] because of his friendship with two of the city's outstanding mayors." Few photos, no bibliography, but heavily footnoted, mostly to newspaper reports.

Inbau, Fred E., and John E. Reid. *Lie Detection and Criminal Interrogation.* Baltimore: Williams & Wilkins, 1942. Includes origins and development of the polygraph.

Inciardi, James A. *Reflections on Crime: An Introduction to Criminology and Criminal Justice.* New York: Holt, Rinehart and Winston, 1978.

———. *Careers in Crime.* Chicago: Rand McNally College Publishing, 1975.

Inciardi, James A., and Ann E. Pottieger, eds. *Violent Crime: Historical and Contemporary Issues.* Beverly Hills, Calif.: Sage Publications, 1978. Little history, except for a stiffly academic chapter disputing traditional views of frontier crime and law enforcement.

Irey, Elmer L., with William J. Slocum. *The Tax Dodgers: The Inside Story of the T-Men's War With America's Political and Underworld Hoodlums.* Garden City, N.Y.: Garden City, 1948.

One of the government officials—not Eliot Ness—who actually nailed Capone tells the story. With chapters on Johnny Torrio, Murray "The Camel" Humphreys, Waxey Gordon, Moe Annenberg, Tom Pendergast, Enoch "Nucky" Johnson and other casualties of the federal tax laws.

Jacobs, Timothy. *The Gangsters.* New York: Mallard, 1990. Thin but attractive coffee-table book with good pictures. Classic dust jacket "family photo" of Birger gang armed to the teeth, and (on the back) police photo of a sour-faced Vito Genovese. Chapters on Capone, Luciano, Dillinger, Floyd, Nelson, Barkers, Kelly, and Bonnie and Clyde include many errors, such as confusing the Shelton gang of southern Illinois with Ralph Sheldon gang of Chicago.

Jenkins, John H., and H. Gordon Frost. *I'm Frank Hamer: The Life of a Texas Peace Officer.* Austin, Tex.: Pemberton, 1968. Biography of the ex-Texas Ranger who led the ambush of Bonnie and Clyde and whose version differs from accounts of others on several major points.

Jennings, Dean. *We Only Kill Each Other: The Life and Bad Times of Bugsy Siegel.* Englewood Cliffs, N.J.: Prentice-Hall, 1968. The best biography of Siegel.

Johnson, Curt, with R. Craig Sautter. *Wicked City: Chicago, From Kenna to Capone.* Highland Park, Ill.: December Press, 1994. Well-researched softcover as readable as Asbury's *Gem of the Prairie,* with new information from many sources and much original material on Diamond Joe Esposito.

Johnson, David R. *American Law Enforcement: A History.* Arlington Heights, Ill.: Forum Press, 1981. Good descriptions of the evolution of U.S. police work.

Johnson, Lester Douglas. *The Devil's Front Porch.* Lawrence: University of Kansas, 1970. History of the state prison at Lansing written by a former inmate who resided there in the '20s and '30s. Johnson knew Alvin Karpis as a boy in Topeka, and served time with him, Fred Barker, Harvey Bailey and Wilbur Underhill, witnessing the escape of the Bailey-Underhill gang in 1933. Long on information, short on confirmation, but includes Jake Fleagle and Ray Majors in brief histories of other Kansas gangs.

Johnson, Malcom. *Crime on the Labor Front.* New York: Putnam, 1950.

Johnston, James A. *Alcatraz Island Prison.* New York: Scribner's, 1949. By the first warden of Alcatraz, when it was opened for the benefit of Capone, Kelly, Karpis and other celebrity criminals as a symbol of the first federal "war on crime."

Jones, Ken. *The FBI in Action.* New York: New American Library, 1957. Includes J. Edgar Hoover's flattering version of his "personal" capture of Alvin Karpis, who insists he was unarmed and already surrounded by G-men when Hoover was summoned from an alley to perform the arrest.

Jones, Peter D'A., and Melvin G. Holli. *Ethnic Chicago.* Grand Rapids, Mich.: William B. Eerdmans, 1981. Indirectly assesses criminality associated with immigrant communities.

Kaplan, George. *Big-Time Criminals Speak!* New York: Maximum Exposure Advertising, 1980. Hardly a useful source. Commentary by Kaplan is awkward and highly inaccurate, with movie stills used to illustrate the chapters on featured subjects: Capone, Dillinger, Bonnie and Clyde, Ma Barker, Mad Dog Coll, the Mafia and Prohibition. Includes Mary McElroy's account of her kidnapping, and snatches of Cornelius Vanderbilt's *Liberty* interview with Capone. "Bonus Section," titled "Sick Chicks," seems mainly devoted to plugging the psychotic film character, played by actress Mimsy Farmer, to whom the book is dedicated. Interesting mainly as a curiosity.

Karpis, Alvin, with Bill Trent. *The Alvin Karpis Story.* New York: Coward-McCann & Geoghegan, 1971. Karpis's version of his life of crime, from taped interviews. Karpis's memory is sometimes faulty, or his coauthor careless at filling in gaps. Has Dillinger killed on Chicago's North Clark Street (site of the St. Valentine's Day Massacre); and Karpis taking his girl to see *Manhattan Melodrama* (the movie attended by Dillinger). Karpis understandably puts himself elsewhere when murders were committed. Still, many interesting anecdotes on the Barker-Karpis gang and other criminals, much of which is corroborated in FBI files. Karpis scoffs at Hoover's account of his arrest, and states that Ma Barker served only as old-lady camouflage for him and her sons. Published in Canada by McClelland and Stewart, Toronto, as *Public Enemy Number One: The Alvin Karpis Story.*

Karpis, Alvin, with Robert Livesey. *On the Rock.* Don Mills, Ontario: Musson/General, 1980. Karpis's account of his long stretch on Alcatraz, published after his death. Interesting and surprisingly candid.

Katcher, Leo. *The Big Bankroll: The Life and Times of Arnold Rothstein.* New York: Harper, 1959. The most fully researched biography of Rothstein, written with the benefit of history and hindsight.

Katz, Leonard, *Uncle Frank: The Biography of Frank Costello.* New York: Drake, 1973. Mostly Costello anecdotes and trivia that make the mob boss sound like a jolly good fellow.

Kavanagh, Marcus. *The Criminal and His Allies.* Indianapolis, Ind.: Bobbs-Merrill, 1928. Criminals and corruption denounced by a hanging judge of the times.

———. *You Be the Judge.* Chicago: Reilly & Lee, 1929.

Keating, H.R.F. *Great Crimes.* London: Weidenfeld and Nicholson, 1982. Gangster chapter includes sketchy biographies of Capone, Dillinger and Bonnie and Clyde. Accepts Nash's bizarre theory that Dillinger wasn't killed at the Biograph. Coffee-table book reprinted by Harmony in New York, and General Publishing in Canada.

Keeler, Eloise. *Lie Detector Man: The Career and Cases of Leonarde Keeler.* N.p.: Telshare Publishing, 1984. Development of polygraph testing and Keeler's work with Col. Calvin Goddard at the country's first scientific "crime lab" privately established in Chicago, with mentions of the Jake Lingle murder and the gift of one of the two St. Valentine's Day Massacre machine guns to the president of Zenith Radio Corporation. [Both guns eventually were returned to Michigan's Berien County Sheriff's Department, which had discovered them in a raid on the house of Fred "Killer" Burke.]

Kefauver, Estes. *Crime in America.* Garden City, N.Y.: Doubleday, 1951. Organized crime in America, described by the U.S. senator who made "Mafia" a household word and Frank Costello's hands a TV star when Costello wouldn't allow his face to be broadcast.

———. *Senator Kefauver's Crime Committee Report.* New York: Arco, 1951. Published in hardcover as *Kefauver Hearings on Organized Crime.*

Kelly, George "Machine Gun" [John H. Webb], with Jim Dobkins and Ben Jordan. *Machine Gun Man: The True Story of My Incredible Survival into the 1970s.* Phoenix: UCS, 1988. Author claiming to be George "Machine Gun" Kelly was actually a fraud named John H. Webb. Mostly fiction, in company with Audett and Bilbo.

Keylan, Arleen, and Arto DeMirjian, Jr., eds. *Crime as Reported by the New York Times.* New York: Arno, 1976. Full page reprints, story continuations and follow-up articles on famous crime stories published in the *New York Times* from 1870s to 1970s. Includes murders of Arnold Rothstein, Legs Diamond and Dutch Schultz, St. Valentine's Day Massacre, killings of Bonnie and Clyde, John Dillinger, Pretty Boy Floyd, Ma and Fred Barker, and capture of Alvin Karpis.

King, Hoyt. *Citizen Cole of Chicago.* Chicago: Horder's, 1931. Battles against crime, vice and corruption by a Chicago reformer, who was marginally effective but largely forgotten.

King, Jeffery S. *The Life and Death of Pretty Boy Floyd.* Kent, Ohio: Kent State University Press,

1998. Like Robert Unger in his recent *Union Station Massacre,* King finds plenty of circumstantial evidence that Floyd was involved in what was more commonly called the Kansas City Massacre. His extensive research covers Floyd's criminal career in general, has him joining up with the Dillinger gang in their last robbery at South Bend and gives additional credence to the story of Floyd's summary execution by G-men as later revealed by the last surviving local lawman, Chester Smith, whose account has been privately supported by others over the years. Together, the King and Unger books are probably the last word on Floyd, going much deeper than the 1992 Wallis book (*Pretty Boy: The Life and Times of Charles Arthur Floyd*), which also is well researched but focuses more on Floyd's early years, questions his involvement in the massacre, and largely accepts the FBI's tidy version of his death on October 22, 1933.

The unidentified "fat man" described in King's report on the South Bend robbery turns out to have been Jack Perkins, a boyhood pal of Baby Face Nelson. Perkins was tried but acquitted, although he later spent time in Leavenworth for harboring Nelson following the death of Dillinger on July 22, 1934, and remained "in the rackets" as a slot machine collector for the Chicago "outfit" for another 30 years.

Kirchner, L.R. (Larry). *Triple Cross Fire: J. Edgar Hoover & the Kansas City Union Station Massacre.* Kansas City, Mo.: Janlar, 1993. Extensively researched, well-illustrated, but highly speculative softcover effort to pin the Kansas City Massacre not only on Vernon "Vern" Miller, but also on William Weissman, Harvey Bailey, Wilbur Underhill, Bob Brady and Ed Davis, while exonerating Pretty Boy Floyd as a patsy put on the spot by J. Edgar Hoover for reasons of publicity and pursuit.

Kirkpatrick, E.E. *Crimes' Paradise: The Authentic Inside Story of the Urschel Kidnapping.* San Antonio, Tex.: Naylor, 1934. Detailed account of the case by a family friend who delivered the ransom money to the Oklahoma oilman's kidnappers, including Machine Gun Kelly.

———. *Voices from Alcatraz.* San Antonio, Tex.: Naylor, 1947. Essentially a reprint of *Crimes' Paradise,* with additional chapter on Kelly and his "gang" in prison.

Klockars, Carl B. *The Idea of Police.* Newbury Park, Cal.: Sage Publications, 1985. Describes the gradual and sometimes grudging acceptance of legally constituted law enforcers in place of defensive measures and do-it-yourself crime control.

———. *The Professional Fence.* New York: Free Press, 1974.

———, ed. *Thinking about Police.* New York: McGraw-Hill, 1983. An investigation of popular attitudes drawn from both factual and fictional sources.

Kobler, John. *Capone: The Life and World of Al Capone.* New York: Putnam, 1971. The first (and in some ways still the best) effort at a comprehensive Capone biography after Fred Pasley's work in 1930, while Capone was still Chicago's crime king.

———. *Ardent Spirits: The Rise and Fall of Prohibition.* New York: Putnam, 1973. Good social history of Prohibition.

Kohn, George C. *Dictionary of Culprits and Criminals.* Metuchen, N.J.: Scarecrow, 1986. Less than impressive in writing style and production quality but otherwise fairly comprehensive and well-researched biographies of gangsters, outlaws, murderers and other criminals up to modern times.

Kooistra, Paul. *Criminals as Heroes: Structure, Power and Identity.* Bowling Green, Ohio: Bowling Green State University Press, 1989. Scholarly study of American "social bandits who enjoyed considerable public support," including Dillinger, Pretty Boy Floyd and Bonnie and Clyde.

Kuhlman, Augustus Frederick. *A Guide to Material on Crime and Criminal Justice.* New York: Wilson, 1929. Reprint, Montclair, N.J.: Patterson Smith, 1969. A boat anchor of a bibliography more for the professional than the public; includes a vast number of articles and books on crime and crime-control published through 1927, some reflecting contemporary views of antisocial behavior that now seem naive and uncomprehending if not totally bizarre.

Lacey, Robert. *Little Man: Meyer Lansky and the Gangster Life.* Boston: Little, Brown, 1991. Contains a wealth of new and well-documented information on Lansky, including his probable true birthdate. Disputes claims of Meyer's wealth in his later years and argues that the only gangsters who died rich were those who eventually went straight.

Lait, Jack. *Put on the Spot.* New York: Grossett & Dunlap, 1930. Potboiler by one of the more sensational crime reporters of the period.

Lait, Jack, and Lee Mortimer. *New York Confidential.* New York: Ziff-Davis, 1948.

———. *Chicago Confidential.* New York: Crown, 1950.

———. *Washington Confidential.* New York: Crown, 1951.

———. *U.S.A. Confidential.* New York: Crown, 1952. Lait's "Confidential" series was popular, lurid and sometimes ridiculous.

Landesco, John. *Organized Crime in Chicago* (Part III of the Illinois Crime Survey). Illinois Association for Criminal Justice: Chicago, 1929. Published also as a hardcover book by University of Chicago, 1968, and Patterson Smith, 1968. Scholarly and fascinating study of Chicago's Prohibition-era crime. Essential.

Laurence, John. *A History of Capital Punishment: With Special Reference to Capital Punishment in Great Britain.* London: Samson, Lowe, Marston, n.d. With index and an extensive bibliography through 1931.

Lavine, Emmanuel H. *The Third Degree: A Detailed and Appalling Expose of Police Brutality.* New York: Vanguard, 1930.

———. *Gimme.* New York: Vanguard, 1931. Includes an account of the shooting of Legs Diamond at the Hotel Monticello in New York in 1930.

Lee, James Melvin. *History of American Journalism.* Garden City, N.Y.: Garden City, 1917; rev. ed., 1923. Good history of U.S. newspaper publishing, with discussion of efforts to deal with issues of crime reporting and Prohibition.

Letts, Mary. *Al Capone.* London: Wayland, 1974. Skimpy 95-page biography, but heavily illustrated.

Levell, Mark, and Helmer, Bill. *The Quotable Al Capone.* Crestwood, Ill.: Chicago Typewriter Co., 1990. Wisecracks and philosophizing by Big Al on nearly everything, plus commentary and names of gang members.

Levine, Gary. *Anatomy of a Gangster: Jack "Legs" Diamond.* Cranbury, N.J.: A.S. Barnes, 1979. A good biography of Diamond, well researched, with rare photos.

Lewis, Lloyd, and Henry Justin Smith. *Chicago: The History of Its Reputation.* New York: Harcourt, Brace, 1929. Contemporary view of Chicago's image problem, at its worst.

Liggett, William, Sr. *My Seventy-Five Years Along the Mexican Border.* New York: Exposition, 1964. Memoirs include a chapter on "Arizona Lawmen," which discusses Dillinger.

Lindberg, Richard. *Chicago Ragtime: Another Look at Chicago, 1880–1920.* South Bend, Ind.: Icarus, 1985; Rev. ed., *Chicago by Gaslight,* 1996. Well-researched and entertaining, with astute observations on Chicago's culture, crime, cops and politics, which combined to gain the city worldwide notoriety during the Roaring Twenties.

———. *To Serve and Collect: Chicago Politics and Police Corruption from the Lager Beer Riot to the Summerdale Scandal: 1885–1960.* New York: Praeger Press, 1991. Exceptionally detailed, brilliantly written, regrettably scarce, but reprint planned by Southern Illinois University Press.

Linn, James Webber. *James Keeley, Newspaperman.* New York: Bobbs-Merrill, 1937. The interesting and often dark side of Chicago, and of newspaper journalism generally, told through the biography of an equally interesting reporter and editor who deserves more recognition.

Liston, Robert. *Great Detectives.* New York: Platt & Munk, 1966. Children's book includes chapters on Elmer Irey and J. Edgar Hoover that focus on Al Capone and the Barker-Karpis gang.

Longstreet, Stephen. *Chicago: 1860–1919.* New York: David McKay, 1973. Setting the stage for Chicago's Roaring Twenties.

———. *Win or Lose: A Social History of Gambling in America.* New York: Bobbs-Merrill, 1977.

Look editors. *The Story of the FBI: The Official Picture History of the Federal Bureau of Investigation.* New York: E.P. Dutton, 1947. Introduction by J. Edgar Hoover.

Loth, David. *Public Plunder: A History of Graft in America.* New York: Carrick and Evans, 1938.

Louderback, Lew. *The Bad Ones: Gangsters of the '30s and Their Molls.* Greenwich, Conn.: Fawcett, 1968. Fairly thorough history of Depression outlaws. Many good photos and original material, but also many errors and some fiction. Has interesting chapters on all the famous "public enemies," but accepts "Blackie" Audett's dubious eyewitness account of the Kansas City Massacre.

Lovegrove, Richard, and Tom Orwig. *The FBI.* New York: Exeter, 1989. Coffee-table history of the Bureau with good, balanced text and many photos. Much on gangster era, including gangster movies.

Lowenthal, Max. *The Federal Bureau of Investigation.* New York: William Sloane, 1950. The first book daring to attack the FBI, extensively and sometimes excessively, with Lowenthal not above taking quotes out of context. Negative bias opposes positive spin of countless other books glorifying the Bureau. Some gangster material, dealing mainly with John Dillinger, Alvin Karpis and Louis "Lepke" Buchalter.

Luisi, Gerard, and Charles Samuels. *How to Catch 5000 Thieves.* New York: Macmillan, 1962. The well-told adventures of a New York insurance investigator who liked police work in and out of state and managed to involve himself in general crime fighting against some notable hoods of the twenties and thirties.

Lundberg, Ferdinand. *Imperial Hearst: A Social Biography.* New York: Random House, 1936. A contemporary look at yellow journalism of the period.

Lustgarten, Edgar. *The Illustrated Story of Crime.* Chicago: Follett, 1976. British author's capsule treatment of pop crime with pictures—international and superficial. American gangsters include Al Capone, Frank Costello, Joe Adonis.

Lyle, Judge John H. *The Dry and Lawless Years.* Englewood Cliffs, N.J.: Prentice-Hall, 1960. Fun, frontline battle stories, usually embellished, by a municipal judge who made Capone-size headlines by harassing Chicago gangsters with vagrancy laws, high bonds, and other dirty tricks, legal or otherwise, but still lost his race for mayor.

Lynch, Dennis. *Criminals and Politicians.* New York: Macmillan, 1932. Similar to Fletcher Dobyns's *The Underworld of American Politics* in blaming police ineffectuality on political corruption.

Maas, Peter. *The Valachi Papers.* New York: Putnam, 1968. Street-level view of organized crime, from the twenties to the sixties, as described (usually from hearsay) by New York mob defector Joe Valachi, whose offhanded expression "cosa nostra" was deemed a synonym for "Mafia," adding to the confusion of crime fighters and book writers alike.

Maccabee, Paul. *John Dillinger Slept Here: A Crook's Tour of Crime and Corruption in St. Paul, 1920–1936.* St. Paul: Minnesota Historical Press, 1995. Excellent in all respects, including photos, addresses, maps and chronology.

MacKaye, Milton. *Dramatic Crimes of 1927: A Study in Mystery and Detection.* Garden City, N.Y.: Crime Club, 1928. Good chapters with new twists on the Birger-Shelton gang war in southern Illinois, and on the first armored-car bombing in Pennsylvania.

Mackenzie, Frederick. *Twentieth Century Crimes.* Boston: Little, Brown, 1927.

Maddox, Web. *The Black Sheep.* Quannah, Tex.: Nortex, 1975. Notorious Texas outlaws, mostly "Old West," but includes chapter on Bonnie and Clyde.

Mandelbaum, Seymour J. *Boss Tweed's New York.* New York: John Wiley, 1965. Full-grown corruption in 19th-century New York, while Chicago was still a juvenile delinquent.

Mark, Norman. *Mayors, Madams and Madmen.* Chicago: Chicago Review Press, 1979. Entertaining, anecdotal and touches all the bases.

Marston, William Moulton. *The Lie Detector Test.* New York: Richard R. Smith, 1938. Origins of a new crime-control tool, before the doubts set in.

Martin, John Bartlow. *Butcher's Dozen: And Other Murders.* New York: Harper, 1945. Revised 1950 edition includes a substantial and interesting reprint of a magazine article on the Shelton and Birger gangs.

Mayo, Katherine. *Standard-bearers: True Stories of Law and Order.* New York: Houghton, 1930.

McCarthy, Pat. *America's Bad Men: Stories of Famous Outlaws.* Middletown, Conn.: Xerox Corp., 1974. Children's book, with illustrations and photos, includes chapters on Dillinger, Machine Gun Kelly and Bonnie and Clyde.

McConaughy, John. *From Cain to Capone: Or, Racketeering down through the Ages.* New York: Brentano's, 1931. Views virtually all professional crime as "organized," from biblical times to Prohibition.

McCormick, Harry, with Mary Carey. *Bank Robbers Wrote My Diary.* Austin, Tex.: Eakin, 1985. In 1935, Houston newspaperman McCormick arranged to be "kidnapped" by bank robber Raymond Hamilton, former Barrow gang member who not only escaped from the Texas state prison's death house but wanted his story to reach the public. Hamilton was later recaptured and executed.

McLean, Don. *Pictorial History of the Mafia.* New York: Galahad, 1974. Scarce in hardcover, common as a thick (nearly 500 pages), profusely illustrated Pyramid paperback crime chronology that suffers from mediocre writing and research.

McPhaul, Jack. *Johnny Torrio: First of the Gang Lords.* New Rochelle, N.Y.: Arlington House, 1970. The closest thing to a detailed biography of Torrio, whom McPhaul regards as the inventor of organized crime, but relies too heavily on the writer's imagination. For example, McPhaul describes Torrio as grief-stricken over the suicide of Longy Zwillman, who lived two years longer than Torrio. Helped out by good photos and chronology.

———. *Deadlines and Monkeyshines.* Englewood Cliffs, N.J.: Prentice-Hall, 1962. Newspapering and crime reporting in Chicago in the Roaring Twenties, reprinted in paperback in 1969, as *Chicago: City of Sin.*

Meskil, Paul. *Don Carlo: Boss of Bosses.* New York: Popular Library, 1973.

Messick, Hank. *Gangs and Gangsters: The Illustrated History of Gangs from Jesse James to Murph the Surf.* New York: Ballantine, 1974. In softcover, with undistinguished chapters on "Dion" O'Banion, John Dillinger and Alvin Karpis. Also, the "Mafia" in pre-1900 New Orleans and the San Francisco tong wars.

———. *The Only Game in Town: An Illustrated History of Gambling.* New York: Crowell, 1976.

———. *Secret File.* New York: Putnam, 1969.

———. *The Silent Syndicate.* New York: Macmillan, 1967.

———. *Lansky.* New York: Putnam, 1971; rev. ed., 1973.

———. *John Edgar Hoover.* New York: David McKay, 1972.

————. *The Beauties and the Beasts: The Mob in Show Business.* New York: David McKay, 1973.

Messick, Hank, and Burt Goldblatt. *Kidnapping, the Illustrated History.* New York: Dial, 1974. Describes gangsters' efforts to help in the Lindbergh case.

————. *The Mobs and the Mafia: The Illustrated History of Organized Crimes.* New York: Crowell, 1972. Reprint, New York: Ballantine, 1973. Pictorial history of organized crime, similar to *Playboy*'s but much skimpier. Some rare photos, including one of Capone with Legs Diamond.

Messick, Hank, with Joseph L. Nellis. *The Private Lives of Public Enemies.* New York: Peter H. Wyden, 1973. Messick's books generally contain much good information but little documentation, many errors and too much invented dialogue.

Meyer, George H., with Chaplain Ray and Max Call. *Al Capone's Devil Driver.* Dallas, Tex.: Acclaimed Books/International Prison Ministry, 1979. "Alleged wheelman [for the] St. Valentine's Day Massacre" reads the blurb on the cover. "Memoirs" less than plausible, or even possible, but details suggest some personal knowledge of Chicago mobsters.

Mezzrow, Mezz, and Bernard Wolfe. *Really the Blues.* New York: Random House, 1946. Anecdotal material on mob control of nightclubs and performers during Prohibition.

Miers, Earl Schenck. *The Story of the F.B.I.* New York: Grosset & Dunlap, 1965. FBI-approved children's book. Basically an expanded version of the FBI's own booklet, *The Story of the Federal Bureau of Investigation,* with a little more on the gangsters.

Mills, George. *Rogues and Heroes from Iowa's Amazing Past.* Ames: Iowa State University, 1972. Collection of stories about famous and infamous people associated with various Iowa cities. Much gangster material, including Dillinger's Mason City bank robbery, the million-dollar train robbery at Council Bluffs in 1920, and the Cedar Rapids embezzlement trial of Jake "The Barber" Factor, plus biographical sketches of Al Capone prosecutor George E. Q. Johnson, and Tom Runyon, a Depression bank robber and murderer who became an Associated Press correspondent and author while still in prison.

Mills, James. *Underground Empire: Where Crime and Governments Embrace.* New York: Doubleday, 1986. Hefty, contemporary, with some historical background.

Millspaugh, Arthur C. *Crime Control by the Federal Government.* Institute for Government Research, Studies in Administration, No. 34. Washington, D.C.: Brookings Institution, 1937. Examines the issue of the country's new federalized law enforcement, still resisted by many states'-rights advocates opposed to a "national police," and feared by many state and municipal officials as a threat to their corruption.

————. *Local Democracy and Crime Control.* Washington, D.C.: Brookings Institution, 1936.

Milner, E.R. *The Lives and Times of Bonnie & Clyde.* Carbondale: Southern Illinois University, 1996. Primary sources, good documentation, and objective, competent writing give Milner a distinct edge over the many other accounts of the legendary boy-and-girl bandit team.

Mockridge, Norton, and Robert H. Prall. *The Big Fix.* New York: Henry Holt, 1954. Mayor O'Dwyer and Prosecutor Dewey still battling post-Depression graft and corruption in New York City.

Monaco, Richard, and Lionel Bascom. *Rubouts: Mob Murders in America.* New York: Avon, 1991. Chapters on celebrated gang murders, 1929–1990. A few good photos devalued by the usual factual errors and invented dialogue. Despite its apt starting point, barely mentions the St. Valentine's Day Massacre.

Mooney, Martin. *Crime, Incorporated.* New York: Whittlesey House, 1935. One of the earliest books on syndicated crime. Claims a vague national network called "Crime Incorporated" controls "sixteen sinister rackets" across the nation and hints that the FBI will soon be taking action. Though the book opens with an approving letter from J. Edgar Hoover, the director in fact had little authority and no inclination to fight organized crime. Also authored *Crime Unincorporated*.

Moore, Gerald E. *Outlaw's End*. No publisher or date, but probably pre–World War II. Strange "biography" of old outlaw Henry Wells, as told by Wells in warning a fictional character (his "long lost son") against a life of crime. Little is known of the real Henry Wells, other than that he served a term in the Oklahoma state prison for bank robbery around 1915. He later claimed, though, to have robbed banks with Henry Starr, Al Spencer and Frank Nash; to have given Pretty Boy Floyd his start as an outlaw; and to have thwarted Floyd's plan to kidnap millionaire oilman Frank Phillips in 1933. Probably more fiction than fact.

Moore, William T. *Dateline Chicago: A Veteran Newsman Recalls Its Heyday*. New York: Taplinger, 1973. Interesting recollections of the newshounds from glory days of Chicago journalism, when crime stories were front page news.

Morgan, John. *No Gangster More Bold: Murray Humphreys, the Welsh Political Genius Who Corrupted America*. London: Hodder and Stoughton, 1985; (U.S. ed.) *The Prince of Crime*. New York: Stein & Day. Slim but useful biography of Capone gangster Murray "The Camel" Humphreys.

Morley, Jackson, et al., eds. *Crimes and Punishment: A Pictorial Encyclopedia of Aberrant Behavior*. Phoebus Publishing/Symphonette Press, 1973–74. A 20-volume set covering nearly all aspects of crime, illustrated by famous cases, with an A-to-Z listing for the leftovers. Gangster coverage ranges widely from Capone, Dillinger, Ma Barker, Luciano, the Mafia and Bonnie and Clyde to the Birger and Shelton gangs, Louis "Lepke" Buchalter, and Brooklyn's Rubel Ice Co. armored car robbery.

Morris, Newbold. *Let the Chips Fall: My Battles Against Corruption*. New York: Appleton, Century, Crofts, 1955. New York City political reformer's review of political corruption in the U.S., especially New York City, with anecdotal material on mobsters.

Mullady, Detective Frank, and William H. Kofoed. *Meet the Mob*. New York: Belmont Books, 1961. Coauthored by a cop, with a preface by former Kings County, N.Y., district attorney Leo Healy, this slim paperback still ranks as collectible kitsch. Includes chapters on Capone and Jake Guzik, the Genna brothers, Dutch Schultz, Mad Dog Coll, Lepke, Anastasia and the Murder, Inc. boys. Somewhat redeemed by photos, including Bugs Moran in his casket.

Munn, Michael. *The Hollywood Murder Case Book*. New York: St. Martin's, 1987. Includes Thelma Todd and Bugsy Siegel.

Murray, George. *The Legacy of Al Capone*. New York: Putnam's, 1975. Decently researched biography in which a Chicago newspaperman attempts to evaluate Capone's lasting influence on local life and politics.

Nash, Jay Robert, and Ron Offen. *Dillinger: Dead or Alive?* Chicago: Regnery, 1970. Convoluted theory, based on common discrepancies in documents and records, that the FBI shot the wrong man and that Dillinger could still be alive and well in California. Only contribution, besides generating interest in Dillinger, is its wealth of research minutiae agonizingly construed (or conveniently ignored) to support various, sometimes conflicting conspiracy theories.

Nash, Jay Robert. *Bloodletters and Badmen: A Narrative Encyclopedia of American Criminals from the Pilgrims to the Present*. New York: M. Evans, 1973. Vast in scope, with poorly researched biographical entries on countless criminals and gangsters.

———. *Citizen Hoover: A Critical Study of the Life and Times of J. Edgar Hoover and His FBI*. Chicago: Nelson-Hall, 1972. A hatchet job on

Hoover, who ridiculed Nash's conspiracy theories.

————. *Murder America: Homicide in the United States from the Revolution to the Present.* New York: Simon & Schuster, 1980.

————. *Almanac of World Crime.* New York: Anchor, 1981.

————. *Look for the Woman: A Narrative Encyclopedia of Female Prisoners, Kidnappers, Thieves, Extortionists, Terrorists, Swindlers and Spies from Elizabethan Times to the Present.* New York: M. Evans, 1981. Minimal gangster coverage includes inaccurate entries on Ma Barker, Bonnie Parker and Kathryn Kelly.

————. *The True Crime Quiz Book.* New York: M. Evans, 1981.

————. *The Dillinger Dossier.* Highland Park, Ill.: December Press, 1983. Recycled version of *Dillinger: Dead or Alive?* Nash presents more "evidence" of Dillinger's survival in the form of interviews with yarn master "Blackie" Audett, who earlier authored a book of tall tales titled *Rap Sheet.* Original printing of *Dossier* advertised cassette tapes of Nash's interviews with Audett, but if produced they're exceedingly rare.

————. *Jay Robert Nash's Crime Chronology.* New York: Facts On File, 1984.

————. *The Encyclopedia of World Crime.* (6 vols.) Wilmette, Ill.: Crime Books, 1990. This magnum opus, covering all crime in all times, carefully retains every error found in the prolific Nash's previous books.

————. *World Encyclopedia of Organized Crime.* New York: Paragon House, 1993. Extracted from Nash's *Encyclopedia of World Crime.*

Nelli, Humbert S. *The Business of Crime: Italians and Syndicated Crime in the United States.* New York: Oxford University, 1976. Debunks the "Night of the Sicilian Vespers," a staple Mafia myth about the mass purge of old "Mustache Petes" in 1931 supposedly ordered by Luciano to Americanize the country's Italian crime families.

Ness, Eliot, with Oscar Fraley. *The Untouchables.* New York: Julian Messner, 1957. The best-selling book that made Ness an American legend, inspiring the popular TV series starring Robert Stack and the more recent Brian de Palma movie. Probably as much fiction as fact, especially in crediting Ness and his Prohibition agents with toppling Al Capone.

Newman, Peter C. *King of the Castle: The Making of a Dynasty—Seagram's and the Bronfman Empire.* New York: Atheneum, 1979. Many sidelights on the often questionable, sometimes illegal activities of some major booze kings, most of whom eluded U.S. Prohibition authorities and gangland heat to prosper as businessmen and politicians.

Newton, Michael, and July Ann Newton. *The FBI's Most Wanted: An Encyclopedia.* New York: Garland, 1989. Simply a list of all fugitives who have made the FBI's "Ten Most Wanted" list since its inception in 1950. Of little historical interest except for its inclusion of some 1930s bank robbers, e.g., Thomas James Holden and Glen LeRoy Wright (former Barker-Karpis gang associates), John Allen Kendrick (of the old Tri-State Gang), and, of course, Willie "The Actor" Sutton.

Newton, Willis, and Joe Newton, with Claude Stanush and David Middleton. *The Newton Boys: Portrait of an Outlaw Gang.* Austin, Tex.: State House, 1994. Entertaining and long-overdue autobiography of the Newton brothers, Willis, Joe, Jess and Doc, who looted dozens of banks and trains from Texas to Canada before going to jail for the "greatest of all mail robberies" (over $2 million) near Rondout, Illinois, in 1924.

Nicholas, Margaret. *The World's Wickedest Women.* London: Octopus, 1984. Reprint, New York: Berkley, 1988. Includes chapter on Bonnie Parker, with previously published inaccuracies. Paperback reprint has famous cigar-smoking Bonnie photo on cover.

Nickel, Steven. *Torso: The Story of Eliot Ness and the Search for a Psychopathic Killer.* Winston-

Salem, N.C.: John F. Blair, 1989; New York: Avon, 1989.

Nown, Graham. *The English Godfather.* London: Ward Lock, 1987. Biography of English-born New York gangster Owney "The Killer" Madden.

O'Brien, Joseph F., and Adris Kurins. *Boss of Bosses: The Fall of the Godfather: The FBI and Paul Castellano.* New York: Simon & Schuster, 1991. Little original history.

O'Conner, Len. *Clout: Mayor Daley and His City.* Chicago: Henry Regnery, 1975.

O'Connor, Dick. *Headline Hunter: Behind America's News Sheets.* London: John Long, 1938. Includes pieces and illustrations on Capone, Dillinger, Karpis, Barkers, others.

———. *G-Men At Work: The Story of America's Fight Against Crime and Corruption.* London: John Long, 1939.

O'Connor, John James. *Broadway Racketeers.* New York: Liveright, 1928. An effort to steal Chicago's thunder.

O'Sullivan, F. Dalton [Don Sullington]. *Crime Detection.* Chicago: O'Sullivan, 1928. Curious, large (667 pages), wide-ranging work on virtually all aspects of crime, criminality and the new scientific crime detection, including contributions by prominent police officials and a section on outstanding crooks of the day.

———. *Enemies of Industry: Gang Invasion of Business and Industry.* Chicago: O'Sullivan, 1932.

Ottenberg, Miriam. *The Federal Investigators.* Englewood Cliffs, N.J.: Prentice-Hall, 1962. Brief histories of the FBI, IRS, Secret Service, postal inspectors, Immigration Service, other federal investigative agencies. Briefly mentions Dillinger and other Depression outlaws but has more on such organized crime figures as Al Capone, Paul "The Waiter" Ricca and Joe Adonis.

Overstreet, Harry, and Bonaro Overstreet. *The FBI in Our Open Society.* New York: W. W. Norton, 1969. A pro-FBI book, written mainly in reaction to anti-FBI books of Max Lowenthal and Fred J. Cook. Full of nitpicking, but makes some valid criticisms of Lowenthal in particular. Little gangster material, but includes a listing of the 1934 anti-crime laws which enabled the FBI to wage war on the Depression outlaws.

Owens, Collinson. *King Crime: An English Study of America's Greatest Problem.* New York: H. Holt, 1932. Britishers seem more fascinated than dismayed by American gangsters, who make their own hoods look tame by comparison.

Park, Robert E., Ernest W. Burgess and Roderick D. McKenzie. *The City.* Chicago: University of Chicago, 1925. One of the early efforts of the "Chicago School of Sociology" to cover many social, cultural and even journalistic aspects of Chicago when Mayor Dever's reform efforts upset the relatively peaceful corruption enjoyed under Big Bill Thompson and helped trigger a five-year period of underworld warfare.

Parker, Emma, and Nell Barrow Cowan, with Jan Fortune. *Fugitives: The Story of Clyde Barrow and Bonnie Parker.* Dallas, Tex.: Ranger Press, 1934; reprint, *The True Story of Bonnie and Clyde,* New York: Signet, 1968. Bonnie's and Clyde's side of the story, as told by their relatives, often in words added by their coauthor. Thoroughly biased, of course, but the closest thing to "inside" information. Reprint in paperback has a poetic, rambling, interesting but irrelevant foreword by Nelson Algren.

Parker, Robert Nash, with Linda-Anne Rebhun. *Alcohol & Homicide: A Deadly Combination of Two American Traditions.* Albany, N.Y.: State University of New York, 1995. Modern scholarly study with little historical background, but a rare effort to quantify a long-recognized connection between booze and bullets.

Pasley, Fred D. *Al Capone: The Biography of a Self-Made Man.* New York: Ives Washburn, 1930. The first serious Capone biography, written while Al was still in power and probably with his tacit approval, judging from its considerable inside information on the Chicago underworld. Pasley was about the only crime writer of the era to write dispassionately and with intelligence, and it's this book and Kobler's *Capone* that most writers use as their main sources on Capone.

————. *Muscling In.* New York: Ives Washburn, 1931. Pasley on racketeering.

Patterson, Richard. *The Train Robbery Era: An Encyclopedic History.* Boulder, Colo.: Pruett, 1991. Well-researched work on train robbers and robberies in the U.S. in the 19th and 20th centuries. Mainly of interest to western buffs, but covers the later gangster era, including Al Spencer, the Newton brothers and the 1924 Rondout, Ill., train robbery, possibly the largest in American history. Karpis buffs may be disappointed by the omission of the Garrettsville, Ohio, job.

Peterson, Theodore. *Magazines in the Twentieth Century.* Urbana: University of Illinois, 1964. Includes a brief but useful mention of the factual-crime magazines that prospered during the public-enemy era, some attracting a large readership with dramatic but well-researched articles on both crime and crime control.

Peterson, Virgil W. *Barbarians in Our Midst.* Boston: Little, Brown, 1952. Well-informed history of organized crime in Chicago by a former FBI agent who later headed the Chicago Crime Commission. Peterson had been Melvin Purvis's assistant in the '30s, so there's much good material on the Depression outlaws, especially the Dillinger and Barker-Karpis gangs.

————. *The Mob: 200 Years of Organized Crime in New York.* Ottawa, Ill.: Green Hill, 1983. Barbarians in New York.

Phillips, John Neal. *Running with Bonnie and Clyde: The Ten Fast Years of Ralph Fults.* Norman, Okla.: University of Oklahoma Press, 1996. Some interesting new information from outlaw. Fults and kin of Bonnie and Clyde, so probably biased in their favor.

Pitkin, Thomas Monroe, and Francesco Cordasco. *The Black Hand: A Chapter in Ethnic Crime.* Totowa, N.J.: Rowman & Littlefield, 1977. Scholarly account of Black Hand extortion practices in the Italian community, mostly pre-Prohibition.

Plate, Thomas, and editors of *New York* magazine. *Mafia at War.* New York: New York Magazine Press, 1972. One-shot publication detailing Mafia gang wars, mostly in New York, from 1915–72. Capitalizes on the Gallo-Colombo feud that was making news at the time. Combines original material with excerpts from several books, including Maas's *The Valachi Papers,* Tyler's *Organized Crime in America,* and Kobler's *Capone;* includes paintings of famous gang murders (from Big Jim Colosimo's to Joe Gallo's), plus a genealogical chart of New York's crime families.

Porrello, Rick. *The Rise and Fall of the Cleveland Mafia: Corn Sugar and Blood.* New York: Barricade Books, 1995. Good account of Cleveland's "sugar wars" for control of sugar during Prohibition.

Powell, Hickman. *Ninety Times Guilty.* New York: Harcourt Brace, 1939; reprint, New York: Citadel, *Lucky Luciano: His Amazing Trial and Wild Witnesses,* 1975.

Powers, Richard Gid. *G-Men: Hoover's FBI in American Popular Culture.* Carbondale: Southern Illinois University, 1983. Superb study of how the director and his publicists took full advantage of Roosevelt's New Deal policies to cultivate the media, create an image and foster legends that helped deglamorize crime, professionalize police work, and turn most Americans into Junior G-men.

————. *Secrecy and Power: The Life of J. Edgar Hoover.* New York: Free Press, 1987. Detailed and relatively balanced biography of the FBI Director.

Prall, Robert H., and Norton Mockridge. *This Is Costello.* New York: Gold Medal, 1951. Limp biography of New York mob boss Frank Costello, a featured attraction of the Kefauver Senate crime hearings.

Prassel, Frank Richard. *The Great American Outlaw: A Legacy of Fact and Fiction.* Norman: University of Oklahoma, 1993. Scholarly study of outlaws and gangsters in history, literature, films and folklore, including Capone and Dillinger, with a nod to Robin Hood.

———. *The Western Peace Officer: A Legacy of Law and Order.* Norman: University of Oklahoma, 1972. Gradual modernization of Frontier-style law enforcement.

Proveda, Tony G. *Lawlessness and Reform: The FBI in Transition.* Pacific Grove, Calif.: Brooks/Cole, 1990. Useful as an original and balanced examination of the changes in the FBI: its early glory days as proponent of scientific crime fighting and law-enforcement professionalism, its decline into the private army of an aging and increasingly eccentric director and post-Hoover efforts at self-reform.

Purvis, Melvin. *American Agent.* Garden City, N.Y.: Doubleday, Doran, 1936. Purvis's version of his FBI career, including Dillinger, Pretty Boy Floyd, Barker-Karpis gang, Roger Touhy case and others. Lauds the Bureau but never mentions Hoover by name, referring only to "the Director." Occasionally lapses into patronizing racism of the day, as in references to darkies.

———. *The Violent Years.* New York: Hillman, 1960. Paperback "uncensored abridgement" of *American Agent,* published soon after Purvis's death.

Quimby, Myron J. *The Devil's Emissaries.* Cranbury, N.J.: A. S. Barnes, 1969. Interesting book on Depression outlaws, with chapters on Machine Gun Kelly, Pretty Boy Floyd, Ma Barker and sons, Alvin Karpis, Bonnie and Clyde, Dillinger and Baby Face Nelson. Based largely on contemporary newspaper reporting that provides more detail than most other accounts, but also includes many errors, such as giving John Herbert Dillinger's middle name as Herman.

Ray, "Chaplain." *God's Prison Gang.* Dallas, Tex.: Acclaimed Books/International Prison Ministry, n.d. Uplifting if unconvincing stories by Christianized convicts, including former Bonnie and Clyde gang member Floyd Hamilton and a supposed onetime wheelman for Capone (see also Hamilton's *Public Enemy No. 1* and George Meyer's *Al Capone's Devil Driver*). Video version may still be available, featuring prison sermons by the boys.

Reader's Digest editors. *Great True Stories of Crime, Mystery & Detection.* Pleasantville, N.Y.: Reader's Digest Assn., 1965. Collection of short articles includes one on Arthur "Dock" Barker by J. Edgar Hoover, Treasury Agent Frank Wilson's account of the Capone tax case, plus other stories on Brooklyn's famous armored-car robbery in 1934 (Rubel Ice Co. payroll), mail robber Gerald Chapman and Paul "The Waiter" Ricca.

Reckless, Walter. *Vice in Chicago.* Chicago: University of Chicago, 1933. Reprint, Montclair, N.J.: Patterson Smith, 1969. Much statistical data on organized and unorganized prostitution. Predictably dry, but provides a good sense of mob involvement in the city's nightlife during Prohibition, spiced up with pseudononymous interviews.

Reed, Lear B. *Human Wolves: Seventeen Years of War on Crime.* Kansas City, Mo.: Brown-White-Lowell, 1941. Written by a former Hoover-worshiper FBI agent who became Kansas City police chief from 1939 to 1941.

Reeve, Arthur. *The Golden Age of Crime.* New York: Mohawk, 1931. A popular mystery writer of the day examines the newly recognized business crime called racketeering.

Reid, Ed. *Mafia.* New York: Random House, 1952. Early 1950s Mafia book reveals how little was known about nationally organized crime at the time of the Kefauver hearings.

———. *The Grim Reapers: The Anatomy of Organized Crime in America, City by City.* Chicago:

Regnery, 1969. Emphasis on the modern-day mob, but better historical material.

———. *The Mistress and the Mafia: The Virginia Hill Story.* New York: Bantam, 1972. On flimsy evidence, decides Virginia was not just a "dumb broad" mistress to the likes of Joe Adonis and Bugsy Siegel, but a cunning bagwoman and dope trafficker who manipulated the hoods around her.

———. *Mickey Cohen, Mobster.* New York: Pinnacle, 1973. Slim paperback biography of Bugsy Siegel's right-hand man and successor, only slightly more useful than Cohen's own uninformative book. Opens on the 1916 war between rival Brooklyn gangs considered to represent the Mafia and the Camorra, which hardly concerned Cohen.

Reid, Ed, and Ovid Demaris. *The Green Felt Jungle.* New York: Trident, 1963. Best-seller on Las Vegas organized crime typically overstates the role of a post-Depression, Godfather-style Mafia that had come into vogue, but includes the murder of Bugsy Siegel and much on the involvement of hoodlums from Chicago and other cities with interesting criminal histories.

Reith, Charles. *A New Study of Police History.* Edinburgh/London: Oliver and Boyd, 1956. Gradual development of professionalism in law enforcement, from a British point of view.

Reynolds, Quentin. *Courtroom.* New York: Farrar, Straus & Giroux, 1950. Biography of legendary lawyer and judge Samuel Liebowitz. Has material on Al Capone, who turned down Liebowitz's legal advice, and Vincent "Mad Dog" Coll, acquitted of murder through Liebowitz's skilled defense.

———. *Smooth and Deadly.* New York: Farrar, Straus & Giroux, 1953; reprint *I, Willie Sutton,* New York: Paperback Library, 1970.

———. *The FBI.* New York: Random House, 1954. Children's book, with emphasis on gangster era.

———. *Headquarters.* New York: Harper, 1955. New York police cases, as recalled by veteran detective Frank Phillips. Includes Dutch Schultz, Mad Dog Coll, Willie Sutton, Legs Diamond, Two Gun Crowley and the Brooklyn (Rubel Co.) armored car robbery.

Rhodes, Henry T.F. *Alphonse Bertillon: Father of Scientific Detection.* New York: Abelard-Schuman, 1956. Like Cesare Lombroso, a pioneer criminologist whose main contribution was to sell police on the usefulness of science.

Robinson, Henry Morton. *Science Catches the Criminal.* New York: Bobbs-Merrill, 1935. Excitement over new crime-fighting technology.

Rockaway, Robert A. *But—He Was Good to His Mother: The Lives and Crimes of Jewish Gangsters.* Jerusalem: Gefen, 1993. Interesting and original, with a particularly good bibliography.

Roemer, William F., Jr. *Man Against the Mob: The Inside Story of How the FBI Cracked the Chicago Mob by the Agent Who Led the Attack,* New York: Donald I. Fine, 1989. Book that made the late Bill Roemer a local if not national celebrity, even if his law-enforcement colleagues would say his accomplishments (largely through government wiretaps) were not as single-handed as the story implies. Roemer has always maintained, with some credibility based on the taps, that onetime driver for Jack McGurn and eventual mob boss Tony Accardo played a role in the St. Valentine's Day Massacre.

———. *War of the Godfathers: The Bloody Confrontation Between Chicago and New York Families for Control of Las Vegas.* New York: Random House, 1990. Published as fact, but admitted by Roemer to be largely speculative.

Rorabaugh, W.J. *Accardo: The Genuine Godfather.* New York: Donald I. Fine, 1995.

———. *The Alcoholic Republic: An American Tradition.* New York: Oxford University Press, 1979. Well-researched study of national drinking habits that were always excessive and that set the stage for national Prohibition when the saloon came to symbolize drunkenness, especially among working-class immigrants.

Rosen, Victor. *A Gun in His Hand.* New York: Gold Medal, 1951. Slim paperback biography of Francis "Two-Gun" Crowley, and probably more than he deserves.

Ross, Robert. *The Trial of Al Capone.* Chicago, 1933. Rare, self-published paperback account of Capone's tax trial.

Rothstein, Carolyn (Mrs. Arnold). *Now I'll Tell.* New York: Vanguard, 1934. A rare and personal memoir by the widow of slain New York crime lord Arnold Rothstein, which complements the biographies by Donald Henderson Clarke (*In the Reign of Rothstein*) and Leo Katcher (*The Big Bankroll*).

Royko, Mike. *Boss.* New York: E. P. Dutton, 1971. Rise of the Richard J. Daley Democratic machine with commentary on its more spectacularly corrupt Republican predecessors. One of the few books to mention Gus Winkeler as one of the St. Valentine's Day Massacre gunmen.

———. *I Could Be Wrong, but I Doubt It.* Chicago: Regnery, 1968. Collection of Royko's newspaper columns includes an interesting Bonnie and Clyde chapter consisting of interviews with the sons of Barrow gang victims, telling of their disrupted lives.

Rudensky, Morris "Red", with Don Riley. *The Gonif.* Blue Earth, Minn.: Piper, 1970, Autobiography of a former safecracker, robber, hijacker and jailbreaker who also did odd jobs for Al Capone and the Purple Gang, ending up at Alcatraz with Capone and Machine Gun Kelly.

Runyon, Damon. *Trials & Other Tribulations.* Philadelphia: Lippencott, 1947. Reprint, New York: Dorset, 1991. Runyon-style reportage on famous crimes of his times, with entertaining chapters on the murder of Rothstein and the tax trial of Capone.

Runyon, Tom. *In for Life.* New York: W. W. Norton, 1953. Autobiography of a Depression outlaw and convicted murderer, written in the Iowa state prison at Ft. Madison, where he became a best-selling author and even Associated Press correspondent. Died there in 1957, after Erle Stanley Gardner and others had campaigned for his parole.

Ruth, David E. *Inventing the Public Enemy: The Gangster in American Culture, 1918–1934.* Chicago: University of Chicago Press, 1996. Excellent study of the evolution of the concept of the modern-day gangster.

Sabljak, Mark, and Martin H. Greenberg. *Most Wanted: A History of the FBI's Ten Most Wanted List.* New York: Bonanza, 1990. Similar to the Newtons' *FBI's Most Wanted* and just as superficial, but includes a chapter on public enemies of the 1930s.

———. *A Bloody Legacy: Chronicles of American Murder.* New York: Gramercy, 1992. Routine re-run on the St. Valentine's Day Massacre, Bonnie and Clyde, Legs Diamond, Louis "Lepke" Buchalter and Albert Anastasia.

Sanborn, Debra. *The Barrow Gang's Visit to Dexter.* Dexter, Iowa: Bob Weesner, 1976. Locally printed and sold Bonnie and Clyde booklet on the 1933 Dexfield Park shootout in which Buck and Blanche Barrow were captured.

Sann, Paul. *The Lawless Decade.* New York: Crown, 1957. Photo history of the 1920s. Emphasis but nothing original on Prohibition gang wars (especially Chicago's) and St. Valentine's Day Massacre, with chapters on Al Capone, Johnny Torrio and Big Jim Colosimo, and biographical sketches of Dutch Schultz, Owney Madden, Legs Diamond, Mad Dog Coll, Louis "Lepke" Buchalter, Jacob "Gurrah" Shapiro, Lucky Luciano and Frank Costello. Revised and updated version published by Fawcett, Greenwich, Connecticut, 1971.

———. *Kill the Dutchman!: The Story of Dutch Schultz.* New Rochelle, N.Y.: Arlington House, 1971. Interesting (and only worthwhile) biography of Schultz, with many photos and transcript of his delirious deathbed poetics.

Scaduto, Tony. *Lucky Luciano: The Man Who Modernized the Mafia.* U.K.: Sphere, 1976.

Schlosser, Alexander L. *The Gentle Art of Murder, 1934.* New York: Vanguard, 1934. Contains contemporary crime stories, including "Society Teaches John Dillinger A Lesson."

Schmidt, John R. *"The Mayor Who Cleaned Up Chicago": A Political Biography of William E. Dever,* DeKalb: Northern Illinois University, 1989. Reform efforts of the well-meaning Dever actually caused Capone to take over neighboring Cicero and threw the underworld into a state of disarray that made Chicago more violent and notorious than before.

Schoenberg, Robert J. *Mr. Capone: The Real—and Complete—Story of Al Capone.* New York: William Morrow, 1992. Some new information, slightly revisionist, but mostly a rehash of Kobler with greater emphasis on crime as big business. Author would have gotten lost in Chicago without the help of local Capone expert Mark LeVell [aka Levell].

Schur, Edward M. *Our Criminal Society: The Social and Legal Sources of Crime in America.* Englewood Cliffs, N.J.: Prentice-Hall, 1969. Examines crime patterns historically and questions conventional crime-control policies.

Schwartzman, Paul, and Rob Polner. *New York Notorious: A Borough-By-Borough Tour of the City's Most Infamous Crime Scenes.* New York: Crown, 1992. Amazingly dull descriptions of New York's most notable crimes; includes some gangster material, such as the murder sites of Arnold Rothstein and Mad Dog Coll.

Sciacca, Tony. *Luciano: The Man Who Modernized the American Mafia.* New York: Pinnacle Books, 1973. Scaduto and Sciacca books appear to be U.S. and U.K. versions of the same, published under different names. Both dedicated to Ernie "The Hawk" Rupolo, a Mafia informer whose luck finally ran out. Disputes *The Last Testament of Lucky Luciano* by Gosch and Hammer, yet repeats the myth of the "Night of the Sicilian Vespers."

Scott, Sir Harold, ed. *Concise Encyclopedia of Crime and Criminals,* New York: Hawthorne, 1961. Unfortunately scarce, but unusually comprehensive and authoritative, with customary emphasis on American law and lawbreakers.

Seidman, Harold. *Labor Czars: A History of Labor Racketeering.* New York: Liveright, 1938.

Selvaggi, Giuseppe. *The Rise of the Mafia in New York.* Translated and edited by William A. Packer. New York: Bobbs-Merrill, 1978. As told by an Italian journalist, based on interviews with deported gangsters. May have lost much in translation of original Italian language version.

Sharpe, May Churchill. *Chicago May: Her Story.* New York: Gold Label, 1928. More collectible than informational, but an entertaining autobiography of a colorful female scoundrel's international life of crime.

Short, Martin. *Crime Inc.: The Story of Organized Crime.* London: Thames Methuen, 1984. Somewhat simplistic account of U.S. crime families and gangs, derived from the BBC-TV documentary series.

Sifakis, Carl. *The Encyclopedia of American Crime.* New York: Facts On File, 1984. Similar to Nash's *Bloodletters and Badmen,* but far superior in content, writing, accuracy and production.

———. *The Mafia Encyclopedia.* New York: Facts On File, 1974. Comprehensive and well-researched work on nationally organized crime.

———. *A Catalogue of Crime.* New York: New American Library, 1979. Slim paperback, but crammed with historical crime trivia.

Simmons, Lee. *Assignment Huntsville: Memoirs of a Texas Prison Officer.* Austin: University of Texas, 1957. Simmons brought former Texas Ranger Frank Hamer out of retirement to track down Bonnie and Clyde. Author's memory fails him on the date of the Barrow-Parker ambush, but he includes notes of his 1935 interviews with Barrow gangster Joe Palmer shortly before his execution. Some material on Matt Kimes and other outlaws.

Singer, Kurt, comp. *My Strangest Case.* London: W. H. Allen, 1957. Recollections of police notables, including the J. Edgar Hoover version of Ma Barker and the Barker-Karpis gang, titled "Matriarch with a Machine-Gun."

Slate, John, and R.U. Steinberg. *Lawmen, Crimebusters and Champions of Justice.* New York: M & M, 1991. Slick coffee-table companion to Diana Claitor's *Outlaws, Mobsters and Murderers.*

Smith, Alson J. *Syndicate City.* Chicago: Regnery, 1954. Lesser-known but well-researched, well-written, and somewhat revisionistic history of Chicago organized crime.

Smith, Dwight C., Jr. *The Mafia Mystique.* New York: Basic Books, 1975.

Smith, Richard Norton. *Thomas E. Dewey and His Times: The First Full-Scale Biography of the Maker of the Modern Republican Party.* New York: Simon & Schuster, 1982. Covers Dewey's collaboration with reform Mayor Fiorello LaGuardia to clean up a city long ruled by gangs under the likes of playboy Mayor Jimmy Walker, forced out of office by the state-supported Seabury Investigation.

Smith, Sir Sidney. *Mostly Murder.* New York: David McKay, 1959. Wonders of scientific crime detection told autobiographically by a leading British forensic pathologist.

Söderman, Harry, and Chief Inspector John J. O'Connell. *Modern Criminal Investigation.* New York: Funk and Wagnalls, 1935. Major effort to sell backward local police agencies on the latest breakthroughs in scientific crime detection.

Sondern, Frederic, Jr. *Brotherhood of Evil: The Mafia.* New York: Farrar, Straus & Giroux, 1959. Another 1950s Mafia book, displaying that period's ignorance of organized crime. Includes chapters on Capone and Luciano, with Capone's verging on the hilarious.

Spencer, James. *Limey: An Englishman Joins the Gangs.* London/New York: Longman's/Green, 1933. Supposed excursions of an Englishman into the American underworld.

Spiering, Frank. *The Man Who Got Capone.* New York: Bobbs-Merrill, 1976. Describes Treasury agent Frank Wilson's major role in putting Capone behind bars. Spiering has also authored books on Jack the Ripper and Lizzie Borden.

Stead, William T. *If Christ Came To Chicago!* Laird and Lee, 1894. Reprint, Evanston, Ill.: Chicago Historical Bookworks, 1990. Classic expose of Chicago's crime, vice, corruption and opulent depravity that was in full flower long before Prohibition gave rise to the Roaring Twenties "gangster."

Steffens, Lincoln. *Shame of the Cities.* New York: McClure, Phillips, 1903, with numerous later reprints. Probably the most influential "muckraking" expose of corruption, squalor and depravity, city by city, which became a combination bible and guidebook for urban activists during the Age of Reform, and a rich source of material for journalistic attacks on entrenched politicians. In the same vein as Stead's *If Christ Came to Chicago,* but national in scope.

Steiger, Brad. *Bizarre Crime.* New York: Penguin Books, 1992. Poor paperback with gangster section that includes chapters on Big Jim Colosimo's allegedly lost gems, the $200,000 treasure Dillinger supposedly buried at Little Bohemia, and the widely discredited legend of Ma Barker.

Stein, Max. *U.S. War on Crime; "Bring 'em Back Dead or Alive.* Chicago: Stein, 1939. One of several garish booklets in a March of Crime series described as "Instructive Discussions," includes Evelyn Frechette's flimsy story of her adventures with Dillinger. Others describe the Dillinger gang, Bonnie and Clyde, St. Valentine's Day Massacre, etc.

Steinberg, Alfred. *The Bosses.* New York: Macmillan, 1972. Substantial biographies of Frank Hague, Ed Crump, James Curley, Huey Long, Gene Talmadge and Tom Pendergast, the "ruthless men who forged the American political machines that dominated the twenties and thirties."

Sterling, William Warren. *Trails and Trials of a Texas Ranger.* 1959. Reprint, Norman: University of Oklahoma, 1968. "General Bill" Sterling rose through the ranks to become commander of the Texas Rangers in the 1930s. His memoir, privately published originally, includes chapters on former Rangers Frank Hamer, who led the ambush of Bonnie and Clyde, and Gus Jones, who joined the FBI and headed the Kansas City Massacre and Urschel kidnapping investigations, plus a few pages on the Kimes-Terrill outlaw gang of the 1920s.

Stern, Michael. *The White Ticket: Commercialized Vice in the Machine Age.* New York: National Library Press, 1936.

Still, Charles E. *Styles in Crime.* New York: Lippincott, 1938. Potpourri of famous criminal cases, crime fighters, police history, punishment, and whatever else struck the author as illustrative, colorful or bizarre.

Stuart, Hix C. *The Notorious Ashley Gang: A Saga of the King and Queen of the Everglades.* Stuart, Fla.: St. Lucie Publishing, 1928. John Ashley and his gang of notorious bank robbers, hijackers, and bootleggers who terrorized Florida in the 1920s. Includes a few photos and a statement on his criminal career allegedly made by Ashley himself. Possibly the first book on America's new "motorized bandits," but many details open to question.

Stuart, Mark A. *Gangster #2: Longy Zwillman, The Man Who Invented Organized Crime.* Secaucus, N.J.: Lyle Stuart, 1985. Biography of New Jersey gangster Zwillman, marred by invented dialogue. Stuart also falls into the biographer's syndrome (as evidenced by title) of exaggerating the importance of his subject, but had the modesty to rate him second.

Sullivan, Edward Dean. *Rattling the Cup on Chicago Crime.* New York: Vanguard, 1929.

———. *Chicago Surrenders.* New York: Vanguard, 1930.

———. *The Snatch Racket.* New York: Vanguard, 1932. Sullivan was an archetypal Chicago crime reporter who produced two of the earliest books on Capone and Chicago gangs. *The Snatch Racket* superficially describes the gangland practice of holding rivals for ransom and seems to have been a rush job to capitalize on kidnap-murder of the Lindbergh baby. Blames the increase in abductions largely on Prohibition.

Sullivan, William, with Bill Brown. *The Bureau: My Thirty Years in Hoover's FBI.* New York: W. W. Norton, 1979. Important critical book on Hoover and the Bureau, written by a former assistant director of the FBI. Mainly of interest to gangster buffs for its chapters on G-Man Charles Winstead, the presumed killer of Dillinger. In his early years with the Bureau, Sullivan worked closely with Winstead, who also claimed to have shot Ma Barker, though some believe she was killed by her son Fred when capture was imminent.

Summers, Anthony. *Official and Confidential: The Secret Life of J. Edgar Hoover.* New York: Putnam, 1993. As sensational as monumental, maintaining that Hoover was a not-always-closeted homophobic homosexual blackmailed by certain mobsters into denying the existence of organized crime. Provides evidence of some truly bizarre aspects of Hoover, but any writer who accepts the Dillinger survival theory cannot be taken too seriously.

Sutherland, Edwin H. *The Professional Thief.* Chicago: University of Chicago, 1937.

Sutton, Willie, with Edward Linn. *Where the Money Was.* New York: Viking, 1976. Autobiography of New York bank robber, burglar, escape artist, master of disguise, known in the underworld as "Slick Willie" and "Willie the Actor." His career as bank robber (with time out for prison terms) extended from the 1920s to early '50s, when he made the FBI's "Ten Most Wanted" list. Includes material on Dutch Schultz and other New York mobsters. Sutton later denied making the remark that the author paraphrases for the title.

Symons, Julian. *A Pictorial History of Crime: 1840 to the Present.* New York: Crown, 1966. Reprinted by Bonanza, a division of Crown. Extensive if superficial photo history of famous crimes and criminals around the world. Gangster section includes biographical sketches of Arnold Rothstein, Johnny Torrio, Al Capone, Dillinger and the Depression outlaws; plus labor rackets, and Mafia as it relates to the national crime syndicate. Published also by Studio Vista in London, the same year, as *Crime and Detection: An Illustrated History From 1840.*

Tallant, Robert. *Ready to Hang: Seven Famous New Orleans Murders.* New York: Harper, 1952. Not particularly relevant, except for its chapter describing a much-reported killing and lynching incident in 1907 and promoting the largely discredited notion that the Mafia had entered the U.S. by way of New Orleans.

Taylor, Merlin Moore. *The Inside Story of Dillinger: Or, Dillinger's Sensational Story—Inside Dope on Public Enemy No. 1.* Long, detailed account of Dillinger's life and career ends with the battle at Little Bohemia, published on newsprint in August 1934, as an issue of *Star Novels* magazine. Unusually accurate period piece, especially interesting for having been written while Dillinger was still in business. Other stories are clearly labeled as fiction.

Terrett, Courtenay. *Only Saps Work: A Ballyhoo for Racketeering.* New York: Vanguard, 1930. An informative early look at the expansion of bootlegging gangs into business rackets. Title reflects increasing pre-Depression cynicism toward honest jobs and politicians.

Theoharis, Athan G., and John Stuart Cox, *The Boss: J. Edgar Hoover and the Great American Inquisition.* Philadelphia: Temple University, 1988. Anti-Hoover book with error-filled gangster chapter. Theoharis also authored *From the Secret Files of J. Edgar Hoover* (Chicago: Ivan R. Dee, 1991), which is gangsterless.

Thompson, Craig, and Allen Raymond. *Gang Rule in New York: The Story of a Lawless Era.* New York: Dial, 1940. Good popular history of the New York gangs of the twenties and thirties.

Thorwald, Jurgen. *Crime and Science: The New Frontier in Criminology.* New York: Harcourt, Brace & World, 1966. Historical background to modern forensics.

———. *Century of the Detective.* New York: Harcourt, Brace & World, 1964.

Thrasher, Frederic. *The Gang: A Study of 1,313 Gangs in Chicago.* Chicago: University of Chicago, 1927. Important scholarly study of the street-gang phenomenon, but one which failed to appreciate how the enormous profit potential of Prohibition would transform some existing gangs into wealthy and powerful underworld organizations.

Thurman, Steve. [Frank Castle] *"Baby Face" Nelson.* Derby, Conn.: Monarch, 1961. Gangster kitch, but collectible.

———. *"Mad Dog" Coll.* Derby, Conn.: Monarch, 1961. Listed to avoid confusion, as this is a novelization of the movie *Mad Dog Coll,* and not one of the usual Monarch "gangster biographies," which purport to be nonfiction.

Tiffany, Ernest L. *War with the Underworld.* Butler, Ind.: Higley, 1946.

Toland, John. *The Dillinger Days.* New York: Random House, 1963. Heavily researched, delightfully written, comparable to Cromie and Pinkston's *Dillinger: A Short and Violent Life,* but more social history that treats Dillinger himself in less detail because it also covers the other major gangs that flourished during the Depression.

Touhy, Roger, with Ray Brennan. *The Stolen Years.* Cleveland, Ohio: Pennington, 1959. Touhy, convicted of kidnapping Jake "The Barber" Factor, finally convinced the courts that the crime was a hoax perpetrated by Capone to put him out of business. Released in 1959 and murdered a few days later. Includes an amusingly erroneous mention of the St. Valentine's Day Massacre as being committed by Capone gunmen disguised not as cops but as priests.

Train, Arthur. *Courts, Criminals, and the Camorra.* New York: Scribner's, 1912. Attempt by a former assistant district attorney for New York County to sort out criminal organization within the city's Italian-American community.

Treherne, John. *The Strange History of Bonnie and Clyde.* New York: Stein & Day, 1984. Probably the best account to date of Bonnie and Clyde, despite some errors and some claims that others would dispute.

Trekell, Ronald L. *History of the Tulsa Police Department, 1882–1990.* Tulsa, Okla.: Tulsa Police Children's Scholarship Fund, 1990. Good history of police department, but poorly researched chapter on Tulsa area gangsters, including Ma Barker and sons, Alvin Karpis, Pretty Boy Floyd, Wilbur Underhill, and Matt and George Kimes.

Trott, Lloyd. *Mafia.* Cambridge: University of Cambridge, 1977. Bibliography of works on the Mafia.

Trovillion, Hal W. *Persuading God Back to Herrin.* Herrin, Ill.: Herrin News, 1925. Obscure contemporary account of crime and labor violence in Illinois's "Bloody Williamson" County.

Tully, Andrew. *Treasury Agent.* New York: Simon & Schuster, 1958.

———. *The FBI's Most Famous Cases.* New York: William Morrow, 1965. Introduction and commentary by J. Edgar Hoover adds it to the long list of books glorifying the Bureau.

Turkus, Burton, and Sid Feder. *Murder, Inc.* New York: Farrar, Straus & Young, 1951. Best-selling thriller by the assistant district attorney who prosecuted New York's Murder, Inc. gangsters.

Turner, William W. *Hoover's FBI.* Los Angeles: Sherbourne, 1970. Anti-FBI book written by a fired FBI agent. Much good information but also many errors. Most interesting for its inclusion of

filched FBI files diminishing Kathryn Kelly's role in the Urschel case, the Bureau's first and most publicized kidnapping, the files on which are oddly absent from the FBI's reading room.

Tyler, Gus, ed. *Organized Crime in America.* Ann Arbor: University of Michigan Press, 1962. Collection of efforts to distinguish Mafia fact from fiction.

Underwood, Sid. *Depression Desperado: The Chronicle of Raymond Hamilton.* Austin, Tex.: Eakin, 1995. Overshadowed in history by his partners, Bonnie and Clyde, Hamilton is finally rescued from relative obscurity—and frequent confusion with his brother Floyd—in an excellent account of his character and career that set him above and apart from his criminal contemporaries. His blazing escape from the Texas state prison death house only delayed his execution, but should have earned him a more enduring place in the annals of American outlawry.

Ungar, Sanford J. *FBI: An Uncensored Look Behind the Walls.* Boston: Little, Brown, 1976. Mainly deals with the post-Hoover Bureau, but some historical material on the public-enemy era.

Unger, Robert. *The Union Station Massacre: The Original Sin of Hoover's FBI.* Kansas City, Mo: Andrews, McNeel, 1997. Without excluding the likelihood that Pretty Boy Floyd was involved in the Kansas City Massacre, Unger's excellent research demolishes the case that Hoover's FBI was trying to build against him, discussing the turf war between Hoover and a local ballistics expert and Hoover's habitual willingness to supress evidence that would have been favorable to the defense. [See King, *The Life and Death of Pretty Boy Floyd,* and Wallis, *Pretty Boy.*]

U.S. Senate, Permanent Subcommittee on Investigations of the Committee on Governmental Affairs. *Organized Crime: Twenty-Five Years After Valachi.* Washington, D.C.: U.S. Government Printing Office, 1988. Includes the FBI document, "Chronological History of La Cosa Nostra in the United States: January 1920–August

1987." Though long denying the existence of a national crime syndicate, Hoover nonetheless kept tabs on major crime figure under what he called the Bureau's "Top Hoodlum" program, ostensibly as a service to local law-enforcement agencies, which often didn't welcome federal meddling in their local affairs. Valachi's use of the expression "Cosa Nostra" instead of Mafia may have given the FBI a face-saving way (since the Narcotics Bureau under rival Harry Anslinger had been talking "Mafia" for years) to acknowledge the existence of long-established Italian-American "crime families" as "Cosa Nostra" organizations that still could be considered the responsibility of local rather than federal police agencies.

U.S. Senate, Special Committee to Investigate Organized Crime in Interstate Commerce. *Third Interim Report of the Special Committee to Investigate Organized Crime in Interstate Commerce Pursuant to S. Res. 202 (81st Congress), A Resolution to Investigate Gambling and Racketeering Activities.* The Kefauver Committee confirmed the existence of nationally organized crime and popularized the term "Mafia," which became the common phrase for all forms of racketeering that prospered during the country's preoccupation with the Depression-era bank robbers so highly publicized by the FBI. Self-wrapped government report became a nationwide best-seller; later reprinted in hardcover by Arco (leaving out seven pages) and Didier (complete).

Valentine, Lewis J. *Night Stick: The Autobiography of Lewis J. Valentine.* New York: Dial, 1947. Former New York police commissioner covers Arnold Rothstein, Legs Diamond, Dutch Schultz, Coll, Luciano and others, with introduction by former mayor Fiorello H. LaGuardia.

Van Cise, Philip S. *Fighting the Underworld.* Boston: Houghton Mifflin, 1936. Dwells on the Lou Blonger gang.

Van Devander, Charles W. *The Big Bosses.* New York: Howell, Soskin, 1944. ("Jacket blurb: "The story of State and City political machines in New York, Massachusetts, Illinois, Missouri, Pennsylvania, New York, California and the South"). Includes the fall of the Chicago's Big Bill Thompson Republicans, along with Al Capone, and the post-Prohibition rise of the "modern" Kelly-Nash Democratic machine that at least drew a broader line between "honest graft" and unconcealed corruption.

Villard, Oswald Garrison. *Some Newspapers and Newspaper-men.* New York: Knopf, 1923. Commentary on the different papers, reporters and publishers who battled for readership and to promote their personal visions and political agendas.

Vizzini, Sal, with Oscar Fraley and Marshall Smith. *Vizzini: The Story of America's No. 1 Undercover Narcotics Agent.* New York: Arbor House, 1972. Posing as an Air Force major in the 1950s, Vizzini became a confidant of Lucky Luciano in Naples while supposedly trying to make a case against the mobster-in-exile; with material also on Capone, Dutch Schultz and Legs Diamond.

Vollmer, August, and Alfred E. Parker. *Crime, Crooks and Cops.* New York: Funk & Wagnalls, 1937. Routine anti-crime polemic, disappointing in that its primary author was considered a foremost authority on law-enforcement tactics and policies.

Waldrop, Frank C. *McCormick of Chicago: An Unconventional Portrait of a Controversial Figure.* Englewood Cliffs, N.J.: Prentice-Hall, 1966. Biography of the *Chicago Tribune*'s powerful and eccentric publisher in the glory days of yellow journalism.

Walker, Stanley. *The Night Club Era.* New York: Frederick A. Stokes, 1933. History of the gangster-speakeasy scene during Prohibition. Also includes a chapter on freelance crime, including the Urschel kidnapping (which Walker attributes to "Harvey Bailey and his gang"). Indexed, unlike most gangster books of the period.

Wallis, Michael. *Pretty Boy: The Life and Times of Charles Arthur Floyd.* New York: St. Martin's,

1992. First major biography of the Southwest's leading bandit of the 1930s. Much new information, including what really happened to Jim Mills (the man who killed Floyd's father and was often erroneously claimed to be Floyd's first victim); Floyd's connections with the Young brothers, Fred Barker and Bonnie and Clyde, etc. Wallis has done an exhaustive and exhausting job of tracing Floyd's genealogy, and a growing fondness for his subject inclines him to doubt Pretty Boy's involvement in the Kansas City Massacre. However, the other published and unpublished accounts state that Floyd probably was involved, if largely by chance; and researcher Charles Webb has since discovered that Floyd may have acquired his nickname Pretty Boy not from a particular prostitute (as the story often goes) but from police confusing him with a small-time hood called "Pretty Boy" Smith who had also worked with one of Floyd's early crime partners.

——. *Oilman: The Story of Frank Phillips and the Birth of Phillips Petroleum.* Garden City, N.Y.: Doubleday, 1988. Biography of legendary Oklahoma oilman Frank Phillips, whose many friends included celebrities from both sides of the law. One was bank robber Henry Wells and here Wallis repeats Wells's fable of how he foiled a kidnap plot against Phillips by Floyd (see *Outlaw's End* by Gerald E. Moore). Wallis regrets including this, as subsequent research (see above) convinced him that Floyd was not so inclined. The book provides some new material on other Oklahoma outlaws (Henry Starr, Al Spencer, Frank Nash) and on the Shelton gang, who were briefly employed by Phillips as strikebreakers in East St. Louis.

Walsh, George. *Public Enemies: The Mayor, the Mob and the Crime That Was.* New York: Norton, 1980. New York reform Mayor William O'Dwyer and Frank Costello.

Ward, Bernie. *Families Who Kill.* New York: Pinnacle, 1993. Contains a remarkably inaccurate account of the Barkers, largely derived from the faulty research of crime-writer Nash and the fertile imagination of his ex-con friend, Blackie Audett.

Warden, Rob, and Martha Groves, eds. *Murder Most Foul: and Other Great Crime Stories from the World Press.* Athens: Ohio University, 1980. Includes standard accounts of the St. Valentine's Day Massacre and the killing of Dillinger, but covers some new ground on the ambush murder of Chicago's Two-Gun Louie Alterie.

Warren, George. *Gang Wars of the '30s.* Chatsworth, Calif.: Barclay House, 1974. Slim paperback with little new information but some uncommon photos. Contains excerpts from an interesting *True* magazine interview with Bonnie and Clyde slayer Ted Hinton, critical of the FBI, published long before Hinton's book, *Ambush.*

Washburn, Charles. *Come into My Parlor: A Biography of the Aristocratic Everleigh Sisters of Chicago.* New York: Knickerbocker, 1934. Successes, trials and tribulations of two famous madams whose flamboyant operations in Chicago's designated red-light district inspired reforms welcomed by the city's criminal community, which could then take over prostitution.

Watson, Frederic. *A Century of Gunmen.* London: Ivor Nicholson & Watson, 1931. British book covers mainly Old West gunfighters, but could not resist a chapter on Al Capone.

Watson, William P. *Union, Justice and Bonnie & Clyde. A Louisiana Legacy!* Bossier City, La.: Everett, 1989. Strange work purports to be true story of ambush of Bonnie and Clyde, but told in the form of a stage play presenting posthumous trials. Author interviewed Bossier Parish residents, including relatives of Henry Methvin, alleged betrayer of the Barrows, but still makes many mistakes. Includes coroner's reports. Some revisions since original printing, either to correct errors or avoid disputes.

Watters, Pat, and Stephen Gillers, eds. *Investigating the FBI: A Tough, Fair Look at the Powerful*

Bureau, Its Present and Its Future. Garden City, N.Y.: Doubleday, 1973. Proceedings of an essentially anti-FBI conference at Princeton University in 1971. Some gangster material, including Dillinger.

Webb, Walter Prescott. *The Texas Rangers: A Century of Frontier Defense.* Boston: Houghton Mifflin, 1935. Includes Frank Hamer's account of the killing of Bonnie and Clyde. Reprinted in 1965 by the University of Texas, with foreword by Lyndon Johnson.

Weeks, Patrick H., M.D. *The Big House of Mystery: A Physician-Psychiatrist Looks at Ten Thousand Crimes and Criminals.* Philadelphia: Dorrance, 1938. By a state prison doctor at Michigan City, Ind., who confirms that Dillinger did have heart trouble, as discovered during his autopsy. Conspiracy buff Nash cited the rheumatic heart in support of his theory that such a debilitating condition ruled out the Biograph shooting victim as the real Dillinger, whose criminal career would have been too stressful. For what it's worth, Alvin Karpis, who outlasted Dillinger in the same profession, survived another 33 years in prison despite a defective heart (as mentioned in Trent, *The Alvin Karpis Story,* and Quimby, *The Devil's Emissaries*), only to die several years later of a drug overdose, possible accidental.

Wellman, Paul I. *A Dynasty of Western Outlaws.* Garden City, N.Y.: Doubleday, 1961. Traces the connections between different outlaw gangs in Missouri, Oklahoma and Kansas from the Civil War to the Depression. Includes map of outlaw sites, genealogical chart and chronology of southwestern outlaws, with chapters on 1920s gangs (Al Spencer's and Eddie Adams's) and Pretty Boy Floyd. Despite errors, well written by a Wichita police reporter who met many law officers as well as some of the gangsters he wrote about.

Wendt, Lloyd, and Herman Kogan. *Big Bill of Chicago.* New York: Bobbs-Merrill, 1953. Thoroughly entertaining biography of Chicago's clown mayor in cahoots with the city's underworld.

———. *Lords of the Levee: The Story of Bathhouse John and Hinky Dink.* New York: Bobbs-Merrill, 1943. Later editions include softcover reprint retitled *Bosses in Lusty Chicago,* Bloomington: Indiana University, 1971. Lively account of Chicago's institutionalized vice and shameless corruption, which easily weathered sporadic reform movements during much of the city's history.

West, C.W. *Outlaws and Peace Officers of Indian Territory.* Muskogee, Okla.: Muskogee Publishing, 1987. "Indian Territory" here refers to eastern Oklahoma, not to the territorial period alone. Mainly a collection of Muskogee newspaper stories on various outlaws and lawmen through the 1930s, including Pretty Boy Floyd, Alvin Karpis, and Matt and George Kimes.

Weston, Paul B. *Muscle on Broadway.* Evanston, Ill.: Regency, 1962. From outward appearances, an unillustrated, thoroughly ignorable, 50-cent paperback from an obscure Chicago-area publisher, which purports to describe mob rule in New York during the twenties and thirties, carrying the byline of a retired deputy chief inspector of police, but told mostly in first person by an anonymous informant and survivor of the Dutch Schultz gang calling himself "Max." Where Max's story is complemented by the author's commentary is left to the reader to puzzle out, yet the combined effort provides a remarkably interesting insider/outsider collaboration heavy with details (including the murder of Schultz) and an apparent familiarity with the subject, presented from both sides of the legal fence. Outwardly lurid, oddly presented, cheaply produced.

Whitehead, Don. *The FBI Story: A Report to the People.* New York: Random House, 1956. "Authorized biography" of FBI, with foreword by J. Edgar Hoover, includes material on Dillinger, Barker-Karpis gang, Union Station [Kansas City] Massacre, Urschel kidnapping, Jake Fleagle, Capone and the surrender of Louis

"Lepke" Buchalter. Probably a command performance in response to Max Lowenthal's epic attack on the FBI.

Whyte, William Foote. *Street Corner Society: The Social Structure of an Italian Slum.* Chicago: University of Chicago, 1943. Scholarly study of ghetto neighborhoods as breeding grounds of criminals.

Wickersham Commission. *Reports.* 1931. With Mooney-Billings Report. 15 reports in 14 volumes. Reprint, Montclair, N.J.: Patterson Smith, 1969.

Willemse, Cornelius W. *A Cop Remembers.* New York: Dutton, 1933.

Willemse, Cornelius W., with George J. Lenner and Jack Kofoed. *Behind the Green Lights.* New York: Knopf, 1931. Scarce, thoroughly engrossing aubiographical adventures of a New York detective who tangled with some of the city's best-known hoods during his 40-year career as a gangbuster.

Williams, Nathan Glenn. *From Alcatraz to the White House.* Seattle, Wash.: Wiljoy, 1991. Autobiography of a former bank robber and prison friend of Alvin Karpis. Some good Alcatraz stories. Cover shows author shaking hands with President Reagan.

Williams, Roger M., ed. *The Super Crooks.* Chicago: Playboy Press, 1973. Anthology of previously published material on celebrity criminals by various authors.

Willoughby, Malcom F. *Rum War at Sea.* Washington, D.C.: U.S. Government Printing Office, 1964. Official, thorough, and intensely boring account of Treasury Department and Coast Guard efforts to combat rumrunning. Includes list (and disposition) of vessels seized under special contraband laws enacted during Prohibition and still on the books.

Wilson, Colin, Ian Schott, Ed Shedd, Damon Wilson and Rowland Wilson, eds. *Colin Wilson's World Famous Crimes: The World's Worst Gangsters, Crooks, Conmen and Scandals.* New York: Carroll and Graf, 1995. Consolidation of material from previous books by the popular British crime writer, including chapters on his American favorites, from Capone to Bonnie and Clyde, with some elaborating sidebars.

Wilson, Frank J., with Beth Day. *Special Agent.* New York: Holt, Rinehart & Winston, 1965. Treasury agent Wilson's tireless (and successful efforts) to convict Capone of income tax evasion.

Wolf, George, with Joseph DiMona. *Frank Costello: Prime Minister of the Underworld.* New York: William Morrow, 1974. Wolf was Costello's attorney, as well as Luciano's.

Wolf, Marvin J., and Katherine Mader. *Fallen Angels: Chronicles of L.A. Crime and Mystery.* New York: Facts On File, 1986. Includes Tony Cornero, the murder of Bugsy Siegel and speculation on organized crime's involvement in the death of actress Thelma Todd.

Woodside, John R., et al. *The Young Brothers Massacre.* Springfield, Mo.: Springfield Publishing, 1932. Contemporary account of the slaughter of six lawmen near Springfield by minor outlaws Harry and Jennings Young, in which Pretty Boy Floyd and Fred Barker were also suspected. Issued just after the event.

Wright, Richard O. ed. *Whose FBI?* Chicago: Open Court, 1974. Pro-FBI book, written in response to Princeton University conference (see Watters and Gillers, *Investigating the FBI*).

Wright, Theon. *In Search of the Lindbergh Baby.* New York: Tower, 1981. Maintains the Lindbergh kidnapping was committed by the Capone mob in order to get Al out of jail, that Bruno Hauptmann was innocent, that the dead infant found was not Charles, Jr., that the real Lindbergh baby was raised by his abductors and grew up to be one Harold R. Olson of Escanaba, Michigan. Super-revisionist history based by the psychic revelations of Edgar Cayce.

Zeiger, Henry A. *Frank Costello.* New York: Berkley, 1974.

————. *The Hit Parade.* New York: Berkley, 1976. Routine rehash of major gang murders and wars from the 1920s to the 1970s.

Zorbaugh, Harvey W. *The Gold Coast and the Slum: A Sociological Study of Chicago's Near North Side.* Chicago: University of Chicago, 1929. For today's Chicagoans, a lucid and lurid picture of the North Michigan Avenue neighborhood when it included the rich, the wretched, the radicals, bootleggers, and the remnants of the city's literary/bohemian community, before wealthy merchants transformed it into the "Magnificent Mile" for the credit-card class.

INDEX

Boldface page numbers indicate major discussions. *Italic* page numbers indicate illustrations.